THE
EXECUTIVE
DILEMMA

HARVARD BUSINESS REVIEW EXECUTIVE BOOK SERIES

Executive Success: Making It In Management

Survival Strategies for American Industry

Managing Effectively in the World Marketplace

Strategic Management

Financial Management

Catching Up with the Computer Revolution

Marketing Management

Using Logical Techniques for Making Better Decisions

Growing Concerns: Building and Managing the Smaller Business

Business and Its Public

Sunrise . . . Sunset: Challenging the Myth of Industrial Obsolescence

The Marketing Renaissance

The Executive Dilemma: Handling People Problems at Work

THE EXECUTIVE DILEMMA

HANDLING PEOPLE PROBLEMS AT WORK

ELIZA G.C. COLLINS

Editor

JOHN WILEY & SONS

New York · Chichester · Brisbane · Toronto · Singapore

Library of Congress Cataloging in Publication Data:

Main entry under title:

The Executive dilemma.

  (Harvard business review executive book series)
  Includes indexes.
  1. Organizational behavior—Addresses, essays, lectures.
2. Personnel management—Addresses, essays, lectures.
I. Collins, Eliza G. C. II. Series.

HD58.7.E95 1985   658.3   85-613
ISBN 0-471-81519-5

Printed in the United States of America

10 9 8 7 6 5 4 3 2 1

Foreword

For sixty years, the *Harvard Business Review* has been the farthest reaching executive program of the Harvard Business School. It is devoted to the continuing education of executives and aspiring managers primarily in business organizations, but also in not-for-profit institutions, in government, and in the professions. Through its publishing partners, reprints, and translation programs, it finds an audience in many languages in most of the countries in the world, occasionally penetrating even the barrier between East and West.

The *Harvard Business Review* draws on the talents of the most creative people in modern business and in management education. About half of its content comes from practicing managers, the rest from professional people and university researchers. Everything *HBR* publishes has something to do with the skills, attitudes, and knowledge essential to the competent and ethical practice of management.

This book consists of 33 articles that describe the very different kinds of challenges and the range of problems managers face when they must deal with personal issues involving their employees. Neither abstruse nor superficial, the articles chosen for this volume are intended to be usefully analytical, challenging, and carefully prescriptive. Every well-informed businessperson can follow the exposition in its path away from the obvious and into the territory of independent thought. I hope that readers will find these ideas stimulating and helpful in making their professional careers more productive.

KENNETH R. ANDREWS, Editor
Harvard Business Review

v

Contents

Introduction, Eliza G.C. Collins, 1

Part One   When the Job Is the Problem

An Overview, 11
1. *Conflict at the Summit: A Deadly Game*, Alonzo McDonald, 15
2. *Problems of a New Executive*, Edmund P. Learned, 30
3. *Power Failure in Management Circuits*,
   Rosabeth Moss Kanter, 43
4. *When Executives Burn Out*, Harry Levinson, 61
5. *The Foreman: Master and Victim of Double Talk*,
   F. J. Roethlisberger, 72
6. *The Dynamics of Subordinacy*, Abraham Zaleznik, 92
7. *The Subordinate's Predicaments*, Eric H. Neilsen
   and Jan Gypen, 112

Part Two   Sexes and Races Working Together

An Overview, 125
8. *Two Women, Three Men on a Raft*, Robert Schrank, 129
9. *Case of the Valuable Vendors*, Mary P. Rowe, 140
10. *Sexual Harassment . . . Some See It . . . Some Won't*,
    Eliza G.C. Collins and Timothy B. Blodgett, 153
11. *Dealing with Sexual Harassment*, Mary P. Rowe, 184
12. *Case of the Borderline Black*, Theodore V. Purcell, 192

13. *What It's Like to Be a Black Manager,*
    Edward W. Jones, Jr., 210
14. *Managers and Lovers,* Eliza G.C. Collins, 223

Part Three   The Changing Needs of Employees

An Overview, 239
15. *Case of the Suspect Salesman,* Albert H. Dunn, 243
16. *Three Vice Presidents in Mid-Life,* Stanley M. Davis
    and Roger L. Gould, 256
17. *On Being a Middle-aged Manager,* Harry Levinson, 276
18. *A Second Career: The Possible Dream,* Harry Levinson, 291
19. *Don't Call It Early Retirement,* Interviews with Wheelock Whitney
    and William G. Damroth, 303
20. *Can You Survive Your Retirement?* Leland R. Bradford, 327

Part Four   The Executive as a Human Being

An Overview, 337
21. *What Killed Bob Lyons?* Harry Levinson, 341
22. *On Executive Suicide,* Harry Levinson, 369
23. *Managers Can Drive Their Subordinates Mad,*
    Manfred F.R. Kets de Vries, 376
24. *The Abrasive Personality,* Harry Levinson, 390
25. *Must Success Cost So Much?* Fernando Bartolomé
    and Paul A. Lee Evans, 401
26. *The Work Alibi: When It's Harder to Go Home,*
    Fernando Bartolomé, 419

Part Five   Overcoming the Barriers

An Overview, 431
27. *It's Not Lonely Upstairs,* Interview with Renn Zaphiropoulos, 435
28. *When Friends Run the Business,* Interviews with Alan Ladd, Jr.,
    Jay Kanter, and Gareth Wigan, 467
29. *Are You Hearing Enough Employee Concerns?* Mary P. Rowe
    and Michael Baker, 491

30. *Management of Differences*, **Warren H. Schmidt
    and Robert Tannenbaum, 506**
31. *The Interpersonal Underworld*, **William C. Schutz, 521**
32. *The Administrator's Skill: Communication*, **F.J. Roethlisberger, 543**
33. *How Much Stress Is Too Much?* **Herbert Benson
    and Robert L. Allen, 557**

About the Authors, 569

Author Index, 575

Subject Index, 579

THE
EXECUTIVE
DILEMMA

Introduction

ELIZA G.C. COLLINS

In his book *Working*, Studs Terkel interviewed a young man, Ernest Bradshaw, who was the head of the audit department in a bank. In talking about his job, Bradshaw commented:

> That's the thing you get in any business. They never talk about personal feelings. They let you know that people are of no consequence. You take the job, you agree to work from eight-thirty to five and no ifs, ands, or buts. Feelings are left out. I think some of the other supervisors are compassionate, as I think I am. But they take the easy way out. . . . When you write a person as minimal, the person won't get a raise and he's subject to lose his job. . . . This takes away all the pressures. I felt it has to be one way: be truthful about a person 'cause it's gonna come up on 'em sooner or later. I look at people as people, person to person. But when you're on the job, you're supposed to lose all this.*

On the face of it, Ernest Bradshaw has a problem with the way some of his supervisor colleagues rate employees. He implies that they don't really care much about the people who work for them and, rather than look at the whole person and rate him or her accordingly, they take the easy way out and "write a person as minimal."

But if we consider his comments in another way, Bradshaw has a different set of problems. He feels alone in his position, he experiences the job of rating people as pressure, and he feels that where he works management doesn't care about people, himself included. On top of all that, although he doesn't mention it, Bradshaw is black.

But is Bradshaw himself a problem? Is the pressure he feels so great that his boss ought to intervene and offer some guidance? Does Bradshaw's being black make a difference to his attitude? Is it really true that people's feelings are being overlooked, and even if they are, is that important? And why aren't the other supervisors taking the time to rate their employees thoroughly—is the job that stressful?

---

*Studs Terkel, *Working* (New York: Pantheon Books, 1972), p. 398.

At some point in their careers most managers are faced with problems concerning employees and have to make the kinds of assessments that I've just described. For most managers, making these assessments and coming up with an appropriate response is one of the most difficult and challenging parts of their jobs.

Executives have difficulty dealing with people problems for many reasons. For one thing, every person in an organization is different, and he or she comes to work every day with a kit bag of different personal issues. If the employee is a woman, or black, for instance, she may be facing subtle discrimination at work and her performance may be suffering. But are her performance problems caused by discrimination or is training the issue? Is a middle-aged employee going through a mid-life crisis? Is that why he or she acts depressed? Is the young trainee happy at home, is he in the right position, and does he have the right resources to do his job? If so, why isn't he more responsive? Would his attitude change if all these things were corrected? What about the employee who seems perfectly suited to his job and seems to perform well, but no one can stand working with him?

The second reason executives have difficulty is implicit in the individual differences I have just described. It's terribly difficult to diagnose problems that concern people. Are the conflicts a question of values? Is every conflict between people caused by personality clashes? Or are other factors involved?

The third, and perhaps the most difficult obstacle to handling employee problems is that managers lack knowledge about how to help the people who work for them, or how to go about resolving some of the inevitable conflicts.

The articles in this collection explore the kinds of personal issues that managers are likely to face in supervising their employees. Although you could group these articles in many different ways, I've tried to organize them according to the kinds of situations in which problems may arise. The first group deals with situations where the job itself might be the cause of the problem; the second, where the problem might come up when men and women, or blacks and whites, work together; the third, where age affects how an employee performs or is judged to perform; and the fourth, where the issue seems distinctly personal—the result of some incapacity to handle either home or work life.

The final section offers articles that provide managers with ways of thinking about the problems discussed in previous sections, as well as guidelines for handling them.

But before getting to the articles themselves I'd like to explore further why people problems are so perplexing and so difficult to recognize and resolve. Six reasons come to mind:

1. *Much of what is problematic is hidden and subtle.* In his article "The Abrasive Personality," Harry Levinson describes a character, Darrel Sandstrom, who is so aggressive and domineering that although he achieves

considerable success in terms of his department's performance, he alienates everyone around him. It would not be difficult for Darrel's supervisor to see that this employee is a problem. But what if Darrel were not so aggressive and instead undermined his subordinates by subtly sabotaging their efforts?

Many women and blacks report that the toughest part of work for them is dealing with the subtle and covert discrimination or harassment that other employees level at them during the workday. Women who responded to the survey *HBR* sent out to its readers in 1981, described in "Sexual Harassment . . . Some See It . . . Some Won't," reported that although gross forms of harassment, such as direct propositions from supervisors with threats of retaliation unless the victim went along, were gruesome and upsetting, the more indirect and covert forms of harassment were more difficult to deal with.

When a woman walks into her office and finds a prophylactic filled with water on her desk or hears her boss make insinuating comments about her to a colleague, she has few ways at the time to act in her own behalf. Many women surveyed commented that because they could not find an appropriate outlet for the fury and rage that harassment aroused in them, they ended up taking the rage out on themselves. Typically, turning the rage inward, these women felt dirty, sullied, and in some ineffable way to blame for what had happened. If they could see themselves to blame they at least retained control over the situation. Maybe it was something they could fix.

Similarly, blacks and other minorities who suffer subtle forms of harassment turn inward and see themselves in the light that their aggressors cast them in. In his penetrating analysis of a conflict between a supervisor and a worker set out in "The Administrator's Skill: Communication," F. J. Roethlisberger comments that a supervisor's perceptions of an employee will in turn lead the employee to behave in the way that will coincide more and more with the supervisor's original untested assumption. So women may see themselves as dirty and sexual objects, and blacks may see themselves as unworthy and underclass.

Subtlety is not confined to relationships between minorities and their coworkers. Other relationships equally damaging to the organization can be covertly corrosive. In "Managers Can Drive Their Subordinates Mad," Manfred F. R. Kets de Vries described a phenomenon known as *folie à deux* whereby the fixation and obsession of a boss can become a shared obsession between the boss and his or her subordinates. In such cases a suspicious boss slowly and inexorably convinces his subordinates that others in the organization are acting aggressively against him and his department. Kets de Vries cites J. Edgar Hoover as a well-known example of a boss influencing totally the views and objectivity of his subordinates.

The reason this behavior is so difficult to recognize is that what the boss fears could be partly true. When obsession nearly describes reality, it is very difficult for subordinates or outsiders to distinguish between the two. Understandably, subordinates in beleaguered, defensive departments would find it nearly impossible not to see the situation in the light that the boss casts.

A manager confronted with hidden problems like those I've just described would have difficulty resolving them even though it would appear that someone is not performing up to par or that all the senior people in a department are acting aggressively. The true problem is not what the manager sees.

2. *People are masters at covering up their problems; they've been doing it for years.* When people are under stress they tend to resist changing their behavior to adapt to the pressure-filled situation. All of us have patterns of behavior that we've developed over the years that help us deal with the pains and anxieties of our lives at work and at home. The problem is that when a situation worsens and the anxieties push us to the breaking point, we tend to avoid corrective action and resort to the behavior that has stood us well in the past. When the problem is working too much and too hard, for instance, rather than work less, people tend to work even harder and have even less time to relax. When isolation has been their traditional way of fending off fears, rather than seek others out when they feel anxiety, people tend to close themselves off even more.

Two articles by Harry Levinson in this collection, "What Killed Bob Lyons?" and "When Executives Burn Out," illustrate how people continue acting in a programmed way until, in some cases, it is too late to rescue them. Bob Lyons is an extreme example but his case illustrates how people can cover up their problems with behavior that exacerbates it and makes it difficult for managers to intervene.

Bob Lyons was a dedicated manager who thrived on hard work. Working fulfilled his self-image. When given a task he'd rush to complete it with gusto. When he *didn't* have a project that drove him nearly to exhaustion, he was depressed. Ultimately, when he had his department operating smoothly and the number of fires to damp decreased, Bob Lyons slipped into depression and committed suicide. Clearly, the problem of self-esteem was there all along, but his feverish working not only masked his pain to himself but also made it difficult for others to see. By the time it was only too obvious that Bob Lyons was in trouble, it was too late.

None of the articles in this series directly addresses the problems of alcoholic or drug-abusing employees, but these people are also classically adept at disguising their troubles until they are in serious jeopardy of losing their jobs. Alcohol and drugs seem to relieve anxiety. Comprehending the threat to their jobs that their drug abuse poses, employees find it nearly impossible to stop. Instead, they may increase their dependence and find more elaborate excuses for sloppy or unsatisfactory behavior at work.

3. *Managers face organizational taboos against interfering in a subordinate's or peer's private life.* Once upon a time organizational life was much simpler than it is today. In the good old days the people in the executive

suite were, for all intents and purposes, white males. They were married and had three kids and two cars. If the organization asked them to relocate, they packed up the wife and the kids in the two cars and they moved, often within weeks of receiving the request. Divorce was less common than it is today, and even if an executive had marital problems, he was expected to take care of them on his own time.

The understanding was that executives at the top, men in control of vast organizational resources, would control their personal lives and feelings with the same skill and adeptness that they did their jobs. If a manager had marital problems he didn't talk about them at work and he certainly didn't let anyone know he was seeking professional help for any emotional troubles. In this kind of atmosphere, it's not surprising that managers were hesitant to discuss how they felt and even more reluctant to approach a colleague who acted as if he might be in some personal pain. The gesture would be seen as aggressive, not helpful.

Employees not at the top punched time clocks. When they were at work, during the prescribed hours, they were the organization's responsibility, but this covered only the context and the processes surrounding their jobs. Once they punched out, they were on their own. If their personal problems caused trouble at work, they could be let go. Organizations did address some personal problems, of course, but there were unmessy quantifiable problems, ones that employee benefit programs could cover.

Today things are different. For one thing, the demographics of the workplace have changed, causing some problems that used to be left at home to crash through the executive suite door in the form of women and minorities. Also, economic realities have created a world in which the patient wife now has her own position in the work force. She may not be ready to move at the tip of her husband's company's hat.

Moreover, although many people in organizations still are reluctant to let their colleagues know that they are seeing a psychologist, in general people are far more sophisticated about psychological issues and even some chief executive officers (CEOs) have written about their personal troubles. In one of the articles in this collection, "Don't Call It 'Early Retirement,'" both Wheelock Whitney, ex-CEO of Dain, Kalman & Quail in Minneapolis, and William G. Damroth, ex-CEO of Lexington Research and Management Corporation, talk candidly about suffering painful anxieties during their lives. And in "Three Vice Presidents in Mid-Life" by Stanley M. Davis and Roger L. Gould, one of the executives admits to having collapsed at the office from nervous strain.

Despite these changes, the tradition remains strong that executives should not interfere in each other's or their subordinates' personal lives. Part of this taboo is based on good sense; it protects the employee from unwanted interference and coercion. But when it comes to dealing with problems that an executive should be concerned with, the taboo and handy rationalizing shibboleths—"don't rock the boat," "you can't teach an old dog new tricks," "it's not a manager's job to be a psychiatrist"—are no longer functional.

One article in this collection, "Managers and Lovers," is about what happens in an organization when a top man and a senior woman fall in love. In the old days the woman could be gotten rid of and the problem would have been solved. However, today that solution won't work and, because of the potential conflict of interest the affair might create, the executive supervisor of the pair has to become involved.

The taboo can be dangerous, too, when it inhibits managers from acting even when they feel deep concern for a fellow employee or for their boss. Some months after *HBR* published "On Executive Suicide," by Harry Levinson, we received a letter from an executive who, upon reading the article, had decided to alert his superiors that one of his colleagues might be in serious personal difficulty. The *HBR* reader had felt there was no one in the organization with whom he could raise the issue, and needed outside encouragement—a journal article suggesting it was okay to do so—in order to act.

4. *The organization itself creates some of the problems so unless it is changed the problem will stay.*   If a manager, having diagnosed a personal problem, acts responsibly on it, he or she has every reason to expect that the problem should clear up. This may happen, but then again it may not. Some problems are clearly personal—the employee who drinks too much, the abrasive supervisor—and can be dealt with on a person-to-person level, and the immediate problem may go away. But the window of opportunity is still wide open unless executives recognize that the organization, its structure, and its processes may cause the conditions in which the problem will rise again.

Look at the new executive in the Dashman Company case, for instance, which Edmund P. Learned describes in "Problems of a New Executive." Mr. Post, the new purchasing head at Dashman, was given the job of coordinating all purchasing functions throughout the company. To accomplish this, Post sent a letter informing all purchasing agents at the various plants that any order over a certain size would have to be cleared through his office at headquarters. Post waited, but he received no mail. Looking at the case, we can see lots of things that Post did wrong. His letter was curt and peremptory; he didn't bother to make personal calls on the purchasing agents so he had no knowledge of them or they of him; and his behavior was alienating and uninspiring to his subordinates in the field.

True, Post could stand some training in human relations skills and if we investigated further we might find that he has indeed a problem getting close to other employees and prefers communicating at a distance. But is Post the only problem? As Learned points out in the article, the organization is also partly to blame. A position of power seems to grant power and many organizations reward the position even before they know how it will be filled.

Positions often have reserved parking places and corner offices that go along with them. And a high position seems to endorse or encourage an authoritarian style when it may not be appropriate. For all we know, Post may have been dying to go out and see his men in the trenches but didn't think it correct for someone in his position to do so.

Problems that require an organizational adjustment to remedy them may occur at the top of the organization as well. When top executives are locked in mortal combat, Alonzo McDonald observes in "Conflict at the Summit: A Deadly Game," structural solutions won't work to overcome the personal ambition of executives. It's almost impossible to move an executive vice president of marketing to another position in the company. But unless a top manager institutes some changes, such as creating management teams or multiple CEO roles, the conflict that occurs between people who have real power and influence based on their expert knowledge may continue to rage to the organization's disadvantage.

Other positions in the organization also cause their incumbents to behave in ways that are alienating and offensive to others. In "Power Failure in Management Circuits," Rosabeth Moss Kanter describes how CEOs, staff members, and first-line supervisors are in vulnerable positions because they lack resources, information, and lines of support to get their jobs done.

The organizational hierarchy itself exacerbates problems or at least prohibits their gaining attention. Because of the long reporting chain a piece of information has to go through before it reaches the top, senior management is generally isolated from many of the problems that plague employees. In the *HBR* survey of readers' views on sexual harassment, we asked them if they thought "the amount of sexual harassment at work is greatly exaggerated." Sixty-three percent of top management agreed or partly agreed with that statement while only 44 percent of lower management agreed. Top managers were also likely to take less serious stances toward harassers. It makes sense. If they don't perceive the problem and thus don't see it as serious, then the solution need not be either.

Top managers probably don't see the subtle discrimination aimed at blacks and other minorities nor do they feel the extreme stress that their subordinates might be under. Although they may have felt the stress on their rise to the top, like the pain of childbirth it is better forgotten. And, as "How Much Stress Is Too Much?" shows, although many of the CEOs interviewed by Herbert Benson and Robert L. Allen claimed to understand the debilitating effects of stress, they hadn't taken much action to correct the conditions that caused it.

Finally, as Abraham Zaleznik writes in "The Dynamics of Subordinacy," the organization hierarchy replicates the family structure we all grew up with, where as children we were the subordinates and our parents were the bosses. No matter how mature we are or how much in tune with our innermost fantasies and feelings, we can never completely get over our dependence on superiors or our resentment at that dependence. As long as someone sits at the top of an organization, someone at the bottom is going to dislike it. That dislike may be displayed in subtle acts of aggression against the organization such as absenteeism or malingering or it may be more openly and severely expressed, such as in political moves to displace the boss. It will be there, regardless, in one form or another, as long as organizations retain their classic pyramid shape. In the interview "It's Not Lonely Upstairs," Renn Zaphiropoulos makes it plain that eliminating the pyramid removes many of the organizational and emotional factors that isolate top managers from their people.

5. *Certain patterns of thinking and feeling make it difficult for people both to recognize sticky personal problems and to confront them directly.* Some truths about people are inescapable. Although some of us are better at it than others, in general, we all find it difficult to confront people when their behavior displeases us; we find it painful to live with ambiguity and tend to take extreme positions; and we often interpret a situation to ourselves in an inappropriate context. Let's look at these patterns in turn.

One of the things that makes it difficult to deal with personal problems is that we are afraid of the outcome of the confrontation. If we were all convinced, for instance, that if we went to a colleague who was giving us difficulty at work and told him or her how we felt when he or she acted a certain way, the behavior would change and we'd all live happily ever after, we'd probably do it. But most of us are aware of our own defensive natures and assume that other people would be equally defensive. We see ourselves as less important than we are and seeing ourselves that way, assume that the other person doesn't think highly enough of us to do the hard work of changing. So we retreat, throw up our hands, and try to manage around the person's behavior.

This situation obviously isn't the case when the person doing the confronting is the boss (how can others mistake his importance?), but even bosses have difficulty telling others just how alienating their behavior is. One of the reasons for this, is as Fernando Bartolomé points out in "The Work Alibi: When It's Harder to Go Home," that we focus on the negative consequences of being candid. Bartolomé also points out that people fear rejection: "Not that their love will be spurned but that they will not be loved in return. In truth fear of rejection is that the other will not give us what we need or want." When a boss intervenes, what he or she fears is loss of respect rather than love. For if any axiom holds true for all people it is that we want to be loved and respected. Confrontation can threaten our own perceived sources of love and esteem.

Another reason confrontation is difficult is that we tend to fly to extreme opinions when we are under stress. In his article, "Case of the Borderline Black," Theodore V. Purcell describes a manager trying to decide in a tight budgeting situation whether to let go a black employee whose work was below par or to retain him because he is black and the company has EEO goals to meet. The manager in Purcell's case recognized that it was not an either/or situation and that somehow he had to find a way to accommodate the needs for both performance and EEO.

But Robert Schrank points out in "Two Women, Three Men on a Raft" that even a liberated and nonchauvinist man like himself, when in a perilous situation, readily adopted timeworn views of what women are capable of doing and how they should be treated. In a trip down the Rogue River he and his fellow male companions ended up actually sabotaging the leadership of the women on the expedition because of outmoded male views of female capability.

Because managers facing human problems see them as stressful—and because in times of stress executives respond by taking extreme positions—they tend not to muddle around the middle which is where the solution and the place to communicate about the struggle will be found.

Also, because we don't, generally, have much sophistication about human problems of others or ourselves, when we find ourselves in a tricky emotional situation we tend to both devalue the situation and to interpret it in another context. Stanley M. Davis and Roger L. Gould give a good example of how this can happen in their article "Three Vice Presidents in Mid-Life." They show how one middle-aged manager who clearly is not happy at home and finds work an escape from his unfulfilling private life is plagued with anxiety that he doesn't want to deal with. In not seeing the true nature of his discontent and simply accepting his unhappy personal life as his lot, the executive does not take his own pain seriously.

Another executive in Davis and Gould's study spent two painful years in a job he hated but which he, nonetheless, ploughed through in misery. What he didn't realize at the time was that his mid-life transition turned into a crisis because of the job he hated. He attributed his miserable state to his job and did not recognize the personal nature of his experience. He saw his unhappiness in the context of work, something that he should be able to handle. This executive (the man who I said earlier was candid about his personal problems) saw the truth when he had a nervous breakdown.

6. *The manager himself might be part of the problem.* None of us is completely free of prejudice. We all have values that we hold dear, and understandably, we prefer to see ourselves in the best possible light. It is hard, therefore, for us at times to put our own values, opinions, and self-images aside and see a situation as it truly is. Only when we can do that, however, can we effectively manage some of the perplexing human conflicts that arise at work.

In the previously mentioned "Managers and Lovers," for instance, an illustration is given of a manager confronted with a couple at work who is having an affair. This manager's wife had very strong opinions about extra-marital affairs and he himself was a strict moralist. Because of his values he had difficulty taking an objective position in regard to a situation that called for his action in the company's best interests. What might have suited him personally, namely to get rid of the problem, would not have been the best response for either the two senior managers or, ultimately, for the company. Had he got rid of one partner or simply ignored the issue because it was distasteful to him, the conflict the love affair caused would not have been ironed out and the wound would have lasted.

Edward W. Jones, Jr., in "What It's Like to Be a Black Manager," writes that one of the most troublesome obstacles managers have in dealing with blacks at work is their need to see themselves as good and fair. He asserts that managers are "more guilty of naiveté than bigotry. They could not recognize prejudice, since it would be a blow to their self-images. And this condition is prevalent in the U.S. Industry."

In Kets de Vries' article, "Managers Can Drive Their Subordinates Mad," a boss destructively pulls his subordinates into a web of suspicion and fear. Also, as I noted, in Robert Schrank's revealing piece on the Rogue River trip, we can see how men needing to be in control of a situation in which women are involved can unconsciously but, nonetheless, purposefully undermine the women's efforts to succeed.

Finally, in his article, "The Administrator's Skill: Communication," F. J. Roethlisberger shows how Harry, the supervisor, makes many mistakes in judging his subordinates' behavior. He shows how Harry makes value judgments about Bing, how he doesn't listen to what Bing says, how he assumes things that are not so, and how (which I discussed before in the context of why problems are difficult to detect) he makes his false assumptions about Bing become a reality by treating him as if they were true. All men and women, whether white or black, respond as they are treated. And if they are treated as intelligent, caring, productive employees they will, the exception proving the rule, respond in kind.

Roethlisberger discusses what Harry might do to overcome his problem. He must do what is hardest for us all and what lies at the heart of many of the conflicts in which the characters selected in these articles are involved. Managers need to accept that their feelings of inadequacy are perfectly natural and normal. We are all flawed and need to accept ourselves as such. When we can do that, we neither project our own inadequacies onto others nor demand that others be perfect. We can judge others with the human concern and respect that we all deserve.

WHEN THE JOB IS THE PROBLEM

AN OVERVIEW

The articles in this section describe those organizational situations where a person may act inappropriately but where the cause of the behavior is the job itself, not the person's personality. Of course, just because the environment strongly affects behavior it does not mean that an employee's personality is not involved to some extent. But all things being equal, and assuming a normal amount of individual peculiarities, some jobs seem to give people trouble and cause their incumbents to show their worst colors.

For instance, Alonzo McDonald writes in "Conflict at the Summit: A Deadly Game," that the pressures of top executive positions can lead managers in those offices to engage in "a continuing stream of major and minor conflicts within the power circle." McDonald concedes that all power is not destructive but points out that conflict which is positive is between ideas, not personalities. When the group in the executive suite hits a critical mass of five or six individuals, outbreaks occur because of differences in attitude toward risk and change, and because of different degrees of personal ambition. At this level of the company, it won't work for the CEO to make structural changes; few would be appropriate. Instead he or she will have to experiment with some of the decision-making approaches that McDonald suggests. Ultimately, however, McDonald contends that the image of the power-hungry executive is so alienating to young people entering business and so destructive to the organization, that businesspeople themselves, acting in their own best interests and in the interests of the company, are going to have to act less selfishly.

One of the problems that executives in high positions have is that they act according to how they perceive they should because of the job. For instance, in "Problems of a New Executive," Edmund P. Learned observes that a high position seems to endorse an authoritarian style. Although Learned is not an advocate of "participative management at all cost," he notes that even though some situations may not be suited to participation "others—including the most challenging ones—require it." The problem for executives, then, is to set aside the power-giving aspects of the job and determine which leadership style the task requires. The project, not the position of the person in charge of it, should dictate the approach.

Rosabeth Moss Kanter, in her article, "Power Failure in Management Circuits," describes three jobs in which the incumbent is particularly prone to act in power-hungry ways. Whereas McDonald asserts that people grasp power because the organization encourages it, Kanter asserts that they act that way often because they lack effective authority.

The three types of managers she describes, chief executive officers, high-level staff people, and first-line supervisors, are all often shortchanged when it comes to the requisite lines of support, information, and resources to get their jobs done. Lacking legitimate ways to effect change, people in these roles often resort to manipulation, rules-mindedness, and overcontrolling behavior that others find extremely difficult to bear. Kanter urges top managers, when they sense a powerlessness in the organization, to expand power by sharing it and to open up new avenues of information and support so that isolated employees become more productive and powerful.

One of the most distressing problems a position can cause its holder is burn-out. Harry Levinson describes a number of cases in "When Executives Burn Out" that are due to unrelenting job stress. Burn-out occurs most often to people in jobs that require a lot of contact with other people under conditions of stress. This happens to nurses, mental health workers, and policemen, but it also happens to company employees who always are working in situations that are repetitive and prolonged, engender burdens, promise great success but don't give it, expose managers to attack, and raise deep emotions. Managers of people in these situations need to be alert to the inherent stress of the jobs involved and should consider structural changes. For instance, top managers should not allow their employees to work 18 hours a day, or keep the same people in hot spots time after time. When someone is particularly good at handling a tough situation, the manager should not reward this employee by putting him or her in another difficult job.

One employee who might feel the kind of stress Levinson outlines is a foreman. In his article "The Foreman: Master and Victim of Double Talk," F. J. Roethlisberger describes how the social environment impoverishes the work life of a foreman at the same time that the company expects him or her to deliver the goods. In this "separated" existence, the foreman acts one of three ways: he or she becomes aggressive, obsessive, or seeks a political solution. Roethlisberger puts the foreman's problems squarely at the feet of management. He asserts that only when managers "learn to be responsible for people not merely responsible for abstract and logical categories'' will foremen and other employees in a structural squeeze begin to feel the approval they need to do their jobs well.

Subordinates, whether they be foremen or managers, share some problems by dint of their working for another person. Eric H. Neilsen and Jan Gypen in ''The Subordinate's Predicaments'' assert that all subordinates feel self-protective. They maintain that this behavior is a natural consequence of hierarchy. Abraham Zaleznik, in ''The Dynamics of Subordinacy,'' also holds that the hierarchy brings forth ''a constellation of motives, wishes, and tensions within the individual.'' Neilsen and Gypen look at the subordinate's role in light of the development stages which Erik Erikson holds people go through in attaining individual maturity, and Zaleznik looks at the conflicts the role creates between the wish on the part of the subordinate to control the authority figure and the equally strong wish to be dominated.

While managers cannot function as psychologists for their employees, they can try to create an organizational environment that reduces the employee's need to be self-protective. They can also try to help the employee see the distinctions between the issues that confront him and the conflicts of personal development.

1

Conflict at the Summit

A Deadly Game

ALONZO McDONALD

Intensive conflict at the top-management level of a company is not merely the business of the participants. Just as there is nothing more dramatic than a struggle at the summit, there is no more dangerous or destructive form of organizational disease. Until management is motivated to accept a new code of ethics and conduct for men in the executive suite, this author says, the disease of destructive conflict at the top cannot be cured. His prescription includes comprehensive criteria for executive selection to reduce the likelihood of such conflict.

Napoleon knew how to organize. He forged the Army of France into a precise and superbly coordinated instrument of conquest. He centralized governmental administration and gave it a new orderliness that has shaped French public institutions to this day. In the face of the formidable challenge of reorganizing a nation's social institutions—its educational systems, its hospitals, and its veterans' services—his genius was a match for his audacity; the structures he designed were as sound as they were advanced for their time.

But one organizational worry baffled Napoleon: the egotism of the marshals who commanded his armies. "They owe their appointments and all their honors to me," he agonized in 1813 as the Prussians stood at the gates of Paris. "But how can one organize the marshals of France?"

In the century and a half since then we have not made enough progress on this organizational level to advise him confidently. Leaders are still con-

---

Published in 1972.

sumed with the problem of how to organize the summit. Inevitably, it is the first topic that a newly appointed chief executive officer (CEO) wants to discuss with his or her most trusted counselors and confidants. Although he or she may calmly devote public moments to substantive business issues, his or her private thoughts are centered on how to organize, deploy, and productively utilize the industrial marshals.

Moreover, the CEO knows that the company's record and his or her personal reputation as a leader will largely be formed by his or her decisions and actions vis-à-vis this group. It is known that conflicts among its members are inevitable—conflicts that may range from open clashes over substantive issues to deadly undeclared wars of personal ambition. And he or she knows that failure to manage and control such conflict can fatally handicap programs and imperil the fortunes of the company.

Each of the people closest to the power center know full well that their own career and opportunities are at stake. Below and beyond the corporate summit, alert middle managers, major stockholders, and union leaders are listening for every hint or comment that filters down; and they are watching every action taken by the leadership that could give a clue as to how the drama inside the executive suite is unfolding.

They have good reason to be concerned. Their own fortunes may hang on the outcome; and so, less directly perhaps, may the future of a multitude of others too far from the power center to sense that anything could be amiss. In short, the stakes are higher than the progress of individual executives toward self-actualization, as described by behavioral science. The vital interests of thousands can all too easily be sacrificed to the self-fulfillment of a few.

Intensive conflict at the top is not merely the business of the participants. Just as there is nothing more dramatic than a struggle at the summit (hence our fascination with historical and fictional accounts of such conflicts), there is no game more deadly or organizational disease more destructive.

If the power center at the top is in chaos, what hope has the rest of the corporation for constructive action? Business cannot go on as usual. Limp, anxious, and vulnerable, the organization is unable to react effectively to new threats. As the contagion spreads, even distant departments are soon infected with pettiness, personal rivalries linked to different leaders, and arbitrary rulings of little logic or importance. Esprit de corps and organizational cohesion evaporate. Good people in the middle ranks begin to drift away in disillusion.

The work force in the plant community, whose destiny is often more closely linked with that of the company than they individually would like to admit, can only hope for enough momentum down the line to keep the business going until the crisis is past. Even after the conflict is resolved, the corporate body will still be feverish and weakened by its ordeal. It may take months or years to get back in shape for a tough external fight. Some of its wounds may heal only with the passing of a generation of management, and even then they may leave ugly scars.

Why, in view of its crucial importance, has the organizational problem at the top so stubbornly eluded solution? Perhaps because it looks so simple. Only a few people—usually between five and ten, rarely more than twenty—are directly involved. To people accustomed to organizing and managing thousands, the task seems elementary. But when a person actually shoulders the chief executive responsibility, his or her perspective suddenly shifts. The problem takes on a strange new dimension: it is one of the few that can be intellectually grasped in its full detail; yet he or she cannot seem to get a grip on it for more than a fleeting moment.

Some may say that this is only a question of leadership. In an earlier, less complicated age, they might have been right. But today, with the nature of leadership itself at issue, that answer begs the question. None of the "styles" associated with familiar leadership roles—Max Weber's authoritarian source of directives, Carl Rogers' "facilitator" smoothing the way, or Chris Argyris' melder of corporate and individual goals—really addresses the chief executive's dilemma.

Organizing and leading "the marshals" is indeed a special problem, different in significant ways from the problems of conflict down the line. That is why answers will not be found by studying small-group dynamics on the shop floor. Only by focusing on the small power center at the summit are we likely to perceive the outlines of a solution.

Accordingly, this article first examines the characteristics and motivations of the men and women in the executive suite. Next, it outlines four approaches to management of the summit, noting some important attitudinal differences in their application in the United States and Europe, and showing why no one of them in itself has provided a satisfactory solution to the problem of destructive conflict at the top. Finally, it reasserts management's responsibility to those below, proposes a sense of mission beyond personal gain, and suggests some criteria for executive selection to reduce the likelihood of such conflict.

Inside the Executive Suite

Despite its lure for ambitious people on the way up and the impression of hushed and opulent tranquillity given to subordinates, outsiders, and visitors for lunch, the executive suite is a busy place occupied by anxious, often frustrated men. True, they have the satisfaction of wielding great power. But the pressures, threats, and uncertainties to which they are subjected are part of the price they pay for that satisfaction.

Consider the complex responsibilities of the top-management group today. In the simplest of terms, their job is to guide the corporate organism toward the accomplishment of a complex of elusive objectives that bear little resemblance to the simple performance targets on the shop floor. To move in balance toward these objectives, they must instill enough coherence in their human following to maneuver it successfully past a series of material and third-party constraints, while they are being buffeted by changing external forces. These multiple pressures, bearing in on top management from all sides, can hardly help but generate a continuing stream of major and minor conflicts within the power circle.

Fortunately, all conflict is not destructive; indeed, it can sometimes be more productive than harmony. Properly handled, it can bring forth imaginative alternatives for accomplishing constructive tasks. But conflict is most likely to be productive when it occurs on the substantive level—in the realm of ideas, interpretations, judgments, and action approaches. Here it is broadening and, up to a point, useful. But it can easily degenerate from constructive dialectic into a clash of personalities kindled and fed by competing personal ambitions.

The problems confronting the top-executive group of a company cannot be resolved by manipulating physical or structural mechanisms. At the summit there is only what Harold Leavitt has called the "people valve" to turn in trying to move the organization along.[1] At this point, then, we come face-to-face with the interpersonal relationships and motivations of the men inside the executive suite—their different perspectives, temperaments, working habits and reactions, and personal ambitions.

Three Basic Types

To oversimplify, inside the executive suite we find a handful of strong *leaders*, a few *followers*, and a lot of *neutralists*.

The *leaders* are typically capable, enthusiastic, and highly motivated. They seek power, willingly take risks, and need recognition and applause. In consequence, their motives may often be misunderstood.

It is easy, when observing a highly talented individual who is aggressively achievement-oriented, to mistake an intense sense of mission for political ambition, and to mistake resolution for ruthlessness. Genuine progress entails change, and change is frequently a threat to those in established seats of influence. Hence it is natural for the threatened to question, at least privately, the motives of the aggressor.

In reality, his or her sense of mission may totally outweigh the motivation of personal gain—and then again, it may not. This contributes to another uncertainty that may confuse and delay the chief operating officer in his efforts to unravel the skein of conflict and achieve a constructive resolution.

The *followers* at the top-executive level, although usually quite capable, are far less aggressive than the leaders. The follower wants to see himself as a superb "number two" who is respected by all and revered by many in subordinate ranks. Followers tend to be more conservative, standing back until the lead becomes reasonably visible and the risks have been assumed by the group.

In between are the *neutralists*, who fall into two distinct types. Neutralists of the first type—thoughtful, objective, and open-minded—are invaluable to large, technology-based companies operating in an unstable environment. The second type of neutralist—the politician—resembles the objective neutralist superficially, but his motivation is very different. This individual's whole policy is to remain uncommitted except in situations that he can exploit for personal gain. General de Gaulle, frustrated at the repeated personal maneuverings of some cabinet members and their supporters, referred disgustedly to this type as *"les politichiens."*[2]

Interpersonal Relationships. As soon as the group in the executive suite exceeds five or six, differences in time perspectives and urgency begin to show up. Some executives are on their way up, others at the peak of their careers, and the remainder on their way down. Individual attitudes toward risk and needs for achievement tend to differ with stages in the career cycle.

Members of the top-management group take differing views of change and its associated uncertainties, tending to see one stage more clearly than others. Some remain preoccupied with past experience and practices. Others are absorbed by today's operating habits. And one or two, if the company is lucky, concentrate on modeling the future and finding ways to move the organization more expeditiously in that direction. For them, current corporate practices and strategies always fall short of the demands of the future.

Although the reactions of individuals may show consistent patterns, group responses to an issue vary rapidly and unpredictably over time. At a given moment they resemble the results from a computer simulation model when the variables, each with its individual frequency distribution of probabilities, are stopped at some random instant. One can only speculate as to what combination of reactions would have resulted had the simulation been stopped at another point in time. This is why many executives devote so much time and energy to premeeting briefings aimed at minimizing open conflict when critical decisions are on the agenda.

Violent conflicts are not confined to major issues. They may even be more likely to occur over minor decisions. There is the phenomenon of preoccupation with familiar things and reluctance to deal with difficult new subjects. The minutes to directors' meetings and executive committee sessions are replete with records of long and heated debates over the relocation of executive washrooms or the choice of a color scheme for the reception area, side by side with decisions reached in minutes to approve multi-million-dollar computer installations.

Personal Ambitions. Most of the influences on interpersonal relationships just discussed lend themselves to logical, reasoned resolution. But where personal ambition dominates the motivation of the men and women in the executive suite, individual positions on critical issues can easily become polarized beyond hope of resolution. I shall cite two examples to illustrate this point:

☐ As a frequent discussion partner with members of a management team in a technology-based processing industry, I have watched an intensive conflict building up over the past 18 months. A personal power struggle between two senior executives has sapped most of the innovative strengths and structural effectiveness from the rest of the organization.

One principal in the struggle, a technician in his early forties who joined the company three years ago as president but not CEO, is a thoughtful, knowledgeable man whose managerial achievements and previous technical contributions ideally qualified him for his high post.

His adversary, also a newcomer but in his fifties, heads a major subsidiary absorbed into the group about a year after the young president's arrival. This division head, who was the chief executive of his company before the acquisition, is dynamic, forceful, and very much in personal command of his operations. His leadership style, and the factors that contributed to his personal success, are very dissimilar from those of the president. In view of his age, moreover, the division head must move quickly to put himself next in line for the chief executive post while it is still an attainable career objective.

But consider the dilemma of the present CEO. He recognizes the diverse talents of his two subordinates and hopes to save both for important future contributions to the group. At the same time, he must keep the organization moving ahead. So he works diligently, but with little hope, as a mediator. If he can patch things up, that would be the optimum solution for the company.

More dramatic solutions, such as replacing one of the two, would be costly and time consuming. Even if he knew where to find within his own organization, or outside it, a comparable combination of technical and business talents, a solution would not be assured. With two other men, or a replacement for one, the same problem could easily arise again shortly thereafter. So he bids for time as he struggles to reconcile the adversaries, consoling himself with the thought, "Better the devil you know than the devil you don't."

☐ In another company, I observed not long ago an equally damaging situation. To maintain a unified command and to avoid possible conflict, the new CEO decided to retain for himself, at least temporarily, the chairmanship of a major subsidiary. To his subsequent dismay, this seemingly logical decision transformed one of his most capable subordinates into a subtle adversary.

From the cooperative and reasonable collaborator of a few weeks earlier, the disappointed subordinate has turned into an archskeptic, using an arsenal of technical arguments relating to his own sphere of interest to slow up group decisions and prolong controversies among his colleagues. Yet his reputation, influence, following, and technical knowledge are all such that his opinions and reservations carry considerable weight. But he is walking a fine line, and there are naturally some suspicions about his motivations.

The CEO has watched the change coming about in his subordinate's attitude, but the case is not clear enough for him to move. There is just the chance that Mr. Number Two, with his experience and his long-standing reputation for good judgment, might be right on the given issue. There is also the fact that Mr. Two has a big following at the second and third levels of management. If the CEO should move too hastily to accuse a trusted senior executive of obstructing corporate aims because of frustrated personal ambitions, there could even be adverse director and stockholder reactions.

As these two illustrations suggest, the problems of resolving intensive conflict based on personal ambitions are uniquely difficult to control, and—since they continue over long periods—uniquely debilitating to the organization. Regardless of how they are resolved, the company is the loser; a struggle of personal ambitions yields none of the potential gain that can flow from a constructive confrontation of new ideas and approaches.

Organizing the Top

Of course, the problem of personal conflict at the top will never be totally eradicated as long as men and women relish the pursuit of power. So rather than seeking to eliminate conflict, we need to control and contain it, and to prevent excesses that can endanger the fortunes of the organization and of all those with a claim on it—employees and dependents, shareholders, customers, and others.

It is easy to say that the CEO can curb such conflict by setting a compelling moral example for his or her subordinates. Unfortunately, many CEOs who sincerely see themselves in the role of moral leaders are perceived by others as confirmed and passionate addicts of power. Moreover, even if the moral example is accepted, this prescription begs the issue of who gets to be chief executive, and how. Among adversaries otherwise equally matched, the odds too often favor the least scrupulous.

So we are left with two possible remedies: either raising the moral criteria for admission to the executive suite, or structuring the relationships within the top-management group to reduce the likelihood of destructive conflict at the summit.

At first glance, raising moral standards may seem too utopian. Instead, pushing the ''organization'' button is the normal management reflex. But at the top-management level this does not work very well. Formal organization per se provides no reliable means of averting or resolving destructive conflict; moreover, efforts to organize the top have at best been only partially successful. The fact is that top management does not want to be organized; and when it is organized in any company, it does not stay that way for long.

Formal Patterns

Nevertheless, the working relationships of top management have a definite bearing on the nature and intensity of conflicts within the group. And since the evolution of these patterns shows considerable similarity from company to company, they are worth examining for their conflict-limiting potential before considering a more fundamental approach to the problem.

The four broad patterns of working relationships most frequently seen at the summit are:

1 The absolute ruler with his court.
2 The line/staff division of responsibilities.
3 The multiple chief executive with no personalized final authority.
4 The management team with a primus inter pares who acts when necessary as the ultimate arbiter.

Only a few organizations ever evolve through all four of these working relationship patterns (see Exhibit 1); but, in my observation, this is the sequence in which any two or three of these options are most likely to be tried in a given company.

Either of the first two structures can be well adapted to an authoritarian style of leadership. Both clearly lodge the final responsibility for selecting appropriate corporate goals and strategies in a single leader. Such CEO will typically rely heavily on discipline to secure reasonable conformity with his or her ideas and to control conflicts. If necessary, the CEO will knock heads together.

The other two approaches can be seen as varieties of the "T" or participative organization described by Lawrence E. Fouraker.[3] Both the multiple chief executive and the team structure endow their members with a large measure of independence and a relatively high degree of overall responsibility for the total enterprise. In both of the latter forms, intensive conflicts are harder to control and when deep and persistent can prove totally debilitating.

Absolute Ruler.   The authoritarian pattern, once dominant in a less enlightened business era, is still alive and thriving in a sizable minority of organizations: smaller companies, family enterprises, long-established but only recently diversified European companies, and divisions of U.S. companies. In this structure, the members of the management group are predominantly concerned with problems and tasks the boss has assigned. Their job is to help him or her, and their primary responsibility is to the man or woman above rather than to the organization below. Lateral communications between top managers tend to be minimal; the channels converge, and confrontations are controlled at the top.

Somewhat liberalized versions of this authoritarian approach tend to rely more on strong personal loyalties than on discipline to contain conflict.

Exhibit 1.

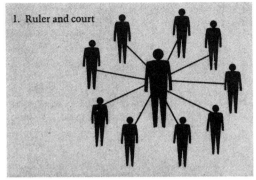

1. Ruler and court

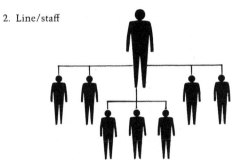

2. Line/staff

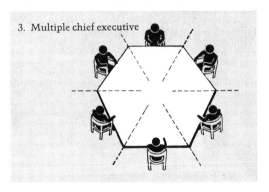

3. Multiple chief executive

4. Management team

This approach is common in U.S. companies, particularly after a change of personalities at the top is followed by a series of new appointments to key posts. The appointees are almost always persons whose loyalty as personal friends and former subordinates is intended to minimize conflict by assuring allegiance to the leader's ideas.

But even this tactic, as Napoleon well knew, offers no lasting solution. To the degree that it does work, imaginative ideas and diversity of opinion are subdued and the potential of valuable individual contributions reduced. The shortcomings that Fouraker has ascribed to the "L" organization—limited vision and sequenced treatment of problems—remain in any case.

Line/Staff. This approach is a favored pattern after the demise without heirs of an absolute ruler; in fact, its value is greatest when a quasivoid exists at the top. If the people moving into the power center have limited experience in overall management, they welcome detailed charters of responsibilities and clear maps of the domains over which they will have to exert leadership.

While everyone is concerned with mastering new responsibilities, the line/staff form usually works well. Those at the top find it exciting to have an important hand in events, and those down below think they know who is in charge. But line/staff delineations, useful as they can be down the line, soon begin to crumble at the summit. When a half-dozen people struggling with the same problems are in near-constant consultation in their efforts to achieve optimum solutions, the legalistic distinctions between responsibilities soon dissolve in the flux of informal working relationships, and the man best equipped—or most willing—to deal with the situation takes the lead.

Multiple Chief Executive. The third structure, sometimes though not always adopted as a successor to the line/staff pattern, is seen much more commonly in Europe than in the United States, although here experiments to organize a "President's Office" with two or more coequal senior executives sharing the power are also under way. In Germany, the law[4] demands a multiple chief executive to prevent the resurgence, even in industry, of the *Führerprinzip.* Similar legal requirements obtain in Holland. Recent legislation in France also permits a *Directoire* to assume collective power as a legal alternative to the all-powerful *Président Directeur Général.*

The multiple chief executive offers, at least in principle, the potential advantages of participative management: breadth of competence, capacity to follow and respond to a variety of pressures simultaneously, and greater balance of judgments on technically complex, uncertain strategic decisions. Its benefits have been amply demonstrated in German industry. Yet, ironically, it has often worked best there when the group includes one powerful personality who is able to command strong personal loyalties and resolve potentially destructive controversies early.

Of all four summit structures, however, the multiple chief executive is the most vulnerable to internal conflict. In many cases, it lacks even the legal basis of a mechanism to secure efficient and equitable resolution of substantive conflict. Where there is no equitable process for resolving them, issues of concept and principle soon lose their positive force and take on a personal character. When this happens, the substantive differences become exaggerated and the decision-making process grinds to a stop.

Management Team. Of growing interest now, particularly to European corporations, is a fourth approach that eliminates the key weakness of the multiple chief executive by providing for a primus inter pares to serve as the final arbiter when needed. The management team is composed of senior executives of diverse talents, experience, and technical knowledge who work together in the manner of an executive committee.

Rather than specific departmental or functional responsibilities in the hierarchical senses, individual team members have areas of special interest— task-oriented in some situations, results-oriented in others—in addition to their overall concern for optimization of corporate efforts. Individual assignments are usually transitory, reflecting corporate priorities for immediate high-level attention and follow-up. At any one time a given team member might have from two to ten such assignments by the decision of the group, to whom he or she would periodically report progress in these areas.

With respect to control of conflict, the management team approach is certainly not an adequate solution, but it does offer a structural alternative between the extremes of enforced conformity and destructive license. And it has the additional merit of harmonizing with many aspects of the informal organization.

Organizational Underside

There is, of course, a perfectly simple reason why none of the formal structures we have been considering can provide an adequate remedy for destructive conflict, and that is the fact of the real power structure, which exists independently of the formal organizational pattern and is rightly the preoccupation of most members of top-management teams. It is the informal organization, not organization charts or job descriptions, that determines the relative power position of executives; and because the informal organization is constantly in flux, these positions are highly volatile.

What, then, are the real sources of power in the informal organization? Lorsch and Lawrence distinguish classical authority, based on delegation of power—that is, "position-based influence"—from "knowledge-based influence," which they define as "the ability of certain persons as persons to influence the commitment of organization resources and to influence the behavior of others, based on the relevance of the information available to them, the soundness of their reasoning, and their reputation for being right in the past."[5]

It is certainly to be hoped that such influence will gain ground in more and more organizations. But within the executive suite, it does not very often carry the day.

"Recognition-Based Influence"?

I would suggest that real power in the informal organization may or may not be partly based on "knowledge" and reason, but does have a variety of important nonrational components. "Recognition-based influence" would perhaps best describe this amalgam. Beyond knowledge and reputation, it is founded on a myriad of impressions, actions, deferences paid, favors received and expected, and observations of the recognition of others by superiors, peers, and subordinates. Each month, in hundreds of conversations, hints of these rankings are passed from one senior executive to another. I am not referring to gossip alone. Often far more important than direct comments are the subconscious communications transmitted by nuance or inflection during discussions of subjects unrelated to personal influence.

Only if he or she knows the location and alignment of the centers of real power can an executive operate effectively in and through the organization. But, as already noted, recognition-based influence is volatile. An executive who is established as one of the two or three most powerful voices in the executive suite may see his or her position erode over a period of weeks. In half a year, the dwindling of power can leave an individual so enfeebled that his or her only remaining options for getting things done are the hierarchical, titular, or administrative crutches he or she can still seize before they too are taken away.

It is the volatility of the real power deriving from recognition-based influence that causes struggles to erupt so easily between executives seeking to distinguish themselves from their peers in the eyes of the organization. Unfortunately, the most appealing approach to formal organization of the summit, the management team, is particularly vulnerable to intensive executive conflict which is motivated by personal ambitions.

Responsibility to Whom?

Performance in the executive suite, unlike performance on the shop floor, cannot be assessed in terms of output. What does count at the top is the quality of leadership and its impact in moving the organization toward its complex of short- and long-term objectives. Moreover, to underscore Leavitt, the problem of motivation is not how to encourage people to work harder; executives are already inclined to overwork. The problem at the summit is how to encourage people to work jointly toward common objectives instead of pursuing competitive individual goals.

Just as the appropriate measure of productivity is different, so are the appropriate means of motivation. At this level, money no longer has the same impact, since increases in compensation will seldom change a senior executive's standard of living. Job security also ranks low as an executive incentive. As for working conditions and fringe benefits, they could hardly be better.

What remains are certain kinds of personal satisfaction deriving from recognition, power, the sense of accomplishing a personal mission. Moreover, for the individual executive in quest of these satisfactions, time is short and opportunity is fleeting. He or she may have reached the last round in a long career struggle to achieve personal career goals and finally prove their worth to their family and intimate friends. The pressures on the individual may be staggering, but the high personal stakes more than compensate—at least for a while. And they are all too likely to render an individual indifferent to the many repercussions that conflict at the summit will eventually have down the line.

A Mission of Service

Most enlightened managers make an effort to empathize with their immediate subordinates. Perhaps what top managers need is to learn how to empathize with the organization as a whole: to perceive and act on the perception that every ounce of status and power must be balanced by a corresponding level of moral responsibility toward the organization and its constituents.

Real acceptance of such an ethic would, of course, mean a basic shift in long-standing cultural attitudes and values relating to material gain, the commercialism of corporate existence, and the resulting tolerance for behavior motivated by personal greed. It would imply acceptance of the proposition that a top-management position now carries such great responsibility that an executive in accepting it must devote himself or herself to the good of the organization and all its members, not solely to achieving his or her own personal aims at any cost to others—conduct still condoned today.

An ethic that ranked the interests of the organization above those of the individual top executive would truly add a dimension of professionalism to the executive career. It would be noble and it would certainly be new. In many executive suites today, talk of "teamwork" or "men of good will" provokes sarcasm or wry smiles. This attitude is crystallized in the proverb, "The road to hell is paved with good intentions." Or, more bluntly still, "Nice guys finish last."

But it is not so simple as that. Where personal ambitions take first place, organizational performance eventually suffers. And today the organization's various constituents, including the public, are no longer inclined to stand back and let top management run the show on its own personal terms, for better or for worse. Accusations of "irresponsible management" are beginning to be heard, and not only from the far left.

Moreover, society's collective willingness to tolerate obvious excesses has aggravated the symptoms of corporate cynicism that repel today's younger generation. In short, even the selfish interests of businesspeople are beginning to push them to behave less selfishly.

What, then, are the prospects for reform? Certainly, the record gives little ground for optimism. Traditionally, there have been few incentives for top managements to avoid destructive conflict by putting professionalism above their personal goals. But as it comes under closer scrutiny and mounting criticism, management may find it has little choice but to impose upon itself a new set of public-service standards. Such standards could provide much-needed evidence of dedication and generous purpose in the motives of the men entrusted with immense power over the working lives and financial welfare of those under their authority. They could foster a new public confidence in business. They could even engender a constructive attitude among our youth, thus enhancing their future contributions to society.

Comprehensive Selection Criteria

The high standards needed cannot be established overnight simply by prescribing new game rules for the present players. New performance measures will have to be linked with a change in the mix of top-management characteristics. The way to launch this evolutionary process is to raise the moral criteria for admission to the executive suite—in short, to reorient the top-management selection requirements.

For many years now, specialist competence and technical skills have dominated the list of qualifications sought in top-management candidates. But with the expanding scope of corporate operations, it is becoming apparent that the final decisions on most questions of technical feasibility and choice of technical processes can no longer safely be taken by general management at the top. The pace of technological advancement today is just too rapid for that.

These assessments are a job for subordinates who are immersed in the new developments in their technical specialties and who can bring a sharply focused, sophisticated understanding to bear on the issues. Top management's task is to weigh and challenge the specialists' assessments of the technical factors involved, and to relate these to the commercial, financial, and human elements that will jointly determine the ultimate success of the undertaking.

Fortunately, this trend makes it practical now to subordinate the technical know-how requirements at the top and give priority instead to strength of character and mature judgment. All the more reason, then, why those responsible for choosing members of the top-management team should begin evaluating candidates against a more comprehensive set of selection criteria.

These are the kind of core qualifications we should now insist on in top-management candidates:

☐ Evidence of personal commitment to carrying out their responsibilities to the whole organization at the highest level of their competence, even at some sacrifice of personal gain.

☐ The maturity and motivation required to deal cooperatively and constructively with their equals as productive members of a top management team.

☐ Sound judgment, open-mindedness, and sensitivity to the human consequences of their actions.

☐ Demonstrated ability and patience to encourage, inspire, and animate subordinates to realize their own potential contributions.

☐ A capacity for thinking strategically, simulating actions and counteractions in the environment, and assessing with a practical eye the associated risks and probable outcomes.

☐ Capability to communicate effectively, particularly in person-to-person situations.

☐ Enough humility to ask for the facts, understand the numbers, and seek the advice and counsel of specialists before making decisions of critical importance.

☐ A keen positive interest in finding at least one way to make things work, rather than exploring in detail all the good reasons why they will not.

☐ Reasonable competence to understand and deal with the factors most critical for success in this company and industry, ideally supplementing the management competences already present.

Concluding Note

To check the deadly game of conflict at the summit, we must evolve a new code of ethics and conduct for individuals in the executive suite. This evolution must be linked to changes in the value standards of those chosen for top management. There is no better way to assure that tomorrow's corporate leaders, entrusted with such power over the well-being of so many employees, shareholders, and their families, will renounce the irresponsible pursuit of personal advantage for nobler and more meaningful objectives.

Notes

1. *Stanford Graduate School of Business Bulletin*, Volume 35, Number 2, Autumn 1966.

2. Philippe Alexandre, *Le Duel de Gaulle-Pompidou* (Paris, Editions Grasset, 1970), p. 40.

3. As summarized by Jay W. Lorsch and Paul R. Lawrence, in *Organization and Environment* (Cambridge, Massachusetts, Harvard University Press, 1967).

4. Aktiengesetz of 6 September 1965, Part 4: Section 1, §§ 76–94 (*Vorstand*) and Section 2, §§ 95–116 (*Aufsichtsrat*).

5. Lorsch and Lawrence, op. cit., p. 173.

2
Problems of
a New Executive

EDMUND P. LEARNED

When executives start new jobs they have trunkfuls of tasks to complete. They have to get to know the people with whom they'll work, get to know the bureaucratic ropes, and find the path of least resistance to these ends. In this article the author gives *HBR* readers two cases that illustrate some of the pitfalls that new executives can fall into in embarking on a new job. In the Dashman Case, when introducing a new procedure the new manager, Post, meets resistance when he needed acceptance. In the Dixie Case, the new executive, Gardner, formulated new policies that no one followed. The author discusses the many problems that the new manager faces but the main issue for the new manager seems to be when to be participative and when not. A high position, the author writes, seems to endorse an authoritarian style when it may be appropriate. The author does not endorse participation at all times, but he maintains that in certain circumstances, particularly when a person is trying to make changes in the organization and is an unknown, the participative style is a requirement of success.

The arrival of a new executive in an established organization is usually an event of considerable importance—both to the person appointed and to the company he or she joins. What is the impact upon the administrative relationships already existing? How can the outsiders find their own place and become fully effective in the executive structure? How should they conduct themselves to achieve that end? And how far should an individual be helped by superiors or others to make the adjustment to the new situation?

These are questions that deserve answers. They represent problems which not only occur frequently in business but are vastly more important in their total impact upon an organization than the frequency of their occurrence would indicate. They afford subtle, yet very real, tests of executive

Published in 1966.

skill, both for the new man or woman and for the organization which he or she joins.

To a large extent the answers to these questions depend on still more fundamental questions as to the executive attitudes and assumptions which characterize the existing administration of the company or which the newcomer brings with him or her. The attitudes administrators reveal in their day-to-day work and the assumptions administrators make or appear to make regarding people and events always have much to do with the effectiveness, efficiency, and morale of the organization. Indeed, there is some evidence that they are often controlling. In the circumstances surrounding the introduction of a new executive they are particularly likely to be critical.

The purpose of this article, however, is not to come to complete and generalized conclusions about the problems of a new executive. Rather, it is to look at some specific business situations that have raised questions along this line, *primarily for the sake of the questions themselves.* If we find some clues to workable suggestions in the process, so much the better.

The situations or "cases" which we shall consider are three in number. (All three cases are disguised to protect sources; all names are fictitious, and dates have been shifted slightly, but the situations themselves are maintained.) The first case, drawn from the Dashman Company, follows upon the introduction of a new central vice president in charge of purchasing into a large manufacturing company characterized by decentralization of management functions. The other two cases are from the Dixie Company—a manufacturer of electrical equipment largely dependent for its success upon the work of specialists in electronics, electrical engineering, and pure physics—one centering on the problems a new product-development manager faces as he seeks acceptance by the top management team of which he is supposed to be a member and by the other departments with which he has to work, and the other describing the behavior of a new chief engineer who must organize a new department and make it useful.

Inasmuch as the purpose and the content of this article may differ somewhat from the usual pattern, several explanatory remarks are in order before we proceed to the substance of the individual cases and to the detailed questions they raise. First of all, the use of cases is not a device whereby I try to inflict *my* answers on you. Nor are the cases merely examples of occurrences which illustrate some point I want to talk about. Rather, they are facts such as almost anyone in a business organization observes firsthand. I hope the article will be a fact-exploring adventure which you and I can share together.

Fact exploring of this kind can be exciting, and I only ask that together we try to observe the reactions and interactions of the people and events unfolded in the three cases, and note the values attached by different participants to the behavior of other people in the situations. I sincerely urge you to reach your own conclusions about the meaning of the events described, and to accept or discard—as you please—such tentative interpretations as I make.

Because an article of this sort cannot reproduce the whole case, it is possible that my selection of data, despite care to make it a fair representation, may prejudice your conclusions. But in any event it is not our purpose to judge a person's total capacity on so limited a sample of his or her executive behavior as is revealed in these cases. We are more interested in grasping the significance of their behavior and attitudes for their organization and in gauging their effect on the people concerned. The hope is that our discussion of the facts will contribute to an understanding of people in organizations and suggest measures for minimizing the frictions which inevitably occur among people who have a job to do together.

Dashman Company

The Dashman Company was a large manufacturer of many types of equipment for the armed forces of the United States. The purchasing procedures of its 20 plants—all located in the Middle West—had never been completely coordinated. The head office of the company, in fact, had encouraged each of the plant managers to operate with his staff as an independent unit in most matters. Late in 1940, when it began to appear that the company would face increasing difficulty in securing certain essential raw materials, Mr. Manson, the company's president, appointed an experienced purchasing executive, a Mr. Post, to assume a new vice presidency in charge of purchasing.

One of Post's first decisions was to begin the immediate centralization of the company's purchasing procedures. He decided that he would require each of the executives who handled purchasing in the individual plants to clear all purchase contracts in excess of $10,000 with his office. He felt that if the head office was to accomplish coordination helpful to each plant and to the whole company, he should be notified that the contracts were being prepared at least a week before they were to be signed. He talked his proposal over with the president, who presented it to the board of directors. The board approved the plan.

Although the company made purchases throughout the year, the beginning of its peak buying season was only three weeks away at the time this new plan was adopted. Post prepared a letter to be sent to the 20 purchasing executives of the company. The letter follows:

Dear ———:

The board of directors of our company has recently authorized a change in our purchasing procedures. Hereafter, each of the purchasing executives in the several plants of the company will notify the vice president in charge of purchasing of all contracts in excess of $10,000 which they are negotiating at least a week in advance of the date on which they are to be signed.

I am sure you will understand that this step is necessary to coordinate the purchasing requirements of the company in these times when we are facing increasing difficulty in securing essential supplies. This procedure should give us in the central office the information we need to see that each plant secures the optimum supply of materials. In this way the interests of each plant and of the company as a whole will best be served.

Yours very truly,

Post showed the letter to an assistant and invited his comments. The assistant suggested that since Post had not met more than a few of the purchasing executives, he might like to visit all of them and take the matter up with each of them personally. Post dismissed the idea at once because, as he said, he had so many things to do at the head office that he could not get away for a trip. Consequently, he had the letters sent out over his signature.

During the two following weeks replies came in from all except a few plants. Although several executives wrote at greater length, the following reply was typical:

Dear Mr. Post:

Your recent communication in regard to notifying the head office a week in advance of our intention to sign contracts has been received. This suggestion seems a most practical one. We want to assure you that you can count on our cooperation.

Yours very truly,

During the next six weeks the head office received no notices from any plant that contracts were being negotiated. Executives in other departments who made frequent trips to the plants reported that the plants were busy and the usual routines for that time of year were being followed.

Looking behind the formal acquiescence of the plants, can you see difficulty in the plant managers' accepting Post's move as a part of the standing company policy? Had they expressed a need for centralization of purchasing procedures? Did they realize that such a need existed? Did such a need in fact exist? Or why did Post receive formal replies which were never followed up by the kind of action he wanted? Was this request ignored merely because of the imminence of the peak buying season?

The attitude of the plant managers seems significant. The very simple decision to rearrange procurement procedures and policies in order to make ready for a special war emergency in plenty of time may have been the act of a forward-looking president, but it may also have been a bombshell for his organization. The plants were the doers, and they were relatively autonomous. Suddenly one of the bastions of their independence—the freedom to act independently in purchasing—came under attack from the home office. Without prior consultation the home office assumed the responsibility for policy and operation in this area. The plant managers may have been uncertain about what their future relationship to their own purchasing agents was to be. The plants had experienced no need for the new position. If any of them had been stymied in their jobs and had already been brought face-to-face with the need for help in the higher echelon of management, they surely would have welcomed the chance occasioned by the letter to lay their problems before Post. They presented nothing to him.

What about Post's assumptions? He may have assumed that the president and the board understood his purchasing problems when they approved his plan. Perhaps they did not. He may have thought that the approval of his plan by the board gave him effective authority to put it through, that a statement of that authority would result in obedience. Apparently, he further assumed that the interest of each plant would be the same as the interest of the company as a whole. He did not seem disturbed by the possibility that a one-way communication in a letter at this stage of acquaintance with the organization might not be so good as a two-way communication made possible by a personal conference. He underestimated the task of getting started. He sent out instructions with a minimum of explanation.

In replying to his assistant's suggestion that he go into the field, Post assumed—if we may presume to put it in words for him—that "what I think is important actually *is* important." Is this an attitude of arrogance, or is it solely an indication that he had many things to do? Whatever the answer, the effect on the receiving end of the communication is fairly clear.

Post may have assumed also that a major break in the continuity of the decentralization policy would be understood correctly by plant managers without explanation. No matter what Post's assumptions were, a serious breakdown of communication occurred in the actual situation. The plant managers and the plant purchasing agents had, as a whole, not indicated actual acceptance of any of the functions which Post, with the concurrence of his superiors, had laid down for himself.

Examination of Post's actions presents additional assumptions that may have prompted his ineffectual behavior and reveals certain of his underlying attitudes. This list may be unkind and perhaps unfair, but it is suggestive of some of the reasons he did not get better results.

Post behaved as if he thought he knew what the purchasing problems of this company were and would be. He did not ask for the opinions of experienced subordinates who had been in full charge of the purchasing function in their respective plants. Post assumed that he had the right answers for these problems, that a dollar dragnet would bring them to his attention for solution, and that his new subordinates in the plant had nothing to contribute either to the statement of problems or to their solutions. *In other words, he thought he needed no help.*

Furthermore, Post acted as if he believed that subordinates would accept his authority and follow his instructions; that purchasing agents and plant managers would have the same conception of Post's job that Post had; that a week's warning on contracts of $10,000 or more was enough notice to make him useful to the purchasing agents. Or Post may have assumed that all purchasing agents worthy of their hire would know that a week's notice was only a way of getting background information to the new boss: that they would immediately supply the information in order to help the new executive.

This type of behavior reveals an attitude of self-importance and a failure on Post's part to recognize that individuals of top stature and responsibility have pride in their work and want an opportunity to show their capacity in the company. It also demonstrates his complete lack of comprehension of the major change in policy involved in the new relationships.

Dixie Company I

Starting years ago as a small business, the Dixie Company had prospered because of the reliability and dependability of its products. The management had grown up with the company. The corporation, ably supported by its own director of research, had benefited by the technical revolution. Like its competitors, the company had grown rapidly during the 1930s and spurted ahead during the war period.

The top management organization consisted of Mr. Eaton, the president; the vice president in charge of sales; the vice president in charge of production; and the treasurer, who also was a vice president. The rapid growth in business had increased the burden of coordinating the major departments. The top officials were unable to initiate and follow up all the necessary research on market potentials, manufacturing costs, or margins involved in appraising fully the desirability of adding a new item to the company lines. Nor could they devote the requisite time and energy to the multitude of administrative details involved in expediting a product through all steps of experimental design, full-scale production and promotion, up to the time when the product could be considered firmly established in the company's manufacturing and marketing departments.

Product development at Dixie was complicated by continuous pressure from the sales department to gain an initial competitive advantage by being the first to make a new item available. This eagerness was countered by the cautious insistence of the research staff that a thorough, time-consuming experimental job be completed first. To resolve such conflicts and to deal with all the related problems the management decided to establish a new "product development" department.

To head the new department the Dixie top management chose a highly successful line executive from a company in another industry, Mr. Gardner by name, who had extensive experience in market research, sales promotion, and product development. Gardner's department was to report to the president, and was to carry the responsibility for coordinating the development of products. But Gardner was not made a vice president of the company.

In his initial interview, the president explained Gardner's duties to him as follows:

> Your principal function will be to coordinate and expedite all the phases of the business related to these new products. When a product proposal gets to the point of putting money into plant facilities, we of the Management Committee want to turn to you for a balanced appraisal from a top management point of view regarding the project. It is not your job to originate projects, but to study them on our behalf from the standpoint of scientific basis, stages of experimental development, end uses, market surveys, competition, plant investment, profit margins, and the like. You will be coordinating the work of the staff and line departments on product developments until a project is approved. After a product is authorized, you will expedite its development, manufacture, and sale until it is going commercially.
>
> Your activities will cut across the work of all departments, but you will not absorb their responsibilities. You will take authority and responsibility on behalf of the top management for getting a project through. You will examine the basic problems, fix responsibility for their solution or for recommendations, coordinate the work of all agencies, and do this without upsetting the organization. Your work may be resented by some who fail to see at first the function you are performing and feel that you are encroaching on their responsibilities, but we'll solve those difficulties when we come to them.

The new product development manager needed to reflect upon the president's directive. In order to assess his assumptions and attitudes we too should try to interpret Eaton's directive. What does the job involve? What does Eaton mean by "coordinate," "expedite," "appraisal from a top management point of view," "not your job to originate or . . . absorb . . . responsibilities [of other departments]"? What does he mean by: "You will take authority and responsibility on behalf of the top management for getting a project through. You will examine the basic problems, fix responsibility for their solution or for recommendations, coordinate the work of all agencies, and do this without upsetting the organization"?

The new job is obviously a tough one, requiring the highest degree of administrative, as opposed to technical, skill. If administration is primarily the process of getting work done through the integration of many hands, then Gardner's mission is primarily administrative. He must fit together the work of others with respect to policies, products, facilities, procedures, investments, inventories, training, and devise schedules so paced that profitable products are manufactured to meet present and potential market demands.

Questions which Gardner might have asked himself when he undertook this particular assignment are: Do members of the top management committee have a common understanding about the functions of the new department? How will I find out? Do I make product policy or preside over its making? With whom will I work, and on what? How many of the vice presidents and department heads are informed about the purpose of the new department and its relationship to their duties? How can they contribute to the success of the company's program? How can I fit together the work of others without doing the original work?

Note that Gardner was instructed by the president only in general terms. He was left to make his own way over uncharted territory in which many conflicts would have to be brought into balance with or without the consent of the department heads accustomed to operating without a product development department. When numerous people have overlapping interests in a project, different opinions among them may retard cooperation. The depth of feeling and the extent of departmental loyalty may make resolution of conflicts difficult.

Another danger which Gardner had to guard against was his own background as a line executive. He was accustomed to making final decisions. It is not easy for a man to shift from a position of authority for making policies into a pattern of leading a group to joint recommendations or decisions. Gardner could find it difficult to refrain from giving orders to the expert heads of departments who knew more about their own jobs than he did. When such department heads desire to make their contributions to the company their own way, and when seniority has given them ideas about their importance and status in the company, a newcomer is likely to have trouble if he or she does not give weight to their points of view. As a former line executive now leading a group, Gardner might well be required to equip himself with a new set of administrative practices made appropriate by the combination of logic and sentiment in the new situation.

Let us examine some of Gardner's first moves. He began at once to organize and staff his own department. Making use of the company's organization manual department, he prepared a complete list of his functions for publication in the manual. Without ado he announced by this means that he would, among other things, *correlate and direct* all matters related to the establishment of new products by the company, *survey and analyze* sales possibilities and *determine* sales potentials, make *initial sales* of new products before relinquishing them to the sales department, *steer* new products through the company, and *integrate* the efforts of all company departments concerned with new products. Gardner decided, furthermore, that it was desirable to work out product policies for classes of products before taking up any product within a class.

During the months devoted to these activities, other departments complained to top management that Gardner had taken action without clearing it with them. Gardner himself believed that he could not make progress in his job until a fully detailed list of procedures—equivalent to the functions already published—could be worked out and put into force by the management. Six months after his appointment he had by no means achieved companywide acceptance of himself and his department, and the development of new products was no more under control than before.

Did Gardner's first moves contribute to his lack of success? The forthright phrasing of his departmental functions in the organization manual prior to much actual work on specific projects with other departments could easily have led to misunderstandings which might not always be stated. The phrase *"correlate and direct . . .* the establishment of new products" could easily cause a loyal subordinate of the production or sales vice president to say: "The new guy thinks he's the whole cheese. My boss made this company. We got along before he arrived, and we can get along after he leaves. We'll see how far he gets in *directing.*"

Some of Gardner's other phrases could well have raised departmental eyebrows. "Determining sales potential" could properly be a function of the marketing department rather than the work of a coordinator. Gardner may have ignored existing routines in the organization and the ambitions of people in various departments.

Gardner made no genuine effort to obtain the assistance of other major department heads in formulating the list of functions for the new department. He was unaware that these other department heads might consider the new department as overlapping their activities. These departments had been "in business" many, many years; they had established routines of doing work; and in all probability the senior heads of these departments expected the newcomer to seek their advice and cooperation. Gardner made no effort to understand the activities of these departments and their relationship to his office but, instead, worked relatively alone in listing his own department's functions. He may have made trouble without knowing it and created resistance to what others felt as usurpation when that was not intended.

Why, we may ask, did Gardner insist on formulating policies before handling particular cases cooperatively with other departments? Will a general policy determine the best way to handle an individual product, or should the "best" way to handle particular products eventually build up a general policy? Should one work from the abstract policy to the detailed application, or should one experiment with specific cases in order to formulate a broad, overall policy? Gardner followed his own logic to the limit and thereby disturbed other executives who were devoted to their particular logics and routine patterns of doing things. His adherence to his own views on procedures and on methods of getting things done left him essentially helpless. His pet ideas of administration did him no good.

Gardner's attitudes toward other people were a genuine handicap. He conveyed a sense of authority and position and did not reveal an attitude of humility which inspires cooperation. His *early* quest for authoritative policies, procedures, and clear definitions of functions, though easy to understand, may not be well founded in experience. The attitude which he took toward his fellow executive seems to have had a very substantial bearing on their reaction to him and on their willingness to cooperate wholeheartedly in determining and carrying out company policy with respect to coordination of product developments.

Dixie Company II

Contrasting assumptions and attitudes were held by a new chief engineer in the Dixie Company. His approach was quite different from that of Gardner. These differences reveal the significance of assumptions and attitudes to management accomplishments.

As a result of the growth of the company, the management decided to enlarge and reorganize its engineering activities. The new chief engineer, a Mr. Kirkland, had to merge the electrical engineers, formerly responsible to the director of research, with four other engineering departments, which previously had reported individually to the vice president in charge of production. These four were the industrial engineering group, the mechanical engineers, the construction engineers, and the maintenance engineers. One man had headed two of these departments. Two more men had headed the other two. All three men and their organizations were assigned to the new chief engineer. The problem was further complicated by the fact that the electrical engineers had not wanted to join the department; their transfer had also been opposed by the director of research. Each engineering group was impressed by its contribution to the company, but the electrical engineers plainly regarded themselves as the élite.

When Kirkland was employed as chief engineer, the president gave him very broad, general instructions. He was to avoid duplication of effort, to improve the previous lack of coordination and poor allocation of work. Eaton said, "We want to accomplish changes by evolution rather than by revolution. We can't be sure of each step toward our ultimate goal, and to freeze a procedure or policy before it is seasoned would be bad business."

What is the significance of the president's behavior in assigning both Gardner and Kirkland to their jobs with high-level blessings but general and possibly vague directives? Was Eaton deliberately requiring his new executives to demonstrate their mettle by undertaking themselves the concrete definition of their responsibilities and obtaining acceptance thereto from their working colleagues?

Whatever the president's design in giving both Gardner and Kirkland broad areas of responsibility, his behavior in doing so is not at all unusual. Its consequence, at least for these two new men, was a freedom from the handicap of specific instructions which might have prejudiced their developing sound working relationships in the process of solving the problems which would soon come into their purview. However, a company may run a very considerable risk that the new people will not make smooth adjustments to the organization. True, as a hard-boiled way of developing executives the method used by the president may be wholly satisfactory. The person who can make the adjustment on their own is likely to be better than the one who needs assistance. On the other hand, such tactics can lead to serious disruption of activities and much frustration on the part of all executives involved in cooperative work and adjustment.

With the stated purpose of creating a competent organization, the chief engineer physically consolidated all the engineering functions. The newly merged departments moved into a new building. Minor problems of adjustment to the new space setup appeared at once. The head of the industrial engineering group, whom Kirkland placed in charge of laying out the new offices, planned to avoid the use of cubicles for individual engineers. Although the use of glassed-in space was common in other company office buildings, he thought it a waste of limited room and, in addition, believed that more work could be accomplished in the engineering group without such obstacles to informal communication.

The electrical engineers had enjoyed unusually good office space in the research building; the loss of those physical comforts had been one of their objections to the consolidation of the engineering departments. After a discussion of several weeks and in spite of his inability to give enclosed offices to other engineers, the head of the industrial engineers gave the electrical engineers the office arrangements they desired. Kirkland did not question or overrule this decision.

Do you agree with the apparent assumption of Kirkland that physical consolidation would encourage interaction among the engineering groups? What is the hazard implicit in deferring to the electrical engineers' assumed superiority and tacitly allowing them to acquire offices denied to the other engineers? Was the head of the industrial engineers astute in his decision to recognize the sentiments of the electrical engineers and give them enclosed space, or insensitive to the impact of this decision on the other engineering groups? What steps should Kirkland have taken to minimize this impact?

Kirkland set out to complete unification by developing and promoting departmental and professional pride, by establishing yardsticks for appraisal of results, by providing incentives for outstanding work, and by personally and forcefully presenting the point of view of the combined engineering groups in all top management discussions which involved engineering functions. He held numerous dinner meetings at a downtown hotel, at which all engineering employees were present, and he discussed departmental engineering issues with the groups at this time. He made daily effort to become acquainted with all the engineers, with the plant and its procedures, with the key men and women in the research department and in the factory; and he dealt personally with situations which caused confusion and conflict.

What is the significance of these various moves by Kirkland? How are they different from Gardner's? Was Kirkland proceeding on the assumption that his job was to lead, not to direct, to review suggestions and not necessarily orginate them, and to bring about a meeting of minds both within and without the department? He seems to have assumed that his subordinates were technically capable of contributing to the company and that his job was primarily to give them a chance to do so. If a defect in the organization temporarily prevented them from so contributing, it was their joint task to find a way to break the jam. Perhaps he assumed, as well, that his people wanted as much as he to be productive and efficient. He gave individuals opportunities for personal development and recognition and enabled them to preserve their individuality while working within a group.

Kirkland arranged frequent joint conferences with his four subordinate engineering heads. He discussed the problems that arose in their work, and together they reviewed the areas in which inefficiency and disagreement had arisen in the past. They attempted to formulate the best procedures to follow in the future. He took them all completely into his confidence with respect to departmental problems and proved himself receptive to the ideas and opinions of other engineers. Outside the department he followed up faithfully the decisions reached in departmental conferences. He required his group leaders to help clarify the interrelationships between the engineering groups. He made it clear that the achievement of all the engineers would be recognized and made the basis for promotion, and he tried to get to know the engineers personally.

Kirkland seems to have assumed that collaborative effort on statements of policy and procedure would yield better results than individually conceived directives of the chief. He betrayed a genuine humility in the presence of his subordinates, and he showed a willingness to listen to and accept their contributions toward the objectives of the group. Perhaps he knew the effect on morale of such an attitude. He seems to have been aware that genuine interest by supervisors in subordinates has a positive effect on the individual and on the organization.

In addition to the problem of merging the engineering groups, Kirkland faced immediately the need for proper division of responsibilities for experimental production among the engineering, production, and research departments. There had long been a question in the company regarding the responsibility for experimental production. When should the production department and the engineering group take over from the research department? Kirkland and the director of research spent a considerable time together in the experimental laboratory and factory discussing ways and means of translating new products into full-scale factory production. When a specific issue arose in a day's work, the subordinate engineers and the subordinate research physicists brought it to the joint attention of the two chiefs who, if possible, tried to formulate a plan from the one event that might be applicable to future situations. They both realized that the research group had the assigned responsibility of development until products were being smoothly produced in the factory and that the engineering groups were obligated to furnish services required by the research people in carrying out their jobs.

Conflicts between engineering and research could easily have arisen from differences in the backgrounds and basic interests of the groups concerned. Instead of trying, as Gardner did, to resolve the differences in advance in terms of abstract policies and to mark out clearly defined areas for each department, Kirkland and the director of research built from particular situations toward general rules. They focused their attention on getting particular jobs done, allowing the problem being solved to determine the specific responsibilities and rules for each group. They worked perhaps on the assumption that by solving together particular difficulties their groups might better understand the place that each deserved in the whole. Thus, final lists of functions and responsibilities growing out of this type of relationship could be based on experience rather than theory.

Summary

We have been exploring the actions of three new executives, all presumably intelligent men. Many questions have come to mind, which perhaps have seemed quite obvious. But they apparently were not uniformly asked by the men concerned. We, as readers, have had the advantages of simplification and objectivity. That is why it can do no harm, and why rather it may be of much help, to become conscious of the kind of questions which need to be asked in these or similar circumstances. Once he is conscious of the problems involved, and of their significant relation to underlying attitudes and assumptions, the intelligent executive is far on his way to achieving desirable solutions.

It is in the same spirit that the following questions, by this time also quite obvious, are made explicit by way of conclusion:

□ Can there be any doubt in your mind that Kirkland is a more successful executive than either Gardner or Post? What do you think is the basis of his success? Is it the difference in the assumptions he makes regarding other people? Is it a difference in the attitude which he takes throughout—in speaking, in writing, and in behavior?

□ Does it seem desirable to take an interest in other people or groups with whom one must work? Is it wise to take account of their status in the organization and of their attitudes toward oneself and toward each other? Does it seem important to consider the assumptions upon which they appear to be working, as well as to consider one's own?

□ Does the comparative study of these cases give *you* any clues as to how executives, department heads, or staff groups like to be treated? Do these accounts of others' experiences give you an insight into the ways of developing cooperative efforts between people and departments?

3
Power Failure in Management Circuits

ROSABETH MOSS KANTER

When one thinks of "power," one often assumes that a person is the source of it and that some mystical charismatic element is at work. Of course, with some people this is undoubtedly so; they derive power from how other people perceive them. In organizations, however—says this author—power is not so much a question of people but of positions. Drawing a distinction between productive and oppressive power, the author maintains that the former is a function of having open channels to supplies, support, and information; the latter is a function of these channels being closed. She then describes three positions that are classically powerless: first-line supervisors, staff professionals, and, surprisingly, chief executive officers. These positions can be powerless because of difficulties in maintaining open lines of information and support. Seeing powerlessness in these positions as dangerous for organizations, she urges managers to restructure and redesign their organizations in order to eliminate pockets of powerlessness.

Power is America's last dirty word. It is easier to talk about money—and much easier to talk about sex—than it is to talk about power. People who have it deny it; people who want it do not want to appear to hunger for it; and people who engage in its machinations do so secretly.

Yet, because it turns out to be a critical element in effective managerial behavior, power should come out from undercover. Having searched for years for those styles or skills that would identify capable organization lead-

Published in 1979.

ers, many analysts, like myself, are rejecting individual traits or situational appropriateness as key and finding the sources of a leader's real power.

Access to resources and information and the ability to act quickly make it possible to accomplish more and to pass on more resources and information to subordinates. For this reason, people tend to prefer bosses with "clout." When employees perceive their manager as influential upward and outward, their status is enhanced by association and they generally have high morale and feel less critical or resistant to their boss.[1] More powerful leaders are also more likely to delegate (they are too busy to do it all themselves), to reward talent, and to build a team that places subordinates in significant positions.

Powerlessness, in contrast, tends to breed bossiness rather than true leadership. In large organizations, at least, it is powerlessness that often creates ineffective, desultory management and petty, dictatorial, rules-minded managerial styles. Accountability without power—responsibility for results without the resources to get them—creates frustration and failure. People who see themselves as weak and powerless and find their subordinates resisting or discounting them tend to use more punishing forms of influence. If organizational power can "ennoble," then, recent research shows, organizational powerlessness can (with apologies to Lord Acton) "corrupt."[2]

So perhaps power, in the organization at least, does not deserve such a bad reputation. Rather than connoting only dominance, control, and oppression, *power* can mean efficacy and capacity—something managers and executives need to move the organization toward its goals. Power in organizations is analogous in simple terms to physical power: it is the ability to mobilize resources (human and material) to get things done. The true sign of power, then, is accomplishment—not fear, terror, or tyranny. Where the power is "on," the system can be productive; where the power is "off," the system bogs down.

But saying that people need power to be effective in organizations does not tell us where it comes from or why some people, in some jobs, systematically seem to have more of it than others. In this article I want to show that to discover the sources of productive power, we have to look not at the *person*—as conventional classifications of effective managers and employees do—but at the *position* the person occupies in the organization.

Where Does Power Come From?

The effectiveness that power brings evolves from two kinds of capacities: first, access to the resources, information, and support necessary to carry out a task; and, second, ability to get cooperation in doing what is necessary. (Exhibit 1 identifies some symbols of an individual manager's power.)

Both capacities derive not so much from a leader's style and skill as from his or her location in the formal and informal systems of the organization—in both job definition and connection to other important people in

Exhibit 1.

To what extent a manager can—

Intercede favorably on behalf of someone in trouble with the organization

Get a desirable placement for a talented subordinate

Get approval for expenditures beyond the budget

Get above-average salary increases for subordinates

Get items on the agenda at policy meetings

Get fast access to top decision makers

Get regular, frequent access to top decision makers

Get early information about decisions and policy shifts

the company. Even the ability to get cooperation from subordinates is strongly defined by the manager's clout outward. People are more responsive to bosses who look as if they can get more for them from the organization.

We can regard the uniquely organizational sources of power as consisting of three "lines":

1. *Lines of supply.* Influence outward, over the environment, means that managers have the capacity to bring in the things that their own organizational domain needs—materials, money, resources to distribute as rewards, and perhaps even prestige.

2. *Lines of information.* To be effective, managers need to be "in the know" in both the formal and the informal sense.

3. *Lines of support.* In a formal framework, a manager's job parameters need to allow for nonordinary action, for a show of discretion or exercise of judgment. Thus managers need to know that they can assume innovative, risk-taking activities without having to go through the stifling multilayered approval process. And, informally, managers need the backing of other important figures in the organization whose tacit approval becomes another resource they bring to their own work unit as well as a sign of the manager's being "in."

Note that productive power has to do with *connections* with other parts of a system. Such systemic aspects of power derive from two sources—job activities and political alliances:

1. Power is most easily accumulated when one has a job that is designed and located to allow *discretion* (nonroutinized action permitting flexible, adaptive, and creative contributions), *recognition* (visibility and notice), and *relevance* (being central to pressing organizational problems).

2. Power also comes when one has relatively close contact with *sponsors* (higher-level people who confer approval, prestige, or backing), *peer networks* (circles of acquaintanceship that provide reputation and informa-

tion, the grapevine often being faster than formal communication channels), and *subordinates* (who can be developed to relieve managers of some of their burdens and to represent the manager's point of view).

When managers are in powerful situations, it is easier for them to accomplish more. Because the tools are there, they are likely to be highly motivated and, in turn, to be able to motivate subordinates. Their activities are more likely to be on target and to net them successes. They can flexibly interpret or shape policy to meet the needs of particular areas, emergent situations, or sudden environmental shifts. They gain the respect and cooperation that attributed power brings. Subordinates' talents are resources rather than threats. And, because powerful managers have so many lines of connection and thus are oriented outward, they tend to let go of control downward, developing more independently functioning lieutenants.

The powerless live in a different world. Lacking the supplies, information, or support to make things happen easily, they may turn instead to the ultimate weapon of those who lack productive power—oppressive power: holding others back and punishing with whatever threats they can muster.

Exhibit 2 summarizes some of the major ways in which variables in the organization and in job design contribute to either power or powerlessness.

Positions of Powerlessness

Understanding what it takes to have power and recognizing the classic behavior of the powerless can immediately help managers make sense out of a number of familiar organizational problems that are usually attributed to inadequate people:

☐   The ineffectiveness of first-line supervisors.
☐   The petty interest protection and conservatism of staff professionals.
☐   The crises of leadership at the top.

Instead of blaming the individuals involved in organizational problems, let us look at the positions people occupy. Of course, power or powerlessness in a position may not be all of the problem. Sometimes incapable people *are* at fault and need to be retrained or replaced. (See Appendix A for a discussion of another special case, women.) But where patterns emerge, where the troubles associated with some units persist, organizational power failures could be the reason. Then, as Volvo President Pehr Gyllenhammar concludes, we should treat the powerless not as "villains" causing headaches for everyone else but as "victims."[3]

First-Line Supervisors
Because an employee's most important work relationship is with his or her supervisor, when many of them talk about "the company," they mean their immediate boss. Thus a supervisor's behavior is an important determinant

Exhibit 2.

Factors	Generates **power** when factor is	Generates **powerlessness** when factor is
Rules inherent in the job	few	many
Predecessors in the job	few	many
Established routines	few	many
Task variety	high	low
Rewards for reliability/predictability	few	many
Rewards for unusual performance/innovation	many	few
Flexibility around use of people	high	low
Approvals needed for nonroutine decisions	few	many
Physical location	central	distant
Publicity about job activities	high	low
Relation of tasks to current problem areas	central	peripheral
Focus of tasks	outside work unit	inside work unit
Interpersonal contact in the job	high	low
Contact with senior officials	high	low
Participation in programs, conferences, meetings	high	low
Participation in problem-solving task forces	high	low
Advancement prospects of subordinates	high	low

of the average employee's relationship to work and is in itself a critical link in the production chain.

Yet I know of no U.S. corporate management entirely satisfied with the performance of its supervisors. Most see them as supervising too closely and not training their people. In one manufacturing company where direct laborers were asked on a survey how they learned their job, on a list of seven possibilities "from my supervisor" ranked next to last. (Only company training programs ranked worse.) Also, it is said that supervisors do not translate company policies into practice—for instance, that they do not carry out the right of every employee to frequent performance reviews or to career counseling.

In court cases charging race or sex discrimination, first-line supervisors are frequently cited as the "discriminating official."[4] And, in studies of innovative work redesign and quality of work life projects, they often appear as the implied villains; they are the ones who are said to undermine the program or interfere with its effectiveness. In short, they are often seen as "not sufficiently managerial."

The problem affects white-collar as well as blue-collar supervisors. In one large government agency, supervisors in field offices were seen as the source of problems concerning morale and the flow of information to and from headquarters. "Their attitudes are negative," said a senior official. "They turn people against the agency; they put down senior management. They build themselves up by always complaining about headquarters, but prevent their staff from getting any information directly. We can't afford to have such attitudes communicated to field staff."

Is the problem that supervisors need more management training programs or that incompetent people are invariably attracted to the job? Neither explanation suffices. A large part of the problem lies in the position itself—one that almost universally creates powerlessness.

First-line supervisors are "people in the middle," and that has been seen as the source of many of their problems.[5] But by recognizing that first-line supervisors are caught between higher management and workers, we only begin to skim the surface of the problem. There is practically no other organizational category as subject to powerlessness.

First, these supervisors may be at a virtual dead end in their careers. Even in companies where the job used to be a stepping stone to higher-level management jobs, it is now common practice to bring in MBAs from the outside for those positions. Thus moving from the ranks of direct labor into supervision may mean, essentially, getting "stuck" rather than moving upward. Because employees do not perceive supervisors as eventually joining the leadership circles of the organization, they may see them as lacking the high-level contacts needed to have clout. Indeed, sometimes turnover among supervisors is so high that workers feel they can outwait—and outwit—any boss.

Second, although they lack clout, with little in the way of support from above, supervisors are forced to administer programs or explain policies that they have no hand in shaping. In one company, as part of a new personnel program supervisors were required to conduct counseling interviews with employees. But supervisors were not trained to do this and were given no incentives to get involved. Counseling was just another obligation. Then managers suddenly encouraged the workers to bypass their supervisors or to put pressure on them. The personnel staff brought them together and told them to demand such interviews as a basic right. If supervisors had not felt powerless before, they did after that squeeze from below, engineered from above.

The people they supervise can also make life hard for them in numerous ways. This often happens when a supervisor has himself or herself risen up from the ranks. Peers that have not made it are resentful or derisive of their former colleague, whom they now see as trying to lord it over them. Often it is easy for workers to break rules and let a lot of things slip.

Yet first-line supervisors are frequently judged according to rules and regulations while being limited by other regulations in what disciplinary actions they can take. They often lack the resources to influence or reward people; after all, workers are guaranteed their pay and benefits by someone other than their supervisors. Supervisors cannot easily control events; rather, they must react to them.

In one factory, for instance, supervisors complained that performance of their job was out of their control: they could fill production quotas only if they had the supplies, but they had no way to influence the people controlling supplies.

The lack of support for many first-line managers, particularly in large organizations, was made dramatically clear in another company. When asked if contact with executives higher in the organization who had the potential for offering support, information, and alliances diminished their own feelings of career vulnerability and the number of headaches they experienced on the job, supervisors in five out of seven work units responded positively. For them *contact* was indeed related to a greater feeling of acceptance at work and membership in the organization.

But in the two other work units where there was greater contact, people perceived more, not less, career vulnerability. Further investigation showed that supervisors in these business units got attention only when they were in trouble. Otherwise, no one bothered to talk to them. To these particular supervisors, hearing from a higher-level manager was a sign not of recognition or potential support but of danger.

It is not surprising, then, that supervisors frequently manifest symptoms of powerlessness: overly close supervision, rules-mindedness, and a tendency to do the job themselves rather than to train their people (since job skills may be one of the few remaining things they feel good about). Perhaps this is why they sometimes stand as roadblocks between their subordinates and the higher reaches of the company.

Staff Professionals

Also working under conditions that can lead to organizational powerlessness are the staff specialists. As advisers behind the scenes, staff people must sell their programs and bargain for resources, but unless they get themselves entrenched in organizational power networks, they have little in the way of favors to exchange. They are seen as useful adjuncts to the primary tasks of the organization but inessential in a day-to-day operating sense. This disenfranchisement occurs particularly when staff jobs consist of easily routinized administrative functions which are out of the mainstream of the currently relevant areas and involve little innovative decision making.

Furthermore, in some organizations, unless they have had previous line experience, staff people tend to be limited in the number of jobs into which they can move. Specialists' ladders are often very short, and professionals are just as likely to get "stuck" in such jobs as people are in less prestigious clerical or factory positions.

Staff people, unlike those who are being groomed for important line positions, may be hired because of a special expertise or particular background. But management rarely pays any attention to developing them into more general organizational resources. Lacking growth prospects themselves and working alone or in very small teams, they are not in a position to develop others or pass on power to them. They miss out on an important way that power can be accumulated.

Sometimes staff specialists, such as house counsel or organization development people, find their work being farmed out to consultants. Management considers them fine for the routine work, but the minute the activities involve risk or something problematic, they bring in outside experts. This treatment says something not only about their expertise but also about the status of their function. Since the company can always hire talent on a temporary basis, it is unclear that the management really needs to have or considers important its own staff for these functions.

And, because staff professionals are often such as adjuncts to primary tasks, their effectiveness and therefore their contribution to the organization are often hard to measure. Thus visibility and recognition, as well as risk taking and relevance, may be denied to people in staff jobs.

Staff people tend to act out their powerlessness by becoming turf-minded. They create islands within the organization. They set themselves up as the only ones who can control professional standards and judge their own work. They create sometimes false distinctions between themselves as experts (no one else could possibly do what they do) and lay people, and this continues to keep them out of the mainstream.

One form such distinctions take is a combination of disdain when line managers attempt to act in areas the professionals think are their preserve and of subtle refusal to support the managers' efforts. Or staff groups battle with each other for control of new "problem areas," with the result that no one really handles the issue at all. To cope with their essential powerlessness, staff groups may try to elevate their own status and draw boundaries between themselves and others.

When staff jobs are treated as final resting places for people who have reached their level of competence in the organization—a good shelf on which to dump managers who are too old to go anywhere but too young to retire— then staff groups can also become pockets of conservatism, resistant to change. Their own exclusion from the risk-taking action may make them resist *anyone's* innovative proposals. In the past, personnel departments, for example, have sometimes been the last in their organization to know about innovations in human resource development or to be interested in applying them.

Top Executives

Despite the great resources and responsibilities concentrated at the top of an organization, leaders can be powerless for reasons that are not very different from those that affect staff and supervisors: lack of supplies, information, and support.

We have faith in leaders because of their ability to make things happen in the larger world, to create possibilities for everyone else, and to attract resources to the organization. These are their supplies. But influence outward—the source of much credibility downward—can diminish as environments change, setting terms and conditions out of the control of the leaders. Regardless of top management's grand plans for the organization, the environment presses. At the very least, things going on outside the organization can deflect a leader's attention and drain energy. And, more detrimental, decisions made elsewhere can have severe consequences for the organization and affect top management's sense of power and thus its operating style inside.

In the go-go years of the mid-1960s, for example, nearly every corporation officer or university president could look—and therefore feel—successful. Visible success gave leaders a great deal of credibility inside the organization, which in turn gave them the power to put new things in motion.

In the past few years, the environment has been strikingly different and the capacity of many organization leaders to do anything about it has been severely limited. New "players" have flexed their power muscles: the Arab oil bloc, government regulators, and congressional investigating committees. And managing economic decline is quite different from managing growth. It is no accident that when top leaders personally feel out of control, the control function in corporations grows.

As powerlessness in lower levels of organizations can manifest itself in overly routinized jobs where performance measures are oriented to rules and absence of change, so it can at upper levels as well. Routine work often drives out nonroutine work. Accomplishment becomes a question of nailing down details. Short-term results provide immediate gratifications and satisfy stockholders or other constituencies with limited interests.

It takes a powerful leader to be willing to risk short-term deprivations in order to bring about desired long-term outcomes. Much as first-line supervisors are tempted to focus on daily adherence to rules, leaders are tempted to focus on short-term fluctuations and lose sight of long-term objectives. The dynamics of such a situation are self-reinforcing. The more the long-term goals go unattended, the more a leader feels powerless and the greater the scramble to prove that he or she is in control of daily events at least. The more he or she is involved in the organization as a short-term Fix-it person, the more out of control of long-term objectives he or she is, and the more ultimately powerless he or she is likely to be.

Credibility for top executives often comes from doing the extraordinary: exercising discretion, creating, inventing, planning, and acting in nonroutine ways. But since routine problems look easier and more manageable, require less change and consent on the part of anyone else, and lend themselves to instant solutions that can make any leader look good temporarily, leaders may avoid the risky by taking over what their subordinates should be doing. Ultimately, a leader may succeed in getting all the trivial problems dumped on his or her desk. This can establish expectations even for leaders attempting more challenging tasks. When Warren Bennis was president of the University of Cincinnati, a professor called him when the heat was down in a classroom. In writing about this incident, Bennis commented, "I suppose he expected me to grab a wrench and fix it."[6]

People at the top need to insulate themselves from the routine operations of the organization in order to develop and exercise power. But this very insulation can lead to another source of powerlessness—lack of information. In one multinational corporation, top executives who are sealed off in a large, distant office, flattered and virtually babied by aides, are frustrated by their distance from the real action.[7]

At the top, the concern for secrecy and privacy is mixed with real loneliness. In one bank, organization members were so accustomed to never seeing the top leaders that when a new senior vice president went to the branch offices to look around, they had suspicion, even fear, about his intentions.

Thus leaders who are cut out of an organization's information networks understand neither what is really going on at lower levels nor that their own isolation may be having negative effects. All too often top executives design "beneficial" new employee programs or declare a new humanitarian policy (e.g., "Participatory management is now our style") only to find the policy ignored or mistrusted because it is perceived as coming from uncaring bosses.

The information gap has more serious consequences when executives are so insulated from the rest of the organization or from other decision makers that, as Nixon so dramatically did, they fail to see their own impending downfall. Such insulation is partly a matter of organizational position and, in some cases, of executive style.

For example, leaders may create closed inner circles consisting of "doppelgängers," people just like themselves, who are their principal sources of organizational information and tell them only what they want to know. The reasons for the distortions are varied: key aides want to relieve the leader of burdens, they think just like the leader, they want to protect their own positions of power, or the familiar "kill the messenger" syndrome makes people close to top executives reluctant to be the bearers of bad news.

Finally, just as supervisors and lower-level managers need their supporters in order to be and feel powerful, so do top executives. But for them sponsorship may not be so much a matter of individual endorsement as an issue of support by larger sources of legitimacy in the society. For top executives the problem is not to fit in among peers; rather, the question is whether the public at large and other organization members perceive a common interest which they see the executives as promoting.

If, however, public sources of support are withdrawn and leaders are open to public attack or if inside constituencies fragment and employees see their interests better aligned with pressure groups than with organizational leadership, then powerlessness begins to set in.

When common purpose is lost, the system's own politics may reduce the capacity of those at the top to act. Just as managing decline seems to create a much more passive and reactive stance than managing growth, so does mediating among conflicting interests. When what is happening outside and inside their organizations is out of their control, many people at the top turn into decline managers and dispute mediators. Neither is a particularly empowering role.

Thus when top executives lose their own lines of supply, lines of information, and lines of support, they too suffer from a kind of powerlessness. The temptation for them then is to pull in every shred of power they can and to decrease the power available to other people to act. Innovation loses out in favor of control. Limits rather than targets are set. Financial goals are met by reducing "overhead" (people) rather than by giving people the tools and discretion to increase their own productive capacity. Dictatorial statements come down from the top, spreading the mentality of powerlessness farther until the whole organization becomes sluggish and people concentrate on protecting what they have rather than on producing what they can.

When everyone is playing "king of the mountain," guarding his or her turf jealously, then king of the mountain becomes the only game in town.

To Expand Power, Share It

In no case am I saying that people in the three hierarchical levels described are always powerless, but they are susceptible to common conditions that can contribute to powerlessness. Exhibit 3 summarizes the most common symptoms of powerlessness for each level and some typical sources of that behavior.

I am also distinguishing the tremendous concentration of economic and political power in large corporations themselves from the powerlessness that can beset individuals even in the highest positions in such organizations. What grows with organizational position in hierarchical levels is not necessarily the power to accomplish—productive power—but the power to

Exhibit 3.

Position	Symptoms	Sources
First-line supervisors	Close, rules-minded supervision	Routine, rules-minded jobs with little control over lines of supply
	Tendency to do things oneself, blocking of subordinates' development and information	Limited lines of information
	Resistant, underproducing subordinates	Limited advancement or involvement prospects for oneself/subordinates
Staff professionals	Turf protection, information control	Routine tasks seen as peripheral to "real tasks" of line organization
	Retreat into professionalism	Blocked careers
	Conservative resistance to change	Easy replacement by outside experts
Top executives	Focus on internal cutting, short-term results, "punishing"	Uncontrollable lines of supply because of environmental changes
	Dictatorial top-down communications	Limited or blocked lines of information about lower levels of organization
	Retreat to comfort of like-minded lieutenants	Diminished lines of support because of challenges to legitimacy (e.g., from the public or special interest groups)

punish, to prevent, to sell off, to reduce, to fire, all without appropriate concern for consequences. It is that kind of power—oppressive power—that we often say corrupts.

The absence of ways to prevent individual and social harm causes the polity to feel it must surround people in power with constraints, regulations, and laws that limit the arbitrary use of their authority. But if oppressive power corrupts, then so does the absence of productive power. In large organizations, powerlessness can be a bigger problem than power.

David C. McClelland makes a similar distinction between oppressive and productive power:

"The negative . . . face of power is characterized by the dominance-submission mode: if I win, you lose. . . . It leads to simple and direct means of feeling powerful [such as being aggressive]. It does not often lead to effective social leadership for the reason that such a person tends to treat other people as pawns. People who feel they are pawns tend to be passive and useless to the leader who gets his satisfaction from dominating them. Slaves are the most inefficient form of labor ever devised by man. If a leader wants to have far-reaching influence, he must make his followers feel powerful and able to accomplish things on their own. . . . Even the most dictatorial leader does not succeed if he has not instilled in at least some of his followers a sense of power and the strength to pursue the goals he has set."[8]

Organizational power can grow, in part, by being shared. We do not yet know enough about new organizational forms to say whether productive power is infinitely expandable or where we reach the point of diminishing returns. But we do know that sharing power is different from giving or throwing it away. Delegation does not mean abdication.

Some basic lessons could be translated from the field of economics to the realm of organizations and management. Capital investment in plants and equipment is not the only key to productivity. The productive capacity of nations, like organizations, grows if the skill base is upgraded. People with the tools, information, and support to make more informed decisions and act more quickly can often accomplish more. By empowering others, a leader does not decrease his power; instead he may increase it—especially if the whole organization performs better.

This analysis leads to some counterintuitive conclusions. In a certain tautological sense, the principal problem of the powerless is that they lack power. Powerless people are usually the last ones to whom anyone wants to entrust more power, for fear of its dissipation or abuse. But those people are precisely the ones who might benefit most from an injection of power and whose behavior is likely to change as new options open up to them.

Also, if the powerless bosses could be encouraged to share some of the power they do have, their power would grow. Yet, of course, only those leaders who feel secure about their own power outward—their lines of supply, information, and support—can see empowering subordinates as a gain rather than a loss. The two sides of power (getting it and giving it) are closely connected.

There are important lessons here for both subordinates and those who want to change organizations, whether executives or change agents. Instead of resisting or criticizing a powerless boss, which only increases the boss's feeling of powerlessness and need to control, subordinates instead might concentrate on helping the boss become more powerful. Managers might make pockets of ineffectiveness in the organization more productive not by training or replacing individuals but by structural solutions such as opening supply and support lines.

Similarly, organizational change agents who want a new program or policy to succeed should make sure that the change itself does not render any other level of the organization powerless. In making changes, it is wise to make sure that the key people in the level or two directly above and in neighboring functions are sufficiently involved, informed, and taken into account, so that the program can be used to build their own sense of power also. If such involvement is impossible, then it is better to move these people out of the territory altogether than to leave behind a group from whom some power has been removed and who might resist and undercut the program.

In part, of course, spreading power means educating people to this new definition of it. But words alone will not make the difference; managers will need the real experience of a new way of managing.

Here is how the associate director of a large corporate professional department phrased the lessons that he learned in the transition to a team-oriented, participatory, power-sharing management process:

"Get in the habit of involving your own managers in decision making and approvals. But don't abdicate! Tell them what you want and where you're coming from. Don't go for a one-boss grass roots 'democracy.' Make the management hierarchy work for you in participation. . . .

"Hang in there, baby, and don't give up. Try not to 'revert' just because everything seems to go sour on a particular day. Open up—talk to people and tell them how you feel. They'll want to get you back on track and will do things to make that happen—because they don't really want to go back to the way it was. . . . Subordinates will push you to 'act more like a boss,' but their interest is usually more in seeing someone else brought to heel than getting bossed themselves."

Naturally, people need to have power before they can learn to share it. Exhorting managers to change their leadership styles is rarely useful by itself. In one large plant of a major electronics company, first-line production supervisors were the source of numerous complaints from managers who saw them as major roadblocks to overall plant productivity and as insufficiently skilled supervisors. So the plant personnel staff undertook two pilot programs to increase the supervisors' effectiveness. The first program was based on a traditional competency and training model aimed at teaching the specific skills of successful supervisors. The second program, in contrast, was designed to empower the supervisors by directly affecting their flexibility, access to resources, connections with higher-level officials, and control over working conditions.

After an initial gathering of data from supervisors and their subordinates, the personnel staff held meetings where all the supervisors were given tools for developing action plans for sharing the data with their people and collaborating on solutions to perceived problems. But then, in a departure from common practice in this organization, task forces of supervisors were formed to develop new systems for handling job and career issues common to them and their people. These task forces were given budgets, consultants, representation on a plantwide project steering committee alongside managers at much higher levels, and wide latitude in defining the nature and scope of the changes they wished to make. In short, lines of supply, information, and support were opened to them.

As the task forces progressed in their activities, it became clear to the plant management that the hoped-for changes in supervisory effectiveness were taking place much more rapidly through these structural changes in power than through conventional management training; so the conventional training was dropped. Not only did the pilot groups design useful new procedures for the plant, astonishing senior management in several cases with their knowledge and capabilities, but also, significantly, they learned to manage their own people better.

Several groups decided to involve shop-floor workers in their task forces; they could now see from their own experience the benefits of involving subordinates in solving job-related problems. Other supervisors began to experiment with ways to implement "participatory management" by giving subordinates more control and influence without relinquishing their own authority.

Soon the "problem supervisors" in the "most troubled plant in the company" were getting the highest possible performance ratings and were considered models for direct production management. The sharing of organizational power from the top made possible the productive use of power below.

One might wonder why more organizations do not adopt such empowering strategies. There are standard answers: that giving up control is threatening to people who have fought for every shred of it; that people do not want to share power with those they look down on; that managers fear losing their own place and special privileges in the system; that "predictability" often rates higher than "flexibility" as an organizational value; and so forth.

But I would also put skepticism about employee abilities high on the list. Many modern bureaucratic systems are designed to minimize dependence on individual intelligence by making routine as many decisions as possible. So it often comes as a genuine surprise to top executives that people doing the more routine jobs could, indeed, make sophisticated decisions or use resources entrusted to them in intelligent ways.

In the same electronics company just mentioned, at the end of a quarter the pilot supervisory task forces were asked to report results and plans to senior management in order to have their new budget requests approved.

The task forces made sure they were well prepared, and the high-level executives were duly impressed. In fact, they were *so* impressed that they kept interrupting the presentations with compliments, remarking that the supervisors could easily be doing sophisticated personnel work.

At first the supervisors were flattered. Such praise from upper management could only be taken well. But when the first glow wore off, several of them became very angry. They saw the excessive praise as patronizing and insulting. "Didn't they think we could think? Didn't they imagine we were capable of doing this kind of work?" one asked. "They must have seen us as just a bunch of animals. No wonder they gave us such limited jobs."

As far as these supervisors were concerned, their abilities had always been there, in latent form perhaps, but still there. They as individuals had not changed—just their organizational power.

Notes

1. Donald C. Pelz, "Influence: A Key to Effective Leadership in the First-Line Supervisor," *Personnel*, November 1952, p. 209.

2. Rosabeth Moss Kanter, *Men and Women of the Corporation* (New York: Basic Books, 1977), pp. 164–205; and David Kipnis, *The Powerholders* (Chicago: University of Chicago Press, 1976).

3. Pehr G. Gyllenhammar, *People at Work* (Reading, Mass.: Addison-Wesley, 1977), p. 133.

4. William E. Fulmer, "Supervisory Selection: The Acid Test of Affirmative Action," *Personnel*, November-December 1976, p. 40.

5. See my chapter (coauthor, Barry A. Stein), "Life in the Middle: Getting In, Getting Up, and Getting Along," in *Life in Organizations*, eds. Rosabeth M. Kanter and Barry A. Stein (New York: Basic Books, 1979).

6. Warren Bennis, *The Unconscious Conspiracy: Why Leaders Can't Lead* (New York: AMACOM, 1976).

7. See my chapter, "How the Top Is Different," in *Life in Organizations*, eds. Rosabeth M. Kanter and Barry A. Stein (New York: Basic Books, 1979).

8. David C. McClelland, *Power: The Inner Experience* (New York: Irvington Publishers, 1975), p. 263. Quoted by permission.

Appendix A: Women Managers Experience Special Power Failures

The traditional problems of women in management are illustrative of how formal and informal practices can combine to engender powerlessness. Historically, women in management have found their opportunities in more routine, low-profile jobs. In staff positions, where they serve in support capacities to line managers but have no line responsibilities of their own, or in supervisory jobs managing "stuck" subordinates, they are not in a position either to take the kinds of risks that build credibility or to develop their own team by pushing bright subordinates.

Such jobs, which have few favors to trade, tend to keep women out of the mainstream of the organization. This lack of clout, coupled with the greater difficulty anyone who is "different" has in getting into the information and support networks, has meant that merely by organizational situation women in management have been more likely than men to be rendered structurally powerless. This is one reason those women who have achieved power have often had family connections that put them in the mainstream of the organization's social circles.

A disproportionate number of women managers are found among first-line supervisors or staff professionals; and they, like men in those circumstances, are likely to be organizationally powerless. But the behavior of other managers can contribute to the powerlessness of women in management in a number of less obvious ways.

One way other managers can make a woman powerless is by patronizingly overprotecting her: putting her in "a safe job," not giving her enough to do to prove herself, and not suggesting her for high-risk, visible assignments. This protectiveness is sometimes born of "good" intentions to give her every chance to succeed (why stack the deck against her?). Out of managerial concerns, out of awareness that a woman may be up against situations that men simply do not have to face, some very well-meaning managers protect their female managers ("It's a jungle, so why send her into it?").

Overprotectiveness can also mask a manager's fear of association with a woman should she fail. One senior bank official at a level below vice president told me about his concerns with respect to a high-performing, financially experienced woman reporting to him. Despite *his* overwhelmingly positive work experiences with her, he was still afraid to recommend her for other assignments because he felt it was a personal risk. "What if other managers are not as accepting of women as I am?" he asked. "I know I'd be sticking my neck out; they would take her more because of my endorsement than her qualifications. And what if she doesn't make it? My judgment will be on the line."

Overprotection is relatively benign compared with rendering a person powerless by providing obvious signs of lack of managerial support. For example, allowing someone supposedly in authority to be bypassed easily means that no one else has to take him or her seriously. If a woman's immediate supervisor or other managers listen willingly to criticism of her and show they are concerned every time a negative comment comes up and that they assume she must be at fault, then they are helping to undercut her. If managers let other people know that they have concerns about this person or that they are testing her to see how she does, then they are inviting other people to look for signs of inadequacy or failure.

Furthermore, people assume they can afford to bypass women because they "must be uninformed" or "don't know the ropes." Even though women may be respected for their competence or expertise, they are not necessarily seen as being informed beyond the technical requirements of the job. There may be a grain of historical truth in this. Many women come to senior management positions as "outsiders" rather than up through the usual channels.

Also, because until very recently men have not felt comfortable seeing women as businesspeople (business clubs have traditionally excluded women), they have tended to seek each other out for informal socializing. Anyone, male or female, seen as organizationally naive and lacking sources of "inside dope" will find his or her own lines of information limited.

Finally, even when women are able to achieve some power on their own, they have not necessarily been able to translate such personal credibility into an organizational power base. To create a network of supporters out of individual clout requires that a person pass on and share power, that subordinates and peers be empowered by virtue of their connection with that person. Traditionally, neither men nor women have seen women as capable of sponsoring others, even though they may be capable of achieving and succeeding on their own. Women have been viewed as the *recipients* of sponsorship rather than as the sponsors themselves.

(As more women prove themselves in organizations and think more self-consciously about bringing along young people, this situation may change. However, I still hear many more questions from women managers about how they can benefit from mentors, sponsors, or peer networks than about how they themselves can start to pass on favors and make use of their own resources to benefit others.)

Viewing managers in terms of power and powerlessness helps explain two familiar stereotypes about women and leadership in organizations: that no one wants a woman boss (although studies show that anyone who has ever had a woman boss is likely to have had a positive experience), and that the reason no one wants a woman boss is that women are "too controlling, rules-minded, and petty."

The first stereotype simply makes clear that power is important to leadership. Underneath the preference for men is the assumption that, given the current distribution of people in organizational leadership positions, men are more likely than women to be in positions to achieve power and, therefore, to share their power with others. Similarly, the "bossy woman boss" stereotype is a perfect picture of powerlessness. All of those traits are just as characteristic of men who are powerless, but women are slightly more likely, because of circumstances I have mentioned, to find themselves powerless than are men. Women with power in the organization are just as effective—and preferred—as men.

Recent interviews conducted with about 600 bank managers show that, when a woman exhibits the petty traits of powerlessness, people assume that she does so "because she is a woman." A striking difference is that, when a man engages in the same behavior, people assume the behavior is a matter of his own individual style and characteristics and do not conclude that it reflects on the suitability of men for management.

4
When Executives Burn Out

HARRY LEVINSON

The military knows about burn-out—but calls it battle fatigue. To offset its devastating effects, the military routinely schedules its personnel for recreation and relaxation retreats, sends soldiers into combat in groups so they can support and help each other, and limits the number of flights that pilots fly. Managers are not soldiers but, according to this author and others who have researched the subject, they are prone to a similar exhaustion and sense of futility. Like other professionals, mental health workers, and police officers who work under severe pressure in people-oriented jobs for long periods of time—with little support and limited gains—managers are among the prime victims of burn-out. The author describes what burn-out is, discusses why he thinks that modern organizations are good breeding grounds for situations that lead to it, and offers some helpful ways top managers can combat it.

☐ "I just can't seem to get going," the vice president said. He grimaced as he leaned back in his chair. "I can't get interested in what I'm supposed to do. I know I should get rolling. I know there's a tremendous amount of work to be done. That's why they brought me in and put me in this job, but I just can't seem to get going."

Eighteen months before making these comments, the vice president had transferred to company headquarters from a subsidiary. His new job was to revamp the company's control systems which, because of reorganization, were in disarray. When the vice president reported to headquarters, however, top management immediately recruited him to serve as a key staff figure in its own reshuffling. Because he was not in competition with line

Published in 1980.

executives, he was the only staff person who interviewed and consulted with both the line executives and the chief executive officer. And because the top managers regarded him as trustworthy, they gave his recommendations serious attention.

But his task was arduous. Not only did the long hours and the unremitting pressure of walking a tightrope among conflicting interests exhaust him, but also they made it impossible for him to get at the control problems that needed attention. Furthermore, because his family could not move for six months until the school year was over, he commuted on weekends to his previous home 800 miles away. As he tried to perform the unwanted job that had been thrust on him and support the CEO who was counting heavily on his competence, he felt lonely, harassed, and burdened. Now that his task was coming to an end, he was in no psychological shape to take on his formal duties. In short, he had "burned-out."

Like generalized stress, burn-out cuts across executive and managerial levels. While the phenomenon manifests itself in varying ways and to different degrees in different people, it appears, nonetheless, to have identifiable characteristics. For instance, in the next example, the individual changes but many of the features of the problem are the same:

> ☐ A vice president of a large corporation who didn't receive an expected promotion left his company to become the CEO of a smaller, family-owned business, which was floundering and needed his skills. Although he had jumped at the opportunity to rescue the small company, once there he discovered an unimaginable morass of difficulties, among them continuous conflicts within the family. He felt he could not leave; but neither could he succeed. Trapped in a kind of psychological quicksand, he worked nights, days, and weekends for months trying to pull himself free. His wife protested, to no avail. Finally, he was hospitalized for exhaustion.

As in the previous example, the competence of the individual is not in question; today he is the chief executive of a major corporation.

Quite a different set of problems confronted another executive. This is how he tells his story:

> ☐ In March of 1963, I moved to a small town in Iowa with my wife and son of four weeks. I was an up-and-coming engineer with the electric company—magic and respected words in those days.
>
> Ten years later things had changed. When we went to social gatherings and talked to people, I ended up having to defend the electric company. At the time we were tying into a consortium, which was building a nuclear generating plant. The amount of negative criticism was immense, and it never really let up. Refusing to realize how important that generating plant was to a reliable flow of electricity, people continued to find fault.

Now, nearly ten years later, we are under even greater attack. In my present role, I'm the guy who catches it all. I can't seem to get people to stand still and listen, and I can't continue to take all the hostility that goes with it—the crank calls, being woken up late at night and called names. I don't know how much longer I can last in this job.

Before looking in depth at what the burn-out phenomenon is, let's look at the experience of one more executive who is well on his way to burning out:

☐ I have been with this company for nearly 15 years and have changed jobs every 2 to 3 years. Most of our managers are company men and women, like me. We have always been a high-technology company, but we have been doing less well in marketing than some of our competitors. Over the past 10 years we have been going through a continuous reorganization process. The organization charts keep changing, but the underlying philosophy, management techniques, and administrative trappings don't. The consequence is continuous frustration, disruption, resentment, and the undermining of 'change.' You don't take a company that has been operating with a certain perspective and turn it around overnight.

With these changes we are also being told what we must do and when. Before, we were much more flexible and free to follow our noses. These shifts create enormous pressures on an organization that is used to different ways of operating.

On top of that, a continuous corporate pruning goes on. I am a survivor, so I should feel good about it and believe what top management tells me, namely, that the unfit go and the worthy remain. But the old virtues—talent, initiative, and risk taking—are *not* being rewarded. Instead, acquiescence to corporate values and social skills that obliterate differences among individuals are the virtues that get attention. Also the reward process is more political than meritocratic.

I don't know if we're going to make it. And there are a lot of others around here who have the same feeling. We're all demoralized.

Burn-Out—A Slow Fizzle

What was happening to these executives? In exploring that question, let's first look at what characterized the situations. In one or more cases, they:

☐ Were repetitive or prolonged.

☐ Engendered enormous burdens on the managers.

☐ Promised great success but made attaining it nearly impossible.

☐ Exposed the managers to risk of attack for doing their jobs, without providing a way for them to fight back.

□   Aroused deep emotions—sorrow, fear, despair, compassion, help-lessness, pity, and rage. To survive, the managers would try to harden outer "shells" to contain their feelings and hide their anguish.

□   Overwhelmed the managers with complex detail, conflicting forces, and problems against which they hurled themselves with increasing intensity—but without impact.

□   Exploited the managers but provided them little to show for having been victimized.

□   Aroused a painful, inescapable sense of inadequacy and often of guilt.

□   Left the managers feeling that no one knew, let alone gave a damn about, what price they were paying, what contribution or sacrifice they were making, or what punishment they were absorbing.

□   Caused the managers to raise the question "What for?"—as if they'd lost sight of the purpose of living.

Those who study cases like these agree that a special phenomenon occurs after people expend a great deal of effort, intense to the point of exhaustion, often without visible results. People in these situations feel angry, helpless, trapped, and depleted: they are burned out. This experience is more intense than what is ordinarily referred to as stress. The major defining characteristic of burn-out is that people can't or won't do again what they have been doing.

Dr. Herbert J. Freudenberger of New York evolved this definition of burn-out when he observed a special sort of fatigue among mental health workers.[1] Freudenberger observed that burn-out is followed by physiological signs such as the inability to shake colds and frequent headaches, as well as psychological symptoms like quickness to anger and a suspicious attitude about others.

Christina Maslach, who is a pioneer researcher on the subject at the University of California, Berkeley, says that burn-out "refers to a syndrome of emotional exhaustion and cynicism that frequently occurs among people who do 'people work'—who spend considerable time in close encounters."[2]

People suffering burn-out generally have identifiable characteristics: (1) chronic fatigue; (2) anger at those making demands; (3) self-criticism for putting up with the demands; (4) cynicism, negativism, and irritability; (5) a sense of being besieged; and (6) hair-trigger display of emotions.

Although it is not evident from these examples, frequently other destructive types of behavior accompany these feelings—including inappropriate anger at subordinates and family and sometimes withdrawal even from those whose support is most needed; walling off home and work completely from each other; diffuse physical symptoms; efforts to escape the source of pressure through illness, absenteeism, drugs or alcohol, or increased temporary psychological escape (meditation, biofeedback, and other forms of self-hypnosis); increasing rigidity of attitude; and cold, detached, and less emphatic behavior.

Most people, even reasonably effective managers, probably experience a near burn-out at some time in their careers. A 20-year study of a group of middle managers disclosed that many of them, now in their forties and with few prospects of further promotions, were tolerating unhappy marriages, narrowing their focuses to their own jobs, and showing less consideration to other people.[3] Despite outward sociability, they were indifferent to friendships and were often hostile. They had become rigid, had short fuses, and were distant from their children.

Personality tests disclosed that these individuals had a higher need to do a job well for its own sake than did most of their peers, and they initially had a greater need for advancement as well (although this declined over time). They showed more motivation to dominate and lead and less to defer to authority than other managers. While they still could do a good day's work, they could no longer invest themselves in others and in the company.

When people who feel an intense need to achieve don't reach their goals, they can become hostile to themselves and others as well. They also tend to channel that hostility into more defined work tasks than before, limiting their efforts. If at times like these they do not increase their family involvement, they are likely to approach burn-out.

The Breeding Ground

Researchers have observed this exhaustion among many kinds of professionals. As the previous examples indicate, it is not unusual among executives and managers, and under very competitive conditions it is more likely to occur than in a stable market. Managerial jobs involve a lot of contact with other people. Often this contact is unpleasant but has to be tolerated because of the inherent demands of the job.

And one problem with managing people lies in the fact that such a focus creates unending stress for the manager. The manager must cope with the least capable among the employees, with the depressed, the suspicious, the rivalrous, the self-centered, and the generally unhappy. The manager must balance these conflicting personalities and create from them a motivated work group. He or she must define group purpose and organize people around that, must resolve conflicts, establish priorities, make decisions about other people, accept and deflect their hostility, and deal with the frustration that arises out of that continuing interaction. Managing people is the most difficult administrative task, and it has built-in frustration. That frustration, carried to extremes beyond stress, can—and does—cause managers to burn out.

Many contemporary managerial situations, also provide the perfect breeding ground for cases of burn-out.

Today's managers face increasing time pressures with little respite. Even though benefits such as flexible working hours and longer vacation periods offer some relief, for the most part the modern executive's workday is long and hard. Also, as more women join the work force, the support most men used to receive at home is lessening, and women at work get as little, if not less, than the men. To many managers, the time they spend with their families is precious. It is understandable if managers feel guilty about sacrificing this part of their life to the demands of work and also feel frustration at being unable to do anything about it.

Adding to the stress at work is the complexity of modern organizations. The bigger and more intricate organizations become, the longer it takes to get things done. Managers trying to get ahead may well feel enormous frustration as each person or office a project passes through adds more delays and more problems to unravel before a task is finished.

Along with the increase in complexity of organization goes an increase in the number of people that a manager has to deal with. Participative management, quality of worklife efforts, and matrix structures all result in a proliferation in the number of people that a manager confronts face to face. Building a plant, developing natural resources, or evolving new products can often mean that a manager has to go through lengthy, and sometimes angry and vitrioloc, interaction with community groups. Executives involved in tasks that entail controversial issues can find themselves vilified.

As companies grow, merge with other companies, or go through reorganizations, some managers feel adrift. Sacrifices they have made on behalf of the organization may well turn out to have little enduring meaning. As an organization's values change, a manager's commitment and sense of support may also shift. Another aspect of change that can add to a person's feeling burned out is the threat of obsolescence. When a new job or assignment requires that managers who are already feeling taxed develop new capacities, they may feel overwhelmed.

These days change can also mean that managers have to trim jobs, cut back, and demote subordinates—and maybe even discharge them. Managers whose job it is to close a plant or go through painful labor negotiations may feel enraged at having to pay for the sins of their predecessors. Also, a fragmented marketplace can mean intense pressures on managers to come up with new products, innovative services, and novel marketing and financing schemes.

Finally, employees are making increasing demands for their rights. Managers may feel that they cannot satisfy those demands but have to respond to them.[4] And if inflation gets worse, so will these kinds of pressures.

Prevention Is the Best Cure

Top management can take steps to keep managers out of situations where they are likely to burn out. Of course, something as subtle as psychological exhaustion cannot be legislated against completely, but the following steps have been known to mitigate its occurrence:

☐ First, as with all such phenomena, recognize that burn-out can, does, and will happen. The people in charge of orientation programs, management training courses, and discussions of managerial practice ought to acknowledge to employees that burn-out can occur and that people's vulnerability to it is something the organization recognizes and cares about. Personnel managers should be candid with new employees on the psychological nature of the work they are getting into, especially when that work involves intense effort of the kind I've described. The more people know, the less guilt they are likely to feel for their own perceived inadequacies when the pressures begin to mount.

Keep track of how long your subordinates are in certain jobs and rotate them out of potentially exhausting positions. Changes of pace, changes of demands, and shifts into situations that may not be so depleting enable people to replenish their energies and get new and more accurate perspectives on themselves and their roles.

Change also enables people to look forward to a time when they can get out of a binding job. Long recognizing this need, the military limits the number of combat missions Air Force personnel fly and the duration of tours ground personnel endure.

☐   Time constraints on a job are crucial to preventing burn-out. Don't allow your people to work 18 hours a day, even on critical problems. Especially don't let the same people be the rescuers of troubled situations over and over again. Understandably, managers tend to rely on their best people; but best people are more vulnerable to becoming burned-out people.

Overconscientious people, in particular, need to take time off from the role and its demands and to spend that time in refreshing recreation. The military has long since learned this lesson, but for some reason management has not. One way to make sure people break from work would be to take a whole work group on a nominal business trip to a recreational site.

Some companies have set up regular formal retreats where people who work together under pressure can talk about what they are doing and how they are doing it, make long-range plans, relax and enjoy themselves, and, most important, get away from what they have to cope with every day. When managers talk together in a setting like this, they can make realistic assessments of the problems they are up against and their own responsibilities and limits.

I think, for example, of the extremely conscientious engineers in many of the small electronics companies on Route 128 in the Boston area, of those in the research triangle in North Carolina, or in the Palo Alto, California area who have reported feeling that they simply are not developing new products fast enough. They are convinced they aren't living up to the extremely high standards that they set for themselves. Such people need to

talk together, often with a group therapist or someone else who can help
them relieve some of the irrational self-demands they frequently make on
themselves as groups and as individuals.

☐ Make sure your organization has a systematic way of letting people
know that their contributions are important. People need information
that supports their positive self-images, eases their consciences, and
refuels them psychologically.

Many compensation and performance appraisal programs actually contribute to people's sense that their efforts will be unrecognized, no matter
how well they do. Organizational structures and processes that inhibit timely
attacks on problems and delay competitive actions actually produce much
of the stress that people experience at work. If top executives fail to see
that organizational factors can cause burn-out, their lack of understanding
may perpetuate the problem.

It is also important that top managers review people's capacities, skills,
and opportunities with their employees so that, armed with facts about
themselves and the organization, they can make choices rather than feel
trapped.

☐ During World War II, the Army discovered that it was better to
send soldiers overseas in groups rather than as single replacements. It
may be equally effective for you to send groups of people from one
organizational task to another rather than assemble teams of individually assigned people. When Clairol opened a new plant in California,
it sent a group of Connecticut-based managers and their spouses, who
were briefed on the new assignment, the new community, and the
potential stresses they might encounter. They discussed together how
they might help themselves and each other, as well as what support
they needed from the organization.

Some construction companies also create teams of people before undertaking a new project. People who have worked together have already
established various mutual support systems, ways to share knowledge informally, and friendly alliances. These can prevent or ameliorate potential
burn-out that may occur in new, difficult, or threatening tasks.

☐ Provide avenues through which people can express not only their
anger but also their disappointment, helplessness, futility, defeat, and
depression. Some employees, like salespeople, meet defeat every day.
Others meet defeat in a crisis—when a major contract or competition
is lost, when a product expected to succeed fails, when the competition
outflanks them. When people in defeat deny their angry feelings, the

denial of underlying, seething anger contributes to the sense of burn-out.

If top executives fail to see these problems as serious, they may worsen the situation. If the company offers only palliatives like meditation and relaxation methods—temporarily helpful though these may be—burn-out victims may become further enraged. The sufferers know their problem has to do with the nature of the job and not their capacity to handle it.

Those managers who are exposed to attack need to talk about the hostilities they anticipate and how to cope with them. Just as sailors at sea need to anticipate and cope with storms, so executives need to learn how to cope with the public's aggression. Under attack themselves, they need to evolve consensus, foster cohesion, and build trust rather than undermine themselves with counterattacks.

☐ Another way to help is to defend publicly against outside attacks on the organization. In recent months a prominent chief executive raised the morale of all of his employees when he filed suit against a broadcast medium for false allegations about his company's products. Another publicly took on a newspaper that had implied his organization was not trustworthy. A visible, vigorous, and powerful leader does much to counteract people's sense of helplessness.

☐ As technology changes, you need to retrain and upgrade your managers. But some people will be unable to rise to new levels of responsibility and are likely to feel defeated if they cannot succeed in the same job. Top management needs to retrain, refresh, and reinvigorate these managers as quickly as possible by getting them to seminars, workshops, and other activities away from the organization.

As Freudenberger commented after his early observations, however, introspection is not what the burned-out person requires; rather, he or she needs intense physical activity, not further mental strain and fatigue. Retreats, seminars, and workshops therefore should be oriented toward the cognitive and physical rather than the emotional. Physical exercise is helpful because it provides an outlet for angry feelings and pent-up energy.

☐ Managers who are burning out need support from others from whom they can get psychological sustenance. Ideally, those others should be their bosses—people who value them as individuals and insist that they withdraw, get appropriate help, and place themselves first.

In times of unmitigated strain it is particularly important that you keep up personal interaction with your subordinates. To borrow from the military again, generals valued by their troops, like George Patton and James Gavin in World War II, make it a practice to be involved with their frontline soldiers.

Freudenberger points out that the burn-out phenomenon often occurs when a leader or the leader's charisma is lost. He notes that people who join an organization still led by the founder or founding group frequently expect that person or group to be superhuman. They were, after all, the entrepreneurs with the foresight, vision, drive, and imagination to build the organization. "As they begin to disappoint us, we bad-rap them and the result, unless it is stopped, is psychic damage to the whole clinic," he comments.[5] The issue is the same whether it is a clinic, a hospital, a police department, or a business.

Executives who are idealized should take time to publicly remove their halos. They can do that by explaining their own struggles, disappointments, and defeats to their subordinates so that the latter can view them more accurately. They need also to help people to verbalize their disappointment with the "fallen" executive hero.

When the leader leaves, either through death or transfer, when a paternalistic, successful entrepreneur sells out, or when an imaginative inventor retires, it is important for the group that remains to have the opportunity to go through a process of discussing its loss and mourning it. The group needs to conduct a psychological wake and consider for itself how it is going to replace the loss.

Frequently, the group will discover that, though the loss of the leader is indeed significant, it can carry on effectively and contribute to the success of the organization. Failing to realize its own strengths, a group can, like the Green Bay Packers after the death of coach Vince Lombardi, feel permanently handicapped. To my knowledge, few organizations effectively deal with the loss of a leader. Most respond with a depression or slump from which it takes years to recover. Also, and more crippling, is the way people in the organization keep yearning and searching for a new charismatic leader to rescue them. As part of a national organization, Americans have been doing this searching ever since the death of John Kennedy.

Notes

1. Herbert J. Freudenberger, "Staff Burn-Out," *Journal of Social Issues,* vol. 30, no. 1, 1974, p. 159; see also his recent book, *Burn-Out: The Melancholy of High Achievement* (New York: Doubleday, 1980).

2. Christina Maslach, "Burn-Out," *Human Behavior,* September 1976, p. 16.

3. Douglas W. Bray, Richard J. Campbell, and Donald L. Grant, *Formative Years in Business* (New York: John Wiley, 1974).

4. Opinion Research Corporation reports a recent survey that confirms this point.

5. Freudenberger, "Staff Burn-Out," p. 160.

Appendix A: I Read the News Today . . .*

A week before he suddenly quit as president of Pratt, Bruce Torell spoke, a little wearily, of "death throe competitions" which had become the norm, rather than the exception. (In earlier decades, engine makers might compete to determine what engine would launch a new jet; after that was decided, the business seemed assured for decades.)

"Almost as much effort was needed to deal with the critics as with the problems," said Torell in an interview on retirement.

Torell's retirement came as a surprise to most workers at the company. In an interview a week before, he had spoken of the ongoing challenges of his job. He put it this way: "This is a business where the risks are high, the stakes are high, and hopefully the rewards are high."

The week after those statements, the wind seemed to have gone out of him. He had, he said, no plans. "After eight years in a real tough environment, I won't be looking for anything quite so stressful."

*New England Business, September 1, 1979, p. 11. Reprinted by permission.

5
The Foreman
Master and Victim of
Double Talk

F. J. ROETHLISBERGER

The foreman is the classic middleman, the man without a country, the man with no place to hang his hat. As the link between management and the shop floor the foreman does not belong to any group and yet has to work with both. The author of this article, a well-known human relations specialist, writes that as a result of being deprived of real social relationships, the foreman will express his dissatisfaction and take it out on the job in any number of ways. The solution to the foreman's dilemma lies in the hands of his manager. It is the manager's job, the author writes, to become a different kind of administrator: "He will have to learn to be responsible for people not merely responsible for abstract and logical categories." In becoming this new kind of administrator, managers will have to recognize the importance of feelings and treat them as legitimate parts of the work environment.

The increasing dissatisfaction of foremen in mass production industries, as evidenced by the rise of foremen's unions, calls for more human understanding of the foreman's situation. This dissatisfaction of foremen is no new, nor static, problem. It arises from the dynamic interaction of many social forces and is part and parcel of the structure of modern industrial organization. In its present manifestation it is merely a new form and outbreak of an old disease, which management has repeatedly failed to recognize, let alone diagnose or treat correctly. Master and victim of double

---

Published in 1945.

talk, the foreman is management's contribution to the social pathology of American culture.

Some of the reasons cited in the current situation for the increasing receptiveness of foremen to unionization in mass production industries are:

1 The weekly take-home pay of many foremen is less than that of the men working under them; this condition has been aggravated under war conditions in those factories where foremen do not receive extra compensation for working overtime.

2 The influx of inexperienced workers, under war demands, has made the foremen's jobs more difficult.

3 The rise of industrial unions has stripped the foremen of most of their authority.

4 Many union-minded workers have been upgraded to supervisory positions.

5 Many production workers promoted to the rank of foreman during the war expansion face the possibility of demotion after the war and the sacrifice of seniority credits in the unions from which they came for the period spent as foremen.

It would be absurd to argue that these factors, particularly as they are aggravated by war conditions, have not contributed to the grievances which foremen hope to correct by unionization. In a number of companies it is only fair to say that management has recognized some of these grievances and, when possible, has taken corrective steps. But is the correction of these grievances alone enough? Unfortunately, the possibility still exists that too little attention will be given to the underlying situation. The symptom-by-symptom attack that management is prone to take in solving its human affairs will fail to go below the surface. Failing to recognize the hydra-headed character of the social situation with which it is faced, management will cut off one head, only to have two new heads appear.

The major thesis of this article therefore will be that once again "management's chickens have come home to roost."[1] And this question is raised: Can management afford not to take responsibility for its own social creations—one of which is the situation in which foremen find themselves?

The Position of the Foreman

Nowhere in the industrial structure more than at the foreman level is there so great a discrepancy between what a position ought to be and what a position is. This may account in part for the wide range of names which foremen have been called—shall we say "informally"?—and the equally great variety of definitions which have been applied to them in a more strictly formal and legal sense. Some managements have been eloquent in citing the foremen's importance with such phrases as: "arms of management," "grass-roots level of management," "key men in production," "front-line personnel men," and the like. Not so definite is the status of foremen under the National Labor Relations Act, since they can be included under the definitions given both for "employers" and "employees." To many foremen themselves they are merely the "go-betweeners," the "forgotten men," the "stepchildren" of industry. And what some employees call some foremen we shall leave to the reader's imagination.

But even without this diversity of names, it is clear that from the point of view of the individual foreman the discrepancy between what he should be and what he is cannot fail to be disconcerting. At times it is likely to influence adversely what he actually does or does not do, communicates or does not communicate to his superiors, his associates, and his subordinates. For this reason let us try to understand better the foreman's position in the modern industrial scene.

It is in his new streamlined social setting, far different from the "good old days," that we must learn to understand the modern foreman's anomalous position. The modern foreman has to get results—turn out production, maintain quality, hold costs down, keep his employees satisfied—under a set of technical conditions, social relations, and logical abstractions far different from those which existed 25 years ago.

More Knowledge Required

For one thing, he* has to "know" more than his old-time counterpart. Any cursory examination of modern foreman training programs will reveal that the modern foreman has to know (and understand) not only (1) the company's policies, rules, and regulations and (2) the company's cost system, payment system, manufacturing methods, and inspection regulations, in particular, but also frequently (3) something about the theories of production control, cost control, quality control, and time and motion study, in general. He also has to know (4) the labor laws of the United States, (5) the labor laws of the state in which the company operates, and (6) the specific labor contract which exists between his company and the local union. He has to know (7) how to induct, instruct, and train new workers; (8) how to handle and, where possible, prevent grievances; (9) how to improve conditions of safety; (10) how to correct workers and maintain discipline; (11) how never to lose his temper and always to be "fair"; (12) how to get and obtain cooperation from the wide assortment of people with whom he has to deal; and, especially, (13) how to get along with the shop steward. And in some companies he is supposed to know (14) how to do the jobs he supervises better than the

---

*Authors Note: The masculine pronoun was used to preserve the language of this period; it should be read as he or she.

employees themselves. Indeed, as some foreman training programs seem to conceive the foreman's job, he has to be a manager, a cost accountant, an engineer, a lawyer, a teacher, a leader, an inspector, a disciplinarian, a counselor, a friend, and, above all, an "example."

One might expect that this superior knowledge would tend to make the modern foreman feel more secure as well as be more effective. But unfortunately some things do not work out the way they are intended. Quite naturally the foreman is bewildered by the many different roles and functions he is supposed to fulfill. He is worried in particular by what the boss will think if he takes the time to do the many things his many training courses tell him to do. And in 99 cases out of 100 what the boss thinks, or what the foreman thinks the boss thinks, will determine what the foreman does. As a result, the foreman gives lip service in his courses to things which in the concrete shop situation he feels it would be suicidal to practice. In the shop, for the most part, he does his best to perform by hook or by crook the one function clearly left him, the one function for which there is no definite staff counterpart, the one function for which the boss is sure to hold him responsible; namely, getting the workers to turn the work out on time. And about this function he feels his courses do not say enough—given the particular conditions, technical, human, and organizational, under which he has to operate.

Freedom of Action Restricted

Curiously enough, knowledge is not power for the modern foreman. Although he has to know a great deal about many things, he is no longer "the cock of the walk" he once was. Under modern conditions of operation, for example, there seems to be always somebody in the organization in a staff capacity who is supposed to know more than he does, and generally has more say, about almost every matter that comes up; somebody, in addition to his boss, with whom he is supposed to consult and sometimes to share responsibility; somebody by whom he is constantly advised and often even ordered.

To the foreman it seems as if he is being held responsible for functions over which he no longer has any real authority. For some time he has not been able to hire and fire and set production standards. And now he cannot even transfer employees, adjust the wage inequalities of his men, promote deserving men, develop better machines, methods, and processes, or plan the work of his department, with anything approaching complete freedom of action. All these matters for which he is completely or partially responsible have now become involved with other persons and groups, or they have become matters of company policy and union agreement. He is hedged in on all sides with cost standards, production standards, quality standards, standard methods and procedures, specifications, rules, regulations, policies, laws, contracts, and agreements; and most of them are formulated without his participation.

Far better than the old-timer of 25 years ago the modern foreman knows how much work should be done in what length of time; how much it is worth; what the best methods to be used are; what his material, labor, and burden costs should be; and what the tolerances are that his product should meet. But in the acquisition of all this untold wealth of knowledge, somehow something is missing. In some sense, not too clearly defined, he feels he has become less rather than more effective, less rather than more secure, less rather than more important, and has received less rather than more recognition.

Interactions with Many People

Let us explore further this feeling of the modern foreman. Not only does he have to know more than his old-time counterpart about the "logics" of management, but also he has to relate himself to a wider range of people. In any mass production industry the foreman each day is likely to be interacting

1 with his boss, the man to whom he formally reports in the line organization;
2 with certain staff specialists, varying from one to a dozen people depending on the size and kind of organization—production control men, inspectors, standards men, efficiency engineers, safety engineers, maintenance and repair men, methods men, personnel men, counselors;
3 with the heads of other departments which his department relates;
4 with his subordinates—subforemen, straw bosses, leadmen, group leaders, section chiefs;
5 with the workers directly, numbering anywhere from 10 to 300 people; and
6 in a union-organized plant, with the shop steward.

Exploring the interdependence of each of these relationships as they impinge in toto upon the foreman makes it easier to understand how the modern foreman may feel in his everyday life. A diagram may help to make this clear (see Exhibit 1).

Foreman–Superior. In the modern business structure there is probably no relation more important than that of the subordinate to his immediate superior.[2] This statement applies straight up the line from worker to president. It is in the relation between a subordinate and his immediate superior that most breakdowns of coordination and communication between various parts of the industrial structure finally show up. It is here that distortions of personal attitude and emotional disturbances become more pronounced.

Exhibit 1.

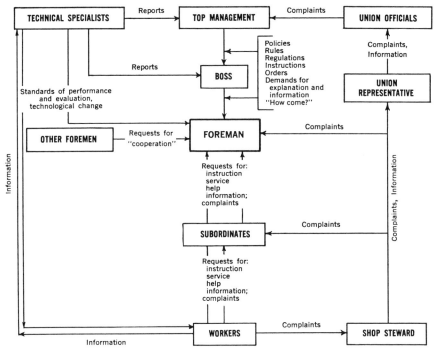

NOTE: This diagram shows only those forces impinging upon the foreman through the actions of other people. It is not designed to show the reaction of the foreman to these actions, in terms of either feelings or overt behavior; or to show the reactions of the workers to management's actions, which in turn become one of the chief forces acting upon the foreman. These reactions will be considered in the text.

Why this relation is so important could be indicated in any number of ways. But it is clear that any adequate analysis would go far beyond the confines of this article, since it would involve a critique of modern business organization and the individual's relation to authority and, in part, an examination of the ideologies held by the leaders and executives of business.[3] It is enough that the importance of this relation and its consequences in terms of behavior, particularly at the foreman level, are matters of common observation; and it will be at this level of behavior and its associated *feelings* that we shall remain.

Personal dependence upon the judgments and decisions of his superiors, so characteristic of the subordinate-superior relation in modern industry, makes the foreman's situation basically insecure.[4] He feels a constant need to adjust himself to the demands of his superior and to seek the approval of his superior. Everything that he does he tries to evaluate in terms of his superior's reaction. Everything that his superior does he tries to evaluate in terms of what it means or implies about his superior's relation to him. Everything that his subordinates and workers do he immediately tries to evaluate in terms of the criticism it may call forth from his superior. In some cases this preoccupation with what the boss thinks becomes so acute that it accounts for virtually everything the foreman says or does and all his thinking about what goes on around him. He will refrain from doing anything, even to the point of dodging responsibility, for fear of bringing disapproval from the boss. Hours at work and at home are spent in figuring and anticipating what explanations or reasons he will need to give the boss. And the boss's most innocent and unintentional acts—failure to say "good morning," for instance—are taken perhaps to imply disapproval.

It is hard to realize how much those who are interested in improving the efficiency of industry have neglected this area. If the manhours spent by subordinates both on and off the job in preoccupation about what the boss thinks were added up, the total hours would be staggering—not to mention the results this phenomenon has produced in nervous breakdowns and other forms of mental anguish. Stranger still, it almost appears as if modern industrial organization, which prides itself so much on its efficiency, has aggravated rather than reduced the amount of this preoccupation, with disastrous consequences for health and thus for efficiency. All this applies to the foreman in particular.

The crux of the foreman's problem is that he is constantly faced with the dilemma of (1) having to keep his superior informed with what is happening at the work level (in many cases so that his superior may prepare in turn for the unfavorable reaction of his superior and so on up the line) and (2) needing to communicate this information in such a way that it does not bring unfavorable criticism on himself for not doing his job correctly or adequately. Discrepancies between the way things are at the work level and the way they are represented to be by management cannot be overlooked, and yet the foreman feels obliged to overlook them when talking to his boss. This makes the foreman's job particularly "tough" and encourages him to talk out of both sides of his mouth at the same time—to become a master of double talk.

Each foreman, of course, resolves the conflict in terms of his own personal history, personality, and temperament. Some foremen become voluble in the face of this situation; others are reduced to stony silence, feeling that anything they say will be held against them. Some keep out of the boss's way, while others devise all sorts of ways for approaching him and trying to direct attention to certain things they have accomplished. And extraordinary are the skills which some more verbally articulate foremen develop in translating *what is* into a semblance of *the way it ought to be* in order to appease their superiors and keep them happy.

But, for the most part, the foreman, being loyal and above all wanting to be secure, resolves the conflict and maintains good relations with his superiors by acting strictly in accordance with his functional relations and the logics of management. In spite of what this may lead to in his relations to workers and other groups, his relations with his superiors at least are not jeopardized.

Thus the foreman, like each individual in the modern industrial struc-

ture, is in effect painfully tutored to focus his attention upward to his immediate superiors and the logics of evaluation they represent, rather than downward to his subordinates and the feelings they have. So rigid does the conditioning of supervisors and executives in the industrial structure become in this respect that it is almost impossible for them to pay attention to the concrete human situations below them, rich in sentiments and feelings. For them, this world of feeling does not exist; the territory is merely populated with the abstractions which they have been taught to see and the terms in which they communicate—"base rates," "manhours," "budgets," "cost curves," "production schedules," and so on.

Foreman–Specialist. Also of extreme importance are the foreman's relations to the technical specialists who *originate* the standards of performance which he must *uphold* and to which his subordinates and workers must *conform.* This experimentally minded group of engineers, accountants, and technologists can become one of the chief sources of change, and rapid change, at the work level; through them changes can be introduced at the work level at a more rapid rate than they can be assimilated by customary shop codes and practices. Through them, also, "controls" can be exercised far more precisely than heretofore. It is one thing for a foreman to know what his cost performance has been; it is another matter to know what his actual costs should be in relation to a standard. What was heretofore a matter of experimental judgment after the fact becomes now a matter of projective evaluation and of constantly shooting at a target—a target whose outlines become increasingly more clear-cut and demanding, at least in one area of his job.

It is little wonder that this group can become (although it does not need to become, as we shall discuss later) a constant source of threat to the foreman's feelings of security. These men of course affect and often make more difficult his relations to workers. They also provide reports to management which can make his relations to his boss exceedingly uncomfortable. The result: more double talk.

It is well to note that these control groups can (as can the union) short-circuit foremen and levels of supervision lower in the line by providing information direct to higher levels of supervision.[5] Whatever the value of this information in evaluating the foreman's performance, it results in certain pressures upon him. Each superior can request explanations from, or give orders to, his foreman based on such information; yet the foreman cannot control it and indeed may be unaware of it until his superior initiates action. Information flowing through the line the foreman can censor before it reaches the boss; but this way the boss can get information at the same time he does, or even before, and the foreman is no longer able to foresee or to gauge the boss's reaction. The results of this in mental anguish, in preoccupations, in worries about what the boss may think or do, in preparation of explanations, "good reasons," and alibis, are tremendous. Because of the subjective nature of the data, the technologists of industry have not as yet decided to study this area or even to give it much attention. But the modern foreman, from the point of view of both his effectiveness and his satisfaction at work, finds the actual phenomena only too real.

Foreman–Foreman.   By the very nature of the closely knit technological processes of a manufacturing organization, the foreman of one department often has to work very closely with a foreman of another department. These lateral relations are not formally defined, and their functioning depends largely upon the informal understandings which exist between foremen. Thus, the kind and amount of cooperation which one foreman is likely to obtain from another foreman is in good part determined by their interpersonal relations. Here again, the boss comes in, because the preoccupation with what the boss thinks may also affect the foreman's relation to his colleagues at the same level.

Although all foremen have equal formal status, they do not, as everyone in a shop situation knows, enjoy equal informal status. The individual foreman's relative status is determined by such factors as age, sex, service, earnings, and social symbols of one sort or another. But the chief determining factor is his direct relation to the boss, i.e., how close he is to the boss. Not only the foreman's need for security but also the closely allied strivings for status and recognition are therefore directed to his superior. He needs to feel "close" to him. Thus he may constantly be comparing his relation to the boss with that of his colleagues. If this comparison indicates his position to be weak, he may enter into competition with his colleagues for recognition from the boss. As can be imagined, such emotional disturbances in the work situation may impede rather than facilitate cooperation among foremen, and they constitute a peculiar kind of "headache" for the superior.

Foreman–Worker.   It is in his relation to the workers, however, with the rise of "scientific" management and with the growth of industrial unions, that the modern foreman's position becomes especially difficult. Here "the straw that breaks the camel's back" is finally reached. Here the problem of getting smooth operation becomes acute because, as we have seen, the foreman according to the logic of industrial organization must (1) *uphold* at the work level the standards, policies, rules, and regulations which have been *originated* by other groups and see to it that the workers *conform* to them and, at the same time, (2) obtain if possible the workers' spontaneous *cooperation* to this way of doing business. As anyone who has been in such a position knows, this is not a very easy task. As a rule, people do not like to conform to matters when they have no say in them, when they do not participate or feel that their point of view is taken into account. This is not a popular way of evoking spontaneity of cooperation; it is not consistent with our basic social values. Yet over and over again both foremen and workers are told, merely told, to conform to conditions over which they have very little or no say—conditions, moreover, which shockingly fail at times to take into account what is of vital importance to them in their work situations.

This state of affairs affects the foreman's personal situation: his strivings to satisfy his needs for security, personal integrity, and recognition in the work situation. Further, it makes his job in relation to his workers very difficult. Again and again, he is put in a position either of getting the workers' cooperation and being "disloyal" to management or of being "loyal" to management and incurring the resentment and overt opposition of his subordinates.

For those who do not fully appreciate the conflicting position in which the foreman is placed, it may be desirable to show the nature of the two contrasting worlds in the middle of which the foreman stands and spends his workaday life. In business, as in any organized human activity, there are two sets of social processes going on:

1.   There are those social processes which are directly related to the achievement of purpose and which result in "formal organization." In business, for example, formal organization leads to such things as practices established by legal enactment or policy, specifications, standard methods, standard procedures, standards of time, output, quality, cost, and so on. They are concerned with those means most appropriate to achieve certain ends. And as such they can be changed rapidly.

It should be noted that these manifestations of formal organization are essentially logical in character. Through formal organization man expresses his logical capacities; in fact, it is one of the chief outlets for the expression of man's logical capacities. It should also be noted that in the past 25 years there has been a tremendous amount of attention given to this aspect of business organization. It is in part because of this that, as we tried to show, the modern foreman's environment is so radically different from the good old days. And yet the foreman, unlike some higher executives, cannot stay only in this logically sheltered atmosphere.

2.   There are those spontaneous social processes going on in any organized human activity which have no specific, conscious common purpose and which result in "informal organization." Informal organization leads to such things as custom, mores, folkway, tradition, social norms, and ideals. In business, for example, it expresses itself at the work level in such things as what constitutes fair wages, decent conditions of work, fair treatment, a fair day's work, and traditions of the craft. It takes the form of different status systems: e.g., old-timers should get preferential treatment; supervisors should get more money than their subordinates; and office workers are superior to shop workers. These are attitudes and understandings based on feeling and sentiment. They are manifestations of "belonging," and they do not change rapidly.

It should be especially noted that these manifestations of informal organization are not logical in character. They are concerned with values, ways of life, and ends in themselves—those aspects of social life which people strive to protect and preserve and for which at times they are willing to fight and even die. It should also be noted that a cursory examination of the periodicals, books, formal statements, and speeches of business executives and business experts shows that little systematic attention has been given to this aspect of business organization. This is indeed a curious state of affairs since, as every foreman intuitively knows, it is only through informal organization and its manifestations that he can secure spontaneity of cooperation at the work level.

Informal organization in any organized human activity serves a very healthy function. It binds people together in routine activity. It gives people a social place and feeling of belonging. It provides the framework for the fulfillment of human satisfaction. It gives people a feeling of self-respect, of independent choice, of not being just cogs in a machine. Far from being a hindrance to greater effectiveness, informal organization provides the setting which makes men willing to contribute their services.

Yet what is management's attitude toward these informal groups which form at the work level? Curiously enough, their appearance makes management uneasy. And sometimes management willfully tries to break them up. Such ill-conceived attempts inevitably produce open hostility to the aims of management. For informal organization cannot be prevented; it is a spontaneous phenomenon necessary wherever coordinated human activities exist.

More important still—for it is more often the case—these informal groups are ignored and not even recognized. Having no representation in the formal organization, which to many an executive is by definition the "reality," they just do not exist. As a result—not from malicious design but from sheer oversight born of overlogicized training—these informal groups at the work level become inadvertently the victims of change, disruption, and dislocation. Technical changes are introduced without any attention to what is happening to the members of these groups in terms of their group associations. New methods of work and new standards are initiated, newcomers are added, someone is transferred, upgraded, or promoted, and all as if this group life did not exist. What happens? There develops a feeling of being "pushed around"—a very uncomfortable feeling which most people dislike and which often provokes the reaction of trying to push the pusher with equal intensity in the opposite direction.

Because their way of life is constantly in jeopardy from technological changes, new methods, raised standards, and constant manipulation of one kind or another by logically minded individuals, these groups in industry take on a highly defensive and protective character. Their major function becomes, unfortunately, the resistance to change and innovation, and their codes and practices develop at variance with the economic purpose of the enterprise. Much pegging of output at a certain level by employees is an expression of this need to protect their ways of life, as well as their livelihood, from too rapid change.

As might be expected, these defensive and protective characteristics of many informal groups at the work level—and they exist full blown in many factories even before any formal union appears—have serious consequences for foremen (not to mention new workers and other individuals). Any supervisor or foreman in charge of such groups has two, if not three, strikes against him to begin with. Anything he does in relation to them is likely to be "wrong." To ignore them completely would be to invite overt hostility; to accept them completely would be to fail in fulfilling his responsibilities to management. Yet the foreman is the key man of management in administering technical changes. He often has the impossible task of taking plans made by the specialists without thought of the realities of human situations and relating them to just such situations.

Foreman–Union. Once these patterns of behavior become formalized in a union, the foreman's debacle becomes complete. Into this situation, now, is introduced a new set of logics, verbal definitions, rules, and regulations, by means of which he is supposed to set his conduct toward the workers. The last vestiges of initiative, of judgment, and, what is perhaps more important, of personal relations with his subordinates are taken away from him. Literally the foreman is left "holding the bag"—a bag containing (1) the maximum of exquisitely logical rules, definitions, procedures, policies, standards that the human mind can devise, by means of which he is now supposed to do his job, and (2) the minimum of those relationships and their associated feelings through which he can obtain the wholehearted cooperation of people. Standing in the middle of a now formally bifurcated situation, where one half is trying to introduce changes and improvements into the factory situation and the other half by habit and conditioning is trying to prevent or resist them, the modern foreman is expected to "cooperate."

The Foreman's Situation Summarized

The salient features of the foreman's situation should now be clear. In very broad outline—tentatively and approximately formulated—the failure on the part of top management, in mass production industries in particular, to understand the social implications of its way of doing "business" has resulted in the development of certain rigidities which do not make for cooperation in the industrial structure:

1. At the bottom of the organization there are people called *employees* who are in general merely supposed to *conform* to changes which they do not originate. Too often the attitude is that employees are merely supposed to do what they are told and get paid for it. Directing them there is—
2. A group of *supervisors* who again are merely supposed to *uphold*—"administer" is the popular word—the standards of performance and policies determined by other groups, one of which is—

3. A group of *technical specialists* who are supposed to *originate* better ways and better standards through which the economic purpose of the organization can be better secured and more effectively controlled by—

4. A group of *top management* men who in their *evaluation* of the workers' behavior assume that the major inducement they can offer to people to cooperate is financial (i.e., that they are merely providing a livelihood, rather than a way of life); that informal organization is either "bad" or not "present"; and that authority comes from the top, so that no attention has to be given to that authority which is a matter of individual decision and comes from the bottom. This group's whole explicit theory of human cooperation—but not necessarily the practice of it—dates back to the eighteenth century: (a) society is composed of a rabble of unorganized individuals; (b) these individuals are only interested in the pursuit of profit and pleasure; and (c) in the pursuit of these ends the individual is essentially logical.[6]

These rigidities in operation make people in one group feel that they are excluded from the activities of other groups and prevent the wholehearted participation of all groups in the full attainment of the organization's objectives.

These rigidities in the industrial structure also have serious consequences for the satisfactions of individuals. Man's desire to belong, to be a part of a group, is constantly being frustrated. Things that are important to him seem to be disregarded. Opportunities for personal and social satisfaction seem to be denied. Yet, contrary to the assumptions made by management, all the evidence of modern investigation shows:

1. Society is composed of people related to each other in terms of group associations.

2. The desire to belong, to be a part, the desire for continuous and intimate association at work with other human beings, remains a strong, possibly the strongest, desire of man.

3. In the pursuit of these ends man is essentially nonlogical and at times irrational, i.e., willing to die or, as management should know only too well, to "cut off his nose to spite his face."

As a result of being constantly deprived of real social (not logical) interrelationship and of those basic human satisfactions which come from it, the worker becomes restless and dissatisfied, if not openly resentful and hostile. And like any human being he expresses his dissatisfaction in a number of ways: by being absent, by quitting, by pegging output, and by joining a union where he hopes to satisfy the needs for self-expression that his job no longer provides.

In this environment the foreman stands—victim, not monarch, of all he surveys. And what does he survey? On the one hand, a monument of technical achievement such as no civilization has seen before, and, on the other hand, what Elton Mayo likes to refer to as "the seamy side of progress," a bleak and arid human scene scorched dry by the babel of words and logics which have long ceased to have any power to motivate or fill with renewed hope and vigor the hearts of men. Separated from management and separated from his men, dependent and insecure in his relation to his superiors and uncertain in his relations to his men, asked to give cooperation but in turn receiving none, expected to be friendly but provided with tools which only allow him to be "fair"—in this situation of social deprivation our modern foreman is asked to deliver the goods.

One only needs to add to this picture the more recent complications of expanded war industries, the influx of new workers—some of them women, untutored and inexperienced in the ways of the factory; some of them Negroes, equally inexperienced and untutored but also apprehensive of their place in this "white man's heaven"—and we have the picture of the social environment of our modern foreman.

In this predicament, how does this foreman feel and behave? In one of three ways:

1.   He "stews in his own juice" and, like Sir Hudibras's rusty sword, "he eats into himself for lack of something else to hew and hack," i.e., becomes obsessive.

2.   Or as current newspapers and periodicals have kept us informed, he joins a union, i.e., becomes aggressive.

3.   Or he too—who knows?—may go to Washington to be delivered from his social isolation and logocentric predicament, i.e., may seek a political solution for his social void.

So at the foreman level do the "mills of God" grind out the three major ills of our industrial civilization.

The Administrative Process

The purpose of the article thus far has not been to prove a thesis; it has been to present and interpret as vividly as possible—*from the point of view of feelings and relationships*—the foreman's situation in mass production industry. No examples have been given, but countless could be cited by any person who has had intimate contact with a war plant during the past five years. The final evidence, however, it is well to remember, exists in the minds of foremen and in their behavior, not in this article; and for those who doubt, let them go out and look and listen for themselves.

But a "distortion" has crept into our discussion, and it needs to be clarified. In dealing with the nuances of social relationship existing in a factory situation, the author has perforce been generalizing at a level somewhat removed from but not unrelated to the concrete and the particular. And although concerned with "a moving equilibrium" and the social forces working both for and against it, nevertheless up to now he has paid almost exclusive attention to those social forces operating to upset stability—simply in order to bring out inescapably the fact that the forces making for unbalance do exist, in latent if not in active form, in *every* mass production industry. The picture presented thus far has been therefore a picture of the inexorable grinding out of the social forces and logics that modern technology has unleashed—in the raw, so to speak, and uncontrolled by the "administrative process." But we must not forget that there is, often equally present and equally strong, the compensatory function of the "administrator."

In the last analysis the forces acting upon the foreman, as upon any other individual in the industrial structure, are the actions of other people. It was for this reason that the actions of the principal people with whom the foreman has relations in his working environment were examined. It should be clear, however, that the actions of these different characters are not always the same. Bosses, technical specialists, foremen, workers, and shop stewards differ in their behavior, sometimes very radically. This fact cannot be ignored; indeed, its implications are tremendous. And if *management's* actions are different, foremen's reactions are likely to be different.

In business (and in unions too) there are not only "men of goodwill" but also men with extraordinary skill in the direction of securing skill in the direction of securing cooperative effort. These men, at all levels, perform an "administrative" function the importance of which is too little recognized. Much of their time is spent in facilitating the process of communication and in gaining the wholehearted cooperation of men. Many of them are not too logically articulate, but they have appreciation for a point of view different from their own. Not only can they appreciate the fact that a person can be different from themselves but, more important still, they can accept his right to be different. They always seem to have the time to listen to the problems and difficulties of others. They do not pose as "experts"; they know when to secure the appropriate aid from others.

Such "administrators," selfless and sometimes acting in a way which appears to be lacking in ambition, understand the importance of achieving group solidarity—the importance of "getting along," rather than of "getting ahead." They take personal responsibility for the mixed situations, both technical and human, that they administer. They see to it that the newcomer has an effective and happy relationship with his fellow workers, as well as gets the work out. Accomplishing their results through leisurely social interaction rather than vigorous formal action, more interested in getting their human relationships straight than in getting their words and logics straight, more interested in being "friendly" to their fellow men than in being abstractly "fair," and never allowing their "paper work" to interfere with this process of friendliness, they offer a healthy antidote to the formal logics of the modern factory organization previously described.

The importance of the "administrative" functions these men perform for the smooth running of any organization is incalculable, and fortunately industry has its fair share of such men. It is the author's impression that a greater proportion of them are found at the lower levels of management, because the logics of promotion in business organization seldom recognize their skills. Were it not for them, it is the author's opinion that the unleashed forces of modern technology would spin themselves out to doom and destruction. Aware of the twofold function of industrial leadership, i.e., the social organization of teamwork and the logical organization of operations, they maintain that healthy balance which makes for individual growth and development and, ultimately, for survival of the organization.

Yet, curiously enough, the theories of administration, as frequently expressed by business leaders, experts, and teachers, bear little resemblance to the functions these men actually perform and give little justification to their actions. As a result, they sometimes suffer from feelings of inferiority and lose confidence in themselves, an unfortunate consequence for them as individuals and also for the organization they serve. It is not comfortable to think that industry may depend for its stability on the personal and intuitive skills of a few such gifted people. Can the "administrative" skills they practice, the skills of getting action through social interaction, be made explicit and communicated?

What Is the Solution?

In the author's opinion, the foreman's dissatisfaction in large part results from actions of management. These actions of management are not the expression of maliciousness, bad faith, or lack of goodwill on the part of business executives. Far from it; they are merely the inexorable working out of the social forces which modern technology has produced and which we have not learned to recognize or control. They are the result of our ignorance and of our failure to pay as much explicit attention to the social organization of teamwork as to the logical organization of operations in our modern industrial enterprises.

The solution of the problem, therefore, seems to depend on a better realization of the "administrative process" as it operates to secure the cooperation of people in the furtherance of the economic objectives of business organizations. More than anything else, the modern world needs men who understand better the nature of, and give more explicit attention to, the social systems they administer. This is the challenge the modern world presents to business leadership; this is the great adventure for the coming generation. The business leaders of today and tomorrow, like the foremen, are facing a new "society," a streamlined "adaptive" society, a world which modern technology has produced and which is far different from the "established" society of their forefathers.[7] For their effectiveness, as well as for their survival, the coming "administrators" must be given new skills and new insights.

Can this job be done? The signs of the times are promising. In all quarters of business there are resolute young men who "when hope is dead will hope by faith," who will build the new world. In this connection it is well to remember that man's enormous capacity for adaptation, readjustment, and growth is his most striking characteristic, and it is upon this strength that we can hopefully rely.[8] In business and educational institutions, a fresh breath of life is beginning to stir. The possibilities of new courses and new methods of teaching and training are being explored.

A New Concept of Administration

Can the outlines of this new "administration" be even dimly envisaged? What will these new "administrators" be like, and in what skills will they be trained? Here we can only guess and express some personal opinions and hopes.

1. The new "administrator" will need to know and understand better the nature of "organization"—its structure and dynamic interrelations. It is indeed a strange remark to make, in the year 1945, that an executive will have to know something about "organization," the very phenomenon with which he daily deals. But strange as the remark may seem, the average executive knows little or nothing, except for what is implicitly registered in his nervous system, about the "social organization" of his business. Most of his explicit concern, most of his logical thinking, is only about "formal organization." About the other aspects of organization, he only stews, frets, and gets stomach ulcers.

2. "Administrators" of the future, to do their new jobs effectively, will have to develop a common language structure which represents accurately the interdependent realities of the phenomena with which they deal—technical, economic, organizational, social, and human. Too many different and often times conflicting "languages" riddle present business. No longer can the human beings who contribute their services to a business organization be regarded as "so many beads on a string." For the new world a new language has to be created which will keep together in words, rather than keep separate by words, those things that are together in the territory. This will be a language of mutually interdependent relations, of togetherness, of equilibrium, of adaptation, and of growth.

3. The new "administrator" will have to understand better the problem of communication—and not only the aspect of communication which by persuasion attempts to sell one's own point of view, but that which tries to understand and has respect for another's point of view. In the systematic practice of taking into account another person's point of view as the first step in obtaining that person's cooperation—a most difficult skill—he should have daily and continuous drill. He should be taught to listen, in addition to being logically lucid and clear. He should learn to practice the "democratic method" *at the level of daily interaction* in the work situation.

4. New methods and new skills will have to be developed whereby change can be introduced into the work situation without provoking resistance. About no urgent and pressing problem of modern industry is there so little systematic knowledge—so little understanding and so much misunderstanding. In no area has it been so convincingly demonstrated, again and again and again, that people refuse to cooperate in meeting a standard of performance when they have not been allowed to participate in setting it up or, many times, even to "understand" it. In no area are the ordinary methods of "salesmanship" so woefully lacking.

For this particular aspect of "administration," the introduction of changes into the shop, we shall need to exercise and practice new insights regarding human motivation. These insights will have to envisage how technological progress and improvement can go hand in hand with individual and social development. Technological change will have to be introduced at the work level so that the group affected will see it, in North Whitehead's phrase, as "an enlargement of its own way of life rather than as an interruption to it." And for the working out of these new methods and skills, more time and more effort will have to be given, more ingenuity and more understanding will have to be exercised.

5. The new "administrator" will have to understand better the dependent relation of the subordinate to the superior in business organizations and the feelings of insecurity this dependence arouses. He will have to learn new methods and techniques of assuring his subordinate of those minimum conditions of security, not merely financial, without which the subordinate's position becomes intolerable. For this he will have to learn something about the principles of individual growth and development through active participation and assumption of responsibility, and these principles he will have to learn to practice in relation to his subordinates in an atmosphere of approval. He will have to learn to be responsible for people, not merely responsible for abstract and logical categories.

We will not obtain this type of "administrator" merely through verbal definition, i.e., by defining what his formal responsibilities and duties are. He has to be fostered and made to feel secure, allowed to grow and, occasionally, to make mistakes and thereby learn. He has to be nurtured like a plant; and, like a plant, the environment in which he grows, the care and human understanding he gets will determine whether he flourishes or withers, gets bugs, and so on. Unlike our present foremen, who have suffered from too many logical definitions and too little human understanding, he must not be allowed to "wither" and be forced to join a union in order to recapture the zest of growth and life again.

6. The new "administrator" will have to learn to distinguish the world of feelings from the world of facts and logic. And for dealing effectively with this world of feelings, he will have to learn new techniques—which at first may seem strange, after having been ignored and misunderstood for so long. Particularly, of course, he will have to learn about "informal organization,"

that aspect of organization which is the manifestation of feeling and senti-ment. Only by paying as much attention to informal organization as to formal organization will he become aware of what can and cannot be accomplished by policy formulation at the concrete level of behavior. He will have to learn new techniques of "control." He will see clearly that "feelings" cannot be verbally legislated out of existence; that, as a first step in their "control," they need to be expressed and recognized.

These and many other new methods and skills the new "administrator" will have to learn. He will have to learn to "control" the future by first learning to "control" the present. He will have to learn to formulate goals and ideals which make the present in which we live more, rather than less, meaningful. And to achieve these new levels of insight and practice, he will have to throw overboard completely, finally, and irrevocably—this will be difficult—the ideologies of the "established society" of the eighteenth and nineteenth centuries. This new representative of a new "adaptive society" at all cost must not be the representative of an "ism." For he does not represent any particular way of life: he is only the guarantor of the "ways of life"—plural—that are important to many different people. In this task he can only represent what Elton Mayo calls "polyphasic methods" of dealing with the complex human, social, economic, and organizational prob-lems of our industrial civilization.

Can we develop a group of such "administrators"? This of course is a matter of opinion. To the author it seems that, if only ½ of 1% of the time, effort, and money that have been spent in the direction of technological improvement were to be devoted to seeking better and improved methods of securing cooperation, the accomplishment would be considerable—and that is an intentional understatement. It just does not seem sensible to sup-pose that man's ingenuity, if given free scope, would fail in this undertaking. The task is tremendous; the challenge is great; the stakes are high; but only by traveling some such arduous road, in the author's opinion, can business leadership face up to its real social responsibilities.

Notes

1. See Clinton S. Golden and Harold J. Ruttenberg, *The Dynamics of Industrial Democracy* (New York, Harper & Brothers, 1942).

2. See B. B. Gardner, *Human Relations in Industry* (Chicago, Richard D. Irwin, Inc., 1945).

3. See Chester I. Barnard, *The Functions of the Executive* (Cambridge, Harvard University Press, 1938), pp. 161–184.

4. For an excellent statement on this point, see Douglas McGregor, "Conditions of Effective Leadership in the Industrial Organization," *Massachusetts Institute of Technology Publications*

in Social Science, Series 2, No. 16 (from the *Journal of Consulting Psychology*, vol. VIII, no. 2, 1944).

5. Discussed more fully by B. B. Gardner, op. cit.

6. These assumptions are taken from Elton Mayo, *The Social Problems of an Industrial Civilization* (Boston, Division of Research, Harvard Business School, 1945).

7. For an elaboration of this distinction between an "established" and an "adaptive" society, see Elton Mayo, op. cit.

8. On this point, see Carl R. Rogers, *Counseling and Psychotherapy* (Boston, Houghton Mifflin Company, 1942).

6

The Dynamics
of Subordinacy

ABRAHAM ZALEZNIK

At one time in his or her life everyone who works has been a subordinate. And everyone knows just how difficult being a subordinate can be: no matter how hard you try not to, at some point you get angry at your boss and engage in activity that the better part of you knows is simply inappropriate. The author of this article, who is a psychoanalyst, looks here at the behavior that subordinates can display and unravels the basic dynamics of subordinacy conflicts. He maintains that subordinacy conflicts exist in a person as responses to inner tensions that the organization's hierarchy sets off. In pursuing the underlying explanation of these problems, the author examines the psychological dimensions, relates these to their origins in individual development, then offers guidelines that managers can employ in overcoming the conflicts that their subordinates naturally fall into, including knowing one's own mind, objectifying the conflict, identifying and addressing reality, and maintaining contact with the subordinate.

Published in 1965.

My purpose in this article is to go beyond the superficial symptoms of superior-subordinate troubles and grasp the basic dynamics of subordinary conflicts. Through understanding of the dynamics we may come to achieve greater sensitivity and judgment in this important area of human relationships. We, hopefully, in turn may learn to avoid precipitous breaks in communication between authority and subordinates.

I hope to show that subordinacy conflicts exist in the person as responses to inner tensions. These tensions usually lurk below the surface of conscious awareness but, like a dormant volcano, may erupt into patterns of behavior with deep emotional content. This emotional intensity overloads communications in the transactions between superior and subordinate.

In pursuing this underlying explanation of subordinacy conflicts I want to: examine the psychological dimensions which assume prominence in the inner conflicts of the subordinate (Part I); relate these inner conflicts to their origins in individual development (Part II); and suggest guidelines that seniors and subordinates can use in resolving subordinacy conflicts (Part III).

The president of a large, aggressive company came to me one time with an experience that had left him stunned. He had undertaken a program to select and train promising juniors for promotion to supervisory and staff jobs. He talked personally with many individuals and helped in the selection and preparation for promotion. The promotions were announced and followed almost immediately by a wildcat strike led by dissatisfied subordinates who felt they had been overlooked.

What shocked the president was the fact that his intention to open new opportunities, to help people design a future for themselves in his organization, had misfired. He wondered where he had miscalculated the motivations of subordinates. He was on the verge of disillusionment with the younger generation.

This example from business is repeated in countless organizations, although not necessarily with the visibility and dramatic impact of strikes and demonstrations. More subtle forms of the discontents of subordinacy are widespread. For example:

☐ There is the individual who is unable to hold a job—who moves from one situation to the next expecting the grass to be greener elsewhere. The problem of "job hopping" is not restricted to any one segment of society. One suspects, for example, that executive placement firms thrive on the discontents and illusions of people who are willing to live perennially out of a suitcase.

☐ The instances of sudden attitude reversal are equally instructive. Some individuals characteristically begin a relationship with an authority figure by overidealizing their boss, overestimating his or her strengths and capabilities. There soon follows the opposite extreme of depreciation and underestimation. In listening to persons who polarize their feelings toward authority, one soon becomes aware of the crucial role of their fantasy in creating and then destroying unrealistic images of other persons. The persistence of fantasy and the willingness of individuals to act upon it at the expense of reality attest to the strength of the emotional conflicts in subordinacy.

☐ Another manifestation of the problems in subordinacy is the recurrence of defective work performances. I refer here to individuals who are unable to follow through on assignments, who display promise but fail to complete, who are excellent critics but faulty performers, who may be verbally adept but are substantively inept.

☐ Then there is the highly dependent individual who accepts projects initiated by others but does not initiate any. The amount of responsibility such a person can assume reliably is quite limited. His or her superiors may count on this person for a quality of initiative which psychologically is not there. This type of individual seems to have little available energy for work, and lacks the capacity to stand in the limelight or make decisions in full view of everyone. Instead, they will tend toward anonymity and compliance.

These symptoms of defective adaptation to positions of subordinacy in organizations by no means exhaust the range of problems. Individuals on both sides of the vertical authority relationship could add countless other descriptions of the difficulties of mastering the challenges and conflicts of the subordinate role. For the *senior* executive these difficulties may cause concern about the nature of subordinacy, about how and why individuals in junior positions in organizations respond to their relationship with authority figures. *Juniors* must avail themselves of opportunities to learn from assessing consequences so that, as they mature and assume increasing responsibilities, their response to pressures will be seasoned by judgment and experience. Otherwise, we face the prospect of a severe discontinuity in the quality of leadership in business and all segments of society.

PART I. PATTERNS AND DIMENSIONS

The eruption of subordinacy conflicts into behavior, whether through group-supported rebellion or more individualistic actions, occurs as a response to the vertical relationship. This vertical relationship reflects, and is reflected in, the constellation of motives, wishes, and tensions within the individual. At the risk of oversimplifying, we can single out two trends in this constellation of motives for special attention.

One trend deals with the polar issues of *dominance* and *submission*. The potential source of conflict here is the balance achieved in the individual between his or her (1) wishes to control and overpower authority figures, and, at the other extreme, (2) equally strong wishes to be dominated and controlled by these same figures. The theme of dominance and submission achieves a unity because both extremes aim at a single outcome: to secure the sole possession of figures who regulate and dispense life-sustaining rewards and punishments. This aim accounts for the intensity of reactions in the subordinate role, since the game is real and the stakes high. In the case of business organizations, the stakes are often related to chances for promotion and career success.

The second trend deals with the balance achieved between *activity* and *passivity* in the individual's characteristic patterns of behavior. At one extreme, the individual initiates and intrudes into their environment. At the other extreme, he or she characteristically waits for others to initiate action and behaves in response to the stimulation from outside. The active-passive modes are usually well established as character traits of the individual, having special significance in his or her personal economy. The personal economy reflects the tensions of reward and deprivation, of energy expended and gratifications realized, of risks which come from frustration and the need to defend against these risks.

We can use the combination of these two trends to describe four patterns of subordinacy, particularly to illustrate types of inner conflict (see Exhibit 1). Let us examine each of these types in turn.

Exhibit 1.

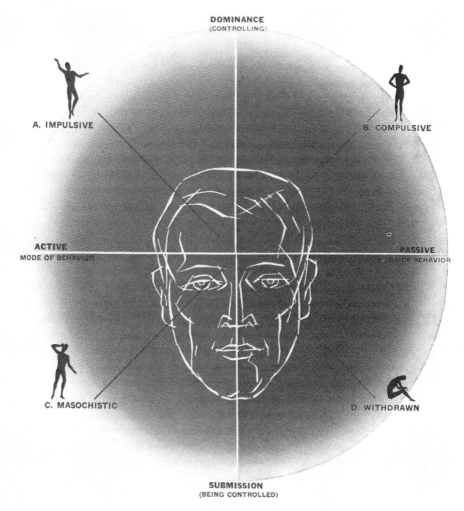

Impulsive Subordinate

The main feature of subordinacy that aims to dominate relationships with authority figures through active means is rebellion. The effort is to overthrow authority and flout its symbols, usually with the unconscious aim of displacing the father.

This theme of rebellion is evident in the group formations of adolescence but can continue for a long time beyond this period of life. In work situations certain forms of rebellion lead to the inability to hold a job and to diffused conflict with superiors. Other forms of rebellion are more constructive in that they overcome complacency and the status quo.

This pattern of subordinacy is shown in the A quadrant of Exhibit 1.

Dynamics of Rebellion

In a study of interpersonal relations and job satisfaction that I conducted in the mid-1950s,[1] I observed the nature of overt rebellion and its significance:

> One of the workers, a highly gifted individual, taunted his supervisor by placing notices on the bulletin board that demanded to know why certain kinds of tools were unavailable in the shop. The notices quoted authorities who recommended these tools, and after each quotation there followed a challenge to the supervisor and the management as a whole.
>
> The supervisor arranged to forbid the posting of notices, but the employee took this as a challenge and built a private bulletin board near his workbench on which he continued to post notices. One day the supervisor called the employee to talk to him. The employee became rude, told his supervisor to "go to hell," and found himself fired.
>
> Inquiry into this employee's situation indicated a history of job hopping. In fact, the man told me he expected to be fired, that "it always happens." This mechanism of predicting dire events in the future stood as a "self-fulfilling" prophecy. The individual made a reality out of a fantasy through his own behavior.

The fantasy involved in this case includes a struggle with powerful authority figures in which the subject ultimately loses, but only as a means of escaping from authority. The job hopping can be viewed as impulsive action to break off contact where the fantasy of the struggle becomes too painful to endure.

The overt aim is to dominate through activity, but beneath this aim is the fear of taking control. This mechanism explains partially why rebels frequently have difficulty controlling and managing affairs even when they assume power. The process of rebellion as an expression of a fantasy is significant. The fantasy relates to prowess, like the story of David and Goliath; a seemingly weak individual overpowers a much stronger opponent to assume control and dominance. In real life, however, such fantasies usually result in injury and frustration to the hero.

The impulse to act can thus be seen both in its outer form as very aggressive behavior and in its inner form as a fantasy involving a rival.

Much impulsive behavior is associated with painful loneliness. The rebel may very much want to be close to others but finds such closeness difficult to sustain because of interfering fantasies of being dominated and controlled by others. The employee in the tool shop case just described lived a lonely existence as a middle-aged bachelor with no friends. He enjoyed one activity—chess competition. And he was a very gifted player, which in itself was revealing because it indicated that his main human relationships existed within a ritual of combat in the two-person relationship of victor and vanquished.

Role of Self-Control

Impulsiveness and rebelliousness do not necessarily make a subordinate's behavior bad. When the impulsive individual assumes control of his or her fantasies, highly constructive behavior appears. Take the spontaneous and courageous subordinate as an example. This individual may use rebellion to speak frankly and assert their views constructively in discussions of work problems. He or she avoids compliance and conformity, not only out of impatience but also out of the urge to create and achieve. Such constructive use of dominance and activity makes it possible for individuals in subordinate positions to influence events. They are highly appreciated by strong authority figures, who themselves tire of endless experiences with yes-people.

But the line between impulsivity as a constructive and a destructive character trait is difficult to draw. Similar dynamics underlie it in both cases; the difference resides in the degree of individual self-control. The constructive rebel knows how to use his or her urge to dominate and acts in appropriate ways. The destructive rebel exerts no self-control and finds himself or herself dominated by their own fantasies.

Compulsive Subordinate

Compulsive subordinacy aims to secure dominance and control, but through *passive* means. It is represented by the B quadrant of Exhibit 1.

The dictionary distinction between compulsiveness and impulsiveness often leads to confusion between two psychologically different characteristics. Whereas the impulsive type acts without thinking, the compulsive type acts under the effects of overelaborated thought processes indicating a powerful conscience and strong guilt feelings.

Compulsiveness leads to rigid behavior that seeks to expiate guilt through a number of mechanisms. The individual who acts but then reverses out of a sense of uncertainty is often dominated by guilt. Or the person who is indecisive, who can only think in endless riddles without reaching conclusions, is also operating under the burden of guilt.

The guilt is connected with the wish to dominate and control authority figures; the hesitation, doubt, and rigidity are connected with the defense against these wishes and the force of conscience that exerts so much pressure on the individual. The origin of the wishes—that is, the guilt and the primitive conscience—is tied to the early experiences of the individual.

Compulsivity has a strange and intriguing quality about it, largely resulting from its use of passive behavior to control situations. Passivity consists of indirect and manipulative attempts at influence where the actor himself may be unaware of the aim of his behavior. The clearest illustration of control through passivity is in the case of the hypochondriac:

> All indications point to illness and suffering as an experience that the victim endures passively. Yet the effect, as members of the hypochondriac's family know, is to control the behavior of those close to the "victim." The entire family experience may be organized to meet the needs of the victim, and, in point of fact, this is the unconscious wish underlying much of the suffering. The restrictions the victim lives by

become the controls that dominate the lives of others. In other words,
"misery loves company"—but by unconscious design rather than accident.

Control Through Passivity

The hypochondriac's behavior presents an extreme and clear instance of
control through passive means. But compulsivity exists in more subtle forms.
The following case example illustrates especially such characteristics as
doubt, attitude reversal, and hidden aggression combined with denial of
responsibility:

> *Dr. Richard Dodds, a newly hired physics research worker in a company
> laboratory, entered the office of his superior, Dr. Blackman, and showed
> him a letter. This letter was from Professor Wilkin of another research
> institution, offering Dodds a position. Blackman read the letter.*

Dodds: *What do you think of that?*

Blackman: *I knew it was coming. He asked me if it would be all right
if he sent it. I told him to go ahead if he wanted to.*

Dodds: *I didn't expect it, particularly after what you said to me last
time. I'm really quite happy here. I don't want you to get the idea that I
am thinking of leaving. But I thought I should go and visit him—I think he
expects it—and I wanted to let you know that just because I was thinking
of going down, that did not mean I was thinking of leaving here, unless, of
course, he offers me something extraordinary.*

Blackman: *Why are you telling me all this?*

Dodds: *I didn't want you hearing from somebody else that I was
thinking of leaving here, because I was going for a visit to another institution.
I really have no intention of leaving here, you know, unless he offers me
something really extraordinary that I can't afford to turn down. I think I'll
tell him that, that I am willing to look at his laboratory, but unless there is
something unusual for me, I have no intention of leaving here.*

Blackman: *It's up to you.*

Dodds: *What do you think?*

Blackman: *Well, what? About what? You've got to make up your
mind.*

Dodds: *I don't consider too seriously this job. He is not offering
anything really extraordinary. But I am interested in what he has to say,
and I would like to look around his lab.*

Blackman: *Sooner or later you are going to have to make up your
mind where you want to work.*

Dodds: *That depends on the offers, doesn't it?*

Blackman: *No, not really; a good man always gets offers. You get a
good offer and you move, and, as soon as you have moved, you get other
good offers. It would throw you into confusion to consider all the good offers
you will receive. Tell me, isn't there a factor of how stable you want to be?*

Dodds: *But I'm not shopping around. I already told you that. He sent me this letter; I didn't ask him to. All I said was I think I should visit him, and to you that's shopping around.*

Blackman: *Well, you may choose to set aside your commitment here if he offers you something better. All I am saying is that you will still be left with the question. You've got to stay some place, and where is that going to be?*

Dodds *(after some discussion of how it would look if he changed jobs at this point):* "*Look, I came in here, and I want to be honest with you, but you go and make me feel all guilty, and I don't like that.*

Blackman: *You are being honest as can be.*

Dodds: *I didn't come in here to fight. I don't want to disturb you.*

Blackman: *"I'm not disturbed. If you think it is best for you to go somewhere else, that is OK with me.*

Dodds *(after another lengthy exchange about what he really wants and how his leaving would look to others):* "*I don't understand you . . . All I wanted was to show you this letter, and let you know what I was going to do. What should I have told you?*

Blackman: *That you had read the letter and felt that under the circumstances it was necessary for you to pay a visit to Wilkin, but that you were happy here and wanted to stay at least until you had got a job of work done.*

Dodds: *I can't get over it. You think there isn't a place in the world I'd rather be than here in this lab. . . .*

Recurring Themes

In going through the case illustration, I hope that you watched especially for the four qualities or themes of compulsiveness in the behavior of the person in the subordinate position which I called attention to in introducing it—(1) doubt, (2) attitude reversal, (3) hidden aggression, (4) denial of responsibility.

Throughout the entire interchange *doubt* appears, reminiscent in many ways of Hamlet's obsessional doubting. Instead of "to be or not to be," the doubting in our research case centers on the dilemma of a career: where and when does one "settle in" and forgo imaginary (or half-real) opportunities? Every person launching his or her career is susceptible to hesitation and concern over opportunities lost. In work, lingering thoughts over the "other job" intrude into the optimism that accompanies fresh experience, just as, in marriage, they occur over the "other man or woman." Where other individuals stake a claim on a career, then pursue their line of work, the compulsive individual continues to doubt. As in the preceding case, he even provokes his environment to keep the doubting alive.

The stubbornness that underlies compulsive doubting is suggested again and again in our example by the inability or unwillingness of the subordinate to "hear" direct advice on the importance of ending doubt and undertaking work.

Attitude reversal, the second theme, consists of rapid oscillation between positive and negative feelings in human encounters. In the preceding case, the subordinate would not think of leaving the laboratory, "unless, of course, he [Wilkin] offers me something extraordinary." The technical term for attitude reversal is ambivalence, suggesting the simultaneous influence of both positive and negative emotions toward a single object or event. It goes hand in hand with doubting, and together they serve to maintain a steady level of tension in the individual's human relationships and work activity.

The third theme of *hidden aggression* is unavoidably present in an otherwise passive pattern of behavior. The hidden aggression appears in the illustration in accusing comments like: "All I said was I think I should visit him, and to you that's shopping around." Despite Dodd's disclaimers (e.g., "I didn't come here to fight; I don't want to disturb you"), his underlying intention is to provoke arguments and verbal tugs-of-war. This underlying motive springs from the uneasy balance between dependent and independent wishes frequently at the core of conflict in the compulsive subordinate.

The fourth theme is *denial of responsibility.* If one detects a note of frustration in supervisors who work with compulsive subordinates, it is because of the tendency to get impaled on the horns of the dilemma on which the subordinate rides. Doubting, attitude reversals, and hidden aggression are ordinarily tough to take, but the "last straw" presents itself in the denial of responsibility. Our case evidenced this theme most poignantly in the subordinate's statement at the end: "I don't understand you. I came in here to be honest with you, and you make me feel guilty." This states the essence of dominance through passivity—that conflict, problems, and nasty emotions exist in the outer world, and are infused from without rather than generated from within.

Much of the literature on management calls for authority with responsibility. I would suggest that of equal importance is the need for *subordinacy* with responsibility, a kind of response absent in the compulsive pattern just described.

Masochistic Behavior

Masochism (shown in the C quadrant of Exhibit 1) consists of the quest for pleasure through the endurance of pain. True masochism is a serious emotional disturbance, but it also exists as a purposeful element in character. In the case of the subordinate who desires pain, it is an active attempt to submit to the control and assertiveness of the authority figure. Here, again, this particular dynamic of subordinacy is to be understood as an aspect of unconscious motivation.

The pattern of subordinacy that seeks to evoke aggression from an authority figure is basically a means of guarding against one's own aggressive tendencies. The individual fears their own aggression and the prospect that, once they begin to show aggression, the destructive potential will get beyond control. Instead of hurting others, this individual will hurt himself or herself through provoking others. The aim is self-destructive.

Typical Manifestations

The most common manifestation of this pattern of subordinacy occurs in the case of the accident-prone employee: he or she may mean to get mad at the boss, as a representative of authority, but only hurts himself or herself through lapses of attention or taking undue risks. A side effect of this self-punishing behavior is the evoking of sympathy and attention from others. At the same time, it invites control from others and the abdication of personal responsibility.

A more subtle form of masochism occurs when the individual invites criticism and shaming by sheer inadequacies in his or her output. The explanation for these inadequacies does not lie in lack of ability or experience, or even lack of hard work. All of these attributes for good performance may be present; but they are not utilized and directed, because to perform well means to accept praise and responsibility while the underlying motivation is to endure persecution and shame at the hands of an imagined aggressor. To take another example:

> We observe, from time to time, individuals in organizations who "identify with the underdog"; they are quick to see injustice in the actions of authority figures and sense oppression in the lives of others who have little power and influence. Apart from the reality of oppression and the existence of the "underdog," the identification with the helpless and the weak against the powerful and the strong reflects this masochistic bent in personality. By identifying with the underdog, the subordinate aims to become a target of attack from powerful authority figures. Submission is the sought-after end, while the active-aggressive behavior is the means.
>
> A subordinate who reflects this tendency acts sometimes like an older son in the family who takes the side of the younger siblings against imagined oppressive actions of parents. This type of subordinate suffers vicariously, and perhaps simultaneously finds an outlet for pent-up aggression. The target is the oppressor, who stands in the place of parents who were the original authority figures.

It is very useful to attack oppressors, but our concern is with those who see oppression where none exists. Instances where standards of performance are enforced in an equitable way may be attacked as vehemently as arbitrary discipline. The ability to discriminate between real and imagined inequity is absent in the individual who organizes his or her experience around identification with the oppressed.

The masochistic pattern, as with the other extremes, continues a dynamic that originated in the early years of the subordinate's experience. The hidden desire to endure suffering at the hands of a powerful aggressor re-creates the infantile wishes used to solve, although tenuously, the dilemmas of early development. It is remarkable to observe the degree to which history repeats itself in the life of the individual. The repetition, however, does not occur through impersonal forces or the whims of chance, but rather through inadequate mastery of inner conflicts.

As I shall try to show later, one way of responding intelligently to the provocations of the masochistic personality is to avoid the game. The masochistic subordinate seeks pleasure in becoming the target of aggression. Avoidance of aggressive response can break the cycle and return the issue to the place where it belongs: within the individual. In this sense avoidance of the reciprocal (the sadistic response to masochistic provocation) holds open the possibility of learning lessons from experience.

Withdrawn Pattern

The fourth pattern, withdrawal (see the D quadrant of Exhibit 1), represents an outcome of successively turning interest and attention from the outer world toward one's self. The pattern is a form of submission because the individual no longer cares about the orientation and content of his or her work. Their behavioral mode is passive in that energy from within is released only sparingly.

This kind of withdrawal through passive submission is in its extreme form a serious human disability that comes about because of lack of trust. The world is seen as malevolent and ungiving; therefore, the individual withdraws from it. But even in its less severe forms, withdrawal presents a difficult problem in superior-subordinate relationships. The subordinate's lack of trust, interest, and involvement make him or her unsusceptible to influence. They will acquiesce and do what they are told, but without orientation and interest. They contribute little to the interchange and thinking necessary for innovative work. They may handle routine tasks well enough, but do little beyond the necessary demands of their job.

The withdrawn subordinate presents other paradoxical features. In many cases, he appears loyal and accepting of existing standards. To illustrate:

In a current study of professional scientists and engineers in a research and development center, some colleagues and I discovered a type of career adjustment with features very similar to the withdrawal pattern described above. Over an interval of about two years during which we collected data, no individual of this type left the company. All other types of career adjustment showed a small, but readily apparent, turnover, including some individuals who left because they were dissatisfied with their work and others who left for better opportunities elsewhere.

The apathy evident in the absence of any turnover was supported by further evidence. There existed, for example, an interesting contradiction in response. On the one hand, the withdrawn type expressed personal disappointment in his career, a feeling of fatigue presumably neurotic in origin, some anxiety, and depression. On the other, individuals in this group tended to evaluate favorably their company, supervisor, and work colleagues. They expressed little desire to move elsewhere or to seek opportunities in other types of work.

Unlike some points of view that attribute withdrawal and apathy to oppressive conditions in an organization's authority structure, the evidence supports the view that their genesis lies in the individual's developmental history. This history typically includes a perception of a passive, withdrawn father and a cold, hostile mother, with the consequence of marked inability to mobilize and use constructively aggressive impulses. The withdrawal and apathy are themselves a consequence, along with depression, of the turning of aggression inward.

Interpreting the Patterns

To sum up at this point, we have seen that one dimension in the continuing development of the individual from infancy through the career years is control (see the vertical axis in Exhibit 1). Here, the polar issues of dominance and submission, in controlling and being controlled, exist in the fantasy and thinking process, both conscious and unconscious. The problem of control exists, so to speak, inside the skin of the person. It is not, therefore, obvious or easily described from the outside.

Fantasies about control range in the extreme, from a sense of omnipotence in relation to the environment to complete expectation that forces outside the self determine one's destiny. The range is from a kind of pathological insertion of one's self into all manner of events and circumstances to the absence of any area in which will and direction can have some influence over one's own activity and environment.

In speaking of control over environment, I refer not only to inanimate forces but also to the significant world of other persons. It is here, in the realm of human relationships, that the issue of control cuts most deeply. What the individual has had done to him or her in the past, in reality and in fantasy, becomes the foundation for the later attitudes toward figures both of love and authority at work and in the family.

The second dimension in this analytic structure is behavioral and *does* exist as readily observable material in everyday interaction. The dimension of activity-passivity (horizontal axis in Exhibit 1) refers to the structure of individual character traits—the surface of one's self presented to others. I should note in passing that while character traits are indeed presented quite openly, the existence of these traits and their persistence in interaction *may be quite out of the awareness of the actor—the individual subordinate whose behavior we are observing.*

The reason for this seeming paradox is in the very nature of character. Character traits serve to guard the balance of motivations in the personality by presenting a patterned, habitual, and reasonably consistent mode of behavior to the environment. In this sense, character or behavioral traits exist as "armor" to protect the inner world of the person in relation to the outer world.

The dimension of activity-passivity is, of course, an oversimplified way of talking about complex behavioral acts. But it will do for our purposes. In observing individuals interacting with their environment, one can differentiate between two extremes:

☐ The active consists of a pattern of initiation or outward thrust. The individual stimulates the environment by directing energy outward.

☐ The passive mode typically directs a low amount of energy outward. Behavior is in *response* to stimulation from others.

Activity-passivity is seen quite clearly in group meetings, for example. Some individuals initiate, talk a great deal, and direct their energy toward other persons. Other individuals are quiet, talk little, speak only when spoken to, and release little energy in the process (even though the situation seems to invite their more active participation).

The combination of the two dimensions of inner motivation and external behavior establishes the four patterns of subordinacy. In the descriptions and interpretations of these patterns, I have emphasized the more extreme representations. I have also tried to present a process rather than, necessarily, a particular person. While individuals in the subordinate role usually tend toward one or the other of the four patterns, they are not rigidly fixed in a category. There is a measure of flexibility and variation depending on the person's dispositions, the time, the place, and the particular individuals with whom relationships develop.

PART II. IMPACT ON DEVELOPMENT

As I have hinted earlier, the problems a person experiences in subordinate positions are usually the end product of a long historical process for him or her. Developmental experiences in successive stages of the life cycle, particularly in the family, lay down the basic patterns of subordinacy.

In Adolescence

The direct and conscious confrontations with the problems of authority and subordinacy usually occur during the adolescent stage of development. This period is fraught with pain and anxiety for parents and adolescent alike. To a great extent, subordinacy conflicts in the business organization represent the prolongation or continuation of the adolescent life crises.

The essential task of adolescence is to achieve independence from the family and assume the responsibilities of an adult. This task, in reality, is never fully completed, yet we usually acknowledge its completion when the individual begins his or her work career, marries, and becomes the head of a family.

The difficulty in adolescence stems from the presence of opposite forces in the personality. There is both a "push" toward rapid maturation, for which the person may feel inadequately prepared, and a "pull" toward the securities in the earlier close relationships with the parents. Yet the pull has to be overcome or there would be little basis for severing the old ties and establishing the new ones of adulthood.

This simultaneous push and pull accounts for much of the bizarre quality of adolescent behavior. The individual, let alone those who care for him or her, may not know whether to respond to the push of development or the pull of security and comfort in the family circle. Both aspects have to be defended against until they have been assimilated within the personality.

To make matters even more difficult for the developing adult, the crisis of adolescence reawakens and reactivates a series of conflicts from the earlier stages of development. We owe a great deal to psychoanalytic psychology for revealing the dynamics of development from birth onward, especially in its demonstration of the importance of the infancy years. Of particular significance here is the reactivation during adolescence of the conflicts of (1) *intimacy,* in the relationship between mother and child, and (2) *initiative,* in the triangle of mother, father, and child.

Intimacy and Dependency

The pull confronting the adolescent is toward restoration of the primary love and dependency relationship with the mother. During the earliest period of development, well before the child begins to acquire the capacity to use words and concepts, all of his or her life-giving needs are secured in the intimacy of the primary pairing with the mother or some substitute figure. In many ways, this initial intimacy prepares the child for the experience of intimacy as an adult, but it contains danger as well. The danger comes from two sources:

1. *Separation.* Separation from the primary relationship of intimacy usually generates considerable anger and even rage. This anger must somehow be dissipated and channeled into constructive ends during development; otherwise, it remains as a destructive potential in one of the four patterns of subordinacy described earlier.

2. *Desire to restore intimacy.* This regressive pull acts very strongly on the developing individual. If the pull becomes strong enough, and the individual gives in to it, he or she may remain markedly dependent all their

life and unable to take the steps necessary for mature adulthood in work and family.

Evidence of the strength of the pull toward restoration of the earlier security is available in adult disturbances such as alcoholism, depression, and stomach ulcers. These symptoms in the adult reflect the desire for the primary intimacy relationship and also guard against the rage and anger caused by separation from it. I would take the current interest in "the angry young man" theme of contemporary novels and films such as *Saturday Night and Sunday Morning* or *This Sporting Life* as a reflection of the problems posed by the pull toward passivity in the male, which they describe effectively.

Initiative and Competition

Conflicts of initiative are also reawakened during adolescence, as a result of the dangers imagined in the push toward maturation. Here, again, the problem is not experienced for the first time during adolescence but is instead a reactivation of earlier dilemmas in development. In this case, the dilemma is spun out in the structure of the triangle of mother-father-child. The triangle is relevant in all life situations and is fashioned along the lines of the early rivalry for supremacy, the desire to be number one.

Sigmund Freud noted the importance of the triangle in observations of emotionally disturbed patients who appeared anxious, guilt-ridden, and dominated by undefined fears of attacking and being attacked. He correlated the adult disturbances with a conflict in infancy occurring between the ages of three and six, which he called the "Oedipus complex," after Sophocles' tragedy, *Oedipus the King*. The triangle in this Greek tragedy consists of Oedipus, his mother, and his father. Oedipus unknowingly kills his father, marries his mother, and becomes the king. Oedipus blinds himself in the first flood of his remorse and is cast out of the community.

The appeal of this tragedy, as of many similar dramatic portrayals of the eternal and fateful triangle, is that members of the audience can be aware of the conflict while remaining in a safe position; as members of a collective body they are at a distance from their own oedipal anxieties. Studies of normal as well as pathological human development indicate that the oedipal period is a common growth phase. Here the young male child has a strong longing for the sole possession of his mother and treats his father as a rival. The longing and rivalry are contained for the most part in fantasy and play activities of the child. But their strength and significance should not be underestimated.

The child, while experiencing this longing and rivalry, is aware of the superior strength of the father and fears retaliation for his wishes. This fear springs from the tendency of the child to attribute or project his own inner fantasies onto the father. This attribution becomes a feeding ground for anxiety; when strong enough, it becomes displaced in the form of phobias and related anxiety symptoms. Among the most important symptoms are work inhibitions, especially the inability to exert initiative and to perform.

The Oedipus complex is initially resolved in the child's capacity to test reality through the eyes of loving parents. He identifies with his rival and delays the gratification of infantile wishes: "If I cannot substitute for Father, I will try to be like him." This formula for identification becomes the dynamic for subsequent development, including the capacity to learn and assume, at an appropriate stage in life, the position of a responsible man.

But it would be a mistake to view the Oedipus complex as a piece of finished business at the time the child enters school. For many individuals the issue is not so simply resolved and may lead to a frozen position in the developmental tasks of life or a retreat to an earlier stage of development. Even without marked failures in the mastery of the Oedipus complex, one finds the reopening of the classic problem of the triangle during subordinacy crises of adolescence and adulthood.

The individual functions in the role of subordinate through most of the adolescent and career years. The oedipal strivings may continue to exert a strong pull toward immature behavior and account for many of the problems of subordinacy that we observe in everyday life. The overanxious subordinate, the poor performer, the indecisive man—for these and other types of people, personality conflicts involving subordinacy reflect the impact of the Oedipus complex.

Learning Through Conflict

The conflicts of intimacy and initiative are inherent in the process of development. They are not to be viewed as negative experiences by themselves, since all development from infancy onward takes place within a matrix of conflicting forces—the push toward maturity and the pull toward restitution of earlier gratifying situations. Instead, the main test of development is in the kind and degree of learning through inner conflict.

The objective of learning remains central to our interest in resolving the conflicts of subordinacy. And with this idea in mind, let us turn to some conclusions based on the preceding analysis.

PART III. IMPLICATIONS

There are presumably two points of view involved in the question of how to resolve subordinacy conflicts—not only that of the individual in the midst of personal subordinacy conflicts, but also that of the authority figure on the other side of the vertical relationship. How can the person who exercises authority in relation to other individuals help minimize these conflicts and aid his or her subordinates in their efforts too grow and mature?

Actually, these two points of view are interrelated. In examining the personal and interpersonal problems of any individual in an organization, it is impressive to note the fact that no one is ever separated from the role of subordinate, no matter how high their position in the hierarchy. Everyone has one or several authority figures whose evaluations and responses are of great personal significance. Simultaneously, however, there are subordinates who look to this same person for direction, guidance, and evaluation.

Self-management

The fact that authority and subordinacy conflicts exist within a web of human relationships does not minimize the importance for the individual of learning to assume responsibility for his or her own behavior. Whether looking at the relationship from above or below, one has to learn to separate their reactions from those of other persons and to achieve appropriate self-management. This attitude of self-management contradicts the tendency to attribute blame to others for the personal predicaments of immediate experience.

One important practical implication of self-management is the awareness of how frequently one tries to relive old conflicts from the past in the present. All too often bosses in organizations become shadowy father figures from the past and are used as objects for the transfer of unresolved conflicts. The subordinate should learn to recognize his or her tendency to overload present relationships in terms of personal history, and seek to mediate and govern his or her reactions so that they accord with reality. It is unrealistic, for example, to overidealize one's boss, just as it is usually unrealistic to depreciate the boss' authority and competence.

Superior and subordinate alike can experience considerable help in viewing the conflicts of subordinacy as conditions of development. Subordinates, in fact, do learn from experience, provided they are not excessively overburdened with the unfinished business of past relationships with their parents. In cases where the indications are massive that a subordinate's past has taken over the present reality in his mind, then it pays to understand that, by and large, little change can occur in the superior-subordinate work relationship.

The superior is not in a position to act as therapist for his or her subordinates. He or she should not try to do so, and should be sufficiently knowledgeable to sort out the realistic issues in their work relationships from the neurotic conflicts of personal development. Focusing on the realistic issues helps to remove the edge of guilt from human relationships in work situations, and frequently serves to remove much of the static that impedes communication.

Both superior and subordinate can learn from experience when they are reasonably free of past conflicts. Growth and change do occur, but only very slowly, and more readily for those individuals who are building on a strong foundation of personal competence. For those who cannot so learn— for whom lessons learned in the past obstruct the capacity to function in the present—reeducation is necessary. This reeducation takes place best within a professional relationship, and it is usually wise to seek out a specialist in psychoanalysis and psychiatry for such help.

Guidelines

What guidelines will help to govern the transactions in superior-subordinate relationships? Here are some ideas and suggestions.

1. *Know your own mind.* It is important for both superior and subordinate to know where they stand on issues of work or personal conflict. We usually hear that it is important to listen to the other person and understand their point of view. This is good advice as far as it goes. What gets left out, to the misfortune of all concerned, is the fact that competent behavior depends on the ability of the individuals to know where he or she stands and what he or she would like to see happen. In particular, the authority figures may find themselves tyrannized by their own vacillations. If the subordinate is confused and torn by mixed feelings, it will do him or her little good to find the boss equally confused. In this sense, knowing where one stands and being prepared to take a position have a salutary effect on human relationships.

2. *Avoid the disabling reciprocal.* In every interpersonal relationship there is usually a balancing effect that takes place. A particular pattern of behavior of the subordinate implies a reciprocal pattern of behavior on the part of the superior, and vice versa. If one individual talks, the reciprocal role necessary to balance the transaction is that of the listener. The relationship is unbalanced in this case if both individuals talk at the same time.

But a balanced relationship is not always desirable, either. It is especially undesirable to play the reciprocal to a subordinate strongly characterized by one of the four patterns of subordinacy earlier described. Each of these patterns tends to evoke a kind of reciprocal response that reinforces the conflict and creates a vicious circle. For instance, the masochistic subordinate seeks to evoke aggression and punishment. If the individual succeeds, their behavior is reinforced.

A reciprocal may in some cases be the opposite behavior; in other cases, the reciprocal is a similar response. For example:

☐ The compulsive doubter evokes doubt and guilt in others as the reciprocal response. The avoidance of the reciprocal in this case means to present a firm and decisive stance to break the chain of doubt. Similarly, avoidance of the reciprocal for the masochistic subordinate would mean refraining from punishment; this would break off the transaction that they hope to induce and require him or her to think again.

☐ But when a subordinate's behavior is impulsive, the tendency is to take the reciprocal and give in. The proper response, in this case, is to avoid the reciprocal, maintain authority over him or her, and stay in control of the relationship.

The reciprocal cannot be avoided if the individual pondering these guidelines for behavior is a poor observer of human interaction and emotion.

To choose, or to avoid, the reciprocal with intelligence requires the ability to observe and understand human behavior. A good way to start cultivating this ability is to try to read accurately one's own behavior.

3. *Watch for the resonance effect.* There is a strong tendency in human relationships for individuals to experience the feelings that others have in the course of face-to-face interactions. In this sense we tend to resonate in response to the tones of feeling originating in other persons. In the positive, resonance may yield the quality of empathy, the capacity to sense what is going on in the other person. However, there is also a negative to resonance that is worth watching.

In no case should the origins of emotions be confused. The compulsive subordinate lives with guilt and, by the process of resonance, tends to generate guilt in others. Trouble can be avoided when one identifies the resonance effect and clearly separates the origin of the feeling from his or her own reactions. Once the sources of the feelings are properly located, the individual is free to respond in terms of their own evaluation of what is needed. Exercising freedom of response provokes rethinking and learning as opposed to the deadly repetitive patterns encountered so frequently in superior-subordinate relationships.

4. *Objectify conflict.* When conflict arises in superior-subordinate relationships, a potential for deterioration arises. It is not useful to increase this potential by dealing with the emotional bases of the conflict head on. For one thing, it may not be at all clear in the minds of the individuals concerned just what the emotional factors are. For another thing, the emotions may be too painful to bring into the transaction.

The potential for deterioration gets minimized when, in the course of communication, ways are discovered for objectifying the conflict. This means that issues are broken down into components and that procedures are discovered for dealing with them. The size and scope of the conflict are reduced to manageable proportions as ways are found for exploring particular concerns. The effort, in other words, is directed toward partial answers rather than toward the heroic attempt to solve total conflicts once and for all.

5. *Identify and address reality.* Work relationships are governed and judged in the final analysis by their contributions to purposes. There are always present, therefore, practical issues and realities to which attention can be addressed. The purpose of superior-subordinate relationships in most organizations is to identify those problems that require solutions in order to move the organization closer to its goals.

The orientation to reality does not require coldness or insensitivity. On the contrary, the search for real problems can be conducted with considerable enthusiasm and regard for feelings. But, at the same time, warmth and sensitivity are not substitutes for problem solving and other attempts at dealing with reality.

6. *Maintain contact.* There are times in organizations when the going gets tough for authority figures and subordinates alike. The temptation to

withdraw is great during these painful experiences. As a temporary measure, withdrawal may be quite necessary and constructive—for instance, as a prelude to forming and consolidating a new position. But withdrawal fails as a permanent stance.

Withdrawal in the face of injury breaks contact with reality. If the withdrawal persists, fantasy can take over, leading to a whole host of incorrect ideas about the situation in which one finds one's self. This in turn leads to difficulty in introducing the corrective mechanisms associated with learning, particularly where authority relations are concerned.

There are many ways known to all of us to maintain contact in the face of injury. The main problem is to avoid the temptation to withdraw when it is unconstructive.

Recognizing Reality

In reviewing and thinking about these guidelines for resolving the conflicts of subordinacy, one principle stands out. This is the need for superior and subordinate alike to recognize the truth when they see it. I refer here not to abstract truth, but to the concrete reality of that which exists in human relationships.

Before change can occur in one's self and others, recognition must be given to the reality. It is here that observation and understanding play a very important role in human relationships. It is in this sense that a description and explanation of patterns of subordinacy can be useful to both seniors and subordinates in modern organizations.

Notes

1. See Abraham Zaleznik, *Worker Satisfaction and Development* (Boston, Division of Research, Harvard Business School, 1956).

7
The Subordinate's Predicaments

ERIC H. NEILSEN and JAN GYPEN

How can subordinates improve relations with their superiors? And how can superiors help their subordinates feel comfortable in what is often a tense relationship? These questions have usually been dealt with only indirectly in management circles. Yet the relationship is so threatening to many subordinates that they react in ways that are damaging to themselves and their organizations. Drawing heavily on the work of psychologist Erik Erikson, the authors present dilemmas that commonly confront the subordinate. They point out that being aware of these dilemmas can make them more manageable and then offer advice to superiors to aid subordinates in handling such situations.

Nearly everyone in the administrative world is subordinate to someone else. Thus getting along with superiors is critical to career success.

Managers, however, tend to approach the topic only tangentially by talking about effective leadership (the other half's responsibility in the relationship) or by striving to get out of the subordinate's role and into the superior's. Ignored is the fact that most managers will always be working under someone else and that being an effective subordinate is just as important a professional task as being an effective superior.

But being a subordinate means dealing with special tensions that often result in debilitating self-protective responses, as the following examples illustrate:

☐ A senior manager of a major retailing company returns to the home office after spending 15 years developing new divisions all around the country. He is made executive vice president and told that he will succeed to the presidency within a couple of years. But after a year at

Published in 1979.

headquarters, he comes to realize that his mentor has no intention of retiring and, more important, deals with people in a manipulative and domineering way. His inability to confront his boss creates discomfort and finally an emotional crisis. He takes a position at another business and leaves the retailing company without an heir apparent.

☐ A former army officer is hired as an administrator by a large company because of his experience in managing large-scale projects. Although his competence is valued, he clings to a bureaucratic style that served him well in the army. The more informal system his new boss prefers makes him so uncomfortable he refuses to adapt to it, and eventually he is dismissed.

☐ A project manager of a research group feels threatened when her boss assigns to the group's staff someone who is both talented and competitive. When asked how the new woman is fitting in, the manager compliments her but fails to discuss the newcomer's weaknesses and the concerns the manager has about her own future. Eventually she resigns out of fear that the new woman will soon replace her. The boss cannot explain what has happened. He was just about to assign the new woman to another project and had no intention of replacing the project manager at all.

One might argue that all three cases are examples of ineffective subordinates whom superiors should be happily rid of. But in another sense, each of the subordinates' actions is quite understandable as an attempt to maintain personal integrity, remain competent, or prevent embarrassment. What superior would not admit that these are legitimate needs in professional life?

How to meet the organization's need for an appropriate amount of hierarchy and at the same time meet the subordinate's need for protecting his or her own identity has always been a problem in organizations. Recent research on power dynamics suggests that a subordinate's effort to be self-protective is a natural consequence of hierarchy itself. That is, the power the superior holds frequently leads him or her to attempt to manipulate the subordinate and to lose sight of the fact that the subordinate has important feelings and emotions, not to mention important abilities.

The research indicates that this manipulation happens because of the structure of the superior-subordinate relationship, not because of the personalities of the superiors.[1]

Indeed, what manager acting as a superior has not had the experience of looking at a project in retrospect and admitting, if only to himself or herself, that his or her role was not as critical as he or she felt at the time and that his or her subordinates' contributions were probably greater than he or she has cared to recognize? And what manager acting as a subordinate has not felt that a superior has not given due credit for effort and that looking out for oneself is a necessary, though perhaps degrading, fact of organization life?

Dilemmas of Self-Protection

If one admits that hierarchy can corrupt superiors but assumes that hierarchy is necessary to organization life, one must also accept the premise that subordinates are justified in becoming self-protective. The issue for those concerned with the effective management of the organization as a whole, then, is not to try to rid subordinates of self-protectiveness but instead to create an environment that reduces their need to protect themselves.

A first step in this direction is to clarify the ways in which self-protectiveness is evoked. Few managers acting as superiors or subordinates are aware of just how pervasive the self-protective urge is and, therefore, of how many aspects of the superior-subordinate relationship it affects. We suggest that the situation be conceived of as a series of dilemmas that subordinates must resolve in dealing with superiors, as follows:

- ☐ Alliance vs. competition
- ☐ Clarifying expectations vs. second guessing
- ☐ Initiative vs. dependence
- ☐ Competence vs. inferiority
- ☐ Differentiation vs. identification
- ☐ Relating personally vs. relating impersonally
- ☐ Mutual concern vs. self-interest
- ☐ Integrity vs. denial

We have derived these dilemmas largely from the theory of individual development formulated by Erik Erikson, the pioneering psychologist who wrote *Childhood and Society* and other books on human development.[2] Our contention is that the same issues which, according to Erikson, every individual must face in finding a meaningful role in society are recreated in the superior-subordinate relationship. The superior in a sense represents what Erikson describes as the pressures of society.[3]

In each dilemma, we shall first consider the consequences of the subordinate's choosing either option and then examine situations in which the dilemma tends to be most important.

Alliance vs. Competition

To view the superior as a trustworthy ally or as a competitor to be on guard against.

How a subordinate handles this dilemma is especially important because the consequences of a poor choice can be disastrous. Distrusting the superior when he or she is really well intentioned can lead to hurt feelings and missed opportunities for all concerned. Of course, trusting the superior and then being taken advantage of can create difficulties as well because the subordinate's lower position makes retaliating difficult.

Obviously, the superior also has to make a choice about whether to view a subordinate as an ally or as a competitor, but a superior can redress a poor choice fairly easily because of his or her power.

This dilemma arises frequently for subordinates, regardless of an organization's dominant management philosophy, as we found recently in a company with a reputation for being sensitive to its employees' needs. A female personnel manager reporting directly to a male division head had risen rapidly through the ranks to become one of the organization's senior female managers. Although she had worked effectively to remove sexual bias in promotion, she sensed that she had not been totally successful.

Her feelings were confirmed when the company passed over a woman and promoted a male candidate to fill a management position. The woman who was not promoted complained to her superiors, and so they called a meeting of the managers involved in the case. The female personnel manager felt that the complaining woman was justified in feeling discriminated against; nevertheless, the boss asked the manager to defend the division's promotion practices at the meeting.

Should she voice her convictions at this meeting and risk generating the wrath of her superior? Or should she go to him directly and share her concerns with him? Either choice might reduce her chances of successfully documenting her case and supporting her female colleague if her superior proved to be unsympathetic or unwilling to examine the issue objectively.

After much agonizing, she chose to confide in her boss. Her superior was sympathetic to her concerns and after further consideration decided to support her position.

The same sort of choice arises when, in order to test the waters, a superior asks a subordinate to advocate a controversial position that the superior has yet to support publicly, when a subordinate is assigned the task of defending an unpopular cause, or when a subordinate is asked to sign papers and relay messages he or she does not really understand. Such situations abound in the day-to-day life of organizations. No one gets hurt as long as there is mutual trust up and down the hierarchy. Nonetheless, events like these place the subordinate at a disadvantage if the superior proves untrustworthy and if, at the time of the act itself, it is the subordinate who must make the critical choice.

Clarifying Expectations vs. Second-guessing

To seek explanations of what the superior wants or to stay uncertain about the superior's expectations and to risk misinterpretation.

Delegating authority so that both the superior and the subordinate are comfortable is critical to the overall relationship. Even then, a certain amount of tension can be expected to reappear because conditions frequently change. The accessibility of each party to the other may change as one person begins to travel more or moves to a new office. New projects may lend themselves to different patterns of delegation.

The subordinate who copes with these changes by regularly seeking clarification of what the superior expects increases his or her ability to sense what results the superior really wants. The subordinate can thus develop clear ideas about what to do when unforeseen events arise. He or she can enjoy open-ended assignments and at the same time feel good about taking issues to a superior that either cannot or should not be handled alone.

Seeking clarification about expectations as conditions change can, however, be a threatening process for a subordinate. New conditions may cause the superior to demand more delegation than the subordinate is ready for, triggering anxiety and self-doubt, which can lead to ineffective job performance. Certain situations may cause the superior to tighten control, leaving an independently inclined subordinate with a sense of being boxed in. Thus second-guessing the superior's changing expectations and avoiding direct clarification may be seen as the best available strategy. The most common results of such an approach are misunderstandings that lead to poor performance and misgivings on the part of all concerned.

The earlier example of the executive vice president who left his company rather than confront his mentor about his retirement date and operating style is a case in which several important changes occurred concerning delegation that were not dealt with effectively. When the subordinate was out establishing new divisions, communication was sporadic and focused on critical results. When he returned to headquarters, however, communication was continuous and dealt with operating details. Out in the field he had been delegated clear-cut matters involving technology and costs. Back at headquarters, where differences in the management styles of the two men were more apparent, the president also monitored and controlled the vice president's operating style.

While the subordinate was in the field, he was still a young manager on the way up. On his return, he was in his fifties and eager to take the reins, but his mentor was in his seventies and becoming concerned about hanging on to control. Clearly, each man's personal growth and changing developmental needs were adding fuel to the fire. The various changes led to a situation in which the subordinate thought his autonomy unfairly reduced, and yet he was unwilling in the end to confront his superior about this.

The fact that the subordinate in the example left the company when he was so near the top and after such a long career shows how this dilemma can linger throughout a manager's career. The clarification of expectations is inevitably an imperfect process. Superiors do not always know what they want. Often they find out too late. What a superior wants and how well a subordinate understands it are rarely in perfect balance. At some point, however, the subordinate must clear the air or face the consequences.

Initiative vs. Dependence

To suggest and promote ways to achieve the organization's goals and enhance one's own development or to wait for the superior to take charge and modify personal aspirations.

Most managers value initiative in their subordinates for achieving the organization's goals and developing as individual contributors, but they vary considerably in how they distinguish between initiative that supports their work and initiative that is competitive. The latter breeds competition in return, and unless the subordinate has other powerful supporters, he or she is likely to lose out because of the superior's power.

A subordinate who works at taking the initiative until he or she finds areas where it is welcome can feel free to make suggestions that will fit in with his or her own aspirations without fear of being blocked.

When the subordinate fears that taking the initiative will be fruitless or will invoke retaliation, he or she is likely to shy away from such behavior and also to take the blame for failures that arise from poor guidance. This pattern may heighten his or her feelings of dependence and encourage him or her to refrain from making suggestions when he or she could indeed be helpful. The superior thus sets the direction without the benefit of the subordinate's input.

Deciding whether to take the initiative or to rely on the superior for setting new directions is especially difficult for a subordinate whose talents are rapidly developing and who many people are beginning to identify as a valuable resource. Then the risks of arousing competitive feelings in the superior and the chances of finding new opportunities the subordinate would like to exploit are both on the rise. Consider the case of a personnel manager who had completed a training program in organization development and was just putting his new skills to work:

> As soon as I completed the diagnosis for the data processing group and word got out that the managers involved were really pleased, I started getting phone calls from other department heads. Within three weeks, I had lined up enough work to keep me busy for a year.
>
> But then my boss got cold feet. He knows about organization development, but I think he's basically afraid of it. He made me cancel almost all of the jobs because, he said, he wanted me to develop the rest of the EEOC program. I think the real reason was that he didn't want us to become known as an OD group. Then he would have had to play the expert, which he knows he isn't, or rely on me, which he's not about to do, or get more training, which he's afraid of.

Whenever a subordinate has an opportunity to increase his or her own status at the expense of the superior, this dilemma arises, yet change and innovation on the part of both are critical to the success of any organization.

Competence vs. Inferiority

To feel capable in one's work given one's experience and training or to feel inept and out of step with one's colleagues.

Subordinates who view their own skills as adequate compared with the skills of others at their level are likely to learn from feedback concerning their performance. They can also feel free to ask for feedback at appropriate times. They welcome challenging new tasks and expect rewards for good performance. Their interest in how the superior views their skills encourages collaboration on mapping out career development steps.

Subordinates who have doubts about their skills are apt to avoid feedback, to misinterpret performance criteria, and to be devastated by critical evaluations. They are also unlikely to initiate new activities that would improve their skills. The subordinate's desire to retrace steps or elect safe courses of action for fear of falling farther behind adversely affects the relationship with the superior.

The decision about how open to be with the superior about competence comes up whenever subordinates face yearly reviews, budget analyses, contract decisions, progress meetings, or major promotion points. These periods are especially stressful because of the rewards and punishments that can result. Viewing oneself as competent and being open to evaluation and feedback facilitates indepth review, but poor evaluations can harm an entire career. Classifying oneself as out of the running beforehand or as not in a position to be given a fair hearing can save face with colleagues and reduce emotional turmoil, but the chances of being seen as unwilling to cooperate may also be heightened.

Unfortunately, this dilemma is frequently complicated by organization politics. While avoiding negative evaluation is sometimes legitimate, it can become intertwined with avoiding evaluation by those whom subordinates incorrectly assume are biased against them.

Consider the case of a project leader in an engineering firm who developed a very close relationship with the senior partner, the person most responsible for hiring him. Aware that several others had opposed his selection, the project leader generally avoided contact with them but invited evaluation from the partner. Shortly before a major promotion decision, the senior partner died of a heart attack. The other partners felt quite justified in passing the project leader over because of their past relationship with him.

Being passed over put the manager at a disadvantage with competing colleagues. His relationship with the other partners never did improve, and his performance declined. Eventually he left the company for another position.

Differentiation vs. Identification

To come across as being very different from the superior in terms of skills, aspirations, values, and professional concerns or to identify with the superior as someone to emulate.

One critical task facing every subordinate is deciding what kind of image to project vis-à-vis the superior. This task is addressed partly by the ways in which the previously discussed dilemmas are resolved.

The subordinate's dilemma whether to define himself or herself as similar in approach and outlook to the superior or as uniquely different hinges on the extent to which the superior is an attractive role model.

Unlike the other dilemmas, we do not see any of the choices in this dilemma as necessarily ideal for the organization. A distinctly different identity for the subordinate compared with the superior's may be just as valuable to the organization as a highly similar one, depending on the circumstances. Likewise, neither choice is necessarily ideal for the subordinate. At one point in the subordinate's career, he or she may find it especially beneficial to identify with his or her superior and to use the superior as an important role model. At other times, the subordinate may find that differentiating himself or herself clearly from his or her superior is important for improving his or her own self-image.

Nonetheless, the dilemma is an important one because its resolution can affect the overall tone of the relationship. To see oneself as different from the superior encourages an emphasis on contrast. To identify with the superior emphasizes like-mindedness and invites a teacher-student type of relationship. What is important for the subordinate is to clarify his or her choice early in the relationship so that he or she can make the most out of it and resist pulls in the opposite direction.

The identity issue comes to the foreground every time a manager gets a new leader. Frequently managers entering midcareer use such leadership changes as opportunities to strike out on their own. Here is what a 37-year-old production superintendent said about his change in bosses:

> I moved into this position when Bill was division manager. He had held my position previously and that, along with our similarities in backgrounds, made it easy for me to use him as a model. I did to the fullest. People used to tell me that I even answered the phone the way he did, used the same phrases, and told the same jokes. More important, when I was in a tight spot, I would often ask myself what he would do in my shoes.

When Roger took over from Bill, I made an important decision. Roger is a very charismatic manager. It would have been easy for me to use him as a model in the same way as I did Bill. But I chose not to. I needed time to figure out on my own who I am.

I talked with Roger about my career interests, and he has been quite supportive in helping me tie them into his own objectives without pressuring me to adopt his style.

Relating Personally vs. Relating Impersonally

To view the superior as a fellow human facing similar problems in managing family and career and in developing friendships or to view the superior's world as different and distant and thus to relate to him or her on a utilitarian basis only.

Our business culture has a bias against close friendships among managers, especially in large corporations. The bias appears to stem from fears that nonjob-related ties might jeopardize objectivity and also from frequent transfers, which discourage people from developing close ties to a place.

Nonetheless, taking the time to inquire into family life, share nonjob concerns, and listen to each other's personal problems are types of intimacy that are becoming more permissible in today's management world.

Deciding whether to treat a superior as a fellow human or as just a functionary in a business role is difficult for subordinates who have been unable to resolve the previously discussed dilemmas satisfactorily. Relating to the superior as an individual opens the door to expressing one's feelings of competition, self-doubt, dependence, and inferiority. But owning up to these feelings in a business relationship could easily be interpreted as a sign of weakness.

Even when the preceding dilemmas have been resolved satisfactorily, the choice to relate personally or impersonally has important consequences. Subordinates must recognize that few superiors act strictly as role players all the time. They have temper tantrums, playful moments, idiosyncrasies, and periods of depression or elation because of what is happening in their personal lives. Any of these states can intimidate, confuse, or frustrate a subordinate who chooses to relate on strictly impersonal terms.

Subordinates who treat their superiors as adults with common interests and problems can tolerate their superiors' moods and idiosyncrasies, resist their irrational behavior without fear of permanently damaging the relationship, and accept whatever friendship develops.

Relating personally can help a subordinate understand the interplay between the superior's emotional needs and his or her business behavior. Consider the case of an engineer in a large manufacturing plant:

I had had 18 years of experience in industrial engineering when I came on board here, and when I first began to work with Howard, my superior, things were very rocky. I could see right away that I had a lot of things to contribute, but every time I suggested something, Howard would turn me down. Somehow I was always wrong. He'd tell me the idea had been tried before and hadn't worked, or the cost of doing this was not worth the effort, or production people wouldn't buy that.

It wasn't until I got to know him that I realized Howard says no to everything the first time. He does it in management meetings. He does it with his secretary. He did it with his kids when I was having drinks at his house.

Two things eventually became clear. First, Howard doesn't forget. He'll bring your idea back to you if he's interested, and he'll give you credit for it and help you act on it. Second, I realized I didn't like starting out with a no. I confronted him, and he's improved a lot. I can see him catching himself when he starts to be negative, and we joke about it. Sometimes he does it anyway, but now I get along pretty well with him because we both know it's 'just his way.'

Mutual Concern vs. Self-interest

To keep the superior's welfare and development seriously in mind or to be totally preoccupied with one's own success.

Superiors are frequently rewarded for how well they develop their subordinates, but the reverse tends not to be true. And yet, subordinates who can look beyond their self-interest and aid their superiors' performance can help their relationships and themselves. Superiors are likely to work at developing subordinates who willingly share their expertise in areas where the superior is weak and who show concern about the company's welfare.

The risk is, of course, that few formally sanctioned rewards exist for helping develop a superior, and the chance always remains that the superior will exploit the relationship by taking undue credit for something that the subordinate has actually accomplished.

Nonetheless, we have found that superiors respond positively to subordinates who have something important to contribute to their superiors' development and who are willing to share it. For example, while interviewing a white marketing executive about his key subordinates, we found he was closest to a black product manager. When we asked him why this particular relationship had worked out so well, he explained that for the first time he had found a black manager who was willing to share the day-to-day experiences of being black in a white-dominated organization. The insights helped the white superior evaluate his own behavior, deal with black colleagues more effectively, and identify important problems in race relations within the company.

Thus we suspect that the most successful superior-subordinate relationships are those in which both parties can identify and use important resources in each other. These resources can be skills, knowledge, charisma, or simply the capacity to help in articulating commonly held values.

Integrity vs. Denial

To accept the relationship with its limitations or to reject or misrepresent it.

Toward the end of one's life, according to Erikson, one must decide how the whole affair has come off. To pass the later years with a sense of integrity is to accept the past for what it has been, to admit to both the good and the bad, and to appreciate one's total experience as something that cannot, need not, and should not be changed. Wisdom is gained from emotionally integrating what has happened and from faithfully passing on one's ideas to the next generation. The lack of such integration leads to despair. People caught in despair become bitter and attempt to rewrite their histories by engaging in new ventures that are impossible to complete.

Most subordinates do not come to grips with this dilemma until they retire, but on a smaller scale it comes up every time a subordinate moves on to another position or undergoes evaluation. He can treat the relationship with his superior either with a sense of integrity or with a sense of denial, which is the counterpart of despair.

Subordinates who are honest with themselves accept the relationship for what it is and has been. In discussions with others, such subordinates are candid about both the strengths and weaknesses they see in the superior, but they are also likely to consider the superior's experience and to evaluate the implications for their own futures. Subordinates with this turn of mind see the facts of the past as a sound framework for understanding the present and envisioning the future.

For example, a manager who had just left an employer of many years described the meeting at which he announced his decision to leave:

> Kenneth is often short on words. When I told him I was leaving, he said only three. First, he smiled and said, 'That's great!' Then he paused for a minute, looked at me with a sad face, and said, 'Nuts!' That was all he needed to say. We had both been working to get me a promotion within the company that would fit my talents and interests. The right slot simply wasn't available. We both knew I was valuable in my old position, but it was clear that I couldn't stay there forever. So this was a good move. Kenneth was a good boss.

Subordinates who are unrealistic about their relationships with superiors are often unwilling to accept the responsibility for what has occurred. They see the relationships as having been unsuccessful or at least as not having lived up to their expectations. In their eyes, failure lies mostly with the superiors. It is the superiors who should have been wiser or more caring, more sharing, more competent.

From the viewpoint of a third party, there might be a grain of truth in these accusations. The superior is indeed more powerful than the subordinate and can have a greater impact on their relationship. Nevertheless, it takes two people to make a relationship.

Certainly a subordinate has some responsibility to confront a superior who does not live up to the subordinate's expectations. This is not to say that continuous confrontation around all the dilemmas we have discussed is the best way of relating to a superior. But a subordinate who wishes to maintain a sense of integrity must accept personal responsibility for failing to face a difficult situation.

Taking Action

Simply recognizing the various dilemmas that subordinates face is a first step in dealing with the problem of self-protection. A second step is to use the dilemmas as a tool for discussing problems and concerns. Of course, the nature and outcome of such discussions partly depend on how both subordinates and superiors have previously resolved the dilemmas.

Subordinates who see their superiors as competitors are unlikely to be candid with them. Those who lack self-confidence will be preoccupied with what the superior wants to hear. Those who are afraid of taking the initiative will not speak from their hearts. Those who feel inferior will steer the conversation toward trivial issues. Those who rely on their superiors to define their identities will be unable to take consistent positions. Those who insist on maintaining a strictly task-oriented relationship will reject the exercise as out of place in the work setting or will fail to grasp its relevance to the total situation. Those who are self-centered will not listen to the superior's needs, and those who lack integrity will paint pretty pictures of themselves and place the total burden for change on the powerful superior.

Superiors who have similarly failed to resolve the dilemmas are likely to respond in kind, despite their more protected positions. The dialogue is likely to end up being a lot of talking about talking that leaves nothing resolved.

While the dilemmas are actually the subordinate's, it is the superior who has the greater power to act, and so we feel it appropriate at this point to address him with several suggestions.

Introspection.   Keep the dilemmas in mind when dealing with a subordinate. What kinds of self-protective behavior are you most likely encouraging, however inadvertently, by your actions? A subordinate will appreciate your sensitivity and will thus be able to make known his or her concerns.

Empathy.   Let your subordinate know how you would react if your own superior were discussing the same important issues with you. While you and your subordinate may be very different, letting the subordinate know you have thought the issues out in such a way is a sign of your respect for him or her, which is likely to encourage open discussion.

Preparedness.   Occasionally, discuss issues of self-protection directly at training sessions or retreats, after mutually shared successes, or at the beginning and end of major tasks. Make the most of such occasions by clarifying to yourself in advance what you think the most important issues are and how you might begin discussing them.

Commitment.   Once dialogue about an issue has started, do not let it drop until some resolution has been reached. Important issues can rarely be resolved in one session. Take the time to follow up and to consider new approaches. Failing to follow up can be just as damaging as initially failing to confront an issue.

Hope.   Interpersonal relationships are rarely ideal from both parties' perspectives simultaneously. Unless you can accept and share the fact that both of you are working for an unachievable ideal and are willing to accept that premise, both of you are bound to become disillusioned.

The need for self-protection is an enduring consequence of the superior-subordinate relationship. The need cannot be eliminated, but each party can examine the costs of self-protective reactions to the other and can make choices that reflect the stake they have in the larger organization.

Notes

1.   See David Kipnis, "Does Power Corrupt?" *Journal of Personality and Social Psychology,* January 1972, p. 33; and Philip G. Zimbardo, Craig Harvey, W. Curtis Banks, and David Jaffe, "A Pirandellian Prison: The Mind Is a Formidable Jailer," *New York Times Magazine,* April 3, 1983, p. 38.

2.   New York: Norton, 1964.

3.   Erik Erikson summarizes his theory in *Identity and the Life Cycle* (New York: International University Press, 1959).

PART TWO
SEXES AND RACES WORKING TOGETHER

AN OVERVIEW

Once the organizational world was the purview as well as the province of white males, so how to behave and what was expected was understood. This understanding eased communication as well as structural processes such as performance appraisal and career planning. With the increase of the numbers of women and minorities in the upper ranks of management, however, top managers have found it difficult to apply the same old sets of assumptions. As the old ways have had to give way to the new, the old guard has understandably, tried to force the newcomers into their mold. Meanwhile, the new arrivals are trying to shape their own roles. Conflicts are inevitable.

In his article "Two Women, Three Men on a Raft," Robert Schrank, in a highly personal story of a raft trip, explores how men feel the need to impress women with their maleness and form a covert understanding that women need protecting. This seemingly gentlemanly and supportive behavior, Schrank comments, actually undermines women's confidence in their own leadership abilities and forces them to reassume an inferior role. Schrank notes that just as he and his raft colleagues, tried to keep canoeists on the Rogue River from learning that the raft with the women on it had tipped over, men at work are afraid of being laughed at by other men for working for a woman who makes mistakes. Schrank maintains that this fear leads men to need to be in control all the time, even when they are not the boss. A boss who observes a woman having a difficult time running her shop should not assume that she's incapable of leadership until he first determines that her subordinates are not trying to sabotage her.

In "Case of the Valuable Vendors," Mary P. Rowe describes the effects of subtle discrimination on women. In the case on which *HBR* readers were asked to comment, Harry, a veteran salesperson, works with Gwen, a young trainee who is important to the company. He treats her as if she were either just a pretty fixture or his mistress. In discussing the case, Rowe points out that "incidents of subtle discrimination may produce a negative Pygmalion effect. If Harry assumes Gwen is an ornament or a sex object, she may begin to behave like one." When cases like these arise, Rowe asserts, each party has to be counseled. But managers need to understand that women and men *have* to work together in an atmosphere that is neither hostile nor intimidating. Separating people is not the answer: it gives credence to the attitude that men and women can't work together, and this is the attitude that the hostile Harry is portraying in the first place.

Managers might well ask just how prevalent sexual discrimination and its uglier form, harassment, is in organizations and how often men like Harry are harassing women like Gwen. If *HBR* readers are to be believed, it happens fairly often; at least 10 percent of the respondents whose opinions were reported by me and Timothy B. Blodgett in "Sexual Harassment . . . Some See It . . . Some Won't" had heard of cases where a woman who refused to have sex with her superior received a poor evaluation as a consequence. Perhaps the most important finding in this article, however, is that sexual harassment is an issue of power. It is in some ways a response of the old timers to the encroachments of the new.

In her article "Dealing with Sexual Harassment," Mary P. Rowe offers superb advice both to women who have to deal with a harassing male colleague, and to managers who want to institute company policies to erase this most offensive symptom of power struggles. The occurrence of sexual harassment might also signal managers to check out how embattled some of their male employees feel. It might be possible to attack the problem by offering more power, as Rosabeth Moss Kanter has suggested.

The next two articles in this section, "Case of the Borderline Black," by Theodore V. Purcell, and "What It's Like to Be a Black Manager," by Edward W. Jones, Jr., deal with some of the same issues of subtle discrimination and harassment that people in organizations can level at blacks and other minorities. Both authors agree that managers have to take extraordinary steps to ensure that companies are truly committed to furthering the careers of blacks. Jones writes that "a moral commitment to equal opportunity is not enough. If a company fails to recognize that fantastic filters operate between the entry level and top management, this commitment is useless." Purcell echoes Jones' sentiments in his article which describes how a manager tries to decide whether to keep a marginal black employee during a budget cut. He states, "Ultimately, the issue is whether corporate economic power should be used to end economic discrimination in the United

States." The stand these authors take is strong but it matches the tightness of the barriers that they maintain that blacks face in corporate America.

Finally, sometimes, of course, relationships between coworkers are neither coercive nor intimidating, but this doesn't mean they are any less troublesome for the manager. In "Managers and Lovers," I described the conflicts of interest that can arise in an organization when two top-level people fall in love. The problems that the senior manager faces in such a situation concern not only the couple itself but also other people in the organization. A powerful romantic twosome represents a threat to others and, because it involves love, it can stir up emotions at very basic levels. At the very least it sets up a tension in an office that can be, but is not necessarily, disruptive. Regardless of what the senior executive does to ensure that the organization is not suffering, he or she has to step very carefully because deep feelings are involved.

Two Women, Three Men on a Raft

ROBERT SCHRANK

The day was cold and gray. Under the pines that towered over their heads, 20 people assembled on the banks of the Rogue River in Oregon. They were members of a special group invited by Outward Bound to take a trip down the river on a raft. There would be five rafts, each holding four participants and one Outward Bound staff member. Raft No. 4 was the only one that had two women and three men. When the trip started, all that the participants knew was that there would be rapids with fearsome names; that each was responsible for doing his or her share of the cooking, tent pitching, ground clearing, supply hauling, and paddling; and that their teamwork or lack of it was what would make their trip a success or a failure. They knew nothing of each other, their Outward Bound staff member, or what a week on the river could really be like. This is one participant's story of how Raft No. 4 fared on the Rogue and what the experience taught him about the relationships between men and women at work.

One afternoon in June, I left the cloistered halls of the Ford Foundation and within 36 hours found myself standing on the pebbled banks of the Rogue River in Oregon with three other uncertain souls who had embarked on a week of "survival training" sponsored by Outward Bound. It was a cloudy, cold day, and as we pumped up our rubber raft and contemplated the Rogue, we also wondered about each other.

Before embarking on a Greyhound for the raft launching site, we had gathered the night before at the Medford Holiday Inn. That night, the Outward Bound staff had distributed individual camping gear and waterproof sleeping/storage bags to the 20 of us, almost all novices, and had given us a short briefing on the perils of going down the Rogue River on a raft.

Published in 1977.

As they explained the nature of the trip, the Outward Bound staffers reminded me of seasoned military men or safari leaders about to take a group of know-nothings into a world of lurking danger. Their talk was a kind of machismo jargon about "swells," rattlers, safety lines, portages, and pitons. Because they had known and conquered the dangers, it seemed they could talk of such things with assurance. This kind of "man talk" called to a primitive ear in us novices, and we began to perceive the grave dangers out there as evils to be overcome. In our minds, we planned to meet "Big Foot" the very next day, and we were secretly thrilled at the prospect.

If the Outward Bound staff briefing was designed to put us at ease, its effect, if anything, was the opposite. Hearing the detailed outline of what would be expected of us increased our anxiety. "You will work in teams as assigned to your raft," said Bill Boyd, the Northwest Outward Bound director, "and you will be responsible for running your raft, setting up camp each night, cooking every fourth meal for the whole gang, and taking care of all your personal needs."

The staff divided the 20 of us into four groups, each of which would remain together for the week on the raft. How we were grouped was never explained, but of the five rafts on the river, No. 4 was the only one that ended up with two women and three men. One of the men was a member of the Outward Bound staff, a counselor and guide who was considerably younger than his four charges.

The four of us on Raft No. 4 were all in our middle fifties. Each of us had experienced some modicum of success in his or her life, and Outward Bound had invited each of us in the hope that after a week of living on the Rogue River we would go back from that trip as Outward Bound supporters and promoters.

Outward Bound exists because of the surprising fact that during World War II fewer younger men survived being torpedoed on the Murmansk, Russia convoy run than older men. Dr. Kurt Hahn, C.B.E., an emigrant German educator living in England, had observed that the older men did things to help themselves survive, such as collecting rain water for drinking, building shelters in the lifeboats, catching and eating raw fish, and learning to care for each other.

Dr. Hahn found that many of the younger seamen, by contrast, tended to sit and wait for somebody to come and rescue them. If no one came, which was often the case, they died just sitting there. Dr. Hahn felt that these seamen must have lacked a certain self-confidence or an awareness that they could take action that would result in survival, and founded Outward Bound to help young people learn that they can take charge of their own survival and lives.

The worldwide organization has been operating in the United States for 14 years; its 35,000 graduates attest to its popularity. During this time, however, Outward Bound has evolved into more of a learning institution than a survival training organization. It now operates under a variety of different notions, one of them being that industrial man has lost and should regain the art of living with nature. The organization believes that the wilderness can teach people about themselves by providing a different backdrop against which they can gain insight into their day-to-day behavior.

This article is about what happened to two women and three men on a raft for a week on the Rogue River in Oregon.

On the River

Like most of the other 19 people on the trip, at the outset I had little or no idea of what to expect. I had participated in a few human growth encounter workshops, so I was prepared for, although again surprised at, how willingly people seem to accept the authority of a completely unknown group leader. Most people seem able to participate in all kinds of strange and, in many instances, new behaviors with no knowledge regarding the possible outcomes. This group was no exception. All of us had some notion of Outward Bound, but we knew nothing about each other, or our raft leader John, or the Rogue River.

Even though their preembarkation talk was filled with the machismo jargon I mentioned, the staff did not describe what we might actually expect to happen, nor did they talk about the many other river trips they had been on. I suppose the staff leaders assumed that the best way for a group of people to learn about themselves and each other is to let the experience talk to them directly.

The two women assigned to Raft No. 4 were named Marlene and Helen. Marlene was a recently divorced mother of five kids from Washington, whom a number of us had observed in her pink bikini in the Holiday Inn pool when we had arrived. Most of us acknowledged that because of that build we would love to have her along. Marlene used to wear her red ski suit at night and talked a lot about times she'd spent on the slopes. A top-notch skier, she said she divorced her husband because she was tired of making believe he was a better skier than she was.

Helen, a big blonde woman with a fierce sense of humor and a divorced mother of two grown boys, was at the time of our trip the president of the Fund Center in Denver, a coordinating body for local foundations, as well as a political activist. She and I became each other's clowns, and one night at a campfire she leaned over and asked me, "Bobbie, is this just another plaything of the bored rich, or can we really learn something out here in this God-forsaken wilderness?" I told her I wasn't sure but we ought to give it a chance, which we did.

One of the two other men was Bill, a very successful lawyer from Darien, Connecticut. He was the only one of the four passengers who was still happily married, since I too was divorced. Bill was a busy executive, but he managed to find time for hiking, skiing, and fishing. While Outward

Bound took care of all our food requirements and most of our medical needs, ·
Raft No. 4 had its own supply officer in Bill. His backpack was organized
like a Civil War surgeon's field kit. He had all his changes of clothing scheduled, and when it rained, his extra plastic rainjacket kept me dry since mine
leaked like a sieve. Though he and Marlene were obviously attracted to each
other from the start, it was clear from his "happy family" talk that nothing
was going to change, and it didn't.

The other man was John Rhoades, our heavily mustached, vigorous
leader, in his early thirties, who saw himself as a teacher, educator, and
trainer. As a progressive educator, John was overdedicated to the notion
that no one can learn from anyone else since learning is a singular, unique
experience. At night John slept away from the rest of us under a very fancy
Abercrombie and Fitch drop clotch which was made to be strung up in many
different ways. Trying a new fancy pitch, John would say to Bill and me,
"Be imaginative in how you pitch your tarpaulin." As we had nothing but
pieces of plastic as tarpaulins, we would greet John's injunction with amused
silence.

The men and women of Raft No. 4 were a warm, friendly, outgoing
bunch, each of whom helped create a nice supportive atmosphere.

When we arrived at the river, each was anxious to pitch in and do his
or her part. The staff distributed the rafts, each of which had a small foot
pump, and Bill and I, with instruction from John, proceeded to inflate ours.
It was one of our first chores, and we did it with a machismo fervor that
suggested either previous knowledge, or that it was man's work, or both.
Marlene and Helen carried food bags, buckets, and ropes. It was a cold day,
a gray mist hung over the towering Oregon pines, and I had a feeling that
at least some of us, given a choice, would have opted for going back to the
Holiday Inn. There was a lot of forced joking and kidding, with which we
attempted to overcome some of our anxieties—we were whistling in the
dark.

John gave each of us a Mae West type life preserver and instructed us
on how to use it. He told us, "You are not to go on the raft without it."
Now with all of us bulging out of our Mae Wests, a Richter scale applied
to anxiety would have registered eight or a full-scale breakdown. Postponing
the inevitable, we shivered, fussed, and helped each other get adjusted to
our life jackets. The trip down the Rogue was beginning to have a serious
quality.

The rafts we used were small, about 10 feet long and 4 feet wide. The
passengers sit on the inflated outer tube with their feet on the inside. Everyone is very close together with little or no room to move around. Also, unlike
a boat, a raft has no keel or rudder mechanism, which means that it tends
to roll and bobble around on top of the water. Unless the occupants work
as a team and use their paddles in close coordination, it is very difficult to
control.

While we were still on shore, John perched himself in the helmsman position at the back of the raft and said, "OK, I am going to teach you how to navigate the Rogue. When I say 'right turn,' the two people on the left side of the raft are to paddle forward and the two on the right are to backpaddle. When I say 'left turn,' the two people on the right are to paddle forward and the two on the left are to backpaddle. When I say 'forward,' I want everyone digging that paddle in like his life depended on it, and when I say 'backpaddle,'everyone paddle backward. When I say 'hold,' all paddles out of the water. Now you got it, or should we go over it again?" We pushed the raft out over the beach pebbles and paddled out into the Rogue, which at this point seemed like a nice pond. John barked his commands, and the team did just fine in the quiet water.

John told us that we were Raft No. 4 of five rafts, and it was important to everyone's safety that each raft maintain its position so that we could make periodic personnel checks to make sure no one was missing. John gave the command "forward," and because No. 3 raft was already far ahead of us and out of sight, Marlene, Helen, Bill, and I paddled vigorously.

As we proceeded down the river, John announced, "Each of you will take turns at being the helmsman." After some comment by Helen, this term was quickly corrected to conform to the new nondiscriminatory linguistics, as well as for the EEOC, to "helmsperson." John said that this person would be in charge of the raft—steering from the stern and issuing the commands.

As John talked, my mind drifted. I was suddenly overwhelmed by the grandeur and beauty of this great wilderness river road we were traveling. In awe of the hugeness of the trees, I did not hear nor respond to a command. John, a very earnest fellow, was somewhat annoyed at my daydreaming and upbraided me saying, "Look, we all have to concentrate on our job or we will be in trouble." And then he explained the nature of the rapids up ahead.

He told us how to recognize a rapid's tongue (entrance), how to avoid "sleepers" (hidden rocks), and then how to ride the "haystacks" (the choppy waves that form at the outlet of the rapids) as you come through the rapids. He said that the most important art we would learn would be how to chop our paddles into the waves as we rode the haystacks. Since a raft has no seat belts, or even seats for that matter, unless you chop down hard the rough water can bounce you right out of it.

As we paddled through the still calm waters, trying to catch up with Raft No. 3, Helen began to complain that she was already getting tired. "I'm just not used to pushing a paddle, but I'm damn good at pushing a pencil," she said. I too was beginning to feel the strain of the paddle, but rather than admit it, I just laughed saying, "Why this is nothing, Helen. You should canoe the St. John in Maine. That would teach you." Bill chimed in with "Yeah, this is nothing compared to climbing Pike's Peak."

As we moved down the river a faint distant roar broke the silence of the forest. And as we drew nearer to it, our excitement grew bigger. One might have thought that rather than a 4-foot rapids, Niagra Falls lay dead ahead. I was relieved when, some distance before the rapids, John told us to head for the bank where we would go ashore and study the rapids. As a team we would then decide what kind of a course to take through them.

We had been on the river now for a few hours, and, as it would be many times during the trip, getting on dry land was a great relief. Life on a small rubber raft consists of sitting in ankle-deep cold water, anticipating a periodic refill over both the side of the raft and one's genitals. If there was not time to bail out, we would just sit in the cold water. And even if there were time we would still be soaking wet and cold from the hips down. Though this was our first chance to escape the cold water treatment, we quickly learned to look forward to such opportunities. The physical discomfort we felt together on the raft was overcoming our sense of being strangers; by the time we disembarked that first time, we were a band of fellow sufferers.

At that point on the river, the bank was very steep, so we had a tough climb up a high rock cliff to get a good look at the rapids. Just before the rapids, the river makes a sharp 90-degree bend creating an additional danger. The swiftly running river could pile the raft up on the bank or into a hidden rock. After considerable discussion, during which Bill and I tried to demonstrate to Helen and Marlene our previous if not superior knowledge of boating, we agreed on taking a left course into the tongue while at the same time trying to bear right to avoid being swept onto the bank.

Coming up and down the steep river bank Bill helped Marlene over the rocks, holding her elbow. A ways behind them Helen commented to me, "Honestly, Bob, Marlene isn't that helpless." As we climbed into the raft, Bill helped Marlene again, and I, smiling sheepishly, offered my arm to Helen. I said, holding the raft, "Well, if we go, we all go together, and may we all end up in the same hospital room." Sitting herself down, Helen said, "Who will notify next of kin since no one will be left." After they were seated, Bill and I huddled and agreed that if anything went wrong, he would look after Marlene and I would look after Helen.

Once back on the river, with John at the helm, we paddled into the rapid's tongue, where the raft picked up speed. Staying to the left but maintaining our right orientation, before we knew what had happened, we were roaring through the tongue, roller coasting through the haystacks, screaming with excitement. Flushed with our first real achievement, the raft awash with ice-cold water, we patted each other on the back on our first great success. While bailing out the raft we paid each other compliments and convinced ourselves that we could master the Rogue River.

But this was our first set of rapids, and while John assured us that we had done well, he also reminded us of the meaner rapids yet to come with such potent names as Mule Creek Canyon, Blossom Bar, Big Bend, Copper Canyon, and Grave Creek. My God, I thought, did we really have to go through all of those terrible places?

Life on the Rogue included many other things besides shooting rapids. We pitched tarpaulins every night, lugged supplies in and out of the raft, and became accustomed to the discomforts of having no running water and of being absolutely frozen after sitting in cold water for a whole day. Nothing cements a group together like collective misery, and the people of Raft No. 4 had a *real* concern for each other as mutually suffering humans.

Each raft carried a watertight supply bag of sleeping bags and personal clothing. The bag was strapped to the front of the raft and had to be carried to and fro every morning and night. When we tied up at our first campsite, Marlene and Helen each took an end and started to carry the bag from the raft up the bank. Bill ran after them yelling, "Hey, hold it. That's too heavy for you," and grabbed the bag. Throwing it over his shoulder, he said, "You shouldn't try to do that heavy stuff." Marlene smiled and said, "Bill, anytime, be my guest." Helen, who was a little annoyed, commented sarcastically, "Well, it's great to have these big, strong men around now, ain't it though?"

When we came off the raft at night, most everybody instantly undressed to put on dry clothes, caring not one fig for a leaf or modesty. But even though on the surface it looked as though the physical sex differences had disappeared, the emergency nature of things exerted a different pressure, forcing each of us to "do what you know best."

Bill and I, for example, would pitch the tarpaulins each night and haul water, while Marlene and Helen would make the beds, clean the ground, and arrange the sleeping bags. Our mutual concern was evident; it was a beautiful experience of caring for one's fellow sisters and brothers, and I loved it.

After pitching our plastic tarpaulins (which were not much bigger than queen-size beds) as protection against the rain, the four of us would wiggle into our sleeping bags for the night. The first night Helen said she thought we were "four wonderful people gone batty sleeping on the hard cold ground when they could all be in soft feather beds." We laughed and helped each other zip up, arranged sweaters as pillows, and made sure we were all protected. Raft No. 4 was a real team.

During the days, I was beginning to learn some basics about rafts and rapids. Once the raft starts down the river and enters a swiftly moving rapid, the helmsperson must give and the crew respond to commands in quick succession in order to avoid hidden rocks, suck holes, boulders, and other obstacles, which can either flip the raft over or pull it under, bouncing it back like a ball.

As we approached the second rapids, we again went ashore to "look over our approach." It was a bad situation as the rapids planed out over a very rocky riverbed. Helen suggested that we let John take the raft through while we watch. "Now, Bob," she said, "do we really care about this damn river? I don't care if we can squeak through these rocks or not. Hit your head on them or something and you could really get hurt." Bill, John, and I cheered us on.

When I became helmsperson, I discovered quickly how difficult it is to steer a raft. The helmsperson can have some effect on the direction in which the raft goes, and because Bill and I had some boating experience, we were at least familiar with the idea of using the paddle as a rudder. Neither Helen nor Marlene seemed to understand how to use a paddle that way, nor did they have the experience.

When one of the two women on our raft, more so Marlene than Helen, was the helmsperson, she would chant, "I can't do it; I can't do it." Each time they cried out neither Bill nor I would answer right away, but we would eventually try to convince them that they could. Typically, Marlene would say, "I don't know right from left. One of you guys do it; you're so much better."

At Copper Canyon we needed a "hard right" command. With Marlene at the helm, we got a "hard left" instead. Bill and I looked at each other in utter disgust.

He asked Marlene, "What's the matter, honey?"

She said, "I don't know right from left. You be the helmsperson."

He said, "Why don't we write on the back of your hands 'right' and 'left'?"

Bill was kidding, but the next thing I knew, they were doing it.

Helen was mad and said to me, "Is it really necessary to make a baby out of her?"

"No," I said, "of course not. But she really doesn't know right from left."

As Marlene would say, "I can't do it," Bill and I would say, "Of course you can do it. It's easy; you're doing just fine." All the time we were speaking, we were thinking, "Ye gods! When is she going to give up?" Each time either Marlene or Helen would be helmsperson, we'd have the same conversation; each time Bill's and my reassurances would be more and more halfhearted. Before long we weren't responding at all.

As the days wore on, Bill and I proceeded subtly but surely to take charge. The teamwork was unraveling. When we approached a tongue, if either Marlene or Helen were helmsperson, Bill and I would look at each other, and with very slight headshakes and grimaces we would indicate agreement that things were not going well at all. Once we had established that things were not going well, we then felt free to take our own corrective measures, such as trying to steer the raft from our forward paddle positions, an almost impossible thing to do. Not only is running the raft from the front not at all helpful to the person at the helm, but also if the helmsperson is not aware of the counterforces, the raft can easily turn around like a carousel. The unaware helmsperson is then totally out of control. When that would happen, Marlene would say, "I just don't know what's wrong with me," and Helen would echo, "I don't know what's wrong with me either." Bill's and my disgust would mount.

Eventually, John became fed up with the inability of the bunch on Raft No. 4 to work together, which was mainly a result, he said, of the two "captains" in the front. As a last resort he ordered each one of us to give a single command that he or she would shout as needed. My command was "hold," Bill's command was "left," Marlene's was "right," and Helen's was "backpaddle." John's teaching objective was to get the four of us working together, or else. Needless to say, "or else" prevailed.

On the fifth day, Marlene was helmsperson. Bill and I were in the bow, silently anxious. Even voluble Helen was silent as the raft approached a fast-moving chute. At that time only a clear, concise, direct command and a rapid response would be of any use at all.

Instead of a "hard right" command, we had no command. Marlene froze, the raft slid up on a big boulder, and in an instant we flipped over like a flapjack on a griddle. The current was swift and swept the five of us away in different directions. As I splashed around in the cold water, cursing that "Goddamned dumb Marlene," I spotted Bill nearby. The two of us began together to look for Marlene and Helen, whom we found each grappling with paddles and gear they'd grabbed as the raft had gone over. We assured each other we were OK and expressed relief at finding each other.

Cold, wet, and shivering uncontrollably, we made our way out of the river. To warm us and to keep us moving, John chased us around the bank to get wood for a fire. He stuffed us with candies and other sweets to give us energy. As we stood around the fire, chilled and wet, unable to stop shaking, we talked about what had happened, and why.

There was mutiny in the air now and a consensus emerged. The four of us were furious at John and blamed him for our predicament. John retreated, but finally we were agreed that we would not have any more of this kind of thing. Regardless of John's wishes, anyone who did not want to be helmsperson could simply pass. Marlene was certain that she wanted no part of being at the helm, and Helen, though less sure, was happy to say, "Yeah, I just want to stay dry. Let you guys take the helm."

After becoming somewhat dry, sober, and a bit remorseful, the crew of Raft No. 4 returned to the river to resume our run down the Rogue. We had lost our No. 4 position, the other rafts having run past us. John was helmsperson. Helen and Marlene were settled into their backpaddle seats. Bill and I, miffed over our mishap, felt self-conscious and fell silent thinking of the inevitable joshing we'd receive from the other rafts.

We slowly overcame the tensions of our crisis, and as the trip came to an end, we were friends again; the fifth day was forgotten. As we climbed out of the raft for the last time, Marlene said, "Well, the next raft trip I take, it will be as a passenger and not as a crew member."

That last night on the Rogue, we celebrated with a big party. The women dressed up in improvised bangles and baubles. I was the maître d', and none of us thought much about what really had happened on Raft No. 4.

Deliverance

What really happened on the river? Why did the raft flip over? Not until I was back in the comfort of my office did I begin to understand, and the realization of the truth was as shocking as any of the splashes of cold water had been on the Rogue. It became clear to me that not only had I been unhappy with a woman as helmsperson, but also that Bill and I had subconsciously, by habit, proceeded to undermine the women. When one of the other two men was in charge, I was comfortable, supportive, and worked to help him be a better helmsperson. When a woman was at the helm, I seemed to direct my activity at getting her replaced rapidly by one of the men.

A most revealing part of the raft experience, however, was not so much the power relationship between the sexes, which I think I understood, but how Bill and I unconsciously or automatically responded to protect our power from female encroachment. When the trip started, I knew that I might have some difficulty accepting a woman at the helm, but I did not realize that the threat would be so great that I would actually desire to see her fail. On that trip I did something new: I actively tried to sabotage Marlene's and Helen's efforts to lead.

Bill and I were unconsciously building on each woman's doubts about herself with negative reinforcement of her leadership role. The effect of our male, sabotaging behavior was to increase Helen's and Marlene's doubts about themselves as leaders. For each of them, their lifelong conditioning that a woman ought to be a passive sweet thing came into play, and they gave up the helm because men ''do it better.''

If the reader thinks males are just threatened in the outdoors, look what happens to us indoors. First there is the machismo business, which is a cultural way of granting power to males. To the macho male, it is his role to take care of the woman, particularly in the face of imminent danger, and, in the course of things, he should never yield any power. In most organizational settings the male need to be in charge in the presence of females may be subtle, which may make it harder to identify than on a raft on a swift-flowing river. If all the male readers of this article would write down just one way to undermine the budding woman executive, there would be quite a list.

Judging from firsthand experience and others' reports, I believe that what happened on Raft No. 4, Inc. occurs in most organizations when women enter positions of leadership. An exception might be organizations that have been run by women from their inception. Because organizations are usually designed as pyramids, the moving-up process entails squeezing someone else out. The higher up the pyramid, the more the squeeze. As women enter the squeezing, men are doubly threatened; first, the number of pyramid squeeze players is increasing; second, because the new players are women, our masculinity is on the block. The resentment of men toward women managers is also exacerbated by the shrunken job market.

As more women become managers in organizations, there will have to be a shift in power. The men who hold that power in fierce competition with each other will not expand the competition by encouraging women to become part of the battle without considerable changes in their own consciousness. In a wilderness setting, all decisions, either one's own or the group's, have immediate consequences, such as being dumped out of the raft. The rightness or wrongness of decisions in organizations is not so obvious since a decision may have no perceptible effects for days or even months. It is during this time lag that the male unconscious activity can occur to undermine the female.

Will women in administrative positions be supported, ignored, or subconsciously sabotaged by men who find their power threatened? As most experienced administrators know, a major problem in running an organization is directly related to the level of subordinate support. How should the organization go? Straight ahead, hold, turn left, or turn right? These decisions are judgments that may be tough, but the leader must make them; and unless they are supported by the subordinates, they might as well never have been made.

A command of "hard right" can be executed as hard-hard, half-hard, and soft-hard, the last one being equal to just a facade of cooperation. That situation is the most dangerous one for the leader who presumes that orders are being executed, while in fact the raft is foundering. I suspect that one of the reasons that a woman has trouble is because the lack of support she receives from one man gets reinforced by others; it is a collective activity. Things might have been different on Raft No. 4 had we been willing to confront each other. It might have spoiled the fun, but we all might have learned something.

At first I thought there might not be much of an analogy between navigating a river and a big bureaucracy. Now I think there is. The requirements turn out to be different, and yet the same. The river is more easily understood: how it flows, its hydraulics, its sleepers, or its chutes, and women, like men, can learn these things. A big organization also has sleepers and chutes, but recognizing their existence is a far more political than intellectual task. Women trying to navigate most organizations may find them more complex than the Rogue, but they need to look for similar hazards. The sleepers and chutes will be vested groups of men, who, when their power is threatened, will pull any woman down for tinkering with their interests.

9

Case of the Valuable Vendors

MARY P. ROWE

If asked to rate their most taxing problems at work, most managers would probably put those involving managing people at, or near, the top of their list. One reason "people problems" are so difficult is that every individual is different, no problem is the same, and destructive behavior is hard to diagnose and cure. But another major role is that the manager may also be part of the problem. Incidents of subtle discrimination in organizations because of sex (or race) have all the foregoing difficulties and more, in that by definition they are hard to recognize. But small and petty as they may seem, they can have serious and destructive consequences. *HBR* sent this case to a selection of subscribers for their opinions on the issues it raises and on how to deal with them: Who is to blame in such incidents? Are they a serious problem? Is there anything management can do to prevent subtle discrimination? In the commentary following the case, the author discusses the respondents' replies as well as tactics managers can use to deal with such problems when they occur.

Harry Fenway is one of the best computer salesmen on the eastern seaboard. He sells equipment for Data-Run Corporation, one of the largest computer manufacturers in the world. His sales record is impressive. The company, which has lagged in recent years because of growing competition, is just ready to test-market a minicomputer model with which it hopes to recapture its share of the market. The company expects big things of Harry for this project launch; to top management he is nearly indispensable.

Gwen Barrett is an up-and-coming junior salesperson whom the company hired in a trainee program specifically to increase the number of women employees in sales. The computer industry has historically been a good employer of women, especially in systems analysis. Lately, Data-Run head-

---

Published in 1978.

quarters had decided there should be more women in sales and had made it a high-priority development program for division managers. One of the main reasons for this emphasis, aside from EEO goals, is that recently more women have been found in buyer positions in companies acquiring new computer equipment; Gwen has really hit it off with one such buyer already.

One hot, steamy day, Gwen asked to see the division manager, Sam Finch. She and Harry had just returned from a sales trip to a large manufacturing company in Connecticut, United Chemicals, Inc., where they signed a contract they had been trying to get for months. It was a great coup; Finch, very pleased, thinks "they obviously work well together." When Gwen asked to see him, Finch got ready to welcome a happy worker. What greeted him was an unhappy woman.

Harry, Gwen says, is the worst kind of macho, male chauvinist pig. His symptoms, she reports, are offensive: he berates his wife; he makes too many inquiries into her (Gwen's) personal life; in front of senior personnel they meet on the trip, he acts as if she were his property; he is patronizing; he tells dirty jokes to other men in her presence; and he interrupts her when she talks. Twice he has failed to introduce her to people they meet.

Gwen complains that she'd tried to stay reasonable and calm about it and had overlooked Harry's behavior because he was such a good salesperson and she felt she could learn about the business from him. But, she tells Finch indignantly, she feels alternately invisible and like a showpiece. Up to now, she had accepted the situation, but on this last trip she overheard a UCI buyer asking Harry why on earth Data-Run would send out a woman. Gwen hoped Harry would mention her *magna cum laude* as a math major and her excellent sales record. Instead, she heard Harry insinuating to this buyer that he had been sleeping with her. That did it. She insists that she would not work with Harry again. She wants to be transferred.

Sam Finch listens to Gwen and then asks Harry to come in, telling Gwen he'll see her later. Much to Sam's surprise, Harry does not get defensive at all. In fact, he is astounded that Gwen has asked for a transfer. He thinks she's overreacting to a few one-liners that maybe were a little blue. But, he says, she's a big girl and if she's going to play in the big leagues, she's going to have to take it like a man. Harry laughs. He thinks Gwen is a really sweet kid and brightens things up a lot, but he wouldn't worry if he were Sam. He advises Sam just to talk her up, and she'll come around.

Sam talks to Gwen again. "No way", she says; Harry is a dyed-in-the-wool MCP and it just isn't worth it to hang around. She can find a job elsewhere, there's no problem with that. The computer industry is wide open for someone with her capabilities and training; she has had a number of job offers already. Sam tries more persuasion. She responds that he doesn't really understand either, does he? It's not only she, she adds, the women buyers don't think Harry's patter is so great either; she's talked with a number of them and they, too, find Harry offensive.

In fact, Gwen says to Sam, she bets that in the future Harry's sales record will not be as great as it has been in the past. And it's just possible that the minicomputer test launch could be affected. Think it over, Sam, she says, and let me know how it comes out. I'm flexible, but some things just aren't worth it.

What can Sam do? He needs Gwen for the sake of his EEO record, as well as for the simple fact that she is an excellent salesperson. He needs Harry for his experience, and he also needs to test that new product. What would you do if you were Sam?

The purpose of the "Case of the Valuable Vendors" was to raise questions about subtle discrimination as a management problem. Most major U.S. corporations have been managed primarily by white males, many of whom have been working very hard to open opportunities to others. And many of these managers are still struggling to employ women and minorities more effectively. But minority and female newcomers to these corporations frequently complain of the "coldness of the atmosphere" and of prejudice, even when management feels certain that no overtly illegal discriminatory practices persist. Puzzled top managers have begun to ask, "What, if anything, is subtle discrimination?"

The case then asks the reader: Is there a problem here? Is Harry behaving in a sexist fashion? Is Gwen just imagining discrimination? The management concerns are several:

1   is this situation serious;
2   what is it about, and whose problem is it; and
3   what should be done?

(Although the case raises questions about sexism only, it could as easily have dealt with issues of race, religion, handicap, age, or national origin—all of which are very frequently raised in allegations of prejudice. In my experience, however, discrimination because of race or sex is by far the most common.)

HBR sent this case to 250 male and 250 female subscribers, in New York, Chicago, and Los Angeles, for their anonymous comment. The 42 women and 61 men who responded were not intended to be a "representative sample" of U.S. managers. Analysis of the readers' comments, therefore, simply suggests the opinions and feelings of contemporary management.

First, I present the respondents' opinions on the case, with some analysis of the similarities and differences between male and female responses. Second, I discuss the issues, the case, and the comments, from the perspective of having dealt with and consulted on several thousand similar cases.

HBR Readers Comment on the Critical Issues

Before discussing the readers' comments as a whole, let us look briefly at how they feel about the three main issues the case raises.

1. *Is the issue between Gwen and Harry a serious management problem?* Nearly all respondents think Data-Run management has a serious problem on its hands. However, readers vary widely in defining that problem. About one-fourth believe the case is mainly about a personality conflict or lack of professionalism. Many comment simply that Data-Run is facing an incident of discrimination; about three-quarters mention the "equal opportunity" aspects of the case. However, that phrase generally connotes different things to different people. Some people think in terms of EEO goals; many people think in terms of lawsuits.

In this case, many of the respondents believe that the environment for women will affect Data-Run's ability to meet EEO goals. But only a few raise the possibility that Gwen might go to court. There is, then, an overall view that the story represents some kind of serious problem, with equal opportunity aspects. But within this broad consensus there is wide disagreement about the kinds of questions the case presents.

2. *What kind and whose problem is it?* Most readers think that, at base, Harry is in some way seriously at fault. These readers find him "a bully," "a super-pig," "monumentally insensitive," "an MCP," "deficient," "inadequate," and "unable to cope with women." Many readers find Harry's behavior "typical," but conclude that since times are changing, Harry's behavior is insupportable. Although some male readers suggest that Harry's personalized, joking salesmanship used to be effective, readers of both sexes think he is very quickly becoming obsolete.

Respondents also widely blame Gwen for her behavior in this situation, for her "defensiveness" and "immaturity," and for not having dealt directly with Harry. However, women, far more than men, blame Gwen. On the average, by the time the case came to Sam, readers had found both Gwen and Harry at fault. About half the women and one-fifth of the men also find fault with Sam. Some of these respondents feel that if Sam had been on his toes, the problem would not have arisen. Others think Sam made the problem worse by his handling of it.

Nearly all readers feel Harry is *initially* the most seriously to blame. However, only one or two criticize Harry's handling of the complaint as voiced to him by Sam. That is, though most think he had misbehaved on the road, few find fault with his manner of discussing the problem with Sam. It is Gwen and Sam who get the blame for the *handling* of the situation; almost nobody thinks that Gwen or Sam acted correctly. However, male and female readers vary somewhat in their analyses of Gwen and Sam.

The women's responses are generally quite critical; most are concerned with analyzing behavior. Nearly half of the women strongly criticize Gwen's handling of the case. Half also criticize Sam's behavior. Female responses are typically: "Gwen should have worked out her Harry problems with Harry"; "Sam should not have let Harry tell him what to do."

Most male respondents are much less critical of the protagonists and simply concentrate on what should happen now. On the other hand, male respondents who *do* criticize Gwen or Sam tend to couch their criticisms somewhat differently from the females. Men are much more likely to describe the personal attributes of Gwen and Sam than to analyze their behavior. This is especially true with respect to Gwen, who received the more frequent comments. Thus the most typical male criticism is in the form: "Gwen is a women's libber," or "Sam is an inadequate manager."

Women respondents tend, first, to recognize Harry's objectionable behavior and, second, to criticize Gwen's and Sam's handling of the scene. Most women then make suggestions about what Sam and Gwen should do now. Most male respondents, first, either simply prescribe a general solution or point out Harry's offensive attributes and, second, criticize Gwen's inadequate attributes. Finally, most men then prescribe specific solutions for Sam.

3. *What should Data-Run do?* Nearly all readers comment very thoughtfully on how to handle Gwen and Harry, and many carefully give the rationale for their suggestions.

The responses vary somewhat between men and women respondents; the variety within each sex is, however, considerable. Male readers' responses range from "Good-by Gwen!" to "Tell Harry to shape up, and he will." From women came comments ranging from "Profit-making means get rid of Gwen" to frequent suggestions for assertiveness training workshops for Gwen and sensitivity training for everyone in the company.

Perhaps the most striking difference in the responses lies in whether a given reader is hopeful or hopeless about Gwen and Harry being able to work together. Both male and female respondents express a range of opinions about whether Harry and Gwen could or should continue to work together, and whether Sam should deal with them at the same time.

Only one-third of the respondents counsel sitting down with Gwen and Harry together. Most of the rest (and especially men) think Sam should meet separately with each. One-fifth of the men and half the women would thereafter firmly reassign Gwen and Harry together, "for the good of the company," after attempts either to mediate or to lay down the law. Others would at least "give it a try." But most men and some women think that Harry and Gwen would be absolutely unable to work as a team. (Some men further counsel that Gwen should deal with women buyers; Harry with men.)

The women are more apt than the men to suggest that Sam seek outside advice in handling this problem. Many women characterize subtle discrimination as extremely pervasive and tenacious and comment frequently on the high personal price they have paid and still pay from having to deal with subtle sexism. Such women seem to feel it will take a long-term effort to create an equal opportunity environment at Data-Run.

The male readers more often recommend that Sam simply give a warning to Harry to shape up. Many men appear to believe that such advice might actually work. Many also note that "times have changed; American business is simply not going to be sexist in the future."

In many ways, male and female responses are similar. Both sexes call for Sam to check out the facts, to "examine his own motives and feelings," to "take a position of leadership." And both look forward to a future with many more women buyers and salespeople.

Men and women contributed equally eloquent and caring letters about the strong feelings cases like these arouse in them, and they share the single most common response: "Of course Harry is an MCP, but Gwen will meet many more." Both sexes appear basically to feel that managers must deal with these issues and not run away from them or pretend they do not exist.

Also, men and women respondents equally mention the anger, bewilderment, and fear people experience from recent changes in women's roles, and many contribute good ideas for companies to deal with these changes. These ideas include strong statements of commitment from the top, in-house and out-of-house training programs, specific training for people like Harry, continued monitoring by people in Sam's shoes, and various in-house, equal opportunity support systems, such as the building of a women's network.

Subtle Discrimination in Organizations

The majority of respondents conclude that this case is serious and that it has important equal opportunity aspects. I agree. I also agree with those who think that personality conflict and professionalism are important components of the case and deserve Sam's concern. However, the equal opportunity issues seem to me the most critical. And I think U.S. corporations need to get to the point where these unequal opportunity problems are dealt with by managers, rather than by judges and government agencies.

In my six years at MIT, I have come to believe that though the law plays a legitimate role in achieving equal opportunity, the most critical problems are not and should not be covered by the courts. Regulations and legislation that cover affirmative action and equal opportunity open doors and set limits to abuse. And this kind of regulation is needed (although it could be vastly improved). But the law is not and cannot be sufficient to guarantee freedom from subtle discrimination, which I am persuaded is now the major equal opportunity question facing large corporations and institutions in the United States.

But by its nature subtle discrimination is very difficult to address. One can define discrimination. For the purposes of this article, let me define it as the damaging stereotyping of an individual with respect to irrelevant characteristics of any group, race, or sex to which the individual may belong. Subtle discrimination refers to covert, nonobvious, or "petty" behavior, most of which could never be taken to the courts because it seems so trivial or is so difficult to prove. Defining this problem in the abstract is, however, much easier than recognizing it in practice.

When minorities and women (or white males) feel they are being discriminated against, people of goodwill may differ completely in their judgments of what is happening. The courts are currently wrestling with major, relatively clear-cut discrimination issues, with no social consensus in sight. Subtle and apparently petty discrimination problems are all the more difficult. If it is so difficult a problem to recognize, why then do we need to look at it?

Damaging Effects of Subtle Discrimination. Women (and minorities) have said for years that in very subtle ways white-male work environments can be extremely difficult for non-traditional members. Several writers and analysts suggest that "micro-aggressions" and "micro-inequities" *in the aggregate* constitute formidable support to racism and sexism.[1]

The damage done by these incidents occurs in varying ways and for varying reasons. Among the most damaging patterns that I have observed is that such incidents, if unchecked, often lead to yet worse behavior. In addition, unlike some other work problems, discriminatory incidents are unpredictable and catch women and minorities off guard. Since they have to be ignored, denied, or dealt with, they take up time and psychic energy. Also they may prevent something better from happening; for instance, Harry should have been training Gwen.

Incidents of subtle discrimination may produce a negative Pygmalion effect: if Harry assumes Gwen is an ornament or a sex object, she may begin to behave like one. These incidents may also produce negative role modeling: if women buyers see Gwen passively accept Harry's offensive comments, they may lose confidence themselves. Because the experience of each race and sex is so unique to itself, subtle incidents of discrimination simply emphasize the differences and sustain systematic barriers between people of different races and sexes. These barriers can be serious for management. For instance, I often see evidence that it is hard for men and women, minority and nonminority, to judge accurately each other's performance.

These incidents cause damage for a number of reasons: they are so subtle the victim may work in constant uncertainty, often in emotional turmoil, often blaming himself or herself. People judge such incidents so differently that dealing with them may worsen communication still further, and there are few institutionalized, appropriately weighted forms of redress for such subtle and petty incidents. It is, as some readers comment, "too much" for Gwen to go to Sam. But, unhappily, as she doesn't know how to seek appropriate redress at Data-Run, Gwen imagines going still further, in effect, to leave.

Subtle incidents of sexism and racism may appear insignificant to white males, but their apparent pettiness can be misleading. When white males get harassed and mistreated, as they do, they are generally aware of it and see it as unjust and as unrelated to themselves. But the difference with subtle discrimination is that it is made up of incidents all hitting the same sore spot, a spot that cannot be changed.

In case you are a white male reader who has read this far but cannot understand why subtle discrimination is important, try this idea. Think back to your childhood and adolescence, and remember the one thing you were most sensitive about. Were you always being compared to your older brother? Were you touchy about your nose, your skin, your muscles, your "cowardice" in some situation? Let's say you still are touchy about this personal problem.

Now try to imagine that everyone around you at work knows this is your weak spot and keeps referring to it obliquely and directly, consciously and unconsciously. Now imagine that every professional mistake you make and every professional shortcoming is still attributed to your failure to be as good as your brother (or whatever you saw as your weak spot). Imagine that your brother, or people you saw as better than you, are *always* in positions over you.

If you were ever sensitive in this way about something irrelevant to performance that you could not change, you perhaps can appreciate how threatening Harry appeared to Gwen, and how damaging was his behavior.

Coping with Discrimination. By and large most respondents feel that though Harry is the original problem, Gwen must deal with it. She should, as some readers say, have "tried with tact, and humor" to "earn Harry's respect." She should have taken a firm stand, for instance, about introducing herself. As one reader comments, Gwen "should not have tried to overlook Harry's behavior, when she realized she was really becoming upset." She should have tried instead to find an appropriate time to lay out to Harry her concerns, and if necessary she should have spoken with him several times.

I would not, myself, have suggested the direct confrontation some readers recommend (several say, "Let him have it"). Gwen should first have tried a gentler, straightforward approach. But I agree with those who comment, "Gwen *must* learn to handle this herself"; "Gwen will meet people like Harry everywhere; there is no place to hide."

Many people who work with women's problems in organizations think that if women are going to succeed, they have to be able to earn the respect of colleagues who harass them. Most believe that this is best done by excellent work and maintaining a professional demeanor. But it isn't easy to take on the responsibility of dealing in a mature way with someone who is harassing you. And some women and minorities are offended by what they see as further injustice in this prescription for success, since it requires a victim to bear the original aggression and then seek her or his own redress as well.

Many blacks and women might be perfectly willing to try to defend and assert themselves, but at the same time they know that they will pay for their self-defense. Many white males expect a subtle deference from minorities and women, not assertiveness. One has to be willing to be called aggressive, bitchy, uppity, castrating, and humorless—and, understandably, many people hate being thought of in these ways more than being pushed around. In any case, any reader who wishes Gwen were more assertive needs to be prepared for what happens when she actually is.

Let us imagine that Gwen pleasantly, humorously, firmly, gently, consistently, and, if neccessary, repeatedly objects when Harry is aggressive. If Harry is sufficiently able and emotionally healthy, he will try to change. Gwen will learn to trust him, Data-Run will be well off, and the good model of male-female relations will tend to spread.

But imagine Harry is not in such good shape. When they sense competition from a woman, some men begin to sexualize work relationships in order to reestablish traditional male-female dominance patterns. If Harry was beginning to do this and sees Gwen as "rejecting" him, he may become hateful and angry, even (consciously or unconsciously) vengeful. At the least, he may be simply bewildered, back off, and spread the word that she is a prickly bitch. Sam, in this scenario, might have been met not by a fuming Gwen but by a hostile, grouchy Harry. Or Sam might have heard about it first when other salespeople refused to work with other junior women, since Gwen was seen as "castrating."

It is also possible that Harry, who has never before had a female peer, let alone one out on the road with him, was afraid of becoming friendly with Gwen. Perhaps Harry had been holding Gwen at arm's length, in his locker-room way (the only way he knows), so his wife would not murder him for his wandering eye or thoughts.

If Gwen is "assertive" and successfully establishes a respectful relationship with Harry, he may find himself sincerely attracted to her. Even though Gwen might know nothing of Harry's esteem, Sam might hear of "the affair" from Mrs. Fenway or other salespeople. In that case, Sam will have to have the wit to backtrack, find out what happened, and then help support Gwen in having been assertive in the first place.

Obviously, Gwen needs to hold her head high and explore the possibilities for making a place for herself. And, plainly, U.S. corporations need the largely unexplored talents of women. Although no one can anticipate the consequences of corporate "Gwens" becoming independent adults, all of us in U.S. corporations and institutions are going to have to deal with them.

As it happened, Gwen went to Sam. She may have felt proud of herself for not quitting outright—for "hanging in." Or she may have been taught as a child that when she was harassed, she should appeal to authority rather than fight for herself. Then again, she may have decided to grin and bear it, as long as she could. And then, perhaps feeling that her behavior was strong, she went to Sam, not to ask for help like a weak female but to "take an independent stand."

What Gwen cannot see, however, is that she needs support to deal with the kind of harassment to which she was subject. She cannot see that asking for help is not being weak and that what she was doing was not strong.

Gwen probably can not see clearly what she could have been doing, what options were open to her.

Sam's job at this point is very important. He needs to understand why Gwen came in and to help her see that asking for help may be a first step in being appropriately assertive and not the last before going out the door. Sam also needs both to help Gwen become more assertive and, at the same time, to not undermine her independence or make her feel unsupported. How can Sam do this?

I agree with those respondents who think that Sam should initially have tried to find out exactly what was going on. Then he should have taken hold of the situation in a more assertive way himself. Many readers feel that "Harry was calling all the shots" and resent Sam's lack of leadership before and during this incident. This is a critical point.

If two requirements for equal opportunity are that women and minority employees should strive for excellence and assert themselves, another is clearly that top management should take a strong, consistent, outspoken stand on opening doors and preventing abuse.

Sam and his supervisors should all along have been talking casually and firmly about equal opportunity and Data-Run's need for all the talent it can find. They should have been making their opinions and policies on equal opportunity so well known throughout the company that Harry would have been immediately uncomfortable about his behavior, when called on it. And they need to affirm to women and minorities, many of whom have been taught not to be assertive with white males, that reasonable self-expression will be supported.

In the case situation, Sam has good strategies open to him. The first is to work with Gwen at length so that she will feel she can handle Harry herself. Sam could discuss with her possible ways to stick up for herself. He could role play with her how she will respond next time and should let her know that he will back her in every reasonable and responsible action she takes.

In counseling both supervisors and supervisees, I have found this tactic very effective. It is incumbent on any manager who wants minorities and women to handle incidents of discrimination effectively themselves to be very explicit about such a policy. But it is sometimes difficult for managers to convince their employees to try to assert themselves responsibly. If Gwen is reluctant to try, Sam will have to try to convince her that she *has* to help herself, because she will find "Harrys" everywhere. Sam's other major strategy may be to find mentors and advisers for Gwen.

Obviously, Sam needs to talk further with Harry, as well, to discuss the real meaning of equal opportunity, of decent manners, and of the changing world. Sam could also explicitly ask Harry to train Gwen well and then role play with *him* how he could do it. One reader suggests that Sam should get Harry and Gwen to prepare a skit to present at the annual meeting, which would help teach others about male-female training situations. Other readers point out that Harry could make a real name for himself as a successful innovator if he would learn how to train newcomers. These suggestions may help Gwen and may also help Harry feel that he has something to gain (besides protecting his job) from changing his behavior.

Sam might also encourage Gwen to seek out other women for support. More and more managers are learning that responsible women's networks are a powerful aid to furthering nonpolarized equal opportunity. In-house women's luncheon groups tend to give fanatics (if any) a place to let off steam, while giving leverage and support to responsible women with responsible concerns.

Like many other management people, I am no longer interested in academic debates about role models versus mentors. I see daily evidence that minorities and women thrive best when supported and inspired by a variety of mentors and models, male and female, black and white, peer and superior. What Sam can do is to mobilize any available support for Gwen, including himself.

I would not encourage Sam to separate Gwen and Harry until he has tried hard to help them both to work together. Until Sam decides that Harry cannot change, he should presume that "equal opportunity" means that in the long run we *have* to get along by race and sex and that each good example breeds the next.

If Harry turns out to be in really bad shape, Sam must remember that it is not legal to retain a supervisor so racist or sexist that he could not place a black or woman with him. If Harry's sexism has deep emotional roots, Harry may need clinical help and Sam may need to support him to get it. Of course, Sam may need some support himself. He should probably keep his top management informed of his EEO concerns and seek their advice. And if Sam comes in for advice, his supervisor should commend Sam for seeking counsel with his problem. As the responses from some readers illustrate, Sam is an easy scapegoat for anger, when much of the actual source of anger is tension about changing sex roles.

Learning from Readers' Responses

What can managers learn from the respondents' opinions? One point of relevance to top management is that different managers will react to these cases in extremely diverse ways. If a company wants to have a reasonably well-integrated policy in this arena, management will have to work hard for it.

If the respondents to this case are at all representative, many U.S. managers are becoming aware of subtle equal opportunity problems, and many are committed to solve them through creative personnel management. However, the respondents were much more sophisticated with respect to outside training programs and consultants than with respect to direct fostering of assertiveness in women. Fostering assertiveness may then be an important subject for top managers to discuss among themselves with an eye toward forming company policy in this area. If top management is committed to equal opportunity, it will insist that support for women and minority employees come directly from line managers, not just from consultants.

Do male and female managers' responses we received vary with respect to this case concerning a woman? There are apparent differences, but it is hard to tell from these data whether they represent systematic differences in management style. Men appear to have identified mainly with Sam, women with both Gwen and Sam, which makes sense because of the story. This fact may explain the women's greater interest in analyzing the past and in the much longer responses they sent in.

Women also appear to have experienced the whole case as more painful. This might help to explain why fewer women responded. More women may want just to deny or forget the problem. But those who did answer might have had good reason to want to work out some particular part of the case (including the occasional woman who felt "Gwen should just go").

Several hypotheses could be put forward about the overall significance in the differences between male and female responses, but they need judicious consideration.

It may be that in general men are more willing to stereotype people— or it may be true in this case only because the subject appeared to be sexism.

Similarly, women may be more likely to analyze behavior—but they may also be more prone to stereotype *men* in a reverse-sexist situation. It is interesting that male respondents were less likely to assign blame and more likely just to "get on with it." Again we do not know if women managers systematically blame more, or only in cases so close to home.

The male respondents were more likely to imagine Sam could solve the problem just by ordering Harry to change. More women imagined that Sam, Gwen, and outside helpers need to address the problem in some depth. Perhaps this difference reflects a male delusion of power, or an unwillingness to deal with the emotional complexities of the case. Or perhaps it simply reflects the different experiences men and women have had in dealing with male-female situations and their different perception of likely outcomes to Gwen's and Harry's conflict.

That is, male managers may correctly perceive that many men like Harry will change their overt behavior if Sam takes a hard enough line. Female managers may correctly perceive that Gwen will also have to deal with Harry's real feelings as well as his overt behavior, and that Gwen and Sam need all the outside help they can get because it takes so long to change feelings and attitudes.

Men were more likely to feel that Gwen and Harry would have to be separated. Perhaps men feel this way because they have not had as much experience in *having* to get along with women colleagues in work situations.

Women (especially *HBR* readers) have had a great deal of experience in having to get along with male colleagues. And they know at a personal level that it can and needs to be done.

More female than male respondents found fault with the way Gwen handled the situation. Perhaps more men find Gwen's behavior "normal"; possibly fewer of them see that Gwen should have handled Harry directly. Or it could be that many more women than men expect women to be perfect superwomen, able to handle every situation, including harassment, on their own. Perhaps they simply believe Gwen will *have* to be a superwoman, in order to succeed in our unequal environment.

Perhaps the major point to be learned from the readers is how much support middle managers actually need in dealing with these new personnel questions. Many are still very unsure how they will be expected to react to the real-life situations they face.

Company presidents and chief executives should, therefore, be sure that commitment to equal opportunity is explicit, frequently voiced, and frequently discussed when managers are evaluated. They should make sure that their managers have all the resources they need, such as in-house and out-of-house training programs, films, skits, and workshops. A chief executive can do much to support responsible minority and women's networks (joining them for lunch, offering a small budget to help them with recruitment, helping to sponsor an outside speaker, seeking their representation and advice on committees, and so forth).

Finally, top management should exemplify the mentorship role with blacks and women. And it should review, strengthen, and support procedures that are obviously important to equal opportunity (such as the grievance procedure and posting systems). But most of all, top management should support its managers as they step off into a new world. They need counsel if they blunder and praise and a bonus if they do well.

Notes

1. Margaret Campbell, *Why Would a Girl Go into Medicine?* (New York: Ann O'Shea, 1973); Chester Pierce, "Offensive Mechanisms," in *The Black 70's,* ed. Floyd Barbour (Boston: Sargent, 1970, p. 265); Wesley Profit, "Blacks in Homogeneous and Heterogeneous Racial Groups: the Effects of Racism and the Mundane Extreme Environment," unpublished PhD. dissertation, Harvard University, 1977; Mary P. Rowe, "The Saturn's Rings Phenomenon: Micro-Inequities and Unequal Opportunity in the American Economy," *Proceedings* of the NSF Conference on Women's Leadership and Authority, University of California, Santa Cruz, Calif., 1977; Jean-Paul Sartre, *Anti-Semite and Jew* (New York: Schocken Books, 1965).

10
Sexual Harassment
. . . Some See It
. . . Some Won't

ELIZA G.C. COLLINS and TIMOTHY B. BLODGETT

In the spring of 1980, *Redbook* magazine invited *HBR* to conduct a joint survey on the issue of sexual harassment in the workplace. Among the questions that needed to be addressed: How critical is the problem? Is it pervasive? How difficult is it for top management to spot and prevent harassment? Will it be easy to implement the newly issued EEOC guidelines? We surveyed more than 7,000 *HBR* subscribers, of whom 25% responded. (In its March 1981 issue, *Redbook* published a separate article on the survey.)

The major conclusions discussed include the following. Most people agree on what harassment is. But men and women disagree strongly on how frequently it occurs. The majority correlate the perceived seriousness of the behavior with the power of the person making the advance. Top management appears isolated from situations involving harassment. Many women, in particular, despair of having traditionally male-dominated management understand how much harassment humiliates and frustrates them, and they despair of having management's support in resisting it. Most people think that the EEOC guidelines—although reasonable in theory—will be difficult to implement because they are too vague.

The survey clearly shows that management should address this problem, which affects the morale, self-confidence, and efficiency of many workers. On a positive note, respondents suggest specific policies and approaches for management to confront the issue.

Published in 1981.

Authors' Note. We thank Grace L. Mastalli, Linda Bose Lord, and Mary Rowe for their help and encouragement and thank the respondents to the survey for their thoughtful comments and opinions.

This entire subject is a perfect example of a minor special interest group's ability to blow up any 'issue' to a level of importance which in no way relates to the reality of the world in which we live and work. *A 38-year-old plant manager (male) for a large manufacturer of industrial goods.*

A vice president of the company where I worked made overt advances following a company banquet. This included stroking my buttocks and continually rubbing himself against me. At one point he got me alone—away from the group—and put his hand down my dress. I finally managed to get rid of him. For several weeks afterward he kept calling me at work. When I talked to my supervisor about it, his only reaction was amusement. A few months later, my supervisor started making advances. When I found another job, I left. It's much better where I am now. *A 27-year-old computer specialist (female) in a large public utility.*

In my own circumstances, sexual harassment included jokes about my anatomy, off-color remarks, sly innuendo in front of customers—in short, turning everything and anything into a sexual reference was an almost daily occurrence. I have just left this company [a big chemical manufacturer] partially for this reason. *A 34-year-old first-level manager in environmental engineering (female) for a large producer of industrial goods.*

I'm baffled by this issue. I used to believe it was a subject that was being exaggerated by paranoid women and sensational journalists. Now I think the problem is real but somewhat overdrawn. My impression is that my own company is relatively free of sexual harassment. But I don't know the facts. *A 53-year-old senior vice president (male) of a medium-sized financial institution.*

Is sexual harassment a manufactured issue? Is it widespread? Should it concern top management? To try to answer these and other questions, the editors of *HBR* and *Redbook* magazine surveyed 7,408 *HBR* subscribers (1,846, or nearly 25 percent, of whom responded) in the United States. (See Appendix A for a complete description of how the survey was conducted.)
Our major findings are:

☐ Sexual harassment is seen as an issue of power. In four out of six situations that we described to readers, they rate a supervisor's behavior as considerably more serious and threatening than the same action by a coworker.

☐ Men and women generally agree in theory on what sexual harassment is but disagree on how often it occurs. Nearly two-thirds of the men, compared with less than one-third of the women, agree (or partly agree) with the statement, "The amount of sexual harassment at work is greatly exaggerated."

☐ Top management appears isolated from occurrences of harassment, and middle-level managers are somewhat less aware of misconduct than lower-level managers.

☐   Most respondents favor company policies against harassment, but few organizations have any policies to address it. For example, 29 percent of respondents work in companies where top executives have issued statements to employees disapproving of sexual misconduct, but 73 percent favor such statements.

☐   In general, most see the Equal Employment Opportunity Commission (EEOC) guidelines issued in 1980 as reasonable and necessary and agree that they will not be difficult to follow. But the returns show that the mildest and most pervasive forms, such as innuendo and dirty jokes—to many women the most obnoxious forms—are harder to prove and often impractical to take action on, even though the guidelines cover them.

☐   Most respondents think sexual harassment can be a very serious matter. Ten percent report they have heard of or observed a situation as extreme as the following in their organizations: ''Mr. X has asked me to have sex with him. I refused, but now I learn that he's given me a poor evaluation.''

Regardless of the perceived seriousness of the problem, however, the findings cannot reveal how pervasive sexual harassment is. Obviously, those who were most interested or involved completed the questionnaire; we do not know about the experiences of others who did not answer or who were not included in the survey.

☐   Finally, many people—nearly one out of three—took the time to write about their concerns and uncertainties regarding this issue. In their comments, many women despair of gaining top management's understanding of how harassment damages them.

Until recently, consciousness of sexual harassment has been low. But people have become aware of it as more women have arrived at levels of authority in the workplace, feminist groups have focused attention on rape and other violence against women, and students have felt freer to report perceived abuse by professors. (Although the survey was designed to investigate mainly women's experiences, we recognize—and the answers to the questionnaire make clear—that harassment of men by women and homosexual harassment do occur, also with distressing consequences to the victims.)

In the last five years, other studies have also shown that sexual misconduct is a big problem. For example, in a recently published survey of federal employees, 42 percent of 694,000 women and 15 percent of 1,168,000 men said they had experienced some form of harassment.[1]

In November 1980, the EEOC adopted its final guidelines for employers to deal with the problem. The new guidelines define sexual harassment as ''unwelcome sexual advances, requests for sexual favors, and other verbal or physical conduct of a sexual nature'' that take place under any of the following circumstances:

1   When submission to the sexual advance is a condition of keeping or getting a job, whether expressed in explicit or implicit terms.
2   When a supervisor or boss makes a personnel decision based on an employee's submission to or rejection of sexual advances.
3   When sexual conduct unreasonably interferes with a person's work performance or creates an intimidating, hostile, or offensive work environment.

According to the EEOC, employers have "an affirmative duty" to prevent and eliminate sexual abuse. Additionally, the guidelines make the employer responsible for misbehavior by supervisory personnel, their assistants, co-workers, or outside personnel. (See *Appendix B* for the legal issues.)

Top managers, middle and lower-level managers, women, and men do not always agree on what constitutes harassment or even whether it is prevalent. But because so many perceive it as a problem, and because the EEOC has issued guidelines and raised the prospect of stepped-up litigation by employees, top management of for-profit and nonprofit organizations clearly should pay attention to the issue.

In this article we explore what some of our readers think sexual harassment is and how much they think it occurs in their organizations. In doing so, we report what they think about the EEOC guidelines, company policies, and, more personally, how they feel when harassed.

What Is It and How Much?

I attended a meeting of department heads (only two women were classified as department heads). There, 40- to 45-year-old men—department heads and elected officials—were tossing a prophylactic back and forth, with the usual comments accompanying the tosses. I don't know if this show was for the benefit of the two women present or if they just found out what the item was used for. We tried to ignore their behavior. Another department head suggested they pay attention and grow up. *(female)*

Constant 'small' examples show lack of awareness, such as from a boss: 'You deserve a pat on the fanny for a good job.' *(female)*

I have heard much 'joking' about sex in regard to women's bodies in the office. I have seen this going on for years. Since it is supposedly said in jest, it is apparently supposed to be ignored. But most of the female employees get very uncomfortable when these remarks are made. The men enjoy every minute of it and it seems to amuse them even more if the women get embarrassed. This has happened in one-on-one situations and in group situations. *(female)*

There is a great deal of fondness in my company, particularly my division, but I'm confident it does not include the necessary element of harassment, that is, indebtedness. Maybe I'm naive. Better yet, maybe my businesslike deportment prevents any encouragement of innuendos or allows me to be 'one of the boys.' There is an unusually high comfort level among the men and women in our company. I attribute most of that to the age of the group (30 to 35) and the fact that they've been brought up in a more aware time. *(female)*

I have supervised many women and have found them very sensitive especially to biases of their male bosses. Many times their sensitivity is more acute than my own—that is, I saw nothing obvious but they were quite sure of the bias. As a result, I am unsure whether accusations of sexual bias are not just disguises of—or poorly stated initial reactions to—some other underlying management problem (or perception). *(male)*

Not surprisingly, respondents to our survey agree about which extreme situations constitute sexual harassment but differ over the more ambiguous cases. For instance, 87 percent think that the following statement definitely indicates abuse: "I have been having an affair with the head of my division. Now I've told him I want to break it off, but he says I will lose out on the promotion I've been expecting." (Exhibit 1 shows the 4 instances of 14 we described that most people think constitute misconduct.)

Opinions on these extreme cases differ little between men and women and between top and lower-level management. For example, 89 percent of the men and 92 percent of the women think the first statement in Exhibit 1 is harassment ("I can't seem to go in and out of my boss's office without being patted or pinched"). Nearly 87 percent of top management and 91 percent of lower-level management also think it is.

In other, less extreme situations, however, people are less certain about the interpretation but still consider the behavior quite offensive (see Exhibit 2). An average of 40 percent say the situation where a man starts each day with a sexual remark and insists it's an innocent social comment is harassment; an average of 48 percent say it is possibly; 8 percent say it is not; and 4 percent don't know. According to many readers, a situation where a man often puts his hand on a woman's arm when making a point is even more innocent (see Exhibit 2).

The perceived seriousness of the harassment seems to depend on who is making the advance, the degree of interpreted intent, and the victim's perception of the consequences. The amount the victim appears to suffer, however, does not necessarily vary with the perceived seriousness. In many comments, for instance, the writers seemed more vexed by persistent low-level misbehavior, which, although covered by EEOC guidelines, is impractical to do something about and is often harder to prove than more extreme forms.

A 26-year-old female market research analyst for an industrial goods manufacturer wrote: "It is not easy for a smart woman to avoid sexual harassment. Case in point—a male in our DP department continually makes comments and gestures to me. I reacted at first by being 'cool and silent.' When this did not have any effect, I requested that he stop, as I found it offensive. I must deal with this person professionally, and I feel that our

Exhibit 1. Views on Extreme Behavior

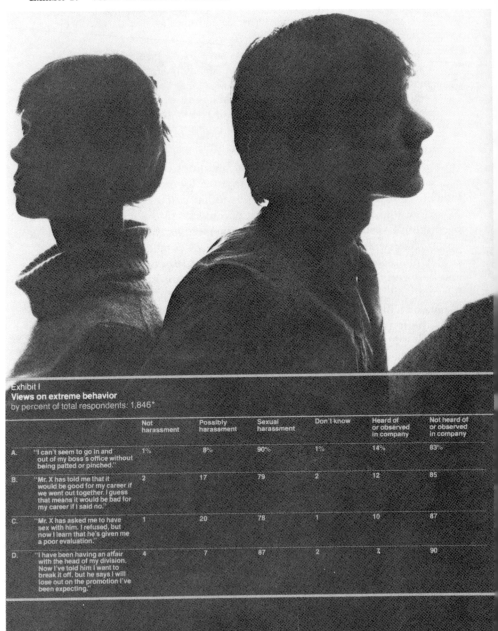

Exhibit I
Views on extreme behavior
by percent of total respondents: 1,846*

		Not harassment	Possibly harassment	Sexual harassment	Don't know	Heard of or observed in company	Not heard of or observed in company
A.	"I can't seem to go in and out of my boss's office without being patted or pinched."	1%	8%	90%	1%	14%	83%
B.	"Mr. X has told me that it would be good for my career if we went out together. I guess that means it would be bad for my career if I said no."	2	17	79	2	12	85
C.	"Mr. X has asked me to have sex with him. I refused, but now I learn that he's given me a poor evaluation."	1	20	78	1	10	87
D.	"I have been having an affair with the head of my division. Now I've told him I want to break it off, but he says I will lose out on the promotion I've been expecting."	4	7	87	2	7	90

*In some cases, throughout the exhibits, not all people answered all questions.

Exhibit 2. Views on Less Extreme Behavior According to Supervisor/Coworker Split Sample

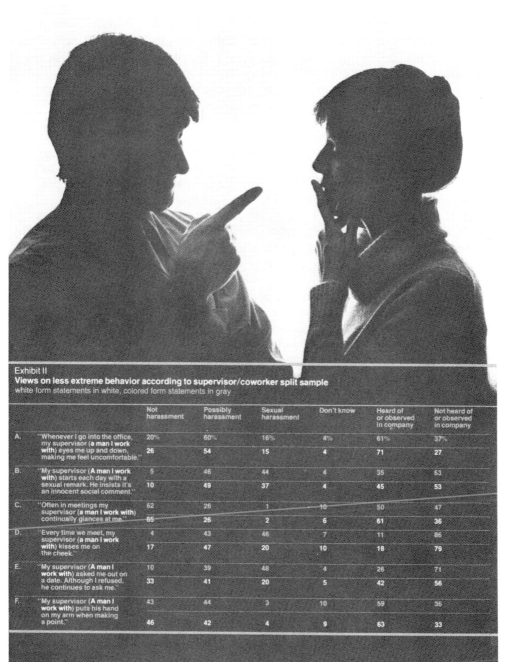

Exhibit II
Views on less extreme behavior according to supervisor/coworker split sample
white form statements in white, colored form statements in gray

		Not harassment	Possibly harassment	Sexual harassment	Don't know	Heard of or observed in company	Not heard of or observed in company
A.	"Whenever I go into the office, my supervisor (**a man I work with**) eyes me up and down, making me feel uncomfortable."	20%	60%	16%	4%	61%	37%
		26	54	15	4	71	27
B.	"My supervisor (**A man I work with**) starts each day with a sexual remark. He insists it's an innocent social comment."	5	46	44	4	35	53
		10	49	37	4	45	53
C.	"Often in meetings my supervisor (**a man I work with**) continually glances at me."	62	26	1	10	50	47
		65	26	2	6	61	36
D.	"Every time we meet, my supervisor (**a man I work with**) kisses me on the cheek."	4	43	46	7	11	86
		17	47	20	10	18	79
E.	"My supervisor (**A man I work with**) asked me out on a date. Although I refused, he continues to ask me."	10	39	48	4	26	71
		33	41	20	5	42	56
F.	"My supervisor (**A man I work with**) puts his hand on my arm when making a point."	43	44	3	10	59	36
		46	42	4	9	63	33

relationship has been hindered. We both found each other's actions and reactions offensive."

Harassment is not, of course, limited to the office. Wrote a 30-year-old male foundry materials manager for an industrial goods producer: "When secretaries walk through the shop, there are whistles and catcalls. However, management has not seen this as a problem. It does not interfere with promotion or pay, but I find it an offensive situation."

To test whether a supervisor's behavior is seen as more threatening and serious than a coworker's, the survey included a split sample in which we asked readers' opinions of statements made by female employees about male coworkers and supervisors (see Exhibit 2). For example, the colored survey form, sent to half the subscribers polled, stated, "Whenever I go into the office, my supervisor eyes me up and down, making me feel uncomfortable." On the white form, which was sent to the other half, "my supervisor" became "a man I work with" (Exhibit 2, part A).[2]

In four of these six less extreme cases, a higher percentage view the supervisor's behavior as worse than the coworker's. Quite clearly, the perceived seriousness of the action correlates with the power of the person making the advances. (The two situations where the coworker is seen as more blameworthy—continually glancing at the woman, part C, and putting a hand on her arm when making a point, part F—are rather ambiguous, and the behavior is certainly less threatening in relation to work but more repugnant because it constitutes unwanted intimacy.)

Many people commented on how power influences perceptions of harassment. As one reader put it, "The indebtedness increases the harassment's potency." Some of our male readers were very aware of the implications of power differences: "There is a male code of silence regarding harassment of females that has to be broken, particularly in the area of male 'power' figures and females without power," said the 38-year-old vice president of marketing in a large insurance company. "Either too many men never recover from being high school jocks or they understand that corporate power can be a new way to be attractive. Having suffered through both lessons, I feel free to comment."

The power phenomenon is not necessarily restricted to men, either. "The more power people have, the more able they are to let go of their inhibitions and act on their desires," testified a 36-year-old government administrator. "As a woman manager, I must admit to temptation! It is when the overtures are unwanted, persistent, and *power* based that they are unhealthy organizationally."

In five of the six split-sample cases, more women than men consider the behavior offensive, whether the statement is about a supervisor or a coworker. For instance, in the situation where the man eyes the woman up and down (Exhibit 2, part A), 24 percent of all women, compared with 8 percent of all men, think it is harassment. (Since it was not possible to include all the survey data in the exhibits, here and in a few other instances, the data have been extrapolated.)

In the remaining split-sample case—where the man kisses the woman every time they meet (part D)—somewhat more men than women, proportionately, rate the action objectionable whether by a supervisor or a fellow worker. Perhaps women are often more conscious of social formalities and tend to accept this kind of behavior from supervisors, whereas men are more likely to consider it merely an encounter between the sexes.

In response to two other statements that were more conventionally social—where the man often offers to drive the woman home and where the married man and the woman have dinner together and go to a nightclub while on a business trip—slightly more men than women also think these are possibly harassment.

Additionally, as all the split-sample responses in this section testify, top managers say that the behavior by supervisors is more blameworthy than the same behavior by coworkers.

Answers to the split sample clearly demonstrate that the power relationship implicitly carries a coercive threat. But what about coworkers? Why do only a third of top managers who completed the white form think that being greeted each day with a sexual remark from a coworker is harassment?

Throughout the survey we found answers that could be explained only by a "that's the way men are" assessment on the part of both men and women—resignation or acceptance bred of recurring experience. Perhaps the more one sees behavior like that we described, the less one is stirred to call it misconduct.

How Much?

Except for the incident where the man kisses the woman on the cheek every time they meet (Exhibit 2, part D), all the situations in Exhibit 2 have been heard of or seen by many people. For example, an average of one-third say that they have heard of or observed persistent requests for a date by men in their organizations.

The four activities our sample considers the most objectionable (Exhibit 1) they have seen or heard of the least. Understandably, these are the least likely to occur, be detected, or be admitted to.

In general, of those who have knowledge of certain sexual behavior in their organizations, a higher proportion assert that such behavior is not harassment. For example, 10 percent of the people who have seen or heard of someone starting each day with a sexual remark say it is not harassment, compared with 5 percent of those who haven't heard of or seen such behavior.

The spread appears greater when we look at the coworker/supervisor split sample. In cases where the supervisor makes the advance, people are much more likely to call it harassment when they have no knowledge of its occurrence in their own organizations. (Does familiarity breed contempt?) In all these cases, however, interpretation of intent may cloud the statistics.

The most striking finding on the question of how much abuse actually takes place is the difference in perception between men and women and between high-level and lower-level management. (Because most high-level managers in our survey were men and more lower-level managers were women, the two sets of responses often parallel each other.) The answers to the statement, "The amount of sexual harassment at work is greatly exaggerated," are:

	Agree or partly agree	Disagree or partly disagree
Top management	63%	22%
Middle management	52	30
Lower-level management	44	40
Women	32%	52%
Men	66	17

In most instances substantial differences appear in men's and women's perceptions of how frequently sexual harassment occurs. For example, one-third of the men, but a full half of the women, have witnessed or heard of a case where the man starts each day with a sexual remark that he insists is an innocent social comment (Exhibit 2, part B).

How can we explain the differences in viewpoint? Sexual harassment may not take place when male managers are around to observe it; and even if it does, they may not "see" it as women do. Consider this account from a 30-year-old female project leader in the finance department of a large company:

> Not a day passes without my boss either sharing a particularly lewd joke with me or asking me what I did with my boyfriend the night before—complete with leers and smirks. My requests for him to cease have fallen on deaf ears; he seems to enjoy my discomfort and chides me for being a 'poor sport.' Prior to my divorce he was totally inoffensive.

That such an attitude on the part of male managers is discouraging for women is evident from many comments we received. Typical was this remark from a 32-year-old financial officer in a small company: "I was the victim of harassment and it was a miserable experience. When I voiced complaints to my so-called feminist male boss and male colleagues, I was made to feel crazy, dirty—as if I were the troublemaker." Another woman wrote, "Sexual harassment eats away at the core of a woman's being, destroys self-confidence, and can contribute to a lowered feeling of self-worth."

Even though men generally agree in the abstract with women about what harassment is, the gap in perception of what actually happens is real and significant. From the comments in the returns, a visitor from another planet might conclude that men and women work in separate organizations.

One factor that may help explain the difference in perception is social conditioning. For example, 44 percent of the women view the statement about the man who starts each day with a sexual remark (*Exhibit 2*, part B) as only "possibly" misconduct. "Many incidents go unnoticed by both parties because of conditioning," wrote a 30-year-old female radio station manager. "Men are 'expected' to do such things, women are 'expected' to have to cope with that type of behavior." Perhaps some women, accustomed to accept such incidents as a price of survival in the business world, have lost sensitivity. They, as well as men, suffer from sexual astigmatism.

One reader, a 30-year-old female vice president of marketing in a large financial institution, wrote, "Senior people are the wrong people to ask about such behavior because they may not know much. The 'little people' are afraid to complain." The survey corroborates her observation, perhaps because the "little people" are afraid of exposure, embarrassment, and retribution.

In extreme cases, higher-level executives report that they are generally unaware of what's going on. Perhaps one of the worst examples of abuse in our survey is epitomized by Exhibit 1, part C—where the man gives the woman a poor evaluation because she refuses to have sex with him. Ten percent of all respondents have heard of or observed this situation. The response by management level breaks down this way: top management, 5 percent; middle management, 9 percent; lower-level management, 13 percent; persons other than managers (a small number), 19 percent.

As in other situations, more women than men testify to knowledge of the situation described in Exhibit 1, part C—16 percent against 5 percent. Whether conditioning, denial, or lack of awareness explains these disparities, the gap in perception between different levels of management and between men and women poses a serious problem for policymakers.

What Would You Do?

Men in my company are not penalized for sexual encounters with co-workers, whereas women are. You feel [helpless] trying to confront silent accusations and using the company complaint channels where the men you talk to share a common, somewhat negative philosophy about women. *(female)*

I have worked successfully in good positions all my life. Since I was both attractive and smart, [the problem] was always the boss. I either had to learn to say no graciously, or lose every good job I got. I find that a woman must defend herself every day, and I don't believe you can find rules for the top men. The world is made of men and women who either get along or don't. If they do get along, the men invariably try to have a physical attachment. I think it's inborn in a man. *(female)*

I was in an elevator along with the president and some other men. One man made a dirty comment, and the president came back with a remark

telling this employee to keep his locker room comments to the locker
room and not make them around any women in the firm.   *(female)*

The problem of disparities in perception appears throughout the survey. To
probe differing attitudes, we sent two different versions of four vignettes in
our split-sample questionnaire. In one we asked readers to say what they
would do as managers in these situations; in the other, what typical managers
would do (see Exhibit 3). One can draw many conclusions from the answers,
but three disparities in perception stand out:

1   the differential treatment men and women employees receive after
    an unwanted advance,
2   how women should handle themselves, and
3   how responsible managers ought to act in the workplace.

Perceived Differential Treatment

The responses to the vignettes show that men and women hold very different
opinions on how top managers will act in an ambiguous situation. Their
opinions also differ depending on whether the victim is a female or male
executive, a female executive or secretary, and on who is making the advance.

For example, in the first vignette a company president walks into his
sales manager's office and finds him standing near his secretary, who looks
upset and flustered (Exhibit 3, part A). On the colored questionnaire we
asked what the typical president would do, and on the white form we asked
what "you" would do. Nearly two-thirds of the women who filled out the
colored form believed that the typical president would do nothing—being
unaware of what happened or unwilling to confront the sales manager on a
personal matter—while fewer than half the men voted this way.

In thinking that the typical president would do nothing, most of the
women chose avoidance of confrontation as the motivation, while most men
selected ignorance as the reason for inactivity. Women, it seems, tend to
think that male executives take an uninvolved stance even when they know
what is happening (and even when it is addressed in the guidelines). "Unless
women make an issue of harassment, management will be more than willing
to bury their collective heads and say they have no problem," wrote a 31-
year-old female manager of training and development in a petrochemical
services company.

This assumption by women of how male executives will behave reveals
itself in another vignette. We described a scene in an elevator where a male
executive makes a remark about a female occupant's body to another male
executive (Exhibit 3, part B). In the white form one man was senior; in the
colored form the two executives were peers.

Of the women who answered the colored questionnaire, 41 percent
asserted that the second executive, the peer, would share the first's amusement, while only 14 percent of the men chose this option. On the white

form, 23 percent of the women decided that the senior executive would join in the joke, while only 7 percent of the men said that he would find the remark amusing. Instead, 37 percent of the men who filled out the white form asking them what the senior executive would do said he would express verbal disapproval when alone with the other executive (option f). In contrast, the prime choice of men who returned the colored form asking what the peer executive would do was option c, where he would remain silent.

Given the same facts, men and women expect vastly different reactions from senior executives and even from two peer males together. On both forms, "share the joke" received more votes from women than any other choice. Here is a representative view from a 32-year-old female manager of customer services in a large insurance company: "Our CEO thinks sexual innuendo, risqué jokes, and flirtations are a natural part of male-female relationships inside and outside the office."

We wonder whether the disparity in perception stems from women's cynicism or from their realism. Are things really as bad as women think? Are the men who answered our questions realistic or are they unaware?

In another vignette, we asked readers who got the white forms to say what they would do if confronted by a female secretary complaining about unwanted advances from a boss (Exhibit 3, part C). In the colored form, a woman executive complained.

The responses to this vignette clearly show that women take harassment more seriously than men. In the case of the secretary, almost two-thirds of the female respondents voted to inform the boss that if his behavior continues, it will harm his career—while only 48 percent of the men selected that action. (In response to a question about the impact of harassment on the workplace, 75 percent of the women had "quitting or firing" as one choice, while 62 percent of the men selected that severe outcome.)

The responses to this vignette also reveal perceived differential treatment of executive women and secretaries. Women disapprove of the activity slightly more when the victim is a secretary (40%) than when she is an executive (36%). One-quarter of all our respondents would express their disapproval to the secretary's boss, while one-fifth would do so on behalf of the executive. If secretaries are unprotected, executive women are even more so, although more respondents say they would give advice on how to deal with the behavior to executives than to secretaries (11 to 6%).

Whatever the sources of this difference, it crops up again. In another vignette, the white form featured a male executive and the colored form a female, receiving unwanted advances from a client of the opposite sex. When asked to rate what the typical division head would do, the male and female respondents differ sharply in their answers (see Exhibit 3, part D).

In both variants, most male readers assume that the typical manager would advise the executive—whether male or female—to handle the client with tact, regardless of the consequences. Most women, on the other hand (perhaps reasoning that the typical division head would regard the client as

Exhibit 3. Split-sample Responses to Four Vignettes*
white form statements in white, colored form statements in gray

	Male	Female	Top Management	Middle Management	Lower Management	Other
Number responding, colored form	489	412	245	332	289	62
white form	470	391	192	277	347	61

A. The president of a company walks into the office of his sales manager to congratulate him on setting a new record in sales. When he enters the office, he finds the sales manager standing very close to his secretary, who looks upset and flustered. When the president and sales manager are alone, what do you think the president would do—if he were typical of company presidents you have known or heard about? (If you were the president, what would you do when you were alone with the sales manager?)

	Male	Female	Top Management	Middle Management	Lower Management	Other
a. He (I) would do nothing, not knowing what had happened.	33% 30	30% 25	30% 27	33% 30	32% 29	35% 15
b. He (I) would do nothing, not wanting to confront the sales manager on a personal matter such as this.	13 1	36 1	20 1	24 1	26 1	29 2
c. He (I) would suggest to the sales manager that even the appearance of sexual behavior was unwise.	47 61	3 66	42 63	39 61	37 63	27 77
d. He (I) would express strong disapproval to the sales manager.	4 4	2 4	4 4	3 5	2 3	3 3
e. He (I) would tell the sales manager that if such behavior continued, it would have an adverse effect on his career.	2 2	3 3	3 4	1 1	2 3	3 2

B. Two middle-level male executives (A senior executive and a junior executive) enter an elevator. One of them (The junior executive) turns to the other occupant, a female employee, and makes a suggestive remark about her body. Then he winks in amusement at his companion (the senior executive). If the companion (senior executive) were typical of those in your company, what would his response be?

	Male	Female	Top Management	Middle Management	Lower Management	Other
a. He would share the first executive's amusement.	14%	41%	17%	25%	33%	36%
	7	23	6	12	20	18
b. He would feel neutral, believing that if the woman objects, it's up to her to say so.	19	21	21	25	18	36
	9	17	13	13	13	13
c. He would remain silent because it's an embarrassing issue to raise.	23	21	24	22	19	24
	7	14	8	10	12	10
d. He would indicate disapproval by his coolness or aloofness.	22	8	17	15	16	11
	30	20	26	26	24	30
e. He would express disapproval within the woman's hearing.	4	5	6	4	2	7
	8	6	9	7	7	8
f. He would express disapproval when he and the other executive were alone.	17	5	16	10	12	8
	37	18	37	30	24	21

Exhibit 3 (*continued*)

C. A female executive earning $40,000 a year is one of the most promising executives of either sex in her insurance company. She complains to the executive vice president in charge of her division (A secretary complains to the vice president in charge of her division) that her boss has been making unwelcome and persistent sexual advances to her. The vice president has reason to believe her even though, in a private talk, her boss insists that the woman has mistaken his "innocent" remarks and gestures. If you were the executive vice president, what would you do?

	Male	Female	Top Management	Middle Management	Lower Management	Other
a. I would wonder about the woman's ability to handle interpersonal relationships.	4%	2%	4%	3%	3%	3%
	1	1	1	1	1	2
b. I would advise the woman on how she might better deal with such behavior.	20	20	15	23	20	18
	12	11	14	13	9	10
c. I would offer the woman a transfer to another division.	2	4	2	3	4	3
	9	5	6	8	9	3
d. I would express my strong disapproval to the boss.	25	16	23	21	18	13
	29	21	27	27	25	26
e. I would inform the boss that if such behavior continued, it could have an adverse effect on his career.	45	56	52	47	52	58
	48	60	53	49	55	59
f. I would discreetly arrange a transfer for the boss.	3	3	3	3	4	3
	1	2	1	1	1	0

D. A female (male) executive with a large manufacturing company has been the object of persistent sexual advances from the male (female) vice president of a major customer. She (He) has tried to discourage these advances tactfully, but in the course of negotiating a new contract, the customer has suggested that she (he) might lose the contract if she (he) were not "friendlier." The woman (man) discusses the problem with the head of her (his) division. What do you think the typical division head would do?[†]

	Male	Female	Top Management	Middle Management	Lower Management	Other
a. Offer to transfer the woman (man) from the account.	23%	35%	27%	24%	30%	42%
	15	18	16	16	18	21
b. Encourage the woman (man) to parry the advances without offending the client.	21	32	23	26	25	36
	28	36	26	35	33	34
c. Encourage the woman (man) to be tactful but firm, regardless of the consequences.	45	28	43	38	34	31
	33	26	35	29	28	25
d. Send a team to future negotiations with the client.	33	30	36	29	32	34
	24	33	27	29	27	31
e. Indicate disapproval to the client.	7	3	4	6	6	6
	1	2	1	2	1	0
f. Other	6	4	7	6	6	2
	9	9	7	7	8	7
g. Don't know.	2	4	3	3	4	2
	6	9	5	6	10	8

*Throughout the four sections of this exhibit in order to determine readers' intuitive responses to the vignettes, we did not include as an option the correct legal approach—starting a full investigation in each situation depicted.

†Respondents were not limited to a single choice.

more important than the employee), believe that the boss would encourage the male executive to parry the advances and, most important, would offer to transfer the female from the account before doing anything else.

If we look at the order of options that our female respondents think a typical division manager would choose in the case of a woman executive, we see a discouraging picture of how much support women think management will give them in the face of sexual harassment. Rather than buttress them with a team (their next-to-last choice), back them regardless of the consequences, or encourage them to parry the advance, women assume that the division managers would want to transfer them. Whether women fear this most as the outcome or base their opinions on personal experience, their perceptions of how management would act should ring alarms for top officers.

What Can a Woman Handle?

Do men and women hold different views on how women should or can deal with sexual advances? Women disagree among themselves here. Some think that women, to survive in the business world, have to handle whatever comes their way. A 43-year-old female office manager in a small transportation company wrote:

> Women should stop feeling sorry or deprived, trying to play both sides to get the career they want, and act more like business people—as men do. Furthermore, the so-called liberated women are probably the ones who are causing this commotion after all. It would be better for everyone if women would start acting more like people.

Other women think that harassment within organizations is too much for any person to handle alone. The following comment by a 34-year-old administrative assistant in an average-sized consumer services company is representative of many made by women:

> In every incident in my organization, every woman has been fired, encouraged to resign or transfer, or demoted. Never has a man been in any way disciplined or punished for sexual harassment. Even when a complaint is won, the work situation continues to be uncomfortable. It is far easier to change jobs.

We asked our readers whether "a smart woman employee ought to have no trouble handling an unwanted sexual approach." Fifty-nine percent of the women disagree or partly disagree and the same proportion of men agree or partly agree. Men seem to think that women can overcome sexual overtures through tact, as in the vignettes of the female executive with the client (*Exhibit 3*, part D) and the female executive and the secretary who complain about their bosses' advances (part C). In other words, it's her problem. That fewer women chose sanctions against the two female executives' bosses than against the secretary's boss indicates that some women think female executives *should* be able to or can handle more.

Most women are less sure that they can deal with an unwanted sexual approach and, in fact, they wonder whether *anything* they do would make them safe from such behavior in the workplace. A full 78 percent of them disagree with the statement, "If a women dresses and behaves properly, she will not be the target of unwanted sexual approaches at work."

The same proportion of women, however, agree or partly agree with the statement, "Women can and often do use their sexual attractiveness to their own advantage" (compared with 86 percent of the men). As one woman who is a 55-year-old supervisor in a large financial institution noted: "Although I do not side with sexual harassment from *any* source at the office, many young women invite this sort of response by their behavior and the type of clothing they wear. Whether it is intentional makes little difference. When dealing with the human factor, you (male or female) should know what can happen and avoid it on the job."

Although we cannot assume that the opposite of the statement—"If a women dresses and behaves properly, she will not be the target of unwanted sexual approaches at work"—is true, the strong female disagreement with it indicates that women feel vulnerable on the issue. If they cannot avoid unwanted advances themselves, what is the manager's duty here? What do our respondents and the top managers among them think about managerial responsibility?

How Much Can a Manager Know?

In dealing with the ambiguity in part A of Exhibit 3—where the company president finds the sales manager standing very close to his secretary, who looks upset and flustered—63 percent of high-level managers who answered the white form said they would "suggest to the sales manager that even the appearance of sexual behavior was unwise." On the colored form, 42 percent indicated that the typical president would choose that option. However, 30 percent of this latter group feel that the typical president would do nothing because they think the executive would be ignorant of the facts or their importance—or of the EEOC guidelines.

Although top managers are convinced that they themselves *would* do something, apparently many people see real problems for most presidents in reacting to the ambiguity. Also, most think top managers are in no position to know about misconduct if it occurs; half of them disagree with the statement, "A good manager will know if it's happening in his or her department." Not surprisingly, lower-level managers and women are in even greater disagreement (56 percent for both groups).

The 27 percent of top managers filling out the white form who pleaded ignorance about part A of Exhibit 3 by marking option a—doing nothing, not knowing what had happened—were playing it very safe considering that they also had option c—suggesting to the sales manager that even the appearance of sexual behavior was unwise. This situation may or may not be harassment, but it should be confronted regardless.

Do women and lower-ranking managers—who may have heard of and observed much more sexual harassment than men and upper-level managers—really know how difficult it is for top managers to be aware of the problem? Does high-level management deceive itself about the difficulty of detecting abusive behavior? Are top managers aware mainly of the grosser forms and less knowledgeable about the daily "accepted" forms that annoy our female readers?

In part D of Exhibit 3, in which the executive faces unwanted advances from the client, top managers' first choice (43%) was a tactful response, when a woman is the object of the advances. Lower-level managers also selected tact first (34%) but spread themselves much more evenly among the other options.

Given that two-thirds of high-level executives agree or partly agree that the reported amount of sexual harassment at work is greatly exaggerated, it might follow that for the *perceived* seriousness of the problem, "tact" would be a sufficient response. But since so many of our women respondents think tact is insufficient, what can a manager do? Will the new EEOC guidelines solve the problem? Should company policies and procedures address directly the subtler, varied, and more covert forms of misconduct that (although covered by the guidelines) are difficult to take action on or prove? If so, which policies would work?

EEOC Guidelines and Company Policies

The guidelines will be hard to implement because of 41,000 years of habit. *(male)*

We have several store managers involved with women and harassment issues. We have a company policy which allows managers who find the need to transfer to another unit. Counseling is available. We don't want to lose people, but if a harassment charge is proven correct, we terminate that management person. Within the last year we have had to terminate three managers for harassment. Interestingly, the problem continues to plague us. Heart-to-heart, man-to-man talks, policy statements, and a proven corporate response have been no visible deterrent. *(male)*

I do not know of a significant incident of sexual harassment at the company recently. The issue came up at seminars on male-female relationships run by the company in January and February 1980—much to the surprise of most males attending (including me). The general issue was problems of atmosphere—sexual remarks, innuendo, etc. As a result, management took a clear position on proper behavior at a series of meetings of all management personnel. I believe the situation has improved, but it is not the type of problem that is ever going to be solved by one action or policy. *(male)*

This is a middle-western conservative work force, stable, with little turnover, and closely managed [20,000-plus employees]. Any individual having a problem could quickly and easily get support through peer relationships or by contacting another manager. Any manager demonstrating such immaturity and insecurity would immediately find his career declining and would be told the reason. This would be done without publicity. *(male)*

Women would have to be brought under a new and stricter dress code. *(male)*

As one might expect, the degree to which people see the EEOC rules as reasonable and necessary correlates closely with the degree to which they think sexual misbehavior is a problem at work. Exhibit 4 shows opinions on the guidelines.

In their comments many respondents maintain that, while the guidelines are reasonable in theory, it is unreasonable to expect much success in implementing them. These people consider them vague and unworkable because so much male-female interaction is ambiguous, private, and varied.

A 31-year-old man who manages special projects in a small trade association observed:

Too much of whatever harassment and/or sexual activity that occurs between employees is subject to interpretation. While employees who are clearly harassing others can be disciplined, I suspect that clear-cut cases will be hard to identify or prove.

Consistent with their perception of the seriousness of the problem, most male managers (68%) think the guidelines will be "not difficult" to implement. Others expressed concern that the guidelines will "become a crutch for disgruntled employees." Asserted a 35-year-old advertising promotion manager for a very large manufacturer of consumer goods, "It could be used as a smoke screen to defend against legitimate performance reviews."

A number of the men agree with a 44-year-old CEO who declared that his bank could "take care of misconduct without government snoopervision." Even more men (and a few women) expressed sentiments like the following from the 40-year-old personnel director of a large health care enterprise: "The guidelines are procedurally okay, but people are reluctant to change deep-seated, culturally reinforced attitudes."

Replies to a question on company policies again show how lack of experience with them, as much as experience, affects opinions on the issue. For instance, although 68 percent of the men and 58 percent of the women think the EEOC guidelines will not be difficult to implement, few work for companies that have any rules governing harassment. As Exhibit 5 shows, a significant gap also exists between what most people favor as policy and what their organizations actually have. (Implementing such rules can sometimes mitigate corporate liability but is not an absolute defense as far as individual liability is concerned.)

The policies listed in Exhibit 5 received substantial support, except for the management statement disapproving of office flirtations. The lukewarm reception for this is consistent with the concern, expressed by younger

Exhibit 4. Opinions on Whether the EEOC Guidelines Are Reasonable and Necessary and Whether They Will Be Difficult to Adjust to

Exhibit IV
Opinions on whether the EEOC guidelines are reasonable and necessary and whether they will be difficult to adjust to

	Highly reasonable, very necessary	Reasonable, necessary	Reasonable, unnecessary	Unreasonable, very unnecessary	Not difficult
Total	15%	57%	16%	7%	63%
Male	5	51	27	11	68
Female	27	64	4	2	58
Top management	9	44	27	14	69
Middle management	13	59	17	6	64
Lower management	19	62	11	4	61

people particularly, over legislation against love affairs and condemnation of camaraderie. Elsewhere, some 20 percent of the sample expressed neutrality, rather than agreement or disagreement, on the statement, "A little flirtation makes the workday more interesting." The 51-year-old male vice president of a large company wrote, "I do not favor any legislative attempts to interfere with natural female-male forms of communication. Vive la différence!"

Exhibit 5.   Opinions on Company Policies

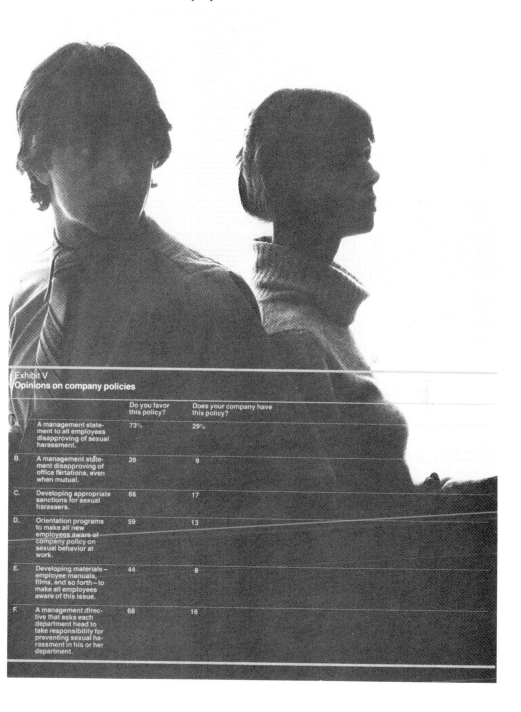

Exhibit V
Opinions on company policies

		Do you favor this policy?	Does your company have this policy?
A.	A management statement to all employees disapproving of sexual harassment.	73%	29%
B.	A management statement disapproving of office flirtations, even when mutual.	28	9
C.	Developing appropriate sanctions for sexual harassers.	68	17
D.	Orientation programs to make all new employees aware of company policy on sexual behavior at work.	59	13
E.	Developing materials— employee manuals, films, and so forth—to make all employees aware of this issue.	44	8
F.	A management directive that asks each department head to take responsibility for preventing sexual harassment in his or her department.	68	16

Judging from many comments, smaller organizations rely more on peer pressure and informal controls to deal with misbehavior. Since such organizations, in general, do not suffer from the impersonal atmosphere of those with thousands of workers, they perhaps feel less need for written and formally enunciated rules. (Whether they ought to is another issue.) Wrote the male president of a professional service firm with fewer than 50 employees, "We wouldn't tolerate sexual harassment any more than we would lying or theft. However, we don't have formal procedures for dealing with any of these forms of misconduct."

That many companies fail to communicate to employees the directives they do have is clear from the responses. And we found a significant difference in men's and women's opinions as to whether their companies even have certain policies. The difference is described in the following table (the letters refer to the list in Exhibit 5).

Policy	Percent of respondents who say their company has this policy	
	Men	**Women**
A	33%	25%
C	20	14
D	15	11
F	19	14

Why this difference? Do respondents really understand whether the policy exists, or have some answered according to their perception of whether the policy is working? Women, who are predominantly in the lower echelons of organizations, may not know what company policy is—especially the sanctions developed for sexual harassers (policy A) and management directives asking department heads to take responsibility for preventing harassment (policy F). And managers may just assume that the policies exist or are working.

Which policies and approaches work? Which really promote an understanding of harassment, its damaging effects on employees, and its divisiveness? And which support women and men in their stands against such abuse? Here are respondents' suggestions:

☐ Make known, in a firm but subdued manner, the chief executive's attitude about sexual misconduct.

☐ Install an all-purpose procedure, bypassing any union channels, that allows people to voice their concerns—including complaints of harassment—confidentially.

☐ Hold in-house consciousness-raising seminars to inform managers of the consequences of misbehavior.

☐ Assign responsibility for cases of harassment to a high-level person—a vice president or assistant to the chief executive. This person should be seen to have the ear and respect of senior management and have credibility in other issues as well.

☐ Foster strong peer relationships among women employees.

☐ Encourage women to confront harassers by letter, after a confidential consultation with an appropriate officer of the company.

The last suggestion is clearly crucial because no enunciated or implied policies, however firmly and evenly applied, can be effective unless victims attack the problem themselves. Also, the situations are so varied that they need individual responses. Sometimes harassment calls for forthright action, such as that recommended by the 56-year-old female treasurer of a small manufacturer of industrial goods: "I have been in the work force for 40 years and find that the female visual and verbal attitude of 'hands off' works. When I was an airline stewardess in 1946, I perfected a devastating hands-off look that still works today. 'Develop the look' is may advice to my daughters and employees."

At other times, a casual confrontation is more appropriate and effective. A 33-year-old woman, the general manager of a management consulting firm, wrote, "My boss has a habit of making sexual innuendos and jokes to female managers. We have not filed a complaint but have instead raised his consciousness. We immediately offer to take him up on his suggestion. I've said, 'Okay, let's get on with it if you're that hot to trot.' He is generally a good guy and this embarrasses him and improves his behavior."

Numbers of men indicate that they don't know "where the line is"—don't know when a joke that is funny to them is offensive to women. They believe it is up to women to tell men when a remark is not funny. In our opinion, by failing to take action right away, the woman risks letting the harasser think that it is welcome. Before women feel safe enough to speak up, however, managers must promote a supportive atmosphere through enforced company policies that make clear what behavior is not permitted.

A Complex Problem

A lot of women hesitate to report sexual harassment because women: (1) don't think they'll be believed; (2) will be punished by smaller raises or cruddy jobs; (3) will be ostracized by male and female employees; (4) will be accused of inviting the advance; (5) have guilt feelings that perhaps it was invited subconsciously; (6) fear publicity; (7) are unsure exactly what is harassment and what is just interaction of people. *(female)*

The problem is not just an artificiality created by the numbers and the varying responses to our probing; it is real. We give the last word to the 37-year-old director of communications for a large financial institution. She wrote:

Sexual harassment is corporate rape and, as with rape on the streets, many people see the victim as responsible. Most of the time the victim who complains falls under suspicion and is thought of as 'dingy.'

Our company has a formal complaint system that allows employees to take problems to the chairman of the board without retribution. This procedure should be adequate to deal with complaints of sexual harassment, but it is not. It puts the burden of action on the victim, forcing her to complain and continue complaining until something is done.

Always the 'real world' issue surfaces. Women can't expect protection from confrontations that are offensive to them in one way or another. Can we hope to achieve in the workplace what we have never been able to achieve anywhere else in society? Women have to take responsibility for managing the conflicts in their lives. Most of us do.

Something that occurred in my office illustrates the problem for women and managers. A male employee who worked for me recently resigned his position. After he left, four women came forward and complained about his sexual overtures, which included statements about his ability to help them in their jobs. One of the women reported directly to him. All four had handled the situation deftly themselves.

The story points up a serious issue. If no one complains, how can management know? Here I sit, a female executive appalled by the idea of sexual harassment, while a male manager who reported to me was practicing it. (All of this is complicated, of course, by the fact that what one woman thinks is sexual harassment, another may never notice.)

Some evidence exists that the situation is changing but, regardless, I think it is extremely difficult for a man to understand the demeaning nature of sexual harassment to a woman and to investigate it objectively. Men don't understand what it is, and I find this to be true without exception. It is hard to recognize something as negative when it has been part of your own way of thinking, and harassment has survived in corporate locker room attitudes for a long time.

A man's view will always be colored by the way he behaves toward women and what he finds acceptable. . . . I do not mean to malign the motives of men, but simply to say they cannot understand what they have never experienced or been educated about. The more we women educate them, the better they'll be able to deal with this subject.

Notes

1. Merit Systems Protection Board Report on Sexual Harassment in the Federal Workplace, given before the Subcommittee on Investigations, Committee on the Post Office and Civil Service, U.S. House of Representatives, September 1980. See also Frank J. Till, "Sexual Harassment: A Report on the Sexual Harassment of Students," National Advisory Council on Women's Educational Programs, U.S. Department of Education, August 1980; Catherine A. MacKinnon, *Sexual Harassment of Working Women* (New Haven: Yale University Press, 1979); and Claire Safran, "What Men Do to Women on the Job," *Redbook*, November 1976, p. 149.

2. The exhibits in this article show the white form statements in white and the colored form statements in gray.

Appendix A: Survey Approach

This survey, conducted jointly by *Redbook* magazine and *HBR,* aimed to measure opinions on and awareness of the issue of sexual harassment in the workplace. We mailed a questionnaire to 7,408 *HBR* subscribers in the United States and tabulated 1,846 replies, a 24.9 percent response. (A further 234 completed questionnaires were returned after the cut-off date and could not be included.)

To serve as a benchmark for respondents and give them a certain amount of information as a starting point, we listed the EEOC guidelines on sexual harassment in the introduction to the questionnaire.

We divided the survey into three sections. In the first, to elicit definitions and attitudes we offered readers 11 statements and asked whether they agreed with them or not. We also listed 14 comments that have been made about the behavior of men toward women at work and asked whether the behavior described constituted sexual harassment and whether people had heard of or observed this behavior in their organizations.

In the second section, we described four vignettes and asked what action to take. The third set of questions concerned EEOC guidelines and company policies, and the fourth section was statistical.

In the first section we split the sample in half to get at differing attitudes that might not otherwise be revealed. Of the 14 comments on behavior, 8 differed between the white and colored forms. The four vignettes in the second section were also worded differently between the two forms.

In examining the data, we discovered a certain amount of conditioning. In the eight split-sample statements on behavior, the aggressor in the colored form was always a supervisor, while in the white form he was a coworker. In the other six questions in the group that were the same in both forms, those who returned the colored questionnaires were more likely to term an action harassment than those who returned the white ones.

We excluded all non-U.S. subscribers (22 percent of *HBR*'s total number of subscribers) from the sample because we wanted to probe the issue from a strictly American viewpoint. We also skewed the sample another way: to ensure a representative response from women, we mailed a questionnaire to virtually every female subscriber, for a male/female ratio of 68 to 32 percent. This bias resulted in a response of 52 percent male and 44 percent female (and 4% who gave no indication of gender)—compared with *HBR*'s U.S. subscriber proportion of 93 percent male and 7 percent female.

The administrative levels of the survey group broke down as follows: top management, 24 percent; middle management, 33 percent; lower management, 34 percent; and other, 7 percent. Nearly three-quarters of the group were in the 25 to 45 age bracket. The breakdown was: under 25, 3 percent; 25 to 35, 42 percent; 36 to 45, 32 percent; 46 to 55, 15 percent; 56 to 65, 6 percent; and over 65, less than 1 percent; 1 percent did not answer.

The salaries of about one-quarter of the group fell into the $20,000 to $29,999 range, another one-quarter in the $30,000 to $39,999 range, while 11 percent earned less than $20,000, and 6 percent more than $100,000. Some 49 percent held graduate degrees and 35 percent, college degrees.

The sizes of the organizations for which the individuals worked were spread widely, the most significant categories being 1,000 to 9,999 employees (23%), more than 20,000 (16%), and under 50 (13%).

On average, the survey group was at a lower management level than our U.S. subscribers overall. Respondents were generally younger and earned less but were about as well educated. We ascribe the differences between respondents and *HBR*'s subscriber group to the fact that our sample was skewed to include more women, who have not reached the higher echelons of U.S. corporations in great numbers.

Appendix B: The Legal Context

by Grace L. Mastalli

The law provides a variety of means by which victims of sexual harassment in the workplace can seek redress through legal action against their employers, directly against the harassers, or (as is often the case) against both.

Title VII

The primary basis for action against employers is Title VII of the 1964 Civil Rights Act (as amended), which prohibits discrimination on the basis of sex in employment and provides the legal authority for the final interpretive guidelines on sexual harassment issued by the EEOC.[1] The final guidelines provide that:

"Unwelcome sexual advances, requests for sexual favors, and other verbal or physical conduct of a sexual nature constitute sexual harassment when (1) submission to such conduct is made either explicitly or implicity a term or condition of an individual's employment, (2) submission to or rejection of such conduct by an individual is used as the basis for employment decisions affecting such an individual, or (3) such conduct has the purpose or effect of unreasonably interfering with an individual's work performance or creating an intimidating, hostile, or offensive working environment."

The guidelines impose absolute liability on employers for the acts of supervisors regardless of whether the conduct was known to, or authorized or forbidden by, the particular employer.

---

[1]"Guidelines on Discrimination on the Basis of Sex" (Washington, D.C.: Equal Employment Opportunity Commission, November 10, 1980).

The standard of employer liability for the acts of coworkers is somewhat less stringent. An employer is responsible for such acts if the employer knew, or should have known, of the conduct in question—unless the employer can demonstrate that it took immediate and appropriate action to correct the problem on learning of it.

Similarly, under the guidelines an employer may be liable for acts in the workplace committed by nonemployees if the employer knew, or should have known, of the conduct and failed to take appropriate corrective action. Moreover, a controversial section of the guidelines states that an employer may be held liable for sex discrimination against qualified third parties who have been denied opportunities or benefits granted to another who provided sexual favors to a mutual supervisor.

In addition to establishing standards for imposing liability, the guidelines make employers responsible for developing programs to prevent sexual misconduct in the workplace. The elements of an adequate prevention program are not specified, but they would probably include the adoption and dissemination of a strong policy statement prohibiting sexual harassment, presentation of the subject in employee training materials and orientation sessions, and development and publication of procedures for handling complaints in the organization—including a range of sanctions and remedies and information about employee rights.

Under the guidelines, an employer must also thoroughly investigate all complaints alleging sexual harassment and all instances potentially constituting harassment that come to the employer's attention through means other than formal complaints. Following an investigation, an employer is required to take immediate and appropriate corrective action to remedy any illegality detected and prevent its recurrence. Failure to do so constitutes a violation of Title VII as interpreted by the EEOC.

Although the guidelines in and of themselves lack the force of law, the courts accorded them some weight while they were still in interim form, and courts are likely to rely on them substantially in the future. In fact, to a large extent the guidelines only restate and amplify the evolving line of Title VII cases establishing employer liability for the sexual harassment of employees by other employees. For example, in a leading Title VII case on the issue of employer liability, *Miller* v. *Bank of America,* the U.S. Court of Appeals for the Ninth Circuit held an employer to be liable for the sexual harassing acts of its supervisors, even if the company has a policy prohibiting such conduct and even if the victim did not formally notify the employer of the problem.[2]

This is also the standard articulated by the guidelines. However, in the provisions concerning any conduct that is offensive, conduct by coworkers and nonemployees, and third-party rights in the guidelines, the EEOC went beyond what the courts had established as harassment constituting sex dis-

---

[2]600 F.2d 211 (1979).

crimination under Title VII. Pending further litigation, it is difficult to assess whether the courts will adopt or qualify the EEOC's broad assignment of liability for and liberal definition of sexual harassment. However, in what may be a bellwether case, the guidelines recently received significant support from the U.S. Court of Appeals in Washington, D.C. In January 1981, the court ruled in effect that sexual harassment in and of itself is a violation of Title VII. The court said that the law does not require the victim to prove she resisted harassment and was penalized for the resistance. According to the decision in *Bundy* v. *Jackson,* employers are liable for sexual harassment in the workplace because it creates an offensive "discriminatory environment" by "poisoning the atmosphere of employment."

(Incidentally, employer reliance on the guidelines provides a defense to charges of discrimination where the acts of alleged discrimination were taken in reliance on the EEOC's interpretation.)

Civil Suits

Victims of sexual harassment are not limited to a Title VII cause of action; they may combine the sex discrimination claim with other civil charges against an employer in order to obtain a more extensive remedy and/or damages. Common law doctrines on assault, battery, and intentional infliction of distress—as well as actions for breach of contract—may be used to establish employer liability for sexual harassment in some circumstances where the elements of a *prima facie* Title VII case may be lacking.

The wide range of compensatory relief, including damages, available through common law actions, combined with what may be more easily met standards of proof, has encouraged victims of employment-related harassment to seek recovery directly from their harassers and, under the tort law doctrine of *respondeat superior,* to hold employers liable for the misconduct of their workers. (*Respondeat superior* is the theory that an employer is liable for all the acts of an employee committed "within the scope of employment.")

Case law suggests that the courts may broadly construe what constitutes "the scope of employment" in order to establish employer liability for acts of sexual harassment. In such cases, however, some damages could be mitigated by the existence of a strong employer-sponsored harassment prevention program.

Sexual harassment that results in the wrongful dismissal of the victim and economic loss may also provide the basis for a suit against the employer for interference with an employment contract or breach of contract. In such cases an employer may be liable for back pay and conceivably even for damages awarded for mental suffering that the harassment causes. (As a rule, courts do not award damages for mental suffering in breach of contract actions unless the breach is of such a kind that serious emotional disturbance is to be expected or likely.)

Similarly, although litigation of this issue is not complete, employers may be subject to liability for breach of contract involving sexual harassment in instances where the victim is unable to demonstrate the degree of harm required under tort law.

Criminal Actions

An extreme instance of sexual harassment in the workplace may also constitute a criminal offense—ranging from criminal assault and battery to self-exposure to rape or other sexual assault—and may subject the perpetrator to prosecution. The nature of such actions varies with state jurisdiction but normally would not involve employer liability. Under certain circumstances and in some jurisdictions, however, employers may be subject to civil liability related to such criminal actions for failing to provide a safe and secure work environment.

Summary

The combination of Title VII, as broadly construed by the EEOC, and the availability of a wide range of other civil actions provides a multitude of ways to establish employer liability for sexual harassment in the workplace. The courts can fashion remedies involving substantial victim compensation for harassment without making a finding of discrimination. Moreover, the flexibility afforded by this combination means that one or more claims against the employer could emerge from the factual circumstances surrounding almost any charge of work-related sexual harassment.

The employer's sole protection against liability is prevention of harassment. In those cases where prevention proves impossible, the employer's actions will, at least under common law, help limit damages.

Appendix C: Unforgettable Quotes

"My department is financial, rather staid. The creative side of the business might well be rife with cases of sexual harassment." (female)

"I married a subordinate. I believe there was no coercion involved." (male)

"Have not had any experience in this area. Too busy working." (male)

"I have never been harassed but I would welcome the opportunity." (anonymous)

"I filled this out with my personnel manager, who is a female (and I harassed her to give me the answers I wanted)." (male)

"I know of no such incidents; two of our top four managers are active churchgoers." (male)

"I am very nearsighted, so when I look at someone (male or female) I give the appearance of staring or ogling. What do I do?" (male)

Dealing with Sexual Harassment

11

MARY P. ROWE

As the recent attention in the press and on television attests, managers are encountering sexual harassment problems more and more frequently. Although by now many corporations have investigated the legal side of these issues and have adopted appropriate policies, reaching an easy resolution in such cases is difficult for the following reasons:

☐ People cannot agree about how to define the problem. In sexual harassment cases, managers will find the widest divergence of perceptions that they ever encounter.

☐ There is usually little evidence to substantiate anyone's allegations. The employer often feels that something ought to be done but can think of no action to take that does not infringe on the rights of one side or the other.

☐ Although third-party intervention often heals other kinds of disputes, such action in a sexual harassment case usually triggers wider disagreement between the original actors, who then persuade bystanders to take sides.

☐ No matter how carefully worded the corporate policy concerning sexual harassment is, new kinds of cases arise, and in such variety as to prevent any precise anticipation of problems.

☐ Those offended may be unwilling to report sexual harassment if they think that public exposure of the situation and mandatory punishment of the offender will follow. Often they will talk with the manager only under an agreement that no public action will be taken. (It is rare, in my experience, for a complainant to ask for any kind of

Published in 1981.

retribution; nearly always this person simply wants the harassment to stop.)

☐ The most serious aspect of almost all reported cases is the power relationship between the alleged offender and the offended person. (I believe that most sexual aggressiveness that occurs *outside* a power relationship is simply ignored or adequately dealt with by the offended party.) In any case, reports of harassment usually involve fear of retribution because of the supposed power of a particular group of co-workers or of a supervisor. In fact, most reported cases do involve a supervisor-subordinate relationship; hence, productivity is threatened.

Some Practical Approaches

I offer three recommendations for addressing these problems. First, complainants can be helped to help themselves. Second, such conflicts can usually be resolved most effectively through procedures designed to deal with all kinds of complaints, not just sexual harassment. Third, corporations should confront the issue of power differences in the troubled relationship.

An employer must give unmistakable signals that action will be taken against proved offenders, if the complainant will agree, and also that proved targets of harassment will be protected from retaliation. But those who deal with offended employees should first explore the possibilities of helping them to help themselves when there is no proof and, of course, when the complainants prefer this method.

The sections that follow may be of special interest to offended persons whose companies do not yet have policies and structures to support them.

What Can the Individual Do?

Complainants must be willing to take action themselves in a rational and responsible way. To many people this may seem unjust since it appears to put a double burden on the offended person. This concern makes sense. But I recommend such action because it works and because nothing else really works as well.

Moreover, it helps offended persons to focus their anger outside themselves instead of becoming sick or depressed, which often happens otherwise. Finally, such measures may be the only way to obtain evidence for management (or the courts) to act on.

The aims of individual action are:

☐ To give the offended and offender a chance, usually for the first time, to see things the same way. Since neither person may have any understanding of how the other sees the problem, discussion may help.

Entry of a third party at this stage usually further polarizes the views of the opposing persons.

☐ To give those who are wrongly accused the chance to defend themselves.

☐ To give those who are correctly, or to some extent correctly, accused the chance to make amends. (This may not be possible in serious cases.)

☐ To provide some evidence of the offense, since usually there is no substantive evidence at all. This step is vital if management or the courts must later take action.

☐ To give aggressors who do not understand what they were doing a fair warning, if this is appropriate.

☐ To provide the offended employee a chance to get the harassment stopped without provoking public counterattack, experiencing public embarrassment, harming third parties, damaging the company's reputation, or causing the aggressor to lose face. In my experience, these points are almost always considered important by the aggrieved person.

☐ To provide offended persons a way to demonstrate that they tried all reasonable means to get the offender to stop. This step may be convincing later to supervisors, spouses, and others who become involved.

☐ To encourage ambivalent complainants, as well as those who have inadvertently given misunderstood signals, to present a consistent and clear message.

☐ To encourage those who exaggerate to be more responsible.

Writing a Letter. One method that works quite consistently, even when many verbal requests have failed, is for the offended person to write a letter to the accused. I usually recommend a polite, low-key letter (which may necessitate many drafts).

The letter I recommend has three parts. The first part should be a detailed statement of facts as the writer sees them: "This is what I think happened. . . ." I encourage a precise rendition of all facts and dates relevant to the alleged harassment. This section is sometimes very long.

In the second part of the letter, writers should describe their feelings and what damage they think has been done. This is where opinions belong. "Your action made me feel terrible"; "I am deeply embarrassed and worried that my parents will hear about this"; "You have caused me to ask for a transfer (change my career objectives; drop out of the training course; take excessive time off; or whatever)." The writer should mention any perceived or actual costs and damages, along with feelings of dismay, distrust, revulsion, misery, and so on.

Finally, I recommend a short statement of what the accuser would like to have happen next. Since most persons only want the harassment to end, the letter might finish by saying so: "I ask that our relationship from now on be on a purely professional basis."

Someone who knows that he or she contributed to the problem does well to say so: "Although we once were happy dating, it is important to me that we now reestablish a formal and professional relationship, and I ask you to do so."

If the letter writer believes some remedy or recompense is in order, this is the place to say so: "Please withdraw my last evaluation until we can work out a fair one"; "I will need a written answer as to the reference you will provide from now on"; and statements of that type.

What Happens Next?   The complainant should, if possible, deliver the letter in person to know that it arrived and when it arrived. When necessary, a plainclothes police officer, security person, or some other protector and/or witness should accompany the writer or be present when the letter is delivered. The writer of the letter should keep a copy.

Usually the recipient simply accepts the letter, says nothing, and reforms his or her behavior. Sometimes there is an apology, an astounded opening of discussion, or a denial. Rarely will the recipient reply in writing to "set the record straight." Nearly always, the alleged harassment stops.

Obviously, it is now more dangerous for the recipient of such a letter to harass the employee. The letter constitutes an attempt to settle the problem peaceably.

A good letter is useful if the complainant later feels the need to appeal to high-level management, especially if the writer can prove it was delivered. It can also, if necessary, constitute invaluable legal evidence. Such letters are usually enough to stop a mildly disturbed aggressor—for example, someone who importunes with sexual innuendo and suggestions for sexual activity.

Even if a written order or request to stop harassment does not succeed, in my experience the complainant is always better off for having tried to stop the offense in a direct and unambiguous way.

Finally, and possibly most important, taking action in this or similar ways often has a powerful effect on all participants. Taut nerves relax as victims learn they can protect themselves. Insomniacs get needed sleep. Productivity improves.

Both persons are likely to feel better about themselves. Aggressors sometimes turn for help, through which their self-esteem may rise. They may also stop harassing people, thus sparing those who could have become victims; this often matters greatly to the person who takes action.

For all these reasons I strongly encourage persons who feel harassed to take action themselves if possible.

Employer's Role

By what I have said so far I do not mean to imply that employers should place all the burdens on those who are offended. Employers can and should encourage employees to take the measures already discussed. They may need to protect their employees from retaliation from a group of coworkers or a supervisor and also to offer strong emotional support.

If significant evidence of wrongdoing is available, the employer may also wish to reprimand the offender, deny a promotion or raise, require attendance at a training program, or transfer, demote, or fire the offender.

What about persons who are too bewildered, frightened, and unsure even to write a letter? Obviously it helps them to talk things over, in confidence, with one or two responsible and supportive people.

If, as frequently happens, an offended employee is suffering physical consequences, such as anorexia, sleeplessness, or anxiety-induced pain, he or she may need medical help. Some victims will want to talk things out with a social worker, psychologist, psychiatrist, Employee Assistance person, or other company counselor, if such people are known to be discreet and supportive.

Special Measures

It often helps the offended person to keep a diary, a careful log of events and feelings. This can serve to affirm the sanity of the writer, who otherwise may begin to doubt the reality of the situation, especially if coworkers are unaware or unsympathetic.

Writing in a diary will help to turn anger outward and will provide clues for responsible action by the offended person and by management. It can provide legal evidence as well. Keeping a diary may also resolve ambivalence (''*Am* I interested in him?'') or demonstrate later one's lack of ambivalence to a doubting observer. A careful diary is always useful later if it seems wise to write a letter of the sort I described earlier.

Persons who feel victimized should do whatever they can to get together with others who will understand. Women's networks can help a great deal. If the company has no such structure, a woman should try to form one with the knowledge and approval of management. Management stands to gain from such groups since in-house women's networks usually give strong support to orderly and responsible change. Outside the workplace, there are compassionate and responsible organizations like the Alliance Against Sexual Coercion, the Working Women's Institute, and the National Commission on Working Women.

Cases of sexual harassment in which the complainant is a man are rare but especially painful. The typical offender is also male, and a male target often feels alone because he is too embarrassed to discuss his problem. As with most female victims, the principal problems for men may be to overcome bewilderment and the immobilizing effect of violent fantasies. They, too, need to muster courage and take action.

Here again, there is no substitute for discussing the problem with discreet, sympathetic, and responsible people. The man who feels sexually harassed should make every effort to find help. (Senior supervisors and commissions against discrimination are often helpful.) In the meantime, a male who feels harassed should keep a diary and consider writing a letter.

Effective Complaint Procedures

Sexual harassment problems have illuminated the general need for better complaint procedures. Union grievance procedures should be reviewed to see if they really work with respect to this class of complaints.

Companies should also have explicit general complaint procedures for employees not in unions. To deal adequately with sexual harassment, nonunion complaint procedures must apply to employees and managers at every level. In my experience, the degree of sexual harassment is about the same at every level of employment. Studies show that many top managers are poorly informed about sexual harassment: usually people do not misbehave in front of the boss. It is *not* true, however, that sexual harassment is relatively rare near the top.

Nonunion complaint procedures should be as general as possible, admitting every kind of employee and every kind of concern.[1] Several harassment cases will represent only a small percentage of the problems brought in, but the grievance procedure will enjoy a better and wider reputation and will operate more effectively if it works well with every kind of employee concern. In such procedures, it should be unnecessary to give a label to every problem, especially a very controversial problem, before management can help.

With poorly defined and controversial problems like sexual harassment, mediation-oriented procedures work best, at least in the first stages; usually the first hope is to help people help themselves. Initial contact with the procedure must, of course, be completely confidential.

The complaint procedure should include both women and men, minorities and nonminorities, as contacts at some point in the process to ensure that different people feel free to come in. It is also essential to establish a procedure for bypassing one's supervisor in a case where that person is the offender. Finally, nonunion complaint procedures should be okayed by the CEO or someone else near the top.

The Power Relationship

Employers may find it helps in dealing with sexual harassment problems to confront directly the general issue of sexual relationships in the supervisory context.

Many people feel strongly that the private lives of employees have nothing to do with company business. However, sexual relationships in the context of supervision often present management with problems that affect company interests. This may be true even in the case of mutually consenting relationships.

When a senior person makes sexual overtures, a junior person may experience and allege coercion, exploitation, intimidation, and blackmail, and may fear retribution. Such reactions are common even when the senior person would be shocked to learn that the overtures were unwelcome. Neither sex can know for sure what the other experiences, and each is likely to misinterpret the feelings of the other.

Also, consenting relationships frequently break up. If the senior person then continues to make overtures, the junior person may complain of harassment. Then the senior person may be outraged, especially if he or she believes that the junior person "started it." The relationship may then disrupt the work environment.

Third parties sometimes complain bitterly about sexual relationships involving a supervisor. Spouses may be outspoken complainants; employees may resent real or perceived favoritism; and the morale of the senior person's subordinates may drop sharply. In consenting relationships that involve a junior person who is trading sexual favors for advancement, management's interests are jeopardized, especially if the junior person is not the employee most deserving of promotion.

Sexual relationships between supervisor and subordinate are frequently very distracting to these two. Also, the existence of widely known consenting relationships sometimes encourages other supervisors to make unwelcome sexual overtures to other employees.

Some companies act on the principle that all sexual relationships between supervisors and their subordinates may conflict with company interests. Where genuine loving relationships do arise, the supervisor should be expected to take steps quickly to deal with the conflict of interest. Sometimes supervision of the junior employee can be transferred to another manager. Or the senior member of the pair might discuss the situation with management.

This kind of policy may serve another purpose. The supervisor who is a target of unwanted seduction attempts, as well as the employee who is unhappy at being propositioned, is often reluctant to hurt the other person's feelings. And often it may not be clear whether unwelcome sexual overtures should be considered harassment.

It can help in such situations for the beleaguered party to have a company policy to fall back on so that it becomes unnecessary to define a proposition as harassment or to tell someone that he or she is not an attractive partner. It is simpler to say, "We can't."

Finally, a company policy against sexual relationships in supervision may be critical to the success of mentoring programs for women. It is absolutely vital to the success of women that they be seen to advance on the basis of the quality of their work and that they receive the same guidance and sponsorship that men receive.

Successful mentor alliances require men and women to work closely together. Thus men must feel free to encourage and criticize the performance of women without innuendo from others and without provoking suspicion. Programs for advancement, for men as well as for women, can succeed only in an atmosphere where neither harassment nor the fear of it exists.

Notes

1. For models of procedures, see Ronald Berenbeim, *Non-Union Complaint Procedures* (New York: Conference Board, 1980); also see Mary P. Rowe and Clarence G. Williams, "The MIT Non-Union Grievance Procedure: An Upward Feedback, Mediation Model" (Cambridge: MIT, 1980).

12
Case of the Borderline Black

THEODORE V. PURCELL

Preferential treatment of minority employees is a problem that few corporations have come to grips with successfully. This is an actual case (though disguised) in which management finds that one of the few eligible candidates for a required reduction in force happens to be a black with a so-so record of performance.

David Kimball stood by the window of his Philadelphia office, looking high out over the Schuylkill River Valley. He was waiting for his Design Engineering manager, Paul Kelley, to arrive for a 10:30 conference. In his hand was a memo Kelley had sent him after the meeting of section heads the day before. It read:

> I have considered the alternatives, and clearly LSI circuits is the program to cut back. I recommend letting two of our engineers on that project go. But I thought you ought to know that one of the two is Thomas Rawlins, the only black engineer we have in Design. What do we do about that?

Kimball, a trim and athletic 51, was manager of the Engineering Department of Industrial Computer Products, the largest division of multinational Inter-

Published in 1971.

With comments by Frank S. Jones, Ford Professor of Urban Affairs in Civil Engineering, M.I.T., John A. Lang, Manufacturing Manager, Analog Devices, Inc., William C. Musham, President, I-T-E Imperial Corporation, Leon H. Sullivan, Chairman of the Board, Opportunities Industrialization Centers, Inc., and Frank J. Toner, Manager, Employee Relations Management and Practices, General Electric Company.

Author's Note. Considerable credit for the preparation of this case and its interpretation goes to my research assistant, Miss Irene E. Wylie.

national Business Systems, Inc. He had risen far in the company and hoped to go farther.

As he gazed out the window, Kimball thought back to his student debate-team days at Cornell, when he had spoken passionately about the race question in 1940, years before the general acceptance of civil rights causes. And he remembered his satisfaction three years ago when Tom Rawlins became his first black engineer.

The sight of a jet plane arching steeply up from the Philadelphia airport brought Kimball's thoughts back to the present. He lit a cigarette to clear his mind for the conference coming up with Paul Kelley. Systematically, he assembled and sorted out his thoughts about the meeting two days ago when his boss, Harold Page, vice president in charge of the division, had announced the cutback.

Page, 60 and a product of the Depression, was a hard driver with a brilliant mind, devoted to the rapid expansion of the industrial computer business. He demanded a lot from his managers. At the meeting Page had quoted part of a memo from the executive vice president, Louis Kagan, which read:

> The Automation Group of International Business Systems must take serious action. We have reviewed the rate of incoming orders and projected our expense levels from the last two quarters. I am convinced that for the balance of this year we are going to have to trim expenses throughout the Group. A 10 percent reduction is a reasonable target for the Industrial Computer Products Divison.

The cutback was inevitable, of course, in light of the current recession, Kimball remembered thinking. IBS had grown into a successful company not only through its alertness in moving in on new technology, products, and markets, but also through its skill in controlling costs, adjusting to changing business conditions, and quickly trimming fat and eliminating unprofitable products.

But Page wanted to go further than Kagan. He had continued:

> I've reviewed our incoming orders rate, our inventory, our backlog, and our cost structure, and I'm convinced that ICP can and should reduce costs 15 percent. I want each of our departments to take a long look at how we can cut back.

The department managers, although not surprised by Page's higher goal, had reacted negatively, for cost cutting is not easy and letting employees go is one of the hardest tasks a manager faces. Both Kimball and Toby Marotta, employee relations manager, had protested the 15 percent target. But Page had said, "We're determined to go beyond the demands of the New York office. I'm sorry, but you're going to have to cut your costs 15 percent for the next two quarters. Find ways and means to do it."

Later Kimball had called a meeting with the managers of his five sections—Software Applications, Design Engineering, Production Engineering, Drafting, and Model Shop—to inform them of Page's decision. He had talked to each about where the cost reductions should be made.

To Paul Kelley of Design Engineering he had suggested, "I think we might stretch out that LSI circuit program, Paul, don't you?" Kelley had said, "Well, I'll see what I can do about it, Dave. I think we can."

"But I didn't know," said Kimball now to himself, "that it would mean that Tom Rawlins has to go. Well, let's see what Kelley says."

"Come in, Paul." Kelley strode in and eased his big frame into a chair by Kimball's desk. Just 40, likable, craggy-faced, he looked more like a football coach than an engineer.

"Thanks for your memo," said Kimball. "I'm asking Toby Marotta from Employee Relations to sit in with us. We need advice on this." Just then Marotta came in.

At 38, Marotta was young for an industrial relations manager, but he had had broad experience in three different locations of the IBS Automation Group, and was once in operating management.

"Thanks for coming, Toby," said Kimball. "Here's the problem. In order to meet that cutback, I've asked Paul Kelley to take two engineers out of Design Engineering. Paul and I agree that the program to slow down is large-scale integration circuits. LSI circuits is a development program for our next-generation computer, so we can slow it down without hurting any systems now in production or on the market.

"But Paul tells me that one of the two people who should be cut from that project is Tom Rawlins, who, you know, is the first black engineer we hired, a few years ago. I'd like to keep Rawlins, but we're in a tight spot. Think you can help?"

Marotta smiled and shrugged. "You know me. No miracles. Just difficult questions."

Kimball turned to Kelley. "Fill us in, Paul, on your reasons for recommending that Rawlins be laid off."

"Sure, Dave," said Kelley. "I hate to do it. I've gotten to like the guy myself, but I don't see any way around it. We have three men on the LSI program. One is Jack Martin, a real hot-shot engineer. I can cut back on the program, but I can't cut back on Jack Martin. He's the center of it. The other two are Rawlins and a white fellow, Longworth Smith. Neither of them have been with us long, and neither are going to become really great engineers. And they couldn't keep LSI circuits going alone. Martin can."

"But you have about 35 engineers in Design," Marotta interjected, looking at the roster. "Couldn't you let any of them go in place of Rawlins?"

"Hold on! It's 29, not 35; I've already lost 6 men and I'm pressed. But I did think of the alternatives. If I move Rawlins to another project, I'll have to take a more experienced man off it. I'm afraid Rawlins wouldn't be able to pull his own weight, and we can't afford to get behind in production now."

"Could you spell that out a bit, Paul?" asked Kimball. "What makes you think that Rawlins wouldn't cut it?"

"Let's face it," Kelley replied. "It's rough for any man to pick up a new job. It would take time before he knew it as well as someone who has been on the job nine months. I'm just not sure he would be able to catch on fast enough to maintain our schedules.

"And then there's the problem of backlash. If Rawlins bumps a white fellow, there's going to be talk of preferential treatment. As a matter of fact, there was some bad feeling several months ago among my engineers when there were rumors that some blacks over in the Manufacturing Department were favored during a layoff. If the men are resentful, they won't help Rawlins much. It would mean hours lost in poor morale."

"How do you think Rawlins would react to a situation like that?" asked Marotta.

"Well, he's a pleasant fellow—no chip on his shoulder," Kelley said. "And he's pretty well liked now. He might be able to win them around eventually, but you can't tell. It's a risk I don't feel I can take. And, frankly, I'm not sure Rawlins is really worth it. If he were white, I wouldn't even have brought it to your attention."

Kimball frowned and made a few notations on a pad. "We'd better have a look at Rawlins' background," he said.

"Rawlins is 34 years old," said Kelley, looking at his notes. "He got a B.S. in electrical engineering from Brooklyn Poly after a stint in the Army. His grades were fair. Let's see. . . . His previous job was an electrical engineering position with a construction company, and before that he did designing of telephone equipment.

"As you know, Dave, we hired him in 1968, and I was the one who did the hiring. As I think I told you then, he did seem marginally qualified for a job in this department. After all, our men are a cut above average. I'll be honest: if he'd been white, I don't think we'd have taken him on. But he seemed to have a good attitude and real potential."

"I remember," said Kimball. "That was about the time we began to ask, 'If a person isn't perfectly qualified now, is he qualifiable?' Black engineers were hard to come by, and '68 was a good year. We could afford to take a gamble on a man who might make it. But I seem to recall that there were some problems with Rawlins at first."

"Yes, there were," Kelley said. "Rawlins had some difficulty on a design. We had a complaint from the Manufacturing Department a couple of years ago on one of his projects. He was catching his mistakes late, Toby, and he had to send through quite a few alteration notices. Then Manufacturing was sore because it slowed down their production and raised their costs."

Marotta, looking up from the notebook on which he was doodling, asked, "What's your experience with other new engineers, Paul? Have other men had this kind of problem?"

"Well, even our experienced men send through alteration notices once in a while. But this was a bad case. Sure, I've had others that bad—some that eventually turned out well—but we worry about them."

"You were able to straighten Rawlins' problem out, as I recall," said Kimball.

"Well," Kelley went on, "he is doing much better now, but the situation got worse before it got better. Part of the problem was the Drafting and Model Shop men. You know what they're like—no engineering degrees, but they know an awful lot about their particular job, and once they find an engineer like Rawlins who isn't very sure of himself, they're going to give him a hard time. Then, of course, Rawlins being black didn't help matters.

"After that problem project, some of them didn't want to work for him at all. But I had a talk with Rawlins. I told him that when he is talking to these technicians, he should take a position and hold on to it. I spoke to the men too, and told them that no one is going to refuse to work for the man I assign him to."

Marotta broke in. "Let's go back to Dave's point about qualifiability, Paul. Do you think Rawlins really has the aptitude for an engineer's job in this unit? Were you able to do anything about his problem with design?"

Kimball looked up from his note pad and said, "I remember authorizing a two-week training program for Rawlins up in New York. That helped, didn't it?"

"It did," Kelley answered. "I also thought it would help to put him on this LSI project so that Jack Martin, the engineer I was telling you about, could kind of work along with Rawlins and bring him out a bit. He's been on LSI circuits ten months now and he's doing all right. He's developing, though slowly.

"But when I think how well he's responded to what we've demanded of him, it's gratifying. In the long run, Rawlins may be as good as some of the fellows I need to keep because of their experience on important jobs. But I have to remind myself that I'm not running a vocational training school; I'm managing a design unit in a highly competitive business. I really have no alternative but to recommend that he and Smith go."

Kimball turned to Marotta. "Toby, your business is 'people business.' What are your reactions?"

"Just a few comments, Dave. Paul's right in hesitating to let Martin or any other really bright young guys go. You need to grow talent for Design Engineering. The service picture of these men doesn't help much, either. Rawlins has only been with IBS three years, and I doubt that you have many other people with less service."

"I have a couple," said Kelley, "but they're in key positions. I can't do without them."

"Okay, let's try another tack," Marotta said. He turned to Kimball. "Could you use Rawlins in the Production Engineering Section, Dave?"

Kimball leaned back in his chair, lit a cigarette, and looked at Kelley and Marotta. "Well, fellows, of course I've thought of that, but it's impossible. I've asked the Production Engineering manager to cut back too, and I couldn't ask him to take on a new man who has no working knowledge of the products and isn't familiar with the factory end of it, not at a time like this."

Marotta nodded. "I can see that would be rough, Dave. But at the same time we've got to consider our affirmative action commitments. Let's look at the statistics. If you let Rawlins go, that means no blacks at all in the Design Engineering Section.

"But let's talk about the whole Engineering Department, which is your biggest concern, Dave. You supervise some 150 professionals and 90 nonprofessionals."

"That's right."

Marotta looked at his notebook. "Your nonprofessionals are 6.6 percent black. That's not too bad. But if you let Rawlins go, that brings your minority percentage for professionals down from 2.6 to 2 percent. That's low when you consider Philadelphia's large black population. That cut will certainly be noticed in our next federal contract compliance review."

"But it's not just a question of flak from the examiners, Toby," Kimball put in. "I personally feel that New York management was right in urging us to build up our black proportions in IBS, and I'd like to do what I can in our department."

"But at the same time, Dave," Kelley interrupted with some heat, "you're telling me I've got to cut two men to meet our cost reduction target. Now, the only two men I can see to let go, in all honesty, are Smith and Rawlins. We'll both be in trouble if we get our production schedules snared up."

"That's the key problem, isn't it?" said Marotta. He opened a small blue pamphlet. "Take another look at our IBS affirmative action policy: 'You should recognize that we are all expected to fulfill our Equal Employment Affirmative Action responsibilities while at the same time achieving our profitability goals. It's not an either/or situation, and one does not give relief from the other.'"

Kimball snorted. "Well, that helps a lot, doesn't it!"

"It does give you the parameters anyway, Dave," Marotta said. "Those aren't just empty words in that policy. Well, I guess the ball is in your court. It's your decision. I can't give you a pat answer."

Kimball snuffed out his cigarette and said with a sigh, "Well, thanks, fellows. I'll let you know tomorrow."

Kimball sat at his desk, solitary, concerned, puzzled. mechanically he jotted down on a pad of paper the issues to be balanced, to be judged. The pros and the cons. The decision was his, all right.

He had to cut costs. LSI was the program to be cut in Design Engineering. He respected Kelley's judgment. He wanted to retain Rawlins, but he did not want to hurt Engineering's production by preferring Rawlins over some better qualified white engineer. He considered going to Page, but promptly rejected it because he knew that Page would be unsympathetic.

He thought of the excellent reputation of the Engineering Department. He thought of his own reputation and his future. Once you got soft on one decision, you could easily get soft on any decision. But was it really getting soft?

Kimball recalled the phrases of the IBS policy guide that Marotta had read: ". . . expected to fulfill our Equal Employment Affirmative Action responsibilities while at the same time achieving our profitability goals." Big help. "It's not an either/or situation." Big help. "One does not give relief from the other." Big help.

Yet what else could those policy makers in New York say? The decision was his.

For a strange moment he saw himself at the tiller of his ketch, plunging through waves off the Maine coast. Easier to sail a boat than manage a department under pressure. You could be pretty sure of the wind and the sea and a boat you knew.

Kimball got up from his desk. He walked over and stood alone by the window of his Philadelphia office, looking out over the Schuylkill River Valley.

Query to Readers

Suppose you were standing in Kimball's place by the window. What would you do about Thomas Rawlins? Would you fire him? If so, what justification would you offer? Would you keep him on the LSI circuit project and let Martin go? Transfer him to another project in Design Engineering? Or Production Engineering? Are there other alternatives? How would you evaluate Paul Kelley's position? Toby Marotta's role?

And finally—the broadest questions—would you consider it preferential treatment to keep Rawlins anywhere in the department? Do you think that a company should practice preferential treatment? Should International Business Systems establish a policy to handle cases like this one? Could the company have done something to prevent this situation from arising?

After you have formed your opinions on these questions and any others that may come to mind, compare your views with those of the commentators and the author that follow. The commentators are five men selected for their experience with minority manpower. One is the president of a large international electrical company; another is a prominent leader of the black community; the third set up the equal employment opportunity and minority relations department in a major electrical company; the fourth is manufacturing manager of a small, fast-growing company employing a number of blacks; and the fifth is a former paper company executive, now a professor of engineering and urban affairs at M.I.T.

What Should Kimball Do?

One of the commentators has no doubts at all that Rawlins should be retained. Three others think that Kimball should keep Rawlins, at least until all alternatives have been explored. But John A. Lang, Manufacturing Manager of Analog Devices, Inc., who is a strong liberal on the race question, differs:

> It is painfully apparent that Tom Rawlins is at best a marginal performer. Launching a rescue operation for this man at the sacrifice of a major contributor like Jack Martin would create substantial personnel problems which would eventually cripple the LSI project and IBS's competitive position in this field.

> Paul Kelley reacted as a responsible unit manager. He had to maintain an adequate level of talent to uphold the reputation of the department. He arrived at the only logical conclusion after considering his schedules and the job he had to accomplish. Kelley did everything he could to help Rawlins by sending him to a two-week training course and placing him with a highly competent engineer like Martin.

Reverend Leon H. Sullivan, founder and Board Chairman of the Opportunities Industrialization Centers of America (black-run training organizations) and a member of the Board of General Motors, disagrees with Mr. Lang both in his evaluation of Rawlins and in his advice:

> Kimball should hold on to the black man. He could shift him to another job. Or he could build him into the budget another way, make a job for him; Kimball supervises a system there with over a hundred workers. Or maybe he ought to make him an administrative assistant to make his workers more sensitive to the black-white problem in America and to keep some 'color' in the place.

> It is significant that this black man had an engineering degree during the 1960's, when there were few blacks willing to go into engineering because they didn't see opportunities there. The fact that this man was motivated toward this kind of vocation is significant. People seem to get along well with him, and he's grown. They took him to a training session; Kelley said he improved somewhat. Maybe they ought to take him to some more training sessions. If holding on to him means shifting him, they should do that. If it means creating another job, do that.

> I'm sure this manager is going to get a pat on the back from the guy at the top for working out the problem, because all big businesses are sensitive to black employment now. As a matter of fact, if IBS lets this man go, and he goes to the NAACP, they'll file a suit against IBS and have the whole company looked at.

Kimball should even do more. He should find a way to get more blacks in his section. And you will find, if this thing is done right, they're not going to cut down on profits.

Not Whether, But How.   There is no doubt either in the mind of Frank S. Jones, Ford Professor of Urban Affairs in Civil Engineering at M.I.T.:

> Given the facts in this case, the question is how, rather than whether, Thomas Rawlins should be retained.
>
> The situation calls for an evaluation of all 150 professionals in the department on some common scale. Rawlins may be No. 2 (or is it 3?) to Jack Martin, but how does he relate to the remainder of the professionals in the department? I am aware of Kelley's statement, 'If he'd been white, I don't think we'd have taken him on.' Nevertheless, Kelley has already let six engineers—presumably all of them white—go. Can't we assume that Rawlins was at least as qualified as they?
>
> If necessary, Kimball should go to Page with this argument: 'cutting back 15 percent, instead of 10 percent, may hurt our ability to compete tomorrow. Moreover, it could mean letting Rawlins go. Is it worth exceeding Kagan's goal of 5 percent, when simply meeting it or exceeding it by a lesser amount could mean better balance between the long and short term as well as economic and social considerations?
>
> The company could seek the engineers' reaction to a proposed salary cut progressive with higher salaries and ranging from 5 to 10 percent on the part of all professional personnel.

William C. Musham, President of I-T-E Imperial Corporation, thinks that Kimball has not investigated the situation adequately:

> Despite his confidence in Kelley's judgment, Kimball should satisfy himself that the facts are as stated. He can do this through discreet personal interviews and checking of performance records to make sure some prejudices do not exist which he himself may not recognize.

If the facts are as stated, what can Kimball do? In Mr. Musham's view:

> While none of the alternatives to laying off Rawlins that are presented in the case seems tenable, it is inconceivable to me that in a company as large as this one there does not exist a wide range of alternatives to those under discussion. Among them are transferring Rawlins to another division of the company, assigning him to a lengthy company-sponsored training program, and finding him another kind of job.

Because of the serious organizational and policy problems that Mr. Musham sees at IBS (which will be discussed later), it may be impossible to adopt any of these alternatives. But Mr. Musham agrees strongly with Mr. Jones that Kimball must go to Page:

Distasteful as it may be, Kimball should face up to Page, so that the situation is clearly understood at that level. If Kimball doesn't inform Page, he is not fulfilling his full responsibility as a manager. Problems like this should not be swept under the mat in a lower-level manager's office; they should be highlighted.

If Page properly understands the situation, it may well be possible for him to find other alternatives, even perhaps to the extent of holding Rawlins for another six months with the real chance that some other opportunity may arise to use him.

What "Affirmative Action" Means. Frank J. Toner, Manager of Employee Relations Management and Practice at the General Electric Company, also questions the resourcefulness of IBS in making use of Rawlins' abilities:

Were any efforts made to cross-train Rawlins, to enhance his basic skills so that he could be moved into other areas?

Affirmative action does not simply mean hiring a Tom Rawlins and being a little patient with his design problems. Providing training to assist the individual toward full qualification and upward mobility is basic to affirmative action—as is restructuring jobs and responsibilities to fit his talent, background, and experience.

Judging from the low minority participation rates at IBS compared with the city, the attitude of management, and the perceived reactions of employees, it does not appear that many of these affirmative action considerations were factored into the decision-making process.

If, however, top management has thoroughly explored the alternatives, examined the tradeoffs, and found that the affirmative action tests have been met, laying Rawlins off would be a proper course of action. In that case, the affirmative action policy would require an effort to place him elsewhere in a position where he could make a contribution.

Management Deficiencies

The commentators' advice for Kimball leads directly to criticism of IBS top management. As Mr. Musham points out:

The company's bureaucracy is saddling Kimball with a problem that top management should come to grips with. The issuance of a broad policy statement subject to wide interpretation is simply not enough. It is manifestly unfair to put the burden on a lower-level manager whose decision can then be 'Monday-morning quarterbacked' all the way up the hierarchy.

Marotta, who should be able to help, unfortunately confines his contribution to quoting company policy and a few statistics. The Industrial Relations Department should be in a position to make a more positive contribution and, through its staff connections, keep top management advised of this and similar situations.

It may be possible, for example, to establish a small review board in the office of the Vice President of Industrial Relations to check the progress of all blacks of professional or managerial status. Before such a person was to be laid off or discharged, his case would be referred to this board.

It may also be desirable for each black professional or manager to have a long-term professional or managerial employee as a personal adviser. This adviser, as in the case of the Japanese system described by Peter F. Drucker,[1] would be outside the immediate chain of command affecting the individual he is advising. This counselor's assistance might well be crucial to the person's ultimate success.

Mr. Toner agrees that top management has an important stake in Kimball's decision, and he implies that Kimball's problem may be symptomatic of other organization problems:

Top management should use this situation as an opportunity to evaluate its performance in providing affirmative action in the broadest sense, and should hold its managers accountable for the ultimate decision. For example, I would ask of the employee relations man, 'What about Rawlins' performance appraisals? Is the company's manpower system providing for personnel development? Doesn't this case point up certain faults in the manpower system?' Shouldn't Marotta reevaluate the system and try to make a more positive contribution to the solution of the problem?

Rev. Sullivan and Mr. Lang agree that Toby Marotta is weak. The latter points out:

Whether an affirmative action policy is merely an apple-pie-and-motherhood thing or gets turned into a useful tool depends a great deal on communication from the personnel department.

Constructive Action. Beyond the negative aspects of top management's performance, there was comment about positive action that IBS could undertake. Mr. Musham says:

I find disquieting the company's use of flat percentage targets to reduce expenses and meet the declining volume situation. Kagan has set a goal of 10 percent, and Page, perhaps to make himself as well as the division look good, goes a little further. No one can quarrel, of course, with the need for prompt, effective, and ruthless cost cutting in a crisis.

However, the upper levels of management must go well beyond flat setting of broad targets by establishing priorities and suggesting alternatives to reach stated goals. For example, it was primarily Kimball's decision to cut back on LSI circuit development—a decision that may or may not have been consistent with other company goals.

In regard to resolution of apparently conflicting goals, Mr. Jones makes an important point:

> Beyond the case facts, the issue might be defined as how IBS, or any other company, should implement its policy of achieving its profitability goals, and at the same time fulfill its equal employment affirmative action responsibilities.

All of the commentators believe that both goals must be met. While Mr. Toner and Mr. Musham stress the resources available within the corporation, Mr. Jones stresses the resources available in its industry, reasoning that a company that overburdened itself in helping minority workers could be overwhelmed by the competition. He makes the following comment:

> Aggressive individual initiative is needed to stimulate aggressive industrywide action. For instance, IBS could initiate with the IBMs, Honeywells, and Digital Equipments a proportional assessment, the proceeds to go toward training of blacks as electrical, mechanical, and other engineers. These companies could collaborate with the M.I.T.s and Cal Techs, as well as the Howards and North Carolina A&Ts, to identify and train blacks, providing them with summer internships, and so forth, to expand the pool.

> Likewise, when cutbacks become necessary to maintain profits, companies should try imaginative plans, such as that proposed by Walter Reuther for the automotive industry. For example, lay off first some of the people protected by government and industrial benefit plans, rather than the recently trained and hired.

Mr. Lang, concerned with the problems of introducing minority group members to the industrial setting, has a different, but similarly long-range, perspective:

> If IBS is truly concerned about the plight of minority groups in America today, it should cooperate with self-help training programs administered by community groups in the ghetto and thereby take the first steps in attracting minority group members to industry.

> An investment like this will have little immediate effect upon the company's ability to attract qualified minority professionals. The gains are extremely long term. These programs are essentially aimed at getting people off the street and into the factory. But if you can get one generation off the street, there is hope that the second may finish high school, and maybe the third will get a college degree and become engineers.

> Working through local groups is very important because it allows a man to feel that he is improving himself through an organization administered by his people and in his neighborhood. Unless he is able to identify with the program, communication will not be effective and the program will not succeed in exposing people in the ghetto to industry.

Underlying Issue

While policy alone can be merely rhetoric, policy obviously is essential. And the underlying issue in formulating a policy for this kind of situation is the question of preferential treatment. Rev. Sullivan wants frank and unashamed preferential practices in favor of minorities:

> In the first place, International Business Systems has been guilty of de facto segregation and discrimination against black workers, as have 99 percent of the industrial institutions in America. Any organization that has grown to the size of IBS and only in 1968 hired one black man in this particular department has been guilty of de facto discrimination.
>
> Someone might object that there were not sufficient blacks who were trained as engineers. That is begging the question. Many of these large businesses assisted in training whites for engineering positions. Many colleges and universities have engineering programs underwritten by large industrial institutions.
>
> The whole industrial and engineering system in America is geared together. IBS has an obligation, as part of a democratic industrial system, to encourage, support, supply, and in every way possible provide for more blacks and minorities in the engineering field.
>
> A big question in all this is: Do you want to show preferential treatment to black people? The answer is *yes*. If a black man has to be upgraded over a white man to fill a certain category, where an insufficient number of blacks have been employed, there should be discrimination for him. There should be discrimination against white people in upgrading a black over a white into a job classification where blacks have been excluded or were employed in an insufficiently large number.
>
> In time, that white man will be promoted into the higher job classification anyhow. Black people have been waiting for a hundred years; white men can wait for a few months.
>
> Should you fire white people to hire black people? No. However, I would fire a white person to hold on to a black person, particularly in a situation where there's only one black man in a department. Even in a recession, I would look favorably on maintaining black workers because there are so few.

The Department Black?   Mr. Lang, on the other hand, thinks that a policy that includes preferential treatment is bound to fail. He makes these observations:

> In facing similar problems, my goal has been to exercise color-blind objectivity as much as is humanly possible. I do not believe one could evolve a separate policy for minority group layoffs without generating a multitude of secondary backlash problems—certainly not in a small or medium-sized company with an uncomplicated bureaucracy that gives you nothing to hide behind. If I exhibited color preference in my layoff

decisions, I would be failing in my basic commitment to maintain a viable manufacturing facility.

The man who is treated preferentially is just as aware of the situation as one who experiences discrimination. A company could not continue this unrealistic policy very long without facing substantial problems with both its white and black employees.

The basic point is that Tom Rawlins was the 'department black.' The real problem IBS should address is the conditions that discourage minority group members from reaching professional employment status.

Mr. Toner tends to agree with Rev. Sullivan, although he prefers the phrase "affirmative action" to the word "preferential":

The painful but inevitable consequence, in the face of declining sales, a pinch on profits, and the need to reduce expenses, is manpower cutbacks. Yet the need for companies to maintain a positive approach to affirmative action cannot be set aside because of a business downturn.

Affirmative action means more than providing equal employment opportunity—it also means living up to the law of the land, in response to Presidential executive orders and Title VII of the Civil Rights Act. Affirmative action means creating the proper climate to gain management and employee understanding of the need for extra effort and special training to combat problems that minorities may encounter because of institutional and societal discrimination.

Affirmative action means seeking out individuals whose potential has not been developed, with the objective of assisting them to meet employment standards. Affirmative action also includes finding additional sources of applicants who can become qualified, utilizing appropriate training to assist them toward full qualification, and developing programs to ensure upward mobility when they become qualified.

Mr. Musham supports special treatment for blacks, but points out that this is not necessarily preferential. In his words:

Most people will agree that some kind of special treatment is necessary to stimulate upward mobility for those blacks who are able and willing to pay the price for advancement. It is wrong to think of this as preferential treatment, which, of course, implies discrimination against someone else. The employment of blacks in professional and managerial jobs can be handled by most companies on a constructive basis without the overtones of discrimination against whites.

Toward Qualification

Retaining Rawlins by firing a better qualified white man is clearly preferential treatment. To justify preferential practice, this important condition must be made: the black person who receives such treatment is either qualified now for the work required or can become qualified after a reasonable period of time.

To help someone merely because of his identity with a certain race, with no reference to ability, robs him of his self-respect. It is actually a kind of paternalistic racism in disguise. Surely a black man, or any person, wants to be hired or promoted eventually because he is valued as a person who can do the job.

Preferential practices for black Americans at work are not something necessary forever. Eventually such special attention will become unnecessary. In time we should not have to notice a man's race in hiring him, promoting him, or laying him off. But now we do.

Furthermore, in considering preferential practices, we should never forget the place of *individual* attention to any person on the job. Apart from race, sex, age, or length of service, the employee is an individual. Ideally, management should look at him as an individual, and as far as possible deal with him as an individual.

What About Backlash?   One of the fears of managers about preferential treatment (and the main reason they do not use the term) is that it may arouse fierce white backlash.

But this fear can be exaggerated. Rev. Sullivan writes:

> White backlash? Wait until paycheck time comes! When management
> holds on to black fellows, white backlash lasts for a couple of paychecks.

In our field studies for *Blacks in the Industrial World* we found integration accepted much better than expected in two plants in Virginia and Tennessee. Preferential hiring of a small number of disadvantaged blacks in two Northern plants and very rapid, though nonpreferential, black hiring at a plant in Chicago were also achieved with little significant resentment.

The key to acceptance seems to be a firm management stand. As Mr. Toner points out, part of a manager's affirmative action responsibility is helping create a climate where employees can learn to understand the need for special efforts on behalf of blacks.

"Some More Equal Than Others."   Many believe that preferential practice for Negroes in this country is not only impractical and conducive to white backlash, but also un-American and unconstitutional. It seems to be an attempt to punish today's white workers because yesterday's were not fair— discrimination in reverse. But when we look at the myths of equality, or rewards by merit, in American society, we are reminded that "all men are equal, but some more equal than others."

The American economy, though based on competition, is replete with instances of government intervention to favor one group at the expense of other groups. To name a few, there are land grants to the railroads, depletion allowances to extractive industries, subsidies to farmers, tariffs favoring certain industries, the Social Security program with weighted benefits, and civil service preference to war veterans.

Preferential practice among private groups has often been the rule. Consider, for instance, law firms that prefer Harvard or Michigan law school graduates, craft unions that discriminate in favor of sons or nephews of union members, reciprocal purchasing agreements between companies, "WASP" company managements that choose their associates because of family ties or name, and non-WASP companies that exclude WASPs. Favoritism is not so uncommon.

What the Law Says. The Civil Rights Act of 1964 neither requires an employer or labor organization to give preferential treatment nor forbids it, except insofar as the tenor of the law is equal treatment with respect to race.

However, the Office of Federal Contract Compliance goes far beyond the Civil Rights Act. Its Order No. 4 requires that a government contractor remedy any *underutilization* of minority people in his company. Underutilization means having fewer minority workers in a given job category "than would be reasonably expected by their availability."

Expectations are formulated by looking at the minority population, the minority unemployment, and the minority work force in the area, including the degrees of skill that could be reasonably recruited, and finally by looking at the promotability of minority people already employed. The contractor is also expected to deal with outside training institutions and consider what training he could reasonably provide to build up his minority work force, guided implicitly by percentages of available persons in the area.

Order No. 4 makes no mention of preferential practice. It does not set inflexible quotas but, rather, uses "targets" as one measurement of the "good faith effort" applied to an affirmative action plan. The directive also asserts that it is "not to be used to discriminate against any applicant or employee [presumably whites] because of race, color, religion, sex, or national origin." But the order implicitly calls for a certain amount of preferential practice.

Justifying Preference

Discrimination and segregation have separated Negroes as a group from the rest of American society, leading to lower per-capita income, often inferior education, and a constellation of sociological and psychic disabilities for many, although of course not for all, blacks. Collectively, blacks have been alienated from the rest of American society not by any innate inferiority but by white racism.

Because humans are social beings, inevitably shaped by the social and economic structures within which they live, justice is not achieved simply by ensuring the rights of persons as individuals. Justice also requires just socioeconomic institutions.

When encrusted patterns of education, employment, and housing put one group at a disadvantage, we are obligated to change those institutions. Whites have a moral obligation to help reform those institutions and make them open to all Americans.

Since preferential practice gives a specific advantage to a black person over a white, however, each situation must be looked at carefully, with a balancing of the needs of those concerned. There might be cases where the white worker would have such a great need for a certain job or a certain promotion that the argument on behalf of blacks would not prevail.

The choice before us may be rapid integration and upgrading of blacks or an escalation of the turmoil and polarization of the 1960's and early 1970's. Unless radical change takes place, blacks and whites may grow farther apart, rending the very fabric of American life.

Such reasoning is not intended to be a "law and order" argument. It is more important to have a just social order than to have a peaceful one. Life in the plantation days of slavery was tranquil enough, but it also represented a shocking violation of the human dignity of almost half its citizens. Peace under justice involves not only blacks but *all* Americans; our entire community is entitled to the peace and order necessary for a stable and happy society.

In Kimball's Shoes.   Since I pressed the five commentators, I must give my own judgment as if I were standing in Kimball's shoes by the window. Rawlins should be retained and efforts made to find a place for him. IBS has a long way to go to strengthen its efforts for minorities. Given the proper precautions, preferential treatment for Rawlins or any other minority employee is justifiable and desirable.

Let two of the commentators state the author's thesis—a thesis, incidentally, as relevant for unions, universities, and hospitals as for business—emerging from "Case of the Borderline Black." First Mr. Jones:

> Ultimately, the issue is whether corporate economic power should be used to end economic discrimination in the United States. Blacks do not have 11 percent of the things worth having, economic or political or social, in a country whose tendencies cluster around having.

> What combination of elements of wisdom and fear are needed to stimulate the private power interests, whose power has been used immorally in regard to the powerless condition of blacks, to use that power to promote a more equitable distribution of income and net worth?

And now Mr. Toner:

> A new measure of management is emerging in this decade of the social seventies. We will be measured by the success with which the enterprise

reconciles its return on investment with its social responsibilities. It's no longer either/or, but both in tandem. Growth alone is no longer a valid corporate objective. Now the goal must include growth and social responsibility or, better still, growth through social responsibility.

Notes

1. See his article, "What We Can Learn from Japanese Management," *HBR* March–April 1971, p. 110.

What It's Like to Be a Black Manager

EDWARD W. JONES, JR.

This author contends that most companies fail to recognize the crucial difference between recruiting blacks with executive potential and providing the much-needed organizational support to help them realize this potential. He cites his own experience in a large company to illustrate the type of lonely struggle that faces a black man in the absence of such support. Then he draws some lessons from this experience that should help management to overcome the subtle ramifications of racial differences within organizations.

When I was graduated from a predominantly black college, I was offered a job in one of the largest corporations in America. On reporting for work, I received a motivational speech from the personnel officer and acknowledged that I agreed with his opinion: the job was going to be challenging in its own right; however, the added burden of prejudice could make it unbearable. In a tone of bravado I said, "I promise you that I won't quit; you'll have to fire me."

At the time, I did not know how important that promise would become. For I was about to begin the most trying experience of my life—the rise to middle management in a white corporation. During those years, I found myself examining my actions, strategies, and emotional stability. I found myself trying desperately to separate fact from mental fiction. I found myself enveloped in almost unbearable emotional stress and internal conflict, trying to hold the job as a constant and evaluate my personal shortcomings with respect to it. At times I would look at myself in a mirror and wonder whether I had lost my mental balance. Somehow I always managed to answer positively, if not resolutely.

Published in 1973.

I think that my experiences should prove helpful to companies that are wrestling with the problem of how to move black employees from the entry level into positions of greater responsibility. I say this because the manner in which many companies are approaching the problem indicates to me that a number of well-intentioned efforts are doomed to failure.

Failure is likely because most companies merely substitute blacks in positions formerly filled by whites and then, acting as if the corporate environment is not color-sensitive, consider their obligation over. In short, U.S. business has failed to recognize the embryonic black manager's increased chances of failure due to the potentially negative impact of racially based prejudgments. Gaining acceptance in the organization, which the embryonic white manager takes for granted, can be a serious problem for his black counterpart.

The Job Offer

My story begins when I happened to bump into a recruiter who was talking to a friend of mine. On gathering that I was a college senior, the recruiter asked whether I had considered his company as an employer. I responded, "Are you kidding me—you don't have any black managers, do you?" He replied, "No, but that's why I'm here."

I did well in a subsequent interview procedure, and received an invitation for a company tour. Still skeptical, I accepted, feeling that I had nothing to lose. During a lunch discussion concerning the contemplated job and its requirements, I experienced my first reminder that I was black. After a strained silence, one of the executives at our table looked at me, smiled, and said, "Why is it that everyone likes Roy Campanella, but so many people dislike Jackie Robinson?"

I knew that this man was trying to be pleasant; yet I felt nothing but disgust at what seemed a ridiculous deterioration in the level of conversation. Here was the beginning of the games that I expected but dreaded playing. The question was demeaning and an insult to my intelligence. It was merely a rephrasing of the familiar patronizing comment, "One of my best friends is a negro." Most blacks recognize this type of statement as a thinly veiled attempt to hide bias. After all, if a person is unbiased, why does he make such a point of trying to prove it?

In the fragment of time between the question and my response, the tension within me grew. Were these people serious about a job offer? If so, what did they expect from me? I had no desire to be the corporate black in a glass office, but I did not wish to be abrasive or ungracious if the company was sincere about its desire to have an integrated organization.

There was no way to resolve these kinds of questions at that moment, so I gathered up my courage and replied, "Roy Campanella is a great baseball player. But off the field he is not an overwhelming intellectual challenge to anyone. Jackie Robinson is great both on and off the baseball field. He is very intelligent and therefore more a threat than Roy Campanella. In fact, I'm sure that if he wanted to, he could out-perform you in your job."

There was a stunned silence around the table, and from that point on until I arrived back at the employment office, I was sure that I had ended any chances of receiving a job offer.

I was wrong. I subsequently received an outstanding salary offer from the recruiter. But I had no intention of being this company's showcase black and asked seriously, "Why do you want me to work for you? Because of my ability or because you need a black?" I was reassured that ability was the "only" criterion, and one month later, after much introspection, I accepted the offer.

Initial Exposure

I entered the first formal training phase, in which I was the only black trainee in a department of over 8,000 employees. During this period, my tension increased as I was repeatedly called on to be the in-house expert on anything pertaining to civil rights. I was proud to be black and had many opinions about civil rights, but I did not feel qualified to give "the" black opinion. I developed the feeling that I was considered a black first and an individual second by many of the people I came into contact with. This feeling was exacerbated by the curious executive visitors to the training class who had to be introduced to everyone except me. Everyone knew my name, and I constantly had the feeling of being on stage.

The next phase of training was intended to prepare trainees for supervisory responsibilities. The tension of the trainee group had risen somewhat because of the loss of several trainees and the increased challenges facing us. In my own case, an increasing fear of failure began to impact on the other tensions that I felt from being "a speck of pepper in a sea of salt." The result of these tensions was that I began behaving with an air of bravado. I wasn't outwardly concerned or afraid, but I was inwardly terrified. This phase of training was also completed satisfactorily, at least in an official sense.

At the conclusion of the training, I received a "yes, but" type of appraisal. For example: "Mr. Jones doesn't take notes and seems to have trouble using the reference material, but he seems to be able to recall the material." This is the type of appraisal that says you've done satisfactorily, yet leaves a negative or dubious impression. I questioned the subjective inputs but dropped the matter without any vehement objections.

Prior to embarking on my fist management assignment, I resolved to learn from this appraisal and to use more tact and talk less. These resolutions were re-emphasized by my adviser, who was an executive with responsibility for giving me counsel and acting as a sounding board. He also suggested that I relax my handshake and speak more softly.

On the Job

A warm welcome awaited me in the office where I was to complete my first assignment as a supervisor. I looked forward to going to work because I felt that subjectivity in appraisals would now be replaced by objectivity. Here was a situation in which I would either meet or fail to meet clearly defined numerical objectives.

There were no serious problems for three weeks, and I started to relax and just worry about the job. But then I had a conflict in my schedule. An urgent matter had to be taken care of in the office at the same time that I had an appointment elsewhere. I wrote a note to a supervisor who worked for another manager, asking him if he would be kind enough to follow up on the matter in the office for me.

I chose that particular supervisor because he had given me an embarrassingly warm welcome to the office and insisted that I "just ask" if there was anything at all that he could do to help me. I relied on the impersonality of the note because he was out on a coffee break and I had to leave immediately. The note was short and tactfully worded, and ended by giving my advance "thanks" for the requested help. Moreover, the office norms encouraged supervisory cooperation, so the fact that we worked under different managers did not seem to be a problem.

When I returned to the office, the manager I worked for called me in. He was visibly irritated. I sat down and he said, "Ed, you're rocking the boat." He stated that the supervisor I had asked for help had complained directly to the area manager that I was ordering him around and said he wasn't about to take any nonsense from a "new kid" in the office.

In a very calm voice, I explained what I had done and why I had done it. I then asked my manager, "What did I do wrong?" He looked at me and said, "I don't know, but whatever it is, cut it out. Stop rocking the boat." When I asked why the note wasn't produced to verify my statements, he said that it "wasn't available."

I left my manager's office totally perplexed. How could I correct my behavior if I didn't know what was wrong with it? I resolved that I had no choice except to be totally self-reliant, since one thing was obvious; what I had taken at face value as friendliness was potentially a fatal trap.

The feelings aroused in this incident were indicative of those I was to maintain for some time. While I felt a need for closeness, the only option open to me was self-reliance. I felt that my manager should support and defend me, but it was obvious that he was not willing to take such a stance. Worst of all, however, was my feeling of disappointment and the ensuing confusion due to my lack of guidance. I felt that if my manager was not willing to protect and defend me, he had an increased responsibility to give me guidance on how to avoid future explosions of a similar nature.

For some months I worked in that office without any additional explosions, although I was continually admonished not to "rock the boat." During a luncheon with the area manager one day, I remember, he said, "Ed, I've never seen a guy try so hard. If we tell you to tie your tie to the right, you sure try to do it. But why can't you be like Joe [another trainee the area manager supervised]? He doesn't seem to be having any problems."

The Appraisal Incident

I directed my energies and frustrations into my work, and my supervisory section improved in every measured area of performance until it led the unit. At the end of my first six months on the job, I was slated to go on active duty to fulfill my military requirements as a lieutenant in the Army. Shortly before I left, my manager stated, "Ed, you've done a tremendous job. You write your own appraisal." I wrote the appraisal, but was told to rewrite it because "it's not good enough." I rewrote the appraisal four times before he was satisfied that I was not being too modest. As I indicated earlier, I had resolved to be as unabrasive as possible, and, even though I had met or exceeded all my objectives, I was trying not to be pompous in critiquing my own performance.

Finally, on my next to last day on the job, my manager said, "Ed, this is a fine appraisal. I don't have time to get it typed before you go, but I'll submit this appraisal just as you have written it." With that, I went into the service, feeling that, finally, I had solved my problems.

Six months later, I took several days' leave from the Army to spend Christmas in the city with my family. On the afternoon of the day before Christmas, I decided to visit the personnel executive who had originally given me encouragement. So, wearing my officer's uniform, I stopped by his office.

After exchanging greetings and making small talk, I asked him if he had seen my appraisal. He answered, "yes," but when his face failed to reflect the look of satisfaction that I expected, I asked him if I could see it. The appraisal had been changed from the one that I had originally written to another "yes, but" appraisal. The numerical results said that I had met or exceeded all objectives, but under the section entitled "Development Program" the following paragraph had been inserted:

> Mr. Jones's biggest problem has been overcoming his own impulsiveness. He has on occasion, early in his tour, jumped too fast with the result that he has incurred some resentment. In these cases his objectives have been good, but his method has ruffled feathers.

I asked the personnel executive to interpret my overall rating. He answered, "Well, we can run the business with people with that rating." I then asked him to explain the various ratings possible, and it became clear that I had received the lowest acceptable rating that wouldn't require the company to fire me. I could not see how this could be, since I had exceeded all my objectives. I explained how I had written my own appraisal and that this appraisal had been rewritten. The personnel officer could not offer an explanation; he recommended that I speak to my old area manager, who had had the responsibility to review and approve my appraisal, and ask him why I had been treated in that manner.

A Bleak Christmas

I tried to sort things out on my way to see my former area manager. My head was spinning, and I was disgusted. The appraisal was not just unfair— it was overtly dishonest. I thought of standing up in righteous indignation and appealing to higher authority in the company, but I had always resisted calling attention to my blackness by asking for special concessions and wanted to avoid creating a conflict situation if at all possible. While the 15-minute walk in the cold air calmed my anger, I still hadn't decided what I was going to do when I arrived at the area manager's office.

I walked into a scene that is typical of Christmas Eve in an office. People were everywhere, and discarded gift wrappings filled the wastebaskets. The area manager still had on the red Santa Claus suit. I looked around at the scene of merriment and decided that this was a poor time to "rock the boat."

The area manager greeted me warmly, exclaimed how great I looked, and offered to buy me a drink on his way home. I accepted, and with a feeling of disgust and disappointment, toasted to a Merry Christmas. I knew then that this situation was hopeless and there was little to be gained by raising a stink while we were alone. I had been naïve, and there was no way to prove that the appraisal had been changed.

I was a very lonely fellow that Christmas Eve. My feelings of a lack of closeness, support, and protection were renewed and amplified. It became obvious that no matter how much I achieved, how hard I worked, or how many personal adjustments I made, this system was trying to reject me.

I didn't know which way to turn, whom to trust, or who would be willing to listen. The personnel executive had told me to expect prejudice, but when he saw that I was being treated unfairly, he sent me off on my own.

"What do they expect?" I thought. "They know that I am bound to run into prejudice; yet no one lifts a finger when I am treated unfairly. Do they expect a person to be stupid enough to come right out and say, 'Get out, blackie' we don't want your type here'? This surely wouldn't happen— such overt behavior would endanger the offending person's career."

After the Christmas Eve incident, I went off to finish the remaining time in the Army. During that period, I tossed my work problems around in my mind, trying to find the right approach. The only answer I came up with was to stand fast, do my best, ask for no special favors, and refuse to quit voluntarily.

New Challenges

When I returned to the company, I was assigned as a supervisor in another area for five or six weeks, to do the same work as I had been doing prior to my departure for the military service. At the end of this uneventful refamiliarization period, I was reassigned as a manager in an area that had poor performance and was recognized as being one of the most difficult in the company. The fact that I would be responsible for one of three "manager units" in the area was exciting, and I looked forward to this new challenge.

I walked into my new area manager's office with a smile and extended hand, anxious to start off on the right foot and do a good job. After shaking hands, my new boss invited me to sit down while he told me about the job. He began by saying, "I hope you don't, but I am pretty sure you are going to fall flat on your face. When you do, my job is to kick you in the butt so hard that they'll have to take us both to the hospital."

I was shocked and angry. In the first place, my pride as a man said you don't have to take that kind of talk from anyone. I fought the temptation to say something like, "If you even raise your foot, you may well go to the hospital to have it put in a cast."

As I held back the anger, he continued, "I don't know anything about your previous performance, and I don't intend to try to find out. I'm going to evaluate you strictly on your performance for me."

The red lights went on in my mind. This guy was making too much of an issue about his lack of knowledge concerning my previous performance. Whom was he trying to kid? He had heard rumors and read my personnel records. I was starting off with two strikes against me. I looked at him and said, "I'll do my best."

More Appraisal Troubles

The area's results failed to improve, and John, the area manager, was replaced by a new boss, Ralph. Two weeks after Ralph arrived, he called me on the intercom and said, "Ed, John has your appraisal ready. Go down to see him in his new office. Don't worry about it; we'll talk when you get back." Ralph's words and tone of foreboding made me brace for the worst.

John ushered me into his office and began by telling me that I had been his worst problem. He then proceeded to read a list of every disagreement involving me that he was aware of. These ranged from corrective actions with clerks to resource-allocation discussions with my fellow managers. It was a strange appraisal session. John wound up crossing out half the examples cited as I rebutted his statements. At the end of the appraisal, he turned and said "I've tried to be fair, Ed. I've tried not to be vindictive.

But if someone were to ask how you're doing, I would have to say you've got room for improvement.''

Discussion with Ralph, my new boss, followed as soon as I returned to my office. He advised me not to worry, that we would work out any problems. I told him that this was fine, but I also pointed out the subjectivity and dishonesty reflected in previous and current appraisals and the circumstances surrounding them.

I was bitter that a person who had just been relieved for ineffectiveness could be allowed to have such a resounding impact on my chances in the company. My predecessor had been promoted; I had improved on his results; but here I was, back in questionable status again.

The Turning Point

About six weeks later, Ralph called me in and said, ''Ed, I hope you make it on the job. But what are you going to do if you don't?''

At that moment, I felt as if the hands on the clock of life had reached 11:59. Time was running out very rapidly on me, and I saw myself against a wall, with my new boss about to deliver the coup de grâce. I felt that he was an honest and very capable person, but that circumstances had combined to give him the role of executioner. It seemed from his question that he was in the process of either wrestling with his own conscience or testing me to see how much resistance, if any, I would put up when he delivered the fatal blow. After all, while I had not made an issue of my ill treatment thus far in my career, no matter how unjustly I felt I had been dealt with, he was smart enough to realize that this option was still open to me.

I looked at Ralph and any thought about trying to please him went out of my mind. Sitting up straight in my chair, I met his relaxed smile with a very stern face. ''Why do you care what I do if I don't make it?'' I asked coldly.

''I care about you as a person,'' he replied.

''It's not your job to be concerned about me as a person,'' I said. ''Your job is to evaluate my performance results. But since you've asked, it will be rough if I am fired, because I have a family and responsibilities. However, that's not your concern. You make your decision; and when you do, I'll make my decision.'' With that statement I returned to my office.

Several weeks after this discussion, a vice president came around to the office to discuss objectives and job philosophy with the managers. I noted at the time that while he only spent 15 or 20 minutes with the other managers, he spent over an hour talking with me. After this visit, Ralph and I had numerous daily discussions. Then Ralph called me into his office to tell me he had written a new appraisal with an improved rating. I was thrilled. I was going to make it. Later, he told me that he was writing another appraisal, stating I not only would make it but also had promotional potential.

After Ralph had changed the first appraisal, my tensions began to decrease and my effectiveness began to increase proportionately. The looser and more confident I became, the more rapidly the results improved. My assignment under Ralph became very fulfilling, and one of the best years I've spent in the company ensued. Other assignments followed, each more challenging than the previous, and each was handled satisfactorily.

Lessons from Experience

My point in relating these experiences is not to show that I was persecuted or treated unfairly by people in a large corporation. In fact, after talking to friends in the company who knew me during the period just described, I am convinced that many of the lack-of-tact and rock-the-boat statements were true. I am also convinced, however, that the problems I experienced were not uniquely attributable to me or my personality and that it is important for companies to understand what caused them.

The manager to whom I reported on my very first assignment made some informal notes which help illustrate my conviction:

> I discussed each case with Ed. As might be expected, there is as much to be said in his defense as against him. He isn't all wrong in any one case. But the cumulative weight of all those unsolicited comments and complaints clearly shows that he is causing a lot of people to be unhappy, and I must see that it stops. I don't think it is a question of what he says and does or a question of objectives. It is a question of voice, manner, approach, method—or maybe timing. No matter what it is, he must correct whatever he does that upsets so many people.

These are not the words of a scheming bigot; they are the words of a man searching for an explanation to a phenomenon that neither he nor I understood at the time. I was not knowingly insensitive to other people or intent on antagonizing them. What this man and others failed to realize was that, being a black man in a unique position in a white company, I was extremely tense and ill at ease. Levels of sensitivity, polish, and tact which were foreign to me were now necessities of life. The world of white business presented me with an elaborate sociopolitical organization that required unfamiliar codes of behavior.

Abraham Zaleznik refers to this phenomenon in *The Human Dilemmas of Leadership*:

> The anxiety experienced by the upwardly mobile individual largely comes from internal conflicts generated within his own personality. On the one hand, there is the driving and pervasive need to prove himself as assurance of his adequacy as a person; on the other hand, the standards for measuring his adequacy come from sources somewhat unfamiliar to him.[1]

My personal pride and sense of worth were driving me to succeed. Ironically, the more determined I was to succeed, the more abrasive I became and the more critical my feedback became. This in turn impelled me to try even harder and to be even more uptight. As a result, I was vulnerable to pre-judgments of inability by my peers and superiors.

The Lens of Color

What most white people do not understand or accept is the fact that skin color has such a pervasive impact on every black person's life that it subordinates considerations of education or class. Skin color makes black people the most conspicuous minority in America, and all blacks, regardless of status, are subjected to prejudice. I personally was not as disadvantaged as many other blacks, but to some extent all blacks are products of separate schools, neighborhoods, and subcultures. In short, black and white people not only look different but also come from different environments which condition them differently and make understanding and honest communication difficult to achieve.

Many whites who find it easy to philosophically accept the fact that blacks will be rubbing shoulders with them experience antagonism when they realize that the difference between blacks and whites goes deeper than skin color. They have difficulty adjusting to the fact that blacks really are different. It is critical that companies understand this point, for it indicates the need for increased guidance to help blacks adjust to an alien set of norms and behavioral requirements.

The Informal Organization

One of the phenomena that develops in every corporation is a set of behavioral and personal norms that facilitates communication and aids cohesiveness. Moreover, because this "informal organization" is built on white norms, it can reinforce the black-white differences just mentioned and thus reject or destroy all but the most persistent blacks.

The informal organization operates at all levels in a corporation, and the norms become more rigid the higher one goes in the hierarchy. While this phenomenon promotes efficiency and unity, it is also restrictive and very selective. It can preclude promotion or lead to failure on the basis of "fit" rather than competence.

Chester Barnard recognized the existence of the informal organization in 1938. As he stated,

> This question of fitness involves such matters as education, experience, age, sex, personal distinctions, prestige, race, nationality, faith. . . .[2]

I believe that many of the problems I encountered were problems of fit with the informal organization. My peers and supervisors were unable to perceive me as being able to perform the job that the company hired me for. Their reaction to me was disbelief. I was out of the "place" normally filled by black people in the company; and since no black person had preceded me successfully, it was easy for my antagonists to believe I was inadequate.

I am not vacillating here from my previous statement that I was probably guilty of many of the subjective shortcomings noted in my appraisals. But I do feel that the difficulties I experienced were amplified by my lack of compatibility with the informal organization. Because of it, many of the people I had problems with could not differentiate between objective ability and performance and subjective dislike for me, or discomfort with me. I was filling an unfamiliar, and therefore uncomfortable, "space" in relation to them. Even in retrospect, I cannot fully differentiate between the problems attributable to me as a person, to me as a manager, or to me as a black man.

Toward Facilitating "Fit"

Because of the foregoing problems, I conclude that business has an obligation to even out the odds for blacks who have executive potential. I am not saying that all blacks must be pampered and sheltered rather than challenged. Nor am I advocating the development of "chosen" managers. All managers must accept the risk of failure in order to receive the satisfactions of achievement.

I do, however, advocate a leveling out of these problems of "fit" with the informal organization that operate against black managers. Here are the elements vital to this process:

☐ *Unquestionable top management involvement and commitment—* The importance of this element is underscored by my discussions with the vice president who visited me during my crisis period. He disclosed that his objective was to see whether I was really as bad as he was being told. His conclusion from the visit was that he couldn't see any insurmountable problems with me. This high-level interest was the critical variable that gave me a fair chance. I was just lucky that this man had a personal sense of fair play and a desire to ensure equitable treatment.

But chance involvement is not enough. If a company is truly committed to equal opportunity, then it must set up reasoned and well thought-out plans for involvement of top management.

☐ *Direct two-way channels of communication between top management and black trainees—*Without open channels of communication, a company cannot ensure that it will recognize the need for a neutral opinion or the intercession of a disinterested party if a black trainee is having problems.

Clear channels of communication will also enable top management to provide empathetic sources of counsel to help the new black trainee combat the potentially crippling paranoia that I encountered. I didn't know whom to trust; consequently, I trusted no one. The counsel of mature and proven black executives will also help mitigate this paranoia.

☐ *Appraisal of managers on their contributions to the company's equal opportunity objectives*—The entire management team must be motivated to change any deep beliefs about who does and doesn't fit with regard to color. Accordingly, companies should use the appraisal system to make the welfare of the black trainee coincident with the well-being of his superior. Such action, of course, will probably receive considerable resistance from middle- and lower-level management. But managers are appraised on their ability to reach other important objectives; and, more significantly, the inclusion of this area in appraisals signals to everyone involved that a company is serious. Failure to take this step signals business as usual and adds to any credibility gap between the company and black employees.

The appraisal process also motivates the trainee's superior to "school" him on the realities of the political process in the corporation. Without this information, no one can survive in an organization. After upgrading my appraisal, Ralph began this process with me. The knowledge I gained proved to be invaluable in my subsequent decision making.

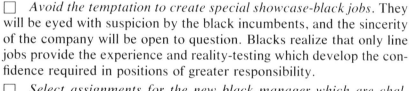

☐ *Avoid the temptation to create special showcase-black jobs.* They will be eyed with suspicion by the black incumbents, and the sincerity of the company will be open to question. Blacks realize that only line jobs provide the experience and reality-testing which develop the confidence required in positions of greater responsibility.

☐ *Select assignments for the new black manager which are challenging, yet don't in themselves increase his chances of failure.* My assignment with John was a poor choice. He was a top-rated area manager, but had a different job orientation and was struggling to learn his new responsibilities. So naturally he would resent any inexperienced manager being assigned to him. Moreover, the fact that he had never seen a successful black manager reinforced his belief that I could not do the job.

These basic steps need not be of a permanent nature, but they should be enacted until such time as the organizational norms accept blacks at all levels and in all types of jobs. The steps will help mitigate the fact that a black person in the organizational structure must not only carry the same load as a white person but also bear the burden attributable to prejudice and the machinations of the informal organization.

Conclusion

In relating and drawing on my own experiences, I have not been talking about trials and tribulations in an obviously bigoted company. At that time, my company employed a higher percentage of blacks than almost any other business, and this is still true today. I grant that there is still much to be done as far as the number and level of blacks in positions of authority are concerned, but I believe that my company has done better than most in the area of equal opportunity. Its positive efforts are evidenced by the progressive decision to sponsor my study at the Harvard Business School, so I would be prepared for greater levels of responsibility.

There are differences in detail and chronology, but the net effect of my experiences is similar to that of other blacks with whom I have discussed these matters. While prejudice exists in business, the U.S. norm against being prejudiced precludes an admission of guilt by the prejudiced party. Thus, in my own case, my first manager and John were more guilty of naïveté than bigotry—they could not recognize prejudice, since it would be a blow to their self-images. And this condition is prevalent in U.S. industry.

My experience points out that a moral commitment to equal opportunity is not enough. If a company fails to recognize that fantastic filters operate between the entry level and top management, this commitment is useless. Today, integration in organizations is at or near the entry level, and the threat of displacement or the discomfort of having to adjust to unfamiliar racial relationships is the greatest for lower and middle managers, for they are the people who will be most impacted by this process. Therefore, companies must take steps similar to the ones I have advocated if they hope to achieve true parity for blacks.

Equal job opportunity is more than putting a black man in a white man's job. The barriers must be removed, not just moved.

Notes

1. New York, Harper & Row, Publishers, 1966, p.111

2. *The Functions of the Executive* (Cambridge, Harvard University Press, 1938), p. 224.

14

Managers and Lovers

ELIZA G.C. COLLINS

If the world—and the human beings who live in it—were perfect, romance between executives in the same company, like that between any two lovers, would achieve the positive results promised by myriad poets and songwriters. Other employees in the company would be better off somehow—more content perhaps, or renewed in some way. At the very least, the impact of a newly discovered love would be neutral.

But love is an emotion that can evoke as many negative as positive feelings, and it can affect not only the lovers but also their coworkers above, below, or on the same organizational level. The impact of a love relationship between top executives can be as vast as the power they wield and the company itself.

This author argues that such love threatens the organization's stability, and she urges top management to view it in that light. Through four case histories, she shows how the threat manifests itself, how it plays itself out throughout various parts of the company, and what top managers must do to preserve the organization and ensure that top employees remain motivated to work toward that preservation.

Two executives, a man and a woman, arrived back at the office after a three-week business trip. Feeling quite pleased with their work, they looked forward to the next day's operations committee meeting, at which the senior executive was to present a report summing up their progress on this first phase of a year-long project. But the pair was not prepared for the reception they met.

The senior executive's briefing got much less attention than did the particulars of his time away from the office. The junior executive's input,

Published in 1983.

Author's Note. I am in great debt to Fernando Bartolomé, John J. Gabarro, and Mary P. Rowe for their comments on an earlier draft of this article.

which she was sure would be good for her career, was practically ignored. While the two executives had been away, the project had become an office joke.

It was clear that everyone believed "something" had happened on the trip. In this case, "something" had not happened, but because of others' reactions, the two executives decided not to travel together again, even though the project would take longer to complete and might not turn out as well. Other, bigger, things were at stake: the project and their careers.

Many executives might have handled the situation differently. With the influx of women to high managerial positions, it becomes increasingly likely that something will happen on a business trip or during a long night's work. Most often it will be a brief sexual encounter that the two will gladly forget. Although a sexual liaison may be considered immoral, unless it leads to harassment it presents a minor problem to the organization. But on occasion an encounter will develop into a love relationship, which constitutes a threat to the business.

Organizational life has not been known for its abundance of close personal relationships. To maintain objectivity and avoid conflicts of interest, managers have learned to keep a protective distance from the people they work with. Even when executives run into people with whom they share common interests and points of view, they tend to keep their personal likes and dislikes separate from their professional judgments. If they cannot maintain that distance, their business lives are in trouble long before the most difficult of personal relationships intrudes: that of romantic and sexual love.

It is not immediately apparent to some that love between two people in the same company can be either a problem for top management or a threat to the organization. After all, love is a positive emotion that is supposed to make the world go 'round, not under. It is negative emotions, like jealousy or feelings of inferiority, that usually cause the messy personal relationships between people working at the same place.

However messy these kinds of relationships, usually everyone understands who has the most power when the relationships are between bosses and subordinates or peers in an organization. Love between managers is dangerous because it challenges—and can break down—the organizational structure. (The accompanying insert describes what I mean by "love.") For instance, even in this day and age, when a man and a woman fall in love, the relationship often takes on a traditional cast; the male is superior to the female. In a company where the two are high-level managers who are supposed to work together as equals, love's old sexist hierarchy is disruptive. Also, because the lovers are managers, their romance affects the organization's power alliances.

In the past, organizations defended themselves against love's buzz saw. In most companies, executives indulging their power in a sexual way lost not only the esteem of others and credibility but also their jobs. Where sexual liaisons did arise at work, most male executives tacitly agreed that

these relationships were only for sexual gratification and that if they threatened the organizational order, the woman could go. Today, because of several factors, neither the abrupt dismissal of the man nor the class-sanctioned
attitude toward the woman will work.

One factor is the changing status of, attitudes toward, and numbers of
women at work. Another is men's growing awareness and acceptance of
how adult males develop and how their needs change. For these reasons,
relationships between men and women will more and more concern love
between powerful managers, not merely sex or love only between lower-
level peers. Executives will need new ways to think about this phenomenon;
neither the old sex-laden concepts nor simplistic policies will apply to what
is already occurring and will continue to occur in organizations.

Of course, wherever a diversity of people congregates, a diversity of
relationships will spring up. In corporations the possibilities are numerous;
what develops depends on the characteristics of the partners. There can be
intimate relationships between heterosexuals or homosexuals. They can be
based on friendship, sex, or love and be between peers, persons at different
levels, or persons of different marital status. Here I am concerned with
relationships between men and women who both have some authority over
others. When one or both of the partners is married, the impact on the
organization is likely to be more intense.

How should management react when a man and a woman, both competent and successful executives, fall in love? Should a top executive intervene and discuss the relationship with the participants, and, if so, what
should he or she propose?

Before answering these questions, let's look first at a few of the cases
that have led me to decide that love between two executives can create a
problem in the organization because of what happens to the people involved.
I base my observations on actual situations that severely threatened careers
and organizational effectiveness. I do not mean to imply that every outcome
I describe in the following paragraphs will occur when a high-level man and
woman in the same company fall in love, but that some of the same patterns
will emerge and their repercussions will be great.

Opportunity and Need

People generally fall in love and marry others who are like them in some
important ways. In the old days, most male executives who had sexual
relationships with women at work did not consider them potential mates. In
all likelihood, the differences in the men's and women's actual or aspired-
to social status ruled out marriage; any alliance was seen as play.

The ambitious young man in search of a place in the sun was more
likely to fantasize about the boss's daughter than about the girl next door
who became a secretary. When the college-educated careerist married the

girl of his dreams, she didn't go to work. She had the option to stay home and raise a family, and almost invariably chose to. Of course, numbers of male executives did marry their secretaries and have lived very happy lives. But the lingering perception that it is OK for men—but not for women—to sow a few wild oats reinforced the notion that men at work were on the lookout for ripe fields to cultivate.

Because the mythical female at work was unlikely to be a mate and was not taken seriously, the office relationships that occurred were, for the most part, short-term sexual sprees. Only under a few conditions would an affair lead to an important long-term commitment: when the woman's social class outside the company was higher than her class role inside or when she was extraordinarily attractive or talented.

What Has Changed?

Today things are different. Regardless of their backgrounds, women are less willing to accept the playmate role in which the man invests less in the relationship than they do. Even if she starts out as a willing partner, a woman may not just go quietly away when an affair becomes disruptive; she may sue, file sexual harassment charges, or simply make the executive's workday a series of unpleasant confrontations and embarrassing moments.

Through education, acceptance by industry, and affirmative action, more working women have jobs that are equal, or nearly equal, to men's, and they are more often seen as appropriate partners for long-term relationships. Four cases highlight these changes. In each, the woman involved has a higher status than she might have had in the past, when her position would have been filled by a man:

□ At a large diversified company, a group manager, Daniel Brown, fell in love with a woman, Sheila Murray, who reported to one of his vice presidents. Although not on the same organizational level as Daniel, Sheila was close to his and was well educated, so her social eligibility was not in question.

□ Sam Dunn, a high-level executive in the headquarters of a bank, fell in love with a woman, Judith Green, who was a vice president.

□ A woman who was being considered for a top executive post in a large company fell in love with an executive in another division.

□ A female associate in a large law firm fell in love with a partner in the firm.

The dynamics of any relationship in which the woman is an equal of the man outside the company and has enough status inside to be a colleague are very different from those of a relationship between unequals. It is more probable that sexual attraction between two people will lead to genuine love; for instance, many of the characteristics of a good working relationship between superiors and subordinates—frequent interaction, mutual respect and trust—can contribute to the development of a romantic attachment.[1] When two managers experience this interaction and have close contact, they have to consider the possibility of a long-term relationship, and recognition of the possibility increases the probability.

While, for example, group manager Daniel found Sheila, the assistant to the vice president, very attractive, he probably wouldn't have approached her if he had been merely looking for a sexual fling. The office affair has many mundane as well as moral constraints. Anyone looking for a good reason not to act out sexual fantasies or satisfy lust inside the organization can find one. One reason is practical: it usually doesn't work very well. Another is that it is frequently actionable.

But Daniel did approach Sheila for the most compelling reason of all; like the men in the other cases, he was emotionally receptive. He had reached a time in his life when a desire for intimacy outweighed his need to achieve.

Transitions

During a man's 30s, work is often far more important than any other thing in his life.[2] Such a man relegates other aspects of his life, such as concern with relationships, feelings, nurturing, equality, and love, to his wife. All the men in the four cases had at one time or another been married. The group manager was married when he met the assistant to the vice president; the bank executive was also married; the division executive had been married but divorced three or four years before meeting the female executive; and the lawyer was divorced.

In all these examples, the men were or had been married to women who might be characterized as conventional—they played a traditional, passive role so that their husbands could move up in their organizations. The marriages came apart because *both* parties in each decided it was over.

As men approach their 40s, work may suddenly lose its emotional hold, and they start caring more about a personal life. If a man turns to his wife at this time he may find nobody at home. In these cases, the men were in mid-life transition when they became involved with women at work; the youngest was 39 and the oldest, 46. Early in their careers they had made choices about the dreams they wished to pursue, had achieved them, and were reevaluating the fundamental values by which they were going to live. With organizational status came the realization that they could choose what they did all day long. A top executive has freedom, power, and money and, with them, the potential for emotional affluence. Richer in resources, he can ask more of life.

Available and willing, the men in these cases became involved with senior females who were not passive but powerful equals. The women were not only sources of acceptance and love but also people who understood—and did not try to pull them away from—the executives' worlds.

Even if both the man and woman knew that love in the office was a dangerous thing, they could not avoid each other. In all the cases their jobs required frequent contact; opportunity and need eventually wore down prudence.

The Love Affair

Love is blind, so they say, and older lovers are only slightly more perceptive than younger ones. Both are blind about the persons they love and about the reactions of other people. This blindness makes the lovers unaware of their impact on others and of possible repercussions on them and their careers.

After a few months of unplanned and then planned encounters, the two executives in the first case arrived at the point where sexual activity is not merely gratifying but also loving. Despite occasional feelings of intense guilt (he was married) and anxiety, they saw their affair as loving. Like most lovers, they thought they were essentially innocent and under love's protective umbrella. The two were first blissfully unaware that anyone noticed and, as no news to the contrary came, that anyone cared. Ultimately, however, people came to know about the affair, and trouble began.

Warning bells finally rang out when the lovers attended a presentation ceremony dinner along with the company's top people. Using Sheila's job as a justification, group manager Daniel arranged to have her go along. During dinner somebody suggested to him that it was inappropriate to bring Sheila, whose formal status was not the same as that of the other guests. So the first objection to the affair was couched in organizational terms. Daniel remembers hearing the objection and thinking, "Can't they see that this is different? Organizational politics have nothing to do with it."

In his innocence about his feelings, Daniel misinterpreted the depth of others' anxiety. From the organization's point of view, however, the actions and feelings of others had not become as important as those of the lovers themselves.

Anxious Outsiders

In the first place, others in the organization hadn't been as blind as the lovers. Almost from the beginning they'd been aware that something was going on. In all the cases the female executives expected surprise when they finally discussed the affair with their immediate superiors but instead found that the superiors had not only known but had also been deeply disturbed. People in love look different. They glow. But those on the outside don't always see the glow as love; sometimes it appears to be a stigma left by the seamiest kind of sex. Particularly in one case some onlookers projected their own nonloving sexual fantasies onto the lovers. Through a filter of lust, they saw the romance as a danger to the social order.

The degree of organizational anxiety is determined by a number of variables. Whether the male executive's leadership style is such that he has close, warm relationships with subordinates and peers or is coolly distant, his coworkers are likely to be made quite anxious by such an affair. If they fancy themselves as protégés, they will see any redirection of the executive's affection—to a woman or to anyone else—as a loss. If they feel removed from the executive, they will see anyone getting close as an extra threat. They will be jealous and angry and feel abandoned. To alleviate these feelings they'll politicize them and assert that the affair disrupts the social order. In all these cases, subordinates and peers started making moral judgments, such as, "He shouldn't do this at work" and "It isn't right."

The second source of anxiety is the way the affair threatens the home lives of others, especially if one or both lovers are married. When executives of a company and their spouses get together on social occasions and the lovers appear, couples whose marriages are shaky can become anxious and angry. To avoid dealing with the problems in their own marriages, coworkers and their spouses may project their anxiety onto the executives who are in love.

Open about the fact that they were becoming very close, bank executive Sam Dunn and vice president Judith Green made a fellow vice president, Jim Silver, exceedingly uncomfortable. Judith would sit in Sam's office and chat during part of the day, and the couple frequently spent evenings with people from the bank. Unfortunately, Jim Silver's wife, Alice, was one of Sam's wife's closest friends. The two married couples had socialized often and lived near one another.

The lovers' relationship progressed at work, but Sam's wife, Marie, did not know about it. Alice knew about the affair, however, and felt disloyal to Marie. She felt she was being asked to live a lie—at least by omission. When Marie finally expressed concern that something was very wrong with her marriage, Alice didn't know what to say. In her distress she blamed Jim for being friends with "such a man" and asserted that she would be the next wife to go. Pots on the back burner began to bubble over.

Outsiders also fear that the formal and informal communication networks of the organization will be crossed by pillow talk. If the male executive has a higher position than the female, his immediate subordinates as well as her peers can fear that their own confidences have been broken. The subordinates begin to fantasize:"Does she know something about me?" "Is she smirking?" "How does the boss see me?" "I've got to be careful with her; whatever I say might get back to him."

In one case, the female executive was one of a group that met regularly to air complaints by grousing to one another at lunch. Whereas before the group could openly complain, "We can't figure this out because the old man doesn't know what the hell he wants," now they fell silent. In the silence, they withheld other information as well; the organization's informal communications network started going awry.

The fourth source of pain relates to the third. In the case of the affair in the bank, Judith's male colleagues engaged in some outrageous behavior.

Having difficulty imagining that the relationship might proceed toward love, they saw it as smut. The male peers saw the banker, "papa" (who was enormously respected, competent, and much liked), take up with a colleague who was not only attractive but also unabashedly sexy. Her peers did not know how to handle their own relationships with her; she was unusual, both assertive and sexual, and very threatening. A few coworkers fancied that she was attracted to them and became angry and hostile when the affair became public. Judith received a number of hate notes in the interoffice mail and on at least one occasion was insulted by an angry peer. Over time such incidents caused unbearable tension, even for many who were not directly involved.

Another source of subordinates' anxiety is the possibility that the male executive will lose power and the ability to influence on their behalf. To many, love flies in the face of power, and power may lose. We want our leaders to be pleasant but also tough when they have to be. We fear that a manager who loves a person we consider taboo has lost his or her judgment and may stop exercising authority. In the bank, people saw their boss losing power to a woman who was also very threatening. Some assumed that equity would go and she would receive special consideration. The organization began to tremble.

As the affair ripens into something important, more and more people learn of it and anxiety becomes widespread. People may really care about the man, be glad that he's having what appears to be a wonderful experience, and hope it will be important to his life. They may also care about the woman and feel the same things. In the bank case, however, subordinates were so threatened that they became increasingly ambivalent and suffered the pain this emotion brings. Because it wouldn't go away, they tried to resolve the conflict by driving out what they saw as its source.

The Woman as Scapegoat

In the bank case, Judith suffered attacks from within the organization. Men began to look at her and think, "How could Sam possibly fall for that one? She's a pushy, aggressive broad." They began to make comments about the old man being "off his rocker" for falling for someone "who's a real bitch." (Other women in the organization may also try to sabotage the female executive.[3]) In picking up on these attacks, Judith realized her worst fears, and her self-doubts began to surface.

At the beginning of an affair, a woman, like a man, is in a state of heightened sensual awareness, loses critical faculties, and almost willingly gives up judgment and reason. As reason, like knowledge in the garden of Eden, returns she will question whether others know, and curiosity about other people's knowledge represents a real wish to tell them, to go public.

In these cases, for example, male peers and superiors expressed subtle hostility, first marked by withdrawal. They didn't ask the women to lunch as often, stopped conversations when the women approached, and tinged their smiles with sarcasm. The women were being iced, and they knew it. Because they were cut out, they felt illicit, immoral, or dirty. At the worst times, these women believed what others implied: that they were no better than the secretarial meat of the corporate-caveman era.

As a rule, members of minorities look over their shoulders with caution; many executive women think "there but for the grace of God go I" about the secretarial pool. A terrible double bind underlies many problems women have in organizations. To get in the arena with men, many women believe they must pretend to be comfortable playing a lot of roles, roles they—or any other woman—have never played before. The affair threatens to reveal the pretense: that she is just a woman after all. Making the affair public legitimizes the woman's position again; at least she doesn't have to worry about being taken for a ride.

When the affairs I'm discussing went public (As most eventually do), the female executives thought they should be included in the settings that were important to their lovers. Intellectually, the women understood that they did not hold the same organizational status as their men. In one case the woman agreed to skip the annual meeting functions and attend only social events, where she would behave very much like a wife. But playing a part that they had ruled out irritated the women, especially because they thought they had brought knowledge of the business and some power to the relationship.

At the same time these female executives agreed to play the wifely role, they were aware that the men in the company didn't want them at social or business functions. These assertive, powerful women who had risen to high levels were not going to be snubbed without fighting back. Survivors, they first became angry at their peers and their peers' wives and, finally, the company.

The women were mainly angry, however, because others viewed them as playthings. That made them afraid; it raised suspicions that they were risking their careers for nothing. Each woman had sacrificed a personal life for her career; now they seemed near to sacrificing their careers for threatened relationships. They felt victimized. In anger, the women in these cases turned to their men and confronted them with the insensitivity of the louts they worked with. Like the organizational outsiders who projected their fears on the women, the women turned theirs onto the onlookers. The male lover was then in the middle.

The Male Executive's Quandary

Caught between loyalty to his subordinates and peers and to the woman he loves, the male executive begins to feel something he hasn't felt for a long time: out of control. The organization is threatened in another way.

If the female executive escalates her demands that she be with him and he capitulates, he may begin to think his fellow executives are unworthy and unfair. That can produce organizational chaos. If he says, on the other hand, "Wait a minute, I have to put the organization first," she will automatically feel slighted. Their relationship may suffer, since they began it in part because they were equals.

In one case the male executive decided that it would be better that the female executive not join him on a business trip even though she had a good business excuse. The female could see the point—in part. But once he had gone, she decided he cared more about his work than about her, that his love was contingent and had limitations. She remembers that she began to see every option as a catastrophe; her emotional needle swung between extremes of abandonment and submission.

In such predicaments, the male executives become angry that they cannot protect the women they love. In the four cases, all the male managers felt indignant and guilty that the women had to take the risks and pay the prices while they could do nothing. They lost not only a sense of control but also their view of themselves as protectors.

Ultimately the lovers may turn their anger at the corporation onto each other; as they begin to doubt the relationships' value, they lose confidence in it and begin to treat each other differently. One man remembers beginning to believe what his subordinates had hinted—that his lover really was a bitch. The female executive's response was to subscribe to a lot of feminist rhetoric about powerful males. Innocent attraction became organizational and emotional turmoil.

From Death to Life

Because the lovers are blind and others around them are anxious, resolution of the conflict falls into the hands of the top manager to whom both executives ultimately report. In the long run, the most fragile thing is probably not the corporation or the people but the love relationship. The top manager must decide whether and how to act and needs to keep one inescapable reality in mind. Regardless of what the manager does, it will be judged at a deep emotional level by others, and most harshly if the relationship suffers. Despite fears, ambivalence, and anxiety, everyone still loves a love affair.

At the outset the decision to intervene seems to pose the thorniest problem. An unwritten rule states that managers do not become involved in the private lives of their subordinates, especially high-level subordinates. Most managers are inclined to look away from a subordinate's personal problem and hope it will clear itself up.

In the case of purely sexual, transitory affairs, that attitude has worked and may still. A manager can reasonably assume that a high-level executive, whether male or female, will soon tire of a romp. Even if a transitory sexual liaison has organizational repercussions, no one doubts what comes first or what the solution will ultimately be if it doesn't stop.

But when genuine love is involved, the solution isn't so obvious. Can a manager afford to ignore the situation? I don't think so. Ignoring the problem means the top manager has no control over the outcome. Moreover, others will feel the loss of control and resent the fact that he or she has not acted in a situation that causes them pain and disrupts work.

In the case of Sam and Judith, the pair first decided that he would leave the bank despite his superior position. They thought he had a better chance to obtain a good job elsewhere. But most important, they wanted to take a stand that would explicitly favor the woman, whom they both saw as more the victim. They presented their decision to the bank's CEO, who remembers thinking: "I can't afford to lose him. This couple understands my position but won't accept it."

The CEO was so upset about losing Sam that he called him into his office and said, "You work it out; I'm not going to take any action." In effect, he pushed the problem down into the organization. Sam eventually decided to stay, but the repercussions of the CEO's inaction were vast. Jim and Alice Silver felt such stress that they had to get outside help and were understandably very angry at the CEO for not dealing with the problem. Jim was unable to talk to either Sam or Judith about his difficulties. A friend of both, he thought they had enough problems of their own.

The question of when to intervene is easier to answer: as soon as the manager knows about the relationship. If the rule is that the person at the top is the last to know, by the time he or she does, you can assume that everyone else has known for weeks or months. Repercussions have already been felt. Of course, the superior must rule out the possibility that the relationship is simply a long-playing dalliance. A short discussion with the senior member of the pair will make the affair's status apparent. If it is merely a sexual liaison, a word of warning will most likely be sufficient to stop it.

What to do in the case of real love is more difficult to say. The manager's task is to protect the interests of the corporation and preserve the careers of the two people if possible. It is a difficult juggling act.

Much depends on how managers deal with their subordinates. If the chief is open and can talk candidly, he or she ought to arrange to discuss the affair with the couple as soon as organizational consequences are apparent. In any case, the boss's attitude and conduct of the meeting are crucial to the outcome. Here are some guidelines that may help:

1. *Treat the relationship as a conflict of interest.* In deciding what to do, a top manager needs to understand how the pain is distributed. When two vice presidents love each other, the other vice presidents who compete for remaining resources and power may feel outweighed. They are now up against a coalition. Also, if the two departments supervised by the two executives often conflict, resolution becomes more and more difficult. The couple's respective subordinates may have trouble being candid with their bosses, and the couple may be unable to confront one another even when it's necessary to protect their people.

The top manager needs to be clear in his own mind before he can help the two people see that their love affair represents a conflict of interest in the organization. In talking to couples, managers must stress that they are going to deal with the romance as they would any business problem—as equitably as possible.

This stance has two virtues. First, it is realistic. The love affair between two executives with status and at least some power is a conflict of interest. They cannot be, and should not be expected to be, objective in their decisions when someone they love might be hurt or put at a disadvantage by the outcome. Second, this point of view takes the focus off the romance, puts it on the business issue, and does not force the two managers to go on the defensive about the affair.

The top manager should not attack the love relationship. Ultimately both the corporation and the people involved will survive, but the relationship may not. Because of its fragility and because both executives will fight to protect it, the boss must not denigrate it.

It may be difficult for top managers to be supportive. They may feel that the affair is immoral, especially if one or both partners is married. Bosses may judge people against their own interpretations of God's law. Top managers' spouses may also feel threatened and try to convince the managers to take a judgmental position. Or the spouse may become so vexed that the executive takes the discomfort at home out on the couple.

Even for the boss whose principles are offended, it is more humane to deal compassionately with the tendency to "sin" than to judge harshly. All of us have principles we hold dear. But to act on them in a business situation may be unwise. In approaching what has become a business decision, executives often have to subordinate personal moral stances to resolve organizational conflicts fairly. If bosses can see the relationship in a light not cast with purple overtones, they will give the couple a chance to decide what they want to do, free of organizational pressures.

Another difficulty is that the manager may simply be unable to imagine the experience. The top manager in the diversified company where Daniel and Sheila worked admitted that he couldn't "catch" the feelings, couldn't remember the innocence, the luminosity, the clear restructuring of what is important in life. After talking with the couple and suspending his own belief system, however, he was able to see that perhaps the liaison was not silly and that the couple was enjoying one of life's great experiences.

2. *Advise the couple to get outside help.* Because the boss is a member of the organization, the executives may not trust his or her assessment of the situation no matter how good their personal relationship. Their hackles raised, the two executives will be unable to accept their boss's judgment on the messiness of the situation. They see it as yet another attack. A specialized counselor can help the couple see the situation more clearly and understand that what happened makes emotional sense. The boss needs to realize that the primary relationship is between two people; of itself, the feeling they share is not an organizational phenomenon. First the pair needs a chance to determine whether their relationship can or should survive.

3. *Persuade the couple that either the person least essential to the company or both have to go.* Coming to the recognition that someone must go is painful but, I regret to say, inevitable. To some this resolution may seem obvious and straightforward. But real cases like the ones I've been discussing raise so many personal and difficult issues that no solution is obvious or easy.

In the first place, many younger women and men simply will not understand that letting the less important person—in almost all cases a woman—go is the fairest action. Younger people are committed to equality; they would see a love-related termination as pure recidivism. Though I arrived at it with great reluctance, the conclusion is inescapable. At present, most people in organizations are not trained to handle such relationships or their own responses to them. That makes it improbable that a high-level love relationship will survive in today's organization.

In collegial, nonhierarchical, or professional organizations, where power and communications networks are less important, the relationship may survive, especially if the couple marries. I know of places where it has happened—not always smoothly, but with everyone still in one place. Love may also survive organizational tensions if it arises between two people in divisions that don't interact often, but it is unlikely that executives in those divisions will meet often enough to begin a love affair. In a large organization where resources are scarce and power is important the chances of both partners staying with the company are minimal, no matter how equal their status.

In cases of two equals, one must leave, and I recommend that it should be the less effective person from a business point of view. If both really are equal, the woman should stay and the man go because although it might not be sexist to let the woman go, it can appear that way. When the status is unequal, however, the lower-ranking person must leave. Taking this stand is difficult and often heartbreaking. But bosses must not be swayed by emotion or think they are merely clearing up misunderstandings between subordinates or between subordinates and themselves. No matter how much everyone understands the beauty of a love relationship, it can't survive if the less valuable person stays.

If the couple chooses to stay and live through the consequences and doesn't have the power to change the organizational structure, I can predict how the relationship will end. It will come under more stress; she (assuming the lower-ranked lover is a woman) will start seeing the organization as the enemy; he will resent how others in the organization are treating her; he will start to resent her for attacking people he cares about. If the affair ends, others in the organization will move in for the kill. She will be cut out of power and may end up a skeleton in the organizational closet. At that point she has no option but to leave if she wants to save her relationship and nurture her career.

One woman became aware that she simply couldn't handle the hostility of her peers. Friends to whom she had looked for help and support withdrew.

Increasingly she realized she couldn't even go into her lover's office for support. Finally, she knew she had to get out. Once she had left, the company gradually returned to normal. It took a while for people to forgive him and for him to forgive those who had been mean to her. But he gradually understood that her perception of the events may not have been exact.

If the male executive insists on going, the female may become an outcast. Most likely she'll lose much of her influence. Her superiors will blame her for the loss of an executive they see as more valuable. Very often, if the higher-status person leaves, the lower will soon go as well.

The simple fact is that for the business's purpose, the most valuable person ought to stay, and in today's organization, considering seniority and time as investments, that person is probably the man. Managers need to believe in the inevitability of this outcome because they will have to counter endless entreaties and pleas for fairness.

The woman who has fought her way to an executive position may think she is being asked to leave simply because she's a woman. She doesn't like that, doesn't want to get out, doesn't want to transfer. She has relationships and friends she wants to keep, especially if the love affair is not at a point where she's certain she wants to stay with him forever. She faces an enormous career risk without knowing whether it will be worthwhile. Of course the man takes a risk that even after the woman goes, others may think that he is in the wrong. He may lose respect and never regain it.

4. *Help the ousted executive find a new and perhaps better job.* The top manager must help the person asked to leave because of a romance. Any boss should want to resolve a conflict of interest to everyone's advantage. Moreover, the top manager will want to boost the ego of the person departing, especially if the organization has treated the couple as if they had committed a crime instead of as valuable contributors.

Finally, the manager should not ignore the feelings of the executive who stays behind or of those who have witnessed and taken part in the decision. Regardless of how right they think they are, everyone but the most callous will, after the threat is removed, feel guilty. To assuage those feelings, the top manager must assure everyone that the organization has done everything it can to make certain the departing executive is not tossed out on the street.

A Happy Ending

Let's look at the outcome of the cases to find out if fairness is really the most important consideration.

It became clear to group manager Daniel Brown that he must seek a divorce. He did and moved out of his home, while the assistant to his vice president, Sheila Murray, got a good job in another company. Their subsequent marriage seems quite stable and satisfying.

In the bank case, Judith Green, the female vice president, also quit. Uncertain about the maturity of their relationship, Judith and Sam Dunn decided not to live together for a while. She wanted to keep her independence in case things didn't work out. Judith got a job that was as good as, if not better than, the one she left. For six months before deciding to marry, they spent a lot of time in one place or the other. Eventually they married, bought a new house together, and began a new life.

Once Jim Silver stopped agonizing about Judith and Sam and his wife stopped fantasizing about being deserted, things calmed down. Jim and Alice were able to spend more time with each other and found out how much more they needed one another.

The two executives in the large company are also married now. She has a job with another company and received a major promotion in the past year.

At the law firm the outcome was equally bright. The woman was on the track to a high-level job when she and a partner in the firm decided to marry. She informed her boss and he helped her find a good job with another firm, where she is now on her way to becoming a partner. Colleagues in the original firm are still friends.

'Tis Better to Have Loved

The issues cases like these raise are numerous, but I'd like to summarize those I see as most important:

☐ Until more women are at high executive levels, the woman will usually be the prime victim when two executives fall in love, even if she is a senior member in the organization. Although it is realistic that the least valuable person leave, because that person is so often a woman, it is a sexist solution. Organizations should, therefore, try to defuse the gender issue. In part, they should deal with the problem as a conflict of interest. Increasing the numbers of women at high levels will make it more likely, though in no way guarantee, that resolutions are not sexist.

☐ Male executives attracted to lower-level female executives will be in a painful and serious dilemma. To begin a flirtation, to see her outside of work and expose her to gossip, could be to end her career in that company. The female executive also has some responsibility, but it is less onerous because she will mainly hurt herself. Both have to be aware of the impact their affair will have on the employment policies of the company.

☐ The "gentlemanly" hands-off way of approaching personal matters disrupts the goals of the corporation. Such love relationships will not go away if ignored; they will most likely lead to organizational stress. Executives must learn to deal with these messy human problems. In fact, the way they approach sensitive issues like love and sex will influence in part the way people view management.

Sadly, most people lack the skills to deal with these issues. More people will need to be aware of the effect of the love affair on the organization, its implications if it lasts, and their own likely responses to it. Until people reach this level of sophistication, even close, platonic friendships between men and women will be affected. As more women enter higher levels in organizations these issues will surface and have to be dealt with. Ultimately we will all be less squeamish, and male-female friendships will form without arousing suspicion.

Until then, clear-cut company policies should outline the conflicts and probable consequences of these romances. Explicit policies wil make executives understand that to break a taboo, a relationship should be worth the price they will pay. Moreover, a policy allays the fears of others in the organization that things will get completely out of control and will mitigate some of the potential organizational chaos.

Top managers have to take the lead in dealing with these complicated situations. Regardless of how clumsy their attempts, it is better to have tried and failed than never to have tried at all.

Notes

1. According to James G. Clawson and Kathy E. Kram, "Managing Cross-Sex Developmental Relationships." *Business Horizons*, forthcoming.

2. Daniel H. Levinson, *The Seasons of a Man's Life* (New York: Knopf, 1978).

3. Robert E. Quinn, "Coping with Cupid: The Formation, Impact and Management of Romantic Relationships in Organizations," *Administrative Science Quarterly*, March 1977, p. 34.

PART THREE

THE CHANGING NEEDS OF EMPLOYEES

AN OVERVIEW

As I indicated in my introduction, one of the difficulties a manager has when faced with a troublesome or troubled employee is figuring out what the problem is and whom it concerns. As we've seen, female and minority employees may present difficulties but the most likely path to resolution is not one the employee can walk alone. Often the problem is a supervisor or the general attitude of others in the organization. The articles in this section concern the problems employees present managers because of their age. Here too, it is not always easy to determine the cause of the conflict; whether it is the stage of life of the employee or of the organization, or whether, in fact, what is happening should be seen as a problem at all.

In the "Case of the Suspect Salesman," Albert H. Dunn describes a situation in which a young salesman who performs superbly for the company gets into trouble with his superior because of his approach to the job. The conflict is one of values. The young salesman is a product of the 1960s' generation—he dislikes authority, likes to work independently, and sees his time as his own. Even though he appreciates the work done, the supervisor is a rules-minded traditionalist who interprets his subordinate's off-hand and carefree ways as a personal affront and a sign of instability. What is responsible and imaginative behavior to one is misbehavior to the other.

The problem here is the older man. By trying to squeeze the younger person into a traditional mold he runs the risk of either forcing the salesman to quit or turning him into a withholding bureaucrat. Neither would be good for the company. Faced with the coming flood of young people with different but nonetheless productive values, senior managers need to educate supervisors and middle-level managers about the needs of young employees. The trick is to help these managers see the difference between supervision and management. With the former they control and with the latter they oversee, keeping in mind the desired outcome, namely, good performance.

Managers may think that older employees are easier to manage. Here at least are people who share the same values and orientations toward work as themselves, people who are mature and loyal to the company. In many cases, this is correct. But even older employees have their own sets of concerns that can derail their careers and confound their bosses. The next two articles in this section, "On Being a Middle-Aged Manager," by Harry Levinson and "Three Vice Presidents in Mid-Life," by Stanley M. Davis and Roger L. Gould, describe some of the concerns that face employees as they pass through the midpoints of their lives and suffer increased symptoms of aging. Often, according to Levinson, work styles and points of view change with time as do personal goals. The employee who was once hard driving and aggressive may slowly become complacent and passive.

A manager needs to be aware of the kinds of changes to which middle-aged employees are prone and, as Davis and Gould point out, see these changes as opportunities for growth rather than as problems. In their article, Davis and Gould give three case histories of men in mid-life change. The two who used the turmoil they experienced to deal with old anxieties, progressed and became more mature. The man who denied the experience, didn't. Managers may want to revise the reward and promotion systems in their organizations to accommodate their aging employees' changing priorities. But most important of all, they need to see people undergoing the trauma of transition not as disabled but as individuals in the process of growth.

People at mid-life often consider changing their careers. Sometimes a new start would be for the good, but the desire to move can also signal that a person is running from some difficulty that he or she finds too painful to face. Executives considering a career change would do well to read "A Second Career: The Possible Dream," by Harry Levinson carefully. He describes a process managers can use to determine whether their dream fits their talents and their personalities, and whether they have considered the costs, both personal and financial, of giving up their present jobs. Two executives, Wheelock Whitney and William G. Damroth, both made career switches during the midpoint of their lives. In "Don't Call It 'Early Retirement'" they describe how they felt strangled and dead-ended in their jobs before making a change, and how afterward they found new energy and direction in their lives.

In the last article in this section, "Can You Survive Your Retirement?"

Leland P. Bradford discloses some of the pains and promises of finally leaving the work life. Retirement means not only giving up a structured routine that gave a person a sense of purpose in life, but it also means reforming a relationship with a spouse. The transition from busy executive to man of leisure was not an easy one for Bradford, and he offers top managers some pointers on how they can help their older employees make the step less painful.

15

Case of the Suspect Salesman

ALBERT H. DUNN

In one sense, this case is about a sales manager who is unhappy with one of his young sales reps. In another sense, it is about a conflict that goes on increasingly between the managers and young subordinates. Indeed, it is likely that the commentators, though their main experience has been in sales management and marketing, mirror the opinions that commentators from other management areas might have supplied. As in the past, *HBR* invites readers to study the case, consider the kinds of questions the commentators were asked, and then compare their own opinions with those in the analysis.

Jim Lee graduated from college in June of 1975 with a major in business administration. He was hired by the Casco Drug Company in September as a sales representative trainee and assigned to Sal Lucci's district.

Sal was the Exeter district sales manager for the Casco Drug Company (see *Exhibit 1*). His 11 sales representatives covered New Jersey, parts of Delaware, and Pennsylvania as far west as Lancaster. The district was considered an important revenue producer for the company.

Like the other 300 Casco sales reps, Jim Lee sold a wide line of prescription and over-the-counter drugs to doctors, hospitals, drug retailers, wholesalers, and chains. Sales reps called on doctors to introduce new products and to remind them of old items with the objective of having the doctor prescribe Casco brands. With retailers, wholesalers, and chains, the reps

Published in 1979.

Comments by: Warren C. Gray, Southeast Region Operations Manager, Taylor Instrument Company, Division of Sybron Corporation; Billy J. Rollins, Vice President/Sales, Ivan Allen Company; and Albert V. Willett, Retired Manager, E.I. du Pont de Nemours & Company.

Exhibit 1.   Casco Drug Company

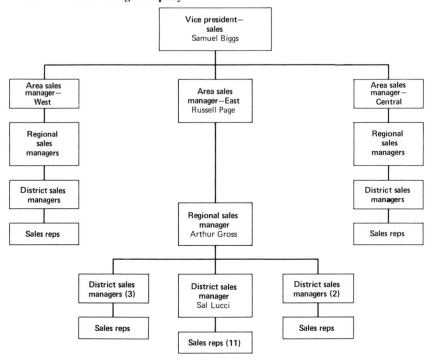

checked inventory, introduced new products, and sold items being specially promoted.

The performance of the reps was evaluated primarily on the basis of sales in their territories. However, consideration was given also to the number of calls per day, number of products presented per call, the supervisor's assessment of their work, and their success in following the current sales promotion plan.

As a sales rep, Jim could improve his sales primarily in two ways: by increasing the number of calls he made in a week and by improving the quality of his relationships with doctors and middlemen. For example, he might make additional calls on some doctors who were in their offices on Saturday morning, he might schedule presentations to hospitals for Saturdays and holidays, or he might take extra time to advise wholesalers and retailers on inventory and promotion.

Like all Casco sales recruits, Jim Lee first worked his way through the sales orientation schedule (see *Exhibit 2*). For those reps who showed outstanding management potential, after some time in the field there was a sales management development program.

Each year three to five of the most promising reps joined the headquarters sales staff in Chicago. Here they were exposed to a variety of

Exhibit 2.   Sales Orientation Schedule

Week	Activities
1	District assignment; beginning company orientation and territory indoctrination.
2-5	Full time at Sales Training Institute (Chicago): product information, sales policies and procedures, work in selling skills and techniques.
6-17	Work-assigned territory, traveling one week each with two training coaches* and district manager; biweekly correspondence instruction; regular quizzes and evaluations from the institute.
18-21	Full time at the institute: advanced instruction in product specifications, use, and performance; sales techniques.
22-27	Work the territory; biweekly correspondence instruction, regular quizzes, and quiz scores from the institute for the last six weeks.

*Senior salespeople from the trainee's district.

management problems, indoctrinated in the corporation's promotion strategies, and given the opportunity to assist headquarters staff in decision making.

After about two years, those who were successful in this program returned to the field as assistant managers in large districts or as managers of smaller districts.

The Problem Unfolds

As part of his sales orientation training, Jim was sent in October 1975 to the Casco Sales Training Institute in Chicago for an intensive one-month indoctrination in the company's products, sales procedures, and selling techniques. In the regular summary report to Jim's district manager, the director commented on the young man's month in Chicago:

> Jim's bright, very bright, learns quickly, and retains well. But he certainly has his own ideas about how we should run things! Some of his ideas are good; in fact, we've implemented several of them here, but the others are a waste of everybody's time. This is probably just a function of his inexperience. He'll learn fast and be a winner!

When he read this comment, Sal recalled some recent experiences with other young salespeople and noted in the margin, "Another young revolutionary???"

In November, Jim was assigned to his territory and worked it for three months, traveling a week each with two training coaches and Sal. During this period he prepared the regular correspondence assignments from the institute and took examinations on the material. He went back in February for another month at the institute and in March returned to his territory and completed his training with six weeks of correspondence instruction from the institute.

Jim Throws a Party. In the late fall of 1976, Jim stopped by Sal's office to invite him to a party the following Sunday. "There are a bunch of us who hang around together, watch TV, play golf—you know," Jim said. "We're going to watch the Jets and the Giants on Sunday, and we'd like you and Mrs. Lucci to join us at our house around 1:30."

This invitation was a new one for Sal. He couldn't remember one time when he and his wife Betty had been asked to an informal party by one of his junior people. Sal didn't like pro football, and he preferred to read the paper on Sundays. Also he didn't like having to shave and put on a tie over the weekend. But he thought it would be impolite not to accept Jim's invitation.

When Sal and Betty drove to the Lee's home, they noted that the house, though small, was located in the most desirable and expensive neighborhood of the city. Several of the cars parked in front of the house were sports models. "Damn well not company cars," Sal muttered.

In addition to Jim and Carol Lee, there were five other couples. Among them were two of Sal's reps, a lawyer, a physical therapist, and an assistant professor at the university. The Cutlers were the only other couple from Sal's generation—Tom Cutler was Sal's office manager.

The party centered around a large color TV, where the game was in progress. The volume was set high, but nobody seemed to listen except the professor who sat as close as possible to the set. Everyone talked loudly over the noise. The conversation was liberally laced with obscenities. All the young people were casually dressed; only Sal and Tom Cutler wore ties. The lawyer and the professor had full beards.

The guests drifted between the living room and the kitchen for drinks; someone had started a pyramid of empty beer cans in a corner. The guests kidded with each other in easy familiarity. The lawyer was "Judge," the professor "Specs," and the salesmen "Huckster."

Carol Lee took Betty Lucci on a tour of the house, and during the halftime intermission the Lees set up a cold buffet. The Luccis and the Cutlers left midway through the fourth quarter. On the drive home, Betty said, "I don't know what Jim Lee makes and I don't care. But I know what we're making and how we can afford to live. That house! Wall-to-wall carpet, expensive furniture, microwave oven, color TV, stereo to all the rooms— and in the best section of town! I'd say they've got a rich uncle somewhere."

Sal replied, "From what I know about Jim's finances, it's more likely they've got a lot of mortgages, IOUs, time payments, and no insurance."

Sal Gets Irritated. By May 1977, Jim's sales performance was clearly superior, and Sal wrote him a personal note congratulating him on his "outstanding selling record." A few months later Jim's expense account included an item of $83.60 for "dinner and entertainment for Doctor and Mrs. Link and self at Pine Grove Inn." Professor Charles Link was perhaps the leading scholar-researcher in the world in the field of targeted delivery of encapsulated agents and was on the faculty of a local prestigious university.

Tom Cutler disallowed his expense item on the ground that Dr. Link had no direct influence on Casco sales in Jim Lee's territory and that contact with academic researchers was the sole responsibility of the corporation's new product group, not of the territory reps. Jim challenged this decision in a memo to Sal:

> Dr. Link is tops in the world in targeted delivery. We're into it too. Who knows what his work will produce next month or next year? We might want to know about it or have a shot at it. It's a pleasure to talk to him about his research. And what in hell does an office manager know about selling anyway? Sal, I protest in the strongest terms. Explain to Cutler how it is!

Sal agreed with Cutler and was angry at being caught between his office manager and one of his best sales reps. Over the weekend he called Jim to discuss the matter and found him still upset. Sal explained that Cutler was only applying corporate expense policies as he was required to do. After some further discussion, Sal said he considered it a one-time incident from which Jim had learned something important about Casco's expense account policies. He asked Cutler to allow the expense.

Casco's national sales report for the quarter ending March 31, 1978 showed Jim Lee to be second in the Exeter district and fifth nationally.

Every other Friday afternoon Sal's people met to discuss mutual problems and to receive new information and instructions. Without advance notice to Sal, Jim was absent from one of these meetings in May. Sal inquired if he was ill. An assistant in Sal's office said she had coffee with him that morning and he was fine.

Sal was annoyed. The meetings were not a life-or-death matter, but for Jim to be absent without an explanation struck Sal as a breach of discipline. Also, the success of the Friday meetings depended on full participation. Asked later about his absence, Jim said he had had an emergency problem with an important customer. This turned out to have been the case, but Sal was still not satisfied with how Jim had handled the matter.

In the summer of 1978, Sal was traveling with veteran salesman Howard Cohen. At lunch Cohen related a recent experience. Three weeks before on a Saturday afternoon, he and Lee had teamed up to make a presentation to a group of specialists in a large hospital on the border of their territories. Cohen thought the presentation had gone excellently and told Jim so. But Jim persisted in asking for criticism and feedback on his part of the presentation and on his preparation for it. The older salesman went on:

> Hell, he should worry! Number two in the district and number five in the country. I should be asking *him* for tips! But he's all over me for suggestions—won't let go. Doesn't seem right. Why does he do that, do you think?

Sal replied, "I get the same reading, Howard, when I'm out with him.

Always wants criticism—I just don't know. Frankly it's really beginning to bug me."

A Question about Jim's Honesty.   In February 1979, while Sal was traveling with Jim, they called on the purchasing agent of a large drug chain. Jim went to the warehouse to check stock, leaving Sal with the buyer. The buyer was enthusaistic about Jim's work for them, citing several innovations Jim had suggested in buying and inventory procedures. The suggestions had saved the chain considerable money.

Several months later Sal received a letter from Samuel Biggs, the sales vice president, commending him "on the fine job you are doing in developing Jim Lee." Attached was a carbon of Bigg's letter to Jim congratulating him on "being number one in your district and number two in the whole country."

In June, Sal was invited by an important customer to golf at his club on Tuesday afternoon. When he was on the 14th tee, Sal saw Jim in the distance with three other men. They were obviously enjoying themselves, more interested in jokes and horseplay than in serious golf.

Sal was furious that one of his reps would play golf on a workday afternoon. The question of what he should do about it occupied Sal's mind more than his golf game for the rest of the round.

That evening, Sal called Lee, saying he had seem him on the course that afternoon. "What gives?" Sal asked.

"Those are some pretty important people," Jim replied.

"You mean important to us?"

"Could be. You never know."

"Are they customers?"

"No. Not right now, but they could be someday."

Sal decided Jim was not telling the truth, but he thought he had gotten the message over to him, and for now this was enough. Sal said, "Okay, just wanted to be sure there wasn't anything fishy going on. Thanks."

Sal Blows a Fuse.   Wednesday, August 22, 1979 was a scorcher. By the time Sal got to his office he was soaked. The air conditioner did not help either his perspiration or his temper. For Sal, Wednesday was "crap day" because he was chairbound all day to sign letters and do the other paperwork he so thoroughly despised.

Late in the morning there was a noisy greeting in Sal's outer office, and in came Arthur Gross, the regional sales manager (see Exhibit 1). Sal was not expecting him. They chatted for a while about Gross's golf game, then discussed some business problems. Finally, Gross explained his unannounced visit:

"Had some business up the line and since I'm here, I came in to talk to Jim Lee. Sam Biggs let Russ Page [area sales manager—East] know he's very interested in Lee for this year's management development program. Thought I'd talk to Lee about this because I'll have to make the recommendation to Russ. Can you get us together? I've got a 6:40 flight out of LaGuardia."

Sal asked his secretary if Jim had called in, as all reps did each day before noon. It was 11:45; he had not called in.

As he left for lunch, Gross said he'd call about 1:30 to see about the meeting with Jim in the afternoon.

Sal tried not to show how furious he was. Where was that young jerk? At noon Sal left for his appointment—still no word from Jim. He told his secretary, "Find Jim before 1:15. Check his weekly call program and call customers if you have to! I don't give a damn if you have to call out the Marines—find Jim Lee!"

An hour later Sal was back. His secretary's note read:

"Got Jim's wife. He's a Big Brother—you know that social service stuff. He's taken his 'little brother' to a ball game. Gone all afternoon. She said he does this sometimes so the kid won't think he's just a weekend Big Brother. I've gone to lunch. Jenny."

Sal balled the note up and threw it against the wall. He stared out the window. He was mad. How would he look to Gross when he couldn't find one of his men? "Jim's a great salesman and a great pain in the behind!" he thought.

Gross's call came all too soon. Was the meeting with Jim Lee set up? Sal debated whether to lie or tell it like it is. He decided to cover for Jim. No, the meeting wasn't set up, Sal told the regional sales boss. Jim was home with the flu, but he was interested in being considered for the management development program. Maybe when Jim got back on his feet, he could come out and see Gross. Gross said that was a possibility. He would think about it. After a few pleasantries, he hung up.

Sal was beside himself. "That damn kid can't get me in this mess! He knows better! Taking company time for golf or Big Brother or whatever else he damn well wants to—covering up. Thinks he knows how to run the company—making his own rules. This has got to stop!"

He told Jenny:

"Tell Jim to be here at 8:30 tomorrow morning. I don't want any crap from him. Get that bastard in. I want to see him tomorrow, *here*!"

Before you read farther, ask yourself the six questions *HBR* asked the commentators, whose opinions appear in the next section:

1 Why is Jim behaving as he is?
2 Why is Sal behaving as he is?
3 Do you find yourself sympathetic to Jim? To Sal? Why?
4 What do you expect Sal will do in his meeting with Jim?
5 Do you think Sal's probable action is the right action for him to take? Why do you think so?
6 Ideally, what do you think Sal should do?

How the Commentators See the Problem

With a few exceptions, commentators Warren Gray and Billy Rollins perceive the problem in much the same way. At some points, Albert Willett takes a different view. But despite some variance in their analyses, the commentators all agree that the situation presented in the case is of great concern to managers in every area of corporate operations, as is shown by their comments:

    Gray: *The problem is realistic and similar to what a manager runs into today with younger account managers.*
    Rollins: *This problem is very real in sales management.*
    Willett: *This is an excellent example of the conflict between the value systems of senior managers and of young people in business.*

Why Jim and Sal Behave as They Do.   All three commentators see Jim's behavior as normal and appropriate for a young go-getter who wants to grow in his job and improve his sales performance. Rollins suggests that Jim believes his success "frees him from some of the management controls Sal must exercise" and adds that Jim is testing Sal and the company to see how far he can go, "a characteristic of many good salespeople." Willett says that Jim is being completely consistent with his own value system and understanding of the world.

Gray and Rollins take a dim view of Sal's behavior, citing his petty jealousy of Jim, lack of imagination, frustration, inability to interact effectively with young people, and poor office and personnel management procedures.

Willett, however, contends that Sal is behaving as he *must* behave, that he is completely consistent with his value system and what he believes the aims of business and selling are.

Where the Commentators' Sympathies Lie.   Gray and Willett are attracted to Jim. They perceive him as ambitious, mature, and anxious to improve—an open and growing person who knows who he is and where he is going. Gray adds that Jim is handicapped by Sal's poor management techniques and personal weaknesses.

Rollins is sympathetic to Sal; he says Sal has been blinded by his emotions—Sal is uncertain if his superiors will judge his performance by results or by adherence to operating procedures.

Willett feels sorry for Sal. He reads Sal as a "closed, cold, narrow, immature, uncertain person." This manager is a man who is "going nowhere and probably knows it"; he has probably progressed in the company beyond his capabilities, without the understanding or skills needed to resolve the problem with Jim. Willett feels Sal is more to be pitied than blamed.

What Will Sal Do?   The commentators all make the same forecast for Sal's meeting with Jim. Sal will come down hard on Jim. His emotions will prevail. One commentator states, "Sal will roar at Jim, eat him out. He'll tell Jim to follow all the rules without variation, regardless of the reason. Quit wasting time with noncustomers and don't miss any meetings. He might go so far as to say, 'Even if you are our best salesman, we've got to have discipline around here. I won't put up with your actions anymore!'"

Is Sal Right?   Gray and Rollins say that what Sal will probably do is the wrong thing to do. They believe that Sal would be acting in anger, that such behavior would accomplish nothing, and that he will destroy what little rapport he has with Jim.

In part because of the treachery of language, Willett argues that Sal's probable action is the only *right* action for him to take. How else could Sal act and be consistent with his principles? Any other behavior would not be Sal. Willett adds:

> If Jim has as much sense as I think he has, he'll immediately resign and hire on with a competitor or valued customer. Sal will be left holding the bag; he'll lose one of his best salesman to a position resulting in future loss of business to Casco.

Ideally, What Should Sal Do?   Rollins and Gray assert that Sal should meet with Jim in an objective and constructive atmosphere, explain the need to adhere to established procedures, and "set up rules that allow certain liberties, but based on results." Sal should emphasize that Jim can contribute a lot to the Friday meetings and point out to him that, if he has aspirations for a management position, conforming to company policies and procedures will help his career.

Willett sees Sal as incapable of taking the "ideal" action. Sal's value system and his conception of "how things are" won't allow him to be understanding and tactful with an "undisciplined" subordinate, especially one he has had to cover for.

Willett writes, "Another, more perceptive manager would tell Jim of Gross's visit and the reason for it. He would tell Jim he was very embarrassed in front of Gross when he could not locate Jim but later deliberately lied to protect him. He'd let Jim know that, despite this episode, he will put in a strong recommendation for Jim for the management training program. The perceptive manager might even make a plea for help: 'Please don't get me into such an embarrassing mess again.'"

How I See the Problem

As is expected of three experienced business managers, each commentator sees the problem of Jim and Sal and its resolution somewhat differently. As is probably also expected of a professor, I see the case in yet another light. It is the shorthand statement of a serious, prevalent, and ongoing problem that is *the* challenge facing managers today. If a solution is not found, and expeditiously, the practice of business management will soon change substantially, not necessarily for the better.

The Two Different Work Ethics. A personal work ethic is formed by an individual's experiences, education, and value judgments about himself, his company, his job, and about business and the world in general. On the basis of this work ethic, he takes actions, makes decisions, and is satisfied or dissatisfied with his job.

For the past 20 years, two often-conflicting work ethics have been interacting in management and business operations. Appendix A illustrates the two contrasting work ethics—the *traditional,* which Sal subscribes to, and the *new,* which Jim follows. The ways in which Sal and Jim behave are consistent with their individual work ethics.

In the superior-subordinate relationship, the traditional and the new value systems constantly interact. In some of these interactions, the two work ethics are in agreement, making cooperation easy. In other important respects, they are opposed to the extent that subtle or direct conflict results, causing frustration, lowered morale, and poor performance.

Sal—and other managers—might hope that the new work ethic will just go away. But it will not, nor can the traditional values be forced on young achievers. The new work ethic has been irrevocably trained into them by virtually every cultural and educational encounter that they have had in their lives.

If Jim Lee—the achiever—were to adopt the traditional ethic, he would be ruined. His behavior might become even more traditional than Sal's, but his inner turmoil would tear him apart. Such an achiever would become a bureaucrat, withholding his ideas, creativity, and extra effort. He would be restless, unhappy, and prone to ulcers. And a valuable corporate asset would be lost.

The primary concern of the good manager is for the achievers among his subordinates—the Jim Lees. Those without ambition, perception, or special talents will perform adequately if they are well *supervised,* but the achievers must be *managed.* They are the future of business and of the company and, if well managed, will reflect credit on their managers. But this is very difficult to do for someone who is as invested in the traditional way as Sal is.

How do we manage when the business world is populated by Sal Luccis and Jim Lees? Indeed, how do we manage the interaction of the new and traditional work ethics so that it accommodates the needs of both and exploits their best assets? This question is the present and primary challenge to all managers.

Unfortunately, we are hampered by the newness of this conflict—until recently the traditional ethic always prevailed. In the infrequent event of a conflict of values, traditional-prone managers resorted to some form of force, propaganda, or bargaining and eventually won out. But now these two strong and divergent work ethics are so well matched that none of the usual techniques of resolution are feasible.

All of the commentators, in one way or another, suggest one possible approach that merits careful consideration. After a problem or issue crops up, the perceptive manager can use it as a launching pad to discuss conflicts and make mutually satisfactory modifications.

In this instance, Sal—ideally—could bring up the broader topics at issue in his meeting with Jim. Through such interactions based on shared experiences, over time a third work ethic could emerge that would accommodate the important values of the new and the traditional systems; and it might be far more realistic for both senior managers and young achievers than either system now in use.

When issues like the ones in this case arise, communication, respect, tolerance, and cooperation will be difficult if not impossible unless managers and subordinates give in a little (or sometimes a lot) and bear in mind where the other person is coming from.

It would be wonderfully satisfying—for the commentators, readers, and myself—to be able to resolve this critical problem with a universal formula or general set of rules. But this is not possible. Instead, this analysis can only end with a plea that those who can effect change in the business world will seriously seek answers to the questions presented here and will recognize this as the management problem of our time.

Appendix A: Traditional Work Ethic Versus New Work Ethic

Event	Sal's view (*traditional*)	Jim's view (*new*)
Director's report on Jim's training in Chicago	Casco's success shows that the company has known how to do things right for a long time. A trainee's job is to learn how we do it, certainly not to offer suggestions without adequate experience.	The company wants fresh ideas and points of view from everybody—new, old, experienced, inexperienced. The company gains from these ideas; communicating suggestions for improvement is an important responsibility of all Casco employees.
Dinner with the Links	The salesman's job is to sell to established customers; development of new business is a specialized corporate group. Salesmen stay out! Expense policies are clearly stated and must be adhered to.	Sales reps are managers in their territories; as such they should be concerned with everything that does or might relate to Casco business in their territories. A sales rep makes his own decisions; as manager of his territory, he is expected to exercise his discretion on how he spends the company's money.

Jim missing the Friday meeting	A manager's job is to manage. There are good reasons for these meetings, and the manager doesn't need to explain them. he knows what's best for his people—absences must be approved, and there must be discipline.	As manager of his territory, a salesman sets his own priorities—the office should recognize this.
The Lee's party	People dress carefully for a party on Sunday; men don't use foul language in front of ladies (and ladies *never* use it).	Standards of personal conduct aren't the same at work and at home. The company doesn't *own* you!
The Tuesday golf game	The company pays for work they specify. This means doing Casco's work during working hours, and unauthorized variations are not allowed.	Casco's management doesn't tell salespeople what holidays and weekends to work; the company should be result oriented, not procedure oriented or schedule oriented.
Jim as a Big Brother	The business of business is business; on company time employees pursue only those activities directly related to the company.	Business and the people in business take profit from our society, so business and its people have important social responsibilities.
The Lee's standard of living	First you earn your luxuries, then you enjoy them.	You can enjoy luxuries while you earn them.

16
Three Vice Presidents in Mid-Life

STANLEY M. DAVIS and ROGER L. GOULD

Some fast-track managers with high potential glide through their careers as if the track were smooth as silk. Others have a bumpy ride but arrive at their goals nonetheless, while still others hit the skids and never recover. What accounts for these differences? One possible explanation is the degree to which each manager has developed personally. People go through numerous phases of development, one of the most crucial of which occurs in mid-life—usually during the early forties. During that time a person may achieve a balance between home and work, become his own authority, and give up the myths of childhood—or he may not develop at all. In any event, this transition period can be a time of crisis that erupts at work. To see how the passage through mid-life manifests itself at work, the authors interviewed more than 50 executives in major corporations and present here three of those interviews. The subjects talk about how their mid-life development affected their work lives, and vice versa, and whether they are content with the outcome. What stands out in these interviews is that in order to grow, people have to be willing to give up many of their old ways of dealing with the world and their beliefs about it and to accept their own mortality.

> I get the willies when I see closed doors. Even at work, where I am doing so well now, the sight of a closed door is sometimes enough to

Published in 1981.

Author's Note. See notes 3–7 for related reading.

Author's Note. We wish to express our appreciation to the Center for Career Development, Columbia University, and to Eileen Morley for their support during part of the research for this article.

make me dread that something horrible is happening behind it, something
that is going to affect me adversely. . . . I can almost smell the disaster
mounting invisibly and flooding out toward me through the frosted panes.
My hands may perspire, and my voice may come out strange. I wonder
why.

The opening words of Joseph Heller's novel, *Something Happened,*
are the 43-year-old hero's account of what many people experience in real
life, namely, a mid-life crisis.[1] A mid-life crisis is an extreme case of the
normal process of mid-life transition.

All lives unfold in steps and stages. For both individuals and organizations, transition points are inevitable and necessary. The mid-life transition
is a particularly powerful period of change and is distinguishable from other
natural transition periods by the nature of the development task that individuals must perform.

At mid-life a person often gives up old dreams and hopes but realizes
new capacities and talents instead. A person may give up youth and reck-
lessness but accept the notion of his own aging and eventual death. Regardless, a taking stock, a reckoning, and a reorientation occur, which can
be painful. (See Appendix A for a detailed discussion of the current thinking
on adult development and on how the stage of life a person is in can affect
his work.)

Because most of the corporations in our society are run by men in their
mid-lives who will undergo or have undergone a transition, we wanted to
examine how this phenomenon mainfests itself in the context of corporate
life. To do so we conducted interviews with more than 50 male executives
in several major corporations.[2]

All people react differently to a period of change. Some work at changing daily and silently and end the transition without knowing that they did
any development work. They just know they have changed. Others, like
Heller's hero, go through hell before they can say they have changed. Still
others avoid the painful task altogether, only to find themselves eventually
in another kind of hell—they are older and sadder instead of older and wiser.

We illustrate these three reactions to the mid-life transition with three
of the interviews we conducted. The subjects are typical of those we interviewed. They are not psychiatric cases but well-paid and successful officers
of major corporations who have all been on the fast track.

What follows are Bob, Larry, and Tom's stories about what happened
to them between their mid-thirties and mid-forties. After each interview we
discuss what we think the nature of the transition was, how the individual
coped with it, and how it affected his work life.

We think it important that managers not mistake a transition period
for failure or catastrophe. Transitions are "critical" decision periods between progress and stagnation. Not all development, personal or otherwise,
is a series of crises. Significant change also occurs in people's lives during
periods of general stability. It is during turning points, however—during

important transitions—when managers need to view crises the way Chinese ideograms define them: not as failures but as dangerous opportunities.

Bob works for an organization on the *Fortune* list of major corporations. He is among the top 5% of the roughly 50,000 employees in the company and is typical of many of the managers we interviewed. He has been with his company for more than 20 years, spending most of that time as a functional specialist in a variety of positions in corporate headquarters.

People who work with Bob and for him speak about him as one of the most seasoned and responsible people in the corporation: "He's the kind of guy you want on your side when you have to go to the mat." Bob's transition began about the time when, as a successful vice president with a good reputation inside and outside the organization, he received an offer of a new assignment within the company.

BOB: An announcement was made that two vice presidents were switching jobs. This was the first they or anyone had heard of it. Three weeks later it was clear that management was scurrying around looking for a replacement for one of the vice presidents. Apparently the team above him was making him lose his breakfast in the morning. So they came to me: "Wouldn't it be nice if you took the job?" I said, "No way." So somebody laid a hand on my shoulder and said, "You know, I really would like you to do that." And it was a voice I couldn't say no to. I said, "I think it's wrong for me, but I'll try."

You have to understand. They came to me and said, "Take a job because nobody else wants to take it." And I said, "There's nothing in it for me. I have a better job than the one you're asking me to take, and you're asking me to go into an area that other people don't want." But somebody asked me to do something for the company. And I did it.

There was nothing at home that detracted seriously from my performance on the job or that caused me any problems. But it was the wrong job for me, and it ended in disaster.

Still, if you asked me, and if I knew what I know now, "Would I repeat the performance?" my answer would be yes. Because I was in that position when everything was happening, I got a far greater understanding of what was going on in the corporation than anybody else around today.

My new boss was the only guy I've ever worked for who made me feel uncomfortable about my conceptual abilities. He was so quick on his feet and so broad in his knowledge. He'd ask questions I couldn't even think of. But we had no rapport at all. It could have been a real turn-on and I could have grown with him, but there was no invitation to grow. He treated me as if he was saying, "I want to show you how dumb you are, kid," even though I was a few years older than him.

It was a crucible, and it put my career back considerably. I was clearly in turmoil, but I didn't know it was happening. I was not in pain or wondering. But one night, after 15 months, they found me unconscious in my office.

Later, the president called me at home and said, "Is it getting too rough for you?" I said, "No, not for me." My boss saw my collapse as a great opportunity for us to part company nondestructively. You know, he didn't want to jeopardize my health and all that bullshit.

After that, they created a lousy job for me that was lower than the one I had. I was a loser. I went through a period of absolute stagnation. I could go to work and sleep for six hours a day. It was such a lousy job—acting as a kind of floating ambassador—you could get a kid to do it. But it looked impressive on paper.

That was the only occasion when I've gone through a bad personal time. I really suffered a loss. I was questioning my competence, my ability: Could I ever do it again? Was it a mistake to begin with? And you've got to work your way out of that yourself. You get no help. No one came with any help at all. Not one query.

A lot of the time I walked around feeling lost. On the job, sometimes I tended to play it safe and wouldn't speak up. You keep your mouth shut.

Did you feel you had to hide it?

BOB: Hell, yes. Absolutely.

What kinds of outlets did you seek during that period?

BOB: Beat the system. Beat the system. I thought, if they wanted me to do a nonjob, I'd give them a total nonjob and convince them it was a real job. My thinking almost reverted to that of a production line worker who says, "If all I'm supposed to do is screw the bolt, screw the job." I did that for a while and then realized that it was counterproductive. I began to size myself up. The important turnaround happened when I came to the conclusion, "Okay, it's happened. I can't change the fact; that's the style here." Then I decided, "Let's see if I can work myself out of here. If I can't, then I'll leave." You build yourself up by taking an affirmative step toward ending the stagnation.

What did it feel like at the lowest point?

BOB: I wanted to cop out. I thought, "Why the hell do I want to work in a company like this to begin with? Why don't I run a hot-dog stand and get out of organizational life? This isn't the place it used to be anyway. Its value system is no longer there. I can't do anything about it, so why bother?"

Then what happened?

BOB: After about two and a half years, a new boss came in. I said, "Oh, boy, this is going to be the crowning thing now." But it turned out that he and I were able to work with each other, which was super from my point of view. We built a degree of trust very quickly. He offered me a new job and said it would provide an avenue for rebuilding as well as exposure that I didn't have to another part of the organization. The only problem was that the head of the group didn't want me.

I told my new boss, "Great, I'll take it." I didn't care. The first six months were rough. It was a deal-oriented culture, where none of my previous experience did much good. But I built my credibility in a group that seemingly had no use for the type of skills that I brought. I didn't even understand how they made money. Still, I could transfer skills and apply them successfully.

So you spent about four and a half years falling off the track and living through what you describe as purgatory. What was going on during that time in your personal life?

BOB: It was not as full and rich a family life as we should have had. But there was no real strain. My wife was very good about it. The kids were good. In the last year or two, though, I've spent more time with them, more fun time, than I spent in all that four and a half years.

As we hear it, you didn't enjoy your work life for four and a half years either.

BOB: No, wrong. I enjoyed the first 15 months of that period. It wasn't a great turn-on, but neither was it a great chore. The chore was the nonjob. If you ask me about stress, I will tell you that it is more stressful not to be occupied than to be too occupied. I didn't have trouble getting up in the morning during the 15 months. But I did during the two and a half years in the nonjob.

I know I'm not a singular case. I can walk through our company dining room and point out five senior vice presidents who have come within an inch of being fired. One person comes to mind who is probably one of the most well-thought-of senior vice presidents in the place. At one point he came so close to not making it. During that time we met at a bar on the other side of town, and I said, "Hang in there. It can't last. Just stay in there."

You think they're terrific guys. You don't know that somewhere along the line in the past five years they got into a tribe, or a subculture, that tried to reject them, and they made it by the skin of their teeth.

We'd like to propose an alternative interpretation and would like to hear your reaction. What you have described seems typical of a mid-life crisis.

BOB: Oh, yes, the male menopause.

Is it perhaps functional to have a nonjob during a period when you're working through a life crisis? At that time your focus was internal, and having a nonjob gave you the time to resolve those issues. Would you have seen any job as engrossing during that period?

BOB: I buy it. I've thought about it, and I've concluded that I wouldn't have changed anything. It may have been for the best—in retrospect—though it was hell while I was going through it.

Bob's Transformation

Mid-life crises do not occur in a vacuum but in certain situations. Bob's experience could have occurred when he was any age. Given an offer he couldn't refuse, Bob agreed to take a tough job that nobody wanted and then found himself with a boss who was more interested in competing with others and proving himself than in being effective or nurturing his staff. As the boss was the better politician, Bob walked away with the label of loser.

That part was situational. The rest of what happened occurred because Bob was in mid-life. At 25 or 30, a person who loses a political battle and ends up labeled a loser can leave the organization, transfer to a distant part of it, or expect to be given another chance because he is still young. But during mid-life, a person doesn't have these options and is vulnerable even when the work is going well. When the world seems to validate a person's self-doubts with the label of loser, the mid-life transition abruptly turns into a mid-life crisis.

Bob vividly describes what he went through and, in response to our question about the mid-life crisis, indicates that something profound happened to him during those years of "being all screwed up." At the end of four and a half years, he had a different basis for his self-confidence. By overcoming his own worst self-doubts, Bob achieved a knowledge of his capabilities that the organization with all its labels could not bestow on him. His new self-confidence came from within rather than from without.

A person does not need to go through a crisis like Bob's to reap benefits from the mid-life transition. Bob was an unfortunate victim of a number of forces, many of which could have been avoided. But his experience is not unique, and others may get comfort from it. From an observer's dispassionate perspective, these events and emotions are not only predictable in a general sense, they are also desirable. Although happiness is part of the process of living rather than the goal, growth is more often the outcome than part of the process itself.

We shrink from assigning causality to the interplay between the person and the organization. The situational reality of the corporation and the psychic reality of the mid-life passage are distinct, but for some individuals the rough spots in each reality occur at the same time.

Periods of crisis—during which a transformation often takes place—

seem to last for two to four years. An event may lead to a person's reha-
bilitation back into the mainstream of organizational life. Often the arrival
of a new boss or someone who knows the person from his or her earlier
career serves as a catalyst to put the person back on track.

The reader might well ask, "Can't I finesse this difficult mid-life transformation? Isn't it possible to change and grow without experiencing and
manifesting extreme difficulties?" In fact, many people pass through mid-
life this way and often receive rewards from their organizations. But do they
escape unscathed?

The answer to that question is both yes and no. Our next two examples,
Larry and Tom, went through the mid-life transition without a crisis. Larry
is paying a heavy price for his apparently smooth ride through the transition.
Tom confronted the pain directly, did his work, and gained the benefits
without a crisis.

To the world at large, Larry is the ultimate success story. He blends
the professional with the company man. He has served in line positions in
a diverse set of businesses in a single corporation to which he is ultimately
loyal. If a seasoned executive in the company needs the counsel of an even
more experienced professional, then Larry is often the person he'll speak
with. Larry is also a mentor to many of the new generation of fast-track
managers in their twenties and early thirties. Ten minutes into the interview,
Larry revealed his private world.

LARRY: I'm 49. I came to work here in 1960, so I've been with the company
for 20 years. Before that, in my college years, I thought it was important to
do something for people. Then I found out that the Ivy League doesn't have
schools of social work. I had a pretty good life, rotating through my assignments here and abroad. I've always had an interesting job; it's always been
challenging. I haven't had any personal crises with the company.

I'm an unabashed enthusiast for the place. I've never worked for anyone I really didn't enjoy there. I've never been jammed into one of those
two- or six-year stints where you have to work for some son of a bitch you
can't stand or you feel isn't interested in you. I feel well acquainted with
senior management. I've worked for two of the three top guys for extended
periods, which does a lot to give you the feeling that you're part of the
enterprise, that you're wanted and cared for. I've always had that feeling,
and I worry that it's probably impossible to give the same sense to people
today.

I'm reasonably good working with people and, in this crazy organization, I'm considered a useful, cohesive force. I have a reasonably broad
perspective on what we're doing. So if I have a theme, it's that I do like
and believe in the organization.

**The theme we hear is "good news." Through two decades, you've enjoyed
what you do, and every so often you've been pleasantly surprised to find**

yourself up one more notch with another great assignment. Is that how you see it?

LARRY: Well, my satisfaction with my business life is high, though I feel my personal life is much too submerged by my business, and I give myself substantially lower marks outside the company. My family life is at best average. Most of my kicks come from the organization. I get up at 5:30 to jog, hit the train at 7:00, come into work charged up, run my battery right down to zero, and by the time I get home, between 7:00 and 8:00, I'm not ready for anything but a scotch, dinner, a game of Ping-Pong with my kids, and bed.

I'm fairly athletic, but I don't really have any intellectual or social interests outside the company. My energy is mainly directed toward the company, which my wife resents. I don't know whether my kids resent it, but that's the way it is.

I'd say my wife and I have a mediocre relationship. I accept my marriage as not being very good. I'm afraid there's not much I can do about it. It's not bad enough to leave, and what satisfaction I get comes from my kids. I enjoy them, and for the few years left that they'll be around, I want to maintain my home. So I think I see myself pretty clearly. I've made peace with myself, and I think I'm much more of a realist than I was earlier when I was in perpetual motion.

When I was younger I worked my ass off, and I was a confirmed optimist. I just kept moving, overcoming things by sheer energy and commitment, but with a fair amount of tension, and anxiety—which just drove me to more effort, kept me flailing away. That's a costly way to go about doing something, and it blots out everything else. You burden yourself, you burn up all your energy with that attitude.

So I wish that 15 or so years ago I'd been more mature. I might have oriented my outside life better and might have had a chance at the policy board—which is a long shot now unless the chief decides that they ought to have an old man there.

What do you think you're running from?

LARRY: Running from? The personal dissatisfaction with my nonbusiness life, I guess. The company saved me. If I hadn't joined the company when I was younger, I would have slowly gone crazy. I was wandering around in the woods, and the focus, direction, and concreteness of the company oriented me. Yes, my work is a defense against the void in my life outside the company; but, on the other hand, the company and I have grown up together.

You're saying the company has been a much healthier family for you?

LARRY: But it's not entirely healthy. For example, pleasurable contact with people is limited to the company, and that's bad. And I'm cast in that role now. I fly around trying to keep the "people equation" going, as well as looking at the business. I like to do those things. I found out last night that the wife of a guy in the company is coming to town, and we're supposed to have them at our house. My wife does not like business entertaining; I'd do a lot more if she did. I'm at the point now where she could travel with me if she wanted to, but she doesn't like to. And she's right. Why the hell should she be a prisoner of the company I work for?

She's struggling to find something to do now. That's her problem. She doesn't have any profession. At age 45, she's worrying about what's in the game for her, particularly when in two or three years the kids will be gone.

Is she as lonely as you are?

LARRY: More so. I think she has less insight into her problems, and she's very, very uptight. It's a very difficult period for her, and she's not much fun to be with because she's so negative. And she resents my success in the company.

It's as if there is an unresolvable problem and the best you can do is to shelve it and get as much as you can out of work—as if that might be a good way to adapt to the situation.

LARRY: I think that's right. Absolutely. Maybe I don't have as much insight as I think I do. I think the company is monochromatic to most people. The success ethic is rampant here, and we expect people to hit the track running fast and faultlessly. We are helpful to people in a state of crisis. We always know if the guy is getting divorced or if he's got cancer, and we do fine in those cases. But I don't think we're too patient with the slow starter, and guys can get lost fairly fast. It's very hard on people down in the ranks who are not fast achievers. It wasn't like that before.

How would you like your life to have gone?

LARRY: My fantasy is to be supersuccessful and have a good outside life. My ideal is to be a senior vice president, at the least, who works about nine hours a day and has 18 other things outside. But I've lost that. Once you acquire the success ethic here, if you're not supersmart and very mature when you hit the track and just function like crazy, then you have to work like hell and kill yourself.

That was true when I came up, and today—Jesus, the younger generation, the really good ones, eat you alive. It's murder out there in the jungle, and nobody's going to get my job who isn't twice as capable as I was. The performance requirement will be brutal, and it will chew up those people who aren't naturally gifted and focused. They are going to have to commit themselves 100% to the struggle. And that will make their lives pretty bleak.

You're 49. What are your thoughts about the future?

LARRY: I don't really think about the future. I have no other life. I'm locked into this. And really, I'm quite unhappy and unsatisfied, so the whole future seems screwed up. But I'm running from that. A week from tomorrow I catch a plane to Argentina, then to Brazil, then to Mexico. I'll have a good time, along with anxiety.

Larry's Transformation

By his own admission, Larry is a success only in the eyes of others. Because he has never ceased to fulfill strictly organizational criteria for success, the company continues to reward him. The bitter irony is that the rewards he receives from work have become less and less meaningful to his sense of success.

If in response to the questions of an inner voice, a person creates a closer and better fit between his needs and his career during his mid-life decade, then he satisfies his questioning and continues his work as a labor of love. If, on the other hand, the inner questioning does not lead a person to change during this period, the issues and emotions he suppresses may instead lead to an internal schism. By refusing to balance inner with outer needs, family with work, a person sacrifices integrity.

Because Larry was unable to tolerate anxiety, his anxiety became a permanent feature of his life. Living with irony and paradox, with ambiguity and confusion, is necessary to negotiating the mid-life passage. The most difficult part of the mid-life transition is facing one's mortality without flinching and living through and enduring the experience that Heller's hero describes: "I can almost smell the disaster. . . ."

The reward for facing up to the ugliest fact of life, one's own death, is relief from the addiction to any illusion—including the addiction to work. Having accepted the inevitable, a person no longer needs to hide from it.

An executive in Larry's company who had broken his addiction to work described himself this way:

> All I can tell you is that I deal with work pressure so differently now. It still excites me, I still work hard, but it doesn't eat at me anymore. And besides that, I look forward to my weekends, and I'm no longer tense on vacations.

Larry's kind of addiction to work is a disease and needs to be distinguished from simple hard work. If a person is addicted, it "eats at" him, and he can't take time off without being nervous and overeager to get back. When getting to work is a relief, it is also an addiction. Transforming the work experience from a relief that eats at you to a labor you happen to love is one of the goals people struggle toward during mid-life. Larry fantasized about freeing himself from work but dulled the fantasy's impact by immediately talking about the need to survive in the jungle.

In order to grow, people have to discover they were wrong about something they took for granted or modify some rule or regulation they imposed on themselves too rigidly. Despite the pain, Bob allowed himself to do this; Larry did not.

The most critical and poignant aspect of the struggle to grow is the attempt to balance family and work. During their apprenticeships, people tend to work excessively long hours and to use work as a way to avoid intimacy at home. Forty-year-olds, however, generally no longer have to work that hard. The choice is theirs alone—either to let go of work as a defense against intimacy and achieve a better balance between the two; or else to avoid this major task, as Larry did, and slip irretrievably back into domination by old themes.

During the mid-life period, people urgently need to finish the work on personal themes that have been familiar companions through life. As children, people surrender to the fears and anxieties that inhabit the recesses of their minds. As people grow, they learn to cope with these fears and push them aside. They may be almost free of their effects for long periods.

At mid-life the themes resurface, as if asking once more to be attacked directly and resolved—this time by a mature adult mind. Bob tried to avoid the struggle, failed to do so, and in the ensuing painful time laid many of his ghosts to rest. Larry was more successful in avoiding the demons and as a consequence failed to balance his work and family lives.

With Larry's case we've illustrated how, by not wrestling with the development task, people can avoid a mid-life crisis. The price they pay is the maintenance of their addiction to work and the bleakness of their personal lives. Now, with the case of Tom, we're going to illustrate how, by confronting the development task, a person can successfully deal with a mid-life transition. By completing this task, a person breaks his addiction to work and achieves a balanced life in its place.

Tom also is a vice president in a large corporation. He has always had line positions, first as a functional specialist, then as a general manager in larger profit centers. Tom has reached the position of a one-star general in his company and is likely to stay there. At this station he leads a balanced personal and work life. He does not let his work dominate his life to the extent Bob or Larry do. Yet one gets the feeling that it cannot quite all be as fine as he makes it sound. Even for Tom there is no free lunch, although it is harder to see the price tag.

TOM: I've been with the company for almost 20 years, most of the time in the same group. I'm a department head now. I haven't spent any time overseas, which I would love to. I got divorced 10 years ago when my kids were still fairly young. I told my boss that, everything else being equal, I would prefer to stay here until they went away to college. I think I passed up a couple of good opportunities, but I knew that was the risk I ran. So I hope that in the next couple of years, if the right opportunity comes along—like running a foreign operation—that I could do that for four or five years.

I got married about 20 years ago, and I've lived since then in the country, about 50 miles north of here. During my whole career I've commuted back and forth. My ex-wife and I live five miles apart, so the kids are very close by; they are an important part of my life. I see a great deal of them.

Outside the company, I'm mainly interested in outdoor sports. I love fishing and camping and hiking and hunting; I love golf and tennis.

You present a very balanced, well-rounded picture. A whole range of interests outside the job, an active family life before and after your divorce, and what sounds like stable, almost routine, progress on the job. How do you feel about it?

TOM: I find the company an exciting place to work. I have been very fortunate to work with really good people. I like what I'm doing, I like the idea of dealing with large companies and also the international flavor. The strength of the company is its people. You can't type the people around here. They come in all different shapes, colors, and sizes. More than 50% of my staff are not American, which gives me a tremendous challenge. So I can say that I am very happy in the company.

As long as I get up in the morning and am challenged, excited, and well paid, then I'll stay. When that stops, I'll leave. I can do any number of things, though I probably would not go to a competitor. I've been offered a lot of jobs.

The view you take of your job as well as your personal world is intriguing. Some people feel they've burned their bridges and don't have options, while you seem to feel that you've got practically a whole lifetime ahead of you. What helped you to look at your life this way?

TOM: I am a very positive individual. The job is exciting, and I've never felt stymied. Still, I could have been in a more responsible job with a bigger title if I had not wanted to stay here until my kids grew up. But that was a decision I made.

Another thing is, whom do I have to impress? I've been in the company for 20 years, and everybody knows who the hell I am. I'm a known quantity.

So you regard what could be seen as negative events, as an end to growth and new job opportunities, instead as generating alternative forms of getting rewards. Could we hear about the difficulties a bit more? What was happening to you during your divorce? Did it affect your work?

TOM: First of all, I always knew there wouldn't be any animosity between my about-to-be ex-wife and me about the kids. I knew she wasn't going to move away. Neither of us was getting a divorce because we loved someone else.

I also had a challenging, interesting job at the company. I wasn't getting on the train in the morning burdened with a whole lot of personal problems around the breakup of my home life that I took to a job that I hated. Instead, my life was positive at both ends.

Can you tell us a little bit about your youth?

TOM: I grew up in the country. I had a very, very happy home life. I had a fantastic father who was 50 when I was born. He lived until he was 75. He and my mother were very happy. If you plotted all of my immediate family's emotional charts, they would be reasonably even. There was not much divorce. Everybody was healthy and liked the outdoors. I had a secure, strong, positive base.

My ex-wife's family was just the opposite. If I had been a kid in that situation I might have ended up a real nut. Her parents were alcoholic; each divorced and remarried several times.

You portray yourself in such a positive, well-rounded way that one can't help but think, "What went wrong in your marriage?"

TOM: I was married to a wonderful woman, but I was unable to cope with the emotional problems. In looking back on it, I probably was the worst person to be married to her. She and I had some strong mutual interests, but I found it very difficult to cope with the roller coaster. We had children within a year after we married. We should have taken more time to become closer friends. I was not able to cope with her problems, which was frustrating for me. I'd never had any problems like that in my family, and the conflicts caused incredible tension. And our sex life fell apart.

Could we pick up again on the interplay between your personal and work lives?

TOM: My boss called me up one night around quarter to five. He said, "Some of the people who work for you say they are having a hard time communicating with you. You don't make yourself accessible to them. They think you've come down hard on a number of people, unfairly." He said, "It sounds like you don't recognize the problem. Maybe you ought to do something about it."

I recognized I wasn't spending as much time with these people as I should, and I started getting to the office at eight A.M. I made a point of visiting with people and talking about things that had nothing to do with the company.

So I had a happy and exciting job. And I had a disintegrating home life, but fortunately the effects of that were minimal. A number of my friends have gone through divorces, and some of them have had horrendous problems. I know how a divorce can really affect your job.

A lot of my friends don't understand why I didn't just pack up and move into the city. But I said, "I have no desire to live in the city." I love the country. I go out with a flashlight and run five miles every night. I escape when I leave this place. I don't take any of it with me.

I'm also active in the schools where my kids go, and I'm on the board of a school for handicapped children and very active in the church and the community. About six years ago I realized I was doing too much, and so I started to cut back. Now, I'd rather do other things.

How do these other things balance with your work?

TOM: My work is not the overriding part of my life. On a scale of 100, the company would be well below 50. But that doesn't mean I don't work my ass off, because I do. Other things are just more important to me than the company. I look around and see some of the people I call "gray people." Christ, they can't even walk across the street and have a drink without wanting to talk business. I think, "It must be sad." I see people going home on the train, and I wonder, "God, what are they going home to?" Half of them down three drinks and fall asleep on the train and get up the next morning and do the same thing all over again.

The goddamn meeting I went to yesterday was a disaster. A whole bunch of gray people. They all looked like undertakers—200 of them. There wasn't a joke, there wasn't a smile, there wasn't a light line in the whole presentation. I almost went to sleep. They were like automatons. Turn them on, line them up, put them on the stage. They are a bunch of gray people talking about business. I think the company encourages that side of them, and it's too bad, because there are a lot of damn good people here.

Some of them are forever chasing that next place they want to be, the next $40,000, the next promotion, and they are not enjoying anything about getting there. That has not happened to me, and I don't want it to happen to anybody who works for me. It doesn't impress me at all if somebody stays at work until 8 P.M. I would say, "There's something wrong; we're not organized. Let's work hard and get the work out, but boy, let's kid around and have some fun too."

Tom's Transformation

Managers need to look outward. Every occupation has its hazards, and corporate managers risk concentrating so thoroughly on the challenge of bottom-line effectiveness that they avoid developing the human side of their personalities. Managers who devote time to people in the organization as well as to their families at home generally modify the extremes of self-doubt and addiction to work by the time they reach mid-life.

Tom thinks that he has been able to do this. He struggles, he juggles his work and family lives, he copes, he has minor crises, and he makes repairs in his relationships. He's not perfect, and his original vision of life as a secure, tranquil experience is cracked. But he's left with hope, some areas of ease, some bitterness, and a philosophy he proclaims too loudly, one suspects, in order to convince himself by convincing others. He has had his fair share of setbacks and prices he's had to pay—such as a divorce— yet he has emerged intact and fuller for the experience.

The Importance of Balance

Strict adherence to parental codes and regulations allows children to participate in an illusion of absolute safety. Preconceptions, habits, routines, unquestioned values, and fixed images of themselves and powerful others are the psychological underpinnings of a child's illusion. In return for safety, however, these preconceptions constrict a person's ability to learn from experience.

Tom's "happy" childhood is a case in point. His preconceptions of what life ought to be like made it difficult for him to accept turmoil and pain and maybe to form another attachment. Preconceptions and unquestioned values are the deadness in a person's soul and create anxiety when forcibly or even voluntarily disrupted. Both of these live inside every person, every family, and every corporation.

In the early years of a person's career, the demands of mentors and bosses replace parental demands, and the illusion of safety begins to slip away. During their thirties people's assumptions begin to defrost, and more interesting selves emerge. Although most people want to push their careers forward, they also look for ways in which their careers can fall more into line with their expanding selves.

As long as work made it possible for him to avoid some of the fears and myths of his childhood, Larry, for instance, was not capable of totally surrendering the job as a defense. He talked about frantic activity as a way to deal with anxiety and about the company as having relieved him of the struggle to avoid his fears. In return for the illusion of safety, the company provided him with a second family to make demands of him. For Bob and Tom, work became less a defense and more a self-defined, slowly discovered, meaningful activity.

All three men accepted new assignments with more questions than they had asked when they were young, and they more frequently asked themselves whether they really wanted to do such assignments. For Bob and Tom, the illusion of safety finally died, but for Larry the inevitable was still something to avoid.

From interviews with dozens of people like Bob, Larry, and Tom, we have come to believe that the prize for a successful mid-life transition is a liberation from strict adherence to the remaining codes and regulations imposed by the people who formed us—our parents and our bosses, our partners and our colleagues. Bob and Tom seem to have earned their prizes, while Larry backed away from even trying for his.

As Tom's case shows, a wife and children often participate, willingly or not, in defining the balance between home and work. The career-focused man, like Larry, is usually a mixed blessing to other family members. They are proud of him and benefit from the rewards that he brings, but they also want him to share more of their lives and vice versa.

When work is unrewarding, as it was for Bob in his nonjob, the person will probably be more receptive to support from home than at any other time. Sympathy from those at work may be less therapeutic than support from home, which can benefit the individual, his family, and the organization.

People who are going through what has come to be called the mid-life crisis are generally neither unstable nor burned out. Rather than seeing them as exemplifying the Peter Principle, managers would make sounder career and promotional decisions if they saw the struggle as evidence that these people had not yet reached their full potential.

The mid-life transition engages people in a process of reorientation and reintegration that equips them for further and continued advancement, which they would not experience without this upheaval. It is now several years since we first interviewed these three men; each is still with his same company and doing well in his job.

What can managers do when they see someone going through this period? First, since they certainly cannot reward the consequent, often negative, behavior, at least they shouldn't punish it. Second, in many cases managers can do best by doing least—in other words, they can't and shouldn't try to prevent such crises.

However, managers should make professional counseling available to those going through a mid-life transition and do so at arm's length. Two of the three vice presidents interviewed here used their companies' services in this way. A paternalistic involvement by a manager is not desirable, particularly since much of the struggle a person goes through at mid-life is to shed the effects of such controlling influences in his or her earlier life.

Most organizations have different promotion tracks, and many identify fast-track performers, however informally and implicitly. In the language of this metaphor, the career train makes stops or job assignments.

But the metaphor ignores the psychology of the person who's growing. Management can program when individuals should change jobs and how long they should stay in different assignments; but it cannot determine when people enter and how long they stay in different phases of their inner lives. However, it can and should respond to transitions. In a company with such an orientation, someone like Bob might more willingly experience a lateral "promotion" as a realistic opportunity.

Managers of large corporations now commonly look at their companies as portfolios of businesses. To allocate resources appropriately, management arrays the business according to various points in a business life cycle. Young and rapidly growing businesses require resources that are quantitatively and qualitatively different from mature, steady businesses or from those being harvested or divested.

Just as it is inappropriate to regard all businesses as the same, it is inappropriate to use the same measurements for rewarding the performance of managers at different stages of their lives. Some organizations, such as the Chase Manhattan Bank, Heublein, Corning Glass, and Texas Instruments, mesh their strategic planning with their executives' skills and personalities.

Rewards could also be linked to the business life cycle concept. All other things being equal, for example, managing a start-up business might merit some equity participation; managing businesses that are large earners and whose market shares should be protected might call for heavy bonus components; and managing declining business units should probably be rewarded with straight salaries.

Management could also match the kind of manager called for in a particular assignment with the expected and appropriate behavior of people at different points in their lives. Just as top management cannot expect managers in their late twenties to pay much attention to developing the abilities of those who work for them, it cannot expect managers in their late forties to charge up the ladder as they did two decades earlier.

In neither instance should management see the executive as a failure. Rather, it should see each as behaving in ways that are meaningful to the tasks of the particular period in life he is in.

Notes

1. Joseph Heller, *Something Happened* (New York: Knopf, 1974).

2. In our research we interviewed many women and members of minority groups, but because their work situations are often considerably different from those of white males, we did not include interviews with them in this article.

3. Gene W. Dalton, Paul H. Thompson, and Raymond I. Price, "The Four Stages of Professional Careers—A New Look at Performance in Professionals," *Organizational Dynamics*, Summer 1977, p. 19.

4. Erik H. Erikson, *Childhood and Society*, rev. ed. (New York: Norton, 1964).

5. Roger L. Gould, *Transformations: Growth and Change in Adult Life* (New York: Simon & Schuster, 1978).

6. Daniel J. Levinson, et al., *The Seasons of a Man's Life* (New York: Knopf, 1978).

7. George E. Vaillant, *Adaptation to Life: How the Best and the Brightest Came of Age* (Boston: Little, Brown, 1977).

Appendix A: Adult Development

The theory of adult development is also called the theory of transitions. Life cycle research has shown that there are natural transition periods during adulthood just as during childhood. Researchers roughly agree about the kinds of changes that occur, although they disagree somewhat about the exact age demarcations of the transition periods.

In 1950, Erik Erikson spelled out eight stages of the life cycle and specified a sequence of now-familiar adult learning tasks: the *identity* struggle of the teens, the *intimacy* struggle of youth, the *generativity* of mid-life, and the *integrity* of older age. Each period is characterized by the attempt to resolve and integrate these tasks and qualities into an unfolding personality. A crisis may occur during each of these periods, which if resolved leads toward health and if incompletely resolved leads to identity diffusion, isolation, stagnation, or despair.

A *transition* period is a time of disruption and discontinuity that requires the reexamination of an important assumption about life. In the Erikson model, it is a time of engaging the next task and the new priority. The transition may be difficult but still not be a crisis. A *crisis* is a critical turning point. The stakes are a higher- or lower-level adaptation. A crisis is an opportunity with a big downside risk.

Research into this new field of adult development holds great promise for more specific applications to managing, both optimally and intelligently, the human resources in industry. We'll discuss a few of the major theories.

In the 1970s, George Vaillant, Daniel Levinson, and Roger Gould independently reported life cycle research corresponding to Erikson's outline of adulthood and added greater specificity about tasks and age periods to the map of adult life.

Vaillant added "career consolidation" as the task between intimacy and generativity and "keeping the meaning" as the task between generativity and integrity. He demonstrated critical shifts in coping styles that predispose a person to reach a healthy outcome during the mid-life period.

Levinson introduced the concepts of "life structure," "dream," and "mentor" into the adult development vocabulary. Life structure is the basic pattern of a person's life at a given time that is created by commitments to occupation, family, and other valued interests. As one works on single components of the life structure by making choices, the life structure evolves and then culminates in the stage Levinson has outlined. During each stage, an individual deals with the large polarities of life: destruction versus creativity, masculinity versus femininity, and attachment versus separateness.

The dream is an emerging vision of oneself in the world and accounts for the changing motivations during different periods of the life cycle. The mentor is a sponsor on life's journey, most often found in the work situation.

Levinson's life phases are as follows:

Age 16–18 to 20–24	Leaving the family
Early 20s to 27–29	Getting into the adult world
Late 20s to early 30s	Age 30 transition
Early 30s	Settling down
35–39 to 39–42	Becoming one's own person
Early 40s	Mid-life transition
A 3-year period around 45	Restabilization

Gould describes the same sequence as Levinson but defines the nature of the task in terms of the psychological work to be done during each period. The deeper work is the questioning of very specific, ingrained assumptions about the world, learned during childhood. These assumptions interfere with the progression of adult life and are hard to reexamine because they constitute the illusion of safety. Be reexamining key assumptions, an adult can break up rigid patterns of behavior and adopt a more open stance toward learning from experience.

To the degree that the adult makes use of contemporary experience in formulating decisions and interpretations about the complex adult world, he acquires whatever safety comes from having good judgment. This safety is a substitute for the illusion of safety that results from continuing old and worn-out—but familiar—belief patterns. The piecemeal dismantling of the illusion of safety is what makes self-exploratory learning during adulthood so emotional and difficult.

The assumptions people reexamine during the phases of life up to mid-life are as follows:

Age 16–22	**Leaving the family** Major false assumption: "I'll always belong to my parents and believe in their world."
22–28	**Entering the adult world** Major false assumptions: "Doing things my parents' way, with willpower and perseverance, will automatically bring results. But if I become too frustrated, confused, or tired, or am simply unable to cope, they will step in and show me the right way."
28–34	**Opening up to what's inside** Major false assumption: "Life is simple and controllable. There are no significant coexisting contradictory forces within me."

34–45	**Becoming an adult**
	Major false assumption: "There is no evil or death in the world. The sinister has been destroyed. Death can't happen to me."

Gene Dalton, Paul Thompson, and Raymond Price use the life cycle approach to establish and describe four successive stages in a professional career. They have gathered evidence indicating that good performance really means performing well within the frame of reference that each of these stages defines.

	Four Career Stages			
	Stage 1	**Stage 2**	**Stage 3**	**Stage 4**
Central activity	Helping, learning, following directions	Independent contributor	Training, integrating	Shaping the direction of the organization
Primary relationship	Apprentice	Colleague	Mentor	Sponsor
Major psychological issues	Dependence	Independence	Assuming responsibility for others	Exercising power

On Being a Middle-aged Manager

HARRY LEVINSON

Becoming middle aged is the commonplace but crisis event that all executives must face sooner or later. The key to the conflict is the word "middle." Once a person reaches the middle, he or she is inevitably on a descending path. The crisis which follows this seemingly sudden realization is a period of adaptation to shock. The person who fails to mature in this sense becomes a disease that afflicts his or her organization; the one who opts for wisdom becomes an organizational resource. Here the author examines both the personal and organizational implications of being a middle-aged manager, about which little has appeared in print.

For most people, attainment of executive rank coincides with the onset of middle age, that vast gulf which begins about 35 and endures until a person has come to terms with himself or herself and his or her human fate (for no one matures until he or she has done so). It is the peak time of personal expansion, when a man or woman lives most fully the combined multiple dimensions of his or her life. The individual has acquired the wisdom of experience and the perspective of maturity. Their activity and productivity are in full flower; their career is well along toward its zenith. He or she is at the widest range of their travels and their contacts with others. He or she is firmly embedded in a context of family, society, career, and their own physical performance. His or her successes are models for emulation; their failures, the object lessons for others. This individual has become a link from the past to the future, from his or her family to the outside world, from

Published in 1969.

those for whom he or she is organizationally responsible to those to whom he or she owes responsibility. In a word, this person has it made.

And need it all come to a harsh and bitter end? *No.*

A person cannot alter their inevitable fate. But he or she can manage the way they come to terms with it. If they do so, rather than simply letting events take their course, he or she can do much to prolong the richness of their life as well as their years.

Sophocles, who lived to be more than 90, wrote *Oedipus Rex* at 75 and *Oedipus et Colonus* at 89. Titian completed his masterpiece, "The Battle of Lepanto," at 95; he began work on one of the most famous paintings in the world, "The Descent from the Cross," when he was 97. Benjamin Franklin invented bifocals at 78. Benjamin Duggar, Professor of Plant Physiology and Botanical Economics at the University of Wisconsin, was removed at age 70 by compulsory retirement; he then joined the research staff of Lederle Laboratories and several years later gave mankind Aureomycin. At 90, Pablo Casals still played the cello as no other man ever had. Santayana, the philosopher, wrote his first novel, *The Last Puritan,* at 72. Carl Sandburg wrote *Remembrance Rock* at 70. Freud's activities continued into his 80's.

These men are the exceptions, of course. But the fact that many people can mature creatively indicates that there is indeed hope for all of us who are closer to 35. In this article I propose to examine some of the experiences of middle age and suggest ways of maintaining creative potential.

First, however, permit me a brief qualification. I am not arbitrarily splitting businesspeople into under 35 and over 35. That would be unrealistic. The figure 35 is not fixed. It will waver, because I am using it here in the sense of a stage of life, not a birthday.

Indexes of Health

Behind the flowering of middle age, a critical physical and psychological turnaround process is occurring. This is reflected in indexes of health. Statistics from Life Extension Examiners indicate that specific symptoms— such as extreme fatigue, indigestion, and chest pains—rise sharply among young executives just moving into top management. Only one third of the symptoms found in the 31- to 40-year-old management group can be traced to an organic cause, the examiners report.[1] They suggest that these problems come about because of both the manner in which the men and women live and the state of mind in which they work.

Psychological Factors

While some explanations for this increase in symptoms are no doubt a product of the aging process itself, there are more pressing psychological forces. The British psychoanalyst, Elliott Jaques, contends that a peak in the death rate between 35 and 40 is attributable to the shock which follows the realization that one is inevitably on a descending path.[2] This produces what for most men is a transitory period of depression. Depression increases a person's vulnerability to illness. There is much medical evidence to indicate that physical illness is likely to occur more frequently and more severely in people who feel depressed.

Lee Stockford of the California Institute of Technology reports from a survey of 1,100 men that about 5 out of 6 men in professional and managerial positions undergo a period of frustration in their middle 30's, and that 1 in 6 never fully recovers from it. Stockford attributes the crisis to a different kind of frustration: "This is the critical age—the mid-30's—when a man comes face to face with reality and finds that reality doesn't measure up to his dreams."[3]

A number of factors in executive work life contribute to the intensification of these feelings and the symptoms which result:

Increasing Contraction of the Hard Work Period.   The average age at which people become company presidents is decreasing. As it does, the age span during which success can be achieved becomes narrower. The competitive pace therefore becomes more intense. It is further intensified by devices such as management by objectives and performance appraisals which give added impetus to the pressures for profit objectives.

Inseparability of Life and Career Patterns.   For managerial men in an intensely competitive career pattern, each year is a milepost. Time in job or level is a critical variable. If one does not move on time, he or she loses out on experience, position, and above all, the reputation for being a star. This means there necessarily must be repetitive subpeaks of anxiety around time dimensions.

Continuous Threat of Defeat.   When both internal and external pressures for achievement are so high, the pain of defeat—always harsh—can be devastating, no matter how well an individual seems to take it. Animal research indicates that when males are paired in combat, up to 80% of the defeated ones subsequently die although their physical wounds are rarely severe enough to cause death. We cannot generalize from animals to humans, but we can get some suggestion of the physical cost of the experience of personal defeat. When we turn back to the management pyramid and the choices which have to be made, obviously many men experience defeat, and all must live with the threat.

Increase in Dependency.   To cope with competition, the executive, despite personal misgivings, must depend on specialists whose word must be accepted because of his or her lack of specialized knowledge. In fact, John Kenneth Galbraith advanced the thesis in *The New Industrial State* that the technical infrastructure of an organization really makes the decisions, leaving only pro forma approval for the executive.[4] The specialists have their own concepts, jargon, and motivation which often differ from those of the executive. Every executive wants to make good decisions. They are uneasy about decisions based on data they do not fully understand, gathered by people they do not fully understand, and presented in terms they do not fully understand. He or she is therefore often left to shudder at the specter of catastrophe beyond their control.

Denial of Feelings. Commitment to executive career goals requires self-demand and self-sacrifice, and simultaneously inhibits close, affectionate relationships. One cannot get close to those with whom he or she competes or about whom he or she must make decisions, or who are likely to make decisions about him or her. Often the executive bears a burden of guilt for the decisions he or she must make about others' careers.[5] No matter how strongly a person wants the achievement goals, he or she still has some feelings of anger, toward both himself or herself and the organization which demands that sacrifice, for having to give up other desirable life goals. He or she must hold in tightly these feelings of anger, together with the feelings of affection and guilt, if they are unacceptable to him or her or in his or her business culture. Repressed feelings must continuously be controlled, a process which requires hyper-alertness and therefore energy.

Constant State of Defensiveness. The pursuit of executive success is like playing the children's game, "King of the Hill." In that game, each child is vying for the place at the top of the stump, fence, barrel, or even literally, the hill. All the others try to push the incumbent from their summit perch. Unlike the game, in executive life there is no respite. Given this state of affairs, together with the other conditions to which I have just referred, one must be always "at the ready," as the military put it. To be at the ready psychologically means that one's whole body is in a continuing emergency state, with resulting greater internal wear and tear.

Shift in the Prime-of-Life Concept. Western societies value youth. It is painfully disappointing to have attained a peak life stage at a time in history when that achievement is partially vitiated by worship of youth, when there is no longer as much respect for age or seniority. This is compounded by one's awareness of the decline of his physical capacities. Thus, at the height of a manager's attainment, he or she is likely to feel also that they have only partly made it, that they have already lost part of what was sought to be won. Since only rarely can one have youth and achievement at the same time, there is something anticlimactic about middle-age success.

Subtle Changes

The issues having to do with health are only one facet of the middle-aging process. There are also subtle, but highly significant, changes in: (1) work style, (2) point of view, (3) family relationships, and (4) personal goals. Let us look at each of these in turn.

Work Style

Both the mode and the content of the work of creative men differ in early adulthood, or the pre-35 stage, from that of mature adulthood, or the post-35 stage. Jaques pointed this out when he observed:

> The creativity of the 20's and the early 30's tends to be a hot-from-the-fire creativity. It is intense and spontaneous, and comes out ready-made. . . . Most of the work seems to go on unconsciously. The conscious production is rapid, the pace of creation often being dictated by the limits of the artist's capacity physically to record the words or music he is expressing. . . . By contrast, the creativity of the late 30's and after is sculptured creativity. The inspiration may be hot and intense. The unconscious work is no less than before. But there is a big step between the first effusion of inspiration and the finished creative product. The inspiration itself may come more slowly. Even if there are sudden bursts of inspiration they are only the beginning of the work process.[6]

Jaques adds that the inspiration for the older man is followed by a period of forming and fashioning the product, working and reworking the material, and acting and reacting to what has been formed. This is an experience which may go on for a period of years. The content of work changes, too, from a lyrical or descriptive content to one that is tragic and philosophical, followed by one that is serene. Jaques recalls that Shakespeare wrote his early historical plays and comedies before he was 35, his tragedies afterward.

Contrary to popular misconception, creativity does not cease at an early age. It is true that creative men have made major contributions before 40, but it is equally true that those who demonstrated such creativity continued to produce for many years thereafter. In fact, both in the arts and in the sciences, the highest output is in the 40's.

Executives have many of the same kinds of experiences as artists and scientists. Executives report the greatest self-confidence at 40. Though their instrumentality is the organization, younger and older men and women do different creative work with organizations. The younger person is more impulsive, flashy, and star-like with ideas; the older one is more often concerned with building and forming an organization. A conspicuous example is the hard-hitting company founder who, to the surprise of their organization, becomes less concerned with making money and more preoccupied with leaving an enduring company. Suddenly, he or she is talking about management development.

Point of View

Concurrent with the shift in work style or orientation is a shift in point of view. This occurs in political and social thinking as well as in business. It is a commonplace that most people become more conservative as they grow older. It is an unspoken commonplace that they are more bored.

True, many activities are intrinsically boring and become more so with repetition, but others no longer hold interest when one's point of view has changed.

Disillusionment.   Some of the boredom results from disillusionment. Early idealism, the tendency toward action, and the conviction of the innate goodness in people are in part a denial of the inevitable. Young people in effect say, "The world can be rosy. I'll help make it that way. People can be good to each other if only someone will show them how or remove the conditions which cause their frustration."

But in mid-life it becomes clear that people are not always good to each other; that removing the conditions of frustration does not always lead to good, friendly, loving behavior; and that people have a capacity for being ugly and self-destructive as well as good. One evidence for the denial of disillusionment is the effort in so many companies to keep things "nice and quiet." Such companies are characterized by the inability to accept conflict as given and conflict resolution as a major part of the executive's job.

Obsolescence.   Another factor in change in point of view has to do with the feeling of becoming increasingly obsolescent. The middle-ager feels as if they are in a world apart from the young—emotionally, socially, and occupationally. This is covered today by the cliché "generation gap." But there is something real to the distance because there is a tendency to feel that one cannot keep up with the world no matter how fast he or she runs. Thus the sense of incompetence, even helplessness, is magnified. Some of this is reflected in an attitude that middle-aged executives often take.

For example, I once addressed the 125 members of the upper management group of a large company. When I finished, I asked them to consider three questions in the discussion groups into which they were going to divide themselves:

1   Of what I had said, what was most relevant to their business?
2   Of what was most relevant, what order of priority ought to be established?
3   Once priority was established, who was to do what about the issues?

They handled the first question well when they reported back; none had difficulty specifying the relevant. They had a little more difficulty with the second. None touched the third; it was as if they felt they were not capable of taking the action with which they had been charged.

Vocational Choice.   This incident might be excused on a number of bases if it were not for other unrelated or corroborative evidence which reflects a third dimension in our consideration of change in point of view. Harvard psychologist Anne Roe did a series of studies on vocational choice in the adult years. In one study she was trying to find out how people make decisions about selecting jobs.

> The most impressive thing about these interviews, she reports, was how few of our subjects thought of themselves as considering alternatives and making decisions based on thoughtful examination of the situation. . . . They seemed not to recognize their role as chooser or their responsibility for choices. It was, indeed, this last aspect we found most depressing. Even among the executives, we find stress on contingencies and external influences more often than not.[7]

Pain of Rivalry.   The sense of being more distant from the sources of change, from the more impulsive agents of change, and of not being a chooser of one's fate spawns feelings of helplessness and inadequacy. This sense of remoteness is further magnified, as I have already noted, by feelings of rivalry. For children, playing "King of the Hill" may be fun. For men and women, the greater the stakes and the more intense the motivation to hold one's place, the more threatening the rivals become. Yet, in the midst of this competitive environment, one is required to prepare rivals to succeed him or her and ultimately to give way. The very name of the game is "Prepare Your Successor."

I recall a particular corporate situation in which the president had to decide who was to be executive vice president. When he made his choice, some of his subordinates were surprised because, they said, the man he picked was the hottest competitor for the president's job and usually such men were sabotaged. The surprising part of the event, as far as I was concerned, was not the choice, but the fact that the subordinates themselves had so clearly seen what tends to happen to rivals for the executive suite. It is indeed difficult to tolerate a subordinate when the executive senses himself or herself to be, in any respect, on a downward trail while the subordinate is obviously still on his way up and just as obviously is demanding his place in the corporate sun.

This phenomenon is one of the great undiscussed dilemmas of the managerial role. Repeatedly, in seminars on psychological aspects of management, cases refer to executives who cannot develop others, particularly men and women that have nothing to fear, in the sense that their future security is assured and they still have upward avenues open to them. What is not seen, let alone understood, in such cases is the terrible pain of rivalry in middle age in a competitive business context that places a premium on youth. This paragraph from Budd Schulberg's *Life* review of *Thalberg: Life and Legend* captures the rivalry issue in one pointed vignette:

> There was to be a dramatic coda to the Irving Thalberg Story: the inevitable power struggle between the benevolent but jealous L.B. Mayer

and the protégé he 'loved like a son.' Bitter was the conflict between Father and Son fighting over the studio's Holy Ghost. They fought over artistic decisions. They fought over separation of authorities. They fought over their division of the spoils, merely a symbol of power, for by now both were multi-millionaires. It was as if the old, tough, crafty, beach-master L.B. was determined to drive off the young, frail but stubborn challenger who dared ask Mayer for an equal piece of the billion-dollar action.[8]

In this case, the rivalry was evident in open conflict. It could be with individuals at that level and in that culture. However, in most cases, if the rivalry does not go on unconsciously, it is carefully disguised and rationalized. Executives are reluctant to admit such feelings even to themselves. Therefore, much of the rivalry is unconscious. The parties are less aware of why they are quarreling, or perhaps they are more aware of the fact that they never seem to settle their quarrels. Every executive can test such feelings in their own experience by reviewing how they felt when a successor took their place, even though they moved up, particularly when that successor changed some of their cherished innovations.

Thus it is difficult for each of us to see the unconscious battle waged with subordinates, now wanting them to succeed, now damned if they will. Subordinates, however unable they are to see this phenomenon in themselves, can usually see it quite clearly in the behavior of the boss. But then there are few upward performance appraisals to help make such behavior conscious, and the behavior itself indicates to the subordinate that the rival would do well to keep his mouth shut.

Dose of Anger. The change in point of view which throws such problems into relief and intensifies fear (though rarely do executives speak of fear) is compounded further by a significant dose of anger. It is easy to observe the anger of the middle-aged executive toward today's youth—who have more money, more opportunity, and more sex than was available yesterday. There is anger, too, that the youngsters are free to "do their thing" while today's executives, pressed by the experiences of the depression and the constraints of their positions, sometimes find it hard to do what they really want to do.

The anger with youth is most often expressed as resentment because "they want to start at the top" or "they aren't willing to wait their turn or get experience" or "they only want young ones around here now." It is further reflected in such simultaneously pejorative and admiring descriptive nouns as "whiz kids," "jets," and "stars." These mixed-feeling phrases bespeak self-criticism and betrayal.

Every time the middle-aged manager uses such a phrase, they seem also to be saying that they have not done as well or that they have been undercut. One who had to learn how to size up the market from firsthand contact with customers finds that knowledge now useless, replaced by a computer model constructed by a person who never canvassed a customer.

One who thought business to be "practical" and "hardheaded" now finds that they must go back to school, become more intellectual, think ahead conceptually, or be lost. The kids have outflanked him or her. They have it so good, handed to them on a platter, at their expense.

Older generations have always complained that the youth not only are unappreciative of their efforts, but take for granted what they have struggled so hard to achieve. Nevertheless, management has never taken seriously the impact of such feelings on executive behavior. The result is an expensive loss of talent as it becomes apparent to young people that managements promise them far more than companies deliver.

I am certain in my own mind that it is the combination of rivalry and anger which makes it so difficult to create challenging ways to use young people in management. (Certainly it is not the dearth of problems to be tackled.) That in turn accounts for much of the astronomical turnover of young college graduates in their first years in a company and also for much of their subsequent disillusionment with managerial careers.

Family Relationships

The same narrowing which occurs in the cycle of achievement in business has also been taking place within the family. People are marrying at earlier ages, children are being born earlier in the marriage and therefore leaving their parents earlier. In turn, the parents live alone with each other longer (according to latest census figures, an average of 16 years). This poses several problems which come to a head in middle life. By this point in time one usually has lost both his or her parents. Though one may have been independent for many years, nevertheless for the first time he or she feels psychologically alone.

Because an executive can less readily establish close friendships at work, and mobility makes it difficult for them to sustain them in off-work relationships, he or she tends to have greater attachment to their children. He or she therefore suffers greater loss when they leave home, and they usually do not compensate for these losses any more than he or she actively compensates for the loss of old friendships through death and distance.

His heavy commitment to his career and his wife's to the children tend to separate them from each other—a problem which is obscured while their joint focus is on the children. When the children leave home, he is left with the same conscious reasons for which he married her as the basis for the marriage (attractiveness, charm, liveliness) and often the same unconscious ones (a substitute for mother, anything but like mother, a guaranteed nonequal, and other, similarly unflattering, reasons).

But she is no longer the young girl he married. She has aged, too, and may no longer be her ideal sylph-like self of twenty years before. If, in addition, his unconscious reasons for marrying her are now no longer as important as they were earlier, there is little left for the marriage unless the couple has worked out another basis for mutual usefulness.

Meanwhile, for most couples there has been a general decrease in satisfaction with each other, less intimacy, a decline in frequency of sexual intercourse, and fewer shared activities. Wives become more preoccupied with their husbands' health because age compels them to unconsciously rehearse for widowhood. Husbands sense this concern and the reasons (which sometimes include a wish for widowhood) for it, and withdraw even more. This is part of what increases the sense of loneliness mentioned earlier, in the context of the need for greater closeness. These factors contribute to the relatively new phenomenon of the "twenty-year" divorce peak.

Personal Goals

Up to approximately age 45, creative executive effort is largely self-centered. That is, one is concerned with their achievement and personal needs. After age 45, one turns gradually to matters outside himself or herself. As psychologist Else Frenkel-Brunswick has shown, the individual becomes more concerned with ideals and causes, derived from religious or parental values.[9] One also becomes more concerned with finding purpose in life.

For example, a young executive, a "jet" in his company, became a subsidiary president early. And while in that role he became involved in resolving racial problems in his community. Although still president, and likely to be promoted to head the whole corporation, his heart is now in the resolution of community problems. Similarly, another executive has retired early to become involved in conservation. Still others leave business for politics, and not a few have become Episcopal priests.

As part of this change (which goes on unconsciously), there are periods of restlessness and discomfort. There appears to be a peak in travel between the ages of 45 and 50, and also a transitory period of loneliness as one leaves old, long-standing moorings and seeks others.

The restlessness and discomfort have another source. When the middle-aged manager is shifting direction, he or she must necessarily use psychological energy for that task. As a consequence, it is more difficult to keep ancient, repressed conflicts under control. This is particularly true when the manager has managed to keep certain conflicts in check by promising one day he or she would deal with them. As he or she begins to feel that time is running out and as yet has not delivered on the personal promises, he or she begins to experience intense internal frustration and pressure. Sometimes he or she will try to hide such conflicts under a contemporary slogan like "identity crisis."

Not long ago, a 42-year-old executive told me that despite his age, his professional engineering training, and his good position, he was still having an identity problem. He said he really did not know what he wanted to do or be. A few questions quickly revealed that he would prefer to be in his own business. However, the moment we touched that topic, he was full of excuses and wanted to turn away from it. He did indeed know what he wanted to do; he was simply afraid to face it. He wanted to be independent but he could not break away from the security of his company. He had maintained the fantasy that he might some day, but as the passing years made that less likely, his conflict increased in intensity.

Most people will come nowhere near doing all they want to do with their lives. All of us have some degree of difficulty and frustration as a result. We become even more angry with ourselves when the prospect arises that time will run out before we have sampled, let alone savored, much of what there is in the world. But most of us subtly turn our efforts to meeting those ideal requirements.

The important point in all this is that, as psychologist Charlotte Buhler points out, it relates directly to survival.[10] The evidence indicates that a person's assessment as to whether they did or did not reach fulfillment has more to do with their old-age adjustment than literal loss of physical capacities and insecurity. Put another way, if a man or woman has met their own standards and expectations reasonably well, they adapt more successfully to the aging process. If not, the converse holds: while experiencing the debilitation of aging, he or she is also simultaneously angry with himself or herself for not having done what they should have. Anger with self is the feeling of depression. We have already noted the implications of depression for physical illness.

Significant Implications

Up to this point, we have been looking at the critical physical and psychological symptoms of the aging process. Now let us turn to the personal and organizational implications in all this.

Facing the Crisis

First, all of us must face up to the fact that there is such an event in life as middle-age crisis. It is common place; it need not be hidden or apologized for. It frequently takes the form of depressive feelings and psychosomatic symptoms as well as increased irritability and discontent, followed by declining interest in and efforts toward mastering the world.

There is a premature tendency to give in to fate, to feel that one can have no choice about what happens, and, in effect, to resign oneself to the vagaries of chance. This period is essentially a mourning experience: regret, sorrow, anger, disappointment for something which has been lost—one's precious youth—and with it the illusion of omnipotence and immortality. It is necessary to be free to talk about the loss, the pain, and the regret, and even to shed a tear, literally or figuratively. We do indeed die a bit each day; we have a right to be shaken by the realization when we can no longer deny it.

When a middle-aged manager begins to experience such feelings, and particularly if they begin to interfere with their work or enjoyment of life, he or she should talk to someone else about them, preferably a good counselor. This kind of mourning is far better than increasing the intense pace of running in an effort to escape reality. In the process of talking, the wise man or woman reworks their life experiences and feelings until they are all mourned out and no longer afraid of being mortal.

When a manager can take their own life transitions and their feelings about them seriously, he or she has the makings of maturity. In the course of making wine, after the grapes are pressed, the resulting liquid is left to age. In a sense, it continues to work. In the process of aging, it acquires body, color, and bouquet—in short, its character.

Like wine, people who work over their feelings about the aging process acquire a certain character with age. They deepen their awareness of themselves and others. They see the world in sharper perspective and with greater tolerance. They acquire wisdom. They love more, exploit less. They accept their own imperfection and therefore their own contributions. As Jaques has put it, "The successful outcome of mature creative work lies thus in constructive resignation both to the imperfections of men and to shortcomings in one's work. It is this constructive resignation which then imparts serenity to life and work."[11]

The middle-aged manager who fails to take self, crises, and feelings seriously keeps running, intensifies his or her exploitation of others, or gives up to exist on a plateau. Some managers bury themselves more deeply in their work, some run after their lost youth with vain cosmetic efforts, others by chasing the opposite sex, and still others by pursuing more power. An individual's failure to mature in this sense then becomes a disease that afflicts their organization. They lose their people, their grasp of the realities of their life, and can only look back on the way it used to be as the ideal.

The executive who denies age in these ways also denies himself or herself the opportunity to prepare for what is to come, following some of the suggestions I shall discuss in the next section. One who continues to deny and to run will ultimately have to face emptiness when he or she can no longer do either and must still live with self. The wise man and woman will come to terms with reality early: he or she will take seriously the fact that their time is limited.

Taking Constructive Action

Second, a person must act. Only one who acts on their own behalf is the master of self and his or her environment. Too many people accept what is for what will be. They most often say, "I can't do anything about it." What they really mean is that they won't do anything. Check your own experience. How often do you mean "won't" when you say "can't"? Much of psychotherapeutic effort is directed to helping people see how they have trapped themselves this way. There are indeed alternatives in most situations. Our traps are largely self-made.

There are a number of fruitful avenues for action in both personal and

business life. In personal terms, the most important efforts are the rene-
gotiation of the marriage and the negotiation of new friendships. Husband
and wife might wisely talk out their accumulated differences, their disappointments and mutual frustrations as well as their wishes and aspirations.
As they redefine their marriage contract, they clarify for themselves their
interdependence or lack of it. If they remain silent with each other or attack
in their frustration, they run the danger of falling apart in their anger at the
expense of their need for each other.

In social terms, the executive must make a formal effort to find and
cultivate new friends with a particular emphasis on developing companionship. We know from studies of concentration camp survivors and of the
process of aging that those who have companions cope most effectively with
the traumas of life. Those who do not almost literally die of their loneliness.
As a person becomes less self-centered, he or she can devote more energy
to cultivating others. When one individualizes and cultivates the next person,
he or she creates the conditions for others' recognition of him or her as a
person.

In public terms, the executive must become future oriented, but this
time in conceptions that go beyond the self and the job. One invests in the
future when he or she becomes actively involved in some on-going activity
of social value which has enduring purpose. Hundreds of schools, colleges,
hospitals, and community projects—most of them obscure—await the capable man or woman who gives a damn and wants that damn to matter.
Most executives need not look more than a few blocks beyond their offices
for such opportunities.

In business terms, the executive should recognize that at this point in
time he or she ideally should be exercising a different kind of leadership and
dealing with different organization problems. In middle age, the stage Erik
Erikson has called "the period of generativity,"[12] if he or she opts for
wisdom, they become an organizational resource for the development of
others. His or her wisdom and judgment give body to the creative efforts
of younger people. They help turn impulse into reality, and then to shape
and reshape it into a thousand useful products and services. They offer those
characteristics in an executive to be admired and emulated. He or she shifts
from quarterback to coach, from day-to-day operations to long-range planning. He or she becomes more consciously concerned with what they are
going to leave behind.

Organizing for Renaissance

Third, organizations must take the middle-age period seriously in their thinking, planning, and programming. I know of no organization—business, university, church, or hospital—which does. No one knows how much effectiveness is lost.

If one of the needs for coping with middle-age stress is the opportunity to talk about it, then part of every supervisory and appraisal counseling should be devoted to some of the issues and concerns of this state. Company physicians or medical examining centers should provide time for the patient to talk with the doctor about the psychological aspects of their age and their life. Sessions devoted to examining how groups are working together should, if they are middle-aged groups, have this topic on the agenda. Company educational programs should inform both executives and their spouses about this period and its unique pressures. Personnel counselors should give explicit attention to this issue in their discussions.

Obviously, there should be a different slant to executive or managerial training programs for people over 35 than for those under 35. Pre-35 programs should be geared to keeping the younger individuals "loose." They should be encouraged to bubble, to tackle old problems afresh. This is not the time to indoctrinate men and women with rules and procedures, but rather to stimulate them toward their own horizons. Training challenges should be around tasks requiring sparkle, flashes of insight, and impulsive action.

Developmental programs for men and women over 35 should be concentrated largely on refreshment, keeping up, and conceptualization of problems and the organization. Tasks and problems requiring reorganization, reformulation, refining, and restructuring are tasks for people whose psychological time it is to rework. Brilliant innovative departures are unlikely to come from such individuals, except as they are the fruition of a lifetime of ferment, as was the *aggiornamento* of Pope John XXIII.

For them, instead, more attention should be given to frequent respites from daily organizational chores to get new views, to examine and digest them in work groups, and to think of their application to organizational problems and issues. When they move toward the future, they are likely to go in protected steps, like the man crawling on ice who pushes a plank before him. Pushing them hard to be free of the plank will tend to paralyze them into inaction. Rather, training programs should specifically include small experimental attempts to apply new skills and views with minimum risk.

Much of managerial training for these people should be focused on how to rear younger men and women. This means not only emphasis on coaching, counseling, teaching, and supporting, but also time and opportunity to talk about their feelings of rivalry and disappointment, to ventilate their anger at the young people who have it so good—the whole world at their feet and no place to go but up. Finally, it should include the opportunity for them to recognize, understand, and accept their uniquely human role. Instead of rejecting the younger people, they can then more comfortably place their bets and cheer their favorites on. In the youngster's winning, they, too, can win.

For the executive, his or her subordinates, and the company, middle age can truly be a renaissance.

Notes

1. "Clinical Health Age: 30–40," *Business Week,* March 3, 1956, p. 56.

2. Elliott Jaques, "Death and the Mid-Life Crisis," *The International Journal of Psychoanalysis,* October 1965, p. 502.

3. Unpublished.

4. Boston, Houghton Mifflin Company, 1967.

5. See "Management by Guilt" (Chapter 18) in my book *Emotional Health: in the World of Work* (New York, Harper & Row, 1964).

6. Jaques, op. cit., p. 503.

7. Anne Roe and Rhoda Baruch, "Occupational Changes in the Adult Years," *Personnel Administration,* July–August 1967, p. 32.

8. *Life,* February 28, 1969, p. 6.

9. "Adjustments and Reorientation in the Course of the Life Span," in *Middle Age and Aging,* edited by Bernice L. Neugarten (Chicago, The University of Chicago Press, 1968), p. 81.

10. Quoted in Raymond G. Kuhlen, "Developmental Changes in Motivation During the Adult Years," in Bernice L. Neugarten, op. cit., p.134.

11. Jaques, op. cit., p. 505.

12. *Childhood and Society* (New York, W.W. Norton & Company, Inc., 1964), p. 13.

18

A Second Career

The Possible Dream

HARRY LEVINSON

What manager hasn't sat at his desk on a gloomy Monday morning wondering what he or she was doing there and asking himself or herself whether he or she could make it as the skipper of a charter boat in the Bahamas or as the operator of a ski resort in Colorado? Sometimes the manager dreams of becoming a lawyer, sometimes simply of writing a book. Regardless of the dream itself, however, managers need to satisfy a few conditions, this author says, before they can be sure that their choice of a second career is a wise one and not simply a flight from the routine and frustration that is common to all jobs. First managers need to understand their "ego ideals," their hidden images of how they would like to be. Then they need to determine how they prefer to behave in certain situations—whether, for instance, they prefer risk taking on their own or the security of groups. Armed with an understanding of their own visions and behavior patterns, managers are in a position to weigh their career options realistically.

Just two years after his appointment as director of marketing services, 35-year-old Tom Conant started thinking about leaving his job and enrolling in law school. He had fantasies of addressing the bench in an attempt to persuade the judge to side with his position. Tom imagined how it would feel to demolish the opposing lawyer by asking the witness penetrating questions that led inexorably to the conclusion he sought. He couldn't wait to get started.

Tom had joined the company right after business school and in 12 years there had topped one success with another. His marketing acumen, his ability to innovate, do research, and carry through new programs brought the company important new business. In other respects, too, Tom had been a model

Published in 1983.

manager to his superiors and his subordinates. He was marked as a comer. Tom's initial impatience to sink his teeth into new challenges had posed some problems, but as he received new responsibilities, Tom began to relax and seemed to enjoy his work and his colleagues.

When he found himself thinking of a career in law, Tom surprised himself. He had thought that he might be wooed by competitors, but he had never expected to think of abandoning his career. Leo Burns, Tom's predecessor as manager of marketing services and his mentor, hoped to see his protégé follow him to the vice presidency. Tom knew that his resignation would shatter Leo, and that knowledge annoyed him. He didn't want to fight or disappoint Leo.

Anger at Leo slowly mounted. In his fantasy Tom tried to explain to Leo his reasons for leaving, to describe the soul-searching he had done in the last year, but Leo wouldn't listen. He pictured Leo's disappointment turning to irritation. The imaginary drama came to a climax with Leo insisting that Tom leave the company immediately. "Marketing doesn't need you!" Tom imagined Leo shouting. "Just get on with your plans and get out!"

When Tom had these fantasies, he always had second thoughts about making such a move. He had a good career ahead of him. He was a loyal company person, and the company had been good to him. His recent promotion had given him new responsibilities and a reputation in the industry. And he hadn't really been that bored for the last two years.

Yet in calmer moments Tom remembered other managers who had switched careers. An engineer he knew had left a responsible job in product development at the age of 40 to go to law school and was now a patent attorney. He boasted that it was a change he was glad he had made: "I was going to spend the rest of my life putting new faces on old products. Now I can use what I know about engineering to help people who are going to make real changes happen."

Tom reflected also about the many people in the news who were on their second, or even third, careers. California ex-governor Jerry Brown had been a Jesuit seminarian before entering politics; Henry Kissinger had been a professor before becoming a diplomat. Several business school deans had been CEOs, and university presidents have become business executives.

As always, Tom concluded his reverie with a farewell handshake; he was leaving his old friends behind. He imagined them thinking that they, too, should have undertaken second careers.

Almost everyone at some point thinks of a second career. Many people have good reasons. Tom's law school fantasy was based in part on a cool assessment of his own life and the contemporary business situation. He believed that growing consumer movements would force the marketing field to change radically in the next decade. Despite their temporary relaxation, he thought that federal, state, and local regulations controlling advertising and promotion would increase. By combining his marketing experience with a law school education, Tom reasoned he could steal a march on this trend and build a solid future for himself either as an in-house counsel or as a consultant.

As the years pass, most people—regardless of their professions or skills—find their jobs or careers less interesting, stimulating, or rewarding. By midlife, many feel the need for new and greener occupational fields. They yearn for opportunities to reassert their independence and maturity and to express the needs and use the talents of a different stage of life.

Some people feel they are no longer in the running for advancement, some that their talents and skills are not being fully used, and some that they have outgrown their jobs, companies, or disciplines. Others, feeling blocked by being in the wrong company, industry, or position, are bored. Some are in over their heads, while others had merely drifted into their jobs or chosen directions prematurely. One or a combination of these feelings can make a person hate to go to work in the morning and can trigger thoughts of a way out.

The realities of contemporary organizational life also stimulate a manager to think about a second career: the competition is stiffer every year. Even to the young manager, the accelerating pace of change makes obsolescence a threat. Rapid technological changes (which demand higher levels of education and training), more differentiated markets, and unpredictable economic circumstances all make it improbable that a manager will have a life-long career in one field or one organization.

By their middle or late 30s, managers usually know how far their careers will take them. By comparing his or her promotion rate to those of peers, a manager can tell if he had leveled off. If a manager's latest assignments takes him or her out of the organization's prescribed route to the top, the upward movement probably has ended.

Other factors behind the wish for second careers are the effects aging and growth have on people. Although an intense period of skills training, job rotation, long hours of overtime, and much traveling may have satisfied them when they were younger and just beginning their careers, managers as they get older probably find the pace exhausting and the rewards insufficiently attractive to compensate for the loss of other gratifications.

But the reasons for thinking about a second career are not always positive. Some people want to change because they are always dissatisfied with themselves; some are depressed and angry; some have anxiety about death that induces restlessness; and some have overvalued themselves and believe they are more talented and capable than they really are. Some managers can't tolerate bosses. Others think they should have been CEO a long time ago. Some are unwilling to acquire experience, while others are competing with old classmates. Some are just competing—and not as well as they'd like.

Seeking a new career for these reasons is an exercise in futility. If a manager blames the job, the boss, or the company when the source of his or her discontent is really himself or herself, his or her second career is likely to be as disappointing as his or her first. Therefore a manager, before embarking on choosing a second career, must have an honest picture of self and understand the changes he or she probably will go through.

Stages in Adult Development

As middle age approaches, thoughts about a second career intensify.[1] Building on the work of Sigmund Freud, psychoanalyst Erik H. Erikson has outlined three stages of adulthood: intimacy, generativity, and integrity.[2] Each stage has a psychosocial crisis and each has its task.

The first adult stage, intimacy, which lasts from about age 21 to age 35, is the most spontaneously creative period. It is an innovative and productive time. The young adult channels great energies into choosing and launching a career and, usually, into contracting a marriage and establishing a family. The third and final stage, integrity, begins at approximately age 55. Ideally, at this age a person ties together his life experience and comes to terms with his life. At work, he prepares for retirement and reflects on his career.

In between, during the stage of generativity, from about age 35 to age 55, the adult lays the foundations for the next generation. Commonly called the mid-life transition, this is the time of reevaluation. At home, the children are leaving the nest and husbands and wives have to rethink their relationship to each other. At work, the drive to compete and excel is peaking, and executives pay more attention to bringing other, younger managers along.

The transition between intimacy and generativity is, according to Daniel Levinson, the time during which the adult makes his last assertion for independence.[3] Levinson calls this "the BOOM [becoming one's own man] effect." His studies of executives indicate that at about age 37, the adult throws off the guidance or protection of older mentors or managers and takes full charge of himself. Those that are able to make this last stand for independence go on to new heights. They demand more responsibility or start their own companies. Others either don't assert themselves or are rejected when they make demands. The BOOM effect is an impetus for seeking a new career.

In our culture people have opportunities to do many things. In youth they choose one and leave the others behind, but they promise themselves they'll come back to them. Fifteen years out of school, people tend to feel satiated with what they're doing—even if it is something with high status and high pay—and itch to fulfill old promises to themselves. They tend to become restless when circumstances keep them from doing so and become dismayed when they realize that they can't go back and start all over again.

When people are in this stage of life, they need to seek counsel, to talk at length about their reasons, and to listen to others' experiences and perceptions. They also need the support of others who are important to them through this difficult decision-making and transition period. Such assistance can ensure that the manager will make a sound second-career choice rather than flee impulsively from frustration or boredom. It might even result in a wise decision on the part of a promising executive to remain, with renewed enthusiasm, in his organization. A manager who thinks through the issues of a second career also gets ready to help others with the same concerns.

Who Are You?

The most critical factor for people to consider in choosing a gratifying second career is their ego ideal. It can serve as a road map. Central to a person's aspirations, the ego ideal is an idealized image of oneself in the future. It includes the goals people would like to achieve and how they would like to see themselves. At an early age, children identify with parents and other power figures, find out how to please or resist them, and learn to adapt to feeling small and helpless in comparison with them. How they do these things, as well as other unconscious factors, determines how their ego ideals develop. During childhood and adolescence, the young person incorporates rising aspirations built on academic or career achievements into the ego ideal and, as time goes on, also includes successive models, each of which has a more specialized competence.

Throughout life people strive toward their ego ideals, but no one ever achieves it. With successive accomplishments, aspirations rise. But as people feel they are progressing toward their ego ideals, their self-pictures are more rather than less positive. The closer a person gets to the ego ideal, therefore, the better he or she feels about himself or herself. The greater the gap between one's ego ideal and one's current self-image, the angrier one is at oneself and the more inadequate, guilty, and depressed one feels.

When a career helps satisfy the ego ideal, life and work are rewarding and enjoyable. When a career does not help meet these self-demands, work is a curse. In short, the wish to attain the ego ideal, to like oneself, is the most powerful of motivating forces. Delivery on the promises one makes to oneself is an important aspect of choosing a new direction.

Tapping into the Ego Ideal

Because people begin to form their ego ideals in earliest childhood, developing an accurate understanding of them is difficult. A careful review of family history and school and work experiences can go a long way in outlining the needs that are important to the ego ideal. A manager can help the process along by discussing with a listener or a friend answers to the following questions (although this exercise may strike you as off the point, there are very good reasons for carrying it out):

1. What were your father's or father substitute's values? Now what did your father say or do, but what did he stand for? What things were

important to him? What was the code he lived by? And then, what were your mother's values?

2.   What was the first thing you did that pleased your mother? Small children try hard to please their mothers, who are the most important figures in their lives. Every child's earliest efforts to please mother become ingrained behavior. They are, therefore, a significant part of each person's characteristic way of behaving and have an important influence on subconscious goals. Later, children try to please the father, too.

(Sometimes, especially for women, it may be the mother's values that are more important and the activities that pleased father that weigh more heavily.)

3.   Who were your childhood heroes or heroines? Did you idolize athletes, movie stars, or political figures? What kind of people do you now enjoy reading about or watching on TV? What kind of achievements do you admire?

4.   Who are and were your models—relatives, teachers, scoutmasters, preachers, bosses, characters in stories? What did they say or do that made you admire them?

5.   When you were able to make choices, what were they? What elective subjects did you take in high school? What major did you pursue in college? What jobs have you accepted? At first glance, these choices may seem to have been random, but they were not. And when you take a retrospective look at them, a pattern emerges.

6.   What few experiences in your lifetime have been the most gratifying? Which gave you the greatest pleasure and sense of elation? The pleasure you took in the experience was really the pleasure you took in yourself. What were you doing?

7.   Of all the things you've done, at which were you the most successful? What were you doing and how were you doing it?

8.   What would you like your epitaph or obituary to say? What would you like to be remembered for? What would you like to leave as a memorial?

The answers to these questions will help managers sketch the outlines of their ego ideals and give them a sense of the main thrust of their lives.

If you still have some doubts about direction after you've talked these questions through, you might take a battery of psychological tests to complement the definition of your ego ideal. Many counseling psychologists provide interest, aptitude, and values inventories as well as tests of intelligence, reasoning, and other capacities. They can interpret the test results and advise you about their significance for your career choice.

How Do You Like to Act?

The next step is to determine the kinds of occupational activities that fit the way you like to behave, how you like to do your job or deal with coworkers.

The point here is to determine whether you are temperamentally fit for the job you're thinking of moving to. For instance, Tom in the opening vignette had always wanted to take on new responsibilities and challenges and to act alone taking risks rather than in a group, where interdependence is important. If Tom decided to go to law school to become a consultant working on his own, he would be making a choice consistent with how he worked best. He would be choosing an environment in which he would be psychologically comfortable.

In determining how your personality will fit with a job, a listener's or friend's questions and insights will be valuable. Explore the following areas:

☐ How do you handle aggressive energy? Do you channel it into the organization and administration of projects? Are you reluctant to express it? For instance, do you have difficulty taking people to task or confronting colleagues or subordinates? How do you react when someone challenges your opinion?

Channeling aggressive energy into the organization and administration of projects means that the person can comfortably take charge and can focus his achievement effort into organizational achievement rather than personal aggrandizement. A person who is reluctant to express aggression may have difficulty speaking up at the right time or representing himself or herself adequately or analyzing problems and discussions with other people. Difficulty in taking people to task or confronting colleagues is also a product of reluctance to express aggression and usually reflects a good deal of underlying unconscious guilt.

A person who is unable to take people to task cannot take charge as a manager; and one who is unable to confront others cannot give colleagues or subordinates honest performance appraisals.

☐ How do you handle affection? Some people prefer to be independent, while others enjoy working closely with people. Do you need constant approval and encouragement or does the quality of your work satisfy you? Can you praise others or do you find it difficult to express positive feelings?

While some people enjoy the affectionate interchange and camaraderie of working closely with others, some people prefer to be independent. The latter may either deny their need for other people's praise, approval, and affection or simply feel more comfortable keeping a distance.

Many managers have great difficulty telling others when they do good work. It is as if any expression of emotion is difficult for them. For some, this is a matter of conscience: they feel like hypocrites for praising work that isn't outstanding. For others, praise may seem to invite a closer relationship with the person being praised or may violate the picture of stoic self-control they want to present.

☐   How do you handle dependency? Do you have trouble making decisions without your manager's OK? Do you work better when you're in charge or in a number 2 position? Do you work as well independently as on a team? Do you have difficulty asking for and using the help of others?

Although most of us fear becoming helplessly dependent on others, in organizations we are necessarily dependent on a lot of other people to get our work done. But some people can't tolerate this aspect of themselves. They need to do everything on their own. It is all right for other people to lean on them, and indeed sometimes they encourage it, but it is not all right for them to lean on other people. Such people disdain others' advice or guidance, even when seeking professional help is appropriate.

On the other hand, some people do well only when they can lean on somebody else's guidance or direction and panic when they don't have that. And while some people may work well by themselves, they may not accept other people's needs to depend on them. Such people will not be good bosses.

Listeners' or friends' special knowledge of a manager's working habits will enable them to be perceptive in questioning the manager in these areas. In addition, the manager should ask others—friends, coworkers, colleagues—to share with him or her their perceptions of his or her characteristic behavior. Sometimes they can tell the manager about working habits that he or she himself or herself is not aware of. For instance, over a period of time friends might have noticed that Tom, from the opening vignette, enjoyed bearing full responsibility and risk for a project and making it work through his own expertise. This information could help Tom choose whether to join a company as in-house counsel or to become an independent consultant. A friend could point out that given his characteristic working style, Tom would probably enjoy the latter better.

In some cases, of course, friends may not be very perceptive or may have their own interests at heart and not be very helpful. At times like these, managers should definitely seek professional help.

Which Way to Go?

Armed with an understanding of his ego ideal and working style, the manager is now ready to weigh options more wisely. He or she may choose to launch a second career or he or she may decide to stick with his or her course in the organization. Whatever the decision, his or her friends' support and his or her deeper understanding of himself or herself and his or her motivation will equip him or her to attack his or her chosen career with new dedication and enthusiasm.

Second careers are evolutionary. They stem from some interest that has lain dormant or has been abandoned in favor of another occupation.

Asked if he had any idea of what he wanted to do when he left the chairmanship of Dain, Kalman & Quail, an investment banking firm in Minneapolis, for a new vocation, Wheelock Whitney answered, "Yes, really. I thought I'd like to pursue some other things that I cared about." Among these interests was the Johnson Institute, a center studying and treating the chemically dependent. Whitney had become deeply involved in the institute eight years earlier when his wife was undergoing treatment for alcoholism.[4]

Many turn to second careers that extend a previous occupational thrust; they may go into business for themselves in fields they already know. By searching the past for those budding interests they had no chance to flower, a manager can draw a long list of career options. At the same time, a manager can eliminate those that are no longer interesting or pleasurable. In choosing his second career, William Damroth said he switched from the chairmanship of Lexington Corporation because "to me the main thing was that I couldn't continue doing what I enjoy the most, which is the creative role, the intense bringing together of all factors, saying, 'It ought to look like this.' For instance, what I'm doing today is much more satisfying than the long-range planning you have to do for a company. Today's satisfaction is immediate."[5]

After eliminating undesirable options, a manager should investigate what additional training is required for each of the remaining possibilities and how much he can afford to invest. To pick up some careers, managers need to spend years in full-time professional or academic training; others they can approach through a course of reading, night school, or correspondence study. By seeing how the remaining options fit with how he prefers to behave and by understanding his ego ideal, a manager can usually narrow the field to one or two general directions. At this point, a manager considering a career change should again ask a friend or counselor to act as a sounding board, letting the manager talk through options and refine his or her ideas.

Finally, before a manager makes a choice, he or she should consider a number of other critical issues:

1. *Family.* Whom do you have responsibility for—a mother-in-law, an uncle, a grandfather, a handicapped sister or brother? Do these responsibilities limit your options? Do your responsibilities to your spouse and children impose geographic or financial constraints?

2. *Present job.* If a manager comes to a premature judgment or acts impulsively, he risks leaving his present job thinking that the company left much to be desired. Will your peers and boss see the move as a rejection of the company and of your work together? Feeling abandoned, they might attack you. The possibility of anger and disappointment is especially high when you and your superior have worked closely together and when you respect and admire each other. Furthermore, some people, disappointed that they failed to act when the time was right, will be jealous. They may unload on you their anger with themselves. Are you prepared for these conflicts?

It will help you to think about what it means to lose these peers and mentors. Rather than thinking that you are being disloyal, recognize that people who prepare themselves for a second career are doing the organization as well as themselves a favor by making space for younger, talented managers looking forward to promotion.

3. *Status.* One's status in the community is directly related to one's status at work. Choosing another career may well result in changing one's status. How important is that to you? How important is it that you associate with the same people you have associated with before, that you play golf at the same clubs or take part in the same social activities? Because your spouse and children will also be affected, the family must discuss this issue together. The sacrifices may well be severe.

4. *Rebuilding.* If you're thinking of starting a new business or launching a new career, chances are that you will have to build a clientele. Rarely does a person move from one organization to another and take with them all of his or her accounts. For example, a lawyer told me that when he and his colleagues left a large firm to start their own, they expected their clients to follow them. Only a small fraction did, and the new firm had to build its clientele from scratch. Anyone starting his or her own business should expect it to take from two or five years to build a stable of customers.

5. *Freedom v. constraints.* For a mature manager in the BOOM period, the pressure to be autonomous, to do what he or she wants to do, to be free of commitments to somebody else, is very high. Therefore, in choosing an activity or direction, it is important to choose, insofar as you can, something that allows you maximum freedom to come and go, to do as you wish, while meeting the formal obligations of the role. As William Damroth comments:

> My time is my own. I can lie on my back for two hours if I want. Instead of saying, 'This is what I want' and moving toward it, I've said 'This is what I don't like; and I've eliminated it. I've cut away all the things that make life unhappy for me. I don't have any tension headaches in the mornings.

But one doesn't always achieve freedom so easily. As we go through life we aspire to many things—promotions, new roles, different experiences. And we often ask ourselves, "Who am I to want to do that? What right do I have to seek that goal?" Self-critical feelings often prevent us from moving toward aspirations that we have every right to work toward and achieve.

The issue becomes particularly important with respect to a second career. Because a mature manager recognizes, if he or she hasn't before, that he or she has every right to pursue anything he or she wants to, now is the time to act. Anyone is eligible for any aspiration. One may not achieve it, but one has as much right as anybody else to want it and try for it.

6. *Year-long depression.* I have never seen a person make a significant career shift without experiencing a year-long depression. I don't mean that people are down in the dumps for a year but that they feel loss, am-

bivalence, and fear that things may not work out. Caught in an ambiguous situation in which they are not yet rooted, they feel detached from their stable routines.

The longer the manager has been with an organization, the more likely they have come to depend on it; the closer relationships will have been with his or her colleagues, the greater will be the sense of loss. The more his or her family has been tied to the organization, the more profound these feelings are likely to be.

7. *Talk.* All change is loss and all loss requires mourning.[7] Even when promoted, one loses the support of colleagues, friends, and known ways of doing things. To dissipate the inevitable sorrow, you have to turn it into words. To detach yourseslf from old ties and give up old habits, you have to talk about the experience. Feeling that they have to be heroic, some managers, men particularly, either deny that they are having such experiences or grit their teeth and try to plow through them. That way of acting doesn't deal with the depression; it only buries it and makes one vulnerable to physiological symptoms and overreactions when traumas occur.

It is important to have somebody to talk to and to be able to talk to that person freely. But even with the most careful and sensitive support from spouse and friends, you may get sidetracked, spin your wheels and get stuck in the mire. If after such talk you are no clearer about your choice, it may be time to consult a professional. The issues and feelings any careful self-appraisal touches on are often too complex to examine or discuss without professional help.

8. *Joint experiences.* Husbands' and wives' careers often separate them. When one member of the marriage makes a career change, new problems having to do with adult development emerge. Early in a marriage the spouses go in different directions, the husband usually to earn a livelihood and the wife usually to bear children. After her childrearing is done, the wife may return to work, but chances are nevertheless that the two spouses will still go in different occupational directions. Their only common interest tends to be the children or family problems.

Usually by the time a person has reached midcareer, the children are out on their own or close to it. The spouses now have to talk to each other. But if they have gone in different directions, they may have trouble communicating. A second career can help spouses reunite. One couple, for example, became interested in antiques. Together they went to antique shows and searched for old glass. When they gave up their old careers, they decided to run an antique store together. What was originally a shared hobby gave the couple financial security while they worked together.

Sometimes a new career threatens an old relationship. One manager was successful and widely respected in his organization. Although unequal to him in status or earning power, his wife also had professional training. When they decided to have children, she left her job to rear them. During those years, he was a supportive helpmate. When she was able, she went to law school and subsequently entered a prestigious law firm. Her status and income now exceed her husband's. He has taken a backseat to her and, with some feelings of embarrassment, carries on some of the household and family maintenance activities that she formerly handled. He speaks of his new situation with mingled pride and shame and is now considering a second career himself.

9. *Open options.* Even if you have exercised great care in choosing a second career, the change won't necessarily work out. Economic vagaries as well as factors that you couldn't foresee may cut your second career short. If you left your old job on a positive note, however, it may be possible to get it back. Many organizations recognize that a manager who has been tested elsewhere and wants to return is likely to be an even better and more highly motivated employee.

Notes

1. Harry Levinson, "On Being a Middle-aged Manager," *HBR* July–August 1969, p. 57.

2. Erik H. Erikson, *Childhood and Society,* 2d ed. (New York: Norton, 1963).

3. Daniel Levinson, Charlotte N. Darrow, Edward B. Klein, Maria H. Levinson, and Braxton McKee, *The Seasons of a Man's Life* (New York: Alfred A. Knopf, 1978).

4. See "Don't Call It 'Early Retirement,'" *HBR* interview with Wheelock Whitney and William G. Damroth, *HBR* September–October 1975, p. 103.

5. Ibid., p. 113.

6. Ibid., p. 118.

7. Harry Levinson, "Easing the Pain of Personal Loss," *HBR* September–October 1972, p. 80.

19
Don't Call It Early Retirement

Interviews with WHEELOCK WHITNEY and WILLIAM G. DAMROTH

Traditionally, a person who retires early does so for one of two reasons: he or she either wants to go to another job where the chances of advancement are greater, or simply wishes to stop working altogether. There are, however, a few people who have left their jobs not because their way to the top was barred or because they wanted to be inactive, but because once at the top they found their own personal needs were not being satisfied. What happens to them after they leave? Do they find a different and satisfying life, or do they miss the fast-paced business world in which they had clearly been a success? To explore these questions, among others, HBR interviewed two men who have left their businesses after reaching the top. After having been for nearly 10 years chief executive officer of Dain, Kalman & Quail, an investment banking firm in Minneapolis, Wheelock Whitney left in 1972 at the age of 45. He is now teaching a course in management at the University of Minnesota Business School and is chairman of the Johnson Institute, an organization teaching intervention techniques for the chemically dependent. William G. Damroth co-founded the Lexington Research and Management Corporation, a mutual fund and investment counseling firm, in the late 1950s, and after being its president and chairman of the board, retired at age 48 in 1969. He now lives in Sanibel Island, Florida, where he photographs wildlife and works with his own foundation. In discussing why they left, Mr. Whitney and Mr. Damroth comment on the responsibilities of business and the rewards of a private life, on the creative and administrative roles the person at the top plays, and on the dynamics that occur in one's life when a great change is made.

The interviews with Mr. Whitney and Mr. Damroth were conducted and edited by Eliza G.C. Collins, associate editor, and Wanda A. Lankenner, editorial assistant, at the Harvard Business Review.

Published in 1975.

Wheelock Whitney

HBR: **Mr. Whitney, before we talk about why you decided to retire from your position as chief executive officer of Dain, Kalman & Quail, could you tell us something of what your career path had been up to that point?**

Whitney: Yes, but first I want to say I always feel a little bit squeamish about the words "retire" or "early retirement." When I hear them, they send off a little signal; I feel my gut tighten. The reason I get so sensitive about the word "retirement" is that right after I left Dain, I'd walk down the street and these old gentlemen—70, 75 years old—would come up to me, put their arm around me, and say, "Wheelock, welcome to the club. You're going to love it. I wish I'd done it 25 years before I did." After all, I was only 45. I didn't have any intention of "retiring," just shifting my career, doing something different with my life.

What had that career been?

I got out of the Navy in 1946, went four years to Yale, then started work in Minneapolis in the bus business in 1950. After three and a half years of that, I was thinking life was too easy for me. I became restless and curious, and, yes, dissatisfied. I asked myself, "Am I being accepted because of the fact that I'm Wheelock Whitney, and my parents live here in Minneapolis, and I belong to all the good clubs, and I have all of these nice things? What would happen if I went into a community where we didn't know anybody? I wonder if I could hack it." And it weighed on me so heavily that I finally decided, to hell with it, I'm going to do something just to see what would happen if Irene, myself, and the children were on our own.

Were you conscious at the time of this being a big risk, a gamble?

I looked on it more as an adventure. It was an honest effort to try to see if we could make it. What kind of life would it be for us, having to make new friends and having to be taken in as total strangers? So I looked around and got a job in Jacksonville, Florida in the bus business. I started working for them in January 1954.

Being Wheelock Whitney meant nothing?

Nothing in Jacksonville, Florida. Although I think it *came* to mean something, I'm happy to say. We would have stayed there for an indefinite period, but my father became seriously ill. I knew that he had a limited time to live, so we moved back to Minnesota in November 1956.

When I came home, I used to visit my father in the hospital; we'd talk, and I would say, "Dad, I think I'd like to get out of the bus business and find a new career. But I don't really know what to go into or what to do." And he said to me, "I think you ought to do whatever makes you happy." And I said, "Come on, how do I know what will make me happy? That's no help." He said, "Well, I don't know what will make you happy and you don't know what will make you happy. I can't tell you what it will be, but you'll have to stick your neck out, take a chance, and change careers."

How did you choose Dain Company?

At that time, J.M. Dain and Company was quite a small investment firm, and all of my friends in the securities business worked for Piper, Jaffray & Hopwood. I didn't know anybody at J.M. Dain, so after giving it a lot of thought I decided that I would rather work for a place where I didn't know everybody. I went to work at Dain on January 2, 1957 as a salesman.

And when did you become chief executive officer?

I was greatly inspired by the man who was then heading the company. His name was Merrill Cohen; he was a very outstanding person, and suddenly in June 1963 he died of a heart attack. I had learned a tremendous amount from him. He was a great teacher, a great person. And even though I had only been there for six years, the board elected me to take his place.

So why was it at the age of 45, after getting to the top of Dain, Kalman & Quail, that you left? Most people at age 45 are still looking forward to or dreaming about being the chief executive officer.

There are probably at lot of factors spanning many years that went into my decision. In 1963, I had decided that I was going to run for the U.S. Senate against incumbent Senator Eugene McCarthy. I guess one of the reasons I was elected CEO was because none of my partners thought I had a chance to make the Senate. They thought my absence would be shortlived, and they were right, although I did spend a lot of time in the latter part of 1963 and most all of 1964 in politics. But I never dreamed in my worst nightmares that Barry Goldwater would be the Republican candidate. Oh, it was a debacle. Nevertheless, it was a terrific growth experience for me. This has made politics a very important part of my life, of course.

Were there personal reasons as well?

Another even more significant thing happened to me in 1964 that had a tremendous influence on why I wanted to change the course of my life later on. My wife was very sick and a troubled person; I did not know what an alcoholic was in 1964—I knew she drank too much, and I knew that it was a source of great difficulty in our marriage and with our family. She was going to a psychiatrist three days a week and not getting any better, in fact, getting worse. Finally, after many years of trouble, with the help of an Episcopalian minister named Vernon Johnson, Irene went into treatment for alcoholism in March of 1964. That was a great turning point.

Were things at Dain, Kalman, & Quail going well, or was the business itself a factor in your decision?

Things were going fairly well. When I returned in 1965 after the Senate race, it became apparent to me that if we were ever going to be able to be competitive in the securities business, we'd have to grow fast, and not just internally. So over the next three or four years we were involved in a lot of mergers, becoming Dain, Kalman and then becoming Dain, Kalman & Quail. We became a very successful securities firm. Later in 1971, I was elected president of the Investment Bankers Association, and I'd say that was an important year for me because I had a lot of time to think. That was a year when I had to travel all over the country and into Canada. When I was in my office at Dain, Kalman, & Quail, I didn't have two seconds a day to think. But airplanes are good places to think, and I got to doing a lot of it during that year about a number of things.

These were things directly related to your decision to leave?

Yes. By now I was 45 and I'd had the thrill and satisfaction of leading a relatively small securities firm into a really good sized investment banking company. I really felt good about that. I'd had the opportunity—or I was having it—to be the president of our largest national trade association in the investment banking field, and I felt good about that. I felt that I had done whatever I had set out to do, at least in the securities business, and had satisfied my own needs.

Were the goals ones you planned as you went along?

Not really. When I was a kid I knew that my goal in life was twofold. I can remember very well. I wanted to run my own business and I wanted to make a lot of money. I'm not proud of these goals, nor am I ashamed of them, but that's what they were. And there I was 45 and with a lot of luck and hard work, it had happened.

What was it you'd think on the airplanes?

I'd think, now do I want to go back? We had built the company up to a point from where it had been earning $100,000 a year after taxes to where it was earning $2½ million a year after taxes; we had 50 employees when I started and now we had 600. I had to ask myself, "Now, do I want to go back after this year of being president of the IBA and go on to building even more offices, more employees, more sales, more profit? Do I want to see the company make $6 million after taxes and have 1,000 employees?'' I mean, hell, I really didn't want to do that.

At this point, did you have any idea of what you wanted to do?

Yes, really. I thought I'd like to maybe pursue some other things that I cared about. The more I thought about it, the more I knew that I really didn't want to go back. Also, I felt that at 45 I'd be in the way of people coming along in the company. I decided that if I was going to leave, I'd better leave while business was still good. But basically I was motivated to leave to develop a different life style and a different career.

There wasn't time to develop these interests while you were CEO at DKQ?

Exactly. I simply couldn't do it. There were two interests I had that I knew I wanted to pursue. One was politics. I wanted to take a look realistically as to whether I might like to go back into politics again. There was a governor's race coming up in 1974, and this was 1972.

I also had a tremendous interest in the Johnson Institute. After Irene had been well for a couple of years we said to Vern Johnson, ''What about starting an institute whose purposes would be to try to help families, individuals like us who had suffered and waited too long for help?'' We wanted to teach principles of intervention for people who are chemically dependent. We started in 1966 with one employee, and by 1971 we had 25 employees. I was chairman, Vern was president. By 1972 I was getting more and more fascinated with what was going on at the Johnson Institute and anxious to spend more time there. But I simply couldn't because I was so tied down in business.

Were there personal interests as well?

Oh, yes. I had three goals. I wanted very much to learn how to speak a foreign language, which I had never had time for, and to learn how to play a musical instrument. I also wanted to travel. I had been a successful businessman and you would think that I had seen the world, but I hadn't. And I wanted to spend more time with my family, and to teach management principles to college students.

Was the question of business values versus your individual life an issue for you at that time?

Well, partly. I have to admit that I was getting turned off by what I thought were absolutely ludicrous, unrealistic amounts of compensation that were being made by people in our business. When a young person could come into our business at the age of 26 and make $75,000 a year, it was . . . well, it got to me, finally. It wasn't just that they made that kind of money, but that they thought they were worth that kind of money. They not only expected that, but they expected that they should even make more than that.

And this was occurring with some people that I was pretty close to and that I really cared for. I guess I was getting grouchy about it, and I think that was one of the negative reasons I wanted to change.

So it wasn't disenchantment with the business world per se?

No, it had nothing to do with respect for the business world, or the business community, or the securities industry, because I believe in all of those. I have a great abiding faith in the business world.

When you left, were you aware of wanting to shed responsibility?

I think that I enjoy responsibility. I enjoy being a leader. I thrive on it. I did not think how nice it would be if I could just be one of the boys and not have to have all these people counting on me. I was very much aware, though, at the same time, of something I wanted to correct in my life, something I would call excessive loneliness. I think it's very lonely to be at the top of anything; it prevents people from sharing with you, from being honest with you, and from getting close to you. And I missed the closeness. I really didn't have many close friends, people that I confided in, people that I saw a lot of, people that I felt comfortable with.

Was that because there was not time for them?

That was certainly a factor. I had so many interests and I was so busy that it was hard for me to take the time, or I did not choose to take the time, to have close relationships with people. Also, I think it was partly the fact that I was the head of a company. I think that you develop a certain place where people don't avoid you, but either through your choice or theirs they don't get close. In any event, during the 1960s my wife got interested in groups as a part of her therapy and she got interested in feelings. I really didn't know much about that and I pooh-poohed it a lot.

And she persisted?

She kept telling me that I wasn't in touch with my feelings, that I operated strictly out of my head. I used to say, "Sometimes I wish you'd never gone into treatment—you come in with all this crap about feelings and all this strange lingo. I think I'm in touch with my feelings." And she said, "Well, I don't," and back and forth we went. In fact, since we didn't have alcohol to argue about anymore, we picked on this. Finally, she persuaded me to go to the Esalen Institute with her for a week in 1967. I'd never done anything like that before. I operated strictly in the straight world.

This was when T-groups and sensitivity groups were at the height of their popularity.

They were just beginning. I spent a week at Esalen in an encounter group. I can point to that as the beginning of opening up a whole new phase of my life. I became aware of how isolated I was from people. Also, I had a lot of anger in me that I had never gotten out. The next year I went to Esalen on my own, and I have been going for one week a year ever since.

Being at the top doesn't make dealing with anger any easier.

No. For so many years, I was trained to keep it cool. Everyone else can lose his head, but the boss has to keep the peace—pour oil on the troubled waters and stay calm, not rock the boat but bring all these dissident forces together. That was my image of a leader, and my image of myself, and I know that I felt you can't trust somebody who can lose his temper or get angry. I mean, Lord, that's unstable. I didn't realize that I was myself suppressing all kinds of anger.

It sounds like Kipling: "If you can keep your head when all about you/Are losing theirs . . . you'll be a Man, my son!"

Absolutely. I had to keep my feelings in check both in the office and at home. At home I had to be Mr. Stability because when Irene was sick, the kids looked to me as the cool, clear stream of reason. While their mother was in trouble, I had to be the strong man.

So your interest and concern in the human potential movement was actually growing at the same time you were feeling more dissatisfied with your working life?

Yes, I'm sure that some of the things that I learned there and in subsequent years had a lot to do with my willingness to change, to try something new in my life, to experiment more with different fields so that I could be more expressive and freer.

To get back to when you left Dain, what did your associates think? Did they regard your leaving as odd?

I had every kind of reaction. Some said, "Well, you might expect that of Wheelock—he's eccentric—you don't know what he's going to do; I'm not surprised." Some were angry. "What does he mean by turning his back on business—did he forget what got him where he is today?" I remember I was quoted in the Minneapolis Tribune as saying that "the thrill of reaching up isn't there." Some people took great offense at that. They felt that business was having enough trouble without one of its members turning his back on it.

What do you think they thought was so threatening?

I think some were quite threatened for two reasons; one, secretly they would have liked to do it themselves, but for one reason or another hadn't gotten up their courage; or secondly, their wives were going to start nagging them and saying, "For God's sake, why don't you do that? You're in a rut, you know." Of course, some were very, very supportive. They'd say, "Good, I'm glad you did it" and "By gosh, it will make it easier for the rest of us who want to do it."

What about the organization? Was it traumatized?

I think the people there were surprised. I am sure that some people were delighted. I said I was getting grouchy, and certainly some people might have felt I was impeding their progress in the company and said, "Now, I'm going to have a chance." Other people who really thought that I was a good leader and that the firm would suffer, were angry, sad, and really disappointed.

Had you made a general announcement?

I did not choose to go around and share it with everybody in advance; I told the two people in the company who were closest to me in authority what I was going to do, and then I just upped and did it at our annual stockholders' meeting.

Was one of the incentives to get to the top that you had some concept of what you wanted the firm to be? In other words, was it an intellectual as well as a personal issue?

I see myself perhaps more as a creative kind of person than an administrative one, and when I said that "the thrill of reaching up" wasn't there, I meant it. I'd reached up as far as I could and created the thing that I had envisioned. I really felt that the company should go through a period of digestion rather than increased growth and size, and I'm sure that a large part of the measure of fun that I'd had was not only building a concept, but also an organization and people. Just managing that organization wasn't fun anymore.

Can you identify what it is that makes you go at full-tilt or what made it necessary for you to go to the top?

Well, I think curiosity has been a big motivator for me. Curiosity to find a better way to do something. Curiosity to try a new idea, to take a new direction. And I guess I'd have to say I enjoy power. In a position of power I often feel very powerless, but that's not the point. I obviously must enjoy power. I think I have a lot of confidence in my judgment, and I feel as though I am instinctively going to do the right thing. I don't know why that would motivate one to take on more and more responsibility, but I think it does.

But is it so much power over people as it is power to realize a conception or an ideal that you're trying to accomplish?

I don't think that the power over people is it. It is power to change things, the power to make, to create something better, whether it be a business or a social service or a community activity. I'm not aware of enjoying having power over somebody's life—whether I can fire him or hire him. Power has certainly been a motivating factor for me in politics. Politicians are the most powerful of all. One, they have the money and two, they make the laws. And if you have those two things, you have an awful lot of power.

When you left DKQ, you were quoted as saying that you were afraid of wandering, of not finding anything new and meaningful. Did you sink in your own estimation?

I said that mostly for publication. I said that because I thought it would seem more humble. Inside I was as confident as I could be that I had done the right thing. I had made the money that I needed in order to enjoy life. I had achieved what I wanted in my business life. I felt confident that I really was together. I had all kinds of things that I was interested in, so I was extremely confident about being able to make the switch.

At the time you changed, had you discussed it with your wife? What were your family's reactions?

I had a lot of support—from my kids and from my wife. I learned a lot from my kids, too, about risk taking. I think my kids had a lot to do with helping me be more expressive and more open. And my wife was very encouraging and supportive. So there was no concern about, "Gee, what is going to happen to Dad?" or "What will he do?" But they were 100% wrong. I was 100% wrong, too.

What happened to you when you left? How were you 100% wrong?

Well, I soon developed a high degree of insecurity, which I never expected would happen to me. Maybe it was because I had so many things I wanted to do that I couldn't decide which I wanted to concentrate on. Maybe I didn't realize how much the security of an office and a large organization and a staff had meant to me. I had taken it for granted, and suddenly I was on my own. I didn't have power anymore. Suddenly I didn't feel effective. It was as though home plate had just been uprooted and I'd gotten lost. I did in fact become temporarily disconnected. I did lose my bearings. I became depressed and anxious. I had problems with my wife that were reasonably serious during this period of time when my security blanket was removed.

There were no financial problems?

No financial problems at all. It was an identity crisis, not a financial crisis. Certainly one of the things that contributed to it was that at almost precisely that time, my wife took on a full-time job. Suddenly I was confronted with a wife with working hours and all the problems that go with that, and I was free. The way it came home to me was that I would be home, we would have planned dinner for 7:00, and at 7:15 the phone would ring. I knew damn well what was going to happen. It would be Irene and she'd say, "Dear, I'm sorry, you're going to have to eat without me." And I'd say, "What do you mean? I've been waiting here!" And I'd just get absolutely livid with rage.

You were used to having things revolve around your own life?

Lord, yes. It was very hard on me. Just at the time I was losing my own identity, she was really finding hers. It was coincidental, but nevertheless, it was bad for me personally. I probably went for as much as nine months or a year before I finally got things into perspective.

You were not yet working full-time for the Johnson Institute during the bad period?

No, but I was spending a lot of time there. I was also teaching. I was taking guitar lessons. We went on a trip to Scandinavia and on one to South America. I was doing some of the things I wanted to do, but I wasn't zeroed in on anything. What happened was just what I'd said I was afraid of. But I didn't really expect it to happen.

Do you think the feeling of drifting was inevitable?

I would say that part of shifting gears, changing your life style or career goal, or altering your priorities will undoubtedly involve a period of insecurity. I think that if you are prepared for it, it might not hit you as hard as it did me. But I do think that if it hit me, with the financial security that I had and my diverse number of interests, that anybody making a shift like this would have to go through a period of doubting whether or not he had made the right decision. I was very anxious about my life and very distressed about it. It worried me that I should be so unhappy, or that I should need what I had had before.

What brought you out of it?

I think that several things helped me break out of it. I was asked to take and accepted the general chairmanship of the United Way campaign for the Minneapolis area—a huge job. I knew that at some time in my life I'd have to do it, so it was sort of like the sword of Damocles hanging over my head. When they finally asked me to do it, I felt a sense of relief in that now I'd be able to get this behind me. That started in the fall of 1972, and gave me a mission, something clear cut that I wanted to achieve. It required all the skills that I had in organization and leadership to pull off, and I think that helped a lot.

What about politics—weren't you considering running for governor in 1974?

This is a kind of crazy thing to say, but I was in a sense aided and abetted in getting out of politics by Nixon's tragedy. It was so obvious—it became increasingly obvious during 1973 as it wore on—that Nixon's leadership was destroying the Republican Party and with it any chance that I might have of running for public office. And for the future, well, I am getting older. I mean, that's a fact of life. And in Minnesota we like our politicians young.

Do you think that the community-spirited atmosphere of Minneapolis has influenced the road you've taken? Would you have worked for the United Way or the Johnson Institute in any event?

I can't answer that honestly. As an adult, I have never lived in any other place except Jacksonville for a brief period. Otherwise I've lived my whole life here. But I think two things would be true of Minneapolis. Number one: this is what we call a home-office town. This is the headquarters of many large corporations. As a result this is where the top executives live, and they want it to be an attractive place. And how do you make it attractive? By making it a well-rounded community. They all pitch in, and in that sense it's a lot different from a branch-office town.

The second thing is that Minnesota is small enough so that people somehow believe they can get their arms around its problems. Whether it's drugs, prison reform, or minorities, whatever the problem, somehow or other it seems manageable in Minnesota.

Are the rewards you are finding now qualitatively different from the ones you found in business?

Yes. And that's one of the things that I still to some degree wrestle with. How do you measure your impact? How do you measure your results in the world, let's say, that I'm now in as opposed to the one I was in? I liked and appreciated the accountability of business. I knew what the rules were. I knew you were measured in terms, simplistically, of earnings per share. I think profit is an excellent discipline.

You don't have measuring sticks in social service?

In social service work you do not have that discipline, and it is very hard to get realistic measurements. You always think that your cause is the most important, you always feel as though you are doing enormously good things, but it is much harder to judge your results honestly. When I teach my course at the University of Minnesota, I really don't know what kind of impact I'm making on the lives of those students who are taking my class. There ought to be better yardsticks to measure social service work because there is so much of our money and activity, and so many people, going into this field.

Have the personal rewards been what you thought they'd be? Have you found the less frantic way of life that you thought you might?

No. My life has not been less frantic. But I'm happier because I'm doing what I really want to do, and there's a difference. I'm feeling fulfilled in my life now. I don't know how long that will last. I mean, who is to know? In some ways I'm perhaps busier than I was before. I don't have an organization to assign people tasks. Oh, I have the Johnson Institute, but everyone there is so busy that I couldn't assign a task anyway, and if I did, they'd probably tell me to go to hell.

You don't run it the same way that you ran Dain?

Quite differently. There's much more group process in decision making. It's painful for me because it takes so much longer. But I think that the people—because they have participated—are more satisfied with the decisions. I don't know if the decisions are better. It's new for me, and I think that in some ways it's better and in some ways it isn't.

Are you still curious about what comes next for you? Or has that curiosity been channeled?

I see myself as a curious person, but I don't feel curiosity about what I'll be doing three years from now. When I say curious, I'm curious about finding a better way to help people cope with chemical dependency. I'm curious about finding a better way to help raise the money that we need for the United Way. I'm curious about a better way to teach students about the business community and about management techniques. And I'm curious about whether I can learn a new tune on my guitar. I really live mostly in the here and now, which I have learned to do through my activities in and exposure to the human potential movement.

A return to business in the future is out of the question for you then?

It would be a remote possibility that I would consider going back into business. I have felt I owed it to myself to take a look at whether the old competitive and earnings-per-share world would be attractive to me again, and whether the unstructured sort of blue-skied, beautiful, helping professional world might not look as good if I got back into business. But I am beginning to realize more and more that that isn't what I want to do. I am so committed to the field of chemical dependency and so optimistic about what is possible to do in this field that I see a long number of years ahead for me in realizing the dreams that I have for what's possible.

And you don't expect yourself ever to feel that loss of identity again?

That wouldn't be true; I'm sure that if I made a shift again in my life, I would be pretty darn confident—but not as confident as last time. Having had it happen to me before, it wouldn't surprise me if I went through a period of insecurity. Again, I'd warn myself next time to watch out for it. I think the transition is one of the things that if you have a little bit more knowledge about, maybe you can handle more easily.

And there is no looking back?

No. Sometimes my ability to pull a curtain down on things that I have done worries me. When I left the bus business, I never gave it another thought. I haven't been back to Yale. I'm going back for my 25th reunion, but I haven't been at all active in the alumni group. I was mayor of my hometown for six years. I put a lot of my life into that. I was a good mayor. But the night I left the council chambers I never went back. When I left DKQ, I never returned. I left the board—I have not taken any active interest in it. I don't know if that's a good or bad trait, but I know it's me. I burn myself out, putting all I have into something, and when it's over, it's over. It's like snuffing out a candle.

William G. Damroth

HBR: **Mr. Damroth, you ran your own company, and now you're on your own as a wildlife photographer and conservationist. Did you always want to work for yourself?**

Damroth: Yes. A lot of my independent ways stem from an attitude of my father's. He was a very Germanic guy who never went beyond the sixth grade. I loved him but I never pleased him; things were never good enough. No matter what I showed him, such as a footstool I'd made in his basement shop, he's say, "It's all right, but that joint isn't very good. Make it light-tight." Or if I brought home a report card with an eighty he'd say, "What's the matter? Can't you get a hundred?" When I was eight and proud of my grades, he would say things like that, and I would lock myself in the bathroom and cry. I don't like criticism and never did. I tried to avoid it by making myself boss.

Do you think this affected your career path?

Yes. I'd say I had a need to please myself, and a need to overcome financial insecurity. My father was the superintendent of a building on East Ninth Street in Manhattan. We lived on the top floor. My parents had very little money, and that was what bothered me most as a kid. I'd fantasize, "Some-day I want to put my hand in my pocket and say, 'I'll buy it, and I don't care what it costs.'" I wanted to reach that point. I wanted to be a millionaire. I started working as a teenager in Macy's stockroom. After the Air Corps, I ran my own promotion agency, then a small sales consulting firm, and finally the Lexington Corporation. All my life I've really worked for myself.

You started Lexington Corporation yourself?

Not exactly. I had a partner. It was in the late 1950s. I was married by that time. I had three boys, and a good family life. When I was 34 or 35, still with the marketing business, I decided to write a book on "How to Win Success Before Forty." I interviewed about 70 successful people for that, tying each one into some ideas I had about success. The third man I inter-viewed was John Templeton, who was a Rhodes Scholar and a financial genius. He was about six years older than I. After the book interview, he took me to supper and finally asked me what I did. I explained that I was a marketing consultant and he said, "Maybe we could get together because I've got a financial organization and staff. You can market; basically, mutual funds are a combination of these two. Why don't you think about it. Perhaps we could set up a business." Two months later we formed Templeton, Damroth Corporation, the forerunner of the Lexington Corporation. It took 13 years and a lot of sweat, but it was a success.

What size firm was it?

By 1968 we had assets of $150 million in four mutual funds and $300 million in private investment accounts, 100 employees and 360 salesmen.

Why did you want to leave, when you were clearly a success, chairman of the board after having been president?

That has a lot to do with my own philosophy. My own values had changed over the past years. You have to know what you want personally—to focus your own drive. You've got to like what you're doing to work 80 and 90 hours a week. When you begin to dislike your work, you'd better quit the job.

What was it you didn't like at Lexington?

Business got to be a bore. For me the fun is not in arriving at the goal, but in the creative process . . . in the doing. It's the conceiving of something, and finally watching the thing start to fall into place. It's the early stages of a concept that are exciting. After ten years at Lexington, things were routine. To me when work becomes repetitious, it becomes a bore. Salesmen were always wanting a little better commission. Managers wanted better branch offices, more expense money, and someone's shoulder to cry on. I finally said to myself, "What am I doing here? What's the fun of this?" I looked ahead 10 years and all I could see was a 10% increase in profits per year and more of the same gripes. What the hell, I could see the future and I didn't like it.

When did you know you actually wanted to leave?

Well, my itch to leave began about five years before I really did. I had joined the Young Presidents Organization several years earlier and immediately became very active. I guess I was about 40 or 41 at the time. One of the things I can thank YPO for was that it helped overcome my feeling of inferiority about not having gone to Harvard and not having gotten that brilliant business education. Once I met and worked with my peer group, I realized many weren't any sharper than I was. But most significant, it helped me clarify my inner feelings. The group used to hold a week-long annual meeting at which there would be educational courses on business, philosophy, family relations, religions of the world—quite a mix. You could pick whatever subjects interested you. I took the philosophy and religion courses. I didn't attend a single business course.

This decision to leave, then, came in stages?

It built up. I would say it started when I was 42 in 1962, and then grew. At that point I didn't have my financial security. I'd just gone public with my little company. I couldn't sell my stock. The corporation had little value. I had no choice but to hold on in order to build the machine up so I could walk away from it one day. That was my idea from the start.

You were actually trying to build yourself financial security to make yourself an exit?

I've always had the exit in mind. Acquiring financial security opened the door. Not that I knew where I wanted to go with the exit. I only knew I wanted my freedom.

Freedom from what?

From the box. I became a prisoner of my own creation. Business takes away your freedom of mobility. You're obliged to your personnel. You're obliged to your investors, your clients. You're always obliged to something.

What exactly was the burden?

Well, to me the main thing was that I couldn't continue doing what I enjoy the most, which is the creative role, the intense bringing together of all factors, saying, "It ought to look like this." For instance, what I'm doing today is much more satisfying than the long-range planning you have to do for a company. Today's satisfaction is immediate. When I take a trip through the sanctuary and photograph a spoonbill, I can get that proofsheet right away and say, "Really, that's a beauty."

For someone like yourself, who has a conceptual frame of mind, would government intervention, regulations, and consumer boards be a cause of disenchantment?

To a degree. Creating a new fund, or whatever your particular business is, gets to the point where you can conceive of how it *should* be. Then it's nitpicked to death for two years by government agencies, lawyers, and everybody else. By the time an idea would come to reality, I couldn't even recognize my brainchild. Regulation takes a lot of fun out of creativity in business. The reason why you are doing things, why you are driving yourself so hard, is because you enjoy the game. If some nitpicker pulls all the fun out of it, you might as well say, "I'll do something else—I'll sit back and take my blue eyes someplace else." Overregulation does impede. But, then again, in each case you find ways to go along with the rules. It's like choices in life; it is not always, "Which am I going to do—this or that?" The alternatives are thousands, and you pick an alternative that fits with whatever your ideas and your restrictions are.

So what really was bothering you was that you liked creating and not managing.

Yes. I don't like managing people. I like dealing with people when it's on a small, more intimate basis. I like having a viable project in mind and trying to convince somebody to move with me on it. I love that, or a committee, or a whole tableful of people. This is fine. Another thing I didn't like in business was the tension.

What kind of tension?

Oh Lord, every morning I commuted from Tarrytown with an 8 × 13-inch pad. Everyone else was reading his paper, but I was working out all the things I wanted everybody else to be doing. By the time I'd get into the office I'd have ten pages, which I'd hand to the male secretary I had and say, "Get this down to accounting," "Get this down to so-and-so," "Get this down to so-and-so." Then I'd be left with a splitting headache. Everyday it was the same damn thing.

Do you think not liking to manage, liking ideas, is characteristic of most people who make it to the top of their organizations?

Not necessarily, but I think it's a characteristic, to a great extent, of many first-stage entrepreneurs. Usually, though, they have, as I did in my president, an administrator to back them up. My president was happy in his job. He liked holding committee meetings and he liked to maneuver people—all the things that I found very boring.

You couldn't have gone on and created more funds, acquired other interests to make Lexington grow?

No, it seemed impossible at the time. I thought my solution was to be acquired by an insurance company. At least my projections indicated that an insurance company and a mutual fund had to be married. Everybody else in the company was against it. So it was a continual struggle those last few years. Eventually, though, it happened in 1969, at the top of the market.

Did you tell associates at work about how you were feeling?

Some key men knew, but I never talked to them about my personal feelings, my shifting values. You can't in a company; you only end up frightening everybody. It's bad enough trying to talk about it at home. So you keep it quiet, and bottle it up inside you.

So for the last two years at Lexington you were carrying a number of burdens you couldn't share?

Yes, and that became one of the things that got me into psychiatry. It was about a year before the company was finally sold. I was feeling so torn apart I thought it was about time I talked to a psychiatrist; I had never done that.

When I first went to see him, I said, "If I am so successful, how come I feel so bad?" It took two months before I felt any better.

What was the breakthrough?

About the third month of psychiatry, I woke up in the middle of the night and sat bolt upright in bed. My heart was going very fast; I didn't know if I was sick or what. I went downstairs and put all the lights on—didn't want to wake my wife—walked through all the rooms, and still the strange feeling of fear didn't go away. I was praying that dawn would come so I could see the sun. I felt full, as though I was being cramped in my chest. I finally went back upstairs, woke up my wife and said, "I'm scared. This feeling won't go away. I may be having a heart attack." I had never felt so frightened before. And so I said, "Call Ian"—he was my psychiatrist.

Ian came over at 2:00 in the morning. My wife couldn't stand to see me in this terrible state of fright and torment, so she went downstairs to get away. Ian held my hand, sat with me on the bed and said, "Let it out, let it out." And I began to cry. I cried for about two hours. I kept sobbing, "Get off my back, get off my back, get off my back." That's all I could say. But finally I had verbalized all of my fears. When I saw Ian the next day, he asked, "Who put them on your back?" I admitted, "I guess I did." Once you understand *that,* you can take them off.

So you had your own necessity to be the strong and reliable one.

Well, I felt responsible for everyone. For the employees, the stockholders, the investors, the clients, my children, my wife, my mother, and I forgot my own needs. I always felt much more comfortable, if there was something to be done, to say, "Oh, don't worry about it, I'll do it." But when you get into a business over a certain size, you can't do it all. And some day you realize you can't please everyone. I had to let go and that was hard.

When it finally came time to leave, were you afraid?

No, no, no, no. No fear. It was just turbulent turmoil in the last year of the company, when I knew I wanted to get out from under, sell it out, and everybody was fighting me on that. And my wife also knew I wanted to clear out and float free.

How did your wife feel about it?

Any time you make a change, everybody around you is affected by the change. And either they adjust or break away. In this case I was constantly getting freer and freer, and she became more and more worried. She'd cry, "What are we going to do? We won't have any money coming in."

But you had sufficient money by that time.

She knew that. It was the job, the *job*. Her daddy was a dentist; he always stood behind that chair and worked hard most of his life. People had jobs, with a capital J. She trembled whenever I said, "I'm not going to work for a salary any more," or, "I don't care what happens to our income."

Was she able to accept it finally?

She got her own psychiatrist eventually and got stronger. We had great ups and downs that last year. We were in fact more in love than ever. We also got angry, angrier than we ever had before. I would say things like, "Damn it, I won't behave only in ways that make you comfortable." I'd never said that before. We'd always been so nice.

What happened then? Did the marriage get stronger?

Well, no. Everything was happening at one time. I never realized there must have been more going on, more traumatic stuff happening, than I knew at the time. I see now that every change you make is a drain on you. I wonder now that I didn't bust apart. The crisis at home came before I actually quit my job. It occurred when I took off to Africa alone to do my first wildlife photography. That started my wife feeling that I was pulling away from her. And then one evening after I got back from Africa, while we were sitting on the couch, it was my wife who had the guts to say, "Maybe we ought to get a divorce." I said, "OK." The nearest I'd got to thinking about divorce was when I was angry one day and walked into my psychiatrist and said, "I wish I could pension her off."

How did your children feel about your separation? Were they as worried?

They took it remarkably well. The 15- and 17-year-old wondered why we didn't separate a year earlier. The 13-year old was jolted but was OK in a day. Those boys are very independent souls. I remember my third year at Lexington; we had made several films of how the mutual funds operate, and I had brought the films home with me to show the kids what I was doing at the office. My middle son said, "I want your job when I grow up," and I said, "Too late, I'm not going to be there." I said, "I just want to show you what I'm doing, but don't ever think, any of you, that you're going to move into any part of this business. You're going to be on your own."

To get back to when you left, were you afraid of not finding something else that would sufficiently replace your work?

No, but there was an emptiness. At first I missed the camaraderie. So I tried to hold on. I went to luncheons, did things with my old contacts. Then you see that what they're talking about now you're not interested in. So you pull away from that. You wonder about your own identity. You wonder about what you are and who you are. And then you wonder if maybe you should take that job someplace and become president of another company.

So you didn't have anything else in particular that you wanted to do?

No. I didn't know what I wanted out of life. But for the first time I knew what I didn't want.

What about your friends? Were they surprised?

Business associates couldn't understand my action. My few friends did, and were supportive. Despite the miles, my friendship with those men goes on even today.

When you finally decided to walk away, how did you feel?

At times terrible. The trauma really is one of loss of identity. When someone says, ''Hello, what do you do?'' you can say you are president of an investment company, and they smile politely and won't ask any more questions. They've got you framed up there someplace. That's fine. I liked that feeling of being framed up there. But after you leave the business world and somebody says, ''What do you do?'' you say, ''Well, I'm retired,'' and they say, ''Oh, you're too young to retire.'' So you can gloat on that one for about two months, and then the novelty wears off. The next thing you say is, ''Well, I *was* chairman of the board, but now I'm setting up a new company.'' ''That's nice.'' And then that wears off. Finally, after a year of uncertainty, I started doing some serious wildlife photography and then I started saying, ''Well, I'm doing a lot of wildlife photography, but I *used* to be chairman of the board.''

Do you ever consider going back to business?

No. Sometimes I wonder where I can find the elements that I miss. I still enjoy people . . . but on my terms. I've been accused of wanting my cake and eating it, too. Exactly. I would consider an appointment to something at a college or in government, but again, on my terms. I could even see taking over a small foundation, provided I didn't have a big, clumsy board to report to. There are small foundations that are, say, between $5 million and $10 million. And, hell, with some creative ideas you could have a lot of fun with that and do quite a lot of good.

What can large corporations do to keep people like yourself, who have valuable years of experience, but who feel the need for new challenges as well as for excitement?

I think corporations have to accommodate the man with a new direction, or whatever it might take. At the production level, if you set up a system like Volvo's and build cars with different teams, you find that you improve production. It is no different when you go upstairs. The good executive in the corporation also forms his team. The organization wants team men— men who are comfortable being on the team. And they're necessary. The world is full of Indians and very few chiefs. But corporations couldn't continue with a lot of chiefs. They put fires under friends and shoot off in all directions. My God, you would never get a car tuned that way.

But if a guy who really is a potential chief, a steamroller, is in a job where he's simply trying to behave properly to get along, all the power, all the energy is being taken out of him. Before you lose him, somebody should be smart enough to stop this, to offer this man a new direction and gamble with him on a project.

And it takes somebody like yourself to give somebody else his head?

If you like to be your own man, you can see how somebody else would like it. So it takes a particular kind of top executive to take risks with this man, to give him a special project with a special budget. After all, the top executive is the one who is eventually going to have to face the board and say, ''I gambled half a million on this man and backed this project.''

How would you identify these people?

I think every good leader recognizes potential chiefs, the ones who might become discontented. You can tell a certain amount from what people talk about. They're not going to talk about comfortable things; they're talking about a meaningful life, adventure, about risk taking, new ideas, and new directions. You see signs in what they do with their private lives, what they do with their families. Even the way they walk tells there's a dynamic tension. You can tell by looking in their eyes. They usually turn out to be the ones who are almost little irritants. They're not the nice ones who are getting along, who look like they're going to be the next department head. They're mavericks, the guys who wouldn't be very happy even if you handed them a $30,000 raise. They'd say, ''What? That's all?''

Would companies do themselves favors if they establish policies and encourage people to change careers at 45?

Discontent for the maverick can come at any age. If inside redirection isn't possible, then look outside, to a new division, a new acquisition. Also, a challenge for this man could be found in assignments that are not related to business, but that use all of his talents, like the foundation work I've gotten into. Big corporations wouldn't lose, lending executive talent to charitable foundations. A man who is from GM, for instance; contributing six months of an executive's time to the Nature Conservancy would help both organizations.

Were you ever conscious of wanting power?

Being able to dominate lives doesn't give me a kick. I prefer to discover and use my own creativity. Someone says, "Well, you could make another million dollars." Maybe so, but I can't eat it. Accumulating money is like accumulating photographs. Just taking a lot of pictures is no satisfaction. I've got to have the outlet for my creations. If I'm not making posters for some conservation organization or publishing a book or giving a wildlife exhibit to the local schools or doing something different, there's no fun. Photography has to have an end product.

So, the same with money. If I have a way to give it away and enjoy doing that, that's fine. And then it's still working for myself. That's why I started my own foundation back in 1968.

What is the full name of the foundation?

Just me. Just The Damroth Foundation. It's small. I just took some of my winnings, $250,000, and put them aside. Most of it right now has got to do with preserving wildlife through the Sanibel-Captiva Conservation Foundation and The World Wildlife Fund. But I give grants to many worthy causes. The only stipulation is that all of the assets are used before I die. I enjoyed making the money. I want the pleasure of giving it away.

Are you finding the satisfactions that you thought you'd find?

I feel much better about my life. Let's say that I'm not frustrated, except that I'm seeking that new challenge that's waiting for me behind that seventh veil. But my time is my own. I can lie on my back for two hours if I want. Instead of saying, "This is what I want" and moving toward it, I've said, "This is what I don't like," and I've eliminated it. I've cut away all the things that make life unhappy for me. I don't have any tension headaches in the mornings.

What is your social life like now?

I have made a few new friends. But I have no close relationships with anybody down here in Sanibel where I live, although I've lived here three years. People are glad to see me, and we do get together. And when I go into the Conservation Foundation, they want to know, "Where the hell have you been? Let's have lunch and hear what you've been doing," and I give them a new idea and then I disappear. A modest social life. But no, no deep friendships here.

Have you remarried?

Yes, last year. A pretty Swiss miss. She's my vice president. My first wife is remarried, too. Funny, she's now in a decorating business on Martha's Vineyard and getting a real kick out of it.

Do you feel that if you suddenly decided that you wanted to go back into business yourself, that age would stand in the way?

No. I see that as no impediment at all. I can start for myself any time. My credentials are pretty good, and all I have to do is present them. I've done a hell of a lot. I can do a hell of a lot more. But it won't be a business for profit.

Do you miss the fast track?

I miss the pulse of being where things are happening and I'm in the wrong place for that on Sanibel. Two things bother me: one is that I feel I have the power to move mountains in terms of people, but just now that talent has no place to go. Not finding the way to fully use myself is very frustrating. Right now I'm living in these happy surroundings but have no way to use all of my strength. That's bothersome. Second: perhaps it would be better if we spent part of the year in a college town, or in Washington, D.C.— someplace with a pulse, and not limit my horizon to Sanibel. I want to feel the pulse, I want to be with people who talk about the pulse, to recommend creative ideas around that pulse. But I don't want you to hold my hand. And that opportunity is not easy to find.

You don't worry about the road not taken?

No, no. That's dead. Yesterday is dead.

Are you working on anything now?

Lots of things. All through my foundation and my photography. I've even written several children's books, one on sea gulls. Publishers liked the photographs, but not "another" gull story. But I like the idea and think the market is there. In New York I've had these same publishers take me to lunch, talk with me. One children's book editor said, "We've got to find something for you to do." I said, "Fine. But I usually find out what I want to do and I hope you like it." He said, "I've got it. How would you like to do a children's book about termites?'' I said, ''I couldn't care less.'' He said, ''There's not a good book on termites. We could sell it.'' And he would. He would sign a contract and pay an advance, if I would do a book on termites. But I don't *have* to do a book on termites. I don't have to do anything I don't want to do.

20

Can You Survive Your Retirement?

LELAND P. BRADFORD

Until they leave employment at the end of their lifelong work careers, many men and women are unaware of how much the organization means to them. The author of this article, the longtime head of a relatively small enterprise, was delighted to escape the office, move to a warm climate, and rush to the golf course. "How wrong I was!" he writes. He experienced a tremendous sense of loss, futility, and uselessness. Moreover, he was soon bored and began having petty marital arguments. He learned that many retirees, apparently overcome by their feelings of emptiness, die not very long after they have supposedly entered the "promised land." How the author and his wife gained insight into their new situation, worked out their difficulties, and eventually made a comfortable transition into retirement is the basis of this article. Out of his research on the subject in the past few years, he provides guidance to managers and their organizations for surviving the emotional stress of this experience.

I was the chief executive of an organization I had helped found, as well as professional behavioral scientist, and I should have known better. But I didn't. After 25 years of working under the strain of building an organization, of interweaving the ideas and needs of the key staff with a multiplicity of outside forces, I was ready for the beautiful promised land of retirement. I persuaded my wife to leave our lovely Georgetown home and move to North Carolina, where I could golf to my heart's content and enjoy relief from the stress of having to make daily decisions. I thought it would be just wonderful.

Published in 1979.

How wrong I was! The first year was awful. The organization moved on without me. Important decisions I had made were reversed. No one called for advice. As far as I could see, no one cared. I even felt that my professional reputation had vanished. It hurt.

At times I thought with empathy of a friend who had been president of a large multinational company. He had told me, before he retired, that he had everything planned carefully. A year after his retirement, some of his former vice presidents told me he came to the office at least twice a week seeking someone who was free to lunch with him.

I found that golf did not fill a day. The consultation and volunteer work I did was not satisfying. Other interests paled before the challenges I had faced. Life felt empty. I was not aged, just a little older. I had plenty of energy and I felt just as competent as I had been.

When for the umpteenth time I complained to my wife about the emptiness of my life, Martha exploded, ''I've heard enough of your complaining! You dragged me away from the city and home I loved best. Do you know why I don't like it here? Do you know why I've gone to the hospital twice this year for checkups, only to find nothing wrong? It was because I'm unhappy. Did you consider my life in retirement when you retired?'' I hadn't, though I thought we had talked everything over. Maybe I had just talked about *my* retirement. What she said woke me up, and I listened.

Then we talked for days, for weeks, it seemed like months—at breakfast, teatime, the cocktail hour, during evenings when there were no parties. We came to know each other's feelings and problems better. We asked ourselves if we were the only ones to react this way, so we looked about us and talked to many others on the golf course and at small parties. We found we weren't alone, although people usually covered up at first before acknowledging the empty hours they dreaded and their sense of futility and uselessness. (We learned later of a census study showing that many persons die four to five years after retirement, seemingly out of a sense of uselessness. And according to a famous French physician, people can indeed die of boredom.)

Only after we had talked through our own difficulties to our satisfaction did we begin to question why this transition period was so very difficult and so different from others we had negotiated. Was it because it marked an ending or were there other causes? Here are our conclusions.

What One Loses In Retirement

As we thought about what had happened to us and to others, we began to see how organizations inadvertently fulfill a number of basic psychological needs for people. The loss of these gratifications on retirement can be devastating unless effectively accommodated to or replaced.

Acceptance and Socialization.   The organization, for almost all positions, provides colleagues, work groups, teams, committees, units, or departments.

Members perforce feel a sense of belonging that they share with others, whether the cohesive factor is task completion or antagonism within groups or the company. Conflict adequately handled is energizing. Task accomplishment is a mutual gain. Work provides the contacts vital for psychological well-being. Otherwise, there are no correctives for perceptual distortion, no antidotes for loneliness.

I found all this out. I felt the alienation of no longer being a part of groups I had belonged to for 40 or more hours a week for more years than I cared to remember. Even in my childhood, when I had been temporarily ostracized by playmates, I had not felt so keenly excluded, bereft, outside, disposable.

I thought again of my friend who had returned hungrily to the office to seek the companionship of his past subordinates. What was different for him, and now for me, was the apparent lack of an arena offering equal challenges and companionship. I found it harder than I ever expected to say a permanent good-bye to a lifetime work career. It took time and suffering to find an adequate solution.

Goals, Achievement, and Affirmation.   Organizations provide goals and tasks to be formulated and accomplished. During the middle years these are interwoven with personal financial aims and family responsibilities. Goals make achievement possible, sometimes with soul-warming results. Achievement brings affirmation from others and from one's self. Without this periodic affirmation, self-esteem and self-worth diminish. They are intricately interdependent and, oh, how important!

To be without goals is to be purposeless, to have no reason to arise in the morning; for some, even to live. I teetered on the brink of goallessness and it took Martha to awaken me. Also, a perceptive club member said to me, "Do you realize the purpose of our club is to keep useless people alive?" That helped wake me too.

Not long ago I had lunch with a man whom I had known for years. Highly successful in the positions he had held, he was generous, sensitive to others, and a good companion. He had been retired for a couple of years. During the two hours of lunch, I don't think I got in three sentences. He didn't tell me what he was doing, because he wasn't doing anything to talk about, but he did talk about the well-known people who sought him out and the artists and musicians who wanted his company. I left our luncheon saddened. He who had achieved so much was now reduced to seeking affirmation from others in superficial ways. How had retirement so drastically stripped him of his sense of achievement?

Power and Influence.   Companies provide for most employees some degree of power and influence. For top executives, of course, the degree is great, though most would admit to various constraints. Power conveys importance to the person and aids the formation and perception of identity. Power increases the areas in which accomplishments can occur and leads to the gaining of more power.

For executives and others who have known considerable power, its sudden loss at retirement can be an acute deprivation. The shock for many is not only great but also bewildering. Events are less under one's control, and the importance in others' eyes that power gives has evaporated. Must the person who has lost power continue to vie for it, or can the individual find power and importance within himself?

On the board of directors of a local organization of not much significance sit some former executives of well-known companies. The board meets periodically for a stated two hours each meeting. For 5 to 10 minutes real work is accomplished. These executives, before retirement, would have ended a meeting in no more than 15 minutes. Now they are content to spend the two hours. Why? One might guess that, since they have little else to do, two hours fill a portion of a day. One might also hazard a guess that for those two hours power and influence are again theirs.

Support Systems.   Individuals need a variety of support systems for psychological and emotional health. Colleagues, friends, neighbors, clubs, community responsibilities, family, and others serve as support systems providing recognition, admiration, assurance of abilities, reality testing, feedback on behavior, and encouragement.

When retirement comes, and particularly if the couple moves away, many support systems disappear. I wish I had thought to list all my support systems before I retired, then crossed off those I would miss. I could then have gone on more than just intuitive feeling in deciding which ones were crucial to replace.

Routines and Time.   The busy executive with wide-ranging interests and multifaceted decisions to make seldom realizes the stabilizing force of set routines—regular staff meetings, daily agendas on the desk each morning, planned luncheon engagements, organized trips, prearranged social events.

When retirement comes, most of these routines stop. At first it seems heavenly: no clock ruling you, no secretary reminding you of your luncheon appointment, no hurried breakfast, no train to catch. So I found it; but not for long, because habit is strong. Besides, inasmuch as my day no longer had its ready-made structure, I was left with the aggravating necessity of making many small decisions. Therefore, routines need to be set; else why should one get out of bed at all? This is a small but significant change in the transition to retirement.

Where we now live there is no postal delivery. Sometimes during the morning, everyone goes to the post office to meet friends, exchange gossip, make golf dates, and sometimes arrange parties. Gradually routines like this become established, but only if the person deliberately develops them; no longer does the organization create them.

Before retirement, the expenditure of time, like routine, is primarily under the control of the organization, and time spent on nonwork activities is fitted into the slots remaining. During the driving, challenging, responsible work years, time becomes a scarce and precious commodity: it is the duty of secretaries and assistants to ensure that this precious resource is effectively used.

In retirement the reverse is too frequently true. Time must be filled, somehow, to pass the day. Time can lead people into the dangerous wasteland of empty time, where no purpose is present to stir any interest or desire. If empty time recurs each day, the will and motivation to seek new interests dwindle. Boredom joins with apathy to reduce the joy of living and speed psychological if not physical deterioration.

In my early days of retirement I would become irritated on the links if a slow foursome in front held up our play. My partners, longer retired, would say, "What's your hurry? What else do you have to do today?"

For many of us, golf was followed by time at the bar, perhaps some bridge, more cocktails at home or at a party, followed by a dull evening. The intense preoccupation with work and community responsibilities had precluded leisurely reading in former years. Interests and new skills not developed before retirement were difficult to cultivate after retirement.

So the challenging hours of yesterday become empty hours today, often with disastrous consequences.

Problems of the Retired

The very different conditions of retirement create new problems stemming from existing situations. Two are sufficiently common and serious to be critical in a misery-free transition to retirement.

Marital Difficulties

Marriage, as a dynamic process, alters of course with changing conditions. The abrupt passage from work to retirement should require consideration of possible marital adjustments. There are a number of factors leading to this necessity.

The Rights of Each.   I never realized that my work career, title, status, job responsibilities, office, secretary, even desk represented my turf, or territory, and thus largely defined my identity to others and to myself. When I thought of turf I thought of the way animals fight to secure or defend a bit of space. It was only at retirement, when all aspects of my turf were given to another, that the dreadful realization of being turfless struck home. For an awful moment, I became uncertain of my identity. I knew who I had been, but I was not certain who I was. The sudden movement from "I am" to "I was" was difficult to adjust to.

I had always thought of the home as mine as well as Martha's. But now I found that it was her turf. It had been her territory to manage, where she had made and implemented decisions and dealt with a host of people. I had never thought of the time and knowledge she had put into managing the home.

It was not long before it occurred to me that I was intruding on her turf. I managed to be in the wrong place at the wrong time—for example, we kept bumping into each other in the kitchen. It was her domain and I was obviously curtailing her freedom of action. We talked it through and worked out accommodations that gave me some turf without depriving her and allowed us time alone as well as shared time.

We observed how turf-loss and intrusion problems beset other retired couples. Once we were looking at clothes in the downstairs section of a store. Sitting on the steps leading downstairs was a gray-haired man. A woman standing near us saw us glance at him and she felt impelled to speak. "Since he's retired he goes wherever I go. I can no longer shop in peace," she said, with a hostile look toward the stairs. "It's like having a child with you all day long. I don't know how long I can stand it!"

Then there is the extreme where intrusion means control. An acquaintance of ours had always been restless, but his nervous energy had fit well with the demands of his high-level corporate position. He did not slow up even in retirement. No sooner did he and his wife return from one cruise or plane trip, with stops at various cities, than he was planning another. His wife grew more weary with each trip.

Finally she spoke up, saying she couldn't take it any longer. He brushed her feelings aside. "Nonsense," he said. "Travel is broadening. It's good for you." That silenced her; she couldn't stand up to his strong (and insensitive) personality. But finally, for the first time, she complained openly and bitterly to her friends.

Unless the couple can undertake a conciliatory review of their turf-loss and intrusion problem and make adjustments to it, irritations will grow, bitterness will mount, and conflicts will continue. But such a marital review is not easy to make. Talking through the problem requires a sense of self-worth on the part of each so that feedback can be openly given and non-defensively received. It requires respect of each by the other and sufficient self-understanding so that each feels secure.

The turf-intrusion problem is typical of the mutually affecting strains that become especially stressful in retirement, when husband and wife find themselves spending much more time together. The turmoil that one of them experiences upsets the other. Unless each can share the problems and can accept help and support from the other, relations that before were calm become potentially explosive.

Sex Role Questions.   Particularly for the man who has lost his turf, the fear of losing a masculine image is bothersome. He has had an identity as the family provider, the family head, the ultimate judge on major issues. Title and position in the eyes of others bolster one's self-image, and a man tries to project himself to others as a strong and competent person worthy of their respect.

Because a man cannot overtly assert his macho drives, he directs them into various innocent and socially acceptable channels. The individual may only be dimly aware of these drives, but they are strong.

Not long ago Martha and I attended a small dinner party with four other couples, all friends or acquaintances. The host had always appeared to us to be a quiet, unobstrusive man. That night, however, he was assertive and extremely aggressive toward his wife. If she broke in on his conversation, he told her to wait until he was finished talking. He corrected her and instructed her not to talk unless she knew what she was saying. She made no protest, out of good manners or perhaps for other reasons. The other guests looked as embarrassed as we were.

Martha and I talked the matter over when we arrived home. What we had seen was not the couple's normal pattern of relationship. One hypothesis stood out in our thinking: the husband, without realizing it, was endeavoring to show the other men at the party that, though long since retired, he was still a man and master of his home.

Growing Apart.   Over the years sharp differences in work responsibilities may have brought first imperceptible and then palpable differences in the levels of growth of the partners. Because so much of the day was spent apart, these differences may not have been important. But with the closer living of retirement, they become almost unbearable.

One man we know rose far in his company through sheer ability. His frequent new contacts, coupled with his absorbing mind, brought continual expansion of his interests. His wife stayed home and socialized with a tight circle of friends. Then he retired, and he suddenly found they had little in common and even less to communicate about. It seemed they had come out of different worlds, and there was nothing they could do but to live out their lives as best they could. My wife and I agreed that both were to blame—he because he had done nothing to help her grow, and she because she had insulated herself and had made no effort to develop.

So at retirement, couples need to undertake a marital review. Those who have negotiated this transition successfully probably made sensitive adjustments as needs arose without waiting for problems to become serious. But those who think that their relationship will remain the same and make no accommodations are in for trouble.

Societal Attitudes

Formerly individuals retired only when they were incapacitated or too old to work. The myth that this is so persists. To be retired, think many younger people, is to be aged. To be aged is somehow obscene; it is a disease to be avoided. Television advertising tells us so—advertising promotes products and devices to make people appear younger. One advertisement asks, "Why look as old as you are?"

A person who is retiring finds it very easy to accept this attitude and feel disposable, unneeded, and useless. It takes effort and will to reject that attitude and project the true picture—to oneself and others—that vast numbers of retired persons are still energetic and competent.

To counteract society's attitude, the individual must not only reject the concept of aging before the fact, he must also change his own attitudes about himself, recognizing the particular psychological and emotional needs which his work formerly satisfied but which he now (together with his partner) is obliged to satisfy himself. My wife and I agree: many years went into preparing us to enter the world of work but nothing was done to prepare us to leave it.

One day we were having a leisurely lunch with a couple who had been longtime friends of ours. He was retiring soon from a key executive post, so Martha and I asked them what they had done in anticipation of that event. He replied that lawyers had worked out family trusts and special accounts for his wife. We pursued the point. She added that they were already looking for the right place to live. We pursued again. They looked puzzled. We explained some of the emotional problems and their causes that we had encountered. They were surprised; they hadn't thought of those.

What Can Be Done

There is no cookbook recipe for retiring. Some may find it a release from hated work and strain; others, whose focus has been the job, may find it a deprivation. Personalities and needs differ. The answer to successful retirement seems to lie in self-understanding, a feeling of self-worth, and the will and ability to survive emotionally.

Census studies indicate that persons reaching 65 can expect, on the average, 15 more years of life—almost one-fifth of the total life span. That is too big a chunk to waste or to endure without purpose or meaning.

Today well over 400 companies reportedly hold preretirement training programs, compared with only a few dozen five or six years ago. Unfortunately, few of these programs deal seriously, if at all, with emotional problems; they merely stress the importance of remaining active and maintaining a healthy outlook. But some enterprising companies are expanding their traditional preretirement sessions to include extra dimensions. The ruled insert outlines what one employer is doing. Here is a sample of other programs:

☐ Connecticut General Insurance Co. conducts a program over an eight-week period offering a package developed by the American Association for Retired Persons and called AIM (Action for Independent

Maturity). Among other aspects, it deals with marital difficulties and emotional problems. The program's focus is new-career planning, whether that means sitting in a rocking chair or embarking on a different type of job.

This insurance concern offers its 13,000 employees a flexible arrangement by which a person can retire as early as age 55 (or leave as early as 45 with vested pension benefits). The employee can participate in the preretirement sessions up to five years before scheduled retirement.

☐ Moog, Inc., which employs 2,500, has taken the initiative to expand its program covering the "classic" matters of health and safety, finances, legal issues, and recreation. For the last two years, this manufacturer of electrohydraulic controls has conducted a pilot program examining emotional adjustments that retirees and their spouses must make. Each group includes about a dozen employees plus their spouses. Some of the sessions are group affairs, and some involve only a single couple.

The participants are in their last year before leaving employment. To help workers make a smoother transition, Moog management plans eventually to start the program for employees in the 50-to-55 age range. The company will encourage "refresher courses" when the employee reaches age 60 and each year thereafter until he or she retires.

☐ Exxon Corporation's giant U.S. affiliate (40,000 employees) recently launched a pilot program in Houston; the first participants were employees retiring in 1979 or early 1980. The company plans to continue the sessions, scheduled for about two dozen persons at a time, and modify them as experience dictates. Each session starts one evening and lasts the next three days.

Exxon's previous preretirement program had stressed the economic factors and—to an extent—physiological factors of retirement. The new program covers psychological elements, particularly how the person can replace the satisfactions and rewards formerly provided by his work. Developing and sustaining relationships with others is a focus of the program (spouses are invited to join the group in this portion).

As the Connecticut General program stresses, retirement can be the beginning of a new career, and the employer can aid the individual in planning and preparing for it. The reward from a new career need not be money; it can be satisfaction, self-affirmation, and achievement of meaningful goals.

Recent research on adult development stresses that growth and learning can continue throughout the life span. The tremendous increase in continuing education courses offered by colleges, community organizations, and high schools is based on this premise. Acceptance of the concept of a new career, increasingly supported by organizational and societal expectations, makes retirement merely a time when careers change. A career, lest the word seem pretentious, can be any sustained activity whose purpose or goal is meaningful to the person, where motivation is maintained, and where achievement brings affirmation from self or others.

Steps to Take

There is much that organizations can do to help employees to make the transition from the organization to a new kind of life in retirement:

1.   Employees can be encouraged to widen personal interests that can be carried on in later years and to develop the skills necessary for a second or third career, which need not be for monetary gain. A physician friend, for example, had taught woodworking at night while going through medical school. Today, long retired, he joyously spends his time as an expert cabinetmaker for the benefit of relatives and friends.

2.   Training programs can be conducted through the early and middle years of employment for persons who have settled in at the organization. Particularly if such training stresses greater self-awareness and self-acceptance, this can help prepare them for retirement. Many companies offer training programs designed to help each person look backward at accomplishments, assess himself, and look forward to his future life.

3.   Preretirement programs, one to two years ahead of the event, should be the focal point of the organization's efforts. It is very important that spouses attend, particularly during sessions dealing with emotional and marital issues. These sessions can be designed in such a way to permit husband and wife to discover gradually for themselves the problems that may be encountered, test some solutions in small groups, and then reach their own decisions in private. Carefully designed sessions permit the person who is retiring to treat realistically the problems of empty time, loneliness, and feeling useless—then to formulate and discuss practical rather than impossible solutions.

But ultimately the development of a successful retirement plan lies with the individual or couple, whether the retiree is a chief executive or a clerk. The will and initiative to seek new activities and socialization patterns—and awareness that saying "I can't" is a way of saying "I choose not to"—are imperatives for the major achievement of the retired: emotional survival.

PART FOUR

THE EXECUTIVE AS A HUMAN BEING

AN OVERVIEW

Without doubt, a manager is at some time likely to face an employee who is a troubled person. In his article "What Killed Bob Lyons?," Harry Levinson writes:

> Because each of us is human and no one of us has had either perfect heredity or perfect environment, each of us has weak spots. When the balance of forces is such that there is stress where we are weak, we will have difficulty. The incidence of mental illness, then, is not 1 out of 20 or some other proportionate statistic. Rather it is 1 out of 1!

None of us escapes gnawing fear or painful anxiety, and when something at work touches a personal wound, then a weakness can become a problem.

Bob Lyons committed suicide because he couldn't stand the anxiety that *not* working hard on a project brought on. The work didn't kill him; rather it was the too wide gap between his self-image and his ideal and the too great difficulty of bridging it. Harry Levinson uses the case of Bob Lyons as a framework in which to explore the warring drives within all of us and to show how, if our inner forces get out of kilter, we can literally become unbalanced. Levinson gives us a small lesson in Freudian psychology that will help managers trying to understand their seriously troubled employees.

The next article, also by Harry Levinson, "On Executive Suicide," offers executives some guidelines for coping with the threats to the self-image that can become destructive. Levinson also offers some symptoms: loss of appetite, substantial weight loss, sleeplessness or excessive fatigue, heavy drinking, and so forth, that could be the first signs of serious trouble. He concludes by observing that executives, whose self-images are always at risk, are especially vulnerable.

The executives in the articles just described had problems that caused them to take their rage out on themselves. The next two articles in this section, "Managers Can Drive Their Subordinates Mad" by Manfred F. R. Kets de Vries and "The Abrasive Personality," by Harry Levinson, are about characters that inflict their anger on others. Kets de Vries describes personality types who have such a need to control and to preserve the dependency of their subordinates that they create closed communities out of touch with the reality of the organization's environment. Often these people appear rational and forceful, which makes it difficult for others to find fault with their increasingly suspicious attitudes.

Harry Levinson describes an individual that most of us have worked with at one time or another, a person who is extremely intelligent but who has a knack for hitting others on their soft spots. In pursuit of perfection, the abrasive person cannot tolerate anyone around who cannot match his or her standards, and who gets in the way of a goal.

Both of these individuals probably had childhood problems that warped their normal development. The hostile, suspicious person most likely had enormous difficulty establishing a trusting relationship with his parents. The abrasive person is probably driven by the need to attain an ideal because he or she was greatly criticized as a child.

The manager of such difficult personalities is going to have to work very hard. If the employee is suspicious and hostile, the manager will need to try to establish a trusting relationship, solicit the help of interested parties, and reorient the work climate and structure to break the paranoid pattern that the employee has set up. When dealing with an abrasive person, Levinson suggests that the manager be candid about the destructive outcomes of the subordinate's behavior and make it clear that his or her performance has to change. The steps Levinson outlines are good ones for a manager faced with any alienating personality problem.

The last two articles in this section concern employees' emotional problems that spill over from work to home. In "Must Success Cost so Much?" Fernando Bartolomé and Paul A. Lee Evans describe what happens to executives who reach management levels at the expense of their personal lives. These managers cannot successfully cross the line from their jobs to their home lives for several reasons: they don't adapt well to changes in their jobs, they're probably in the wrong jobs, and they don't handle career disappointments very well. When a manager is unhappy at work, his or her negative emotions spill over to the home life making that less and less a source of comfort and support.

Clearly, top management cannot be responsible for every aspect of their employees' lives and the main burden for managing the effects of negative spillover does rightly fall on the executive. Bartolomé and Evans maintain, however, that managers can do a number of things—broaden organizational values, create multiple reward and career ladders, give realistic performance appraisals, and reduce organizational uncertainty—to lessen the likelihood that employees are going to get into pressure-filled situations at work that reduce the pleasure they get from both home and work.

Finally, in "The Work Alibi: When It's Harder to Go Home," Fernando Bartolomé directly confronts the often repeated myth that our home lives are unhappy because we have to work so hard. Bartolomé counts up the numbers of hours a very busy executive spends on work and finds that even the most diligent have as much time available in a week for their families as they do for their jobs. If work is not the reason, what causes unhappiness at home? Bartolomé cites a number of reasons—the assumption that managing life is easy, fear of confronting conflicts in marriage, legitimate distractions such as children, and the tendency we all have to put things off. The core issue for managers is to become authentic human beings, people who are not afraid of admitting either their weaknesses or their legitimate needs. It is managers who can grow into their own skins, as it were, who are likely to be the most happy at home and the most effective at work. It is people who are not afraid to admit their own inadequacies who can tolerate imperfections in others.

21

What Killed
Bob Lyons?

HARRY LEVINSON

Bob Lyons serves as an extreme example of the conflicting forces in all of us. Successful, hardworking, aggressive, he drives himself relentlessly. What happens when he can no longer balance the demands of internal forces with those of external reality? What can we learn from his tragedy about the problems, pressures, and anxieties with which we must deal?

The case and the extensive analysis that follows were originally published in *HBR* in 1963. A penetrating study of some of the possible causes of self-destructive behavior, the article provides insight into an area of human psychology that continues to be of major concern to *HBR* readers. In his retrospective commentary, the author explains why the article has endured. He argues for the validity of Freudian psychoanalytic theory and briefly discusses six major trends in psychoanalysis that provide a contemporary perspective.

Those who knew Bob Lyons thought extremely well of him. He was a highly successful executive who held an important position in a large company. As his superiors saw him, he was aggressive, with a knack for getting things done through other people. He worked hard and set a vigorous pace. He drove himself relentlessly. In less than 10 years with his company, he had moved through several positions of responsibility.

Lyons had always been a good athlete. He was proud of his skill in swimming, hunting, golf, and tennis. In his college days he had lettered in football and baseball. On weekends he preferred to undertake rebuilding and repairing projects around the house or to hunt, interspersing other sports for a change of pace. He was usually engaged, it seemed, in hard physical work.

Published in 1963.

Authors Note. See notes 1–8 for related readings.

His life was not all work, however. He was active in his church and in the Boy Scouts. His wife delighted in entertaining and in being with other people, so their social life was a round of many parties and social activities. They shared much of their life with their three children.

Early in the spring of his ninth year with the company, Bob Lyons spoke with the vice president to whom he reported. "Things are a little quiet around here," he said. "Most of the big projects are over. The new building is finished, and we have a lot of things on the ball that four years ago were all fouled up. I don't like this idea of just riding a desk and looking out the window. I like action."

About a month later, Lyons was assigned additional responsibilities. He rushed into them with his usual vigor. Once again he seemed buoyant and cheerful. After six months on the assignment, Lyons had the project rolling smoothly. Again he spoke to his vice president, reporting that he was out of projects. The vice president, pleased with Lyons's performance, told him that he had earned the right to do a little dreaming and planning; and, furthermore, dreaming and planning were a necessary part of the position he now held, toward which he had aspired for so long. Bob Lyons listened as his boss spoke, but it was plain to the vice president that the answer did not satisfy him.

About three months after this meeting, the vice president began to notice that replies to his memos and inquiries were not coming back from Lyons with their usual rapidity. In addition, he noticed that Lyons was beginning to put things off, a most unusual behavior pattern for him. He observed that Lyons became easily angered and disturbed over minor difficulties, which previously had not irritated him at all.

Bob Lyons then became involved in a conflict with two other executives over a policy issue. Such conflicts were not unusual in the organization since, inevitably, there were varying points of view on many issues. The conflict was not personal, but it did require intervention from higher management before a solution could be reached. In the process of resolving the conflict, Lyons's point of view prevailed on some questions but not on others.

A few weeks after this conflict had been resolved, Lyons went to the vice president's office. He wanted to have a long private talk, he said. His first words were, "I'm losing my grip. The old steam is gone. I've had diarrhea for four weeks and several times in the past three weeks I've lost my breakfast. I'm worried and yet I don't know what about. I feel that some people have lost confidence in me."

He talked with his boss for an hour and a half. The vice president recounted his achievements in the company to reassure him. He then asked if Lyons thought he should see a doctor. Lyons agreed that he should and, in the presence of the vice president, called his family doctor for an appointment. By this time the vice president was very much concerned. He called Mrs. Lyons and arranged to meet her for lunch the next day. She reported that, in addition to his other symptoms, her husband had difficulty sleeping. She was relieved that the vice president had called her because she was beginning to become worried and had herself planned to call the vice president. Both were now alarmed. They decided that they should get Lyons into a hospital rather than wait for the doctor's appointment that was still a week off.

The next day Lyons was taken to the hospital. Meanwhile, with Mrs. Lyons's permission, the vice president reported to the family doctor Lyons's recent job behavior and the nature of their conversations. When the vice president had finished, the doctor concluded, "All he needs is a good rest. We don't want to tell him that it may be mental or nervous." The vice president replied that he didn't know what the cause was, but he knew Bob Lyons needed help quickly.

During five days in the hospital, Lyons was subjected to extensive laboratory tests. The vice president visited him daily. He seemed to welcome the rest and the sedation at night. He said he was eating and sleeping much better. He talked about company problems, though he did not speak spontaneously without encouragement. While Lyons was out of the room, another executive who shared his hospital room confided to the vice president that he was worried about Lyons. "He seems to be so morose and depressed that I'm afraid he's losing his mind," the executive said.

By this time the president of the company, who had been kept informed, was also becoming concerned. He had talked to a psychiatrist and planned to talk to Lyons about psychiatric treatment if his doctor did not suggest it. Meanwhile, Lyons was discharged from the hospital as being without physical illness, and his doctor recommended a vacation. Lyons remained at home for several days where he was again visited by the vice president. He and his wife took a trip to visit friends. He was then ready to come back to work, but the president suggested that he take another week off. The president also suggested that they visit together when Lyons returned.

A few days later, the president phoned the Lyonses' home. Mrs. Lyons could not find him to answer the telephone. After 15 minutes she still had not found him and called the vice president about her concern. By the time the vice president arrived at the Lyonses' home, the police were already there. Bob Lyons had committed suicide.

Why Did It Happen?

This tragic story is not unusual. Probably no other single emotional problem is as disturbing to those who must live with it as is suicide. No doubt Bob Lyons's colleagues and superiors suffered almost as much anguish as his family did. The president and vice president were concerned long afterward. They wondered if, despite their conscientious efforts, they had in some way been at fault or if they could have prevented it. Neither his family nor his colleagues could understand why it happened. Why should a successful man in the prime of his life, like Lyons, destroy himself?

Lyons's problem may have been extreme, but similar problems are not rare in business and industry. Executives, managers, supervisors, industrial physicians, and—to a lesser extent—all employees frequently must cope with emotional problems on the job. Many problems are of lesser proportion than Lyons's was, but all have four factors in common:

☐ They are painful both for the person who suffers from them and for those who must deal with that person.

☐ They are usually destructive to both the sufferer and the organization.

☐ The origins of the problem are almost always more complex than either party realizes; and only infrequently are even the precipitating events clear.

☐ Rarely does the person responsible for dealing with the on-the-job problem know what he or she should do about it.

As a result, few businesses have ways of dealing with these matters even reasonably well, and management actions tend to range from abrupt firing to hostile discipline to, in some instances, procrastination that goes on for years. Often management makes a vacillating series of efforts, accompanied by feelings of guilt, failure, and anger on the part of those who must make the managerial decisions. Emotional problems, then, are contagious. The disturbance suffered by one person affects the emotions of others.

Was It Hereditary?

How can we understand what happened to Bob Lyons and the ways his problem relates to problems with which all of use must deal? The customary commonsense reasons fail us. He had no serious illness. He did not fail in his business activity. There was no indication of difficulty in his family life. The course of the story told by the vice president is too consistent to attribute his death to an accident or to chance. What then was responsible?

Heredity? Can we say he inherited a tendency to suicide? People inherit certain capacities and traits, but these are essentially physiological. They inherit eye color, nose size, and other physical features. In addition, they inherit certain sensory and motor capacities. That is, they will be able to see, hear, or feel physical stimuli—color, sound, warmth—more or less keenly. Newborn infants in a hospital nursery vary widely in their response to such stimuli. Some are calm and placid; an attendant can drop a metal tray with a clang, but these children continue to sleep. Others, however, are startled and awake crying.

The reasons for these differences in reaction are obscure. We have some clues from experiments with white rats. When pregnant rats are placed in crowded cages or in other situations where they experience stress, this stress apparently produces biochemical imbalances in the mothers that affect the rat fetuses. When the baby rats are born, they have greater anxiety and greater difficulty in adapting to the external world than rats whose mothers were not subjected to such stress. Among human beings, the mother's diet, the illnesses she has during pregnancy, and her general physical condition affect the human fetus.

Something Physical?

Apparently people also inherit the capacity to coordinate their muscles with greater or lesser efficiency. A person who inherits excellent coordination potential and develops it may ultimately become a good athlete or a good musician. One who inherits a better than usual capacity for abstracting sights and sounds may have the makings of an artist. People do not inherit athletic or artistic skill, but some inherit such a high level of sensitivity and physiological harmony that they seem to have a "natural bent" toward certain talents.

Some apparently are born with greater general intelligence; therefore, they have the potential for dealing with their environment with better reasoning power and more effective judgment. Others have more specialized capacities: the ability to abstract ideas readily, the ability to remember well, and so on. Such differences, which in some instances appear at birth, bring about different kinds of interactions with the environment. The irritable infant will have quite a different relationship with his or her mother than will the placid child. The child who walks and talks early comes into contact sooner with a wider range of experiences than does another child in the same general environment, in whom these skills develop later.

Heredity, then, to a large extent determines what a person will be— short or tall, intelligent or unintelligent, and with different thresholds of the various senses. People differ in the combination of endowments that they have and in the degree to which those endowments enable them to cope with life's stresses.

Hereditary factors predispose people to behave in gross, or general, ways but have little direct effect on specific behavior. Because of the high level of development of the frontal lobes of the brain, people are capable of both abstract and reflective thinking and are also capable of a wide range of emotions, particularly feelings about themselves in relation to other people. These capacities for thought and feeling make human beings extremely responsive to many nuances of environmental stimulation and also make it possible for them to initiate a wide range of actions in keeping with their thoughts and feelings, as well as to respond to their environment, particularly to others in it.

Family Influence?

Another environmental factor that has an important influence on behavior is the extremely long period, particularly in Western cultures, during which human children depend on their parents. The intimacy of these relationships and the many social pressures that are transmitted through the parents to the children make family influences extremely important in guiding and controlling behavior. The extended period of dependency also presents a psychological problem because each person must then resolve the conflict between the wish to retain the pleasures of dependency and the desire to become an independent adult. No one ever completely gives up the former or completely attains the latter.

Individuals seek some way of being interdependent with others that enables them to depend on others without losing their pride—because others in turn depend on them. Each person has dependency needs to varying degrees, the extent depending on how well each one has resolved this problem. Some who have not resolved it well will always be more dependent than others. Some have resolved it reasonably well and can accept whatever dependency needs they have. Some have rejected or denied such needs and will have nothing to do with situations in which they might have to depend on others.

So, too, different companies will require different degrees of dependency in their employees. People who remain in a stable public utility company for a long time will be more dependent on their company for their security than will itinerant salespeople who sell magazines on commission. The fact that such a range of possibilities is available for fulfilling such needs at work is one of the health-giving aspects of work in business organizations.

Something Inside Him

Thus, we cannot very well say that Bob Lyons committed suicide because of heredity. We might be able to say hereditary factors, interacting with environmental factors, led to his death; but in our present state of knowledge it would be extremely difficult to demonstrate a hereditary predisposition that contributed to his self-destruction. Of necessity, we must call on more purely psychological factors for an explanation. In a way, when people in despair over why someone like Bob Lyons would kill himself cry out, "There must have been something odd inside of him that drove him into doing it," they are partially right. Inside all of us are many emotional drives that seem odd when we do not understand them.

To try to understand these drives, let us return for a moment to the first paragraph of his superiors' description of Lyons. There we find these phrases: "highly successful," "aggressive," "a knack for getting things done through other people," "worked hard," "set a vigorous pace," and "drove himself relentlessly." These phrases speak of drive or energy. The subsequent two paragraphs describe other ways in which he discharged his energy. Some of these ways were highly useful to himself, his company, his family, and his friends. Others had a destructive potential: "He drove himself relentlessly.'' In fact, his difficulties seemed to begin when he could no longer drive himself on his job.

Warring Drives

The theories of Sigmund Freud help us understand the importance of such drives. According to Freud, two psychological drives constantly operate in the personality. One is a *constructive drive* and the other a *destructive drive*. Just as there are always processes of growth and destruction in all biological matter, anabolism and catabolism, so there are similar processes in the personality. These drives constitute the basic, primitive energy sources for the personality.

The constructive drive (sometimes referred to as the *libido*) is the source of feelings of love, creativity, and psychological growth. The destructive drive gives rise to feelings of anger and hostility to others. The twin forces are variously referred to as love and hate, or in terms of Greek mythology as Eros and Thanatos, or sex and aggression. (Used in this way, both of the terms *sex* and *aggression* have a far broader meaning than they do in ordinary usage.)

A major psychological task for every human being is to fuse these drives so the constructive drive tempers, guides, and controls the destructive drive; the energy from both sources may thus be used to further individual self-interests and those of society. If we speak of the destructive drive as the aggressive drive (recognizing that we are using the word *aggressive* according to its dictionary meaning and not as synonymous with assertion as in ordinary usage), we can say that it is far better for a person to use the aggressive drive—tempered by larger amounts of the constructive drive— in the pursuit of a career, the creation of a family, and in business competition than in destroying others as might be the case if the drives were not adequately fused.

Perhaps an analogy will help. Think of an automobile engine. A mixture of gasoline and oxygen serves as the energy source. If there is too much gasoline, the engine will flood, and if there is too much oxygen, it will sputter and die. With the right blend or fusion of fuel—and particularly with considerably more gasoline than oxygen, which is then channeled through a mechanical structure—the automobile engine can serve a useful purpose.

Channeling the Drives

In Bob Lyons's case we saw that his constructive and aggressive drives, and usually more of the former than the latter, were well fused and channeled into his work, his relationships with his family, and community service. But in some areas his destructive drive was dominant, for he drove himself, as the vice president put it, ''relentlessly.''

The two drives are included in a part of the personality (a set of psychological, not physical, functions) to which Freud gave the name *id,* the Latin neuter for "it." In addition to the two basic drives, the id also includes many memories and experiences that the person can no longer recall.

The brain acts like a vast tape recorder. Theoretically, people should be able to recall all of the experiences and feelings about those experiences they have had. We know that under hypnosis, in psychoanalysis, and under the influence of some drugs, people can recall many experiences although unable to do so before, no matter how hard they tried. Many of these memories, feelings, and impulses (impulses are derivatives of drives) are *repressed* or buried in the id. But they are still "alive" because they would be expressed, as we shall see later, if there were not adequate controls. For the id cares little about restraint; it operates on the pleasure principle: "I want what I want when I want it."

Repression, incidentally, is the process of "forgetting" or of making unconscious certain kinds of experiences and information that may be too troublesome or painful to handle on a conscious level. Here is how repression may have worked in Bob Lyons's case:

To judge from his behavior, he may have learned in his childhood that the only way to obtain love from his parents was by good performance. If high performance was the price of love, Lyons may well have resented his parents' attitude. But since such a conscious feeling of anger toward his parents would have been painful to live with, it was repressed. Lyons was no longer aware of his anger toward them, but it remained with him. The id, being unconscious, has no sense of time; it is inconsistent, contradictory, and not amenable to logic or persuasion. Thus, the early experiences that caused Bob Lyons's feelings of resentment were still "alive" and painful in his id.

In speaking of the drives, I have said that psychological growth and survival require more of the constructive drive, implying that individuals differ in the amount of drive energy they have. We don't know how these differences come about, nor do we have any satisfactory way of specifying amount other than grossly and comparatively. We do know, however, that warm, affectionate relationships, especially those between mother and child, give added strength to the constructive drive, while those in which the child experiences severe frustration and hostility from others stimulate more aggression in the child. In general, the same is true of adults: the relationships and experiences that provide affection and gratification bring out the good side of people, while those that precipitate frustration and anger bring out the bad side.

Something Outside Him

Not only did Bob Lyons (as do all of us) have the major psychological task of balancing or fusing his constructive and aggressive drives, but he also had to discharge these drives in socially acceptable ways only. It might have been permissible in more primitive times to hit a man on the head and take his wife, but it is no longer so. There are stringent cultural controls on how love and aggression may be expressed.

These controls on how we may express our basic drives vary from culture to culture, even from one social class to another; but they are transmitted through parents and other authority figures to children. Early in a child's development, the parents control and direct his or her behavior. They permit some forms but prohibit others. As children grow older, they incorporate into their own personalities what their parents have taught them. Children will incorporate these rules and values most effectively if they feel an affectionate bond with the parents and want to be like them. This is one of the reasons the parent-child relationship is so important and why it should be one that enables the child to feel happy and secure.

Various values and rules can be "pounded into" children, but these tend not to be genuinely theirs. They live by them only as long as external pressures require them to and abandon them when the external pressures diminish. Some parents who try to force piety and goodness into their children are dismayed to find them neither pious nor good when they grow up.

Still, Small Voice

When children develop a conscience, they become self-governing. In Freudian terms, they develop a *superego*, which is made up of four parts:

1 the values of the culture as transmitted through parents, teachers, friends, scout leaders, ministers, and so on;
2 rules, prohibitions, and taboos;
3 an ego ideal—the image of ourselves at our future best that we never fully attain and as a result of which we are perennially discontented with ourselves; and
4 a police-judging or self-critical function.

Some theorists separate the superego and the conscience. They limit the superego to the values and the ego ideal (parts 1 and 3 cited), and refer to the rules (part 2) and the self-critical function (part 4) as the conscience. While that distinction is important scientifically, for our purposes we can ignore it. We will consider the conscience to be a part of the superego and include all four factors in the superego, as mentioned.

The superego begins to develop in the child the first time the words "no" or "don't" enter his or her small world. Its general form tends to be established by the time the child enters elementary school, although it becomes further refined and expanded as the person grows up. Some features of the superego, developed early in life, are not conscious. The person is no longer aware of why he or she must live by certain rules and values but knows only that if these are not obeyed, he or she feels uncomfortable or experiences anxiety. Some children, for example, feel that they must be the best in their class. They may not know why; but if they are not always successful, they feel they are no good.

Conscience and Culture

Because the superego is acquired from the culture in which a person lives (principally through the parents and later by incorporating the values, rules, and ideals of others he or she respects), it is reinforced by the culture. The superego may keep a person from stealing, for example, but there are also social penalties for stealing. Cultural changes may, in turn, bring about some changes in the superego, particularly in those aspects of the superego that are conscious. Thus, every older generation contends that every younger generation is going to the dogs. While certain basic values and rules endure, others change with time. This is also why many parents are so concerned about where the family lives and about the beliefs and attitudes of their children's teachers and friends.

Among the directions that the superego provides are those which have to do with how the constructive and aggressive drives may be directed, how a person may love and hate (and under what circumstances), and what kind of an adult he or she should be. For example, a man may love his parents but in a way different from the way he loves his wife. He may not, in Western cultures, love another woman as he loves his wife. In Italy and Spain he may express affection to other men by embracing them but not in the United States. He may express his anger verbally but not in physical attack. He may direct some of his aggressive drive into work, sports, and community activities but not comfortably into those areas that in his culture are commonly regarded as feminine.

There are many variations among families and subcultures that become part of the superegos of people in those groups. Middle-class American families heavily emphasize achievement, cleanliness, good manners, hard work, and the avoidance of open expressions of hostility. Lower-class families, particularly those at the lowest socioeconomic levels, are not particularly concerned about these values. Some fundamentalist religious groups prohibit drinking and dancing. Some groups teach their children they are sinful by nature, others that almost anything their children want to do is acceptable.

"Know Then Thyself"

People's self-images are related to their superegos. One measure of self-evaluation is the disparity between their ego ideals and how they perceive themselves at present. When people are depreciated by others who are important to them, this reinforces the critical aspects of the superego and lowers self-esteem. When self-esteem is enhanced, however, this counteracts the criticism of the superego and neutralizes some of the aggressive drive, thus stimulating individuals to an expanded, more confident view of themselves and their capacities.

It has been said that no wound is as painful as that inflicted by the superego. When people behave in ways not in keeping with the values and rules they have made a part of themselves or when, in their judgment, they fall too short of their ego ideals, the superego induces a feeling of guilt. For most of us guilt feelings are so strong and so painful that we try to make up for violations of the superego by some form of atonement. The religious concept of penance is a recognition of this phenomenon. Restitution is another way to relieve guilt feelings. It is not unusual to see newspaper articles about people who have anonymously sent money to the government because they cheated on their taxes years before. Government officials speak of this as "conscience money."

Because the development of the superego begins early and children are not in a position to judge rationally the relative importance of some of the rules they are taught, it is easy for them to learn to judge themselves more harshly than they should. With their limited capacity to reason, children may blame themselves for events they had nothing to do with. For example, suppose a two-year-old child is severely hurt in a fall. His four-year-old brother, who must inevitably have some feelings of hostility and rivalry toward the younger child, may come to feel he is responsible. As a matter of fact, he had nothing to do with the fall, but for a small child the wish is often tantamount to the act. To wish the younger child to be destroyed may be the same to a four-year-old as actually having pushed him. He may then harbor irrational guilt feelings for many years thereafter, completely unaware that he has such feelings or how they came about.

Since there is love and hate in every relationship, children have considerable hostility toward, as well as affection for, their parents. Usually young children do not understand that their hostile feelings are not "bad" and that parents will not be destroyed merely because their children have such feelings. As a result, most of us carry a considerable load of irrational guilt feelings. One of the major tasks in some forms of psychological treatment for people who are emotionally disturbed is to make such irrational unconscious feelings conscious so that their irrationality may be recognized, and they will no longer plague the person.

The Balance Wheel

The superego, then, becomes a built-in governor, as it were. It is the internalized civilizing agent. Without it, there would be no continuing self-guide to behavior. The superego is an automatic protective device. Because of it some issues are never raised; we never even ask, "Should I or should I not steal?" As a guide to behavior it makes for stability and consistency of performance.

If, however, the values and rules that the child is taught are inconsistent, then the superego will be inconsistent. If there are too many, too

strict rules, then the superego becomes a harsh taskmaster, either constrict-
ing too narrowly the way a person can behave or burdening him or her
excessively with feelings of guilt and demanding constant atonement. But
even without punishment or strict rules, a tyrannical superego can develop—
if performance is the basis for obtaining love and if there are unrealistic
expectations of extremely high performance. In such cases, people's behavior tends to have a driven quality. They feel that there is so much they
should do or must do as contrasted with so much they would enjoy doing.
They feel uncomfortable unless constantly doing what they feel they should—
but without knowing exactly why. Lyons, for example, not only drove himself relentlessly but also usually had to be working hard.

We have seen so far that the constructive and aggressive drives, which
continuously seek discharge, are major motivating forces in the personality.
The superego, with its capacity to induce guilt feelings, not only defines
acceptable ways in which the drives may be discharged but also serves as
a motivating force.

Home and Job

Not everything we do, of course, is completely influenced by our emotional
drives. Environment also plays a part and should be considered in our attempt to understand Bob Lyons's suicide. For, in addition to the task of
balancing or fusing our drives in keeping with the strictures of the superego,
we do have to deal with our external environment. At times, this environment
is a source of affection, support, and security. An infant in a mother's arms,
a woman in a happy marriage, a man enjoying himself among his friends,
an individual building a business, a minister serving a congregation—all draw
emotional nourishment from the environment. Such nourishment strengthens
the constructive forces of the personality.

Looked at closely, *needs for status, recognition, and esteem are essentially needs for love and affection.* Each person, no matter how old or
jaded, wants to be held in esteem by some others. Few can survive long
without giving and receiving love, though often these expressions are thoroughly disguised, even from the self. Status needs have to do with the
constructive forces of the personality as I have described them here. One
who seeks recognition or status symbols simply searches for concrete indications that some others do or will hold him or her in esteem. One way
to describe status needs is to say that the person needs infusions of love
and of gratification to foster his or her own strength by supporting his or
her self-image.

However, the environment may also stimulate aggression: anger and
jealousy, exploitation, competition for various advantages, economic reverses, wars, and so on. Every person has to deal with the realities of the
environment—whether with the necessities of earning a living, the frustration
of an unsolved problem, the achievement of personal goals, the development

of satisfying relationships with other people, or something else. We saw that Lyons was actively involved with all of these things in his environment.

Ego and Reality

Now I have spoken of three sets of forces—id drives, the superego, and the environment—each interacting with the others, which must be kept in sufficient balance or equilibrium so that a person can function effectively. Some mechanism is required to do the balancing task, to serve as the executive part of the personality. Such a component of personality must fuse the drives, control their discharge in keeping with the conditions set by the superego, and act on the environment. Freud gave the name *ego* to this set of psychological functions. We tend to speak of the ego as a thing; actually, the term is merely a short way of describing *the organized executive functions of the personality, those functions that have to do with self-control and with testing reality.*

The ego includes such mental functions as recall, perception, judgment, attention, and conceptual or abstract thinking—those aspects of the personality that enable the individual to receive, organize, interpret, and act on stimuli or psychological and physiological data. The ego develops (not as well in those who are mentally retarded) as the person grows. Like a computer, the ego acquires and stores information in the form of memory images, particularly information and experiences that previously have led to successful solution of problems. When an impulse arises from one of the drives, the ego contains the impulse until, in effect, it has checked with the superego and determined the consequences of acting on the impulse.

The impulse may have to be fully contained or modified to meet both the conditions of the superego and the demands of the environment. The ego presumably checks its memory images to find acceptable ways of refining and discharging the impulse. When the ego can do this well, we speak of a strong ego or of psychological maturity. When it cannot do so adequately, we say a person does not have adequate ego strength or that he or she is immature. *The ego acts on the basis of what is called the reality principle:* "What are the long-run consequences of this behavior?"

The process of checking the memory images and organizing a response is what we know as thinking. Thinking is trial action or a "dry run," as it were. Sometimes it goes on consciously, but much of the time it is an unconscious process. Thinking delays impulses until they can be discharged in the most satisfactory way the person knows how. When a person acts impulsively in minor ways, for instance, in being inconsiderate of another person, we commonly speak of such behavior as "thoughtless."

The ego, operating on the reality principle and obeying the superego, must contain, refine, or redirect id impulses so that the integrity of the personality is preserved. The ego is constantly concerned with the costs and consequences of any action. In other words, the ego is concerned with psychological economy.

Beleaguered Ego

This task puts the ego in a difficult position. This system of psychological functions is always a buffer between the other systems, the id and the superego, and also between them and the forces of the environment. The ego, then, is always under pressure. To carry on its integrating function well requires considerable strength. Strength comes from several sources: the basic inherited capacities, experiences of love and gratification that enhance the constructive forces, the development of skills and abilities that help it master the environment, and the physical health of the person. The ego may be weakened through physical injury or illness—a brain tumor, a debilitating sickness—or by having to devote too much of its energy to repressing or otherwise coping with severe multiple or chronic emotional pressures.

The ego cannot deal with all of the stimuli that impinge on it. It is constantly being bombarded with all kinds of data and would be swamped if it tried to deal with all of the information it had in the form of both past and present experiences. It must be selective. Some data are therefore passed directly on to the id. The ego is never consciously aware of them. Furthermore, it has not been able to successfully resolve all of its psychological problems, some of which are extremely painful. With these it acts on the thesis, "If you can't lick it, forget it." These problems are repressed or "pushed down" into the id. The little boy who erroneously thought he hurt his brother, then repressed his guilt feelings, is a case in point.

Perhaps some other examples will help us to understand these processes better:

☐ Suppose someone walking along the street sees a new car parked at the curb. He has an impulse to take the car and, acting on the impulse, drives it off. We say he acted impulsively, by which we mean he was governed by an impulse from the id and not by rational considerations. To put it another way, we might say that the ego was weak, that it did not anticipate the consequences of the act and control the impulse. The price paid for acting on the impulse, perhaps a jail term, is high for what little momentary pleasure might have been gained. We say such a person is immature, meaning that his or her ego is not sufficiently developed to act in a wiser and less costly way.

☐ A store manager may also be said not to have good judgment if she bought items without thinking through their marketing possibilities or merely because she liked the salesperson. This is another form of impulsiveness or immaturity. Marketers count on the irrational impulsiveness in all of us by creating in supermarkets such a vast array of stimuli to our desires for pleasure that the ego does not function quite as well as it might. Impulse buying results—unless the ego is bolstered by additional support in the form of a shopping list and a budget.

☐   Here is a more personal example. If you observe young children, you see their lives are extremely active. They have many pleasant moments and some painful ones. They remember experiences from day to day and recall exciting events like a trip to the zoo with great relish. Now try to remember your own early childhood experiences, especially those that occurred before you were four or five. Probably you will be able to recall few in detail, if you can recall any at all. Many other experiences of childhood, adolescence, and even adulthood are beyond voluntary recall. Yet under hypnosis they can be recalled. This information, much of it not immediately necessary to solve today's problems, is stored in the id.

     Memory traces of some of these experiences, which might help us solve problems, are stored in the ego, though even they are usually not conscious. A person may be surprised to arrive home, having driven from work while preoccupied with a problem, without ever having noticed the turns, stoplights, or other cars. Obviously, that person used many cues and did many specific things to get home safely but did so without being aware of his or her actions.

☐   A final example illustrates how the ego deals with impulses from the id. Suppose an attractive secretary comes to work in a new dress whose lines are calculated to stimulate the interest of men—in short, to stimulate the sexual impulse. When this impulse reaches the ego of one of the men in the office, the ego, acting within limits set by the superego ("Look, but don't touch") and based on its judgment of the consequences of venting the impulse ("You'll destroy your reputation"), will control and refine the impulse. The man may then comment, "That's a pretty dress"—a highly attenuated derivative of the original impulse. Another man with a more rigid superego might never notice the dress. His superego would protect him by automatically prohibiting the ego from being sensitive to such a stimulus.

Ego's Assistants

If the ego has the job of first balancing the forces from the id, the superego, and the environment, and then of mediating and synchronizing them into a system that operates relatively smoothly, it requires the assistance of two kinds of psychological devices to make its work possible. Thus:

1   It needs *anxiety* to serve as an alarm system to alert it to possible dangers to its equilibrium.

2   It must have *defense mechanisms* that can be called into play,

triggered by the alarm system; these will help it either to fend off the possible threats or to counteract them.

Anxiety's Purpose

We are conscious of the alarm-triggering system called anxiety whenever we are afraid of something. It is a feeling of unease or tension. But a much more subtle and complex phenomenon of anxiety operates spontaneously and unconsciously whenever the ego is threatened. Being unaware of its operation, we may not know consciously why we are restless, tense, or upset. Bob Lyons, we recall, was worried but did not know why. We have all experienced his anxiety. A feeling of tension and restlessness that one person picks up from another is very common. Sensing that the other person is upset makes us feel uneasy for reasons which are not very clear to us. We do not consciously decide that we are threatened, but we feel we "can't relax," that we must be on guard.

Perhaps the work of unconscious anxiety may be likened to a gyroscope on a ship or an airplane. The gyroscope must sense the imbalance of the ship or plane as a result of waves, currents, or storms. It must then set into motion counteracting forces to regain the vehicle's balance. This analogy highlights something else for us. *There is no state of placid emotional stability, just as there is never a smooth ocean or an atmosphere devoid of air currents. There is no peace of mind short of the grave. Everyone is always engaged in maintaining psychological equilibrium.* Even when people sleep, their dreaming is an effort to resolve psychological problems, to discharge tension, and to maintain sleep. The workings of unconscious anxiety may be seen in a number of different ways:

☐   Suppose a three-year-old child, drinking milk from a glass, bites and shatters the edge of the glass. The glass cuts the child's lip, which bleeds profusely. Striving to remain calm, the mother places a compress under the lip and stops the bleeding. But she does not know whether the child has swallowed any of the glass and, therefore, what she should do next. She asks the child if he has swallowed glass. He says he has not. To be certain, she asks again, saying, "Please tell me if you have, because if you have, you might have a tummyache, and we don't want you to have a tummyache." At this point the child says he *has* swallowed some glass. Now the mother does not know whether he has.

Before the mother can decide that she had better take the child to the hospital, he begins to quiver as if shaking from the cold. This shaking is involuntary. Though the child has no conscious understanding of the possible fatal danger of swallowing glass and though the mother has tried to remain calm, unconsciously the child has sensed the inherent threat in the situation. Automatically, emergency physiological and biochemical processes are called into play to cope with the danger. We see the effects of these in the shaking. The manner and attitude of the hospital physician assure the child that there is no threat and gradually the shaking subsides.

☐ Adults may have the same experience in many different ways. Suppose as you drive your car down the street, a youngster dashes out from between parked cars into your path. You immediately slam on the brakes. For a moment you do not know whether you have hit the child. When you get out of the car, you see that you have not; but you find yourself shaking, your heart beating rapidly, your skin perspiring. You did not consciously cause any of these things to happen. The threat to your equilibrium—constituting stress—aroused anxiety, which in turn mobilized your resources for dealing with the emergency. A similar experience is commonplace among athletes. Some of them experience such psychological tension before competitive events that they cannot eat; if they do, they throw up.

Here I am speaking of conscious anxiety at one level. We are aware of certain threats and react to them. But at another, unconscious level, our reaction is disproportionate to the event. There is no objective reason for the driver to continue to be anxious after discovering that he or she has not hit the child. The overt threat is past. Yet the person may continue to shake for hours and may even dream or have nightmares about the event. It is understandable that athletes would want to win a game for conscious reasons. Why the competition should cause such a violent physical reaction is a more complex and obscure problem. They themselves do not know why they must go to such extremes of defensive mobilization that their bodies cannot tolerate the ingestion of food. Unconscious anxiety is at work.

Ego Defenses

If we are to penetrate deeply enough into Bob Lyons's reasons for suicide, we must go beyond admitting that he was undoubtedly anxious and under stress. We need to see why his ego was not sufficiently protected from such a completely destructive attack—why the defense mechanisms mentioned earlier as one of the ego's assistants did not enable him to overcome his anxiety.

A number of personality mechanisms operate automatically to help the ego maintain or regain its equilibrium. These mechanisms may be viewed as falling into three broad classes:

1.   One group has to do with shaping or forming the personality. Included in this category is *identification,* the process of behaving like someone else. For example, a man identifies himself with his boss when he dresses or speaks as his boss does. Women identify themselves with a leading movie star when they adopt her hairstyle. Another device, *introjection,* is a stronger form of identification, although the line between them is hazy. One who

introjects the mannerisms or attitudes of another makes these firmly a part of himself or herself. We speak of introjecting the values of the parents and becoming a "chip off the old block."

2.   Another group of mechanisms is universally used. These devices are required to control, guide, refine, and channel the basic drives or impulses from the id. I have already talked about *repression*. Another mechanism, *sublimation,* is the process by which basic drives are refined and directed into acceptable channels. Lyons, for example, sublimated much of his aggressive drive into his work.

3.   A third group of mechanisms is made up of temporary devices that are called into play automatically when there is some threat to the personality.

Denial, a form of repression, is one of these devices and can be clarified by an example.

Suppose a plant superintendent has five years to go to retirement, and his boss suggests that he pick a successor and train him. But our plant superintendent does not select a successor, despite repeated requests from the boss. He cannot "hear" what the boss is saying and may be forced to select such a man. When the time for retirement arrives, he may then say to his boss that the boss really did not intend to retire him. He cannot believe the boss will compel him to leave. This behavior reflects a denial of the reality of the situation because the ego has difficulty accepting what it regards to be a loss of love (status, esteem, etc.).

Rationalization is another temporary mechanism that all of us use from time to time. In fact, as the following example shows, it provides the subject matter for comedy.

A man's wife suggests that it is time to get a new car because theirs is already eight years old and getting shabby. At first, acting under the influence of the superego, the man doubts if he needs a new car. He cannot justify it to himself. To buy one without an adequate reason would be a waste of money for him. "You're too mature to be so extravagant and to fall for style," his superego says. The guilt aroused by the thought of buying a new car (a form of anxiety) causes the idea to be rejected to appease the superego. The old car still runs well, he says; it gives no trouble, and a new one would be expensive. Soon we see him in an automobile showroom. "Just looking," he tells the salesman. "He thinks he's found a sucker," he chuckles to himself to avoid the condemnation of the superego. Next, however, he begins to complain to his wife and friends that the old car will soon need repairs, that it will never be worth more on a trade-in. Before long he has developed a complete rationale for buying the new car and has convinced himself to do so.

Projection, another temporary mechanism, is the process of attributing one's own feelings to someone else. If, for example, one can project hostility onto someone else ("He's mad at me; he's out to get me"), then one can justify to the superego that hostility toward the other person ("It's all right for me to get him first"). This is one mechanism behind scapegoating and prejudice.

Idealization is the process of putting a halo around someone else and thereby being unable to see his or her faults. This process is seen most vividly in people who are in love or who have identified strongly with political leaders. It enhances the image of the idealized person as a source of strength and gratification.

Reaction formation is a formidable term for the process of doing the opposite of what one wants to do to avoid the threat of giving free rein to impulses. Some people become so frightened of their own aggressive impulses that they act in an extremely meek manner, avoiding any suggestion of aggression.

Another important mechanism is *substitution,* or displacement. This is the process in which the ego, unable to direct impulses to the appropriate target, directs them to a substitute target. In a benign way, this happens when people devote much of their affection to pets or to their work if, for whatever reasons, they do not have satisfactory ways of giving affection to other people. More destructive displacement occurs when a person seeks substitute targets for aggression. For instance, if unable to express anger at his boss to the boss, a man may displace it onto the working conditions or wages. He may even unwittingly carry it home and criticize his wife or children. This is another mechanism behind scapegoating and prejudice. Not only does displacement of this kind hurt others; worse yet, it doesn't contribute to the solution of the real problem.

Compensation is still another mechanism—often highly constructive. This is the process of developing talents and skills to make up for one's unconsciously perceived or imagined deficiencies or of undertaking activities and relationships to regain lost gratification. In certain respects, compensation and substitution are, of course, closely related.

The Defensive Process

These mechanisms need not be elaborated further here. The answer to why Bob Lyons killed himself has necessarily been delayed long enough. Now we see the point, however. When the ego is threatened in some fashion, anxiety spontaneously and unconsciously triggers mechanisms to counteract the threat. If there are too many emergencies for the personality, it may then overuse these mechanisms, and this in turn will seriously distort the person's view of reality or cripple him or her psychologically. To identify with those one respects is fine; to imitate them slavishly is to lose one's individuality. It is one thing to rationalize occasionally, as we all do, but another to base judgments consistently on rationalizations. At times all of us project our own feelings, but we would be sick indeed if we felt most of the time that everyone else had it in for us.

By and large, self-fulfillment has to do with the ego's capacity to function as effectively as it can. When emotional conflicts can be diminished and the need for defensiveness can be decreased, the energy that ordinarily maintains the defenses is freed for more useful activity. In a sense, some of the brakes are removed from the psychological wheels. Furthermore, as threats are removed and the defenses need no longer be used so intensely, one perceives reality more accurately. One can then relate to other people more reasonably and communicate more clearly. A psychological blossoming can occur. When such balancing fails to take place, the ego is overwhelmed for the time being. In Bob Lyons's case, he acted to relieve his emotional pain and killed himself before equilibrium could be restored in a less destructive way. Since this balancing process is the ultimate key to an understanding of Lyons's act, let us make sure we understand how it works and then apply our knowledge directly to his case:

Fusion of Drives Toward Appropriate Target. Suppose a man is called into his boss's office, and his boss criticizes him harshly for something he did not do. The ideally healthy man, if he exists, will listen calmly to what his boss has to say and, in good control of his rising aggressive impulse, might well reply, "I'm sorry that such a mistake has happened. I had nothing to do with that particular activity, but perhaps I can help you figure out a way to keep the same mistake from happening again." His boss, also brimming with good mental health, might then respond, "I'm sorry that I criticized you unfairly. I would appreciate your giving me a hand on this." Together they direct their energies toward the solution of the problem.

Displacement to Less Appropriate Target. But take a similar situation where, however, the man knows his boss will brook no contradiction or is so emotionally overwrought that there is little point in trying to be reasonable with him. This man may fume with anger at the unjust attack but control his impulse to strike back at the boss. His reality-testing ego tells him that such action won't help the situation at all. He takes the criticism, anticipating a better solution when the boss cools off. Nevertheless, he is angry for being unjustly criticized, and there has been no opportunity to discharge his aroused aggressive impulse in an appropriate way toward the solution of the problem.

Because in this situation it seems so rational to control one's impulse (i.e., the boss is upset and there's no point in discussing it with him now), the ego finds this secondary anger an inappropriate feeling to allow into consciousness. The more primitive secondary anger is then repressed. When the employee goes bowling that night, he gets particular pleasure from knocking the pins down, without knowing why. Unconsciously he is using bowling to drain off his excess aggression. Such displacement is a partially constructive way of discharging aggression: it hurts no one and provides gratification. However, it does not contribute directly to resolving the problem itself, presuming that some further action toward solution might be required.

Containment of Drives.   Suppose that another man finds himself in the same situation. This man has learned in the course of growing up that it is not permissible to express one's aggression directly to authority figures. Being human, he has aggressive impulses, but, having a severe superego, he also feels guilty about them and goes to great lengths to repress them. When the boss criticizes him and his aggressive impulse is stimulated, repression automatically sets in, and the impulse is controlled without his being aware of it. However, it is so controlled that he can't speak up to contribute to the solution of the problem.

Because this man constantly maintains a high degree of control to meet the demands of his superego, he is already in a potentially more explosive situation, ready to defend himself from the slightest possible threat. If he has to contain more of his anger within himself, the situation is much like rising steam pressure in a boiler. If this situation is repetitive or chronic, the mobilization and remobilization of defenses almost require of the ego that it be in a steady emergency state. The alarm bells are ringing most of the time. This kind of reaction strains the ego's resources and is particularly wearing physiologically because each psychological response to stress is accompanied by physiological mobilization, too.

Psychosomatic symptoms result. The body is literally damaged by its own nervous system and fluids, leading to ulcers, hypertension, and similar phenomena. This experience is commonly recognized in the phrase "stewing in one's own juice." Clinical data seem to show that there are reasons why one particular organ is the site for a psychosomatic symptom, but often these reasons are obscure.

Displacement onto the Self.   Take another man, who also has learned that aggression should not be expressed to others and who cannot do so without feelings of guilt. In fact, his superego won't tolerate much hostility on his part, so he lives constantly with feelings of guilt. The guilt, in turn, makes him feel inadequate as his superego repeatedly berates him for his hostility. No matter how nice he may try to be, by means of reaction formation, he can't satisfy his superego. Somehow, he himself always seems to be at fault. With such a rigid, punitive superego, this man under the same kind of attack may then respond by saying, "I guess you're right. I'm always wrong; it's my fault. I never seem to do things right." He may also then have a mild depression. Depression is always an indication of anger with one's self, originating from anger toward another, and reflects the attack of the superego on the ego. The aggression is displaced from the appropriate target back onto the self and results in a form of self-blame and self-punishment.

Another form of self-attack or self-punishment is seen in many accidents. Most of them are not actually accidents in the sense that they occur by chance but are unconscious modes of self-punishment. "Forgetting" to turn the motor switch off before repairing the machine or not seeing or hearing possible threats frequently indicates that denial or repression has been operating in order to permit the person to hurt himself or herself to appease the superego. In extreme form, this self-directed aggression is the mechanism behind suicide, and now we are prepared to see what happened to Bob Lyons.

The Reason Why

Driven by an extremely severe superego, Bob Lyons sublimated his drives successfully in his work as long as he could work hard. There was an equilibrium among ego, superego, id, and environment, although only a tenuous one. By driving himself, he could appease the superego's relentless pressure.

Such a superego, however, is never satisfied. Its demands arise from unconscious sources, which, because they are unconscious, probably have existed from early childhood and are to a large extent irrational. If they were not irrational, their terms could be met.

Whenever he reached a goal toward which he had aspired, Lyons got no satisfaction from it, for his superego still drove him. And when he could no longer work as hard as he had, this for him was an environmental deprivation. He could no longer earn love by performing well. His superego became more relentless. The vacation, which placed no demands on him at all, simply added to his guilt and feelings of unworthiness and inadequacy. With sublimations and displacements reduced, given his kind of superego, his aggressive drive had only the ego as a major target.

And, at that moment, the only way that Bob Lyons knew to appease his superego was to kill himself.

Had his superego developed differently, Lyons might have achieved as he did because of ego reasons (the pleasure and gratification he got from his work), with a mild assist from the superego to do well. When his superego developed so strongly, probably because of a heavy burden of hostility in childhood for which he felt irrationally guilty for a lifetime, there was no real pleasure in what he did and nothing more than temporary gratification. The relentless driving of himself was a form of self-sacrifice—just like alcoholism, most accidents, repeated failures on the job, presenting the worst side of one's self to others, and some forms of crime.

We should recognize that a bit of self-sacrifice exists in all of us, just as we can see something of ourselves at times in each of the preceding three examples. The ancient observation that "man is his own worst enemy" is testimony to the self-destructive potential in each person. Bob Lyons differed from the rest of us only in degree and only because of a combination of forces at a given point that precipitated his death. A change in any single force might conceivably have prevented it: more and harder work, psychiatric or psychological treatment, no vacation to add to the feelings of guilt and uselessness, or open recognition by his physician of the seriousness of mental illness.

Groping for Shadows

But how would his physician or friends have recognized early symptoms of Lyons's illness? It would not have been easy. We cannot put an ego under a microscope or locate the id in any part of the body. These are simply names given to what seem to be systems of forces operating in the personality. We cannot see repression—it is only a name for the observation that some things are forgotten and can be recalled only under certain circumstances. The same is true when we speak of something being unconscious. It is not relegated to a given physical organ or place. One is merely not able to call it into awareness.

If the ego has a constant balancing task and calls certain mechanisms into play to carry it out, the ego, being concerned with psychological economy, will develop mechanisms that are preferred because they work best consistently. These become the established personality traits. As individuals we make our preferred modes of adjustment those ways of behaving that are most comfortable (least anxiety arousing) to us.

The consistent modes of adjustment, the personality traits, become the hallmarks by which we are known to others. Even physical styles of behavior become part of this system. If we hear on the telephone a voice that we recognize, we can place it with a name. If we meet a friend we have not seen in 10 years, we will observe that he or she seems to be the same as always—talking, reacting, thinking in much the same way. Some are hail-fellow-well-met gregarious types, others more diffident and conservative. Each has preferred modes of adjustment, preferred ways to consistently maintain equilibrium.

Given these entrenched modes of adaptation, even clinical psychologists and psychiatrists are unlikely to make *radical* changes in people, although they can often help alter certain forces so that people can behave more healthily than they did previously. The alteration of internal forces (superego-ego-id) is the job of the clinician. But individuals often can make a contribution to the alteration of external forces (ego-environment). Even minor changes in the balance of forces can significantly affect how people feel, think, and behave.

The very fact that people do not radically change their styles of behavior makes it possible to detect signs of emotional stress. Given certain characteristic modes of adaptation in the form of personality traits, a person who experiences some kind of emotional stress is likely first to make greater use of those mechanisms that worked best before. The first sign of defense against stress is that a person seems to be conspicuously more like always. A person who is ordinarily quiet may become withdrawn under stress. If like Lyons, his or her first reaction may well be to try to work harder.

Second, if this line of defense does not work well (or if the stress is too severe or chronic for that method alone), inefficient psychological functioning begins to appear—vague fears, inability to concentrate, compulsions to do certain things, increasing irritability, and declining work performance.

We will also see the results of physiological defensive efforts. We saw in Lyons's case that tension, jitteriness, and inability to hold food or to sleep all accompanied his psychological stress. The whole organism—physiological and psychological—was involved in the struggle.

Psychological and physiological symptoms are ways of "binding" or attempting to control the anxiety. They are ways of trying to do something about a problem, however ineffective they may be. And they are the best ways of dealing with the problem that a person has available at the moment, though better ways of coping may be apparent to others who do not have the same psychological makeup. That's why it is dangerous to try to remove symptoms. Instead, it is wiser to resolve the underlying problem.

Third, if neither of these types of defenses can contain the anxiety, we may see sharp changes in personality. A person no longer behaves as before. Lyons felt himself to be falling apart, unable to work as he did previously. A neat person may become slovenly, an efficient one alcoholic. Radical changes in personality indicate severe illness, which usually requires hospitalization.

Conspicuous change in behavior indicates that the ego is no longer able to maintain effective control. If a person is so upset that he or she hears voices or sees things that do not exist, previously unconscious thoughts and feelings are breaking through. Obviously irrational behavior indicates the same thing. There is a loss of contact with reality, seriously impaired judgment, and an inability to be responsible for oneself. In such a state, Bob Lyons committed suicide.

Conclusion

Now that we *think* we understand why Bob Lyons killed himself, it is important that two cautions be raised.

About Ourselves

First, readers newly exposed to psychoanalytic theory invariably fall victim to what may be called the freshman medical student's syndrome: they get every symptom in the book. Everything to which this article refers, average readers will be able to see in themselves. As we were discussing Lyons, we were talking about human beings and human motivation; so it was inevitable that we ended up talking about ourselves. We must recognize this tendency to read ourselves into these pages and compensate for it by consciously trying to maintain an objective distance from the material.

At the same time, does this very experience not make it clear to us that everyone has the continuing task of maintaining an equilibrium? At any given time, any one of us may be listing to starboard a little or trying to keep from being buffeted about by a sudden storm. Despite these pressures, we must nevertheless move forward, correcting for the list as best we can or conserving our strength to ride out the storm. Each will defend himself or herself the best way he or she knows how—the more energy devoted to defense, the less available for forward movement.

Each of us at one time or another, therefore, will be emotionally disturbed or upset. For a few hours, a few days, a few weeks, we may be irritable or angry ("I got up on the wrong side of the bed"), blue ("I'm feeling low today"), or hypersensitive. When we feel these ways, when we are having difficulty maintaining an equilibrium, for that brief period we are emotionally disturbed. We cannot work as well as we usually do. It is more difficult for us to sustain our relationships with other people. We may feel hopeless or helpless. We're just not ourselves.

But just because we are mildly emotionally disturbed does not mean we need professional help or hospitalization. A cold is a minor form of upper respiratory infection, the extreme of which is pneumonia. If one has a cold, that does not mean he or she will have pneumonia. Even if a person does get pneumonia, with present treatment methods most people recover; and the same is true of mental illness. The difference between the mild and the severe is one of degree, not of kind.

Because each of us is human and no one of us has had either perfect heredity or perfect environment, each of us has weak spots. When the balance of forces is such that there is stress where we are weak, we will have difficulty. The incidence of mental illness, then, is not 1 out of 20 or some other proportionate statistic. Rather it is 1 out of 1!

What We Can Do

The second caution has to do with the limitations of this exposition and the reader's preparation for understanding it. This necessarily has been a highly condensed version of some aspects of psychoanalytic theory. Many important aspects of the theory have been omitted, and others have been presented without the many qualifications a serious scientific presentation would require. The reader should therefore look on what is presented only as an introduction to better understanding of psychological problems, should be careful about overgeneralization, and should studiously avoid using jargon or interpreting people's behavior to them.

Without observing these limitations, the inexperienced person will be unable to help anyone. Within these limitations, however, executives can render extremely important help to others in their companies—and to themselves. Specifically, they can recognize that:

☐ *All* behavior is motivated, much of it by thoughts and feelings of which the person is not aware. Behavior does not occur by chance.

☐ At any one time each person is doing the best he or she can, as a result of the multiple forces that bring about any given behavior. A change in the forces is required to bring about a change in behavior.

☐ Love neutralizes aggression and diminishes hostility. "A soft word turneth away wrath," says the old aphorism. Love does not mean maudlin expressions but actions that reflect esteem and regard for the other person as a human being. The most useful demonstration of affection is support that takes the form of:

Understanding that the pain of emotional distress is real. It will not go away by wishing it away, by dismissing it as "all in your head," or by urging the person to "forget it," "snap out of it," or "take a vacation."

Listening if people bring problems to you or if problems so impair their work that you must criticize their work performance. Listening permits people to define their problems more clearly and thereby to examine courses of action. Acting constructively to solve a problem is the best way the ego has to maintain the fusion of drives in dealing with reality. Listening, by providing some relief for distressed people, already brings about some alteration in the balance of forces.

If you listen, however, you must clearly recognize your limitations: (1) you can offer only emergency help; (2) you cannot hold yourself *responsible* for other people's personal problems, some of which would defy the most competent specialist.

Referring the troubled person to professional sources of help if the problem is more than temporary or if the person is severely upset. Every organization should have channels for referral. A person who has responsibility for other people but no formal organizational channels for referral would do well to establish contact with a psychiatrist, a clinical psychologist, or a community mental health agency. Professional sources of guidance will then be available when problems arise.

Finally, we can maintain a watchful, but not morbid, eye on ourselves. If we find that we are having difficulties that interfere with our work or with gratifying relationships with other people, then we should be wise enough to seek professional help.

Notes

1. Charles Brenner, *An Elementary Textbook of Psychoanalysis,* revised edition (New York: Doubleday, 1974).

2. O. Spurgeon English and G.H.J. Pearson, *Emotional Problems of Living,* third edition (New York: W.W. Norton & Co., 1976).

3. Anna Freud, *The Ego and the Mechanisms of Defense,* revised edition (New York: International Universities Press, 1967).

4. Calvin S. Hall, *A Primer of Freudian Psychology* (New York: New American Library, 1973).

5. Karl A. Menninger, *Man Against Himself* (New York: Harcourt Brace Jovanovich, 1938).

6. Harry Levinson, *Emotional Health: In the World of Work,* revised edition (Cambridge, Mass.: Levinson Institute, 1980).

7. Harry Levinson, *Psychological Man* (Cambridge, Mass.: Levinson Institute, 1976).

8. Abraham Zaleznik and Manfred Kets de Vries, *Power and the Corporate Mind* (Boston: Houghton Mifflin, 1975).

Appendix A: Handling the Constructive Drive

In this article, because we are focusing on Bob Lyons's case, we are looking at ways in which the ego deals with the *aggressive* drive by calling into play certain defense mechanisms in order to maintain its equilibrium. But the ego also must deal with the *constructive* drive in order to maintain the proper balance. We see how it might handle sexual stimulation by control and refinement, or even denial, of the impulse. Other examples illustrate how the same mechanisms that are used to cope with the aggressive drive apply themselves to handling constructive drives and, in so doing, often cause us distress as well as relief:

1. *Fusion of drives.*   Fused with the aggressive drive, and dominant over it, the constructive drive is directed toward appropriate targets in intimate relationships with one's family, the solution of work and family problems, citizenship activities, and so on. Idealistic love without an aggressive component might lead to merely fantasized images of a sweetheart rather than marriage, or a person might dream about job success rather than take action toward it.

2. *Displacement to less appropriate targets.*   Like the aggressive drive, the constructive drive may be deflected from appropriate targets. Homosexuality is one such phenomenon whose dynamics are too complex for discussion here. In brief, many psychoanalytic clinicians theorize that the homosexual cannot establish adequate and satisfying relationships with those of the opposite sex. Instead, he or she uses the mechanism of substitution and builds up extended rationalizations to appease the superego.

Some people can invest themselves in causes but not really in other people. Some lavish great affection on animals or houses or hobbies at the expense of personal relationships. Some adults can have affectionate relationships only with young children but cannot tolerate other adults. These targets provide useful channels for love but not the fully satisfying, wide range of relationships enjoyed by most mature adults.

3. *Containment.*   Some people for complicated reasons, learned that it was psychologically safe not to express affection and have repressed their affectionate feelings. These people we know colloquially as "cold fish,"

people seemingly without emotion. They may be highly intellectual or great professional successes, but they have divorced compassion from judgment and feeling from reasoning. Others are known as ruthlessly efficient. They keep their emotions tightly controlled and their feelings of love deeply buried within themselves.

4.   *Displacement onto the self.*   Children rejected by their parents learn bitterly that it is too painful to try to love other people because they will not return love. In adult life, such people become highly self-centered. In conversation they constantly talk about themselves. They give overmeticulous attention to their appearance and revel in self-display. They tend to seek out activities which provide public adulation and become extremely unhappy when they cannot get it. We find such people unpleasant to deal with because they are unable to give anything of themselves to someone else. Often they exploit others for their own gain. Because they cannot love others, they have almost no real friends and often are unable to sustain their marriages.

For these people much of the constructive drive is displaced onto themselves because environmental forces have made identification and introjection difficult, thereby impairing the possibility of relationships with other people. The early conflicts, now repressed, still exist unconsciously. Their egos—remembering early pain—will not open again to the possibilities of rejection and narrowly constrict the constructive drive to a limited target for self-protection. Because of the limited range of attachments their egos permit, such people do not really enjoy life, despite what appears to others to be an extremely sparkling series of social adventures.

Each person must have a certain amount of self-love if he or she is to have self-respect. Overweening egocentricity, however, is ultimately destructive because of the absence of gratification, because of the pain caused other people, and because it diverts energy from social contributions the person could make.

An extreme form of egocentricity is hypochondriasis. Some people invest all of their energy in themselves in an extremely distorted way by being preoccupied with their own bodies. They are never free of aches and pains, often spend years and untold dollars ''doctoring.'' They sacrifice most of life's pleasures to nurse their fancied ills, undeterred by repeated medical reports that show there is no need for surgery or that they do not have cancer, and the like. In some respects, such people commit slow suicide as they cut themselves off more and more from the outside world. In some cases, they will even allow one or more limbs to atrophy from disuse because they claim it is too painful to walk or to move.

22
On Executive
Suicide

HARRY LEVINSON

There are healthy ways and unhealthy ways of reacting to a defeat in a business setting. The executive may recognize the gap between what he or she is trying to accomplish and what he or she has achieved and try to carry on and narrow the gap. They may react in anger, which they will try to suppress, escape (perhaps via alcohol), or vent against somebody. One person against whom he or she may vent the anger (unconsciously) is oneself. The person who blames himself or herself repeatedly for defeats and losses in life may eventually plunge into such a severe depression over seemingly never-ending failures that his or her self-esteem is destroyed and he or she becomes suicidal. This article examines the executive who irrationally sets such high goals for himself or herself that he or she can never reach them.

In recent months two corporate exeutives have made headlines across the nation by committing suicide. One in New York City leaped to his death from his office window. A routine check following his death disclosed that he had authorized a bribe to a foreign official in order to prevent an increase in export taxes which would have harmed his company. In Texas a top executive shot himself. He left behind a note that alleged he had been involved in political wrongdoing on behalf of his superiors.

In each case it was easy to conclude that the man had taken the only way out to avoid the intolerable consequences of guilt. That conclusion, however, is too glib; behind such incidents lie complex mechanisms that make certain executives particularly vulnerable to suicide, especially in times of economic distress. In self-interest, the special nature of these factors should be widely understood in management ranks.

Published in 1975.

Suicide always raises the question, "Why?" The question is especially important during a recession, when the suicide rate always rises. Both of these men were very successful, as their top-ranking positions indicate. Both had strong consciences, or their behavior would not have troubled them. What intense pressures for achievement or approval forced these men to comply with actions that violated their consciences? What rigid self-demands made them think that death was the only way out of their dilemmas? Why do some executives attach so much importance to their roles? Why are their aspirations so high and crucial to them that if they face business reverses, their only solution is to punish themselves with long hours of fatiguing work and perhaps eventually with death?

In this article I want to explore some of these questions, to examine the character of the executive likely to be vulnerable to suicide, and to suggest why suicide can appear as a way out to a dynamic individual. Then I shall discuss ways in which people can recognize the symptoms of severe depression in themselves and in others, thereby, perhaps, preventing suicide.

The reader should appreciate the limitations of a brief presentation. All we can do here is try to understand a little about a very complex phenomenon and hope that understanding may cause someone to cry for help instead of escape to death.

High Aspirations, Low Self-Image

A bright, aggressive, middle-aged corporate controller thought himself to be in line for the position of vice president of finance. He approached the company president and asked whether he would be appointed to that position. The president said that he would not, whereupon the controller left the company and became financial vice president at another company. On the first day in his new post he jumped from the eighteenth-story offices of the company. His suicide was inexplicable. Many years after the event his former employer still blamed himself for refusing the controller his promotion.

In this example are some of the common elements surrounding suicidal behavior: intelligence, ambition, disappointment (and, for those who were close to the person, uncomprehending guilt). These elements are particularly germane for executives.

Executives are men and women of high aspiration. As a rule, they are very ambitious, seeking power, prestige, and money, and nearly always they are competing intensely against other executives. In psychological jargon, they have extremely high ego ideals that revolve around power. They have deep-seated, unconscious pressures for attainment; their conscious goals are merely the tip of the iceberg. People who have such high levels of aspiration are frequently nagged by the feeling of being a long way from achieving their goals. No matter what their achievement, it never seems to be enough. As a result, they always view themselves as inadequate.

All of us try constantly to narrow the gap between the ego ideal and the self-image. The failures of a person with irrationally high self-demands lower his self-image and thereby increase his anger at himself. We experience self-directed anger as depression. While depression is widespread and is usually amenable to treatment, in its extreme form, as we have seen, it often leads to suicide.

Early Traumas

The problems of high aspiration, high ego ideal, and low self-image start very early in life and contain significant components of irrationality. Some infants react to frustrations as the product of a hostile world and take a fighting stance toward it. Others interpret pain and frustration as a product of their own inadequacies and therefore are prone to blame themselves. This is a depressive position and becomes a context for self-flagellation when later frustrations or failures confirm already established belief. Regardless of any achievements, such persons always see themselves as deficient and, according to their logic, deserving of self-punishment.

Among those particularly subject to depression are people who early in life lose one parent or both. And if the parents of a person who attempts suicide were separated from him when he was a child, the separation is more likely to have been intentional (such as through divorce) than natural (such as through death).[1] The consequent loss of love and support in childhood results in anger at the loss. Through primary-process thinking (explained in a moment) children become angry with the lost parent for deserting them—which the children think is their fault because they are unlovable or inadequate. Irrationally, they become enraged with themselves. Although the rage in time subsides, it leaves a psychological bruise, and new losses–such as business losses—can stir up the rage again. The person is now more vulnerable to self-punishment.

A second element of irrationality often underlying depression in later life lies in what is called primary-process thinking. In this state children equate thinking and feeling with doing. When children are frustrated, anger mounts and a wish to attack the frustrating object frightens them. In their anger with parents or others, the children fear that their thoughts alone will destroy them. Simultaneously they feel they are bad for having such thoughts.

In an effort to cope with these feelings, the child frequently develops a pattern of behavior in which he controls the expression of feelings so that they do not show. They become unconscious; he is no longer aware of them. He tries to be so good and so competent that nobody will ever believe he has harbored bad thoughts. This pattern underlies the elevation of ego ideal aspirations to unrealistically high levels; the consequent pressures to achieve perfection follow the person through life, though he does not know why.

Dr. Margaret Prouty, former chief of pediatrics at Jackson Clinic in Madison, Wisconsin, has reported cyclical occurrences of depression among a selected group of children from seven to nine years old. Her profile of these youngsters corresponds strikingly to the problems of the ambitious, depressive adult:

> The majority are perfectionists, have a poor self-image and find that their classmates, parents, and teachers cannot measure up to their expectations. They have much need of affection and approbation, trying hard to please and be good. They have a high incidence of anxiety and dependence and poor ability to express antagonism. . . . One of their chief personality defects is an almost total lack of sense of humor. Life is indeed real and earnest and they have no ability to laugh at themselves or others.[2]

The future will find many of these children, and children like them, in managerial roles and other positions of responsibility and power, where their intensity, seriousness, and drive to perform well will make them high achievers and superior workers.

Through adolescence and adulthood the ego ideal demands are stimulated further by external pressures for achievement, by the expectations of parents and other influential figures, by competition for preferred places on athletic teams, in colleges, for professional training and preferred jobs, and by competition within organizations. In short, those who may be coping with repressed childhood rage this way demand much of themselves, and much is demanded of them.

Threat of Failure

When scholastic, professional, or organizational achievement is a cherished dream, the threat of failure, real or imagined, is a constant companion. By the time they reach middle age, many persons, especially ambitious executives, feel defeated by a lifetime of competition and still others feel constantly burdened by the threat of failure. Intently pursuing high aspirations, they are vulnerable to defeats that move their self-images farther away from their ego ideals, increasing their disappointment in themselves. As this gap increases, they get angry at themselves, become highly self-critical, feel inadequate, guilty, and depressed. These feelings may finally lead some to self-destruction.

For the corporate executive, this depressive pattern is reinforced by a career demanding that they absorb their frustrations and control their emotions ("Don't make waves"), carry on with equanimity regardless of what storms may come their way or be stirred up within them. They must not admit to having problems and must not under any circumstances give way or seek help. In fact, to seek help from a friend or the company doctor is considered a sign of weakness or failure to cope. Moreover, if they seek help from a psychiatrist or psychologist, they are either weak or crazy or both. When a conscientious executive with tremendous self-demands recognizes that they are failing to cope effectively with a situation under circumstances in which they must control intense negative feelings, they may see limited alternatives. If they do not seek professional help, escape from an apparently hopeless situation can seem possible only by developing psychosomatic symptoms, by attacking themselves in the form of accidents, or, in the extreme, by committing suicide.

In an effort to avoid the attack on self, some managers may attack and sabotage their organizations quite unconsciously. They make "stupid" mistakes. They provoke and discharge competent people, reorganize without reason, or go off on what prove to be tangents of diversification. Some try to overcontrol their organizations with rigid systems that allow them to "whip people into line" and punish those who don't "shape up." Sometimes these managers plunge their organizations into bitter, unnecessary strikes or provoke community attacks that ultimately result in their defeat. They ascribe the failure, however, not to themselves but to the organization or someone else.

But people can destroy themselves in many ways other than the physical. Some manage repeatedly to jeopardize or set back their careers, some ruin their marriages or damage their children. Some undermine their own best-laid plans; we have recently witnessed the example of Richard Nixon who, if he had planned it, could not have engineered his destruction more effectively than did his own unconscious will. Even accidents can be psychological in origin.[3] These self-destructive events cannot be ascribed only to those who are "pathological," mentally ill, or crazy. As every clinician knows, these experiences are commonplace. When people are under heavy stress from self-criticism, they may atone unconsciously for their fantasied sins by punishing themselves.

Prevention of Suicide

How can one recognize and cope with threats to the self-image that may precipitate depression and, eventually, self-destructive behavior? Here are some recommendations:

☐ Self-directed aggression occurs with greater intensity in the person who is very conscientious and who has overidentified with his or her profession, business, occupation, or major life interest. The more the person has circumscribed sources of ego gratification and organized their life around one activity, the more vulnerable they are. Defeat or loss in that area can be cataclysmic. Therefore one should cultivate a range of interests to which they can devote themselves. They cannot be equally competent in all of them, but when things go badly in one area, they can always turn to another for gratification.

☐ Accurate, honest, and frequent performance appraisal is important to enable the executive to maintain a perspective on himself. Everyone needs confirmation from others of his performance; statistics do not satisfy this need. While the person who is not performing well may suffer a temporary decline in his self-image, the appraisal opens up alternatives to failure. Information from outside the organization may provide some input; it is useful, for example, for an executive to learn from another company that his peers have similar problems.

The chief executive officer is usually exempt from realistic appraisals, though he may often be criticized. A committee of outsiders on the board of directors, who have the necessary knowledge and detachment, may serve the purpose. In my judgment, a major function of the board is to help the CEO cope with the stress that comes with the job. Of course, board members who view anxiety over problems as reflection of weakness are of no help to him.

☐ When a problem seems insurmountable, it should be broken down into components so that they can be tackled one at a time. Frequently, the advice and consultation of others is helpful in this task. Spouses and good friends have served such a function, and sometimes colleagues in trade associations or other outsiders can help with business-related problems.

☐ In reporting relationships, senior executives should try to relieve irrational pressures of guilt or responsibility that people express—but not by dismissing their expression with words like "Don't let it bother you" or "Forget it." One constructive way to avoid a buildup of pressures is through clarification of what is and is not the subordinate's responsibility. Job descriptions usually include the former but not the latter. It may be helpful if the superior recounted his own past problems and failures in order to help his subordinate accept the human quality of imperfection in himself and others.

☐ Be alert to signs of depression. These include loss of appetite and substantial weight loss, sleeplessness or excessive fatigue, heavy drinking, excessive use of tranquilizers or energizers, inability to complete work because of mental paralysis or reverie, increasing irritability, slowness and dull quality in speech, physical symptoms that have no physical basis, repeated deep sighing, and talk of suicide.

An executive who suspects that a subordinate is depressed should not urge him or her to take a vacation or take time off to "rest." The subordinate would only have greater freedom to punish himself and heighten the depression. The person whose depression does not require hospitalization needs to have an atmosphere in which he or she can work on his or her problems, with the support of his or her superiors and preferably with the involvement of others. Above all, a seriously depressed person must be treated professionally. Superiors, peers, and subordinates may think that the problem is not serious, or that the person will "snap out of it." But such optimism is unfounded unless substantiated by a diagnostician.

Point of Vulnerability

When people suffer a loss or defeat and become depressed, they usually do one of five things:

1. They act positively to narrow the gap between their goals and their present position. This is the best course to follow, obviously, but also the most difficult, especially in cases of serious depression.

2. They become more irritable. They turn their anger against others— spouse, children, subordinates, friends, and even against their business. (Child abuse has reportedly increased as a consequence of the recession.)

3. They seek to escape their feelings of futility and find solace in religion, counsel, or good works. If these avenues fail to bring relief, they may flee to alcohol and drugs. Some people flee by "copping out" or withdrawing in some fashion, others by engaging in a frenzy of social activity or by plunging into work.

4. They try to control or deny their feelings on the assumption that ultimately they will somehow go away or that they can overcome their problems.

5. They atone their supposed failures or sins. They can punish themselves by having accidents or by making "stupid mistakes" in which they set themselves back. If driven to extremes, they can kill themselves.

A person's greatest asset, the wish to succeed, can become his or her point of greatest vulnerability if a significant loss or defeat triggers a torrent of self-criticism. As a matter of self-preservation, each of us must try to temper the irrationality of that torment while at the same time capitalizing on its motivational power—the push to reach high goals. Awareness of these factors will help us remain alert to the danger to ourselves and to others. Executives, whose self-images are always at risk, are especially vulnerable.

Notes

1. Thomas Crook and Allen Raskin, "Association of Childhood Parental Loss with Attempted Suicide and Depression," *Journal of Consulting and Clinical Pathology*, April 1975, p. 277.

2. Margaret Prouty, "Juvenile Ulcers," *American Family Physician/GP*, September 1970, p. 66.

3. See Karl A. Menninger, *Man Against Himself* (New York: Knopf, 1938).

4. *Time*, March 17, 1975, p. 88.

23

Managers Can Drive Their Subordinates Mad

MANFRED F.R. KETS de VRIES

We are all familiar with and horrified by the stories that came out of Guyana about the Reverend Jim Jones and the mass suicide that occurred at Jonestown. After the dust had settled, everyone wanted to know how so many people could have believed in one person so completely that they would commit suicide to please him. It is a horrid but fascinating story. Perhaps one of the reasons it fascinates is that each of us is aware of a small portion of himself or herself that can go a little crazy because of another person. Excessive dependency on another is a state one usually grows out of, but when the dependency is mutual and reality seems to support it, breaking away may be impossible. In some business organizations, the conditions for unhealthy dependency needs to be gratified also can occur with disastrous effects for the parties involved and for the organizations. The author of this article describes the phenomenon called folie à deux—and how what we often term eccentric behavior patterns of people in organizations might be better understood in that context.

Managers, no less than other people, have personality quirks. Little things they do on occasion drive their subordinates "up the wall." In the main, however, subordinates tolerate their manager's quirks because for the most part the manager's style is acceptable and for many subordinates it is much more than that. But what happens to subordinates when a manager seems to be all quirks, when there is no in-between?

As an administrator, J. Edgar Hoover struck many as an erratic autocrat, banishing agents to Siberian posts for the most whimsical reasons

Published in 1979.

and terrorizing them with so many rules and regulations that adherence to all of them would have been an impossibility.[1] Hoover viewed his directorship as infallible; subordinates soon learned that dissent equaled disloyalty. No whim of Hoover's was considered too insignificant to be ignored. For example, nonobedience to participation in an antiobesity program was likely to incur his wrath, and rumor had it that chauffeurs had to avoid making left turns while driving him (apparently his car had once got struck by another car when he was making a left turn).

If it originated from Hoover, a trivial and unimportant order changed in meaning. Even if the directive was unclear, subordinates would have to take some form of calculated action, and, it was said, should expect trouble if they did not take the directive seriously. Nurtured by the organizational participants, these directives often assumed a life of their own. Only appearances of and actual slavish obedience to the rules, and statistical accomplishments such as monetary value of fines, number of convictions, or apprehended fugitives counted. And problems arose if the figures did not increase each year.

Naturally, those agents who embraced the concept of the director's omnipotence were more likely to succeed. To ensure compliance, inspectors would be sent out to field offices in search of violations (the breaking of some obscure rule or instruction). If a "contract was out" on the special agent in charge of the office, a "violation" would inevitably be found. Apparently, the inspector's own future at the FBI was at stake if no violations were discovered because then, in turn, a contract might be issued on *him*. If one wanted to survive in the organization, participation in many of these absurdities was often unavoidable. Many of these bizarre activities seem to have been treated as quite normal aspects of organizational life and were carried out with great conviction.

While Hoover at the FBI, Hitler in the days before the collapse of the Third Reich, and, even more recently, Jim Jones at the mass suicide in Guyana are newsworthy examples of what leaders can do to their subordinates when they lose touch with reality, the effects of dependence also occur in less heralded tales.

The president of a faltering company in the apparel industry seemed increasingly unwilling to face the declining profit position of his company. Even two months before the banks eventually took control, the president held meetings during which nonexistent orders, the development of new revolutionary machinery, and the introduction of new innovative products were discussed. These new developments were supposed to turn the company around and dramatically change its position in the industry. The president ignored the dismal profit and loss picture, inefficiencies in production, and poor sales performance, attributing them to unfair industry practices by competitors, or even sabotage, and assured his managers that change was imminent and the company would be out of the red shortly.

Sadly enough, these glorious ideas were far removed from reality.

While the president seemed to originate most of these fantasies, his close associates not only participated in them but also encouraged his irrational thoughts and actions. The rare subordinate who expressed his disbelief was looked on with contempt, found himself ostracized and threatened with dismissal. Among the small but increasingly isolated group of managers the belief persisted that everything was not lost. Miraculous developments were just around the corner. Only when the banks took control was the spell finally broken.

What is striking about both these anecdotes is the shift of what appear as delusions and unusual behavior patterns from the originator of these activities to one or more others who are closely associated with him or her. These associates not only take an active part but also frequently enhance and elaborate on these delusions. The delusions seem to escalate in intensity when the people involved try to solve problems concerned with an already deteriorating situation. They inevitably aggravate the situation, make it worse, and become correspondingly more and more reluctant to face external reality. Feeling most comfortable in their own chosen, closed environment, they do not welcome the opinion of outsiders, seeing them as threatening the status quo and disturbing their tunnel vision.

Also noticeable in these two examples is just how contagious the behavior of a senior executive can be, and how devastating its effect on his subordinates and his organization. In Hoover's case, the reaction of his subordinates further encouraged him to continue in his dysfunctional behavior. Perhaps the particular mission of Hoover's organization may have contributed to the fact that very few subordinates were willing to refuse to participate in some of these bizarre activities. Regardless, many conformed to his wishes and some may actually have believed in the appropriateness and importance of his actions. In the second example, again the process of mental contagion is central.

In psychiatric literature, mental contagion is a recurring theme. This particular process of influence, which usually goes together with some form of break with reality occurring among groups of individuals, is generally known as *folie à deux*—that is, shared madness. Although folie à deux as a way of interaction has been limited to seriously disturbed relationships between two people, a broader definition of this particular psychological process may be helpful in understanding the interactions between leaders and followers in organizations.

One may gain insight into what is frequently described as an "eccentric" leadership style if one studies emotionally charged superior-subordinate relationships characterized by some kind of impaired ability to see things realistically within the context of folie à deux. One may discover that this phenomenon, with various degrees of intensity, is a regular occurrence in organizations and can be considered one of the risks of leadership.

A senior executive should not underestimate the degree of influence he wields in his organization. Recognizing dependency—need for direction—as one of man's most universal characteristics, a manager should be aware that many of his subordinates will sacrifice reality for its sake, participating in even irrational decisions without mustering a critical stand and challenging what is happening. (For a better understanding of how strong dependency needs are, see Appendix A.)

To preserve the dependency, both subordinates and superiors create closed communities, losing touch with the immediate reality of the organization's environment to the detriment of organizational functioning. When the reality is not abandoned completely, however, this phenomenon is often difficult to recognize. But in view of its damaging consequences, even in a limited form, it deserves serious attention. I will explore this aspect of leadership, hoping to help managers diagnose and prevent the incidence of its potentially disastrous effects.

Dynamics of Folie à Deux

We have seen that folie à deux is marked by contagious irrational behavior patterns, but how does it occur in organizations?

Suppose a senior executive under the strain of leadership, trying to cope with often disconcerting imagery around power and control in addition to the general pressures of the business environment, gradually loses touch with the organization's reality. Also this individual's charismatic personality may once have attracted executives with highly ungratified dependency needs to the organization. Or it may have been the organizational climate itself which was conducive to a reawakening of these executives' dependency needs.

Whatever the reason, during their association with the organization these managers may have become dependent on the senior executive. Although strong, these needs do not at first completely overpower all other behavior patterns. What changes dependency needs into folie à deux? When both senior executive and subordinates become dependent on each other in a situation which offers few outside sources of gratification, their complete commitment to each other can be taken as symptomatic.

At some point, triggered by an event usually associated with a depriving experience of the past, the senior executive may become preoccupied with some delusionary ideas (and this is not necessarily a conscious process), one of which being that his subordinates are taking unfair advantage of him. As a result, he develops a certain amount of hostility. But, at the same time, since the subordinates' expressions of attachment finally fulfill his own dependency needs which have been ungratified for so long, he experiences guilt about this feeling of hostility.

In spite of lingering resentment, therefore, the senior executive is extremely reluctant to give up his relationships with his subordinates. They may be among the few close relationships he has been able to establish. Consequently, to defend himself against his own emerging hostility toward his subordinates, he externalizes it and attributes the hostility to others.

The senior executive absolves the closely associated executives of responsibility for these feelings; it is "the others" who are to blame. This blame can take many forms, eventually encapsulating everything that may be going wrong with the company. The senior executive, who has been the originator of this process, now needs his or her subordinates to support his or her delusionary ideas and actions. He or she needs that support not only because the ideas are his or her defense against hostility but also because he or she may lose feelings of closeness with subordinates if he or she does not get it. There seems to be only one option—namely, to induce subordinates to participate.

If a subordinate resists, the senior executive will become overtly hostile, including him or her in their vision of "the other camp"—the enemy. Naturally, the subordinate's level of anxiety will rise. A double-bind situation develops for the subordinate; he or she will have to choose between the loss of gratification of his or her dependency needs and exposure to the wrath of the senior executive, on the one hand, and the loss of reality, on the other.

In many instances, the subordinate will solve this intrapsychic conflict by giving in to the psychological ultimatum, "identify with the aggressor." He or she thus satisfies his or her own dependency needs and deflects the hostility of the senior executive. Separation from the person who started this process is viewed as much more of a direct, tangible loss than the loss of reality.

Identifying with the aggressor usually implies participating in his or her persecutory fantasies. The shared delusions are usually kept well within the realms of possibility and are based on actual past events or certain common expectations. Because the accusations contain a bit of reality, this process is difficult to discern. Through participation in these fantasies, the subordinates maintain their source of gratification, lower their anxiety and guilt level, and express their anger in a deflected form by directing it toward others. The process is mirrorlike; the actions of the initiator of the process become reflected in those of the subordinates and vice versa and can be viewed as the outcome of an effort to save the alliance from breaking up.

Now let us look at some of these dynamics in greater detail.

Getting Trapped

In organizations, folie à deux can be one of the pitfalls of leadership. Often, however, this dimension of leadership is not seen for what it is, and contagious behavior patterns are more often than not accepted and rationalized as being merely side products of an eccentric or autocratic leadership style.

Take, for example, the behavior and actions of the first Henry Ford, who had been acclaimed not only a mechanical genius but also, after the announcement of the five-dollar day, as a philanthropist. Because of the darker sides of his actions, however, this image eventually changed. While the public merely ridiculed his escapades, for the employees of the Ford

Motor Company the situation was not a laughing matter. His despotic one-man rule and his continuous search for enemies increasingly had repercussions in every function of the company. He began to view Wall Street bankers, labor unions, and Jews as his enemies, seeing each group as supposedly endangering his complete control over the company and obstructing him in his grandiose plans (e.g., the Peace ship mission, his idea to stop the First World War, or his senatorial campaign).

At one point there may have been an element of reality to some of Ford's notions (i.e., the labor union movement), but over time what there was got lost. One can regard the relationship between the senior Henry Ford and his lieutenants Liebold, Sorensen, and, particularly, Bennett in the context of folie à deux. Using a system of intimidation, helped by a large number of Detroit underworld characters, Bennett spread terror in the organization, a process originally instigated by Henry Ford but perfected by Bennett and his henchmen.

Executives who did not participate in the idiosyncracies of Henry Ford and his close associates were fired. The Model T, which carried the company to its original success, eventually became a burden. Regardless, reinforced in his behavior by his close subordinates, Henry Ford stuck to his original strategy of a cheap car to the masses, making even suggestions of modification taboo. Only in 1927, after the Model T had been in production for 19 years, and only after an incredible loss of market share to General Motors, was Henry Ford willing to make a model change.

This example illustrates how contagious a senior executive's behavior can be and how originally functional behavior can become increasingly damaging to the organization and even bring the company close to bankruptcy. Henry Ford's subordinates only encouraged his views, although it remains open to question which subordinates were only conforming and which were truly believing in their actions.

A more contemporary example involves the behavior of a manager of an isolated plant in a mining community who had developed the belief that the head office wanted to close down the production facility. The recent introduction by the head office of a new factory control system started him in his belief, and regular visits by head office staff to implement the new control system only reinforced these ideas, which he communicated to his subordinates and which were widely accepted. Although the production figures were more than adequate, a collusion began to develop among plant personnel. Eventually the plant manager and his subordinates began to falsify information to show the plant in an even more favorable light. Only a spot check by the internal auditor of the head office brought these malpractices to light.

In many of these instances, however, a major question remains. How much of the behavior of the subordinates can be accurately described in the context of folie à deux, and how much is mere compliance to the eccentric leadership style of a senior executive? The latter situation is illustrated by this example:

The division head of a company in the machinery equipment industry would habitually mention the advanced product technology used in his plants to each visitor of the company and at talks at trade association meetings. On promotion trips abroad, he was always trying to obtain license arrangements for his technology. And occasionally he would be successful. But, in spite of the fact that the company was turning out a high-quality product, there was nothing unique about the technology. As a matter of fact, most competitors were using comparable or even more advanced technological processes. Although most of his subordinates were aware of the actual state of affairs, they were unwilling to confront the division head with the facts. Compliance seemed easier than confrontation.

It is worth noting that mere compliance, if continued long enough, can evolve into stronger alliances, possibly resulting in active participation in these irrational actions. These examples also emphasize some of the characteristics of folie à deux; for example, the relative isolation of the actors, their closeness, the existence of a dominant partner, and the emergence of delusionary ideas.

The Search for Scapegoats

Interaction that contains elements of folie à deux can contribute to collusion among subgroups that fosters and maintains organizational myths and fantasies often only remotely related to the reality of the situation. In these instances, for some cliques, the organization's overall objectives and strategies become of lesser interest than tactical considerations. As concern for the maintenance of various irrational notions consumes more energy, there is less congruence between specific actions and available information.

It appears as if the members of these groups live in a polarized world that no longer includes compromise or the acceptance of differences. Everyone is pressured to choose sides. It is also a world where one continuously has to be on one's guard against being singled out as a target for unfriendly actions. In such an organization, scapegoating becomes a predominant activity directed not only toward individuals within the organization but also toward such groups as the government, labor unions, competitors, suppliers, customers, or consumer organizations. What may have been a well-thought-out program may become distorted. For instance, alertness to the environment, which at one time may have been an organizational strength, can turn into a watch for imminent attach—a caricature of its original purpose.

Because of structural arrangements, subgroups frequently overlap with departments or other units. When this happens, people jealously guard areas of responsibility; territorialism prevails. The determination of boundaries between departments can lead to disputes. Seeking or accepting help from other groups may be considered a weakness or even a betrayal.

For example, in a large electronics company a vice president of production development began to imagine that two of his colleagues, a vice president of R&D and a vice president of manufacturing, wanted to get rid of him. He perceived that his two colleagues were trying to reorganize his department out of existence and incorporate it into their own functional areas. At every available opportunity, he communicated this concern to his subordinates and expected them to confirm his own suspicions. Disagreement was not tolerated; resistance resulted in either dismissal or transfer to another department. Gradually, many of his executives began to believe in his statements and to develop a siege mentality which led to a strong sense of group cohesion.

Relationships between this group and members of other departments became strained. What were once minor interdepartmental skirmishes deteriorated into open warfare. Committee meetings with members of other departments became public accusation sessions about the withholding of information, inaccurate data, and intrusion into each others' territory. In addition, because of his recurring complaints about poor quality of delivered material and late deliveries, the vice president's contacts with some of his suppliers deteriorated. (A subsequent examination by a new vice president found that most of these accusations were unwarranted.)

Eventually, managers of other departments began to avoid contact with product development people, thereby confirming their suspicions. Over time, the rest of the company built up a number of separate, fairly informal information systems to avoid any dealings with the product development group. Finally, after the product development group made a number of budgetary mistakes because of distorted information, the president transferred the vice president and reorganized the department.

In this example one can see how excessive rivalry and suspicion can lead people to adopt a narrow perspective of organizational priorities and become defensive and controlling. Without integrating mechanisms to counterbalance their effect, these attitudes can fractionate an organization. Understandably, organizational participants will take refuge in policies and procedures, collusive activities, and other forms of organizational gamesmanship. Cooperation will disappear and priorities will become distorted.

Where elements of folie à deux seep into organizations, conflict becomes stifling, creativity is discouraged, and distrust becomes the prevailing attitude. Instead of taking realistic action, managers react to emergencies by withdrawing or scapegoating. Fear will be the undercurrent of the overall organizational climate. As ends and means become indistinguishable, the organization will drift along, losing touch with originally defined corporate goals and strategies.

Entrepreneurial Dangers

Because of the great intensity and closeness that develop in small isolated groups, entrepreneurial ventures tend to be particularly susceptible to folie à deux behavior patterns. In many instances the venture begins because the entrepreneur tries to overcome his or her feelings of dependency, helplessness, and rejection by adopting an opposite posture, a financial and psychological risk-taking style. In addition, the entrepreneur may have a strong need for achievement, control, and power, as well as an intense concern for autonomy.[2]

The relationship between entrepreneur and enterprise is usually an involved and conflict-ridden one in which the company has great emotional significance for the individual. Frequently, this type of attachment may lead to growth and succession crises, episodes aggravated by developments of a folie à deux nature, as the following example shows:

The president and founder of a medium-size electronics company often expressed concern about the need for more professional management in his company. He liked to state that the entrepreneurial phase had been passed and that the time had come to make organizational changes, prepare to go public, and plan for succession. To that end, he became personally involved in the recruitment of MBAs at various business schools. His charismatic appeal and his strong advocacy of professional management attracted a great number of MBAs. The MBA influx was balanced, however, by a steady exodus of many of the same MBAs who soon realized the difficulties in conforming to the president's demands.

Under the guise of being "a happy family," the founder felt he could intrude into the private family affairs of his subordinates. What he presented as the great deal of responsiblity that he would delegate to the newcomers turned out to be poorly defined assignments without much authority, which frequently led to failure. A person's career advancement depended on his or her closeness to the president, compliance with his wishes, and willingness to participate in often irrational behavior patterns. Exile to various obscure sales offices became the price of resistance. Eventually, the company had to pay a toll for his leadership, but the president blamed the steady drop in sales and profits on government intervention, union activities, and sabotage by a number of singled out employees.

Hoarding of information, playing of favorites, inconsistent handling of company policies, and, generally, creating ambiguous situations constitute a common phenomenon in entrepreneurial companies. Because the company's survival does depend on the entrepreneur, many subordinates are easily drawn into supporting him even when what he does may be irrational. Those unwilling to participate leave, while conformers and ones susceptible to folie à deux relationships remain.

This phenomenon may explain why in so many entrepreneurial companies a strong layer of capable middle managers is missing. In situations of folie à deux-like behavior, those who remain will spend a great part of their energies on political infighting and supporting the irrational behavior and beliefs of the entrepreneur. These activities can become even more intense if members of the entrepreneur's family are employed in the company so that family and organizational dynamics become closely intertwined.

Management of Folie à Deux

Assuming a folie à deux pattern occurs in an organization, what can be done to cope with it? How can managers prevent getting stuck in this peculiar circular process? How can they recognize the symptoms?

Before outlining the steps managers can take, I want to stress that some aspects of what might look like folie à deux are not always organizationally undesirable. As I indicated earlier, in the initial phases interpersonal processes that could lead to folie à deux may be a source of strength contributing to team building, commitment to goals and strategies, or even the establishment of effective environmental scanning mechanisms. Unfortunately, in the long run, interpersonal relationships that in extreme form typify folie à deux may become a danger to the organization's operations and even its survival.

The first steps in the containment of folie à deux are recognizing those individual and organizational symptoms:

1. *Check out your managers.* Managers likely to initiate this type of behavior usually show specific personality characteristics. For example, they may appear to possess a lot of personal charm and seductiveness, qualities that may have been originally responsible for their personal attractiveness. A closer look, however, will reveal that this behavior is often a cover-up for attitudes of conceit, arrogance, demonstrative self-sufficiency and self-righteousness. Individuals prone to folie à deux find it extremely difficult to alter their concepts and ideas; their actions often contain a rigid quality.

Because of their need to dominate and control other people, this type of executive usually stands out. They will deeply resent any form or use of authority by others. They seem to be continually on their guard, prepared to fight suspected, often imagined, dangers. Hyperalertness, hypersensitivity, and a suspiciousness of others tend to become ways of life. Frequently, they are preoccupied with people's hidden motives and searches for confirmation of their suspicions. They evince a great concern about details, amplifying and elaborating on them. Not surprisingly, the creation and maintenance of a state of interpersonal tension in the organization will be one of the effects of such behavior.

Such an executive will easily feel slighted, wronged, or ignored. Lack of trust and confidence in others can make him extremely self-conscious, seclusive, reserved, and moody. Frequently, there is querulousness, insensitivity, and a lack of consideration of others. Dramatic mood swings can be observed. If an attitude of friendliness and companionship temporarily prevails, such behavior will be quickly shattered by the slightest provocation, after which the full force of hate, mistrust, and rage may break loose. A sense of playfulness and humor seems to be lacking.

When behavior of a folie à deux nature starts to spread, the influenced persons may show similar behavior patterns, but in most instances not of such an intensive nature. For all the participants in this form of mental contagion, a key problem remains the existence of highly ungratified dependency needs. It is exactly those needs that the instigators of this process fulfill. By being directive, self-assured, and willing to take complete control, these executives attract those followers who need to be treated this way.

2. *Look at their organizations.* The danger signals of folie à deux can also be detected by looking at possible peculiarities of the organization's culture and ways of operation. One symptom is unusual selection and promotion procedures that largely reflect a senior executive's idiosyncracies rather than a concern for a candidate's overall managerial capabilities. Strange, selective, and unsystematic decision-making patterns, erratic information systems, and excessive control and extreme secrecy can also often be taken as danger signs.

Other indications may be a department's preoccupation with details at the cost of overall company effectiveness, and excessive manifestation of various stress symptoms in the organization, such as a large turnover of executives and a high degree of absenteeism. One can also view frequent changes in organizational goals, and existence of grandiose, unrealistic plans, and insistence on supposed conspiracies, or the actual creation of the latter, as other signs.

Whatever the exact nature of the disturbing behavior pattern or process one notices, one should keep folie à deux processes in mind as a possible cause. Once symptoms are recognized, managers need to take corrective action, as well as to design systems and procedures that will counteract folie à deux:

1. *Establish a trusting relationship.* When folie à deux is in full swing the manager involved is beyond helping himself or herself. For the person who started this process, the route back to reality is particularly difficult. A disposition toward delusional thinking can be difficult to overcome. Appeal to the manager's logic and reality does not help; on the contrary, it might evoke uncompromising, hostile, and aggressive reactions. Rather, in these instances, one has to establish some degree of trust and closeness with the affected manager to make him or her willing to entertain the possibility that his or her assumptions of the organizational environment are invalid.

This change in attitudes is not going to be arrived at easily, but without a change it will not be possible for an affected manager to make a realistic self-appraisal of inner strengths and weaknesses. Substituting reality for fantasies is likely to be a slow and difficult process involving reintegration and adjustment of many deeply ingrained behavior patterns. Because of the intensity of the delusions, in many instances these persons may need professional guidance.

The outlook for the affected followers is more positive and usually less dramatic. Frequently, merely the removal of the closeness with the affected senior executive will be sufficient to break the magic spell. Some form of disorientation may occur at the beginning, but proper guidance by other nonaffected executives will soon help to bring the managers back into more normal, reality-oriented behavior patterns.

2. *Monitor your own susceptibilities.* One way to make the occurrence of this behavior less likely is to be aware of your own susceptibility to it. Most people are to some extent vulnerable. We like to be taken care of at times and do not seriously object when others make decisions for us. It is sometimes easy to relax and not be responsible, to have someone to follow, to guide our behavior. Moreover, an activity such as scapegoating has its attractive sides; blaming others for things you may be afraid of but tempted to do yourself creates not only a sense of moral righteousness but also a sense of satisfaction about your own behavior. Furthermore, as long as the interpersonal interactions retain a firm base in reality, these behavior patterns are not disturbing or dangerous. Unfortunately, the slide into irrational action is easy.

To prevent yourself from entering into a folie à deux pattern you should periodically take a critical appraisal of your own values, actions, and interpersonal relationships. Because it is hard to recognize your own possible "blind spots" and irrational behavior patterns, you might consider getting help in this appraisal process from outside the organization. Also a certain amount of courage is needed to face these confrontations with yourself.

Nonetheless, the executives with the willingness to test and reevaluate reality will be the ones who in the end possess real freedom of choice, acting out of a sense of inner security. Ability for self-examination enhances a person's identity, fosters adaptation to change, and limits susceptibility to controlling influence. Because these qualities form the basis for mature working relationships, mutual reality-oriented problem solving, and a healthy organizational climate, they deter episodes of folie à deux.

3. *Solicit the help of interested parties.* Awareness of the occurrence of folie à deux is of limited help when the instigator is a powerful senior executive who happens to be a major shareholder. Occasionally, however, in such instances, the support of a countervailing power such as the government or a union may be necessary to guide the organization away from possible self-destructive adventures. Naturally, other possible interested parties who could blow the whistle are customers, suppliers, and bankers.

The situation becomes somewhat less problematic when the chief executive officer is not a major shareholder since the board of directors and the shareholders can play a more active monitoring role. One of their responsibilities will be to watch for possible danger signs. Naturally, the possibility always exists that board members will be drawn into the delusionary activities of a senior executive. Such an event is, of course, less likely to happen with a board of outside directors.

Regardless, because boards traditionally follow the directives of the CEO, the possibility of folie à deux indicates how important the selection of board members is. Important criteria in this selection process will be independence, a sense of identity, diversity of background, and reality orientation which can neutralize a folie à deux process.

4. *Reorient the work climate and structure.* Organizational solutions to folie à deux become more feasible when the instigator is not a senior exeuctive officer. Then confrontation, transfer, or, in serious cases, dismissal will be sufficient to stop the process. Also important, however, are the systems and procedures in an organization. For instance, reward systems that promote irrational behavior also give it implicit approval. Thus it is crucial to foster a healthy climate where irrational processes cannot take root.

Supporting individual responsibility and independence of mind in the organization, as well as selecting and promoting managers who behave accordingly, can be a buffer against folie à deux. An organizational culture of mutual collaboration, delegation, open conflict resolution, and respect for individuality will expose a process of mental contagion before it can spread. Such organizational patterns will lessen dependency needs and force conflict into the open, thus counteracting the incidence of vicious circles in interpersonal behavior.

Objective information systems can also assist managers to focus on reality, as can using many different sources for information gathering and processing. Interdepartmental committees and formal control systems can fulfill a similar function.

Contemporary pressures toward participative management, or work democratization, are other ways of preventing, or at least limiting, the emergency of proliferation of folie à deux. These structural changes can reduce the power of senior executives and restrict the advantage they may take of their subordinates' dependency needs.

Notes

1. "The Truth About Hoover," *Time,* December 23, 1975.

2. Manfred F.R. Kets de Vries, "The Entrepreneurial Personality: A Person at the Crossroads," *Journal of Management Studies,* 1977, 14(I), 34.

Appendix A: The Paradox of Dependency

Two French psychiatrists were the first to coin the term *folie à deux*. Other names given to this phenomenon have been *double insanity, mental cata-*

gion, collective insanity, or *psychosis of association.* Folie à deux essentially involves the sharing of a delusional system by two or more individuals. This phenomenon has frequently been observed among family members living an isolated existence.

To better understand this psychological process, let us look for a moment at the early childhood development of a person responsible for instigating this form of mental contagion. One central theme in the origin of this disorder appears to be the degree of success or failure a person has in establishing feelings of basic trust with people (originally with the parents). Lack of basic trust due to the absence of sustained interpersonal care, accompanied by anxiety because of frustrating, humiliating, and disappointing experiences will contribute to a lack of cohesive sense of self, a sense of betrayal, and a perception of the environment as hostile and dangerous. The individual's personality will develop accordingly.

In his dealings with others, such a person will continually take precautions and be on his guard to be ready for any confirmation of his suspicions. In situations of power, as a reactive way of dealing with what he sees as a hostile environment, he will be highly susceptible to grandiose fantasies and prone to delusions.

Apart from suffering the emerging paranoid disposition, a person who lacks trust also suffers an absence of closeness and, consequently, has frustrated dependency needs. For such a person, the world becomes a dangerous place where only a few individuals can be trusted. If an opportunity arises to satisfy these dependency needs, the attachment this person makes to others can become extremely intense, frequently overpowering all other behavior patterns. Because this person's attachment is so important, he will do anything—even sacrifice reality—to preserve it.

The individual to whom this attachment is directed, and who is not without his own dependency needs (though perhaps not of such an intense nature), may enjoy the way the other person is taking care of him and giving him some form of direction and guidance in life. One outcome may be that he will strongly identify with those things for which the other person stands. However, the price for these feelings of closeness becomes the acceptance of the behavior and actions of the domineering person, often without much concern for its base in reality.

This identification process appears to be of a special nature, and contains elements of the defense mechanism sometimes called *identification with the aggressor.* This is an unconscious process whereby a person takes for his own his image of a person who represents a source of frustration. Paradoxically enough, the process is gratifying because it becomes a way of overcoming a sense of inner weakness. Through identifying with the aggressor, the susceptible person neutralizes his own hostile and destructive wishes (which can be viewed as a reaction to feelings of helplessness and dependency on the dominant partner), and fear of retaliation about these wishes. At the same time he gains through the alliance and symbolic merger with the aggressor, rather than allowing himself to be the victim.

24
The Abrasive Personality

HARRY LEVINSON

Not everyone who rises quickly in a company and has good analytical skills and a lot of energy is abrasive, nor are all abrasive people in high management levels, but when the two do coincide, top management has a real problem. The problem is simply how to keep the extraordinarily talented person in a position where he or she can be most effective, and at the same time not sacrifice the feelings and aspirations of the people who work with and for this person. According to this author, managers can cope with this dilemma by helping their abrasive subordinates to understand the negative consequences of their personalities. This method takes time and patience, but it is most likely the only way managers can save such people for the organization.

The corporate president stared out the window of his skyscraper office. His forehead was furrowed in anger and puzzlement. His fingers drummed the arm of his chair with a speed that signified intense frustration. The other executives in the room waited expectantly. Each had said his piece. Each had come to his and her own conclusion about the problem.

Darrel Sandstrom, vice president of one of the corporation's major divisions, was the problem. Sandstrom was one of those rare young men who had rocketed to the division vice presidency at an age when most of his peers were still in lower-middle management. "He is sharp," his peers said, "but watch out for his afterburn. You'll get singed as he goes by." And that, in a phrase, was the problem.

There was no question that Sandstrom was well on his way to the top. Others were already vying for a handhold on his coattails. He had a reputation for being a self-starter. Give him a tough problem, like a failing di-

Published in 1978.

vision, and he would turn it around almost before anyone knew what had happened. He was an executive who could quickly take charge, unerringly get to the heart of a problem, lay out the steps for overcoming it, bulldoze his way through corporate red tape, and reorganize to get the job done. All that was well and good. Unfortunately, that was not all there was to it.

In staff discussions and meetings with his peers Sandstrom would ask pointed questions and make incisive comments. However, he would also brush his peers' superfluous words aside with little tact, making them fearful to offer their thoughts in his presence. Often he would get his way in meetings because of the persuasiveness of his arguments and his commanding presentations, but just as often those who were responsible for following up the conclusions of a meeting would not do so.

In meetings with his superiors, his questions were appropriate, his conclusions correct, and his insights important assets in examining problems. But he would antagonize his superiors by showing little patience with points and questions that to him seemed irrelevant or elementary. Unwilling to compromise, Sandstrom was an intellectual bully with little regard for those of his colleagues who could not keep up with him.

There were complaints from subordinates too. Some resented his controlling manner. Fearing his wrath, they spoke up at meetings only when they knew it to be safe. They knew he would not accept mediocrity and so they strived to attain the perfection he demanded of them. When he said they had done a good job, they knew they had earned his compliments, though many felt he did not really mean what he said.

His meetings were not noted for their liveliness, in fact he did not have much of a sense of humor. On the golf course and tennis courts he was equally humorless and competitive. Playing as intensely as he worked, he did not know what a game was.

And now here he was. The division presidency was open and the corporate president was in a dilemma. To promote Sandstrom was to perpetuate in a more responsible position what seemed to many a combination of Moshe Dayan, General George Patton, and Admiral Hyman Rickover. Sandstrom would produce; no question about that. But at what cost? Could the corporation afford it? If Sandstrom did not get the job, the likelihood was that he would quit. The company could ill afford that either, for his division's bottom line was a significant portion of its bottom line.

Around the table the opinion was divided. "Fire him now," some said; "you'll have to do it sooner or later." "Be gentle with him," others said; "if you hurt him, he'll lose his momentum." "He'll mature with age," said others. Still others commented, "When he gets to be president, he'll relax." And there were those who said, "What difference does it make? He's bringing in the bucks." The corporate president faced the dilemma; Sandstrom could not be promoted but neither could he be spared. None of the options presented gave him a way out; none of them could.

Darrel Sandstrom epitomizes people who puzzle, dismay, frustrate, and enrage others in organizations—those who have an abrasive personality. Men and women of high, sometimes brilliant, achievement who stubbornly insist on having their own way, and are contemptuous of others, are the bane of bosses, subordinates, peers, and colleagues.

In the long run, they are a bane to themselves as well; when they fail, their failure is usually due to their abrasive personalities. Because of their value to their organizations, however, their superiors frequently go to great lengths to help them fit in the organization. In fact, top executives probably refer more managers with abrasive personalities to psychologists and psychiatrists, and human relations training programs in order to rescue them, than any other single classification of executives.

In this article I describe the abrasive personality, trace its origins, and suggest what managers might do to both help and cope with such people.

A Profile

Like the proverbial porcupine, an abrasive person seems to have a natural knack for jabbing others in an irritating and sometimes painful way. But that knack masks a desperation worse than that of those who receive the jabs, namely, a need to be perfect. (For a closer look at how a need to be perfect drives a person to the point where they alienate and cause significant stress to most people around them, see Appendix A.) The person who becomes a Darrel Sandstrom however, is not just someone who needs perfection. They have other characteristics which, combined with that need, create the behavior others find so offensive.

Such a person is most usually extremely intelligent. With a passion for perfection, accuracy, and completeness, they push themselves very hard, and can be counted on to do a job well, often spectacularly. They tend to want to do the job themselves, however, finding it difficult to lean on others who they feel will not do it to their standards, on time, or with the required finesse. They have, therefore, great difficulty delegating even $25 decisions. Such complete thoroughness, however, no matter how good for the company as a whole, tends to leave others figuratively breathless, making them feel that they cannot compete in the same league.

They are often keenly analytical, capable of cutting through to the nub of a problem, but with their need for constant achievement, they are impatient with those who cannot think as quickly or speak as forthrightly as they can. Thus their capacity for analysis tends not to be matched by equal skill as a leader to implement the answers they have deduced.

On a one-to-one basis they are often genial and helpful to people they are not supervising. But despite what they say, they are usually not a good developer of people for, frequently, they feel too inadequate when they have to compare themselves with others. Also, the abrasive person's intense rivalry with others often leads them to undercut others, even though they themselves may not be aware of doing so.

When their competitive instincts overwhelm their judgment, an abrasive person will sometimes crudely raise issues others are reluctant to speak about, leaving them a scapegoat for their own forthrightness. In groups they tend to dominate others, treating all differences as challenges to be debated and vanquished. At the same time that they are domineering to their subordinates, they are fawning to their superiors. If they feel themselves to be exceptionally competent, however, they may try to dominate their superiors also.

Though often in imaginative pursuit of bigger and broader achievements for which they frequently get many accolades, they may well leave their bosses and those around them with no sense of having any input to the task or project. They move so fast and range so widely that even when they have good ideas, their boss will tend to turn them down fearing that if he or she gives an inch, the subordinate will take a mile. The boss feels there will be no catching them, no containing them, and no protecting the stellar subordinate, himself or herself, or higher management from any waves that may be created, the backwash from which might overwhelm them all.

Once reined in by their boss, the abrasive person feels that they have been let down, that their efforts have been in vain. Feeling unjustly treated, they become angry because they were asked to do something and it did not end well. Therefore, they reason, they are being penalized because other people are jealous, rivalrous, or do not want to undertake anything new. Seeing their boss as somebody to be outflanked, rather than as somebody whose step-by-step involvement is necessary for a project's success, they are politically insensitive and often righteously deny the need for such sensitivity.

Although others often perceive them as both grandiose and emotionally cold, the abrasive person has a strong and very intense emotional interest in themselves. Needing to see themselves as extraordinary, they act sometimes as if they were a privileged person—indeed, as if they had a right to be different or even inconsiderate.

At times they see others as mere devices for their self-aggrandizement, existing as extensions of themselves, rather than as full-fledged, unique adults with their own wishes, desires, and aspirations. To inflate their always low sense of self-worth, they compete intensely for attention, affection, and applause. At the same time, they seem to expect others to accept their word, decision, or logic just because it is theirs. When disappointed in these expectations, they become enraged.

To such a person, self-control is very important, as is control of others, which they make total if possible. Thus they overorganize, and cope with imperfections in others by oversupervising them. To them, losing a little control is the same as losing total control. To prevent that, they are rigid, constricted, and unable to compromise. In fact, for them, making a compromise is the same as giving in to lower standards. They therefore have little capacity for the necessary give and take of organizational political systems. This inflexibility is especially apparent around issues of abstract values which, for them, become specifically concrete.

To others the same control makes them appear emphatically right, self-confident, and self-assured. In contrast, those who are not so sure of what they believe or of the clarity of an issue, feel inadequate and less virtuous.

The abrasive person, appearing to have encyclopedic knowledge, is often well read, and, with already a good academic background, strives for more. While subordinates and even peers may strive as well to meet the high expectations of such a person, and some may reach extraordinary heights, many ultimately give up, especially if they beat them down. Thus the legendary Vince Lombardi drove the Green Bay Packers to great success, but all of its members, recognizing that he was the key to their success, felt that the better and more competent he was the less adequate they were. When such a person dies or leaves an organization, those left behind are demoralized because they have no self-confidence. Usually they will feel that they have not been able to measure up and indeed, frequently, they cannot.

If they are compelled to retire, abrasive people will have difficulty. If they are not compelled to retire, they tend to hold on to the very end, and with age, their judgment is usually impaired. In their view, they have less and less need to adapt to people and circumstances, or to change their way of doing things. Thus they become more and more tangential to the main thrust of the business. If they are entrepreneurs, they may frequently destroy organizations in an unconscious effort to keep somebody else from taking over their babies. J. Edgar Hoover, a case in point, ultimately corrupted and very nearly destroyed the reputation of the FBI out of his own self-righteousness.

Solving the Dilemma

Given that you, the reader, have a subordinate who fits the profile I have drawn, what can you do? Corrective effort occurs in stages, and takes time and patience on everybody's part.

First-Stage Techniques
The following steps can be used with any employee who is having a behavior problem, but they are particularly effective in introducing an abrasive person to the consequences of his or her behavior.

☐ Recognize the psychological axiom that each person is always doing the best they can. Understanding that abrasive, provocative behavior springs from an extremely vulnerable self-image, a hunger for affection, and an eagerness for contact, do not become angry. Instead, initiate frequent discussion with this person.

☐ In such discussions, uncritically report your observations of their abrasive behavior. Describe what you see, especially the more subtle behavior to which people react automatically. Ask how they think others feel when they say or do what you describe. How does he or she think they are likely to respond? Is that the result they want? If not, what would you do differently to get the response they want? How would they respond if someone else said or did what they do?

☐ Point out that you recognize their desire to achieve and that you want to help. But tell them that if they want to advance in the company, they need to take others into account, and that their progress along these lines has implications for their future. Ensure them also that everyone experiences defeats and disappointments along the way.

☐ When, as is likely to be the case, their provocative behavior ultimately irritates you, try to avoid both impulsively attacking back on the one hand and being critical of yourself for not responding in kind on the other. Explain to them that although you understand their need to do or be the best, that they made you angry and that others they work with must feel the same. Tell them you get irritated and annoyed, particularly with hostile, depreciating, or controlling tactics. After all, you can say, you are only human, too, even if they think they are not. Let them know how frequently such behavior occurs.

☐ If they challenge, philosophize, defend, or try to debate your observations, or accuse you of hostility to them, do not counterattack. Tell them you are not interested in arguing. Merely report your observations of what they are doing or misinterpreting *at that moment*. Keep their goal the point of your discussion; do they want to make it or not?

☐ If your relationship is strong enough, you might ask why they must defend or attack in situations that are not combat. Point out that to be part of a critical examination of a problem is one thing; to turn such a situation into a win-lose argument is another.

☐ Expect to have to repeat this process again and again, pointing out legitimate achievements about which they can be proud. Explain that goals are achieved step by step, that compromise is not necessarily second best, that the all-or-none principle usually results in futile disappointment, and that perfection is not attainable.

Much good talent can be saved if managers employ these steps with their abrasive subordinates. Of course, some people are less abrasive than others and may be able to modulate their behavior voluntarily and cope consciously with their abrasive tendencies. For those who cannot, however, more drastic measures may be needed.

Further Steps

Sometimes people with unconscious drives cannot see reality despite repeated attempts to show them. Perhaps they are too busy thinking up defensive arguments or are preoccupied with their own thoughts. Whatever, if they do not respond to the gentle counseling I have described, then they should be confronted with what their arrogant, hostile, and controlling behavior is costing them.

Such people must be told *very early on* how their behavior undermines them. All too often afraid to do this, their bosses quickly become resentful and withdraw, leaving their subordinates uncomfortable, but not knowing why. Feeling anxious, the abrasive subordinate then attempts to win back the regard and esteem of the boss in the only way they know, by intensifying this behavior. That only makes things worse.

Abrasive persons can make significant contributions to an organization, but managers need to steer them again and again into taking those political steps that will enable them to experience success rather than rejection. Rather than corral such people, who tend to figuratively butt their heads against restrictions, managers do better to act like sheepdogs, gently nudging them back into position when they stray.

Highly conscientious people, who need to demonstrate their own competence by doing things themselves, are likely to have had to prove themselves against considerable odds in the past. Their demonstration of competence has had to be in terms of what they, themselves, could do as individuals. Thus they need political guidance and instruction in teamwork, as well as support from a superior who will tell them the consequences of their behavior in straightforward terms.

These people will often need frequent feedback on each successive step they take in improving their political relationships. As they move slowly in such a process, or at least more slowly than they are accustomed to, they will experience increasing anxiety. While not demonstrating their individual competence, such people may feel that they are not doing well, and get so anxious that they may indeed fail. When they have such feelings, they then tend to revert to their own unilateral way of doing things.

However, if despite the boss's best efforts the subordinate does not respond, the manager must tell them *in no uncertain terms* that their behavior is abrasive and therefore unsatisfactory. Managers should not assume that their subordinates know this, but should tell them and tell them repeatedly, and in written form. Being told once or twice during a performance appraisal should be enough. My experience is, however, that most superiors are very reluctant to tell people, particularly abrasive ones, the effects of their behavior during performance appraisals.

In one instance, when I was asked to see such a manager, they did not know why they had been referred to me. When I told them, they were dismayed. Showing me his performance appraisal, he complained that their boss had not told them. Rather their boss had commented favorably on all their qualities and assets, and in one sentence had written that their behavior with people was improving. In reality, the boss was so enraged with their subordinate's behavior that he was not promoting them as far as they would have wished.

When the steps I have outlined have been followed to no avail, when the subordinate clearly knows, and he or she is unable to respond by changing his or her behavior, when repeated words to the person and even failures to be promoted have produced no significant improvement, there are two likely consequences. First, the abrasive person will feel unfairly treated, unrecognized for his or her skills and competence, and unappreciated for what he or she could bring to the organization. Second, the superior is usually desperate, angry, and at his wit's end.

If by this point the abrasive person has not already been referred to a competent psychologist or psychiatrist for therapy, they should be. *Nothing else will have a significant effect,* and even therapy may not. Whether it does will depend on the severity of the problem and the skill of the therapist. This is not a problem that will be solved in a T-group, or a weekend encounter, or some other form of confrontation.

The manager should make sure the subordinate understands that when a person is referred to a psychologist, there are two implications. The first is that the person is so competent, skilled, or capable in some dimension of his role that their superiors would not only hate to lose them, but also have reason to expect that the person could flower into a mature executive who can assume greater responsibility. The second is that despite their talent, the subordinate is so unable to get along with other people that they cannot be promoted beyond his present role. Both points should be made emphatically.

These same principles apply equally in dealing with any ineffective or dysfunctional behavior on the job. Some people cannot seem to get their work done. Others have a habit of getting in their own way as well as that of others. Still others manage to stumble their way to work late each morning or produce incomplete or inadequate work. Whatever the case, steps in treating them are essentially the same.

Other Problem Situations

What do you do if the abrasive person is your boss, your peer, someone you are interviewing, or, hardest to face of all, yourself? What recourse do you have then?

The Boss

Let us assume that you are relatively new or inexperienced in a particular area and need a certain amount of time to achieve your own competence. Chances are that because of their knowledge and competence, your abrasive boss will have much to teach. Since their high standards will ensure that the model they provide will be a good one, there will be sufficient reason for you to tolerate their abrasiveness.

But after two years, or whenever you establish your own competence, you will begin to chafe under the rigid control. As you push for your own freedom, your boss is likely to become threatened with loss of control and feel that you are becoming rivalrous. He or she is then likely to turn on you, now no longer a disciple, and, in sometimes devious ways, get back at you. Your memos will lie on their desk, unanswered. Information being sent through channels will be delayed. Complaints, suggestions, requests will either be rejected outright or merely tabled. Sometimes they will reorganize the unit around you, which will fence you in and force you to deal with decoys—nominal bosses who have no real power.

If you are in a safe position, you might tell the boss how they appear to you, and their effect on subordinates. If they are at a high level, it will usually do little good to go above their head. Certainly, you should check out how much concern his or her superiors have about them, how much they are willing to tolerate, and how able they are to face them in a confrontation. Few at higher management levels are willing to take on a bright, combative, seemingly self-confident opponent—especially if they have a record of achievement, and there is little concrete evidence of the negative effects of their behavior.

In short, after you have learned what you can from such a person, it is probably time to get out from under them.

The Peer

If you are the peer of an abrasive person, do not hesitate to tell them if their behavior intimidates you. Speaking of your irritation and anger and that of others, you might tell them you do not think they want to deliberately estrange people or be self-defeating. They might become angry, but if approached in a kindly manner, they are more likely to be contrite and may even ask for more feedback on specific occasions.

The Candidate

What should you look for during an interview to avoid hiring someone who will turn out to be abrasive?

Pay attention to the charming personality. Not all charming persons are self-centered, but many are. Some preen themselves, dress to perfection, and in other ways indicate that they give an inordinate amount of attention to themselves. The more exhibitionistic the person, the more a person needs approval, the less he or she can be thoughtful of others. Also pay special attention to precision in speech or manner. Clarity is a virtue, but a need for exactness indicates a need to control.

Find out how the person gets things done by having him or her describe past projects and activities. How much does he or she report starting and finishing tasks all by himself or herself, even to the surprise of superiors? To do so is not necessarily bad; in fact, it may be good for a person to be a self-starter. But repeated singular achievement might indicate a problem in working as part of a team. How often do they use "I"? How closely did they have to check the work of subordinates? How important was it for them to have control of what was happening? How did they talk to people about their mistakes? How did they go about coaching them?

How did they view the limits and inadequacies of others, as human imperfections or as faults? How much better do they think things could have been done? Why were they not done better? Why could they not do better? What did their bosses say about them in performance appraisals?

You, Yourself

Finally, what if you are abrasive? If you ask yourself the question in Appendix A on this page and find that you answer three of them in the affirmative, the chances are that your behavior is abrasive to the people around you. If you answer six or more affirmatively, it takes no great insight to recognize that you have more problems than are good for your career. Of course, none of these questions taken by itself is necessarily indicative of anything, but enough affirmative answers may reveal an abrasive profile.

If you are the problem and it troubles you, you can work at self-correction. Most often, however, you need the help of a third person—your spouse, a friend, your boss, or a professional. If your behavior causes you serious problems on the job, then a professional is indicated. Managers and executives with naturally heavy orientations to control, need to check themselves carefully for this kind of behavior lest unconsciously they defeat their own ends.

Appendix A: The Need to Be Perfect

If a person's ultimate aspiration, their ego ideal, is perfection, then they are always going to fall short of it—by astronomical distances. And if this person's self-image is already low, the distance between where they perceive themselves to be and the omnipotence they want to attain will be constantly increasing as the feeling of failure continues. They must, therefore, push themselves ever harder—all the time. Others who are or may be viewed as competitors threaten their self-image even further; if they win, by their own definition, they lose. Their intense need to be perfect then becomes translated into intense rivalry.

If a person is always pushing themselves toward impossible aspirations and is never able to achieve them, there are two consequences for their emotion. The greater the gap between their ego ideal and self-image, the greater will be both their guilt and anger with themselves for not achieving the dream. And the angrier a person is with themselves the more likely they are to attack themselves or drive themselves to narrow the gap between their ideal and their present self-image. Only in narrowing the gap can they reduce their feelings of anger, depression, and inadequacy.

However, as the unconscious drive for perfection is irrational, no degree of conscious effort can possibly achieve the ideal nor decrease the self-punishment such a person brings down on themselves for not achieving it. The anger and self-hatred are never ending, therefore, and build up to the point where they spill over in the form of hostile attacks on peers and subordinates, such as treating them with contempt and condescension.

These feelings may also spill over onto spouses, children, and even pets. In fact, the abrasive person's need for self-punishment may be so great that they may take great, albeit neurotic, pleasure in provoking others who will subsequently reject, that is, punish them. In effect, they act as if they were their own parent, punishing themself as well as others. In Anna Freud's words, they become a good hater.[1]

Appendix B: Do You Have an Abrasive Personality?

You might ask yourself these questions. Then ask them of your spouse, your peers, your friends—and even your subordinates:

1. Are you condescendingly critical? When you talk of others in the organization, do you speak of "straightening them out" or "whipping them into shape?"
2. Do you need to be in full control? Does almost everything need to be cleared with you?
3. In meetings, do your comments take a disproportionate amount of time?
4. Are you quick to rise to the attack, to challenge?
5. Do you have a need to debate? Do discussions quickly become arguments?
6. Are people reluctant to discuss things with you? Does no one speak up? When someone does, are his or her statements inane?
7. Are you preoccupied with acquiring symbols of status and power?
8. Do you weasel out of responsibilities?
9. Are you reluctant to let others have the same privileges or perquisites as yourself?
10. When you talk about your activities, do you use the word "I" disproportionately?
11. Do your subordinates admire *you* because you are so strong and capable or because, in your organization, *they* feel so strong and capable—and supported?
12. To your amazement do people speak of you as cold and distant when you really want them to like you?
13. Do you regard yourself as more competent than your peers, than your boss? Does your behavior let them know that?

---

[1] Anna Freud, "Comments on Aggression," *International Journal of Psychoanalysis,* vol. 53, no. 2, 1972, p. 163.

25

Must Success Cost So Much?

FERNANDO BARTOLOMÉ and PAUL A. LEE EVANS

Undeniably, many people who reach executive levels in organizations do so at the expense of their personal lives. They spend long hours at difficult and tension-filled jobs and retreat to their homes not for comfort and sustenance but for a place to hide or to vent feelings left over from a bad day at the office. Yet other executives who endure the same long hours and tension-filled jobs come home full of energy and excited by the day. What distinguishes the two groups of people? After studying more than 2,000 executives and interviewing many husbands and wives, these authors have found that, psychological differences aside, the executives who successfully cross the line from job to private life are able to do three things better than the other executives. They adapt well to change in jobs, they find the right jobs for them, and they handle career disappointments well. The authors discuss these sources of potential negative emotional spillover; then they investigate how organizations might minimize obstacles to coordinating one's private and professional lives.

A good number of executives accept the cliché that success always demands a price and that the price is usually deterioration of private life. This cliché does not always reflect reality, however—some executives seem to be exempt. What distinguishes the executives who pay a heavy personal price for

---

Published in 1980.

Authors' Note. The ideas described in this article are the result of many hours of conversation with executives and their wives. Both of us are conducting research on the relationship between the professional and private lives of male executives; our extensive questionnaire has been completed by 700 international managers. The quotations are taken directly from interviews conducted with 44 executive couples in the United Kingdom and France and from exchanges with more than 2,000 executives of many different nationalities who attended executive development courses and seminars at the European Institute of Business Administration over a period of five years.

their success from those who are able to maintain and develop fulfilling private lives?

In studying the private and professional lives of more than 2,000 managers for nearly five years, we've seen that some very successful executives have meaningful private lives. One thing that does *not* distinguish these executives is professional commitment. (To succeed, individuals have to give their jobs a high priority in their lives.) Nor is it easier for these executives to develop a private life. For everyone, it is difficult.

What *does* distinguish the two groups is this: the executives whose private lives deteriorate are subject to the negative effects of what we call emotional spillover; work consistently produces negative feelings that overflow into private life. In contrast, the other group of executives have learned to manage their work and careers so that negative emotional spillover is minimized, and thus they achieve a balance between their professional and private lives.

After countless exchanges with managers and their wives and after careful analysis of research data, we concluded that the major determinant of work's impact on private life is whether negative emotional feelings aroused at work spill over into family and leisure time. When an executive experiences worry, tension, fear, doubt, or stress intensely, he is not able to shake these feelings when he goes home, and they render him psychologically unavailable for a rich private life. The manager who is unhappy in his work has a limited chance of being happy at home—no matter how little he travels, how much time he spends at home, or how frequently he takes a vacation.

When individuals feel competent and satisfied in their work—not simply contented, but challenged in the right measure by what they are doing—negative spillover does not exist. During these periods executives are open to involvement in private life; they experience positive spillover. When work goes well, it can have the same effect as healthy physical exercise—instead of leading to fatigue, it is invigorating.

If things go right at work, a feeling of well-being places people in the right mood to relate to others. They open up, they are available, they may search for contact. That, of course, does not guarantee that such contact will be successful. A person may not be skillful at it, or there may be deep conflicts from the past that make contact difficult. But when the executive feels good at work, contact at home is at least possible.

We can summarize our findings this way: for an ambitious person, a well-functioning professional life is a necessary though not sufficient condition for a well-functioning private one.

For the time being, our study has focused on male managers only. We have not yet studied female executives, but our exchanges with some women and our reading of the literature on women managers lead us to believe strongly that the ideas we present apply to them as well.

The dilemmas and conflicts women face in trying to manage the relationship between their professional and private lives may be even more difficult than those faced by men. While in many cultures it is acceptable for men to specialize in their professional roles and delegate the main responsibility for private life to their wives, our impression is that even in the more liberal and advanced cultures the married woman who chooses to pursue a career is still expected to be responsible for the quality of the couple's private life.

Women are under more pressure to manage skillfully the boundaries between professional and private life. They are probably more aware of what causes the conflicts than many men. As increasing numbers of women join the work force, these issues are being more openly considered at work.

The Price Some Managers Pay

Even though we recognize that positive spillover exists, for the most part in this article we're going to be concerned with the negative emotions that spill over from work into executives' private lives. What are its sources? How can individuals manage it, and what can companies do to minimize the likelihood that people will suffer from it?

The experience of this 36-year-old manager typifies the spillover phenomenon: "When I started working for my boss four years ago, that affected my family life. He was very different from my previous boss. He was a bit of a tyrant. From working with someone who was terribly easygoing to someone who's an absolute dynamo—that certainly had an influence on my family life. It made me slightly—how can I put it? Well, I'd come home to my wife talking about him, about decisions he had reversed on a certain proposal I'd made. I'd talk it over with my wife, but I couldn't get it out of my mind, because it was such a different way of operating from my previous boss."

All of us have experienced spillover at one time or another in our careers. The problem is that some executives lead life-styles that pave the way for never-ending spillover. Such an executive's wife is likely to react with this sort of comment: "What annoys me is when he comes home tense and exhausted. He flops into a chair and turns on the TV. Or else he worries, and it drives me up the wall."

Work spills over into private life in two ways: through fatigue and through emotional tension, like worry. Fatigue is the natural consequence of a hectic day at the office. But curiously enough, a hectic day—if it has gone well—can make us feel less worn out, often almost energetic. On the other hand, a boring day at the office, when the executive feels he has not accomplished anything, is exhausting. He comes home tired. Home is not a place for private life; it simply becomes a haven—a place to rest, relax, and recharge batteries to survive the next day.

Worrying, the other symptom of negative emotional spillover, is caused by frustration, self-doubt, and unfinished business. One wife puts it this way: "Yes, his mind is often on other things. Yes, he often worries and it *does* disturb the family life. When he is like that he can't stand the noise of the children. . . . He can't stand the fact that the children are tired. In general we have dinner together so that he can be with them. And obviously they chatter, they spill things, they tease each other—and he blows his top. He is tense and uptight—it's disturbing; I can't stand it. I have to try to mediate between them and cool things down. The only thing is to finish everything as soon as possible and get everyone quickly off to bed."

The feelings that spill over from work are acted out at home. Sometimes they are expressed through psychological absence, sometimes through acts of aggression. One loses one's temper with the children. One explodes in fury if one's wife makes a minor mistake. Such aggression is visible and painful, but withdrawal is equally damaging to family relationships. As one wife said:

"My husband is not one of those men who vents all his frustrations on the family. One cannot reproach him for being aggressive or for beating his wife. Instead he closes up like a shell. Total closure. The time he thinks he spends here isn't spent here."

Because psychological withdrawal can make a person blind to what is going on at home, it can have very serious consequences. A 40-year-old executive described the most painful period of his marriage this way:

"It was just after the birth of the third child, eight years ago. The birth coincided with a move to another part of the country and with a complete change in job. And there I have to admit that I was completely unaware of the consequences that all this had for my wife. She was overloaded with work and worries. It went on for some time, and I just wasn't aware of what was happening. Finally she fell ill and had to be hospitalized. It was only then that it began to dawn on me. I was quite unconscious of everything I was doing."

"You were overloaded in your work?"

"Yes. Well, not really overloaded. I was worried about my work. I didn't feel very sure of myself and so was very worried. . . . It was the time of a merger between two companies and a period of great uncertainty. That had led to my new job and the move. And I just couldn't get my work out of my mind. I think back even today—the uncertainties of the time were real. It was normal, but anyway I couldn't get the work out of my mind. Today I'm much more sure of myself. I find it a lot easier to switch off."

When negative emotions spill over, managers often express dissatisfaction with their life-styles and complain of wanting more time for private life. But because their minds are numbed by tension, these people cannot use even their available time in a fulfilling way. Some report needing a double martini just to summon the energy to switch on the television. Many read the newspaper, not because they're interested in world events, but to escape into personal privacy. Some mooch around in the basement or the garden as a way of just getting through the day.

Again and again, the wives of these executives express the same idea: "I don't really mind the amount of work he has to do. That is, if he is happy in his work. What I resent is the unhappiness that he brings home."

Or sometimes they agree with this 42-year-old wife: "The very best moment in our marriage is, without any doubt, right now. We have never before had such a complete life together. The children are interesting to my husband and he is very happy with his work. On the other hand, the most difficult moments have been when he wasn't happy with what he was doing."

Managing Spillover

To have a healthy private life, one must manage the negative emotions that arise at work. When we began our investigation into the work lives and private lives of managers five years ago, we held the biased belief that these two sides of life are in fundamental conflict with each other. During these five years we have gathered more and more evidence suggesting that, among managers at least, individual and organizational interests can be in harmony. Moreover, a healthy professional life is a precondition for a healthy private one.

Job and home can be in harmony and mutually reinforce each other if—and only if—one avoids various pitfalls in the management of self and career and one copes satisfactorily with the emotions that arise at work. Conversely, executives who fail to manage the emotional side of work achieve professsional success at the expense of private life.

Let's look now at what the executive can do to manage the emotional side of work better. We single out three major causes of negative emotional spillover: the problems of adapting to a new job, the lack of fit between a person and his job, and career disappointments.

Coping with a New Job

Without doubt, the most common trigger of spillover tension is the process of settling into a new job following promotion, reorganization, or a move to another company. Since all of us change jobs from time to time, we all experience spillover caused by the problems of adaptation. Having to familiarize ourselves with a new task, learn to work with new people, settle in a different town and environment, and establish new relationships with superiors, subordinates, and peers—all at the same time—overloads our emotional systems.

That work dominates the emotional life of a person adapting to a new job is natural and necessary. It allows him to master major changes. Once that is done, the spillover effects begin to fade away.

What is vital is that the individual assess and recognize how important a change he (and his family) face when he changes jobs. The more new skills the job requires and the more radical the change in environment, the longer the adaptation period is likely to be and the longer the negative spillover is likely to last. To deny this reality in an attempt to persuade a reluctant family that the job change will also be good for them is risky.

Top managers often fail to assess correctly the magnitude of the changes and adaptations they ask of executives and their families. Often individual executives, driven by their own ambition, also fail to assess accurately the difficulty of tasks they accept. Only a realistic evaluation of the degree of change executives and their families will face allows them to come through the process of adaptation relatively unscathed.

In talking to executive couples, we have found too often the case of the ambitious executive who accepted an exciting job in a developing country that sounded like a wonderful opportunity and a major career step. His wife was unhappy about it, but there was no heart-to-heart discussion about the decision. The wife felt that her husband's mind was made up and was reluctant to hold him back. Her fears were half-assuaged by his assurances that the move would be challenging and exciting and that he would be there to help out. They moved.

What executives do not realize is that the change to a new and important job, to a new locale, and to a new culture will create massive amounts of tension. The negative spillover into private life will be immense. For a year or more, they will have minimal psychological availability for private life. If their wives expect and need that availability, its absence will aggravate the adaptation problems that they are undergoing themselves. Far too often, the story ends catastrophically for all concerned.

And yet it doesn't need to happen this way. We have heard executives describe enthusiastically how similar moves brought their families together and how dealing with the difficulties of adaptation as a family was a most positive experience.

What accounts for the difference in experiences? These latter executives analyzed the change carefully with their families before the move, negotiated the decision with them, openly expressed the problems they would all confront, and did not promise what they could not deliver.

Most wives will understand and accept that for some time their husbands will be preoccupied with the job and won't be readily available. If they recognize this in advance and as long as they know that emotional spillover will fade away, they may even support him at this difficult time. But sometimes spillover does not fade away. The new job turns out to be beyond the person's talents or capacities.

If after a reasonable period of time—say, one year—negative spillover is increasing rather than fading away, a misfit situation (where the only way of mastering the job is through sheer brute energy rather than skill) could be in the making. Because wives experience the spillover consequences directly, they are good judges as to whether it is increasing or decreasing. If it's increasing, the time has come to negotiate a move out.

Taking the Right Job

The lack of fit between an individual and a job is the second most common source of negative spillover. Judgments on the "shape" of people and jobs are difficult to make; square pegs are often put in round holes. Top managers may overemphasize skills and experience while ignoring the very important factors of personality and individual goals. Consider the experiences of Jack and Melinda:

Three years ago, Jack was a computer company's research manager, content in his job and very ambitious. Top management offered him a promotion to a job as manager of administrative services. While at first Jack didn't like the position offered him, management persuaded him to accept it by arguing that it would be an important step in his career development. Since Jack's ambition was to become research director, the argument seemed logical. The new job would give him administrative experience that would help qualify him for the post he wanted. Jack accepted the job.

Jack has already spent three years in this job, yet spillover tension is not on the wane. On the contrary, during the past three years it has increased steadily and is now an almost inextricable part of his life. But while he is hurting, his wife Melinda and his two children are hurting even more.

Melinda talks of how Jack has brought nothing but sadness and tension into the family's life since he undertook his new job. Since then, she says, "He hasn't even been interested in talking about our problems." In fact, she has often considered divorce.

For his part, Jack finds it difficult to say anything positive about his job. "You meet interesting people and a wide variety of situations," he says, "but one part of the work consists of acting as the office boy to deal with everyone's banal problems." The other part consists of negotiating with trade union officials on grievances, a duty that Jack finds tiring and frustrating. "You have no authority over anyone," he says, "and what I didn't realize at the beginning is that one doesn't have any real contact with the people in research."

The tension and doubt that Jack feels—and which his wife experiences even more strongly—are growing. At the end of a two-hour interview, he spoke of the feeling of being trapped: "I'm not really content in this job, but if I do well it will help me in my next job in research. It's a thankless task, being at everybody's beck and call. The trouble is that it's getting to me. I can't take the strain much longer. I went to my boss last month and told him that I want to move back to research. He told me that they would take care of that in due time, that I was doing a grand job now, and that they needed me here.

"The trouble is—did he really mean it that I was doing a grand job? I feel that things can only go downhill from here. And I'm drifting further and further away from research."

Lack of Fit

Jack is a misfit. However valid or invalid his reasons for accepting his present job, the work does not suit his personality. It makes him permanently tense without satisfying him. Yet because he took the job as a "stepping stone," he *must* perform.

Lacking deep interest and natural skill for the work, the misfit can only compensate with an overinvestment of energy. This investment may lead to success—but at the price of enormous internal tension, reinforced fear of failure, and the suspension of an investment in private life.

Tension and deep fear of failure are the natural consequences of going against one's grain. People who take jobs for which they are ill-fitted are often afraid that their weaknesses will show, that they will be found out. These inner doubts can be so intense that no amount of external recognition or acknowledgment of success can eliminate them.

For misfits the ultimate irony is that, instead of decreasing with each new success, fear of failure increases. Outward success does not reassure them. Instead, their successes trap them in jobs they do not enjoy. With their bridges burned behind them, they feel snared in situations that create permanent and increasing tension.

Let us define what we mean by the fit between individual and job. A perfect fit occurs when you experience three positive feelings at the same time: you feel competent, you enjoy the work, and you feel that your work and your moral values coincide. To express this in another way, a job should fit not only with skills and abilities but also with motives and values.

A misfit situation occurs whenever one of these three conditions is absent. In the case of the *total misfit,* none of the conditions is fulfilled: they are not particularly competent at what they do, they enjoy few aspects of their work, and they feel ashamed doing things that go against their values or ideals. Jack, the manager we just described, is an example.

Absence of Skill.   The *competence misfit* enjoys their work and is proud of what they do. They work hard enough to keep their job, but they are not sure of their ability to really master the work. For example, a manager in a line position may find it difficult to make decisions, or someone taking a personnel administrator's job hoping to broaden their skills may not work well with people. For the time being, those executives may manage well, but they live with the persistent fear that things will get out of hand. This sense of insecurity tends to diminish their enjoyment of the job and spills over into their private lives.

This "competence misfit" most typically happens to people in the early stages of their careers, when they haven't yet found out what they are good at doing. It is the type of misfit that organizations are most sensitive to, which they try hardest to avoid. But two other kinds of misfit, which most organizations fail recognize, are equally important. We call them the "enjoyment misfit" and the "moral misfit."

Dislike for the Job.   An *enjoyment misfit* occurs when individuals are competent at their job and proud of doing it but do not like it. One executive had the necessary qualities to be a manager and was promoted to a managerial job even though he would have rather remained in a technical position. Despite his preference for individual challenge over the laborious process of working through other people, he succumbed to a sense of duty and to unanimous pressure and accepted the job. He is unhappy in his new job and consequently suffers from negative spillover.

The most frequent cause of "enjoyment misfit" is intrinsic dislike of various work characteristics, but other causes are common as well. Staying in a job too long can transform enjoyment into boredom; persons can be competent but see what they do as predictable variations of a humdrum theme. Having too much work to do can also destroy enjoyment: some people, finding it very difficult to say no to challenges and tasks they enjoy doing, agree to do too much. The consequent stress gradually erodes the intrinsic pleasure of the tasks.

Different Values.   The last type of misfit, *moral misfit*, results when individuals enjoy their work and are competent but do not feel proud of what they do, when they feel they compromise their values. A sales manager we met, for example, was good at his job, but he did not believe in the merits of the product he was selling. He would not have bought it himself and could not wholeheartedly recommend it to others. He used to reassure himself by saying that "as long as there is a market for it, it must be O.K." After a successful and important sale, rather than feeling proud of himself he would come out feeling "thank goodness that's over."

The negative spillover created by going along with unethical business practices (such as bribing foreign officials) has two additional painful twists to it. The person fears potential legal consequences, and he cannot vent his feelings by expressing them to others because the position dictates secrecy.

Each of these ways of not fitting a job is dangerous. If individuals accept tasks for which they lack the competence, they risk feeling continual self-doubt. If they accept jobs for which they are skilled but which they do not like doing, they will be bored. If they accept jobs in which they do not feel pride, they will not feel at peace with themselves.

The incompetent misfit may be the only type of misfit the organization is able to spot; whatever the cause of the misfit, however, the individuals and their families will suffer. For an individual in top management to avoid putting the wrong person in the wrong job, it is essential to understand what causes some of the mistakes.

Why People Take the Wrong Job

We find four main reasons why people are in the wrong jobs: the strong attraction of external rewards, organizational pressure, inability to say no, and lack of self-knowledge or self-assessment. Let's examine each one of these issues in turn.

External Rewards.   We all like and need money and have some healthy needs for status and recognition as well. But because in our Western society having these things implies that one is a "good" person, we sometimes put too much value on them. As a result, many people end up doing what will bring rewards rather than what fits them. They are seen as good members of society but don't feel good about themselves.

Executives we spoke with often justified accepting jobs they didn't really want on the ground that the material rewards the jobs provided were essential to realizing a fulfilling private life. They fail to realize (except in hindsight) that no matter how much they earn, no matter how much status is attached to the position, their private lives will suffer through emotional spillover if the job doesn't fit them.

Organizational Pressures.   When management approaches an individual in the organization or outside it to offer him a job, in most cases it does so after carefully analyzing available candidates. The person chosen is usually the one management deems most competent for the job.

But management pays little if any attention to the two other dimensions of fit—will the person enjoy the job and will he be proud of it? If it assesses these dimensions at all, management will often dismiss any problem as an individual or personal concern. A person's capacity to do the job well is all that counts. Some managers assume that if he does not feel he will like it or be proud of it, then he will say no; some also assume that if he doesn't say no, the personal issues don't exist.

But here is the problem. When management reaches its final decision and offers the person the promotion or the new job, he is no longer simply a candidate for that job. Management has made a statement that he is the best person available. To refuse is to deny management what it wants. Of course, he is free to say no on emotional grounds; but is he really? The pressures to accept are considerable.

Management often adopts a selling attitude that manifests itself in a variety of ways. The rewards and incentives are expressively described, the fact that this is a "unique opportunity" is stressed, and the argument that "this will be good for your career" is emphasized. If the individual points out that he may lack some of the necessary skills for the job, management is likely to say that this is "an exceptional opportunity to develop such skills," expressing vague doubts about the future otherwise. At the end of the process, management often brings the ultimate pressure to bear. It makes it clear that a decision has to be reached quickly, that an answer is expected "let's say, in 72 hours."

By this time many executives will have succumbed to the appeal of external rewards or to the fear of saying no or of showing hesitation. Nevertheless, the best of them will indeed insist on enough time to analyze as thoroughly as possible the intrinsic characteristics of the job and the extent to which it fits them.

These people are deeply aware that their decisions will influence not only every working hour in the years ahead but also every hour of their private lives. And these are the people most likely to avoid becoming misfits and suffering from massive spillover. In most cases, their attitudes are reinforced by a real concern for their families and a deep understanding of the impact that changing jobs may have on them.

Above all, such executives realize that they hold the main responsibility for managing their careers and are unwilling to transfer that responsibility to anybody else.

The Ability to Say No. If learning to ask for sufficient time to think over accepting a job is difficult, learning to say no is even more difficult, particularly in times of economic crisis.

Learning to say no requires, first of all, the ability to estimate realistically the consequences of refusal. Many people assume fearsome consequences that they often are too afraid to test. But one also has to estimate realistically the negative effects of acceptance. Executives we spoke to mentioned they had sometimes made the decision easier by minimizing the difficulties they would face.

Ability to assess consequences realistically is one of the characteristics of highly successful people. They can do this because they have the final and most important quality of people who want to avoid spillover—namely, self-knowledge and the ability to assess themselves accurately.

Self-Assessment. Much of our behavior is rooted in unconscious motives, and it is difficult to know that part of ourselves. Also, as we age we are continually changing and acquiring new experiences. So, even under the best of circumstances, to assess whether one will fit with a new job is difficult.

Self-assessment implies that one can accurately recognize one's competences—acknowledging limitations as well as strengths, identifying what brings pleasure or pain, and knowing what elicits pride or guilt in different work situations. It requires admitting to feelings rather than masking them.

The raw data for self-assessment are past experiences. Because of limited experiences, the task is especially difficult for the younger manager. During one's 20s and early 30s, the only way to assess oneself is to take different jobs in different companies to find out what kind of work one does best, enjoys most, and finds most meaningful. Our research indicates that foreclosing this phase of exploration too quickly may have negative consequences later in one's career.[1]

This exploration, however, does not need to be a blind process. Under ideal circumstances, a mentor successfully guides the younger person in the trial and error stages of his career. The mentor—an older, experienced, and trusted guide (often a boss with whom one enjoys an open and special relationship)—does more than simply provide new challenges and experiences. This mentor also helps the younger manager learn from those experiences what his skills, needs, and values are, and thus speeds up the process of self-assessment.

No matter how well this process of starting one's own career and finding one's professional identity goes, the individual will suffer from considerable tension and stress. Managers at this stage in life are predominantly oriented toward launching their careers, and emotional spillover often pervades private life.

After such a period of exploration and with better knowledge of themselves, some individuals in their mid-30s eventually find jobs or positions that fit them in the three dimensions outlined earlier. The young man assessing a job asks himself above all "Can I do it?" But the more mature man asks two other questions as well: "Will I enjoy doing it?" and "Is it worth doing?" He is likely to accept the job only if all three answers are positive.

People at this stage in their careers turn more toward their private lives. They are no longer content simply with the competence fit. They aim for total fit that ensures minimal spillover and full availability for private life. They can achieve this if they have developed sufficient self-knowledge to guide their careers. This knowledge will also allow them, after having benefited from a mentor in their early careers, to become mentors themselves.[2]

For some people, self-knowledge grows with experience, and consequently they are able to manage their careers and avoid spillover. Others, however, fail to learn from experience and as a result are likely to suffer from the third main cause of spillover—namely, career disappointment.

Learning from Disappointments

Prevention is better than cure. Individuals skilled at self-assessment run a smaller risk not only of finding themselves in the wrong job but also of suffering serious disappointments. But all of us face disappointment at one time or another in our careers. It can have immense psychological impact, especially if work is an important part of our lives.

The most frequent type of disappointment that we have found in our research is experienced by the older manager whose career flattens out below the level he expected to reach. More or less consciously, he recognizes that he has plateaued. Individual signals of the end—a turned-down promotion, a merit raise refused, a bad appraisal, or a shuffling aside in a reorganization—are bitter blows.

When deeply hurt, most of us will automatically react in a defensive way. While some individuals can eventually react healthily and learn from a painful experience, many become disillusioned and turn into bitter, plateaued performers. Often such executives disengage from activity. Abraham Zaleznik suggests that two things are necessary to cope well with disappointment: the ability "to become intimately acquainted with one's own emotional reactions" and the capacity to "face the disappointment squarely." And, he adds, "The temptation and the psychology of individual response to disappointment is to avoid the pain of self-examination. If an avoidance pattern sets in, the individual will pay dearly for it later."[3] In all cases, the danger is distortion of reality.

In our contacts with executives, we have found ample confirmation of Zaleznik's observations. It is indeed difficult for people to face disappointment squarely. The experience often triggers in them strong feelings of loss that they turn into anger against themselves, which sometimes manifests itself as depression or withdrawal. But people cope with such situations in diverse ways. After a short period of mourning their losses, some bounce back (having learned something) and adapt successfully; others get permanently stuck in bitter and self-destructive positions.

Those who do not recover from severe disappointment often find themselves stuck in no-exit jobs that they do not enjoy and are not particularly proud of. They find it difficult to accept that their careers have plateaued in this way. They feel cheated. The emotional tension of an unenjoyable job, now aggravated by bitterness, often spills over into their home lives, where everyone else also pays for their sense of failure. Private life, as well as professional life, becomes hollow and empty. The injury to self-esteem they received in the professional world seems to color their whole experience of life.

Other plateaued managers recover their enthusiasm for their professional and private lives in a constructive way. They may compensate for their disappointment by enriching their present jobs—for example, adopting a role as mentor.

Often this positive compensation comes through developing leisure activities. These activities have, however, a professional quality to them rather than being mere relaxation. One man transformed his hobby of riding into a weekend riding school. Another got involved in community activities. A third broadened his home redecorating pastime into buying, redoing, and selling old houses. In these examples, work became more meaningful in that it helped to finance an active leisure interest; family life benefited since the man recovered his sense of self-esteem.

We can add a nuance to Freud's idea that the main sources of self-esteem and pleasure in an individual's life are work and love. Failure at work cannot be fully compensated by success in love. Failure at work has to be compensated by success in worklike activities. Only when work and love coexist in parallel and appropriate proportions do we achieve happiness and fulfillment.

What Organizations Can Do

We have suggested that the main responsibility for managing a career, reducing negative spillover, and achieving a good balance between professional and private life lies with the individual executive. It makes more sense for individuals to feel responsible for managing their own professional lives (taking care that career does not destroy private life) than to expect the organization to do this for them. Management in organizations, however, bears the responsibility for practices and policies that may make it unnecessarily difficult for the individual executive to manage the relationship between his professional and private lives. We see four things top managers can do to reduce the work pressures.

Broaden Organizational Values

Our first recommendation to managers is likely to be the most heretical. Managers can help their people by encouraging them not to be devoted solely to career success. Many managers attach too high a value to effort, drive, dedication, dynamism, and energy. Managers often take long hours at work and apparent single-minded dedication to professional success as indicators of drive and ambition. Attachment to private life and efforts to protect it by working "only" 45 hours a week are interpreted as signs of weakness in today's middle aged; in younger managers, this pattern signifies an erosion of the work ethic, a symptom of what is wrong with the younger generation.

We find little evidence in our research, however, of an erosion of the work ethic among younger managers. Their professional commitment is strong, but it represents a commitment to what interests them rather than a blind commitment to their companies. They resist simply doing what has to be done and conforming to organizational practices, even if they are compensated by incentives. They are aware that a lot of office time is wasted by engaging in ritualistic, nonproductive "work" and that few people make a real success of activities that fail to excite and interest them. Above all they appreciate that the quality of an individual's work life has an enormous impact, positive or negative, on his or her private life.

Paradoxically, organizations do not necessarily work better when they are full of highly ambitious, career-centered individuals striving to get to the top. As a matter of fact, these "jungle fighters" are often ostracized by their colleagues and superiors because they have too much ambition and too little ability to work with others. What organizations ideally need are a few ambitious and talented high achievers (who fit with their jobs) and a majority of balanced, less ambitious but conscientious people more interested in doing a good job that they enjoy and are adequately rewarded for than in climbing the organizational pyramid.

Organizational practices that overvalue effort and climbing and undervalue pride in one's job and good performance are counterproductive. Economic recessions in years to come will make this even more apparent. As the growth rates of organizations stabilize, the possibilities for advancement and promotion will diminish. People will be productive only if they enjoy the intrinsic value of what they are doing and if they draw their satisfaction simultaneously from two sources—work and private life—instead of one.

Create Multiple Reward and Career Ladders

Since external rewards often pressure people into accepting jobs they don't fit, our second recommendation concerns the reward policies and ladders of organizations.

The reward ladder of most organizations is a very simple, one-dimensional hierarchy; the higher, the more "managerial" one is, the more one is rewarded. People come to equate success with the managerial ladder, which would be appropriate if skilled managerial people were the only skilled people we need. But this is far from the case. Most organizations have relatively few general managerial positions and, while these are important posts, the life blood of the company is provided by people who fit with their jobs in other ways. To encourage these people, reward ladders need to be far more differentiated than they are at present.

Edgar H. Schein shows how managers fit with their work and careers in at least five different ways that he calls "career anchors."[4] While some people indeed have managerial anchors (that is, they aspire to positions in general management), others are oriented toward expertise in a technical or functional area. A desire to be creative is the central motive in the careers of a third group. (And do we not need more entrepreneurs in our large organizations today?) The fourth and fifth groups are anchored in needs for security and autonomy, respectively.

The obvious implication is that organizations must create multiple career and reward ladders to develop the different types of people required for their operations. Some high technology companies that rely heavily on technical innovation have indeed experimented with offering both managerial and technical reward ladders. In the future, we will probably see the development of reward ladders that reinforce creativity and entrepreneurship as well.

The problem with the simple structures of many organizations is that they channel ambition and talent in only one direction, creating unnecessary conflict for the many individuals who are ambitious or talented but do not walk the single prescribed path. We can warn individuals against being blinded by amibition to the emotional aspects of fit; yet we must also warn organizations, not against fostering amibition, but against channeling it into a single career path.

Give Realistic Performance Appraisals

Our third recommendation is that managers help individuals in their own self-assessment, thus reducing the chances that they will either move into positions that do not fit them or be promoted to their "Peter Principle" level of incompetence. To do this, managers need to pay greater attention to their subordinates' performances and also to be honest in discussions of the subordinates' strengths and weaknesses. Managers should also encourage self-assessment. Contrary to standard assessment practices that only emphasize skills and competence, self-assessment should focus as well on the extent to which the individual enjoys his job—both as a whole and in its component parts.

Many researchers have called for accurate and realistic feedback in performance appraisal.[5] We also ask that managers be as concerned and realistic about enjoyment and value as about competence.

Of all managerial omissions, lack of candor about a subordinate's chances for promotion can be most destructive. At one time or another, to one degree or another, most managers have agonized over trying to motivate an individual with the lure of promotion while knowing that the individual does not have much of a chance. Candor may result in employees' short-term unhappiness and even in their leaving the company, but we suggest that the long-run effects of dissembling are far worse. Eventually truth will out, and the negative effects of disappointment are likely to harm not only the individual's performance at work but also, through the spillover effect, his private life—at a time when perhaps it's too late for him to change jobs.

Reduce Organizational Uncertainty

Uncertainty is an increasingly frequent fixture of today's world. Sudden, unpredictable events—like and oil shortage or the taking of hostages in Iran—can have massive impact on the lives of managers in Dallas, Paris, or Bogotá. Economic recession lurks in the background, and no one feels entirely safe. The jobless executive next door makes many a manager aware that "it could also happen to me." Reorganization and restructuring of companies have become almost annual events; and sudden policy changes have vast repercussions on people's lives that create worries and preoccupations and lead to emotional spillover.

Managers can help reduce unnecessary stress and uncertainty by protecting their subordinates from worry about events over which they have no control. A good example of this is the young manager of a foreign exchange department in a large bank. It is difficult to imagine a more uncertain, hectic, anxiety-ridden job. When we asked him how he managed, he answered: "I protect my subordinates and I trust them. When my superiors drop by to tell us how stupid what we did yesterday was and ask who did it, I tell them that it's none of their business. I offer them my job if they want it. That shuts them up quite fast.''

We asked him how he could trust his subordinates in a department that could lose millions in a day. He answered: "I trust them because I have to. And I have learned to show them that I trust them by leaving them alone to do their jobs and helping them only when they ask for help.''

Here we have a "shock-absorbing" manager. However, the price for his courage is enormous. He absorbs a lot of the anxiety around him, acting as a buffer against many pressures. He has an ulcer and no nails, but his subordinates love him.

Top managers cannot expect to have many people like this in their ranks. But they clearly need people who can absorb as many shocks for others as possible. And they owe it to such people to relieve them from positions where uncertainty is too high by systematically rotating these jobs after a certain time. People can protect others from uncertainty and anxiety (to some extent this is part of a manager's job), but only for so long.

Whose Life Is It Anyway?

In managerial circles, there's something almost sacred about the separation between private and professional life. The respect for an individual's privacy is one of our fundamental values. However, no one can deny that work has a powerful effect on private life. The issue is where does responsible behavior stop and where does interference begin?

The individual executive adheres to the principle that his or her private life is none of the organization's business. But today he or she does expect the organization asking him or her to accept a big new job in Latin America to consider as legitimate his or her concerns about, say, his or her three children and spouse with a career of his or her own. In the interest of his or her future performance, the corporation is well advised to listen and respond to his or her concerns.

We do not need to invoke altruism to recommend that organizations make sure their people are in jobs that fit them, that they can cope with the changes the organization may ask of them, and that they have the tools for realistic self-assessment. Doing this is essential to the morale and productivity of the organization.

Responsible behavior on the part of the organization is simply behavior that is in its own best interest. This means recognizing the emotional aspects of work and career. A person's capacity to enjoy doing a job is as important a consideration as his or her potential competence.

Even if organizations choose not to deal with these issues, the changing values and life-styles of younger managers—especially those in dual-career marriages—may eventually force top management to face the impact work has on private life.

Notes

1. See our article, "Professional Lives Versus Private Lives—Shifting Patterns of Managerial Commitment," *Organizational Dynamics,* Spring 1979, p. 2.

2. *Ibid.*

3. Abraham Zaleznik, "Management of Disappointment," *HBR* November–December, 1967, p. 59.

4. Edgar H. Schein, *Career Dynamics* (Reading, Mass.: Addison-Wesley, 1978).

5. See, for example, Harry Levinson, "Emotional Health in the World of Work" in *Management by Guilt* (New York: Harper & Row, 1964), pp. 267–291.

26
The Work Alibi
When It's Harder to Go Home

FERNANDO BARTOLOMÉ

Lack of time is one of the best excuses for not doing almost anything. Because all of us use it, we're all ready to believe it. But if you do some simple calculations, the author of this article points out, you'll find that the amount of time most executives spend at work isn't more than half of their waking hours. If lack of time isn't the cause of the unsatisfactory home lives that worry many of them, what is? The author explores some important contributing factors to a disappointing personal life, such as having the wrong assumptions in the first place, being excessively afraid of confronting conflict, and taking a "mañana" approach to problems. He concludes, however, that the most important factors are a married couple's ability to maintain an ongoing dialogue about their feelings, to ask openly for what they truly need from each other, and to have fun.

In discussions with executives about how they mesh their personal and business lives, I hear versions of the following story countless times:

> We married when we were young. We had very little experience in dealing with personal problems and so we had troubles from the beginning. We didn't know how to talk about how we felt. We'd get angry at each other and sometimes we'd argue, but never constructively. We thought it would get better, but it didn't. When we had our first child, things seemed easier between us. Then we had our second one—a boy. Our marriage still wasn't good—we couldn't talk about our problems—but we loved our kids. Then we found out that the boy had a congenital heart problem.

Published in 1983.

It was just about then that my father retired and I took over the family business. I worked a lot and when we talked, it was always about little Johnny. We stopped even trying to talk about our own problems. The boy got worse. Finally we had to operate, and he died. The pain was terrible. That brought us closer, but still we couldn't talk. I needed something else. I fell in love with another woman. Three years later I divorced my wife.

What I hear so often is a story of the tragedy and waste that can afflict the personal lives of many successful executives because of lack of attention and skill. In these conversations I find executives searching for a solution to difficult and painful problems at home and for ways to reinvigorate their private lives.

In general, executives' private lives are not in terrible shape. Most people, however, have unresolved personal problems that worry them and often a feeling that "something is missing." For some the issue may be a concern with a child. Others feel that their marriages have lost vitality. Many worry about their life style or physical health. It is dealing with such problems that executives often find difficult.

When I ask executives why their private lives are not as fulfilling as they would like them to be, most answer that they lack time and energy for personal affairs because of their devotion to work. And when I ask them how they feel about this, most of them say they feel "guilty." Their use of the word guilty is revealing. It implies that they feel they are at least partly responsible for this situation through neglect.

While in some cases work may contribute to an unsatisfactory family life, in many others it becomes an alibi that executives use to cover up much more important factors.

When Work Is to Blame

Let's talk first about those cases when work does contribute to a poor private life. Strong and persistent negative emotional spillover that a stressful work situation can produce is sure to cause havoc at home.[1] But absence of spillover is not enough to ensure that time at home is happy. A well-functioning professional life is a necessary but not a sufficient condition for a good private life: an executive may be available to family and friends, but availability doesn't automatically make him or her a good parent, spouse, or companion.

Another way in which professional life can have a negative effect on the home is when executives work too much. "Workaholism" is one type of overwork. The word, with its connotation rooted in "alcoholism," implies escape or avoidance of problems through a drug, in this case, work. Despite the similar consequences—an estranged family and impaired health—society condemns alcoholism but condones and even applauds workaholism.

But while many people who work excessively are workaholics, others whose actions may produce the same effects are simply "prisoners of success." The difference between the workaholic and the prisoner of success is that while the former is trying to escape through overinvolvement in work, the latter has simply fallen in love with the job and the rewards it brings. Executives addicted to success don't escape their private lives but simply neglect them.

Popular belief to the contrary, if the executive population I interviewed is representative, workaholics and prisoners of success are the exception rather than the rule.

When I ask executives to estimate what proportion of their waking hours they invest in work, most estimate between 60 and 70% per week. Yet when I do some arithmetic, I usually find a number much closer to 50% (see Appendix A). These figures hold for a great majority of managers and executives, and they would be even lower if I included in my calculations vacation time and holidays. In any event, explaining family difficulties in terms of pressures of work doesn't hold water. The time that most executives have available for their private lives is roughly equal to, if not greater than, the time they devote to work.

For most executives, therefore, the only way work can have a direct negative influence on private life is through negative emotional spillover. But when spillover is absent and an executive's private life is still not as good as he or she would wish, the causes have to be found elsewhere.

If It's Not Work, What Is It?

My discussions with many executives have helped me identify a number of factors that hurt their private lives. These include: incorrect assumptions, excessive fear of confronting conflicts in marriage, legitimate distractions, a "mañana" attitude, and, in general, a lack of necessary skills.

Incorrect Assumptions

The most pervasive wrong assumption executives hold is that managing family life is easy—something they can do with their left hands while their right hands are busy dealing with their professional lives.

Executives have formal traning to be accountants, financial analysts, marketing specialists, or computer experts; many professionals must have a diploma to practice. Yet, despite all the evidence to the contrary, many managers assume that they can learn to be good spouses without thinking about it or developing the necessary skills. People get married with neither full awareness of the problems that can arise in a marriage nor the skills necessary to establish an intimate relationship that is intended to be exclusive and last a lifetime.

When I mention this lack of training to executives, many respond that,

"You can't study those things. You learn them by trial and error." But is this really so? Consider business affairs. Even though management is still largely an art, executives haven't stopped learning analytical concepts and processes that have proved helpful in understanding problems and identifying opportunities. The same should apply to private life.

Some people assume that it is easy to love their children. But while we may not have to learn to feel the emotion we call love, it is often very difficult to learn to love children in the "right" way, or to educate and raise them. We can't learn these things in a hurry when crises arrive; we need to learn them over time in a persistent way, which takes energy, commitment, and the gradual development of necessary skills.

I have seen many competent men and women executives who accept the challenge of professional problems throw up their arms in despair when the solution to a problem with a child doesn't come easily to them. One executive's description of his frustration is typical:

> I feel extremely competent at work, but not at home. At home I feel like a bumbling idiot. For example, I relate very well to one of my kids, almost too well; he is very fond of me and I think he may be excessively dependent on me. He is my oldest. My youngest kid is exactly the opposite. He is very independent and seems to avoid me. When I travel and call home, Bruce can't wait to talk to me. But my wife has to go look for Peter and ask him to come to the phone. Things are okay, but I sense that they're not really right, and I don't have the faintest idea what to do.

This executive has been aware of this "problem" for the last three or four years. He is puzzled, but hasn't done anything about it. He is afraid that he may make things worse if he tries to improve them.

What is intriguing about this all too common situation is that the executive involved doesn't realize that it's difficult to learn to resolve the problems of private life, or that it may take time and, above all, enthusiasm and imagination to learn to identify and enjoy private life's opportunities and pleasures.

Fear of Confronting Conflicts in Marriage

When working with executives in seminars, I ask them to write a list of "issues that you and your spouse do not talk about sufficiently." Each time I get the same response. After a brief pause for laughter, people settle down to write and then become quite serious. Later I ask them to write down the reasons why they do not talk enough about these issues.

The most common reasons given for avoiding discussions are fear of being rejected, facing the unknown (one never knows where such exchanges may lead), having to confront painful decisions, having to change, and showing vulnerability.

At first glance, these reasons will probably appear sensible and, perhaps, familiar. But a deeper analysis will reveal the more important reasons people are immobilized in personal relationships. They show that, for the most part, people focus on the potential negative consequences of exploring issues with their spouses without analyzing equally thoroughly the possible benefits. But, above all, they fail to mention what in my opinion are the main reasons for avoiding such exchanges. Because these exchanges are extremely rare, people don't know how to go about them. When people explain their lack of candor with each other by describing its potential catastrophic consequences, it's likely they are not accustomed to making such disclosures regularly and it is the discomfort of the exchange per se that they try to avoid.

The reasoning many people use when trying to decide whether to explore difficult issues openly often looks like this:

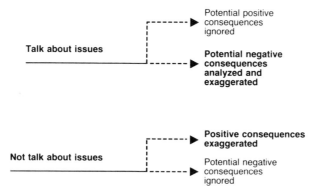

After making such a biased analysis, a person could reach only one conclusion: it is better not to rock the boat. But not confronting difficult issues is no solution. I am not saying, of course, that confrontation is easy or painless. It can be done, however. (I indicate how later on in this article.)

Legitimate Distractions

The persistence of problems in marital relationships is frequently due to what are seen as legitimate distractions for avoiding communication. The literature of family therapy describes the most frequent pattern. The situation that executives, particularly younger ones, find familiar, develops as follows:

A couple gets married. Natural conflicts develop in the relationship. Some of them surface and the couple deals with them in the early stages of the marriage. However, they often perceive deeper issues as too difficult to confront. Both husband and wife may find excessive work a wonderful excuse not to face these issues. Then a natural "solution" arrives in the form of a child. Now the man and woman do not need to talk about their problems; they can talk for hours on end about issues concerning the child. If one is not enough, two children are sure to give them plenty to talk about. Moreover, as children grow they begin to satisfy for each parent some of the needs the other parent fails to meet. The couple continues to postpone dealing with hidden marital conflicts.

THE WORK ALIBI: WHEN ITS HARDER TO GO HOME

Work and children are dangerous distractions from dealings with marital issues. They are dangerous because they are such legitimate, right, and perfect excuses. But, of the two, because they compete directly with the marriage for time and energy that may be necessary to overcome marital problems, the most dangerous distractions are children.

Family therapists often find a fear of confronting marital issues so strong that if a family comes for help with a problem child and the therapeutic intervention is effective, the parents panic. As the distraction disappears, the couple loses an excuse for avoiding confrontation of their marital issues.

'Mañana'

The label says it all.

You are 25, and married. You are young and starting your career. You are exploring your skills, trying to find your professional niche, trying to get on "the fast track." You are busy and decide that you will take care of your private life "mañana."

Mañana—you are 30. You have a 3-year-old child, and you have either found a good track or are still looking for one. If you are doing well, the demands of work keep increasing. If you are doing poorly, you are still struggling to find your way. You decide that you'll take care of your private life mañana.

At 35, you have made it to your first goal. You are vice president in charge of the most important single account in your firm. You relate well to your boss, who has told you that you are on the home stretch. You earn much more than the people you started out with. Yet sometimes you experience a feeling of emptiness and fear. One of the top people in your firm, who is 55, tells you, "You know, I learned all that has to be learned in this industry in the first ten years." Because that's how you feel, it scares you. But you don't know how to deal with that vague feeling of anxiety. You think that you may be hitting the mid-life crisis prematurely. You decide to wait and see if this too will pass.

Mañana—you are 40 and, as happens to many men and women at this age, you want to turn toward your private life. And you decide that *now* is the time.

Many people in all walks of life have experienced a version of this tale. While they are making sacrifices, they keep saying to themselves that they will recapture what they are giving up. This, of course, is impossible. The experience a person misses today can't be had tomorrow. If you don't enjoy your relationship with your spouse when you are 25, the chance to do so is gone forever. If at 40 you divorce and marry someone younger, you will still be 40.

The woman (or man) who decides to invest in a career and postpone a family until she is 30 or 35 may have a wonderful experience. But raising a small child when you are 35 is not the same as doing it when you are 25.

We cannot recover the relationship that we didn't have with our children when they were young. Many parents discover to their regret that they have missed their children's childhood.

People who forfeit the present risk the quality of their future private lives. As in business, you have to invest today to enjoy the returns tomorrow. The parent who tries suddenly to establish a friendship with his or her 16-year-old son or daughter after years of neglect often learns that it is too late.

Turning the Corner

Now that I've outlined the main sources of problems executives have managing their personal lives, I want to focus on potential solutions.

Avoid Saying 'Mañana'

Realizing the futility of thinking that tomorrow we can recapture today and understanding how much is at stake may help executives avoid missing the present. But it is not easy to change habits of thought and behavior.

I mentioned earlier that many executives say they feel guilty about paying too little attention to their private lives. Guilt feelings generally mean a belief of not doing one's duty. As long as people think of private life more as a duty that as a pleasure and an opportunity, they are likely to find excuses to stay longer at work than they need to. On the other hand, when people stop thinking of their home life as one more chore and learn to enjoy it, they may start organizing themselves to leave work on time.

While some people show great creativity in enjoying private life, for many the time they spend with their families is unexciting. For these people their home life is blandly passive; they experience it as a spectator. Developing creative, appealing ways of being with their families is crucial for executives because it determines the force of the pull that their home lives will exert over them.

How, for instance, could the father with the two different sons, one very close to him and the other extremely distant, deal with his problem? Let me give two examples of such a case. The first shows an unproductive way of dealing with such a problem. The second is an example of a creative solution.

In the first case, the executive was sensitive and shy. His son was 12 years old and doing very well at school. He appeared to be happy but he was also shy and seemed to have problems making friends. The executive wanted to have a closer relationship and also wanted to help his son overcome his shyness. One day he proposed that they go camping together. His son agreed, but one week before the camping trip he sprained his ankle while playing tennis. The trip was cancelled. The father waited until the following summer and again proposed a camping trip. Three weeks before the second trip his son broke his leg playing basketball.

What went wrong? It is clear that the camping trip was a bad idea. It meant moving abruptly from great distance to excessive closeness, and the child subconsciously managed to avoid it.

Another father with a similar problem dealt with it more creatively. He noticed that his 13-year-old child was studying botany at school and had a couple of new plants in his room. The father was very proud of the garden he himself tended in the backyard. One day he told his son in passing, "You know, I'm not using all the space in the back. If you want to plant anything, feel free." The son planted melons, and soon he was coming to his father for advice.

In the second case, both the "solution" and the process were right. The father first paid attention to his son's growing interest in plants. Second, he approached his son gently suggesting "in passing," that he plant something; instead of invading his son's territory, the father invited him into his own. Finally, it was their common interest and gradually increasing physical proximity that brought father and child together. It was an elegant solution to a complex problem.

Deal with Conflicts

Paradoxically, before a couple can address its problems, both people have to establish first that the marriage can be improved. People need hope, and this they can gain by determining what does work and what is good in the relationship. When I ask people to list issues that they are not discussing with their spouses, often their lists include only problems: "our disagreements about raising the children;" "the ways in which he or she disappointed or hurt me;" "what we have lost."

But people will only work to solve conflicts if they believe the relationship can be improved and if the atmosphere is right for them to do the necessary work.

Before starting to address problems, people should talk about the opposite side of the coin, about what is good and works well in their marriage— to rephrase the list above: "our agreements on raising the children;" "the ways in which I am proud of you;" "how you have helped me;" "what we have created"—then they'll know that it is worthwhile fighting to improve the relationship and that they have the resources to deal with existing problems. Talking about what is good can help them see not only the potential catastrophic consequences of a dialogue but also the benefits.

Emphasizing the positive can also create an atmosphere of warmth and trust that can make talking about conflicts less threatening.

Dealing with conflict itself requires that people learn two fundamental skills. The first is, as a matter of everyday practice, continuing a dialogue instead of letting emotions accumulate and eventually explode. This means learning to give not only negative but also positive feedback. Many people, particularly men, have as much trouble expressing positive as they do negative feelings.[2]

The second skill is dealing with persistent and deeper conflicts. In most cases, couples who find it exceedingly difficult to handle conflicts have a long history of poor communication marked by sporadic and usually unsuccessful attempts to cope with important issues. As a consequence, a couple with such a track record associates discussing conflicts openly with emotional explosions, hurt egos, and catastrophes. The couple believes "once burned, twice shy."

Here is an example of what such a couple fears when extreme feelings in one or both of the parties necessitate a "conversation." Under conditions of heightened emotion, such a conversation promptly turns into reciprocal blaming, explosion, and withdrawal. In this case, a couple was discussing their children. The exchange started gently, but then the wife told the husband that he was being too rough with 11-year-old Paul, who has having problems in school.

The dialogue, that I witnessed, went something like this:

"You're too rough with him. He's scared of you."

"Somebody has to do the disciplining around here and you don't do it!"

"Okay, but you don't need to be so brutal."

"I am not brutal. The children see me as brutal because you don't confront them at all and leave that job to me. You tell them 'wait until your father comes home!' "

"That doesn't justify your behavior."

"You want me to discipline the children when I come home from the office completely exhausted. How do you expect me to behave?"

"You see, I can't talk with you. You get all upset and start blaming it all on me! . . ."

In this conversation the blaming game is in full bloom. But how can a couple avoid this? One way is to keep track of how the conversation is going and at the first sign of excessive emotional tension, to stop to recover some equanimity and some warmth.

But even stopping to examine what is going on in the conversation to make sure things don't go wrong can become part of the blaming game—"you interrupt me all the time," "you never listen,"—so people have to learn how to talk constructively.

This is no easy feat. But learning how to build a bridge, create a company, or sell something isn't easy either, and people do learn.

Become Authentic

For some people, having fun in a relationship comes naturally. For others, whose lives have become routine, reawakening a sense of excitement and pleasure in a relationship may be difficult. The easy solution is, of course, to go after the greener grass on the other side of the fence. But in most cases the price people pay for straying is very high.

Of course, not all relationships can be revitalized or launched anew. Some may be beyond hope, and the issue a couple faces is how to end it without undue pain and destruction and have what therapists refer to as a "creative divorce." But my contact with executives makes me think that many have relationships that are satisfactory but could be vastly improved.

How can a marriage be revitalized? To build a relationship that satisfies both partners' needs and allows them to have fun, each has to be able to clearly ask for what he or she needs or would enjoy. Some people feel, however, that they shouldn't need to ask, that their partners should know them well enough to realize or sense what they need. This can happen only when a couple is so transparent that they never lie to each other with either words or behavior.

Some people say that they are "afraid of rejection." And by using the word "rejection" they indicate how little clarity and honesty they achieve in their communication. When a person says he or she fears rejection, he or she conveys the idea that the other may reject what is being offered. But, in most cases, when people talk about fear of rejection, what they fear is not that their love will be spurned but that they will not be loved in return. In truth, fear of rejection is a fear that the other will not give us what we need or want. When people fear they won't get what they need and do not ask honestly for it because of that fear, indeed they end up not getting it.

If people are to have true pleasure in relationships, they need to learn both to get rid of excessive fears and unconscious fantasies and to be authentic. A transparent person shows his or her needs and problems—and also shows joy and pleasure. Only when two people own up to their deepest feelings can the true issues between them arise, namely, the extent to which they are deeply and naturally compatible or the extent to which their mutual attraction can motivate them to adapt to each other. The courage to be transparent does not come easily, however. Fears can be very deep. As Erik Erikson has said, hope and trust are basic virtues that people have to develop. This requires intelligent risk taking, courage, and luck.

When behavior is authentic, both partners can learn what the other person needs, how he or she feels, what he or she truly enjoys, and what hurts. The transparency of one partner tends to evoke transparency in the other. And most important, being able to see each other clearly, people learn to trust each other.

How many married people really trust the messages of pleasure that their partner expresses when making love? My guess is that those who really trust their partners are the same ones who, during those times, never lie with words or acts. And what will happen to trust if we don't trust each other in our most intimate moments?

But sometimes being authentic cannot guarantee getting what we need. Then it is necessary to talk. If a couple is transparent on a daily basis, they will find that talk comes easily; what makes communication problematic is the unwillingness to be candid. When people are ready to be candid, communication may involve pain but it is not in itself difficult.

Authentic behavior and clear communication are, together with imagination and playfulness, the doors to pleasure in relationships.

Making It Work

How can executives begin to enhance the quality of their home lives? The first step is to abandon the assumption that having a good private life is easy or that they can easily acquire the necessary skills. Most people find it difficult.

The second step is to abandon the equally incorrect assumption that personal relationships are too complex and difficult to handle and, therefore, people shouldn't even try. In their private lives as in their professional lives, executives need to establish clear, concrete, and achievable goals and to monitor their achievement.

Private goals are often implicit or impossibly vague, and many are extremely unrealistic. People need to ask themselves what they want their marital relationships to be, or what they would like their relationship with a child to be, and what their self-development goals are. If the answers to these questions are general statements—"I want a good relationship with my husband" or "I want to be friends with my children"—it is necessary to ask, "What does that mean?"

To say, "I want to spend more time alone with my husband" is not enough. To specify that "Every week I will make sure that I spend at least two hours alone with him doing something that we both enjoy" is much more likely to work. To say, "I want to have a better relationship with my son" is too vague. To say, "I will first stop and think about what is causing problems between us, and then figure out what we may enjoy doing together" is a more logical way to proceed.

In talking with executives about these kinds of issues, I suggest they select one or two improvement projects at home. These may be taking better care of their health or of their self-development or improving their relationships with their wife, children, or friends. I recommend that the projects have the following characteristics: to begin with they should be *modest*, not revolutionary; they should yield results that are *measurable* so that the executive can notice a difference, and *pleasurable* so that the executive will enjoy the outcome; and, finally, they should *involve another person* who will help the executive persist.

I caution readers not to attempt to address the most difficult issues at the beginning. Because nothing succeeds like success, you should attempt to improve "small" things first, thereby learning new skills and signaling clearly an intention to improve relationships. The results are often surprising.

And finally, I encourage you to suspend your skepticism, although this can be difficult. Recently I talked with a couple who had tried this approach, and the wife assured me that "It has really worked." Small changes can make a significant difference for those who, lacking insurmountable problems, sense that something is missing at home and want to improve the quality of their private lives.

It's Never Too Late

Many people tend to believe that, late in life, it is too difficult to change. Today, adult development research shows that people have a much greater capacity to change and learn through life than was assumed.

Some people argue that personal skills are fully intuitive and either you have them or you don't. But the main component in dealing with many private life issues is interpersonal sensitivity, and my experience is that people have much more sensitivity than they give themselves credit for. I consistently find that what on the surface looks like insensitivity hides, in reality, a deep hypersensitivity. Under the right conditions, people can uncover their hypersensitivity, transform it into sensitivity, and put it to work. With very little prodding, their hope can be rekindled.

Notes

1. For a discussion of research on this subject, see my article, coauthored with Paul A. Lee Evans, "Must Success Cost So Much?" *HBR* March–April 1980, p. 137.

2. Fernando Bartolomé, "Executives as Human Beings," *HBR* November–December 1972, p. 62.

OVERCOMING THE BARRIERS

AN OVERVIEW

If addressing the human problems at work is so difficult, how can managers begin to cope with them? From what we've seen so far, determining the kind of problem you are faced with—whether it is a conflict of races, sexes, values, or personalities—is difficult. And taking the right approach would seem to require the manager have the wisdom of Solomon as well as the tact of a seasoned diplomat.

The following articles offer some ways of determining the right approaches. Some of our earlier selections in Part One, for instance, described the problems of organizational structure and function—the isolation of people at top-management levels, conflicts, and the noxious effect of being subordinate. Here we see how companies can counteract the hierarchy's divisiveness.

Renn Zaphiropoulos talks about one way in "It's Not Lonely Upstairs." Zaphiropoulos, one of the founders of Versatec, Inc., conceives of his organization as a circle rather than a pyramid. No individual in the circle is better than any other, but some merely have a broadened point of view. There are pay differentials at Versatec, but in the main, management is not isolated from its resources and it is not competitive. Because authority at Versatec is spread so wide, subordinates don't suffer the same pains that Zaleznik writes about and Nielsen and Gypen describe in "The Subordinate's Predicaments." It's impossible to argue, of course, that Versatec's organization scheme creates no problems, but it is probably safe to say that these are of a different magnitude and are less destructive than problems caused by hierarchical designs that exacerbate fear of authority.

Another way to overcome some of the effects of the organizational structure, including the stress and pressures of a job, is to find nuturance and support at the workplace in the form of friends. In "When Friends Run the Business," Alan Ladd, Jr., Jay Kanter, and Gareth Wigan discuss the benefits of working with close friends. All three maintain that the friendships they have at work are very important to them and that they probably couldn't do their jobs as well if they didn't feel the support and sense of caring that the friendships bring. If more organizations nourished an atmosphere where people can become friends in the sense that Ladd, Kanter, and Wigan are, we might see less burn-out; people would know if others were in trouble before it was too late; men and women might be able to form friendly relationships without everyone assuming that a love affair was underway; subordinates and bosses might be able to talk to each other without assuming that negative statements will cause the relationship to fall apart; and, finally, with more positive emotions experienced at work, executives would likely spill over some of these at home, enhancing the home life as well.

Part Two of this book features articles about the difficulties men and women and different races have working together. Clearly, managers have to deal with a lot of these issues on a person-to-person level, often quickly, when an employee's behavior may be actionable. But many of the problems that women and blacks encounter have unseen roots. These are problems that may erupt.

In "Are You Hearing Enough Employee Concerns?" Mary P. Rowe and Michael Baker offer a way to make sure that festering problems surface. They describe the benefits to companies of having complaint channels for nonunion employees. With such structures in place, an employee who feels harassed can talk to someone in the organization in complete confidentiality and get help in dealing with a problem. The employee would also feel that the organization cares about the problem. Complaint channels are another way of overcoming the effects of hierarchy. They offer employees who are afraid to go to their bosses—especially when the boss is the offender—an opportunity to seek redress instead of quitting.

Articles in Part Three address the problems that beset employees because of their age as well as the difficulties managers have in understanding the changing needs of employees. In "Management of Differences," Warren H. Schmidt and Robert Tannenbaum explore why it is difficult for executives to handle conflicts and offer a wealth of suggestions for managers who want to turn a conflict into a problem-solving situation. They argue that the most important determinant of success is a manager's objectivity, which he or she achieves only by understanding his or her own motivation. Only then is a manager "in a better position to diagnose a situation accurately and to choose rationally the kind of behavior which is in the best interests of the organization."

In Part Four the selections explore the personal lives of employees and how a conflict of their personalities with the demands of their jobs can result in emotional pain and even death. The final three articles here will help managers understand how an individual's behavior affects the ability of a group to function, what responsibilities a superior has to help a difficult employee, and, finally, how to assess when a person is experiencing too much stress.

In "The Interpersonal Underworld," William C. Schutz offers a theory of interpersonal behavior that managers faced with an abrasive personality or a colleague entering into collusion with his subordinates will find helpful. Schutz writes: "No matter how much people try to keep interpersonal problems out by ignoring them, they will turn up in subtle forms such as loss of motivation, tiredness, or the group member's preoccupation with outside tasks; or they may get entangled directly with the solution of the task and have to be worked out in the body of the problem."

F. J. Roethlisberger notes in "The Administrator's Skill: Communication" that in order to do the job well, a superior needs to see that his or her own imperfections are normal and natural in order not to judge others so harshly. If Bob Lyons or the other executives whom Harry Levinson described could have been helped in the way Roethlisberger suggests, they might not have taken the ultimate punishment out on themselves.

Finally, in "How Much Stress Is Too Much?" Herbert Benson and Robert L. Allen discuss how executives, particularly at middle management levels, are prone to stress and they encourage organizations to help their executives balance pressures with stress-reduction programs. Stress influences the survival of the organization, and as numbers of the articles in this book have shown, drastically affects the work and home lives of employees.

It's Not Lonely Upstairs

An Interview with RENN ZAPHIROPOULOS

In 1969 Renn Zaphiropoulos and four other engineers founded Versatec, Inc. in Santa Clara, California to manufacture electrostatic printers, plotters, and dual-function printer-plotters for computers. Although the fledgling company was a latecomer in its field, it prospered and grew rapidly. In fact, today it outsells all competitors combined. It employs about 900 people in Santa Clara and abroad, and it maintains field services in more than 50 countries. In 1975 Xerox Corporation acquired the company.

In this interview Mr. Zaphiropoulos, president and chief executive officer of Versatec and vice president of advanced product development, Information Products Group, at Xerox, talks about the management philosophy that has worked so well at his company. He describes the organization as a series of concentric circles rather than as the conventional pyramid. He also discusses the value of celebration after achievement, the encouragement of creativity in problem solving, and the emphasis Versatec places on closeness and openness in relationships.

In four succeeding interviews, other employees show how this philosophy works. In the first two, William Lloyd, a vice president and founder, and Ian Turner, director of development and engineering, focus on innovation. In the last two, Bobbette Johnson, manager of employee relations and training, Cynthia Trainer, an assembler, and Vitória Cardoza, a quality assurance inspector, talk about the ambience of the company.

The interviews were conducted and edited by Pamela M. Banks, manuscript editor at *HBR*, and by David W. Ewing, managing editor at *HBR*.

HBR: **What made you and the others want to start this company?**

RENN ZAPHIROPOULOS: In our previous company the environment was frustrating. We were not in the command positions. We had to ask too many

Published in 1980.

questions before we could get going on anything new, so we left to do our own thing.

When we started out, we had two objectives, and the company has grown around them. They are still our objectives. One is to make money because that is a condition for survival. The other is to arrange a situation in which people look forward to coming to work. These two things have to go together. If you are too one-sided about making money, it becomes a sweatshop and people hate your guts. If you are too one-sided the other way, it becomes a country club. You cannot have either objective without the other.

Is it hard to keep this balance as you add new departments and layers of management?

When the general idea is that people should be put in an environment that encourages free communication, there is a de-emphasis of levels and status. We do this here merely by being the kind of people who are comfortable being close to others. These are not the kinds of things that anyone can do by following any sort of formula. You cannot say, "Now it is really important for me to communicate the problem; therefore, I'm going to go out and communicate."

I think what really has happened here is that the company ever since its inception has been fortuitously put together by people who really enjoy our form of management. And therefore, through 10 to 11 years now they have insisted that it continue. When someone comes in who thinks he's above somebody, he's almost immediately exposed. He becomes the kind of a thing that is bad taste.

The differences between people are only relative—man-made differences. We at the top are merely people who, because of our position, are supposed to have a broad perspective: we are supposed to see everything that's going on in the company.

When I'm talking with company people, I sometimes draw the organization as a series of concentric circles instead of as the usual pyramid. That helps to eliminate the notion of levels and status. [See Exhibit 1.]

That's a somewhat unconventional way of thinking about organizational relationships.

The trouble with the pyramid is that it accents up and down, and we attach values to up and down. Up is good, down is bad. If you're down, you're lower. Down is almost always lower in our value systems. It's like other opposites in values—black and white, light and dark. So the pyramid sets people's minds in a prejudicial fashion. They get conditioned to thinking that up is the only way to go.

What we want to say in our organization scheme is that an increase of responsibility is commensurate with a broadening of one's view. Now, the

Exhibit 1.   The Organization as a Series of Concentric Circles

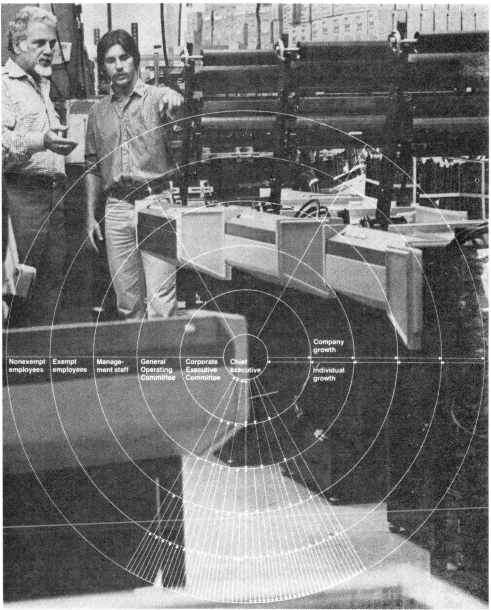

pyramid is legitimate in the sense that the higher you go on it, like a mountain, the more you can see. But in this circular design I look at things another way. It's a way of saying that a company doesn't just start from one point and go up or down. Rather, it starts from one point and radiates in all directions.

The circles are a symbol that all efforts lead to one thing, which is the company's survival.

If you're at the center of the circles, how do you relate to people in the outer circles?

You do it by being interesting. By not being too detailed, not becoming picayunish. Not meeting people only when disciplinary action is necessary. Talking over what is of mutual interest, not just writing memoranda or reports. Celebrating together when we do something right.

Do you publish this scheme for all employees? Is it part of the company literature?

No, we don't advertise it. It is something I have developed myself and use sometimes in talks about management. It is another way of saying we all have joined our fortunes together, and therefore we might as well cooperate. It's a way of looking at the company as a whole. If you look inside each department, you'll see a structure of authority that looks very much like a pyramid, so in that respect we're not radically different from many other companies.

Within this circular scheme there are still promotions and incentives and rewards?

Yes, and with them goes a certain amount of status that attends the person who is very good at his or her job. But no job is higher or lower in importance than another job—that is what we say with the circular design. How do you compare the importance of a salesman who overachieves his quota by 30% with a person who invents something new? You can't. You have to say that their values to the company have no levels or heights.

How do you communicate this idea to people in Versatec?

To begin with, we do it with the building itself. Take our offices. An office can be designed to bring together or to separate. My office here is the same size as the marketing vice president's across the way. Now my office could be bigger, and I could have a very good reason for that—for example, to have a conference room in here. That would be functional, that's okay. But suppose I have a rosewood desk when everybody else has only imitation rosewood. My rosewood desk wouldn't change the functions of my office. It would be designed only to separate me from other people.

What you're saying is, the more psychological separation there is, the poorer the communication.

I want someone coming in here to feel at ease because I like the person. If

I were the kind of person who didn't want to get close to people, I could make this place into a mausoleum so that when they walked in here they would really be afraid. Then I would always have the upper hand. But then I would lose the final game because the final game depends on the employee being enough at ease with me to reveal what he's doing so that I can understand his situation. In our organization circles, I'm not "on top" of others. I can only be on top on a pyramid.

What about the offices that don't have windows?

Oh, there are differences. But what I'm saying is, we try to minimize the differences and make sure that people do not use certain things for status symbols. Now there will be status symbols, no question about it. And there will be differences. But we try to make these things functional. We say the engineer has an office and a desk to put up his feet, while the operator has a lathe. The desk for the feet is very much a tool for the engineer who's thinking through a design, as the lathe is a tool for the operator.

Are there other ways in which you communicate your concept of the company?

Yes. We do as little standing on ceremony as possible. There are no private parking places, and there will never be any here because there's no need for that. Reserved parking, it seems to me, is based on the notion that the president's time is more valuable, which is fundamentally nonsense. What time I spend here is really by own business, and it will not be improved by somebody giving me a parking place in front. That is not a privilege that goes with rank. It's a privilege that separates me from the other people. So if I want to be friendly, I want to be able to talk to someone coming into the parking lot. If I have a white spot reserved where nobody else can park, that removes me from the rest of the people, and that attitude goes right down the line.

You emphasize the simple, everyday physical closeness of people in the company. Could you give other examples of how this promotes the spirit of openness and equal importance?

Many times I answer my own phone. People walk in and out of offices. Starting at four o'clock every Wednesday we have meetings where we spend a lot of time with various groups of people. Some of these are meetings for the whole company—for everyone working here. Off and on we all have drinks together and some food, and we talk. Seeing the top manager in the company is therefore not an event. If it's not an event, people don't think it is extraordinary, and if they don't think it's extraordinary, they don't think of the structure so much as up and down, as being a pyramid.

Isn't it difficult for you, with all the other demands on your time, to make yourself so accessible?

You see, that's the myth. If I want people to talk with me, I have to have relationships with them. Executives who fly around so that nobody sees them don't develop relationships. My own feeling is that most executives, when they begin to make a lot of money, almost feel embarrassed and guilty. They feel they have to do something to make it appear that the money is in the proper place. So they develop the syndrome of appearing very busy and put themselves at the end of a corridor behind a door with a whole bunch of doormen. People say it's lonely upstairs, but that's only if you close the door and stay out of sight.

Your philosophy, then, is that busyness is not good business, or at least, not good management.

The late Alan Watts, the philosopher who popularized Eastern thought in the West, affected quite a bit of my thinking, especially with his concept of the path of least resistance. The essence of any kind of success is to be able to say that a person's talents, natural talents, fit the requirements of the job. This is what I would say is working in an effortless manner. That is, you naturally fit what you're asked to do.

　　If that is the situation, then the person gets out the most for the amount of input he or she puts in. What I'm trying to stress is that people who come in here should really look forward to enjoying themselves. My definition of hard work is to go against your grain. If you are in a position in which things go along with your talents, it is not hard work anymore.

Suppose you have an engineer who is a very good engineer and has the talents you want but perhaps is not good at communicating. Do you tell him, "No, you don't fit," or do you work with him or her to develop skill at communicating?

The requirements of the job may be such that the engineer works individually. In that case, the communication problem isn't a serious one. The question is: If there is much of a disparity between what the person can do and what the job objectives are, what do you do about it? It all depends on how critical this disparity is to getting the work done. There is no way of having people or things be exactly what you want them to be, and I don't care if we're talking about employees, wives, husbands, kids, parents, church members, lodges, or foreign countries. There will always be some sort of disparity between what you want and what occurs with another person. So as a manager or an employee, no one is going to fit the demands of the company completely.

So if what you want from the engineer is a technical contribution, and that is what he can do with the "least effort," it doesn't matter so much if he's not good at communicating?

Yes, let me put it another way. I can never do everything. There are certain things I will overlook or not get to. Ideally, those things won't matter a great deal. What I should do depends on what we call the "critical path," that is, the truly necessary aspects of my job. The critical path is carrying the water when you go across the desert, and you give that job to a very competent person. Now, other things that are not as essential you give to others. What I'm saying is, the fit you look for between people and jobs depends a lot on how critical the jobs are to the success of the company.

For you, then, being accessible and communicating is part of the "critical path."

Absolutely, and that goes for many other managers. There have been people whose employment we've needed to terminate because they would not communicate, and their jobs required them to do so. For example, a large part of what an engineering manager should do is discuss designs with people. If that doesn't happen, the people starve for contact and the whole department begins to falter. So in that kind of situation we have to step in and do something about it.

Is there a corollary here, that sometimes you try to change the job to fit the person?

Oh sure, we are full of eccentrics, from what I'm told, and we just bend to suit their needs. If there's some star inventor sitting in a laboratory creating something important, we bend over backward not to require much communication from him or her. We work around it. But it has to be possible to work around it; that is, it must be possible to sit alone in that lab and stay on one of the critical paths without spending a lot of time talking. If we have to compensate too much, if it gets too tiring to hold hands with the person, we stop doing it.

We have been talking about communication, but the result you want at Versatec is innovation and creativity. How do you relate communication to the innovative spirit?

One of the worst things you can do is put people in situations where nobody cares about what is going on. In a lot of research laboratories, people sit in rooms and nobody pays much attention to what they've developed. The way to keep people innovative—constructively innovative—is to react to what they are doing. Your reaction can be positive or negative. You can say they are failing or they are doing something great. Both statements say that you care. They answer the person's question: "Am I doing something useful that anyone cares about? How am I doing?"

I think it's important to define the problem or need in its least constrained form. Creativity is the process of inventing new combinations of old things. If I have a screwdriver and a hammer, and I put them together in some new way with the screwdriver at one end and the hammer at the other, that's an invention. The hammer isn't new, the screwdriver isn't new, but the combination is original. Now, if I define the problem in a very narrow form, people won't invent anything. If I say, "Look, try to design a bottle this way," I limit the solution too much. I'm not giving enough room for manipulation. I'm not leaving enough risk and uncertainty about how to do it.

How do you present the problem then?

What I need first of all to do is to present a challenge—"Invent a new toner bottle that doesn't leak so that a person can put it on the system without ruining his hands or getting them dirty. You see what I mean? See what you can do. We'll meet in two or three months, okay?" Then, they've got the ball and maybe they'll invent something. It's got to matter to us whether they succeed, and there has to be full confidence that they will succeed, but also there's got to be some risk. They must see that things won't necessarily work out.

You leave them with some anxiety, in other words, as well as freedom?

One has to instill an anxiety about success for people to become productive. But it must be what I call manageable anxiety. It must be a challenge that doesn't break them down but that gives them an interest in living and solving new problems. If there isn't any anxiety, life is too easy and they atrophy.

Do they understand that there are penalties for failure?

It is understood that it is permissible to fail. It is also understood that it is preferable not to. A lot depends on how desperate they are to succeed. If they are very desperate about succeeding, they won't create anything new because of worry about the result. So they have to know that the maximum help will be given to bring about success. Almost everything we do here is very difficult, very risky, new. It goes without saying that the game we play is dangerous. But then it also goes without saying that life isn't worth living without danger. The attitude has to be one of mutual support—"Maybe it will work, maybe it won't, we'll have to do it together."

There is a kind of group pride, then.

The pride of working for an organization that is awake, progressive, that insists on excellence. We talk a lot about competence. We talk a lot about doing the job right, and if the job is not done right, the failure surfaces fast. And when it does, we take action to change the budget, the resource, the engineers—whatever must be corrected. People can feel almost chauvinistic about being members of such a group.

Can you give an example of when people here have felt like that?

Yes, when we got our first order for our wide plotter—it's a big machine, about six feet wide—we had what seemed like an impossible deadline. The order came in in June 1979, and the machine had to be delivered by September twentieth to an industrial show in Philadelphia—the first order for a new piece of equipment, and only a few months to construct it in.

Before the last 30 or so days of the job, I made a handwritten calender of tasks and due dates. We put it in the laboratory and checked off every day until time zero. In the space for certain days we drew little pictures of milestones like "All the parts are here" and "Test begins at this point."

You'd be surprised how eager the people were to come in and scratch off the day each job was done. There was a very strong interest in the approaching deadline. "Time zero is approaching, guys. Have you got everything?" "Is it really going?" "How are we doing?" "Don't tell me tomorrow we didn't do it!" A kind of crescendo built up. It's amazing what incredible things can happen when people tune in. It's like the business of resonance in physics, when all the frequencies match so there can be a transfer of energy.

Is the 30-day chart a technique regularly used?

Oh no. If you do something like that too often, it becomes phony and it won't work, like always smiling at someone.

Were the people who made that prodigious effort on the wide plotter rewarded?

We rode it out in record time—9:30 on a Tuesday night. I invited everybody who was there to my house for a big party that very evening. We played pool, we sang—lots of things. But the reward was in the celebration, in our feelings, you see, not in anything valuable in a monetary way.

You may give a person a bottle of Grand Marnier, you know, if he or she gets a special order the company wants. But the reward is like the ancient Greek wreath for the victor. The wreath was made of laurel, and laurel was a weed which had no value. The idea of the laurel wreath was to remove physical value from the reward. It was the event that was valuable in people's minds. No gold in the award, like the Romans later made it—in Greece the award was pure.

Now, there is a big difference in philosophy between making the award an expensive, gaudy thing and making the idea or event precious. And I believe that most of the people at an organization like Versatec are more grateful if their image is enhanced rather than just their wealth. Therefore, if you improve their image, you meet one of their important needs.

Do you ever get negative reactions to your rewards?

Yes, and I'll give you an example. We have a practice of awarding pins to employees for each five years of service. A lot of companies give five-year pins. When an employee has served five years, I ask the person to lunch with me. The person's supervisor, the vice president for the area, and a personnel department representative usually join us.

But once a lady here said, "I don't want to go to lunch with you." I said, "That's perfectly okay. I would be interested to know why if you want to tell me." She answered, "I think it's sort of a phony thing. Here you don't pay any attention to me for five years, and now it's a five-year pin just because I've been here that long. Big deal!"

I said, "Well, I guess it appears that way, doesn't it? But if I don't pay attention to you at the end of the five years, I pay less than I'm trying to now. And really it would be impractical, you understand, for me to spend time regularly with every employee. At least we make an organized effort once every five years to see you and say, 'Hey, how do you feel about things?' "

Do you think the woman felt she was being typed?

Certain people have a need to be individualistic. They want to be different. So when someone says, "Look, there's the president driving a five-year employee to lunch," their reaction is, "I am not going to be one of those."

My attitude is, "That's fine. I respect that. If you don't want to socialize with me, that's your business. But I am going to make the offer because I have to be true to myself." It gives me pleasure to invite someone to lunch whom I don't see normally and to take an hour or two to sit around and ask how things are going. I know that we could talk in my office, but I think with most people you want to get out of the framework of work and go to some place different and relax.

However, if this seems too mechanical to the other person, I will not argue. I have only made the offer, and in another five years I will make the same offer because that is what I want to do.

You've mentioned how your philosophy may affect a production effort or meeting a deadline. What about an example of innovation?

Well, we had a program called "gorilla." The gorilla project was the development of a very low-cost machine—a small, tabletop model of our standard electrostatic plotter. The project got that name after I wrote a sketchy memorandum to my boss at Xerox saying that we needed funds to produce a low-cost model in two and a half years. Of course we followed up the proposal with a budget, return-on-investment calculation, and so on. Presented with that proposal, the Xerox executive said, "Even a gorilla would think that that is a good plan." So we called it the gorilla project after that.

Gorilla went from me to Bill Lloyd, our vice president of research, development, and engineering and one of the most inventive people here.

Then he brought a fellow we recruited in England into the project—Ian Turner. He's now director of development and engineering after two years at Versatec. The new machine was announced last spring.

What does it do?

What it does is reduce the cost of a printer-plotter by about one-third. Doing this required a great deal of inventiveness because our printers and plotters don't work in a mechanical way but on the basis of semiconductor technology. New semiconductors have become available that are cheaper, and we have taken advantage of that and other innovations to invent a machine that works at much lower cost. It is very successful. Its development is right on schedule.

Earlier today you were out on the plant floor. Was it the gorilla project you were looking at?

I was downstairs looking at how a line of production for another project was doing, and I saw some machines sitting there alone. I asked if there was a problem with people. I was told we have shortages on the line and we cannot work on those machines, that maybe next week we will have the proper people there. I asked how the month was going. Were we going to have a crunch at the end?

Then somebody comes in and brings some Philippine egg rolls, and he says, "Hey, you want to eat some?" So he gives me a napkin and we eat the egg rolls on the line. Bill Lloyd comes down, and he eats an egg roll. And we discuss fishing at the same time. Then somebody nearby has a technical problem, so we go and look at it—the machine's not writing correctly. I am at the production line and everywhere else in the company at least twice a day.

Does the company use any organizational techniques to keep people in touch with each other?

We have what we call the Management Advisory Group—"MAG"—eight people who represent employees from all parts of the company. There's a person from marketing, one from manufacturing, one from cost control, and so on. They meet once a month and talk about the problems of the company.

What power does MAG have?

Advisory, but they can come straight to me or straight to our executive committee members and have a séance with them. MAG doesn't have to go through supervisors or channels.

It is a way for people at the periphery to tell top management how the hell things are going, and when something is wrong, we decide what's to be done about it. For a group to have value doesn't mean it has to make major policy decisions. If what it says is taken very seriously, it has quite a bit of influence.

Where are the policy problems discussed?

The Corporate Executive Committee does that. This group is the half dozen or so people who report directly to me, and they are what we call the inner circle. If you're in the inner circle, we say, you're supposed to have a perspective on the whole company's goals. You're supposed to think about your department—marketing or manufacturing or whatever—but you're also supposed to see how your department ties in with the fortunes of the company, and vice versa. The executive committee worries about general things like what businesses we're in and morale, not so much about operating problems.

And whose concern is operating problems?

Those are for the General Operating Committee, the people who really make things happen, the directors of quality analysis, industrial relations, manufacturing, engineering, field sales, and so on. The rest of the company reports to them. They meet periodically during the month. There are 18 of them. In the circular chart they are shown as the second circle out. Their perspective is one specific field of responsibility rather than what the whole company's doing.

In the Exhibit [see page 437] you have some smaller fields of responsibility shown within a director's field.

The next smaller field is for members of the management staff—about 60 people on this circle. The narrowest fields, shown on the next circle, are 250 or so people who, though not managers, are still exempt. On the other circle are the nonexempts—people like wire weavers, clerical workers, quality controllers.

But the circular scheme isn't really an organization chart.

No. It shows how closely all our functions are connected. It describes an attitude. It is not something we start with. It's something we end up with.

So management still has to resolve conflicts and make rules?

Of course. Business is, you might say, an activity that has rules. If it doesn't have rules, you don't know what the game is. As in tennis, you have to have lines to know what is a good shot and what is a bad shot. So we say we're going to have a structure and have certain people report to certain other people, and this goes clear to the center.

Now this is okay, except that employees have interests that often conflict with what the company wants to do. I can have a game outside of here that has other rules. Say my wife wants me to do something, wants me to be there at 5:30, but the company says we're having a meeting and it's not yet finished. Now the question is, how does one negotiate that? What do you do about conflicts between the games employees play outside the company and the games they play inside the company?

There's a universal game going on. Versatec is not the only game in town. It shouldn't be. What happens is that we must watch that the people who don't do a job right because of other conflicting games do not hurt the people adjacent to them or the people on the next circle. You can have a marvelous setup at the center that says this is the way the company should behave, but that center still must have feedback from the periphery.

What kind of feedback do you look for?

It depends whether you reward effort or results. Needless to say, we reward effort—for instance, an employee who has worked many years for us. But the thing we talk most about is results.

Life is very much responsibility for producing results, and effort does not compensate for lack of results. So if somebody says, "I'm busy," he's talking about effort—it's an activity-oriented statement. But when the person says, "This is what I've done," it's a different story. And it doesn't make any difference how long he took, because the ultimate thing is what he did, what really happened. Of course, the most marvelous thing is to do the least amount and get the most out of it. That's what I want people here to call efficiency.

Suppose you find that a person is not efficient, that he or she is not getting results. Do you feel a responsibility to keep him employed?

If I learn that my understanding of what a person could do is erroneous, that he or she doesn't meet the need, my responsibility is to tell him or her as fast as possible that I think I've made a mistake. It has to happen in a company like this that's growing at a rate of 40% per year.

Suppose we have a manufacturing manager who, let's say, is very good at producing 3 million printer-plotters for shipment per year. As the company grows, the job may totally outgrow him. He may be poor at getting 12 million printer-plotters out the door every year. The monitors and controls he used a few years ago may be useless now.

Or, take the star who does everything by himself, like the financial manager in a small organization. The organization grows, and pretty soon he needs a controller, then a receivables manager, a chief accountant, and so on. He's not right for the job anymore because he has to work through them. He can't be the star. I don't believe that a person is promoted to the level of his incompetence, as the Peter Principle says. What happens is more subtle. What happens is that the requirements of the job change.

Would you try to reassign the person instead of firing him?

Oh, of course, because the role of a manager is to arrange talent. It's the same as with a painting. Here is available talent sitting all around like paints. The question is, how do you put them together so that the composition is right? And then, if the composition isn't right, what do you do? You don't say that the red is wrong or the green is wrong. What you actually say is that the green should be red and that the red should be blue or a different shade of red. So you arrange, and if the arranging isn't right, you try to rearrange.

We have had people who were good engineers, but when they were made engineering managers they were not so good. So they became senior scientists, where they make just as much money but are better suited because of their talents and fears or wishes about communication.

Lots of executives think of being nice to people as quite time-consuming. But you see it as efficiency.

Yes, because if I can explain to people, by virtue of my relationship with them, the position we're in and the problems we have to solve, they'll go ahead and solve them. I don't have to hold their hands or crack the whip or direct their activities. Now, I cannot do that if I am apart from them, separate and distant. Because then, if I go to criticize someone, how am I going to make it possible for him or her to understand that what I'm saying is not hostile?

Is there any hindrance to continuing this management style that you have, this desire to have communication radiating from the center out and from the periphery toward the center?

It all depends on who runs the company in the future. It depends on who the people coming in are, and if top management changes, the company will change. There are many ways to manage people. We, as I say, are the kind of people who enjoy this. I think there are many people here today who believe in the present philosophy—they are very much disciples of it.

> **Bill Lloyd,** *vice president of research, development, and engineering:*
> My reason for wanting to form a company had to do with the thought of developing something new and exciting that would at the same time offer us the opportunity to run an organization in a different way.

I had a strong interest in making a printer product out of the technology I'd been using, and the five of us who founded Versatec wanted more freedom to manage business in our own style.

HBR: **Was it your invention that this company was formed around?**

Well, yes. It developed out of a number of inventions I had in the field of electrography and the product development that followed.

It's been much easier to get new product developments started in our own company. If someone's got an idea he wants to work on, he doesn't have to interface with anyone else or any other group. It's all internal, and within budget constraints we each do our own thing.

In order to have that freedom, we normally budget approximately one-quarter of the research budget every year for what we call "blue sky activities." These are projects that are undefined at the beginning of the year and that are totally controlled by the people in this department.

What have some of those activities been?

About a year ago we decided that using our kind of equipment for color looked interesting. Marketing certainly wouldn't support nor did they want anything to do with color at that point, so we took some money out of our blue sky funds and made some color samples that satisfied our need to see what could be done with this technology. And then we let it lie.

When marketing finally comes around and says, "Hey, we want a color device," we'll be able to talk intelligently about it. This kind of thing is very important to us.

There are other things we've done with blue sky money that have improved our technology. We've looked into different techniques for doing things we've been doing in particular ways for a long time—as an example, the use of hybrid technology. It's an old technology, but we hadn't been using it in high voltage devices. Someone said, "I want to look into the use of hybrids," so he made use of some blue sky funds. As a result, today most of our products are made with hybrids, which save us money and use less board space, and you know, while this may not be a major advance, it is of importance to the company.

Can anybody initiate an idea?

Absolutely. Within the RD&E organization, anyone can come up with an idea and try to promote it within the department and then sell it to management.

What do you have to go through to turn an idea into a regular project, one that's not a blue sky project?

The engineers are the most likely to initiate and promote an idea, but anyone can. Generally that person brings it to one of the managers' attention—the head of research, the head of systems, or the head of engineering—and tries to get funding for it.

One thing this company is very good at, unlike many larger companies, is being so flexible that if we start a program and find that it's a bummer and there's a better one, we can change in midstream and say, "The heck with the other one. It's not the right one. Let's go with this one." We don't get too hung up on pet projects.

Just recently someone spent a lot of his own time at home building a wooden mock-up and demonstrating a new approach to one of our wide plotter projects. He did an excellent job; and we all admired his stamina and ability. When we finally decided which way to go with that product, we decided against his approach. Here was a case of a guy promoting something that lost.

That's not often the case. When people really get turned on to an idea, we usually go along with it, and more often than not, that idea will have something to do with improving our present product line or describing a new product concept.

Normally we try to sell marketing on new ideas. In the early stages of this company almost all new product ideas came from marketing. Today I would say that some new product ideas come from engineering, and some from marketing. Incidentally, I believe that RD&E has been just as successful as marketing in judging the value and even the marketability of products.

This kind of flexibility must've been something you wanted to bring to the company too.

Absolutely. We tend to let people do what they do well the way they want to do it rather than try to influence them to come around to someone else's method of doing things.

The three people that report to me vary tremendously in the way they manage each of their groups. One manages a systems activity, one manages a research activity, and one manages the development and engineering arm. And I don't try to change or influence their behavior. That's up to them.

We have total informality with each other. We have interesting conversations and interplay, and we don't have a structure that would cause anyone to be concerned about telling me, "That's wrong." They say it. We use a lot of very plain language. We don't attempt to be too gentle with one another in discussions about technology or management techniques.

The function of the top management of the company varies from time to time. There are times when we keep our noses out of certain areas that are working well. But if some area has serious trouble functioning, all of us become involved in its support or management.

We're not so structured that I sit up here and say to somebody, "You do down and solve that problem." I get the calls, and I decide whether I should send someone else down to solve the problems or whether I should go down myself. Normally I find that I do a lot of it—partly because I like to and partly because I'm probably best at it because I have the most experience with some of the older products.

What have you found to be most important in managing creative people?

I think a lot of freedom is probably the key element. I think it's very difficult to get creative people to accept someone else's ideas. I think creative people tend to want to do their own thing, and I find it difficult to force my ideas on people.

There are times, of course, when we get to a head-butting stage, where someone has to yield, and more often than not that's me. Occasionally I do win out and get my way. It's difficult to manage creative people. And there is no single formula. I think that everyone I've known who's creative has had a different personality and therefore that a different interface must occur.

Would you say that the company has brought about most of the changes that you were hoping to make in forming it?

I think so. I think that we are probably not as good today at keeping people happy as we were in the earlier days, though.

Oh, why is that?

I think it has to do with what happens as we grow—people don't get the personal attention they used to, and I think creative people demand a lot of attention, no matter what the field. People like to be talked to and feel that they're part of the same team. I think that as we grow people get a little farther apart. That's when you start to feel the need for rewards other than money.

One of the things we can do to supplement financial reward is to have a close relationship with the people who work here. I socialize with the people in my department and with many people in other departments.

I just took a group out fishing on my boat this past weekend. I believe that there is a real benefit to the company and to each of us in this type of socializing in that the next time a business interface with that person occurs it will prove to be more comfortable and very likely more productive.

We try to operate according to what people here want. We're a very people-oriented company.

> *Ian Turner, director of development and engineering:*
> A company needs to have the ability to innovate built right into its structure. Accountability and responsibility should be coincident. What happens in most companies is that the manager says, "I hold you responsible, but I'm going to approve everything you do." Worse than

that, quite often there are large committees of people whose opinions about a new idea must be congruent before any progress can be made. And above that level there is usually nobody. So nobody is accountable. It's a committee with some guys responsible over here and other guys accountable somewhere else. That means that if one person dissents or misses a meeting, you get into a morass with nothing coming out of it.

Versatec understands that problem. What it says is that one person is champion; one person has the responsibility and is also held accountable and is given the tools to make it all come true.

HBR: What kind of tools are you given here?

Freedom. It's everything. It includes powers of signature, the chance to organize, the right to veto other people's ideas and sometimes to be terribly autocratic. You can build teams the way you want to and not have other people second-guessing you. It all comes back to the fact that the guy who does the innovation is seen to be in control of what happens. And you have a power over the system.

Now, as it turns out, I don't use all the power. My own style is very participative. I like to generate agreement as a group. But the point is that there is a way it can be controlled from a single point. We don't have some poor devil down here running this bit, and some other poor devil down there running that bit, and no consistency in the baseline.

How do you generate this agreement?

I think you have to get what's called goal congruence. You have to paint the dream in space so vividly and so realistically that everyone sitting at the baseline will say, "I like that dream too" and "We will all work toward it." The way you specify the dream has got to be sufficiently vague that they don't see conflict with their own activities. Somebody down in the quality assurance department, for example, has to be able to say, "I see what my job is with respect to getting it out the door." And therefore, he becomes a positive rather than a negative power.

The way I do that is that I don't sit in my office very much. I don't usually shut the door. I walk around a lot. I don't use the telephone unless it's absolutely necessary. I walk to people's offices to set up meetings, and I talk a lot.

I talk about the objectives. I talk about the dream. But I talk about it in a semi-nebulous way so that nobody can become a bureaucratic role player and say, "Hey, the plan said this." The concept is what we're hanging onto. It says we're going to try to achieve this goal, and the route toward it is arbitrary to some extent.

So you give the people under you a kind of freedom too?

Yes, it applies all the way down the chain, but they only get freedom if their dream coincides. My job is to watch them work without directly controlling them. Every so often we'll go into a three-hour discussion about the manner in which their procedures differ from what I think should happen. Rather than say "Do this, do that," it's a case of saying, "Aren't we all trying to get to this point?" and "What you're doing doesn't seem to be contributing in the way I think it should." The only thing that I have is a kind of power of veto, but you rarely actually have to use it if you discuss every problem thoroughly.

The management team that works directly for me is very social. We're definitely friends as distinct from co-workers. We're very open about our failings and our strengths. They can attack me on my weaknesses, which I don't defend. I've got weaknesses. Other guys have got weaknesses.

We spend a lot of time making sure that we cover for each other. If I go out of the office for a month, any one of the guys can run the whole show. They may not do it quite the way I would, but they have all the same information at their disposal, so they know roughly where the whole thing is going.

What interested you about coming to Versatec?

I worked in research originally—I was a physicist by training—but I very rarely took a problem to solution and got the chance to make it into a product. I saw coming here two and a half years ago as a chance to innovate and to take the whole thing right through for the first time.

Are you working on inventions of your own now?

Yes and no. I don't make as much technical contributions as I used to. I don't sit down and draw diagrams and compute things. What I do do is sit in brainstorming meetings with other people who have their own points of view. I try to create an atmosphere which lets people be creative. I stop people from shooting each other down too early.

In this kind of team meeting, somebody may say, "But plastic bends" and someone else may say, "Ah, we could use the fact that it bends," and then someone else builds on that, and over a half an hour an idea starts to grow. It's the person who points it out who gets to be considered the inventor, but he doesn't actually invent the thing.

It's very rare that you can point to one person and say, "He did it." I don't believe there's ever been a patent like that that's any good. We deal patents out so that we all get our names on one or more of the patents that are issued as a result of group brainstorming.

In these meetings do you have not only the managers but also the engineers and the draftsmen?

Yes, anybody who's around. We're very informal about it. I don't call a meeting. What often will happen is that an engineer will be working on something and will come to a problem. And I'll go and sit on the end of his desk and say, "How're you going with this?" During the course of the conversation, somebody else will walk past and we'll say, "Hey, what do you think?" Then the meeting kind of grows impromptu. A set of ideas comes in. You watch them crystallize over the next week or so.

I can spend 20 minutes with one of the engineers and then go off to somebody else as a result of what he wants and say, "Why don't you two talk about that?"

Have you had the chance to be innovative that you wanted at Versatec?

Yes, on many levels of innovation. In the case of the V80—the gorilla project, which is the machine I'm most involved with right now—there were no examples to extrapolate from. We looked at things that had very loose connections. When you try to create a solution to a design problem, what you don't do is plan the route to it. Otherwise, you'll get exactly what you expect and there'll be no room for innovation.

For the V80, the specification was to make a graphics output printer that would make marks on paper at two inches a second for a price of about $3,000. Now, there is no easy way to do that. It turns out that the price for existing technologies is $10,000 to $12,000. It needed innovation at the very outset to be successful.

That innovation wasn't one single idea. It had to be a total package that somehow fitted together and that minimized the cost.

How did you get that package?

That's to ask how the design process normally goes.

What we started with was the notion that the product is a set of things that must happen. It's made up of sets of objects—what we call "subsystems." At the very limit there are parts. Some of these parts relate together to do something, and their functions may be overlapped.

The first thing you have to do is get agreement on what the subsystems are and what they must do. The perception of a set of things varies according to the designers working on them. People think their perceptions of the world are right. If you get two guys looking at something differently and they haven't communicated that fact, the communication breaks down, and they don't even know why. So what I do is say, "Let's move to some common ground that says we can at least communicate about what we're doing."

It takes about a month to get agreement on which subsystems to talk about. If you don't do this first step, you'll have all kinds of design problems downstream.

What's the next step as you see it?

Then you sit down with the designers and discuss specific solutions for each subsystem problem. From there on, you come to conclusions about what is critical to the design. You discuss whether A is more fundamental than B and whether B is more fundamental than C. After a while it becomes pretty obvious to all of them which things are going to kill them and which ones aren't, until eventually the team commits. Not only are they committed to the idea of what the subsystems are, to what is special and personal to the team that they're going to deal with, but they've also roughly agreed on the order in which things should go and how important they are from a cost and a design point of view.

Then what you do is look at the numbers of solutions you've got for each subsystem design problem, and there aren't many—probably two or three. Whichever solution you choose is very cost sensitive. It also probably interacts with the rest of the system a lot.

Next you say, "If I pick this one, what's its effect on this other subsystem?" Now, you just beat down these lines of reasoning as far as you've got time, money, effort, and intellect to do. You rapidly see an end to some of these lines. You often find that one's impossible or that another doesn't meet the product specs. Or people will say, "That's terrible. I bet they'll run out of plastic in two years' time" or "That process is unreliable" and so on.

How long does this design process take?

Oh, you spend three, four, or five months sketching things out, doing research on the cost of components, brainstorming for solutions—because now you're actually into the creative phase. That's when you say, "If I'm clever, I can reduce the criticality of this factor or that. I could actually find ten more total solutions by thinking of one idea that may have never been thought up before."

When you've done that, you've really got the whole thing cracked. At that point, you haven't drawn a single design parameter. You've got a few grubby sketches, a few notes, and probably a thousand hours of conversation. But the team is committed to the approach. You don't get people later saying, "Did we decide that? Maybe it was wrong."

For this gorilla project, you went all through this kind of process?

Absolutely, and we found some interesting things as a result. We found that the electrical interconnection between our writing head and the electronics which drive it is critical to the design. That means the wires. Who would have thought the wires so important? But there are 128 of them, each with difficult technical problems, and how to put them together had always been designed last.

It turns out that that component was not only costing a lot, it was dominating a lot of other subsystems in the machine. There had been lots of Band-Aid solutions used to correct the mistakes that had been made.

Gorilla was made possible by finding the criticality of that one component and designing the whole machine around it.

Renn Zaphiropoulos says he likes to think of this company as a series of concentric circles. Have you heard him talk about this?

Yes, and I think that that picture is very accurate. The caliber of a manager is how far out toward the periphery he can retain contact. Companies get quite good but dried up managers who've got six people working for them, and those six people they know well and work well with. But the next level down, nothing—no contact, no communication, no leadership. That guy is a caretaker manager really. He doesn't influence the spirit or the morale of the team. He's the guy who's in his office with a real battle-ax secretary whose orders are to prevent anyone from talking to him unless he chooses.

If you find a manager who is recognized four or five levels down—they speak to him and smile—he really has a talent that's superior to that other person from a human point of view. It doesn't mean attention to detail. It means contact. His leadership influences many people.

Renn, for example, goes right down. He goes very far out to the periphery of this organization. Face-to-face communication with lower-level people is critical.

I get people stomping in here red in the face and saying, "Let me tell you what's going wrong." Probably only 3% of all the grumbles come to me that way, but I respond completely to that 3%. At least that way people feel that the leadership is sensitive.

How do you prevent the company's self-assurance from getting in the way of further innovation?

You don't, unfortunately. There's a dilution that probably occurs anywhere. Take the executive group: it's a unique bunch of people, a rare group to put together in one place—outrageous personalities and talents. They recruit other people who are slightly less outrageous and perhaps slightly less talented for positions below them. And so on down. By the time you get to the lower levels in the organization, it's just a cross section of society.

That's fine because the leadership is still outrageous. But as the company grows, the lower levels start to rise in power without being reselected for the growing jobs that they have. So after a time, you end up with less of the original type of talent at the top levels than you would like. You start to get analysts and the kind of person who shuts his office door. You begin to see a dilution of the company's theme.

What if you have an engineer who feels he has to shut the door because he's trying to work out a design problem? Do you mind if he says, "I really have to concentrate by myself for the day"? Do people feel free to work that way too if they need to?

Yes, in fact the door is a very useful tool. The door shut is a symbol that says "Right now I don't want to be disturbed" without having to direct a secretary to say "Go away" and thus create a barrier between oneself and someone else. If you open the door again, people will put their heads around the door and start talking.

What kind of reward do you find that creative people working under you are most interested in getting?

In my environment, I think 50% peer accolade and 50% approval from me and the other managers. Once they get a competitive salary, money is no longer a driving force for most creative people.

So when somebody here succeeds in presenting an innovative idea, an upgrade in salary is not necessarily used as the reward?

Money is used, but it's expected anyway, so it's not a reward. If you do well, you expect to get more money. That's built into the philosophy of the society; therefore, it goes away as an incentive. It would be negative if you didn't give it, but it's not positive when you do give it.

The day after people get their raises, they feel the same as they did the day before. At the time, they enjoyed the experience of being told; it has no motivational aspects after that. On one project recently some people worked late at night very often, so we wrote up a citation—The "You Want It When?" Award for Insane Behavior. We had them printed up and put into little scrolls. There were about 12 of them.

We took the people out to lunch, gave them a slap-up Chinese meal and then a humorous but full presentation of the scrolls that said in effect, "We appreciate this and you didn't go unnoticed." These are the kinds of rewards that mean the most.

> **Bobbette Johnson**, *manager of employee relations and training:*
> I'm a sort of vocal, "can-do," opinionated person and also a woman, and I have worked in personnel departments where I got silent messages which said, "Sit down, shut up, and don't rock the boat." At Versatec I get verbal messages which say, "It's quite all right to stand up, sound off, and rock the boat." I need that in a work environment for myself. I have had the opportunity to do that, which is why I have stayed with the company for six years.

We at Versatec encourage people to be bold, which suggests that you don't simply sit still for things, or take orders, or do something just because someone in a revered position tells you to do it. You do it because you believe that person to be right or to be just.

We have several recourses here—the Management Advisory Group is one of them—which allow any kind of rules or practices to be challenged and explored. If we were a company that took an authoritarian point of view, we wouldn't bother to create such organizations.

HBR: **Has the Management Advisory Group been created since you've been here?**

Yes, MAG was created about five years ago to formalize something we were already doing informally. Employees have always challenged things here. Management here has always been visible and approachable. The problem-solving path, though, as we get larger is longer, and MAG shortens that path so that comments that come from the outer levels of our organization can go on a direct express to this inner level. MAG is just a formal expression of what we've always done naturally.

Where did the idea for it come from?

It came from Renn.

If you think back over the MAG meetings you've been to, what do you remember MAG challenging and influencing?

Small changes in the company have come as a result of creating an awareness in management that there are problems. For example, the group was instrumental in creating smoking and nonsmoking sections in the cafeteria recently and in establishing a mileage reimbursement increase because of the escalating gas prices.

People wanted a way to voice reactions to the cafeteria that weren't positive, so we created an anonymous hotline. Employees can put reactions into a box. They're gathered and responded to weekly by the cafeteria staff and posted in a public place in the cafeteria. It's this kind of thing that MAG influences.

Another thing that comes to mind is the fact that the Management Advisory Group got together with the Safety Committee and took some photographs of areas that showed aisles that were not kept clear, debris not promptly removed, and so on. People in both of those groups created an awareness on the executive level of how bad and unsafe, from their point of view, housekeeping was.

What did top management do about it?

As a result of that, we instituted tally sheets and formalized reporting procedures by our Safety Committee to make sure that these areas would be kept tidy. And management implemented things that were possible to do, such as having our facilities technician establish gathering points for waste material.

Our product uses a lot of paper, and in testing it we create a mountain of paper. We decided to contract with an outside service to pick it up.

Can anyone at the company serve as a MAG member?

No, only nonsupervisory, nonmanagement people serve on MAG. Our management staff meetings, general operating committee meetings, executive staff meetings, and operations group meetings—which are for everybody who is exempt at the company—are established vehicles for bringing supervisors' and managers' problems to the surface. People who deal in nonmanagement, nonsupervisory areas—people who don't have this communication vehicle—need one, and MAG is it. People in the professional ranks are usually more concerned about issues other than the sort of thing we talk about at MAG.

Everybody in the company has a way of upward communication, of problem identification and reaching a solution. It's the quality thing, I guess. MAG is just offering the same opportunity that one segment has to the other segment, that's all.

One MAG member today introduced himself as a research chemist. Is his membership inconsistent with the others?

Not really, because he was a guest. He may have been filling in for someone who was away, or he may have asked to attend a meeting. At the end of the MAG meeting minutes, we publish an invitation to people to sit in on meetings and to serve as future members. MAG members whose terms in office are over often choose their replacements from among the guests.

Who gets the minutes?

Everybody in the company.

Why is membership arranged this way instead of through election by employees?

They are elected by the MAG members themselves, not by co-workers. The MAG members say, "Yes, I want Joe to become part of this group."

MAG has this arrangement so that the group won't lose credibility.

They can say, "Look, the eight of us who are members know that John Doe, in our collective opinion, is a raving maniac and we don't want him to represent what happens at this group. We don't think that John could correctly repeat one-two-three to somebody without having it come out four-five-six." So rather than the group having to deal with a person it gets stuck with, it has the option of saying, "Yes, we respect John Doe. We think he's going to do a good job. We wish him to join us."

Another reason we don't have election by co-workers is that it seems to suggest unions, and it almost implies that people here need representation, which isn't really the case.

Also, I think it would be administratively burdensome. The MAG members have short terms of office—three months extendable to six. You can see that with eight members and several guests and the many Versatec departments that would be having elections, it would soon become very cumbersome.

What happens is that the member who is about to exit lets everybody in his department know via a memo that says something like: "My term of membership in MAG is about up. I seek the names or the contact of those of you who are interested in exploring the group. Come with me as a guest to see if you want to throw your hat into the ring for three months."

Many members serve three months and then say, "I'm involved in the activities here and I want to see this action item through, so I will opt for another three months."

And can the people in the department say, "No, we don't want you"?

It's possible, but it never has happened.

Why are the terms of office so short?

We used to have six months and a year as terms. The reason that we feel the shorter term is beneficial is that the more people we get to participate, the more points of view the group gets to deal with. It just makes the group more relevant to the needs of everybody instead of just relevant to the needs of a few who have the long tenure.

Where are the MAG meetings usually held?

In our main meeting rooms. One has a fancy table custom-built for this building by Renn and others on the management staff. When I started with the company, all the tables in our conference rooms were homemade. They were built at Renn's house.

Wasn't one of your marketing vice presidents—Milt Reed—at today's MAG meeting?

Yes, executives and directors attend as management representatives because they can be a source of information to the group. They can say things like "Here's what I know about the flex-time decision" and give the straight scoop.

The executive or director also gets information from the group. He learns what people have on their minds and can relay that to his peers when he goes to their meetings, just as Milt did, for example, when he took up the issue of employees feeling so strongly about late performance reviews. The day after the MAG meeting in which this issue came up, there was a management staff meeting in which for 30 minutes Milt discussed the concern that had been brought to his attention through the MAG people.

So now personnel lets Renn know when there is a review that's late. He will then contact the supervisor and say, "If you wish me to make this employee's pay retroactive, then you must tell me why he's getting his performance review late."

Do supervisors ever attend MAG meetings?

No, because supervisors are several management tiers down and are not necessarily in an appropriate place to be able to give information. Our top management is in a place to be helpful to the group. In addition, the supervisors may be part of the problem being brought up.

Is there antagonism generated then among the supervisors when they hear there's a MAG meeting coming up?

Sometimes, yes, because MAG brings up issues that they may not want to deal with.

Do the supervisors have any vehicle for voicing their opinions and complaints?

Yes, the management staff meeting. There they sometimes identify the Management Advisory Group as a problem.

But there are lots of ways to solve the problems that come up here. MAG is just one of many employee options.

Out of all the issues that came up today, which one were you especially glad to hear?

I was glad to hear all of them articulated, especially the action steps we have taken toward issuing reviews on time and reducing the danger of driving into the busy traffic outside our building. The purpose of this group is to deal with problems that affect everyone in the company, not department problems or personal things.

We are all concerned about the traffic, for instance. In the last year and a half, this has become an issue. It was brought up again and again at MAG meetings. Renn said, "It seems ridiculous to me that we can't make any headway. Make sure that a MAG person, myself, and anyone else able to influence the outcome are clued in on when the next City of Santa Clara meeting is held to discuss traffic."

So one of the MAG members took on the role of expediter. He talked with Renn and the personnel director, and they all went down to the meeting together to make a plea to have a traffic light put in at our intersection. The result is that the city has agreed to put a light in a year from now—quick for them, they say.

Do you remember anything coming up in one of the meetings that Renn Zaphiropoulos has called for the whole company which made you feel that the people in this company were working together more than they might have without his leadership?

I guess the last total company announcement that Renn made was last fall. He called us together in the parking lot for what he called a "bold finish" party. It was to create an awareness of where we all were in relation to meeting our goal for the end of the year, where we wanted to be, and the fact that we wanted to work together as a team and with the understanding that all our jobs were different but important to meeting the goal.

How did you find people reacting to what Renn said about this?

The comments I have heard to Renn's addresses, including this one, have been generally favorable. People who are new to our company and who come from companies of comparable size or larger ones tell us that before they came here they rarely saw a company president and that if they did it was by "Hey, that fella crossing the floor way over there is our president." Rarely was there a time when he got out into a parking lot with a band and beer and dancing and tomfoolery as our president does.

I think that Renn's philosophy of quick response to MAG establishes its credibility. Renn sets the tone for it, and I believe that the people who visit this group as management representatives follow that philosophy through. I certainly try to, and I think that that's part of the reason MAG works.

Do you think it could function without Renn being here?

I think that it would function on its own as long as whoever was managing the company at the uppermost levels of it continued Renn's practice of being a living expression of the belief that employees have worth and should be responded to.

I believe that MAG is going strong because it actually solves problems. It really does involve the participation of the workers who have the problems themselves and who represent others like them. I think MAG's a strongly working kind of thing that contributes to the betterment of the company.

You know, I think Versatec is a place of many options that express an individual's preference, an individual's feeling about what's appropriate for tackling issues.

Cynthia Trainer, *chairman of the Management Advisory Group:*
I weave wires onto boards on what we call "the head" in a Versatec machine. That's where the wires that make the marks on the paper connect with the power supply. I've been here six months, and I'm now a head weaver II. The wires have to be woven, soldered, and cleaned. You make mistakes, you fix them, which isn't easy when you have thousands of wires.

Vitória (Vickie) Cardoza, *member of the Management Advisory Group:*
I'm a quality assurance inspector, and I've been here a year.

HBR: **How does someone get to be on MAG?**

VICKIE: You're chosen by MAG. I really wanted to get into MAG, so when one of the MAG members left the company, she asked me if I'd like to take her place, and I said, "Yes, I really would."

Had you been a guest at the meeting?

VICKIE: No, but I had wanted to go. Being a guest is usually how MAG chooses its new members. Each member serves a term of three to six months, and then someone new is chosen from the department he or she represents.

CYNTHIA: At the end of the MAG minutes, which every employee gets in printed form, there's a form you can fill out with your name and department to say, "I'm interested in being a guest at MAG."

How does someone get to be chairperson of MAG?

CYNTHIA: You're elected by the eight MAG members. You're nominated from among the eight members. I was the only person nominated, but I think a lot of people don't want the responsibility. It's a lot of extra work. I put in a lot of my own time that I don't put on my time card. You've got to really want to help, to get things going and be concerned about company problems—not just your own job's, but everyone's.

How do you find out what is of concern to the people you represent?

CYNTHIA: Sometimes people will say, "I want to talk to you," so you meet with them. As soon as the people in the headroom found out I was in MAG, they brought me so many things. "I want this brought up, I want that brought up." You know, they had all these questions and problems.

Also, there's a suggestion box. People can put their concerns in there. Others write their problems on slips of paper and leave them in my tool box.

VICKIE: Most of the time, with me anyway, they approach me and say, "Gee, I've got a big problem. How about helping me out? Can you bring this up at MAG?" I listen to them and take notes and then investigate. Some things I have to do a little research on before I bring them up.

Usually, my way of handling it is to look into the problem myself. If I can't find help or answers to their questions, then I'll bring it up at MAG.

CYNTHIA: A lot of times problems are covered by policies in the personnel manual, which we all have. I also have a log of minutes from day one when the committee was started, too, so I have all these minutes I can go back through and see what the decision was at another time to answer a question, and then it's not necessary to bring it up again.

And sometimes it's just common sense. Somebody once said, "I got a nail in my tire the other day. Take my complaint to MAG." That was really a matter for the facilities crew to clean up.

As you think over yesterday's MAG meeting, what do you remember as being important?

VICKIE: I felt it was a little argumental at times, but that's because we—the MAG members—are pressured by the people. They feel strong about certain subjects, and we try to bring them out the best we can, even if it's just the privilege of playing a radio or requiring that performance reviews be issued on time, as it was in yesterday's meeting. And we ourselves want to be heard too.

If it takes a little bit of argument, you've got to give it to MAG. Otherwise, nothing will be solved.

The things that I was mentioning yesterday—performance reviews being late and radios at work—are little things to some people. I realize that. But they are very important to the rest of the people who are out here working every day, so I try to fight for them.

CYNTHIA: Reviews aren't considered little.

VICKIE: Well, maybe insignificant to other people. But to these people here, it means a lot. And when they come in on Saturdays, they like to have a few more privileges like playing a radio. They are getting extra pay, but then it's the weekend. It's their day off. The company's asked, "Will you help us out?" It's not mandatory, coming in on Saturdays—Versatec is great that way. But we want to make money for the company, we want to make everyone happy, so we say, "Yeah, we're coming in."

So the radios are not unimportant either?

VICKIE: Right, and I don't really think they're a hazard. Not everybody brings a radio. There's usually just one in each department if any at all.

CYNTHIA: The thing is, there's the other side—it depends on your work, and people don't all like the same kind of music.

When I'm working on a wide plotter, if I miss one little tiny wire, I have to go back and find that mistake, and if I've already soldered one side, the whole head is ruined. Any noise where I work is really distracting.

I felt I should cut the discussion short yesterday because it was out of our hands anyway. There's a company policy against radios.

VICKIE: But you should allow people to express themselves in whatever way they can.

CYNTHIA: Right, but when you have so much business to conduct in two hours, you've got to stick to essential business.

Would you say that there was some more essential issue that came up yesterday?

VICKIE: I thought performance review was really the most important issue.

How often are you supposed to get reviews?

VICKIE: Three months after your're hired, and then after that it's every six months. The paperwork gets to the supervisors in plenty of time, so reviews should be given to the employees on time too.

Why don't you like getting them late?

CYNTHIA: Because of the pay. If a review is late, then your raise, if you get one, starts late.

VICKIE: It's not only the pay that's important. It's the supervisor's evaluation of your performance. We like to know how we stand here in the company. How can we improve ourselves? If we're not told this, we'll just continue in our old patterns.

Of course we all like to get a raise at review time. Who doesn't? This is the world, and you've got to make money to survive. Things are getting tighter every day, so it's nice to get an evaluation. Any time your supervisors want to give you their own opinions of your performance, I think it's a great thing.

And if you feel like you need improvement, then, you know, you'll say, "I'm going to get with it because I really like it here and I want to learn and progress."

Renn Zaphiropoulos says he likes to think of the company as a series of circles

because he feels that all of you are working side by side, that you're all more or less on the same level. Does it seem that way to you?

VICKIE: We're on a first-name basis—everyone, even Renn. It's like a friendly family here. You see Renn around and you say "Hi," and he always acknowledges you.

CYNTHIA: You see him a lot in the headroom, too. The headroom, I guess, is kind of a central point as far as manufacturing goes. He takes people through, and he comes around to see what's going on. It's kind of neat, you know. He'll say, "Hello. Good morning. How are you?"

VICKIE: That's something you don't see in very many companies. Usually a president or a vice president or people in high offices will stay in their own areas, but he always comes around and makes us feel very comfortable and happy.

What about the person from management who was at the MAG meeting yesterday?

CYNTHIA: He's one of the ones who's very open. He's there to represent top management, but he also brings his own viewpoint in. In the discussion yesterday, he would explain things and make you understand why something's got to be done a certain way instead of just telling you, "This is it."

VICKIE: He makes sure that if the topic needs working on, he'll get right down to the bottom of it. He won't let things slide, no matter how little they are. If it's important to us, he'll be right there to back us up.

CYNTHIA: That's the way it is here for most things. If I really need something done or have a question, I can demand to be answered and I'll get an answer from somewhere. I know if my managers don't know, I can go to their manager or I can go to MAG. We have so many different places to take problems to.

VICKIE: That's what's good about this company. We have an open door policy, and everyone who works for Versatec can speak through it to their benefit.

CYNTHIA: And if you do speak, you don't have to worry about losing your job.

28

When Friends Run the Business

Interviews with ALAN LADD, JR., JAY KANTER, and GARETH WIGAN

In the summer of 1979, Alan Ladd, Jr., Jay Kanter, and Gareth Wigan resigned their top positions in the motion picture division of Twentieth Century-Fox over, among other things, a major dispute concerning the payment of bonus money to production people. After a few months, Ladd founded The Ladd Company, an independent film production group, in partnership with Warner Communications Inc., where Kanter and Wigan continue their creative roles as heads of production.

A couple of things stand out in this simple chronology. First, the people at the top of a large division—which in 1978 had received 33 Academy Award nominations and which had just produced the largest single money-making film in the industry's history (*Star Wars*)—believed that the people involved in the creation of the product were more important than the company. Second, the relationships between the three of them and those people were themselves important to their success. Quite simply, Ladd, Kanter, and Wigan trust each other, and they are friends.

The link between friendship and managerial success, at least at The Ladd Company, is the climate for encouraging creativity that trust creates. Attributes of friendship, candor, lack of competition among individuals, and deep mutual concern become the attributes of a company. The interviews that follow show how these relationships contribute to making effective decisions and allow Ladd and company to motivate creative people in ways that go against such traditional management practices as MBO and performance appraisal techniques.

Readers may ask how the successful management approach at The Ladd Company and the work atmosphere could apply to other management teams, films being so distinct a product. But the work environment of the film industry is not so foreign to any company where creative individuals need to blend their talents and where the goals are unsure, the means ambiguous, and no one has a blueprint.

The success factors Ladd and company have isolated, aside from sheer ex-

---

Published in 1980.

pertise, should be of interest to peer organizations or professional groups such as architectural and consulting firms, advertising agencies, publishing houses, engineering and scientific groups, and R&D groups even within large companies.

These interviews were conducted and edited by Eliza G. C. Collins, senior editor, *Harvard Business Review.*

Alan Ladd, Jr.

HBR: **We'd like to discuss how important close personal relationships are to your work, mainly relationships with people you work with daily but also with the creative people you select to do a film. For instance, you have been quoted as saying that when you decided to do *Star Wars* you were actually betting on George Lucas.**

That's true. I had seen the two movies he'd done—*American Graffiti,* which I was very impressed with, and *THX,* which is a different kind of movie altogether—and I felt that he had extraordinary talent. I get a lot of credit for taking a big risk on *Star Wars,* but the truth is it didn't scare me as much as a lot of other pictures did.

What made the difference?

Lucas himself and the way he explained what he was going to do and how he was going to do it. He said he had an idea about a space picture that was a throwback to all the old movies we grew up on as kids. Because I grew up in this business and saw every movie ever made, or tried to, and have a great love for film, when he said, "This sequence is going to be like *The Seahawk,* or this like *Captain Blood,* and this like *Flash Gordon,*" I knew exactly what he was saying. That gave me confidence he was going to pull it off. I knew from other people and from spending time with him that he was a dead honest person who knew what he was doing.

Was the same true of Ridley Scott? You had seen only his one film, *The Duelists,* before you chose him to direct *Alien.* Did you get to know him too?

Yes, I did. But I think too, you can see a lot in films about directors—what their attitudes are, how they feel. You can look at a film and get a feeling—just an intuition—that the director is not quite sensitive enough for what you're trying to do, or lacks a sense of humor, or seems to back away from confrontation sequences.

So you have to be on your intuitive toes all the time. Isn't that exhausting?

Yes, it is. That's why you really have to love this business. If you don't, it can tear you apart.

Could you describe what tears you apart?

Well, you're constantly dealing with people who have ideas different from your own, trying to make them feel that you're right, or to let them convince you that they're right. So there's a lot of giving and taking. Also, you have to form quick assessments of people and material because you don't have a lot of time. You have to make quick judgments and decisions. For example, how a film is to be marketed: Is this the right way or the wrong way? Should we go out with a picture in 500 theaters or in just 10? Some films lend themselves to a natural course of decisions, but others don't, particularly the riskier pictures like *Julia* and *The Turning Point*.

Then there's always that final moment whe you say to somebody, "OK, here's $5 million, or $7 million, or $10 million—do what you want to do." And then you look at the daily rushes, sometimes saying, "Wonderful," and sometimes, "Oh, my God." Finally, it's always frightening to go to the first preview when you show the picture to the people "out there." Every time somebody gets up you think, "My God, are they walking out of the theater or are they going to the bathroom?" And you discover yourself getting up and following people to find out. It's a scary feeling, the 10 or 12 times a year you go to the theater and expose a picture for the first time. All you have to go on up to that point is the reaction you get sitting in an isolated little screening room.

What helps you deal with that pressure?

I think having friends around. For example, when we were still at Fox and we began to have trouble with the chairman and the board, I didn't involve anybody else in it. But I think it showed that my relationship with Jay and Gareth was very healthy. Basically, I had to deal with the corporate problem on my own, but there was someone to whom I could say, "God, was this frustrating! Can you believe this new chart that's coming out?" I need that. I like family. I've been married for over 20 years to the same person.

The relationships between you and Jay Kanter and Gareth Wigan seem important to the work you do. How would you describe them?

One thing that characterized us at Fox, which made us distinct from other companies, was that we ran it much like a family. Our personalities, thoughts, and ideas intertwine. This is a business of collaboration; you'll find that among people who make films, certain writing teams are wonderful together and certain directors work better with certain stars. The creative side is a business of input, discussion, and attitude. It's also a business we all work very hard at. In the mornings, Jay picks up the trade papers and we ride to the office together. Generally, we don't leave the office until 7 or 8 o'clock at night. We sit around and talk and laugh and let the tensions of the day wear off. I guess it works.

Do you see a lot of Kanter and Wigan during the day?

A great deal. We're in and out of each others' offices all the time and of course we're required to do certain social things in the evenings—take a writer, director, or producer to dinner, for example. Then our weekends are filled with business, often previewing pictures, which means we're away for the whole weekend. Working this way could be a nightmare if we didn't have good, strong relationships.

 We read volumes of material and we phone to exchange ideas like, "Hey, I read this script; I think it's pretty good." Or if I get the figures on a Fox product such as *The Rose,* and it's doing really well, I'll call Jay and Gareth over the weekend.

You're still getting the Fox figures?

Sure, I left a bunch of films, like children, there; I still want to find out how they're behaving.

Would you call Kanter and Wigan friends?

Oh, absolutely, they're friends. Even if we didn't work together, we'd still be very close friends. There's no question about that. We left many people behind at Fox with whom all three of us are still very close. Last night Joe Graham—who's our vice president of business affairs—and I went out and watched a football game together. And we want the same kind of relationship with anybody who joins us. It's always been my feeling that you work best in a family environment, where you really care about the people you work with. I've just found working that way has always been more productive for everybody.

Would you say the relationships are intimate? Are there areas you feel you can't touch on?

I think we're very close. If something happened to one of my children, I'd certainly tell Jay or Gareth; or if they said, "You seem upset today," I wouldn't hesitate to say, "Well, one of my daughters is fighting with her teacher." And they would tell me the same thing. It isn't as if the only things we talk about are work related.

If you had a personal problem, would you feel that you could talk to them without lessening your authority?

I think being able to talk freely is one of the things that makes it all work. And it's not just the three of us, but the same applies to all the people we've worked with in the past. They always felt they could talk to someone about a problem. Even the people who are still at Fox have no hesitation about calling one of us and saying, "Hey, do you mind if we have dinner? I've got a problem." We've always run a very open situation: people aren't suspect if they have emotions.

Does part of the work you do depend on being very close to your emotions— so that you can feel and trust your feelings?

People have always said that I'm very quiet and laid back and seem unemotional. But that isn't really true. Maybe I don't walk around shouting at people or hang up the phone and cry—but it's still a business of emotions. Reading a script, you have to be able to sit there and laugh. If it makes you laugh, you know it must be funny. Or you must be able to cry—if you can't, everything becomes flat. It's crucial to be able to trust your own responses to material.

Did you look for something particular in choosing Kanter and Wigan to work with?

Trust, basically. That's the first thing. Life is too short to work in an environment where you have to worry about somebody stabbing you in the back. You have to be able to trust a person completely.

How can you tell what somebody is likely to do?

Know the person. I've known Jay for a very long time; he was my father's agent. Then we worked together in London producing a lot of unsuccessful movies. Gareth and I worked together too; in fact, I more or less worked as an agent for him. So when Gareth came to Fox it was because I had known him previously. Sandy Lieberson—he became president of Fox's production after I left, though he left too—and I worked together very closely 20 years ago as agents. I knew I could trust and feel comfortable and safe with him.

What about women?

We've had the same close working relationships with women. Strangely enough, I think half the people at Fox were women—Lucy Fisher, Paula Weinstein, to name two. I knew something about Paula because she dated David Field, and David worked at Fox. I knew from David she was a very trustworthy person.

What does that mean?

That you can communicate with each other, that you care about one another personally, that you can have a good old-fashioned argument without any-body walking out, slamming the door, and pouting.

When conflicts arise, how do you solve them?

It's a collective responsibility to resolve conflicts. We work them out openly, in a healthy manner. I've never gone home at night angry at Jay or Gareth. We might do things differently, but I've never gone home thinking, "They messed up everything; I should have done it myself." It's a business of making mistakes, and we all make them. You don't go in thinking you might be making a mistake, but you sure find out later.

So you don't take personally differences in feelings or opinions about a project— say, choosing a director for a film?

You have to respect those differences. Every Monday morning we have a meeting and discuss the scripts we've read over the weekend. Now one of us might be impassioned about a script, and someone else might hate it. We don't take a vote, but if everybody doesn't hate it, then we'll probably let the person who likes the project take it through the next step. By the same token, we can't expect the entire moviegoing public to like the same movie. Just because I like *Breaking Away* doesn't mean everybody out there is going to like it. Not everybody in the world liked *Star Wars*.

It seems to me enough did! Do the relationships ever become more important than a good business decision? In other words, are there times when preserving the group friendship and cohesion is more important than the price tag on a particular decision?

I don't think the question becomes an issue. If Jay came in and said, "Here's a picture that I'm totally passionate about; I really must do it," and Gareth and others in the company were totally negative, I'd say, "Well, wait a minute. As a friend I'd love to see you do the picture, but you can't put that burden on the rest of the company, because everybody else dreads it." If 50 percent of the people liked it and I didn't, I'd never say we weren't going to do it. But I don't think any of us would say, "I love it and I don't care that everybody else in the company hates it." On the other hand, the rest would never say, "We'll go along and do this because we don't want to hurt your feelings."

How do you appraise friends? Is that a problem with people who are close to you?

No, I don't think so. You don't sit down and appraise somebody on a yearly or six-month basis. We're not making shoes, where you can say, "Your output's lousy." Appraisal is an ongoing, constant thing that happens when you speak openly and freely to one another. When you feel something's going amiss, you say, ''I think you're on the wrong track.'' But you state it at that time, not six months later when the personnel review comes up.

Do you feel it's necessary to say it at the time because you have to have a clear emotional slate to work with?

Absolutely. The worst thing we can do to ourselves and each other is let something fester inside and bother us. It's better to get it out in the open as best you can. And you try to do it tactfully. You just don't burst into somebody's office and say, ''I don't like what you did.'' You don't send a memo and include it in someone's personnel file.

Isn't the confrontation difficult?

Not if you see it as necessary to the team effort, which it is. One thing that has made all this teamwork succeed is that none of our egos are involved. Nobody's ever said, ''This is mine.'' Everything is everybody's. We all share. Nobody's ever said, ''Well, the picture that failed was yours, and mine was the one that succeeded.'' You just can't say that because I made the decision to go with a film, I'm the one who should be heavily rewarded. A whole team of people—the person who comes in with the terriffic ads, the person who develops a wonderful new kind of publicity, the production people—makes something work, not just one individual.

Does feeling part of a team, recognizing that your decision isn't the only thing that's going to make a film work or fail, in some ways mitigate the awesome feeling of being alone at the top?

It does. But the most important thing is working in an atmosphere that makes you happy to get up and come to work in the morning, looking forward to seeing everybody in the hallway as you walk in. It would be horrendous for me to think, ''Here's somebody I *have* to work with. He may be terrific, but I really can't tolerate this human being.'' That's a terrible thought.

Do you think that Kanter and Wigan feel they can come and confront you as easily as they can talk between themselves? Do you have a sense that there are eggshells subtly strewn around your office?

They're just as quick to confront me about something as they are each other. It worked the same with the group at Fox, not just Jay and Gareth. I never got upset when somebody in advertising came in and said, ''I read the script and I don't like it.''

How big a group had access to you?

Hundreds of people, actually. I've always had an open-door policy.

Isn't that distracting?

Yes, but it's important to the quality of work. For instance, at Fox the production and marketing people would come in and openly discuss what they did or didn't like about an ad or a script. But we were quick to say, "We'll do the best we can." And they really worked hard whether they liked a picture or not. If people feel free to say what they don't like, they're more open—and that's important.

You couldn't possibly be a personal friend to hundreds of people. Did some get jealous?

When you work with that many people, as long as they know you care, you don't have to have dinner with them every night to prove it. If they know you're trying to do the best for them in terms of salaries and are working on their behalf, and they know they can come in anytime and have a conversation about anything, they know you care.

Is it important to you that Kanter and Wigan are friends with each other as well?

Yes, because if something were wrong between them I'd be in the middle of it, like an arbitrator. It's best to let them arbitrate their own problems. As friends they can discuss problems openly between themselves. The people I've been close to all get along very well.

One senses the film business is exceedingly risky. When you decided to do *The Turning Point* and *Julia*, numbers of people thought it was a bad idea to put out two so-called female films so close together.

Followed by a third, *An Unmarried Woman*.

With *The Rose* in the background . . .

And *Norma Rae*.

Was it easier to make decisions when you had friends around who respected them?

Not all of the six people or so who were directly involved were thrilled with the possibility of making *Julia* and not everybody was thrilled about *The Turning Point*, but enough people did care about making them that the decisions were easier. And then it gave me a great deal of security to know that those who didn't like them were not going to walk around saying, "The fool."

People who have worked for you—creative people, production people—have been quoted as saying one of the things that makes them want to work for you is that you leave them alone. How do you leave them alone on the day the rushes you've seen make you say, "Oh, God."

Well, there's leaving people alone and leaving them alone; the difference is how you approach your involvement. If I see something in the rushes I really dislike, I don't immediately stomp over to the stage and say that what I saw was terrible. I catch the person at the end of the day and tell him or her, "Something's bothering me here." It's the same when Jay, Gareth, others, and I talk out a problem without getting into confrontations. You talk with the creative people in the same manner; you don't say, "I'm right and have all the answers," because they may be right too.

Are you conscious of trying to make people feel free from pressure?

You try to make them feel free. I don't know the formula, but whatever you do, it just has to be natural. At Fox, I felt I had to keep the pressures off the other executives. There was no need for them to get involved in the complications of the corporate structure. If you're going to assume responsibility, it's your obligation to protect the people involved. You can't go to George Lucas in the middle of *Star Wars* and tell him, "Some of the members of the board of directors don't like your movie." It's not going to contribute anything to what he's trying to accomplish.

What underlay the conflict between you and Fox's higher corporate officers and some of the board members?

Some of the corporate people and some of the board understood charts and MBOs, and I couldn't convince them that people have needs other than getting a bonus or a new car every two years. People don't stop working once they've achieved something. Mel Brooks is not going to make a better picture out of *Young Frankenstein* if you say to him, "Well, you know you'll get a bigger bonus if you make a better picture." He'll say, "I can only do as well as I can; I'll try my hardest." But I couldn't get people at Fox to see that.

Were there other constraints on the creative process at Fox?

Well, yes, the attitudes of the people. Nobody on the corporate side ever came to us and said, "You did a good job," or, "The film division is 85% of the company and we appreciate what you're doing." The year Fox broke all industry records, none of the corporate people ever said, "Hey, you did a nice job."

Do you think if people had made you feel that they gave a damn about what you were doing the friction might have been avoided?

Absolutely, or if they had understood *what* we were doing. A lot of the people on the corporate side thought, "Well, aren't those people lucky? They just look at movies all the time, go to dinner with movie stars, and take flashy trips almost every weekend for previews." What they don't see is the Mel Brooks who walks into my office, loses his temper over a problem, picks up a chair, and throws it across the room. Their attitudes were almost resentful. And when I said I was leaving, not one corporate staff person who worked for Dennis Stanfill came in and said, "I'm sorry you're leaving."

One of the things that seems to suit you is a lot of input—people in and out of your office, lots of data, rushes, financial information—forming a big confusing picture. Do you have a sense of riding with the confusion until the ambiguity becomes clear?

Well, you have to. And it really is a muddle determining what's important and what isn't, hoping to zero in on the most essential things. On an average day I have to juggle 60 or 70 telephone calls. It's like a chess game.

But it seems that the chaos is necessary; you couldn't do without it.

No, you can't. The creative process comes out of the chaos. No book can tell you how to make a good movie. All these involved people and all their ideas make a movie. A good director or producer will try to cast a movie as you might try to cast the people on an executive level. An accountant comes in with some ideas, and so does a script person. Good directors are receptive to that: they listen to everybody, taking a little of this, a little of that.

Would it be too difficult to do all that juggling without the emotional climate in which you work?

By myself, I'd be pretty miserable. Some people would think it was terrific, I'm sure. But it's just that the emotional needs I have are deep down. I need friends around.

Jay Kanter

When you, Gareth Wigan, and Alan Ladd, Jr., left Fox, you were quoted as saying that the MBO forms there had "sent a flash of fear into people." What did you mean?

Those things were absolutely awful. I know what goes into running a big business, or at least I think I do; I realize there has to be some sense of order, responsibility, progression, and ways to evaluate people. General Motors is not a mom and pop business. It's run with great efficiency, and managers have to do certain things along the way. The movie business, the entertainment business—any creative group, I suppose—are not constructed that way. You can't exchange the head of General Motors for the head of production of Warner Brothers. It just doesn't work.

Why do you say that?

It would be wrong for me, and I've been in the industry for years, to have an argument about something that's vital in a producer's or director's mind and not acquaint myself with the facts. If he says, "Listen, you don't know how important this particular location is," and I argue with him and I haven't been to that location to see or don't understand the context, then I'm wrong. I'm just making an executive dictatorial decision that is not based on any firsthand knowledge or experience.

The MBO forms were an example of headquarters not knowing what you were about?

Yes. For instance, Fox headquarters sent them to quite a few people. They went to the legal department, the production department, the music department, me, Gareth, Laddie—all of us. It's one thing to get accounting people to fill them out, but it's quite another to get the head of the music department—strictly a creative force who deals with musicians, conducts orchestras, and knows what the best scoring stages are—to fill one out. He'll look at a thing like this and throw his hands in the air, go home, and spend sleepless nights worrying about what he's going to say on it.

When I received one I had to be more tolerant because I was the head of a department. And yet I would procrastinate, get angry, and generally waste a great deal of time avoiding ever filling it out. For Laddie it was even more of a form of hatred than it was for me. It was frustrating being unable to stop a practice within your division that was a waste of people's time and certainly the company's money.

Do you think the interests of a large corporation, which needs controls, are antithetical then to the needs of a creative unit?

There's a serious conflict, no question. People require some form of discipline and begin to resent their managers when they don't get it, but they also require freedom to do their jobs without feeling that every time they're two days over schedule Big Brother appears.

But it all isn't necessarily a conflict. I must say that in spite of the fact I initially resented the regimentation of the MBO forms, I found it was good to sit down with the head of business affairs and say, "You know, we're having this discussion in both of our best interests, and this is where I think you can improve. And this is where I think I've fallen down in helping you improve." If the discussion was a give-and-take thing, we both got something out of it.

What was the underlying conflict with Fox about paying extra bonuses to production people after *Star Wars* was such a success?

Quite simply, we three—Laddie, Gareth, and myself—were the recipients of an awful lot of money (it's no secret), and we felt that the people in the division should have gotten more. There was a windfall, an absolute windfall. The company was very quick to give the stockholders a special dollar dividend and the stockholders also profited because the value of their shares increased—tremendously. I'm very sympathetic to stockholders—they own the company—but the people who provided those windfall profits were the people in this division. We just felt that their bonuses should have been more, especially since the three of us had had a special bonus.

So you actually shared yours with the people in your division. If fairness was one motivation, was keeping those good working relationships in order another?

That crossed our minds, but I don't think it was what motivated us. It was a way of saying to the company: we're willing to put our money where our mouths are. We asked the people in the company to do it first and they said no. I was very surprised that even after we made the gesture, they didn't decide differently.

Would you say then that having control over rewards is one of the crucial areas of conflict between creative groups and large corporations?

There lies the biggest problem. I told the chairman directly how I felt. It seemed silly to us that Laddie could spend all the production and marketing money—which in itself was in excess of $150 million a year—and nobody would question his decisions. There was no logic to the fact that he could buy $4 million of television network time and nobody would question whether it was a good buy, but he couldn't give somebody a $100, a $200, or a $500-a-week raise.

The chairman told me how he felt, and I was sympathetic to what he said—that he was running a company, was responsible for all aspects of it, and couldn't have people in one division getting rewards so far out of proportion to other divisions. He wasn't wrong about that.

How would you resolve the conflict?

I think one of the things to consider is the individual who's in charge of dispensing the money. Either the person is responsible or he's not. Laddie made salary recommendations, made bonus recommendations, was certainly never known as a giveaway artist, and was always very financially responsible. Our division never went crazy on budgets; we always watched them. Given a reasonable period of time to judge a person's performance, the chairman should or could have come to the conclusion that the individual in charge was not going to give salaries or bonuses which were not deserved.

Was the fact that you knew the people involved personally part of what made you share your bonus money?

Yes, because we could really see a measure of their work. At a certain point in a year you know whether you have earned the bonus, and once you've got it there's no way in the world that anybody can take it away from you. For a couple of years, midway through the year, there was no way the film division was not going to get the maximum bonus permitted. And yet deep into the year the people in the division never coasted—they worked every bit as hard as they had earlier in the year. I didn't expect the corporate staff to be aware of that measure unless we told them, and we did. But you can only feel it if you have a working relationship with your staff as we did.

How would you describe the relationship that the three of you have developed?

We all have special abilities and talents in one direction or another, and we have confidence in our own abilities. Even more important, we don't want to prove a point among ourselves. Competition is a healthy thing. But I regard my competitors as being outside the company, not inside it. We've never been so big, at Fox or here at The Ladd Company, that we'd have to compete with each other to reach certain goals. I've seen that happen in companies where survival is a game, but you have to have the right makeup to work in that sort of environment; we don't have it.

Do you consider Ladd and Wigan friends?

Yes, I consider them friends. I do. That doesn't mean we spend all of our time together; I have other friends with whom I spend an equal amount of time socially. We're not all joined together at the hip.

How personal are the relationships? Are there boundaries you don't cross?

There are people I've very close to personally with whom I enjoy a different sort of relationship, but when the chips are down, you add up the people in the friend column and you've got to really ask, "What is a friend?" A friend really isn't defined by the hours spent together but by your feelings for that person. On that basis I would say that I do have a personal relationship with Laddie and Gareth because they're very close to me. They're people I can depend on. I would trust them with anything. If something were bothering me or I were in serious trouble, I feel that I could go to Laddie or Gareth and say, "Help!" And they could do the same.

Would that affect your work?

Well, it wouldn't reflect on my work; why should it? I don't think Laddie and Gareth feel any differently.

Do you feel you can blow off steam in front of each other if it's necessary?

We're not very demonstrative in that way, and only on rare occasions do we really ever blow up at all, but Laddie's done it, I've done it, Gareth's done it. It's had nothing to do with each other but is always directed at something else. There are times when I'm absolutely so angry that I scream over the telephone. If Laddie and Gareth walked in with a birthday cake it wouldn't calm me down; I'd go right on screaming and yelling. It's not something that is common with me, but I certainly wouldn't be embarrassed doing it in front of them nor they in front of me.

At Fox, Ladd was president, you were senior vice president, and Wigan was vice president. Did the titles make a difference in your relationships?

In many things I think our duties—well, Gareth's and mine—were and are interchangeable. Laddie's responsibilities were much greater than ours. But none of us ever thought it was an important part of our lives to be a vice president. I suppose the first time I became a vice president of anything was very important. It was important to my mother.

Have you ever felt frustrated when you walked out of one of those group meetings where you made a "go" or "no go" decision because it didn't reflect what you wanted?

Of course, there's a feeling of frustration.

Can you resolve that with Ladd? Does it affect your friendship or your work?

No, it really doesn't, because you know that somebody has to be, in the final analysis, responsible. All sorts of disagreements occur in making a movie—what you're going to make, who the writer is, who's going to direct it, who's playing in it. Having all been in this business a long time and knowing the number of opportunities there are for disagreement, we seem to get along and skirt over those problems fairly well. When you do walk out gritting your teeth, swearing that the others are all wrong, at the same time you have to turn around and say, "Look, considering the number of times we go through this process, I'm fairly lucky." We all love our children, but there are those odd times when you're ready to fling them or yourself out the window. You can't base your feelings about the children on those infrequent times they drive you crazy.

Do you feel there is an emotional outcome of working in an environment like this that's important to the work you do?

Yes. I feel that there's an emotional satisfaction. I just enjoy coming to work. I'm very emotionally involved; it's not just a job. We all get paid very well but it's more than that. I get up in the morning and I look forward to seeing the people and exchanging ideas. It's as much the actual way we all work together that is important to me, beyond the product.

Is protecting the group process an end in itself?

We do try to respect each other's feelings, whatever they are, because what we're after is beneficial to the company. There have been things that I felt strongly about over the past few years while this relationship has existed, without Laddie having to make a career of taking me away to Palm Springs for two weeks to help me understand. We don't have the time to do that, and we wouldn't have the kind of relationship that we do if we treated each other like children. We know each other's limits.

Do the sensitivity and tolerance you have, which make it possible to work closely together, affect the creative outcome?

They have a great effect on the people we deal with and the people we try to attract to work with us. A big part of this business, in addition to money, is relationships with other people. If people feel comfortable in a particular work atmosphere, the chances of their coming to you first with a film idea are far greater than if it's just a question of how much money you're willing to pay. I'm not dismissing the value of the money, but in this business it's not leverage.

What do you mean when you say "comfortable"?

People know that with us they can come and have a discussion, that we'll be supportive, that in fact we may even have some good ideas. I think most people who haved worked with us do feel that we have something to offer beyond financing. If writers, directors, and actors feel comfortable in a relationship, feel they're not being dictated to, feel they're being treated with respect as human beings, then they're willing to convey that same respect back.

We take an interest not only in seeing the picture through to the finish, but we also care about the way it's sold. People know that once a film is turned over to the distribution company, we don't lose interest in it. We try to put our money in the screen, not in six limousines waiting all night long in case somebody wants a ham sandwich.

Gareth Wigan

When Alan Ladd, Jr., resigned as president of Fox's film division, he was quoted as saying that wherever he went, you and Jay Kanter would go as well. What do you think makes your relationship so special?

I doubt there are many people in the world who enjoy doing what they're doing more than we do, and I think a lot of that enjoyment is because of our mutual trust. I'm sure, or I hope, that when Laddie said the three of us would go together, he made the decision to move with the two of us out of pure self-interest, that he believed he would enjoy his life more and do what he wanted to do better because we were there rather than because he felt he had to take care of us.

Do you consider Ladd and Kanter friends?

Absolutely. Very much so. How do you define "friend"?

Well, I don't know. I was going to ask you.

One of the ways I would define a friend is someone you can rely on absolutely in bad times as well as good, and by that definition, they are unqualified friends.

You would not feel inhibited about going to either one of them if you were in trouble or needed to talk about something personal?

Would not, did not, and will not. Not in the least. Let me give you a rather roundabout response. One of the characteristics we all share, I think, though it materializes in very different ways, is that all three of us are reticent, un-Hollywoodish people. We are not extroverts at all. I don't honestly know what Laddie and Jay may talk about privately between themselves, but I know what I talk about with them and they talk about with me; we do not, on the whole, overburden each other with our personal problems.

When we reach a certain age, everyone has two or three people to turn to in a crisis who'll sit up all night and listen, and no, I don't think that either Jay or Laddie would be one of those two people for me. Or for any of the three of us. But, for instance, I separated from my wife at the beginning of last year, and since last summer it's been one of the bad times; they're certainly aware of that. I've spoken with Laddie two or three times about it, but not in the same way that one burdens one's other kind of friends.

So in the important ways, yes, I think we are friends. But mostly what we have, I think, is the kind of relationship that straddles civilian and professional life, in a way you can't altogether define, which is in my experience exceedingly rare.

Does this affect the way you work together?

That needs a prologue as well. This is a personality-based business. You're as good as you are. Very few objective qualifications are relevant. You may have a law degree; you may have accountancy or business management qualifications. They're all meaningless, frankly, unless you have the innate ability to relate to and judge people, as well as the innate courage and talent to interpret your own instincts about material. Add to that experience, opinions, and personal obligations, and you have a movie executive. To have a career as a studio executive requires a great deal of ego projection, and it traditionally leads to an immensely competitive spirit and an enormous amount of politics or politicking. We have succeeded in having between us at Fox and here at The Ladd Company—it would be ridiculous to say zero but— as near zero politics as it's practical to achieve. You can't ever totally overcome it, obviously, but for all intents and purposes, no politics—and thus security.

Can you give an example?

Say you're making a film like *Julia*—*Julia* was Jay's project, and traditionally he would probably have meetings with the writer and the producer and not necessarily tell even his colleagues what was going on. He would seek help only when he wanted it. He would be deeply offended if anybody visited the film while it was being made or spoke to the director, Fred Zinnemann, or to anybody else who was involved in making it. And if anybody—and I'm talking about his immediate colleagues—criticized it at any point, he would instantly defend it.

It doesn't work that way for the three of you?

I can remember only once in four years at Fox when we ever had to ask, "Well, am I doing this or are you?" and then only because it happened to be a film produced by somebody with whom I had worked on three films and directed by somebody with whom Jay had worked for years. When I'm away or not available, people in a project I've been closest to will speak to Jay or Laddie; one of them will make whatever decision seems sensible at the time, and there's no problem about it.

So you feel that professionally and personally the relationships are fairly reciprocal. Can you take as much initiative with Ladd as he can with you around the projects that he's working on?

Yes. It's not because we've all worked in England—though that is a coincidence—but our company constitution, like the British Constitution, is unwritten. There is a perfectly clear understanding of where Alan Ladd's prerogatives and responsibilities as president start; I can give examples but I don't think I could define them. *I* just know where the line is drawn and so does Jay and so does he.

Can you give an example of where the line is drawn?

Oh, I consider it really as a continuity of thought, for simplicity's sake. For instance, we would not make a deal with any artist of any substance or a writer or anybody like that without his first being aware of it and approving it, if possible.

But those seem like fairly straightforward decision-making responsibilities; what about the encouragement of ideas when you're sitting together in a meeting discussing film scripts? Are you aware of deferring to him and his ideas because he's president?

The way a meeting occurs, because it isn't "run," is that it is understood Laddie's voice has and should have a greater emphasis and weight than anybody else's. But then he operates in a very individual way. He's one of the great listeners of my experience. He hears everything and forgets nothing that he's heard. When it may appear his thoughts are elsewhere, he still hears everything that everybody has to say. If we're sitting in his office, as we do every Monday morning, talking about things that we've read and there's some divergence of opinion, his tendency is to listen for some time to what everybody's saying and to cull a collective opinion allied with his own. So while his feelings or recommendations don't necessarily represent a consensus, they are colored by what he feels to be a consensus.

How do you feel having your performance appraised by a friend?

I don't enjoy it, who does? But I don't resent criticism from anybody whom I respect, and there are very few people I've known in my life whom I respect as much as Laddie. There've been a couple of times when I'd disagree or I'd think, "Well, I wouldn't do that." But I know a couple of occasions when he has made more than generalized criticism, and both times his judgment was correct.

Part of the art is the way he does criticize?

Well, part of the art is that he's prepared to do it at all and not just brush things under the carpet, or that any of us are prepared to do it. The art—whether it's the art of our being together or just the art of being in business—is being able to say no to people and still retain their respect. On many occasions, Laddie has consulted at length with Jay and myself on whether we thought that so-and-so could do this job, or about situations that might blow up between X and Y and whether they weren't relating to each other as well as before. I think that he values and needs our opinions and judgments, and needs to express his own feelings and be totally confident that what he says won't go any further.

How does he nurture this peer sense in light of his position?

A cynic could say that he chooses people to work with him who are prepared to accept his position, but that's not true. He put together the team at Fox, *that's* true. He probably left a couple of people doing what they were doing and shifted around a couple of other people, but he brought in everybody else—Jay, myself, Sandy Lieberson, Paula Weinstein, Lucy Fisher, the whole creative side. Obviously, like any leader, he chose his immediate subgroup. But leaving that aside, he was very quickly recognized as the best and it didn't and doesn't have to do with his age. His judgments on the whole are sounder and his ability to listen and judge before speaking is better developed than anybody else's. He has lived and breathed and thought and studied film in a way that people are only just beginning to do. George Lucas *[Star Wars]* and Steven Spielberg *[Jaws]* do it, but Laddie did it without ever intending to be a film director, writer, or actor. He does have an encyclopedic knowledge *and* the judgmental wisdom that grows out of that knowledge and out of thinking about film all the time.

Doesn't that set him apart?

No. We work together as a team. We have to accept the bruising of our egos and sometimes we have to compromise, we have to support each other, we have to work—in political terms—in a cabinet fashion. If I love a film but nobody else does, it's no good saying to the outside person who brought in the script, "I loved it but everybody else said no." You have to say to the person, "I like it but the overall feeling was that we really couldn't do it."

How is this sense of loyalty fostered?

Laddie fosters it and also, of course, the group fosters it; if you have the good fortune to experience this way of working, as soon as any member of the group appears to betray the tribal interplay, the rest of the tribe will complain.

So it really is a small culture with its own mores and values.

It's a small culture, but it's curious that it's also pervasive. I think one of the enormous errors that Fox made in considering letting Ladd go, and in what was done at Fox after his departure, was the purblind inability to recognize the depth to which his inspiration had permeated the company. I think Fox management thought that if the three of us went, we would go and that would be it. But apart from Jay and myself, there was another inner circle of maybe 12 more people, then other circles beyond that. The sense of confidence in and tremendous affection for him had gone very deep.

What made it go so deep?

It comes, of course, from success; there's nothing like success. It comes from the fact that our greatest aim is to make terribly good and terribly successful films. You see, they don't often go together. We had the good fortune to make a lot of very good films. Some of them were very successful and some of them fairly successful, and so people have pride in the product— the people on the road who are out there selling it. But more than that, it is Laddie's personal involvement, something that people recognize as his character. He's not an easy man to get to know; he is characterized by a complete lack of bullshit. There isn't a better word for it. He has immense concern, something that all of us have, for sharing.

How does he communicate that? How do you? You must have to communicate it to the people who report to you.

I've always made a practice of talking about people working *with* me and not *for* me. That prepositional change is very important. If it's a reasonable portrayal of an attitude, it carries through into your work. As for Laddie, he's a man who has a lot of pride, as he should, and very little arrogance. Jay has too, and I hope that I have. You see, Laddie is completely different from anybody who has ever done that sort of job before. He's rotten at self-promotion, but his self-depreciation and total refusal to speak in public under any circumstances other than one-to-one or at a table over dinner and things like that set him apart from the normal run of people in charge of a studio. And as soon as people in Dallas or Toronto find that he's not behaving as expected, nor does he tolerate it when other people at any level try to behave in the traditional way, then they think, "Hey, this is something different."

What won't he tolerate?

Anyone saying, "This is mine." To give you an example, the decision to make *The Turning Point* was very difficult. I was totally committed to the film—objectively because I did believe it could be successful, and emotionally because I had had the advantage of seeing Mikhail Baryshnikov dance; I love ballet. And I did believe that Baryshnikov was enough of a superstar to break the barrier of prejudice against this highly esoteric subject. But we had great misgivings because we were making all of these other films with women.

Now since it became successful people have said to me that it was my film. No, it wasn't. I was involved in it, yes, all the way through. I was much more involved than anybody else—too involved at times. And both Laddie and Jay at different times and in different ways expressed quite proper and sensible concerns about the film. But whatever I did, I could not have done without their questions and, of course, their support. And I hope that works both ways.

The relationships made it possible for you to oversee the film you did?

For the film to be made.

And no one ever said to you, "You've got to go handle this; this is your baby"?

It was the group working; the more confidence Laddie feels in one of us, of course, the less he has to get involved. The more confidence we feel in Laddie's support, even if we're sometimes wrong, the more we're united as far as the enemy is concerned. I don't believe that has to be questioned anymore; it's there.

How long did it take to develop this trust?

It happened very quickly, and I don't quite know why. But within a very short time after I joined Fox it was apparent to me and, curiously, to other people in the company that there were an awful lot of things which didn't have to be said or didn't have to happen—a sense there was something strange or unusual in this tripartite relationship.

Do you think that as a group you have ever made a bad business decision because of your friendships?

I think bad business decisions have been made because we are collectively sometimes reluctant to make a tough decision. But not very often. Not more often than most people. But I can think of movies that we've made which we shouldn't have, decisions that have been postponed and postponed because we were reluctant to face up to our responsibility. In the end the thing is done, but it would have been much better to do it sooner.

Is that one of the dangers—groupthink? Because you know each other so well and have worked together so long, might you collectively not see something?

I don't think that's a problem, because we see things in different ways. You see, while I suppose it's interesting to stress the sameness and the unlikelihood of three people coming together who seem to share so many feelings and attitudes and so much trust, it's also important to stress the substantial differences.

What would you say the differences are?

Well, there's a disparity of eight or ten years in age between the oldest and the youngest of the three of us. I'm 47, Laddie's 42, and Jay is 50—something like that. One is a Jew, one's an Englishman, and one's an American, I think Protestant. Not that any of us are religious, but there are those differences.

Laddie has only one passion outside the movie business—football. I'm very ignorant about football. I love music. The kind of music I love is not something in which either of them is particularly interested. I am voluble to the point of being diuretic, I think, and loud. Laddie, as you know, unless you have particularly keen hearing, is difficult to hear—if you can get him to speak.

You said you were all reticent.

In behavior, but in my case, not in speech. I think that I am the most volatile in mood. I do play poker quite well, but apart from that I've had to reconcile myself to the fact that I could never hide an emotion. I walk in thinking I'm hiding it and people say, "What's the matter?" And Laddie—well, there are people who would say he shows his emotions about as vividly as the face of a mountain. I think that when you get to know him, he does, yes, but very little.

You seem to have no inhibitions about people showing emotions and incorporating them into what they do. Is that part of what makes it comfortable here?

What makes it comfortable for me is that the others allow me to show *my* emotions, yes. And I feel much happier to be able to do that. It's a little self-indulgent at times but helps get things out of my system. And I try to make up for that in other ways. I am the scribe of the group, drafting the things that we then rewrite if we need to. I'm not particularly good at it, but it's something that I'm quite happy to do. Neither Jay nor Laddie feels particularly happy doing it. I also don't mind standing on my hind legs and talking to people, while Laddie totally refuses to; Jay will if he's asked but doesn't particularly like to. Jay says he's the one who goes to funerals and functions—and he seems to, but he also does a lot more. There are different things that we do for each other, the kinds of chores of life that are harder for one person to do than another.

Do you think you can explore options more freely in this atmosphere than you might elsewhere and thus make better decisions?

Traditionally, it's terribly dangerous to be wrong in this business. It's bad for your ego and your reputation. It's important that all the mistakes should be somebody else's. So it's very luxurious to be able to be wrong and to make a decision based on merit instead of political reasons. It's very important to be able to change your mind without someone saying, "Yesterday you said something else."

Have you found your way of managing people has changed since you've been involved in this collaboration?

I expect so. I hope that I have contributed to how the enterprise is run, but happily I've found myself working with a man who feels the same way as I do about how things should be run. Certainly, were I running it, there'd be some little things that I would do differently, but only because that would be better for me. There's not one person out of the 15 closest to Laddie at Fox who at one time or another didn't say to him, "When we have meetings couldn't we have them in the room that we have set aside for meetings, instead of four on a couch, two on a stool, in your office? It would be so much more efficient," or "Couldn't we start it and know that it's only going to run an hour and a half instead of sometimes three-quarters of an hour, sometimes four hours?" And his answer was always no, because he works much better that way. When he was away or on vacation and we had a meeting, it was held in a much more orderly or seemingly organized way. But for him to function best and for us to function with him, it has to be done in a certain way.

It needs a chaotic atmosphere?

The ants in an anthill and bees in a hive look totally chaotic, but they're not. The meetings are in fact structured. The structure doesn't always work, but then no structure ever does. But as to how we treat people, I would say that on the whole Laddie is largely apolitical and was not, as far as I know, particularly involved in student politics. I was, and a lot of the feelings that I have about the way people with whom you work should be treated stem from that sort of common effort. I don't know where his stem from but they seem to be the same. He has a very real personal concern for all the people who work with him or for him. And he takes his responsibilities and his personal relationships very, very seriously. You've got a bunch of egos that have to be fostered and encouraged; these are the weapons that the film business uses and that have to be kept sharp.

Like your own ego?

Like my own. The real reason the whole thing broke down at Fox was because the management failed to understand the importance of human relationships, because of all the betrayals, not of us, but of other people in the division.

One pictures a father with his family having the meetings in his office and everybody sitting around and feeling very comfortable. Does this whole process provide something emotionally satisfying to you?

It's difficult to define what it supplies or provides. But yes, it provides something immensely satisfying. It provides an ability to get up early in the morning and go to bed late at night. It provides the fact that people say, "You're looking good." It provides the good things that you do. It fortifies you in the bad times. It makes everything worthwhile. I can say I've had the best four years of my life without any doubt or hesitation whatsoever. And it doesn't have to do with being paid more than I've been paid in my life, or anything like that. I don't know what proportion of the population actually enjoys its work as opposed to having a job. Those of us who love what we do should be profoundly grateful.

You said that with a real sense of affection.

Oh, yes. I don't think we have to be shy. It's possible to speak of loving somebody in that sense of comradeship, joined experience in success and failure; to be able to trust them in the same way that, to be melodramatic, members of a patrol out in the jungles learn to trust and depend on each other. But what's better about our relationship is that it's infinitely broader. Basically, you need to trust your buddies when you're patrolling the jungle so you won't get shot; there's only one goal, which is to get from point A to point B without dying. We have a multitude of other things to consider, and comradeship works at all kinds of levels.

Do you think that any one of you could do your job as well alone?

I have an absolute conviction that I couldn't, and with a sense of relief, I believe the others couldn't either. I hope not. I'd be mortified if I found that they could. I set a very, very much larger store on working with them than either of them probably realizes. They probably don't know how much I depend on it.

As an indication of the importance of the trust and support that come from working in the family-like atmosphere which Ladd created in the Twentieth Century-Fox film division, since these interviews were conducted seven other Fox executives—some of them mentioned in these interviews—have joined Ladd, Kanter, and Wigan. Two other executives, not from Fox, have also joined The Ladd Company team—E.G.C.C.

29

Are You Hearing Enough Employee Concerns?

MARY P. ROWE and MICHAEL BAKER

It looks like there's no solution. A supervisor unjustly gives a poor performance rating and threatens a worker with termination. The employee feels he or she has been wrongly criticized but worries that if he or she goes over the supervisor's head to complain, he or she will lose in the final confrontation. He or she fears that personnel will listen only to the supervisor and sees no way out. Ultimately, the situation becomes too much, and finally, in frustration the employee quits.

Not all employees are treated unjustly and not all supervisors are unjust, but in too many companies, the authors maintain, nonunion employees feel they have no safe, credible, and accessible route to take to have their concerns and complaints heard. The authors describe what nonunion employees go through when they don't have secure complaint channels and then discuss the structures and functions that best protect the rights of employees and managers while dealing with conflicts.

☐   For what seemed ages, Mark Greenfield had been having arguments with a brilliant engineer, Cal Floren, in the successful product-development group Greenfield directed. As he cleaned up a week's worth of papers on his desk, Greenfield reflected on the difficulty he was having resolving tension in the lab. Cal Floren was creative and fit well with the research team, but he would become very angry about pressures—secrecy, keeping ahead of the competition, solving messy

Published in 1984.

technical problems by next Saturday—that others accepted as part of
the job. And it was getting worse. Recently, Cal had been suspicious
and hostile about Mark's presenting the team's work to management.
What had Cal meant when he said Mark was "stealing all the credit"
and "that God knew all about it"? "Whom can I ask for advice?"
thought Mark. "Can a manager go to personnel with a problem like
this?"

As Greenfield answered the doorbell that Friday evening, he caught
just a glimpse of the shotgun before it went off, spraying his face and
shoulders with buckshot. He was never certain of his assailant's identity. The following year, Floren, who had quit the lab, was committed
to a mental institution after fatally shooting his current boss on the golf
course at point-blank range.

☐ Less than a year after joining a prestigious financial firm, Marcy
Lowell is leaving. Along with her will go other women trainees, to
each of whom the firm offered a settlement (Lowell received $25,000)
in a belated effort to avoid costly EEO suits.

Marcy was the object of discrimination in job assignments and
was the victim in several ugly instances of physical and verbal sexual
harassment. On several occasions she was publicly demeaned by a
supervisor using foul language. Her objective, low-key memos to her
boss and to the human resources department received little attention
and no written response. Her boss repeatedly postponed meetings to
analyze her job assignments and to evaluate her performance. Her
supervisor continued to harass her. A fourth, eloquent letter—this time
to the CEO—resulted in a perfunctory analysis of her concerns and
the disclosure that records of her positive performance evaluations had
been "lost."

Marcy's complaint was seen as an isolated problem until other
staff women made their own considerable, personal complaints to the
section head and to a vice president. These complaints covered issues
of pay inequity, harassment, unfair assignments, unethical behavior by
a supervisor, and also "lost" work performance records. Beyond the
precarious legal situation in which the firm finds itself is the long trail
of lost talent and low productivity since the women have banded together.

☐ At a major West Coast company one day, Dr. Zimmer found a
technician unconscious from exposure to a toxic substance. Just a
month or so before, fumes in a nearby lab had also made employees
ill. For the second time, Zimmer, a shy person who found confrontation
very difficult, talked to her boss, the new lab director. She pressed
him to report the incidents to the company health and safety director,
as required by company rules. Once again, she was told it was not her
concern. Dr. Zimmer was both willing to be persistent and unwilling
to go over her boss's head. Knowing no alternative, she tried repeatedly
to force her boss to respect safety procedures and to see the foolhar-

diness of withholding information from senior management and stage agencies. Within six months of the second incident, he fired her unceremoniously.

As a result of Zimmer's unjust-discharge suit against the company, management faces a full investigation in court of incidents and practices that it regards as "atypical" and "not representative of company philosophy."

In these true incidents, respectable companies and valued employees suffered unnecessary losses, and the work of entire units was disrupted for months. The real costs were, thus, far greater than the individual costs or legal settlements might suggest. Yet in each of these cases, the situation had developed slowly and the unpleasant outcome was avoidable. In these incidents, which are dramatic but not unrepresentative of many cases we've seen, either an aggrieved employee or a supervisor in need of assistance had nowhere to turn for effective help in settling a grievance within the company. For nonunion employees and managers, channels through which to express their concerns are a real necessity.

Harassment, inequities, safety problems, and real and imagined grievances are common in all workplaces. Though the sources of their frustration,

Exhibit 1.   Ways Employees May Deal with a Complaint

Unconstructive options		Constructive options	
Doing nothing, bottling it up inside, being apathetic	Being rude to clients, gossiping maliciously and making trouble inside and outside of the company, openly or anonymously harassing supervisors or fellow employees, pursuing petty sabotage	Talking it over with trustworthy people, e.g., family, employee advisor, health care practitioner, or religious counselor	Talking directly with a supervisor or someone else in line management
Taking it out on family and friends		Redirecting frustration toward sports and other creative activities outside work	Working for orderly change with a responsible committee or "network" inside the company
Being absent or late frequently, taking long lunch hours, socializing extensively	Being wasteful, stealing company secrets or other property, presenting fraudulent data, plagiarizing data	Finding another position or project in an orderly manner, going back to school, working hard	Talking with the personnel department
Working slowly, adopting a "that's not in my job description" attitude, urging others not to work so hard	Quitting without notice		Appealing to other designated complaint handlers such as hotline staff, harassment officer, ombudsman, or employee council members
Being depressed, weeping or making angry outbursts, suffering insomnia and being exhausted	Polarizing union activities in and out of the company		Appealing to the CEO or the company directors
Being sick, having accidents, taking drugs and drinking, suffering eating disorders	Making precipitous or premature complaints to regulatory agencies, newspapers, or filing expensive lawsuits—while making little attempt to work things out or to change things inside the company		Making an orderly exit
	Consciously or unconsciously constructing "ambushes": setting up a colleague or oneself for serious mistakes or accidents on the job or project failure, pursuing major sabotage		
	Threatening violence, being violent		

irritation, and rage may differ depending on personal characteristics and position, managers, foremen, secretaries, professionals, and assembly-line workers all experience dissatisfactions. "Unconstructive" options for employees who have a problem or complaint far outnumber alternatives that management would see as constructive (see Exhibit 1).

In this article we first describe the system for and attitudes of employees with complaints that exist in many companies. Then we go on to describe how corporations can handle such problems effectively by listening well and providing a set of constructive options for concerned managers and employees. This response is particularly important now when the boundaries between the rights and interests of nonunion employees and their employers are changing. Effective complaint systems can reduce the friction at these boundaries and foster employee satisfaction and productivity.

Drawbacks of the Conventional Approach

The majority of U.S. companies and institutions have no broad, explicit structures for dealing with employee concerns and no nonunion appeal channels other than the traditional chain of command. When they are unable to resolve disputes with their supervisors, employees at all levels are expected either to drop difficult problems or to take them up the line if they dare.

Managers in some companies claim that an "open door" policy exists, which suggests that it is possible to go over the boss's head or that the personnel department offers an alternative route. But most companies don't have the clear policies and supporting procedures necessary to make these additional routes a credible resource for a broad range of employees and problems. In particular, lower- and middle-level managers rarely feel free to complain on their own behalf or even to seek assistance in handling subordinates' complaints and problems. When companies do respond effectively through traditional arrangements, they must rely on an uncertain supply of supervisors and managers who can listen well and who have unusual tact and judgment.

In addition to the chain of command, most large companies have some kind of special channel for handling discrimination complaints. Conventional companies formally comply with the EEO laws and regulations that apply to them. Many managements tend, however, to see EEO complaints as springing from "isolated" problems and address them, like other grievances, in the manner that "chain of command" suggests—with swift, all-or-nothing decision making. This mode may end the immediate concern but it may also prevent managers from seeing discrimination as a systemic problem that needs systemwide solutions. All-or-nothing decision making may also be inappropriate for discrimination complaints. Often such cases involve a conflict between two different cultural norms, and the company's best bet may be to create some third alternative to the two being presented.

Under traditional arrangements, because management is likely to define an employee's concern as an "accusation" and will see its mere exposure as "causing conflict," employees often find it difficult just to make an inquiry or to explore informally the dimensions of a problem. Even where model complaint and appeal systems for nonunion employees exist, an emphasis on adjudication can produce polarization that both employees and managers find unpalatable.

To design a more effective approach for handling concerns and complaints, it is important to examine common reactions of employees and middle managers to the conventional approach we have been describing.

Fear of Reprisal. Most people try to avoid conflict and shrink from bringing up problems. And most employees—support staff and managers alike—definitely do not want to take a complaint "up the chain" past their supervisor. They understand all too well the taboo against going over a boss's head and they acutely fear reprisal for doing so. For professionals, the fear may not be immediate reprisal but rather of a deferred reckoning that would upset their careers years down the line.

In many companies these fears are well grounded. Many top executives encourage the "middle management macho" ethic and press supervisors to handle things on their own, thereby making them feel deeply undercut when employees' complaints go over or around them. Resistance and reprisal can grow also because the only real power many supervisors have lies in controlling both access to higher levels and the downward flow of information. The chain-of-command system may also prompt managers' fears that they will be punished for any decision found to be so bad that it is overturned.

These fears support the powerful tradition of exit as a solution. When they have an unresolvable dispute with a superior, many executives and other professionals believe it is better to get out than to risk a fight. And even in companies committed to low turnover, middle managers may pass this way of thinking down to subordinates, encouraging exit rather than dispute resolution.

The fear of retaliation also creates diffidence about going to a personnel office. Angry employees often view their problems in all-or-nothing terms, seeing first the supervisor and then the personnel officer as nothing but apologists for management. And because the personnel department keeps a formal file and an informal oral history about an employee, some workers are afraid to make their complaints known. They fear that if they talk to personnel, especially about personal but work-related problems—alcoholism, drugs, love affairs, harassment, divorce—they will suffer retribution.

Loyalty to the Company. Employees who are loyal to their supervisors and work units—and most are—may want to express concerns but not "grievances." One technician we talked to said, "I really was worried about the fumes, but how would my team look if I complained?" Most employees do not want to be litigious and do not have the resources or the psychological orientation—or even the idea—to sue their company.

Many who do sue report feeling that they have no other option. Most instances of whistle-blowing Baker has studied involved employees who were punished, repeatedly rebuffed, or fired for trying to raise an issue *inside* the company. Only when employees receive no support from inside do they take the matter to the courts. Because his or her loyalty "seems to count for nothing" with the company, by the time the suit goes to court the employee is enraged.

Privacy and Personal Control.   The majority of employees want very much to guard their privacy and will do almost anything to avoid revealing certain kinds of problems to fellow workers. Moreover, many employees and managers strongly prefer to act on their own rather than turn to others for help. Most also prefer to resolve a dispute or a problem directly with their supervisors or fellow employees or subordinates. Many people, therefore, will not complain to a superior or to a personnel officer because they fear these people may be indiscreet or may take action on the complaint without permission.

Moreover, some employees mainly want to be heard at the top or seek information that they feel only top management has; these people may not want to go to a supervisor or to personnel. They believe they won't get what they want if they go through intermediaries.

Lack of Skills in Effective Disputing.   No matter what organizational level they are on, employees often lack the knowledge and skills necessary to handle a dispute on their own. If treated unfairly—especially in cases of sexual or racial harassment—many workers know (or believe) that they have too little evidence on their side and are reluctant to get into a "his word against mine" confrontation.

Conflict resolution is difficult also because many people expect much less than employers would find reasonable. And some others expect much more. "Employees-at-will" increasingly believe they are entitled to the full panoply of due process (although this is a term most people cannot define). When they first make a complaint they are surprised to learn the real implications of employment-at-will—that there are relatively few protections for nonunion employees—and, thereafter, they are too resentful to try again constructively.

Supervisors, especially those with little experience, also may have a very limited view of what constructive options are open to them as they attempt to handle a problem with a subordinate.

Belief That It Is Pointless.   Employees at all levels often think that it's useless to complain about certain kinds of problems. Engineers, scientists, and medical specialists often are convinced that managers and personnel officers won't understand technical, safety, or public policy issues. Especially when they are worried about safety issues and ethical problems, managers in particular may feel they can't safely take their frustrations to others.

Problems with coworkers seem particularly hard to complain about. This is especially true if the problem appears bizarre—an office mate is exposing himself, an odd scientific colleague never speaks and naps under his desk, someone is interfering with an experiment—or is one that others might define as trivial, e.g., a close coworker smells, has a bad temper, or smokes.

In our experience, when better options seem not to be available, nearly everyone with a complaint considers using an unconstructive option. Because of the problems we've cited, both executives and employees sometimes even consciously prefer them. Recognizing the costs of not resolving employee complaints earlier and less painfully, many companies have begun to try more innovative approaches.

Accessible, Safe, and Credible

We estimate that perhaps a third of U.S. employers have developed new complaint systems for employees and managers. The major impetus has been to make these systems accessible, safe, and credible. Nearly all these companies have developed innovative procedures for discrimination problems, some also have counselors trained for sexual harassment concerns. Most have established some kind of multistep review system for employee appeals that introduces objective adjudicators. Perhaps 300 to 500 companies and as many colleges and universities have adopted a broad problem-solving approach to complaint handling in which a number of different channels are simultaneously available to employees (typical examples are included in Exhibit 2).

Many employers have increased the *accessibility* of their systems by offering a number of choices for bringing concerns to light. So that people can readily find constructive options and can have backup options where any one route fails, redundant channels are necessary. Some options—hotlines, managers on the shop floor, ombuds offices—should be easy contact points for the employee. Other means—attitude surveys, jobholders' meetings, meetings with people up two levels—provide less immediate but also effective routes.

Companies increase accessibility for minorities and women by making sure that minority and female professionals are employed throughout the complaint channels, especially at senior levels, and by supporting and staying in contact with the informal as well as formal networks of minority and female employees. In similar fashion, it is important that other large populations in the work force—technical and nontechnical, older and younger workers—be represented among complaint handlers. Innovative complaint

Exhibit 2. Typical Structures and Functions in Complaint Systems

Functions	Communication with individuals (may be on a confidential basis)	Counseling with individuals (may be on a confidential basis)	Investigation, conciliation, and mediation	Adjudication	Upward feedback: management information*
Typical structures					
Line supervision	●	●	●	●	●
Personnel/human resources/employee relations	●	●	●	●	●
Multistep appeal systems			●	●	●
Equal opportunity counselors	●	●	●		●
Open-door investigators	●	●	●		●
Ombuds practitioners	●	●	●		●
Work problems counselors	●	●	●		●
In-plant counselors	●	●	●		●
Communications managers	●	●	●		●
Employee coordinators	●	●	●		●
Employee councils					●
Advisory boards					●
Suggestion-processing committees	●				●
Standing working groups			●		●
Jobholders' meetings	●				●
Skip level meetings	●				●
Managers out on plant floor	●		●	●	
Question lines (telephone)	●				●
Question boxes	●				●
Question columns in in-house publications	●				●
Attitude surveys					●
Employee audits					●
Employee assistance		●			●
Employee networks	●	●			●
Health and safety committees			●		●
Mentoring systems	●	●			
Nursing and medical offices		●			●
Performance appraisal systems	●	●			●
Policy advisory committees					●
Quality circles					●
Product safety and liability committees					●

*Data usually offered in the aggregate to protect confidentiality and privacy.

498

systems emphasize access for supervisors and managers so that they can seek advice on supervisory problems and have constructive options for coping with their own problems as employees. Accessibility can be greatly improved by establishing at least one general complaint channel open to all managers and workers regardless of their work location, pay classification, or specialty.

For employees, a *safe* complaint system is one that can provide anonymous or confidential access to responsible human resources professionals. Hotlines, confidential-question systems, employee relations counselors, and ombuds offices should operate with confidentiality and privacy as primary objectives. Confidential discussion of problems offers the employee a chance to plan an approach to resolving the matter or to drop it entirely. A discussion of this kind ensures that the employee has some control over the dispute resolution process.

A safe system encourages effective disputing and forbids reprisal against those raising responsible concerns. Building employees' belief in nonreprisal requires that top management make a serious commitment to preventing retaliation and that it frequently reaffirm its policy. Even so, company pronouncements of "no retaliation" are difficult to enforce. Some senior managers react to complaints with anger or even rage. And sometimes an untrained manager simply behaves in a way management would deplore. At one company a manager fired an employee for putting a suggestion in a suggestion box. (She sued the company and won.) Moreover, unless top management encourages effective disputing, emphasizes its commitment to effective dispute resolution, and works to create a climate where reprisals don't happen, coworkers will often retaliate against a person who voices a concern.

A complaint system that is safe for managers means that they can use it themselves; that their sensible decisions will be backed up; that unfortunate decisions can be reversed in a face-saving way (for example, the complaint handler helps the manager devise a new solution); and that reversal of a responsibly made decision will trigger no action against the manager who made it. Because a good complaint system affirms in whole or in part most managerial decisions and provides safe personnel advice for managers, and because employees who go around their supervisor will most often be helped to resolve the matter with that supervisor, most managers and supervisors who work within a good system come to like it. Indeed, in some systems, supervisors are encouraged to take issues up jointly with the subordinate who initially raised them, to a higher level, an ombuds office, or a special review committee.

Assurances of objective review of concerns and complaints by human resources offices or by other special review channels apart from the line of supervision, greatly enhance a system's *credibility* to employees. To increase objectivity further, a growing number of companies have designated in-house "neutrals," who are counselors, mediators, and sources of formal and informal recommendations. They may be referred to by such titles as work problems counselors or ombuds officers. A few systems allow for outside, nonunion arbitrators.

Where they have broad powers, designated in-house neutrals may investigate complaints, hear concerns, review processes and decisions, mediate among warring parties, and make oral and written recommendations to line management. With very few exceptions, however, they are not arbitrators; they cannot reverse management decisions. They are interpreters among different viewpoints but do not make or change the rules. Typically, an ombudsman can receive complaints from any employee but does not formally review the decisions of other top managers who report to the CEO. Usually enjoying very wide latitude in making an investigation, a neutral can talk with anyone at any level.

The philosophy behind a neutral office is that the long-run interests of the company are congruent with those of a wronged employee, and that the employer may share a partial common interest with each of two employees (for example, supervisor and subordinate) who disagree with each other. This viewpoint is very different from the assumption embedded both in traditional labor-management relations and in the U.S. court system, where disputing parties are seen as adversaries.

Employees see a credible complaint system as responsive. They believe that when they bring concerns forward, management will sometimes change its decisions, in whole or in part. To ensure that the system stays responsive, multiple complaint channels serve as checks and balances for each other.

When management changes from the conventional chain-of-command approach to an innovative, nonunion complaint system, there are often associated changes in language, from "backing up the chain of command" to "supporting and training line supervision," from "preventing dissent" to "effective disputing," from "make-it-stick decision making" to "problem solving," from the idea that "accusations are disloyal" to the ethos that "loyalty requires responsible discussion." To effect this change, management needs new structures with new functions.

Five Functions

Although adjudication will always be a necessary function in an effective complaint system, it takes a back seat to problem solving. Face-to-face communication, confidential counseling with individuals, mediation, and improved management information are more salient characteristics of the new systems approach to handling complaints.

1. *Personal communication.* The commonest need of employees who request assistance is for information. Ways to defuse rumors, clarify policy, and provide accurate information to employees who have misunderstood a work situation are basic to a complaint system.

Supervisors out on the floor, responsible employee networks, and sensitive human resources professionals may perform this function. In many cases it is important to provide ways for employees to request information anonymously or confidentially.

Under names such as "Open Line," "Speak Up," and "Your Voice," the newer approaches use phones or letters to answer general questions about company policy or procedure. Some channels will also get management's opinion on any personal or workplace issue, providing anonymity or confidentiality to the inquiring employee. One such hotline defused potentially damaging rumors about the closing of branch offices. Another handled dozens of calls about an obscure change in benefits that many employees wrongly thought would wipe out an existing benefit.

2. *Confidential advice & counseling.*   Counseling can help address employees' lack of skill and lack of faith in responsible dispute resolution. One of the least dramatic but most effective things that employee counselors accomplish is to help both managers and employees see a problem in perspective, to frame and present it effectively, and to show them what options they have within the organization for resolving it. Most frequently the confidential counselor succeeds by helping a visitor resolve a problem on his or her own. Companies that take an innovative approach to complaint handling for nonunion employees are beginning to allow or encourage some confidential discussion of employee problems by supervisors as well as by personnel staff.

Helpful advice can also come to employees from fellow participants in a formal or informal network and from mentors, if a mentoring system is in place. Employee assistance and health care professionals sometimes extend their mandate to counsel effectively about work problems.

Innovative structures (the professional counselors at NBC, the employee relations managers at Digital Equipment, the resident managers at IBM, and other corporate ombuds offices) usually concentrate on performing this advice function well. One work problems counselor spent many hours with a manager who felt he was racially harassed by his boss. The manager ultimately wrote and delivered a responsible letter asking the boss to desist. The boss did stop and subsequently promoted the manager.

Confidential complaint channels can also help management deal with individual problems in a general way, at no cost to anyone's privacy or individual rights. Mentioning no names, an ombudsman alerted a department head to an allegation of sexual harassment. The department head raised the subject of harassment in a "routine" but thorough way at the next staff meeting. The offending behavior ceased.

3. *Investigation, conciliation, & mediation.*   A modern and creative approach to handling employee complaints stresses dispute resolution rather than adjudication. Many companies have procedures to investigate and mediate employee complaints in a far less polarized and formal manner than companies usually follow in unionized settings or when outside agencies are involved. The employee has to give permission for the investigation, which

should be conducted on a low-key basis to protect everyone's privacy as well as the company's image.

Open-door investigators, sexual harassment and other EEO officers, employee relations managers, and designated neutrals (the ombudsman at AT&T Information Systems, the personnel communications director at Anheuser-Busch, the mediators at Carleton College and at various small businesses) are often able to resolve problems through fact finding and mediation. At one company, dozens of nonsmoking high-tech employees threatened to quit when management introduced a group of smokers into their work space. The employee relations manager investigated and changed air flows, altered desk patterns, and designated smoking and nonsmoking bathrooms. No one quit.

In many companies with such structures, ad hoc mechanisms such as a committee of inquiry, a small group of professional peers, or an appointed investigator known to have relevant expertise mediate disputes among professional and technical employees. An equipment expert came into one publications division, for example, to help resolve a flaming dispute about the choice of highly specialized equipment. Mediating between two angry managers in the division, the expert got them to agree to a two-year plan for phasing in what each wanted.

4. *Adjudication.* Many companies have designed formal complaint and appeal channels for adjudication of complaints. Some are multistep systems designed to serve nonunion employees in unionized environments. As a result, they resemble traditional grievance systems in the scope and structure of their operations. A few such systems involve some form of binding arbitration that includes a neutral party from outside the company as a last step. This feature is said to be a critical aspect of the credibility and effectiveness of employee complaint procedures at companies such as American Electric Power, American Airlines, and TWA.

At Northrop's aviation division, full-time nonexempt employees may press complaints about the application of company policy through a formal grievance system. The steps include going through one's supervisor, the employee relations department, a management appeals committee, and binding arbitration.

Other companies have created alternatives to the union grievance model. At NBC appeals go to a high-level management panel, Security Pacific National Bank created a three-step grievance procedure; with final appeal to a member of the management committee. Some managements—for example, at the Cleveland Clinic and at the First Bank of Oregon, for discrimination complaints—believe that to be credible in their response to employee complaints, they must involve officers and staff who are not in the employee's line of supervision.

Finally, some companies will try to continue a mediation approach until the very last moment. At Control Data, for instance, 80% of the cases about to go to final appeal through the peer review committees have been mediated successfully by an ombudsman.

5.   *Upward feedback*.   Many companies have designed specific structures to provide management with ways of finding out about concerns and complaints. Such companies use employee surveys, advisory councils, and formal and informal employee audits to stay alert to emerging problems. Many other structures can also contribute data. Quality circles can illuminate the employee relations issues that are often at the core of "technical" problems. Health and safety committees (developed voluntarily or by law, as in Washington) can identify supervisors or employees whose behavior poses a special risk. Mentoring arrangements provide a good ear and savvy advice on how the junior employee should approach a problem encountered on the job; a summary of these problems is useful to management. Employee networks can help management understand the problems of special groups.

Performance appraisal systems that involve more than occasional conferences and higher-level review of decisions provide both opportunities and incentives for employee and supervisor to work problems out constructively; management should review summaries of these problems. Research, development, and product-liability review committees are sometimes forums in which professional employees can raise legal, ethical, or professional issues. And nursing and medical offices can sometimes identify personal and work-related problems that underlie the health complaints troubled employees present. It is important that these secondary complaint-handling channels report aggregated data regularly to top management.

Some open-door ombuds officers and investigators—for instance, the personnel communications director at Anheuser-Busch—are charged to bring policy-relevant data back to line management in a way that protects the confidentiality of employees. To monitor for retaliation attempts and to locate trouble spots, IBM, Security Pacific, and Control Data carefully compile statistics on employee complaints.

With good confidential complaint systems in place, top management can head off serious problems. A telephone complaint counselor in a large manufacturing company got an anonymous message: "You guys should check the waste disposal records from the TDR facility!" The ensuing investigation enabled the health and safety director to avert environmental damage and, most likely, heavy government fines.

The Systems Approach

Many companies—large and small—work hard to provide all five functions effectively in a coherent complaint-handling system. At Security Pacific one sees the following mix of approaches: the line of supervision; a telephone hotline for fielding employee questions and channeling problems; a personnel system; a confidential question-response office that answers questions and provides advice on how to proceed without revealing the employee's identity

to management or to personnel staff; and a formal complaint procedure. At
Control Data, the broad approach to problem solving is reflected in the
presence of both telephone and personal access to professional, personal,
and work counselors; a four-step complaint procedure ending with peer
review committees; and a special channel for discrimination complaints.

These approaches illustrate the fact that specific structures and job
titles within systems will vary (see Exhibit 2), but all five functions previously
discussed should be well represented for an innovative system to work. We
believe multifaceted systems offer the best chance for supporting nonunion
employees and for managers to find constructive options for problem solving.
No system will be free of injustice, complaints, and concerns, but some can
teach and exemplify effective dispute resolution.

How might the stories at the beginning of this article have turned out
if the companies had had better complaint-handling procedures in place.

☐ Mark Greenfield reflected on advice given at the group leaders'
meeting: "If you have any unusual problems, talk them over with an
older group leader or with the employee communications manager sooner
rather than later. Remember, you can always go in off the record."
Half an hour later he was referred by employee communications to the
employee assistance office. From there he returned to Cal Floren and
laid out his concerns quietly but firmly. He told Floren that the ugly
outbursts must stop and that if after today's discussion Cal still felt
Mark was unfair, he should take the matter up the line or to employee
communications. If he wanted to talk about being upset, Cal could seek
out the employee assistance office.

Cal glared, stony-faced, and stalked out. A one-sentence resignation awaited Mark the following Monday. The young group leader
felt very troubled about the loss of a pivotal team member and again
sought out the employee communications manager. Several days later,
the manager told Mark she had heard that Cal had been hospitalized
"for a nervous breakdown."

☐ Marcy Lowell looked at the notice on the bulletin board: "Got a
problem? Work problems counselors are at 495-HELP." Her call during lunch break started a long chain of events: almost a dozen talks
with a counselor; a personal letter to the supervisor, which stopped
his offensive language and behavior; a long discussion with her boss
about work assignments, which resulted in more responsibility; and
several tough months when Marcy faced her own shortcomings in order
to do better. Discussions with the work problems counselor and her
boss helped both Marcy and her boss understand how she was going
to get (and to be able to hear) the supportive criticism she needed. The
year ended with a substantial bonus.

Somewhat later, Marcy found herself talking toughly at the staff
women's luncheon in favor of performance appraisals. She laughed at

herself inwardly. Maybe *she* was on her way toward management. But should she have listened more carefully to her colleague's complaint about pay inequity? Marcy phoned Harriet to recommend 495-HELP.

☐ In her methodical scientific way, Dr. Zimmer leafed through the employee handbook, "Safety concerns . . . Talk with your supervisor or see the health and safety director." She'd tried her supervisor; she didn't want to go over his head to the safety office. The cover of the handbook mentioned the ombudsman as another option. "If you don't know where to go, try us!" Zimmer went in as "Ms. X" to discuss her concern. The ombudsman took a sober view, saying, "How can we ignore this?"

He encouraged Zimmer to write a detailed and carefully worded letter to her boss, which she then took in to him personally. She sent no photocopies. He blew up and fired her. Zimmer had been helped to prepare for his anger, but not for a firing. She returned immediately to the ombudsman. The ensuing investigation resulted in Zimmer's return to her bench. Her boss was transferred and subsequently left to start his own company.

30

Management of Differences

WARREN H. SCHMIDT and ROBERT TANNENBAUM

Most managers would agree that certain parts of their jobs give them more trouble than others. But practically all managers would agree that what gives them the most difficulty is handling the conflicts that arise between people. The executive's problem is, simply, to judge the nature of the issue and then to decide what the best course of action is. In this article, two experts on human behavior write that to do these things successfully, managers need first to determine the nature of the difference, see what factors underlie it, and to find out to what stage has the difference evolved. In selecting the right approach, managers should not avoid differences or repress them, they should instead, try to make the differences creative. The final problem managers face is their own feelings. The authors point out that in dealing with conflicts it is natural for managers to be self-interested, and that being aware of their own motivation and needs is the best defense against making biased judgments that can hurt the organization.

The manager often experiences his or her most uncomfortable moments when they must deal with differences among people. Because of these differences, one must often face disagreements, arguments, and even open conflict. To add to the manager's discomfort, he or she frequently finds himself or herself torn by two opposing desires. On the one hand, there is the desire to unleash the individuality of the subordinates in order to tap their full potential and to achieve novel and creative approaches to problems. On the other hand, he or she is eager to develop a harmonious, smooth-working team to carry out the organization's objectives. The manager's lot is further troubled by the fact that when differences do occur, strong feelings

---

Published in 1960.

are frequently aroused, objectivity flies out the window, egos are threatened, and personal relationships are placed in jeopardy.

Toward Effective Management

Because the presence of differences can complicate the manager's job in so many ways, it is of utmost importance that he or she understand them fully and learn to handle them effectively. It is the purpose of this article to assist the manager to manage more effectively by increasing the understanding of differences among the people he or she works with, and by improving their ability to deal with others.

A large part of what follows will focus, for simplicity of exposition, on the differences which occur among a manager's individual subordinates. However, we would like to suggest that the principles, concepts, methods, and dynamics which we discuss throughout much of the article apply to intergroup, to interorganizational, and to international differences as well.

Our basic thesis is that a manager's ability to deal effectively with differences depends on:

☐ The ability to diagnose and to understand differences.

☐ The awareness of, and ability to select appropriately from, a variety of behaviors.[1]

☐ The awareness of, and ability to deal with, his own feelings— particularly those which might reduce his social sensitivity (diagnostic insight) and his action flexibility (ability to act appropriately).[2]

There are two basic assumptions underlying our approach to this problem. Let us examine them before going any further.

1. *Differences among people should not be regarded as inherently "good" or "bad."* Sometimes differences result in important benefits to the organization; and sometimes they are disruptive, reducing the over-all effectiveness of individuals and organizations.

2. *There is no one "right" way to deal with differences.* Under varying circumstances, it may be most beneficial to avoid differences, to repress them, to sharpen them into clearly defined conflict, or to utilize them for enriched problem solving. The manager who consistently "pours oil on troubled waters" may not be the most effective manager. Nor is the manager necessarily successful who emphasizes individuality and differences so strongly that cooperation and teamwork are simply afterthoughts. We feel, rather, that the effective manager is one who is able to use a *variety* of approaches to differences and who chooses any specific approach on the basis of an insightful diagnosis and understanding of the factors with which he or she is faced at that time.

Diagnosing Disagreements

When a manager's subordinates become involved in a heated disagreement, they do not tend to proceed in a systematic manner to resolve their difference. The issues often remain unclear to them, and they may talk *at* rather than *to* one another. If a manager is to be helpful in such a situation, he or she should ask three important diagnostic questions:

1. What is the nature of the difference among the persons?
2. What factors may underlie this difference?
3. To what stage has the interpersonal difference evolved?

Nature of the Difference

Now, looking at the first of these three important questions, the nature of the difference will vary depending on the kind of issue on which people disagree. And there are four basic kinds of issues to look for:

☐ *Facts*. Sometimes the disagreement occurs because individuals have different definitions of a problem, are aware of different pieces of relevant information, accept or reject different information as factual, or have differing impressions of their respective power and authority.

☐ *Goals*. Sometimes the disagreement is about what should be accomplished—the desirable objectives of a department, division, section, or of a specific position within the organization.

☐ *Methods*. Sometimes individuals differ about the procedures, strategies, or tactics which would most likely achieve a mutually desired goal.

☐ *Values*. Sometimes the disagreement is over ethics—the way power should be exercised, or moral considerations, or assumptions about justice, fairness, and so on. Such differences may affect the choice of either goals or methods.

Arguments are prolonged and confusion is increased when the contending parties are not sure of the nature of the issue over which they disagree. By discovering the source of the disagreement, the manager will be in a better position to determine how he or she can utilize and direct the dispute for both short- and long-range good of the organization. As we will indicate later, there are certain steps which are appropriate when the differences are about facts, other steps which are appropriate when the differences are over goals, and still other steps which are applicable when differences are over methods or values.

Underlying Factors

When people are faced with a difference, it is not enough that their manager be concerned with what the difference is about. The second major diagnostic question he should ask is *why* the difference exists. As we try to discover useful answers to this, it is helpful to think in terms of:

☐   Whether the disputants had access to the same information.

☐   Whether the disputants perceive the common information differently.

☐   Whether each disputant is significantly influenced by his role in the organization.

These questions involve informational, perceptual, and role factors. Thus:

☐   *Informational factors* exert their influence when the various points of view have developed on the basis of different sets of facts. The ancient legend of the blind men and the elephant dramatizes this point as vividly as any modern illustration. Because each of the men had contact with a different part of the elephant, each disagreed violently about the nature of the animal. In the same way, when two persons receive limited information about a complex problem, they may well disagree as to the nature of that problem when they come together to solve it.

☐   *Perceptual factors* exert their influence when the persons have different images of the same stimulus. Each will attend to, and select from the information available, those items which they deem important. Each will interpret the information in a somewhat different manner. Each brings to the data a different set of life experiences which cause him or her to view the information through a highly personal kind of filter. The picture which they get, therefore, is unique to them. Thus it is not surprising that the same basic "facts" may produce distinctive perceptual pictures in the minds of different individuals.

☐   *Role factors* exert their influence because each of the individuals occupies a certain position and status in society or in the organization. The fact that one occupies such a position or status may put certain constraints on him or her if the discussion is related to their role.

The concepts we have been discussing can be best illustrated by a concrete case. Such a case is presented in detail in *Exhibit 1*.

Stage of Evolution

Important conflicts among people ordinarily do not erupt suddenly. They pass through various stages, and the way in which the energy of the disputing parties can be effectively directed by the manager depends to some extent on the stage of the dispute when he or she enters the picture.

One way of diagnosing a dispute—the third major question—is to identify it as being at one of these five stages in its development:

Exhibit 1.   Hypothetical Situations Illustrating a Difference

NATURE OF THE DIFFERENCE

	Over facts	Over methods	Over goals	Over values
Expert on office methods	"Automation will save the company money."	"The new system should be installed fully and at once."	"We want a system that gives us accurate data rapidly — whenever we want it."	"We must be modern and efficient."
Head of accounting department	"The new system will be more expensive to install and operate."	"Let us move slower — one step at a time."	"We need most a flexible accounting system to meet our changing needs — managed by accountants who can solve unexpected and complex problems."	"We must consider the welfare of workers who have served the company so loyally for many years."

REASONS FOR THE DIFFERENCE

	Explanation of position of methods expert	Explanation of position of head accountant
Informational (Exposure to different information)	He has studied articles about seemingly comparable companies describing the savings brought about by automation. Representatives of machine companies have presented him with estimates of savings over a 10-year period.	He has heard about the "hidden costs" in automation. He has priced the kind of equipment he believes will be necessary and has estimated its depreciation. This estimated cost is much higher than the salaries of possible replaced workers.
Perceptual (Different interpretation of the same data because of differing backgrounds, experience, and so forth)	He regards the representatives of the machine company as being alert, businesslike, and knowledgeable about the best accounting procedures. He feels that their analysis of the company's needs is dependable and to be trusted.	He sees the representatives of the machine company as salesmen. Their goal is to sell machines, and their report and analysis must be read with great caution and suspicion.
Role (Pressure to take a certain stand because of status or position)	He believes that the company looks to him as the expert responsible for keeping its systems up-to-date and maximally efficient.	He feels responsible for the morale and security of his team in the accounting office. He must defend their loyalty and efficiency if it is ever doubted.

Stage #1—the phase of anticipation.   A manager learns that the company is about to install new, automated equipment which will reduce the number and change the nature of jobs in a given department. He or she can anticipate that when this information is released, there will be differences of opinion as to the desirability of this change, the way in which it should be introduced, and the way in which the consequences of its introduction should be handled.

Stage #2—the phase of conscious, but unexpressed, difference.   Word leaks out about the proposed new equipment. Small clusters of people who trust one another begin discussing it. They have no definite basis for the information, but tensions begin to build up within the organization. There is a feeling of impending dispute and trouble.

Stage #3—the phase of discussion.   Information is presented about the plans to install new equipment. Questions are asked to secure more information, to inquire about the intentions of management, to test the firmness of the decision that has been made. During the discussion, the differing opinions of individuals begin to emerge openly. They are implied by the questions which are asked, and by the language which is used.

Stage #4—the phase of open dispute. The union steward meets with the foreman to present arguments for a change in plans. The foreman counters these arguments by presenting the reasons that led management to decide to install the equipment. The differences which have heretofore been expressed only indirectly and tentatively now sharpen into more clearly defined points of view.

Stage #5—the phase of open conflict. Individuals have firmly committed themselves to a particular position on the issue; the dispute has become clearly defined. The outcome can only be described in terms of win, lose, or compromise. Each disputant attempts not only to increase the effectiveness of their argument and their power in the situation, but also to undermine the influence of those who oppose them.

The power of the manager to intervene successfully will differ at each of these stages. The manager is likely to have the most influence if he or she enters the picture at stage #1; the least influence if he or she enters at stage #5. This range of possible behavior and action changes as the conflict passes through the various stages. For this reason, it is important for the manager not only to assess the nature of the given dispute and the forces affecting the individuals involved, but also to assess the stage to which the dispute has evolved.

Selecting an Approach

After the manager has diagnosed a given dispute (or a potential one) between subordinates, he or she is next confronted by the problem of taking action. And here there are two additional questions that it will be helpful to consider:

1. What courses of action are available?
2. What must be kept in mind in selecting the best one?

Assuming, first, a situation in which the manager has time to anticipate and plan for an impending dispute, we suggest that the general approaches typically available are (a) avoidance, (b) repression, (c) sharpening into conflict, and (d) transformation into problem solving. In deciding which to use, the manager's primary concern should be to select the alternative that will yield optimum benefits to the organization.

Avoidance of Differences
It is possible for a manager to avoid the occurrence of many differences among his or her subordinates. He or she can, for example, staff the orga-

nization with people who are in substantial agreement. Some organizations select and promote individuals whose experiences are similar, who have had similar training, and who come from a similar level of society. Because of such common backgrounds, these individuals tend to see things similarly, to have common interests and objectives, and to approach problems in much the same way. A staff thus developed tends to be a very secure one: the reactions of one's fellows are both readily predictable and congenial to one's own way of thinking and doing.

The manager may also avoid differences among subordinates by controlling certain of their interpersonal contacts. One can, for example, assign two potentially explosive individuals to different groups or physical locations, or choose not to raise a particularly devisive issue because it is "too hot to handle." But let us take a closer look:

When Is This Alternative Appropriate?   Some organizations depend heavily on certain kinds of conformity and agreement among their employees in order to get the work done. Political parties and religious denominational groups are perhaps extreme examples of this. If an individual holds a different point of view on a rather fundamental issue, he or she may become a destructive force within the organization. This approach may be especially important if dealing with somewhat fragile and insecure individuals. Some persons are so threatened by conflict that their ability to function effectively suffers when they operate in a climate of differences.

What Are the Difficulties and Dangers in This Approach?   The manager who uses this approach consistently runs the risk of reducing the total creativity of the staff. Someone has said, "When everyone in the room thinks the same thing, no one is thinking very much." In an atmosphere in which differences are avoided, new ideas not only appear less fequently, but old ideas also are likely to go unexamined and untested. There is genuine danger of the organization's slipping unknowingly into a rut of complacency.

Repression of Differences

Sometimes a manager is aware that certain differences exist among members of the staff, but feels that the open expression of these differences would create unproductive dissension and reduce the total creativity of the group. He or she may, therefore, decide to keep these differences under cover. This may be done by continually emphasizing loyalty, cooperation, teamwork, and other similar values within the group. In such a climate, it is unlikely that subordinates will express disagreements and risk conflict.

The manager may also try to make sure that the potentially conflicting parties come together only under circumstances which are highly controlled—circumstances in which open discussion of latent differences is clearly inappropriate. Or the individual may develop an atmosphere of repression by consistently rewarding agreement and cooperation and by punishing (in one way or another) those who disrupt the harmony of the organization by expressing nonconformist ideas. But once again:

When Is This Alternative Appropriate?   It is most useful when the latent differences are not relevant to the organization's task. It is to be expected that individuals will differ on many things—religion, politics, their loyalty to cities or states, baseball teams, and so forth. There may be no need to reach agreement on some of these differences in order to work together effectively on the job. It may also be appropriate to repress conflict when adequate time is not available to resolve the potential differences among the individuals involved. This might be particularly true if the manager's concern is to achieve a short-run objective and the potential disagreement is over a long-run issue. The wounds of disagreement should not be opened up if there is insufficient time to bind them.

What Are the Difficulties and Dangers in This Approach?   Repression almost always costs something. If, indeed, the differences are important to the persons involved, their feelings may come to be expressed indirectly, in ways that could reduce productivity. Every manager has witnessed situations in which ideas are resisted, not on the basis of their merit, but on the basis of who advocated them. Or they have seen strong criticism arising over mistakes made by a particularly disliked individual.

Much has been said and written about "hidden agenda." People may discuss one subject, but the *way* they discuss it and the positions they take with respect to it may actually be determined by factors lying beneath the surface of the discussion. Hidden agenda are likely to abound in an atmosphere of repression.

When strong feelings are involved in unexpressed differences, the blocking of these feelings creates frustration and hostility which may be misdirected toward "safe" targets. Differences, and the feelings generated by them, do not ordinarily disappear by being ignored. They fester beneath the surface and emerge at inopportune moments to create problems for the manager and his or her organization.

Differences into Conflicts

When this approach is used, the manager not only recognizes the fact that differences exist, but attempts to create an arena in which the conflicting parties can "fight it out." However, like the promoter of an athletic contest, he or she will want to be sure that the differing persons understand the issue over which they differ, the rules and procedures by which they can discuss their differences, and the kinds of roles and responsibilities which each is expected to bear in mind during the struggle. Again:

When Is This Alternative Appropriate?   A simple answer is: "when it is clarifying and educational." Many an individual will not pause to examine the assumptions held or the positions advocated until he or she is called on to clarify and support them by someone who holds contrary views. In the same way, the power realities within an organization can come into sharper focus and be more commonly recognized through conflict.

For example, the manager of production and the manager of engineering may develop quite different impressions of how the board of directors feels about the relative importance of their respective units. Each is sure that the board is most impressed with the caliber of the staff, output, and operational efficiency of their respective departments. When a dispute arises over which group is to get priority space in a new building, top management may permit both departments to exert all the influence they can on the board. During the struggle, the two managers may each gain a more realistic assessment of, and respect for, the power of the other.

Another valuable thing learned is the cost of conflict itself. Almost invariably at the end of a long dispute, there is a strong resolve that "this shall not happen again," as the individuals reflect on the financial costs, tensions, embarrassments, uneasiness, and wasted time and energy it caused.

What Are the Difficulties and Dangers in This Approach? Conflict can be very costly. It not only saps the energy of those involved, but also may irreparably destroy their future effectiveness. In the heat of conflict, words are sometimes spoken which leave lifelong scars on people or forever cloud their relationship.

Because the risks involved in conflict are so great and the potential costs so high, the manager will want to consider carefully the following questions before using this approach:

1   What does he or she hope to accomplish?
2   What are the possible outcomes of the conflict?
3   What steps should be taken to keep the conflict within organizational bounds and in perspective?
4   What can be done after the conflict to strengthen the bonds between disputants, so that the conflict will be of minimum destructiveness to them and to their ongoing relationship?

Making Differences Creative

"Two heads are better than one" because the two heads often represent a richer set of experiences and because they can bring to bear on the problem a greater variety of insights. If the differences are seen as enriching, rather than as in opposition to each other, the "two heads" will indeed be likely to come up with a better solution than either one alone. For example, had the six blind men who came into contact with different parts of the elephant pooled their information, they would have arrived at a more accurate description of the animal. In the same way, many problems can be seen clearly, wholly, and in perspective only if the individuals who see different aspects can come together and pool their information. Here, too, let us take a more specific look:

When Is This Alternative Appropriate? When it comes to choosing courses of action for a given problem, differences among the individuals in an organization can help to increase the range and variety of alternatives suggested.

The channeling of differences into a problem-solving context may also help to deal with some of the feelings which often accompany disagreement—frustration, resentment, and hostility. By providing an open and accepted approach, the manager helps to prevent undercurrents of feelings which could break out at inopportune moments. He or she also helps to channel the energy generated by feelings into creative, rather than into destructive, activities. Whereas conflict tends to cause individuals to see ways of weakening and undermining those who differ with them, the problem-solving approach leads individuals to welcome differences as being potentially enriching to one's own goals, ideas, and methods.

What Are the Difficulties and Dangers in This Approach? To utilize differences requires time. Often it is easier for a single individual (rather than two or more persons) to make a decision. Also, when a rapid decision is required, it may be easier and more practical to ignore one side of an argument in order to move into action. Finally, unless a problem-solving situation is planned with some care, there is always the risk of generating conflict which will be frustrating to all parties concerned.

Enriched Problem Solving

Let us assume that the course of action decided on is the one just discussed—turning the difference into creative problem solving. Let us further assume, now, that the manager enters the picture when the subordinates are already involved in conflict. What are the things that can be done if he or she wishes to transform this conflict into a problem-solving situation?

☐ *Welcome the existence of differences within the organization.*

The manager can indicate that from the discussion of differences can come a greater variety of solutions to problems and a more adequate testing of proposed methods. By making clear the view that all parties contribute to the solution of problems by sharing their differences, he or she reduces the implication that there will be an ultimate "winner" and "loser."

☐ *Listen with understanding rather than evaluation.*

There is abundant evidence that conflicts tend to be prolonged and to become increasingly frustrating because the conflicting parties do not really listen to one another. Each attempts to impose their own views and to "tune out" or distort what the other person has to say.

The manager may expect that when he or she enters the picture, the individuals will try to persaude him or her to take a stand on the issue involved. While each adversary is presenting his or her "case" to the manager, he or she will be watching for cues which indicate where the manager stands on the issue. It is therefore important that the manager make every effort to understand both positions as fully as possible, recognizing and supporting the seriousness of purpose of each where appropriate, and to withhold judgment until all available facts are in.

In the process of listening for understanding, the manager will also set a good example for the conflicting parties. By adopting such a listening-understanding attitude, and by helping the disputants to understand each other more fully, he or she can make a most useful contribution toward transforming potential conflict into creative problem solving.

    ☐   *Clarify the nature of the conflict.*

In the heat of an argument, each participant may primarily focus on either facts, specific methods, goals, or values. Frustration and anger can occur when one individual talks about facts while another is eager to discuss methods. The manager, having carefully listened to the discussion, can clarify the nature of the issues so that the discussion can become more productive.

    ☐   *Recognize and accept the feelings of the individuals involved.*

Irrational feelings are generated in a controversy, even though the participants do not always recognize this fact. Each wants to believe that he is examining the problem "objectively." The manager, recognizing and accepting feelings such as fear, jealousy, anger, or anxiety, may make it possible for the participants squarely to face their true feelings. The effective manager does not take a critical attitude toward these feelings by, in effect, saying, "You have no right to feel angry!" Rather, he or she should try sincerely to communicate sympathetic feelings.

Ordinarily, we do no real service to people by encouraging a repression of their feelings or by criticizing them for experiencing fear, anger, and so forth. Such criticism—whether implied or expressed openly—may block the search for new ways out of the controversy. There is considerable evidence that when a person feels threatened or under attack, they tend to become more rigid and therefore more defensive about positions to which they have committed themselves.

    ☐   *Indicate who will make the decision being discussed.*

Sometimes heated disputes go on with respect to issues over which one or more of the persons involved has no control. When people have differing notions about the formal authority available to each, a clarification by the manager of the authority relationships can go far toward placing the discussion in clearer perspective.

☐ *Suggest procedures and ground rules for resolving the differences.*

If the disagreement is over *facts,* the manager may assist the disputants in validating existing data and in seeking additional data which will more clearly illuminate the issues under dispute.

If the disagreement is over *methods,* the manager may first want to remind the parties that they have common objectives, and that their disagreement is over means rather than ends. He or she may suggest that before examining in detail each of their proposed methods for achieving the goals, they might together establish a set of criteria to be used in evaluating whatever procedures are proposed. The manager may also want to suggest that some time be spent in trying to generate additional alternatives reflecting new approaches. Then after these alternatives have been worked out, he or she may encourage the parties to evaluate them with the aid of the criteria which these persons have developed together.

If the disagreement is over *goals* or goal priorities, the manager may suggest that the parties take time to describe as clearly as possible the conflicting goals which are being sought. Sometimes arguments persist simply because the parties have not taken the trouble to clarify for themselves and for each other exactly what they do desire. Once these goals are clearly stated, the issues can be dealt with more realistically.

If the disagreement is over *values,* the manager may suggest that these values be described in operational terms. Discussions of abstractions often tend to be fruitless because the same words and concepts mean different things to different people. To help individuals become more fully aware of the limitations to which their actions are subject, the question, "What do you think you can do about this situation?" usually leads to a more productive discussion than the question, "What do you believe in?" Because value systems are so closely related to a person's self concept, the manager may want to give particular attention to protecting the egos involved. He or she may make clear that an individual's entire ethical system is not being scrutinized, but only those values which are pertinent to the particular instance.

☐ *Give primary attention to maintaining relationships between the disputing parties.*

Sometimes, during the course of a heated dispute, so much attention is paid to the issue under discussion that nothing is done to maintain and strengthen the relationship between the disputing parties. It is not surprising, therefore, that disputes tend to disrupt ongoing relationships. Through oversight or deliberate action, important functions are neglected which sustain or further develop human relationships—for example, the functions of encouraging, supporting, reducing tension, and expressing common feelings. If a conflict is to be transformed into a problem-solving situation, these functions need to be performed by someone—either by the manager or, through his or her continuing encouragement, by the parties themselves.

☐ *Create appropriate vehicles for communication among the disputing parties.*

One of the ways to bring differences into a problem-solving context is to ensure that the disputants can come together easily. If they can discuss their differences *before* their positions become crystalized, the chances of their learning from each other and arriving at mutually agreeable positions are increased. Having easy access to one another is also a way of reducing the likelihood that each will develop unreal stereotypes of the other.

Misunderstanding mounts as communication becomes more difficult. One of the values of regular staff meetings, therefore, is that such meetings, properly conducted, can provide a continuing opportunity for persons to exchange ideas and feelings.

If the manager wishes the subordinates to deal with their differences in a problem-solving framework, he or she will want to ask, "In what kind of setting will the parties to this dispute be best able to discuss their differences with a minimum of interference and threat?" He or she will exclude from such a setting any individuals whose presence will embarrass the disputants if the latter "back down" from previously held points of view. It will be a setting which reflects as much informality and psychological comfort as possible.

☐ *Suggest procedures which facilitate problem solving.*

One of the key needs in a dispute is to separate an idea from the person who first proposes it. This increases the chance of examining the idea critically and objectively without implying criticism of the person. Techniques like brainstorming, for example, are designed to free people from the necessity to defend their ideas during an exploration period. Another facilitating action is outlining an orderly set of procedures (e.g., examining objectives, obtaining relevant data) for the disputants to follow as they seek a constructive resolution of their difference.

Managerial Objectivity

Thus far we have tended to make the unrealistic assumption that the manager is able to maintain his or her own objectivity in the face of a difference among his or her subordinates. Obviously, this does not easily happen because their feelings also tend to become involved. It is, in fact, not unusual for people to react to differences more on the basis of their own feelings than on the basis of some rational approach to the problem at hand.

A manager may be deeply concerned about the disruptive effects of a disagreement. He or she may be troubled about how the persistence of a dispute will affect him or her personally or their own position in the organization. One may worry about the danger of coming under personal attack, or of incurring the anger and hostility of important subordinates or a superior. He or she may become anxious as another person expresses deep feelings, without really understanding why.

While sometimes personal feelings of this kind are at the conscious level, often they are unrecognized by the manager himself or herself because they lie in the area of the unconscious. This, then, highlights the importance of the manager's own self-awareness. While we do not intend to deal with this topic here, it might be well to note some "alerting signals" to which the manager might pay attention when he or she confronts a difference.

Certain kinds of behavior may indicate that the manager's handling of differences is strongly influenced by their personal needs and feelings rather than by the objective interests of the organization—as, for example:

☐ A persistent tendency to surround oneself with yes men.

☐ Emphasizing loyalty and cooperation in a way that makes disagreement seem equivalent to disloyalty and rebellion.

☐ A persistent tendency to "pour oil on troubled waters" whenever differences arise.

☐ Glossing over serious differences in order to maintain an appearance of harmony and teamwork.

☐ Accepting ambiguous resolutions of differences which permit conflicting parties to arrive at dissimilar interpretations.

☐ Exploiting differences to strengthen his personal position of influence through the weakening of the position of others.

Any of these kinds of behavior could, as we have already suggested, be appropriate in certain situations and actually serve the general interest of the organization. If, however, they represent rather consistent patterns on the part of the manager, then it may be worth his or her while to examine more closely the reasons for his or her actions.

There are times in the lives of most of us when our personal needs are the strongest determinants of our behavior. Fortunately, most organizations can tolerate a limited amount of such self-oriented behavior on the part of their managers. The danger occurs if an individual believes that their actions are solely motivated by the "good of the organization" when, in fact, they are operating on the basis of other kinds of personal motivation without being aware of it.

The manager who is more fully aware of his or her own feelings and inclinations is in a better position to diagnose a situation accurately and to choose rationally the kind of behavior which is in the best interests of the organization.

Conclusion

This article began with the assumption that many managers are uncertain and uneasy when differences arise. Because their own emotions and the feelings of others quickly become involved, they often deal with differences in a haphazard or inappropriate manner. We have attempted to suggest some more systematic ways to view differences and to deal with them. We believe that if a manager can approach a difference with less fear and with greater awareness of the potential richness that lies in it, he or she will better understand the basic nature and causes of the difference. And having done this, he or she will be in a better position to discover and implement more realistic alternatives for dealing with it.

Notes

1. For insightful treatments of the causes and consequences of conflict, and the alternative means of dealing with it—as well as with other expressions of difference—see Lewis A. Coser, *The Function of Social Conflict* (London, Routledge and Kegan Paul, Ltd., 1956); and Raymond W. Mack and Richard C. Snyder, "The Analysis of Social Conflict—Toward an Overview and Synthesis," *Conflict Resolution,* June 1957, pp. 212–248.

2. For definitions and discussions of social sensitivity and action flexibility see Robert Tannenbaum and Fred Masarik, "Leadership: A Frame of Reference," *Management Science,* Vol. 4, No. 1, October 1957; and Robert Tannenbaum and Warren H. Schmidt, "How to Choose a Leadership Pattern," *HBR* March–April 1958, p. 95.

31

The Interpersonal Underworld

WILLIAM C. SCHUTZ

The Interpersonal Underworld, says William C. Schutz, operates beneath the level of people's overt behavior and affects how they work with one another. "No matter how much people try to keep interpersonal problems out by ignoring them," he writes, "they will turn up in subtle forms such as loss of motivation, tiredness, or the group member's preoccupation with outside tasks; or they may get entangled directly with the solution of the task and have to be worked out in the body of the problem."

Although the businessperson must spend a major part of his or her time dealing with other people, he or she has in the past had little help in overcoming the difficulties that inevitably arise when people get together. The terms which have been used to describe these problems—terms like "disciplinary problems," "human relations troubles," or the currently popular "communications difficulties"—have served only to hide the real difficulties, for they are descriptions of symptoms. The real causes must be sought at a deeper level; they lie in interpersonal relations.

In every meeting of two or more people two levels of interaction occur. One is the overt—the play that is apparently being played. The other is the covert—like a ballet going on in back of the performance on the interpersonal stage—a subtle struggle for attention and status, for control and influence, and for liking and warmth. This ballet influences the performance by pushing the overt players into unusual postures and making them say and do unusual things. Thus, the objective, hardheaded executive is overtly very resistant to a splendid idea suggested by the brash young fellow who may someday replace him or her. But this example is much too obvious. The ballet's effect on the actors is usually more subtle.

Published in 1958.

The importance of these covert factors can hardly be overestimated. The productivity of any particular group is profoundly influenced by them. One of the main functions of this article is to attempt to dispel the idea that strong interpersonal differences existing within a group setting can be effectively handled by ignoring them—as if by the magic of closing your eyes you could make problems go away. Rather, interpersonal problems must be understood and dealt with. If ignored, they are usually transformed so that they are not expressed directly as open hostility but find their expression through the task behavior of the group. Failure to allow these group processes to work in a direct fashion will decrease the group's productivity.

The types of behavior that result from interpersonal difficulties are various. In many cases it is difficult to recognize their connection with interpersonal relations in the work situation. To illustrate some of these more subtle connections, I shall describe several behaviors resulting from, or symptomatic of, interpersonal difficulties, and then present a sampling of situations giving rise to these behaviors.

Behavior Symptoms

Generally, interpersonal problems lead individuals to resist each other and each other's influence in various overt, but more often covert, ways. Each individual may oppose, delay, fail to support, or sabotage another. The mechanisms to be discussed here are largely covert, or unconscious; the individual does these things without being aware of their intention to resist or obstruct.

Communications Problems
These days "communications problems" are greatly emphasized as a source of industrial difficulty. This emphasis, however, seems misplaced. For one thing, problems which are caused by communications are due not to *inadequate* communication but to *too adequate* communication, since what is transmitted most accurately between people is how they feel rather than what they say. Thus, if the boss really feels that the research scientist is not very important, that feeling will be communicated to the scientist much more readily than any words that pass between them. For another thing, communications difficulties are primarily the *result* of interpersonal difficulties; they are seldom themselves a primary *cause* of problems. Resisting another person is often accomplished through the medium of communication. Thus:

☐ A person may find it difficult to understand what is being said, or, sometimes, actually not hear what is said. Often a person feels confused; he or she just cannot follow all the things that are going on. Another sign of resistance is incoherent speech, mumbling, not bothering to make a point clear, or not making sure that the listener has heard. All of these occurrences impede the process of verbal communication.

☐ Resistance may also take the form of forgetting to pick up a message that was to have been left on one's desk. Or one may forget to mail a memo or leave a message of importance to someone else; or the message may be garbled, ambiguous, or actually contain a factual error. Similarly, misreading and misinterpretation increase greatly in situations of interpersonal strife.

Individually, these behaviors all appear to be simple human failings and, indeed, in many cases may be only that. However, it is always a good bet, especially when the incidents recur, that they are unconsciously motivated by interpersonal differences. In short, interpersonal problems frequently find expression through the obstruction of valid communication. Excessive communications problems can usually be interpreted as a symptom of interpersonal trouble.

Loss of Motivation

Another expression of interpersonal problems is the loss of motivation to work on a task. In innumerable ways the individual's work becomes ineffective because he or she lacks the desire to produce. The accumulation of many minor inefficiencies amounts to the equivalent of losing the services of a group member or a part of one or more members' resources and abilities. For example:

☐ If a group member is supposed to look up some information which is needed for other members of the group to complete their work, he or she may just miss getting to the company library before Friday night closing time. Therefore he or she will have to wait over the weekend and, in the meantime, hold up two other people who are waiting for the report. Or perhaps some morning they will oversleep when they should be at the committee meeting.

☐ Another individual does only what is required and nothing extra. If he or she works from nine to five, he or she will leave promptly at five, considering the work a chore, a task to be accomplished and nothing more. If something goes wrong because of someone else's error, no effort will be made to compensate for it. If he or she is not very busy and someone else needs a hand, this individual will not lend it. All in all, they will do only the very minimum required to retain his or her job.

☐ Another manifestation of a person's loss of motivation is a sudden realization that his or her outside interests and commitments are much stronger than when the group began. He or she finds that conflicting meetings and other things force him or her to leave meetings early, to arrive late, or perhaps even to miss one. Or he or she may have reports to write that prevent him from coming or working for this committee.

☐ Chronic absenteeism or lateness is still another manifestation of an interpersonal difficulty. Perhaps a group member has an actual illness or some committment at home that prevents them from coming; there may be any one of a large number of reasons for this absence or lateness, many of which are rational. But these situations may happen too often to make the whole pattern a rational one. If a person has a meeting and the snow is heavy, it may be that they cannot make the meeting because of the traffic situation; but if it were a meeting which they really wanted to attend, the snow would not be a great enough obstacle to prevent them from going.

☐ Also, a loss of motivation very frequently expresses itself in an actual feeling of physical tiredness. Handling emotional and interpersonal difficulties is hard work, especially if it involves holding back certain strong feelings. This work actually makes the individual so tired that the individual has great difficulty in bringing himself or herself to work and to persevere on a job once it is begun. It often happens that an individual who feels completely exhausted in one part of their work situation miraculously perks up when a new task comes along or when they go home to a more enjoyable activity. Again, this is not a case of deliberate malingering. The person actually feels tired. When the conflict-inducing situation is removed, the tiredness lifts.

In general, what is happening is that a person suddenly finds that other groups in which their interpersonal relations are happier are more important than the present group, and hence the motivation to work in the situation is reduced. A person will seek a situation in which they are happiest and will attempt to avoid unpleasant situations as far as possible. In other words, he or she escapes the situation by withdrawing their involvement.

Indiscriminate Opposition

Another category of responses to interpersonal difficulties involves direct blockage of action. This mechanism is often quite overt and conscious, but it likewise has many covert and unconscious forms.

A symptom of a bad relationship is resistance to suggestions. It may happen that an individual in the group makes suggestions which are opposed by another member regardless of their merit. As soon as the first member begins to talk, the second person—because they feel hostile to the first—feels a surge of resistance or reluctance to accept anything they are going to hear. This is, of course, not beneficial from the standpoint of the group, because a very good suggestion may be rejected for irrelevant personal reasons.

The manner in which such opposition is manifested is often very subtle. If an antagonist makes a suggestion, rather than use direct attack an individual may say smilingly, "That sounds interesting, but perhaps if we tried this other method it would be even more effective." Another technique is to postpone a decision on an opponent's suggestion. The parliamentary procedure of "tabling" is one formal method, as are setting up investigating committees, considering other matters first, offering amendments, or being unavailable for a meeting to decide on the suggestion. Undoubtedly the experienced businessperson can extend this list indefinitely. Again, it is important to note that, although the techniques are often deliberately used, they are perhaps used even more often without the user's awareness of his motivation.

Operational Problems

There are several ailments of total group functioning that are symptomatic of interpersonal difficulties. In most cases, difficulty in reaching decisions is a sure indication of interpersonal strife. This usually implies that the group is unable to tell anybody *no*, since to make such a decision involves saying *yes* to the proponents of another view. Compromises are then put through that satisfy neither side and that certainly do not accomplish the task as effectively as the group could under optimal conditions. The compromise is really one between the individuals who are in conflict, and not a compromise, essentially, of the issues of the case.

Another symptom of interpersonal problems in a group is inefficient division of labor. If the relationships among the people are poor, difficulties arise as soon as it comes time to assign different roles and divide the labor so that the group can operate more effectively. Strongly held interpersonal feelings prevent the group from saying *no* to somebody who wants to be in a particular position in the group but whom the other members consider unsuited to that position. This person may, therefore, be put into the role anyway, to the detriment of the functioning of the group. For example:

> In one group of marketing personnel there was a man of clearly out-standing abilities regarding ideas for the solution of the group's problem. Because of his strength and dominance in the group he was accepted as the leader. One result of this was that he was not in a very good position to express his ideas, since as the leader he had to assume a conciliator role; thus, his virtue as a member who could contribute to the substance of the group's task was diminished.

> A second result was that he could not act as a good administrator, that is, could not effectively coordinate the efforts of the other group members. So, by not being able to say *no* to this person, or by not being able to discuss more openly the best use to be made of his abilities, the group lost in two very important ways.

Another frequent instance of this difficulty is putting a person who is extremely capable in a subordinate role, with the result that their abilities cannot be utilized by the group. Thus:

In a different group the phenomenon opposite to the previous example occurred, resulting in equal injury to the group's performance. Because of personal hostility from several other members the most competent man was relegated to the role of secretary. There his time was consumed taking minutes, and his stellar abilities were wasted.

In general, then, ability to place people properly within a group is one indication of good basic interpersonal relations, while inability is a sign that there must be something wrong among the people that prevents them from using their resources optimally.

Task Distortions

Interpersonal difficulties are almost invariably reflected in a group's performance on its task, although at times these effects are more obvious than at others. Here are three examples of interpersonal problems being expressed directly in work behavior, taken from groups of eight graduate students working on actual industrial problems at the Harvard Business School:

☐ One of these groups was working on the problem of bringing out a new product for a major manufacturer. The members developed a marketing strategy for this product in which the big stress was on the image that the product would present to consumers. In fact, they put so much stress on the image that they neglected certain other factors.

My observations of this group in operation indicated the reason for the inefficient emphasis. From the beginning certain men were assigned by the group, not to the actual task, but to the presentation to be made to the company at the completion of the work. Some of them became very concerned with the impression *they* would make—in fact more concerned with this than with the impression the product would make. Therefore, they unconsciously sought the aspect of their assigned task which would allow them to work on their interpersonal problem and anxiety and concentrated on it to the consequent neglect of other factors which were also important.

☐ Another group evolved a marketing strategy for bringing out a family of products. On examination, it appeared that this product family was not particularly well integrated. In addition, there was reason to believe that a single product would be more effective.

From interviews with the individual members and from observations of their working as a group, it became clear that the family of products was a compromise solution. Certain members of the group had wanted one product; others had wanted a different one. Instead of trying to work out these differences of opinion in terms of marketing considerations, the group decided implicitly to bring out the whole family as a solution to their interpersonal problem.

☐ Still another group devised a marketing solution with a heavy emphasis on a decentralized distribution system. But the company representatives immediately wondered about the wisdom of using such autonomous distributors, since company-hired distributors should lead to more profits. The group was at a loss to justify its own suggestion.

Again, observations of the group throughout the term indicated a possible reason. The group had had a serious interpersonal blowup at one point, and the members had decided to go their separate ways. The result of this decision was autonomous operation by the individual members of the group. Apparently the group members were unconsciously influenced by the fact that their group could operate more effectively as autonomous individuals.

Interpersonal problems are often worked out on some aspect of the task that closely approximates the relationship which is of concern to the group (company to dealer, company to consumer, and so forth). In this way the tensions generated by the interpersonal problems can be relieved by symbolically displacing them into the work situation. The drawback of this phenomenon is that, although it appears that the group is very task-oriented, its work may in fact be quite inappropriate and inefficient at many points.

Common Issues

We have looked at some of the behaviors which may be considered symptomatic of inadequate interpersonal relations. Certain problem situations that occur in group and interpersonal dealings with great frequency generate these symptoms. As an illustration of the nature of the problems and some of their vicissitudes, I shall now discuss three of them.

Consensus for Decision

In every group, sooner or later, a decision-making apparatus must be agreed on. Whether it be consensus, majority rule, unanimity, or any other method, there must be some *modus operandi* for the group to make decisions. By consensus I mean, here, that everyone in the group is agreed that a certain course of action is best for the group, regardless of whether or not he individually agrees with it. Ordinarily, if the group does not have consensus and a decision goes through, the group pays. For instance:

Let us suppose that a group, perhaps a committee, has gotten together with the task of deciding a particular issue. The issue has come to a vote, and the vote is fairly decisive, say six to two. The two people in the minority, however, do not really feel that they have had an opportunity to express their feelings about the issue. Although they are committed to go along with the decision, they have an inner reluctance to do so. This covert reluctance may manifest itself in any of the symptoms already mentioned. Perhaps the most common symptom is a loss of interest, although this situation could be expected to give rise to any of them.

The question of consensus is central in decision making. In a deeper sense, consensus means that eveyone in a group feels that the group understands their position and feelings about it; and he or she feels, then, that the group should take a particular course of action even though they do not personally agree. If the individual is not allowed to voice their own feelings and reasons for voting against the particular issue, they will, at least unconsciously, resist the efficient functioning of the group from that point on. If consensus is not required, decisions can often be made more quickly (for example, by majority rule or by fiat), but delay will probably result, due to the unacknowledged members having various ways of resisting once the decision has been made and the action is undertaken.

The ability to detect a lack of consensus is, of course, a very important attribute for a group leader. A few rules of thumb might be of help here. The clue is that it is very difficult to find out whether there is a consensus unless each person is allowed to speak; for lack of disagreement does not necessarily indicate that the group has consensus. Frequently people simply are reluctant to raise their objections. However, if each member is asked separately whether or not he assents to the issue, the group leader can usually pick up objections:

☐ He or she may be able to spot disagreement by noticing such things as changes in tone of voice. In one group the leader asked if everyone agreed on a suggested course of action. As she went around the room she got the following responses: *yes, yes, yes, yes, yes, okay.* This leader, being fairly astute, immediately began to question the woman who had said *okay*, because this woman apparently could not quite bring herself to be like the other members of the group with regard to this decision. This inability is usually a good indication of an objection. The individual is reluctant to object directly because of the weight of all the other members disagreeing with her.

After this woman had been quizzed for a while, it became clear that she did have a strong objection. Once she was allowed to talk it out, she went along with the group and was quite willing to say *yes* and, in fact, to pitch in and work with the decision that was finally made.

☐ Another good indicator of lack of consensus is any attempt by a member to postpone a decision by further discussion or by further action of some kind. Comments like, "What is it we are voting on?" or "Weren't we supposed to discuss something else first?" or "I have no objection to that, but . . ." all indicate that the individual is not yet ready to cast a positive vote for a given decision. They probably have an objection that ought to be brought out into the open and discussed.

Allowing the objector to raise their point for discussion is not just a hollow gesture. The objector will be more likely to go along with the final decision—or they may eventually carry the day because they reflect some objections that other people had but were not aware of. Whether the group actually changes its vote or not, it will be more likely to reach a correct decision. This opportunity for the group to discuss a previously covert factor is very important for its effectiveness.

Authority Problem

Another group phenomenon that leads to reduced effectiveness concerns the relationship of the group members to the leader of the group. (The term *leader* will be used loosely to mean the person who is, in the eyes of the group members, supposed to head the group—usually a formal leader, a designated person who has a higher title.) It is the nature of such relationships that members of the group have ambivalent feelings toward the authority figure—both positive and negative feelings. The negative feelings can be particularly disturbing since it usually is hard for people to express such feelings directly, because their jobs may be in jeopardy or because they feel that they should not attack an authority figure.

Since the hostility must be expressed, however, they often transfer it to another member of the group. Some other member, usually one with characteristics similar to those disliked in the leader, will be attacked more than he realistically should be for his behavior in the group. He or she will be attacked not only for what they do, but also because the attack that the group would like to level toward the leader is displaced onto them. The term *scapegoat* is often used for this person. For example, if the group members are dissatisfied because the leader is not giving sufficient direction to the group, the dissatisfaction may be vented toward a silent or nonparticipating member, the member in the group who comes closest to having the characteristic of the leader which the group members do not like. For example:

> In one marketing group the leader offered the group very little direction, far less than most members would have liked. Subsequently, everyone began to get very angry with one group member who did not say much and who occasionally missed meetings because of his other commitments. The group attacked him of his lack of interest and unwillingness to contribute to the group.

> A key to what was really happening is found in the fact that he was actually quite interested and was contributing a great deal, thus making the attack somewhat undeserved; but significantly, the characteristics which angered the group members were precisely those that covertly irritated them about the leader. Apparently they displaced their aggression from the leader, whom they felt they could not attack directly, onto a group member who had similar attributes.

This same mechanism operates when the boss is too *authoritarian*. Somebody in the group who has similar tendencies will be severely attacked, again as a displacement of the attack they would like to level at the boss. With regard to dealing with this phenomenon, perhaps the most useful thing to be said is that there are times when a leader, in order to allow a group to operate more effectively, must become the scapegoat. If he or she can absorb some of the hostility that is really meant for him or her or perhaps in some cases even absorb some of the hostility meant for other group members, he or she can be most useful in helping a group to function more effectively. Of course, in order to do this the leader must be aware that the hostility is not necessarily directed at him or her personally; it is just an inevitable consequence of group activity that hostility does arise. If he or she can absorb the hostility directly, it does not have to be deflected into the group where it is most destructive to the group and to the group's ability to fulfill its purposes. An important part of a leader's role is to be a scapegoat occasionally in order that the group may proceed and operate more effectively. This situation brings to mind an old saying, "A good king is one whose subjects prosper."

The Problem Member

Another frequently occurring group difficulty is the presence of a problem member, one of the most difficult of all interpersonal problems for a group to deal with. Problem members are of two main types—the overactive member and the underactive member. Either can disrupt group functioning, and both are usually difficult to handle.

The overactive problem member dominates the group's attention far more than his abilities warrant. The difficulties arise partly because the apparent intensity of their feelings leads to a general reluctance of the group to hurt the individual while at the same time they cannot curtail his or her destructive activities. To illustrate what can happen in such a situation:

> In one five-man group of military personnel working on a series of tactical problems, Mac immediately took over control of the group. Because he was reasonably competent and highly forceful, he went unchallenged for several meetings. The other group members were not very compatible, so they had a difficult time handling Mac. Gradually some members began losing interest in the group until one discussion of a very trivial topic, the postal rates from Washington to Chicago, came up in one of their rest periods. The exchange that followed was amazing in that Mac was attacked severely and at length by the other group members for his dogmatically stated opinion about postal rates. The group used this topic to vent their stored-up feelings toward Mac. By this time, however, the group had no resources to cope with these strong feelings, and it quickly disintegrated after the conflict.

The optimal solution to the problem represented by this member is to handle him in such a way that he can be retained in the group and his resources made use of and still not be allowed to obstruct the group's functioning:

> Another group had this problem with Bob. But this group quickly deposed Bob and set up a leader of considerably less intellect but with superior

coordinating abilities. For a short time after they had deposed Bob the group made sure he realized he was not going to run the group; then they gradually allowed him back into the group by paying more attention to his ideas. Finally, after about ten meetings, his ideas were highly influential and sought by the group, although he was not allowed to dominate. In this way the group took care of the problem presented by an overactive member and was still able to utilize his abilities. This is an ideal solution and the sign of a strong, compatible group.

Someone who will not become integrated into the group also poses a problem for the group. The lack of commitment of this member, perhaps even a lack of willingness to work, constitutes a serious group problem. One solution is to eject the member from the group. This is a solution only insofar as it removes the source of a difficulty; it does not allow the group to utilize the person's abilities. The problem member often serves a useful function by enabling other members to direct their hostility toward him or her, so that they do not have to deal with the real differences among themselves. Thus, it is not unusual that if a chronically negative member is absent, the group finds that it still has disagreements.

Framework for Behavior

Now that I have described examples of several interpersonal problem situations and various reactions to them, I shall present a brief outline of a theory of interpersonal behavior. In order to deal with interpersonal behavior it is necessary to have an understanding of the *general* principles of this behavior, since formulas for handling *specific* situations are of limited value at best. The following theory is by no means the only one extant in psychological literature, but it is offered as a possible framework for understanding phenomena of the type under discussion here.

Interpersonal Needs

The basis for evolving this theory of interpersonal behavior is the individual's *fundamental interpersonal relations orientation* or, to abbreviate, FIRO. The basic assumption of this approach is that people need people. Every human being, because they live in a society, must establish an equilibrium between themselves and their human environment—just as they must establish an equilibrium between themselves and the physical world. This social nature of man gives rise to certain interpersonal needs, which he or she must satisfy to some degree while avoiding threat to oneself. Although each individual has different intensities of need and different mechanisms for handling them, people have three basic interpersonal needs in common:

1. *The Need for Inclusion.* This is the need to maintain a satisfactory relation between the self and other people with respect to interaction or belongingness. Some people like to be with other people all the time; they

want to belong to organizations, to interact, to mingle. Other people seek much less contact; they prefer to be alone, to interact minimally, to stay out of groups, to maintain privacy.

If a continuum were to be drawn between these two extremes, every person could be placed at a point (or region) at which he or she feels most comfortable. Thus, to a certain degree each individual is trying to belong to a group, but he or she is also trying to maintain a certain amount of privacy. From the other point of view he or she wishes to some degree to have people initiate interaction toward him or her through invitations and the like, and also wishes to some degree that people would leave him or her alone. For each dimension these two aspects may be distinguished: (a) the behavior he or she initiates toward others, his or her expressed behavior; and (b) the behavior he or she prefers others to express toward him or her, their wanted behavior. This distinction will prove valuable in the discussion of compatibility.

2. *The Need for Control.* This is the need to maintain a satisfactory relation between oneself and other people with regard to power and influence. In other words, every individual has a need to control their situation to some degree, so that their environment can be predictable for them. Ordinarily this amounts to controlling other people, because other people are the main agents which threaten him or her and create an unpredictable and uncontrollable situation. This need for control varies from those who want to control their entire environment, including all the people around them, to those who want to control no one in any situation, no matter how appropriate controlling them would be.

Here, again, everyone varies as to the degree to which he or she wants to control others. In addition, everyone varies with respect to the degree to which he or she wants to be controlled by other people, from those who want to be completely controlled and are dependent on others for making decisions for them to those who want to be controlled under no conditions.

3. *The Need for Affection.* This is the need to maintain a satisfactory relation between the self and other people with regard to love and affection. In the business setting this need is seldom made overt. It takes the form of friendship. In essence, affection is a relationship between two people only, a dyadic relationship. At one extreme individuals like very close, personal relationships with each individual they meet. At the other extreme are those who like their personal relationships to be quite impersonal and distant, perhaps friendly but not close and intimate.

Again, between these two extremes everyone has a level of intimacy which is most comfortable for him or her. From the other side, each individual prefers that others make overtures to them in a way that indicates a certain degree of closeness.

To clarify the various orientations in these three areas, *Exhibit I* presents the extreme positions taken on each of the dimensions. Everyone fits somewhere between these two extremes, most of them in the middle.

Exhibit 1. **Extreme Types on the Three Interpersonal Dimensions**

EXPRESSED BEHAVIOR		DIMENSION	WANTED BEHAVIOR	
EXTREME HIGH	EXTREME LOW		EXTREME HIGH	EXTREME LOW
OVERSOCIAL	UNDERSOCIAL	INCLUSION	SOCIAL-COMPLIANT	COUNTERSOCIAL
AUTOCRAT	ABDICRAT	CONTROL	SUBMISSIVE	REBELLIOUS
OVERPERSONAL	UNDERPERSONAL	AFFECTION	PERSONAL-COMPLIANT	COUNTERPERSONAL

Group Compatibility

This theory of interpersonal relations can be very useful to businesspeople in determining the compatibility of the members of a group. If at the outset we can choose a group of people who can work together harmoniously, we shall go far toward avoiding situations where a group's efforts are wasted in interpersonal conflicts.

Our theoretical framework is designed to handle this problem. Suppose we consider in more detail the two aspects for each one of the three interpersonal dimensions. One aspect is what we *do* with relation to other people; let us call this "e" for *expressed* behavior. The second is what we *want* from other people, how we want them to act toward us; let us call this "w" for *wanted* behavior. Then we can use "e" and "w" to try to find out how people will relate to each other in the *inclusion* dimension ("I"), the *control* dimension ("C"), and the *affection* dimension ("A"), as shown schematically in *Exhibit 2*.

If we make a ten-point scale, from zero to nine, and say that in each of the two aspects of the three dimensions everyone has some propensity, some preferred behavior, we can characterize each person by six scores: e^I, w^I, e^C, w^C, e^A, w^A.

In the course of my research I have developed a questionnaire, called FIRO-B (the "B" refers to *behavior*), comprising a check list of 54 statements designed to measure an individual's propensities in each of these six categories; a portion of it is shown in *Exhibit 3*. The resulting scores for each need area can be plotted on a diagram, as in *Exhibit 4*.

Exhibit 2. **Schema of Interpersonal Behaviors**

EXPRESSED BEHAVIOR	DIMENSION	WANTED BEHAVIOR
I initiate interaction with people	INCLUSION	I want to be included
I control people	CONTROL	I want people to control me
I act close and personal toward people	AFFECTION	I want people to get close and personal to me

Exhibit 3. Sample of Questionnaire

GROUP.................................

DATE.................................

MALE............FEMALE............

AGE.................................

NAME.................................

FIRO-B

	I	C	A
e			
w			

Please place number of the answer that best applies to you in the box at the left of the statement. Please be as honest as you can.

1. I try to be with people.
   1. usually 2. often 3. sometimes 4. occasionally 5. rarely 6. never
2. I let other people decide what to do.
   1. usually 2. often 3. sometimes 4. occasionally 5. rarely 6. never
3. I join social groups.
   1. usually 2. often 3. sometimes 4. occasionally 5. rarely 6. never
4. I try to have close relationships with people.
   1. usually 2. often 3. sometimes 4. occasionally 5. rarely 6. never
5. I tend to join social organizations when I have an opportunity.
   1. usually 2. often 3. sometimes 4. occasionally 5. rarely 6. never
   other people strongly influence my actions.
   usually 2. often 3. sometimes 4. occasionally 5. rarely 6. never
   ...mal social activities.
23. I try to g...
   3. sometimes 4. occasionally 5. rarely 6. never
   1. most people people ...h people.
24. I let other people control my actions.
   1. most people 2. many people 3. ...me 4. occasionally 5. rarely 6. never
25. I act cool and distant with people.
   1. most people 2. many people 3. some people 4. a few people 5. ...ly 6. never
26. I am easily led by people.
   1. most people 2. many people 3. some people 4. a few people 5. one or two people 6. nobody
27. I try to have close, personal relationships with people.
   1. most people 2. many people 3. some people 4. a few people 5. one or two people 6. nobody

(See other side)

Exhibit 4. Graphic Representation of Interpersonal Dimensions

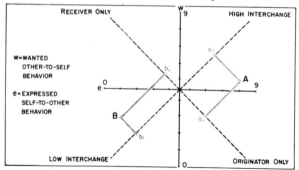

534

Two Kinds

Note that in *Exhibit 4* there are two diagonals, which may be used to explain two different kinds of compatibility—"originator compatibility" (oK) and "interchange compatibility" (xK). Individuals can be located on these diagonals from their scores on FIRO-B.

In popular literature there are at least two well-known and apparently contradictory maxims relating to the bases of compatibility: "Opposites attract," and "Birds of a feather flock together." Considering the diagonals on *Exhibit 4* might aid us in coming to a sensible resolution of these maxims, since there seems to be some truth in each of them:

1. *Originator Diagonal.* Let us take an example in the control dimension and consider the lower right to upper left line. The people who fall in the lower right quadrant are the ones who want to control others and do not want to be controlled themselves. These people can be called autocrat-rebels; they want to be the bosses and do not want anyone else to tell them what to do. In the upper left quadrant we have just the opposite. These are abdicrat-submissives; they want to be told what to do, and they do not want to control anyone else.

For smooth functioning it would appear that if we had one autocrat-rebel, we would not want another one, since they would both want to give orders and neither would want to take them. This is called *competitive* incompatibility. Also, if we had two abdicrat-submissives, a situation would be created wherein both people want someone to tell them what to do and neither wants to do the telling. This is called *apathetic* incompatibility. However, if we have one autocrat-rebel and one abdicrat-submissive, the relationship will probably be harmonious, since one person wants to give orders and the other wants to take them.

2. *Interchange Diagonal.* Now, consider the other diagonal on the diagram. Let us take affection for an example this time. In the upper right quadrant are the people who express a lot of close personal behavior and want the same expressed to them. These are the people of "high interchange," and they can be called overpersonal-personal-complaints. They like an atmosphere in which there is a lot of affection; so, for instance, they would like a party better than a board of directors meeting. In the lower left quadrant are people of "low interchange," who like neither to give nor to receive affection. They can be called underpersonal-counterpersonals. They do not want anyone to get very close to them, nor do they want to get very close to anyone. They like their relations rather reserved, cool, and distant.

Here the complementary idea of the originator diagonal—that opposites attract—does not apply; for, if one person likes to be very close and personal and the other person does not, they are going to threaten each other. One who likes to keep their relations reserved is not going to like it when the other makes overtures; and, in the reverse direction, the one who wants very close relations is not going to be very happy if the other does not. So it seems reasonable that the situation would lead to harmony more readily if the people involved were close on this diagonal, unlike the situation on the originator diagonal.

In the inclusion dimension, again, it would be better if both interacting persons were very close to being either very high or very low on this diagonal so that one would not always want to be with people while the other wanted to stay home and read a book. Hence, on the interchange diagonal the "birds of a feather" maxim seems most appropriate; people should be similar in their values along this diagonal.

Predictable Relations

To exemplify the working of the technique let us consider *Exhibit 4* for the control area:

> From FIRO-B we learn that A has a score of 8 on e^c and 5 on w^c, while B has a score of 1 on e^c and 1 on w^c. These points are plotted on the diagram. Each score, for illustrative purposes, may be divided into two components, one on each diagonal. These components are represented by a_x and a_o and b_x and b_o on the diagram.

> The measure of interchange compatibility (xK) of A and B is proportional to the distance between a_x and b_x. A smaller distance means a more similar orientation toward the amount of interchange of control that should exist in a relation. In the example, A believes that relations should involve a great deal of influence and control, while B's preference is for less structured, more laissez-faire relations. Their incompatibility in this regard is reflected in the relatively large distance between a_x and b_x.

> Originator compatibility (oK) is proportional to the sum of a_o and b_o. Optimal originator compatibility occurs when one score is to the left of the midpoint of the diagonal and the other score is exactly the same distance to the right of the midpoint. In our example this is almost exactly true; thus A and B have high originator compatibility. A wishes to control others but not to be controlled, while B wishes to be controlled but not to control or influence others very much. Hence they complement each other.

> Our conclusion then about this pair is the following: they disagree as to the atmosphere they desire regarding mutual influence and control. A likes structured hierarchies while B prefers more permissive relations. However, when there is a situation of a certain structure, they are compatible with regard to the roles they will take in relation to each other. A will take the influential, responsible position, and B will take the subordinate role.

These psychological considerations can very easily be converted into formulas, and in research work and practical applications this is done. There have been several experiments performed which indicate the usefulness of this approach. These experiments demonstrate that groups of from two to eight can be composed—based on FIRO-B scores—in such a way that their productivity, and to some extent their interaction, is predictable. Much research is still to be done to improve the accuracy of these predictions, but the results are highly encouraging.[1]

Group Development

Another major point in the theory is that every group, no matter what its function or composition, given enough time, goes through the three interpersonal phases of inclusion, control, and affection in the same sequence. To illustrate:

> Recently I was interviewing a member of a group, which had just completed 30 meetings, to get an idea of her feeling about the experience. In response to the question, "How would you describe what happened in this group?" she replied, "Well, first you're concerned about the problem of where you fit in the group; then you're wondering about what you'll accomplish. Finally, after a while, you learn that people mean something. Your primary concern becomes how people feel about you and about each other."

In or Out

First, *the inclusion phase centers around the question of "in or out."* It begins with the formation of the group. When people are confronted with each other, they must first find the place where they fit in. This involves being in or out of the group, establishing oneself as a specific individual, and seeing if one is going to be paid attention to and not be left behind or ignored. This anxiety area gives rise to individual-centered behavior such as overtalking, extreme withdrawal, exhibitionism, recitation of biographies and other previous experience.

At the same time the basic problem of commitment to the group is present. Each member is implicitly deciding to what degree he or she will become a member of the group, how much investment they will withdraw from their other commitments and invest in this new relationship. They are asking, "How much of myself will I devote to this group? How important will I be in this setting? Will they know who I am and what I can do, or will I be indistinguishable from many others?" This is, in short, the problem of identity. They are, in effect, deciding primarily on their preferred amount of inclusion interchange and their preferred amount of inclusion initiation with the other members—just how much actual contact, interaction, and communication they wish to have.

Hence, the main concerns of the formative process are "boundary problems," problems that have to do with entering into the boundaries of a group and belonging to that group. These are problems of inclusion.

Characteristic of groups in this phase is the occurrence of what have been called "goblet issues." The term is taken from an analogy to a cocktail party where people sometimes pick up their cocktail glass, or goblet, and figuratively peer through it to size up the other people at the party. Hence, they are issues that in themselves are of minor importance to the group members but serve as vehicles for getting to know people, especially in relation to oneself.

Often a goblet issue is made of the first decision confronting a group. In some groups discussions leading to a decision about such an issue continue for an unbelievably long time and then never reach a conclusion. But there has been a great deal of learning in that the members have gained a fairly clear picture of each other. Each member knows who responds favorably to him or her, who sees things the way they do, how much he or she knows as compared to the others, how the leader responds to him or her, and what type of role he or she can expect to play in the group. Acquiring this knowledge is the unconscious purpose of the goblet issue.

The frustrating experience of having groups endlessly discuss topics of little real interest to anyone is very common. Every group finds its own goblet issues within the framework of its aim. "The weather" is fairly universal; "rules of procedure" is common in formal groups; "Do you know so-and-so?" often characterizes new acquaintances from the same location; relating incidents or telling stories has a goblet element for business gatherings; and "Where are you from?" often serves for military settings. Mark Twain apparently overlooked the fact that nobody really *wants* to "do anything about the weather"—they just want to use it as a topic for sizing up people. These discussions are inevitable, and, contrary to all outward appearances, they do serve an important function. Groups which are not permitted this type of testing out will search for some other method of obtaining the same personal information, perhaps using as a vehicle a decision of more importance to the work of the group.

Top or Bottom

After the problems of inclusion have been sufficiently resolved, control problems become prominent. *This phase centers around the problem of "top or bottom."* Once members are fairly well established as being together in a group, the issue of decision-making procedures arises. This involves problems of sharing responsibility and its necessary concomitant, distribution of power and control. Characteristic behavior at this stage includes leadership struggles; competition; and discussion of orientation to the task, structuring, rules of procedure, methods of decision making, and sharing the responsibility for the group's work. The primary anxieties at this phase revolve around having too much or too little responsibility and too much or too little influence. Each member is trying to establish himself or herself in the group so that he or she has the most comfortable amount of interchange and the most comfortable degree of initiation with the other members with regard to control, influence, and responsibility.

Near or Far

Finally, following a satisfactory resolution of these phases, problems of affection become focal. *This phase centers on the issue of "near or far."*

The individuals have come together to form a group; they have differentiated themselves with respect to responsibility and power. Now they must become emotionally integrated. At this stage it is characteristic to see such behavior expressed through positive feelings, direct personal hostility, jealousies, pairing behavior, and, in general, heightened emotional feeling between pairs of people.

The primary anxieties at this stage have to do with not being liked or close enough to people or with being too intimate. Each member is striving to obtain their most favorable amount of affectional interchange and most comfortable position regarding initiating and receiving affection—deciding, like Schopenhauer's porcupines, how to get close enough to receive warmth, yet avoid the pain of sharp quills.

Tightening the Bolts

These are not distinct phases. The group development postulate asserts that these problem areas are *emphasized* at certain points in a group's growth, but all three problem areas are always present. Similarly, some people do not always go along with the central issue for the group. For certain individuals a particular problem area will be so personally potent that it will transcend the current group issue. The area of concern for any individual will result from his or her own problem areas and those of the group's current phase. Perhaps a close approximation to the developmental phenomena is given by the tire-changing model:

> When a person changes a tire and replaces the wheel, he first sets the wheel in place and secures it by tightening the bolts one after another just enough so the wheel is in place and the next step can be taken. Then the bolts are tightened further, usually in the same sequence, until the wheel is firmly in place. Finally each bolt is gone over separately to secure it.

In a similar way, the need areas are worked on until they are handled satisfactorily enough to continue with the work at hand. Later on they are returned to and worked over to a more satisfactory degree. If one need area has not been worked out well on the first sequence, it must receive more attention on the next cycle.

Applications of Theory

The next question is: What can we do about these problems so as to utilize this information practically? This is more difficult. The above analysis is derived largely from experience with experimental research on small groups selected for this purpose. Solutions for the problems observed are largely, though not entirely, speculative and can only be offered as suggestions which should be explored carefully in each individual case before being adopted.

More specifically, the interpretations presented here can be looked upon as suggestions for *diagnosis*. The more men and women in business can become aware of the basic factors underlying their interpersonal difficulties, the better they will be able to meet these difficulties. As in the practice of medicine, if the disease is properly diagnosed, the doctor has a better chance of curing it than if it is improperly or superficially diagnosed, even though a correct diagnosis by no means guarantees a cure.

Clearing the Air

Serious interpersonal difficulties that are left covert only smolder and erupt at the expense of efficiency and productivity. The most effective way covert difficulties can be dealt with is by first making them overt. For example:

> In one marketing group, the leader finally told one member that he did not like the way he was acting in the group and that he felt he should contribute more. After a brief but difficult and bitter exchange the two began to tell each other their feelings about the situation. They managed to clear the air, and the situation improved markedly.

When successful, overt discussion is like a cold shower: it is approached with apprehension, the initial impact is very uncomfortable, but the final result justifies the tribulations.

To summarize, "interpersonal problems" include difficulties such as members who are withdrawn from a group; personal hostilities between members; problem members who are either inactive and unintegrated or overactive and destructive; power struggles between group members; members battling for attention; dissatisfaction with the leadership in the group; dissatisfaction with the amount of acknowledgment that an individual's contributions are getting; or dissatisfaction with the amount of affection and warmth exhibited in the group.

If it becomes quite clear to the group members that their difficulties are so severe that their activity is being impaired, then bringing the issues out into the open and talking about them will help. It is somewhat difficult, however, to tell exactly when a problem is so severe that it is holding the group up. Perhaps some of the earlier discussion of symptoms will be useful for assessing the effect of interpersonal factors on the group.

It might be helpful to view groups (including anywhere from two to twenty people) on a continuum—from those that are completely compatible, that is, able to work well together, to those that are completely incompatible, that is, incapable of working together. Any particular group can be placed somewhere along this continuum. To illustrate:

> The members of the group at the extreme compatible end of the continuum are able to work well together within a relatively short time with a minimum of difficulty and can operate effectively over a period of time on a wide variety of problems. They need no training or new awareness.

> The group at the incompatible end, however, cannot work effectively. The interpersonal problems that cause the task difficulties are so deep-

seated in the personalities of the individual members that no amount of outside assistance will be worthwhile. It would take so long before this group could operate effectively that, from a practical standpoint, any kind of training of the group members or any awareness of their problems would be unfruitful.

Between these two extreme types are groups that profit more or less by the kind of awareness which has been discussed. If a group is relatively near the compatible end, with a minimum of awareness and a minimum of discussion of its difficult problems, it will become a smoothly functioning group. If interpersonal problems in a group are very minor, they can usually be ignored without impairing the group seriously; or, if the problems exist between two members, they can often work out their difficulties by themselves outside the group.

With groups near the incompatible end much more intensive work has to be done to get through their problems so that they can function effectively. Such work should probably be guided by someone who is experienced with group process and can help group members to work out their difficulties.

Another advantage of this approach operates more through the individuals than the group. If the individual members can gain the kind of awareness of their own needs in situations as discussed in this article, then this in itself will help them to understand their reactions to other people and, perhaps, to operate more effectively. In addition, it is often helpful to point out to group members that other people have the same basic needs; for, if they understand what other people are trying to do, they may be more tolerant of other people's behavior. Since everyone has these needs, everyone tries to get the same thing from other people, even though each may use difficult adaptive patterns for achieving his ends. To illustrate such a mechanism:

It generally is felt that if an individual has an excessively strong negative reaction to another individual in the setting of a work group, the individual who is irritated fears deep down within that they are like the one who annoys them, that they have the trait that is so annoying. It is threatening for them to see it in some other individual, and he or she must immediately deny it and attack it, almost as if they were trying to deny to themselves that they are like this.

Awareness of mechanisms of this type may help in understanding what is happening in the group and one's own reaction in the situation.

Conclusion

The time seems to have come for the businessperson to make use of some of the social scientists' more recent findings on the unconscious, or covert, factors in human interaction. Since the businessperson does deal so heavily in interpersonal relations, his or her skill and success are dependent on his or her ability to understand interpersonal relations and to deal effectively with them. Thus, it becomes important for him or her to gain a more basic understanding instead of simply trying out panaceas that aim only at the symptoms of the problems and not at the basic problems themselves. He or she must understand the vast interpersonal underworld that operates beneath the overt, observable behavior.

As I have already pointed out, current interest in what are called "communications problems" provides an example of the symptomatic approach, for these problems are symptoms of poor interpersonal relations rather than primary causes of operational difficulties. It is an error, therefore, to try to attack the problems of communication by building more effective physical lines of communication, when the trouble really lies in the relation between individuals. The way to attack the basic problem would seem to be to investigate what is going on among the individuals themselves and try to improve those relations.

If it is true that the unconscious factors are so all-important to understanding groups, then we ought to find out exactly how these factors do affect what the businessperson is usually primarily interested in, namely effective operation. In this article I have tried to illustrate the inadequacy of attempting to operate by ignoring interpersonal difficulties and attending to the task only, since in reality the interpersonal factors somehow find their way into the task and directly affect the productivity of the group. No matter how much people try to keep interpersonal problems out by ignoring them, they will turn up in subtle forms such as loss of motivation, tiredness, or the group member's preoccupation with outside tasks; or they may get entangled directly with the solution of the task and have to be worked out in the body of the problem.

I have offered a theoretical framework which may be of some help in understanding the structure of these interpersonal problems in an attempt to aid in the diagnosis of interpersonal behavior. Such a diagnosis may then leave the businessperson in a better position to deal with what actually occurs. I have tried to suggest possible lines of solution, but these attempts are offered in a much more speculative manner. Although they are based on rather extensive experience with psychological phenomena, they are only suggestions that the individual businessperson must try out and adapt to his or her own needs.

Notes

1. See William C. Schutz, *FIRO: A Three-Dimensional Theory of Interpersonal Behavior*, Rinehart & Co., 1958.

32

The Administrator's Skill: Communication

F. J. ROETHLISBERGER

We know a lot about breakdowns in machines, but we do not know so much about what causes breakdowns in human relations. We know a lot about how to keep a line of hydraulic presses running efficiently, but we are often at a loss to keep the operators from slowing down or going on strike. In short, our progress with the human problems of administration has not kept pace with our technological progress.

This situation has led to growing concern in the business community, with the result that in recent years a number of forward-looking projects have been undertaken at various universities for training and research in human relations. These programs are likely to have a very far-reaching influence on knowledge and understanding; indeed, they have already had a decisive impact, as is indicated by the author shows why friction develops in work situations and suggests some of the principles of an approach by which "misunderstanding can be diminished—not banished—by the slow, patient, laborious practice of a skill."

For some time I have been deeply interested in the process of interpersonal communication within the administrative setting. What is taking place when two people engaged in a common task interact? What do the actors involved perceive is taking place? What is a useful way for the executive to think about these interpersonal proceedings in which he or she is engaged, and what skills can they practice which will make him or her more effective as an administrator of people?

In this article I want to discuss these questions in terms of a specific, down-to-earth case in an industrial plant[1]—a case of misunderstanding between two people, a worker and a foreman. (It is not important that they

Published in 1953.

Author's Note. This article is based on The Alfred Korzybski Memorial Lecture, which I delivered before the Institute of General Semantics, New York, April 24, 1953.

happen to be foreman and worker; to all intents and purposes they might as well be superintendent and foreman or, for that matter, controller and accountant.) A brief review of the case should be useful in providing us with a point of departure as well as a point of return for our questions. And it should make it possible for us to discuss the practical application of some of the recent findings of general semantics and human relations.

A Case of Misunderstanding

In a department of a large industrial organization there were seven workers (four men and three women) engaged in testing and inspecting panels of electronic equipment. In this department one of the workers, Bing, was having trouble with his immediate supervisor, Hart, who had formerly been a worker in the department.

Had we been observers in this department we would have seen Bing carrying two or three panels at a time from the racks where they were stored to the bench where he inspected them together. For this activity we would have seen him charging double or triple setup time. We would have heard him occasionally singing at work. Also we would have seen him usually leaving his work position a few minutes early to go to lunch, and noticed that other employees sometimes accompanied him. And had we been present at one specific occasion, we would have heard Hart telling Bing that he disapproved of these activities and that he wanted Bing to stop doing them.

However, not being present to hear the actual verbal exchange that took place in this interaction, let us note what Bing and Hart each said to a personnel representative.

What Bing Said
In talking about his practice of charging double or triple setup time for panels which he inspected all at one time, Bing said:

> This is a perfectly legal thing to do. We've always been doing it. Mr. Hart, the supervisor, has other ideas about it, though; he claims it's cheating the company. He came over to the bench a day or two ago and let me know just how he felt about the matter. Boy, did we go at it! It wasn't so much the fact that he called me down on it, but more the way in which he did it. He's a sarcastic bastard. I've never seen anyone like him. He's not content just to say in a manlike way what's on his mind, but he prefers to do it in a way that makes you want to crawl inside a crack on the floor. What a guy! I don't mind being called down by a supervisor, but I like to be treated like a man, and not humiliated like a school teacher does a naughty kid. He's been pulling this stuff ever since he's been a supervisor. I knew him when he was just one of us, but since he's been promoted, he's lost his friendly way and seems to be having some difficulty in knowing how to manage us employees. He's a changed man over what he used to be like when he was a worker on the bench with us several years ago.

When he pulled this kind of stuff on me the other day, I got so damn mad I called in the union representative. I knew that the thing I was doing was permitted by the contract, but I was intent on making some trouble for Mr. Hart, just because he persists in this sarcastic way of handling me. I am about fed up with the whole damn situation. I'm trying every means I can to get myself transferred out of his group. If I don't succeed and I'm forced to stay on here, I'm going to screw him in every way I can. He's not going to pull this kind of kid stuff any longer on me. When the union representative questioned him on the case, he finally had to back down, because according to the contract an employee can use any time-saving method or device in order to speed up the process as long as the quality standards of the job are met.

You see, he knows that I do professional singing on the outside. He hears me singing here on the job, and he hears the people talking about my career in music. I guess he figures I can be so cocky because I have another means of earning some money. Actually, the employees here enjoy having me sing while we work, but he thinks I'm disturbing them and causing them to 'goof off' from their work. Occasionally, I leave the job a few minutes early and go down to the washroom to wash up before lunch. Sometimes several others in the group will accompany me, and so Mr. Hart automatically thinks I'm the leader and usually bawls me out for the whole thing.

So, you can see, I'm a marked man around here. He keeps watching me like a hawk. Naturally, this makes me very uncomfortable. That's why I'm sure a transfer would be the best thing. I've asked him for it, but he didn't give me any satisfaction at the time. While I remain here, I'm going to keep my nose clean, but whenever I get the chance, I'm going to slip it to him, but good.

What Hart Said

Here on the other hand, is what Hart told the personnel representative:

Say, I think you should be in on this. My dear little friend Bing is heading himself into a showdown with me. Recently it was brought to my attention that Bing has been taking double and triple setup time for panels which he is actually inspecting at one time. In effect, that's cheating, and I've called him down on it several times before. A few days ago it was brought to my attention again, and so this time I really let him have it in no uncertain terms. He's been getting away with this for too long and I'm going to put an end to it once and for all. I know he didn't like my calling him on it because a few hours later he had the union representative breathing down my back. Well, anyway, I let them both know I'll not tolerate the practice any longer, and I let Bing know that if he continues to do this kind of thing, I'm going to take official action with my boss to have the guy fired or penalized somehow. This kind of thing has to be curbed. Actually, I'm inclined to think the guy's mentally deficient, because talking to him has actually no meaning to him whatsoever. I've tried just about every approach to jar some sense into that guy's head, and I've just about given it up as a bad deal.

I don't know what it is about the guy, but I think he's harboring some deep feelings against me. For what, I don't know, because I've tried to handle that bird with kid gloves. But his whole attitude around here on the job is one of indifference, and he certainly isn't a good influence on the rest of my group. Frankly, I think he purposely tries to agitate them against me at times, too. It seems to me he may be suffering from illusions of grandeur, because all he does all day long is sit over there and croon his fool head off. Thinks he's a Frank Sinatra! No kidding! I understand he takes singing lessons and he's working with some of the local bands in the city. All of which is O.K. by me; but when his outside interests start interfering with his efficiency on the job, then I've got to start paying closer attention to the situation. For this reason I've been keeping my eye on that bird and if he steps out of line any more, he and I are going to part ways.

You know there's an old saying, 'You can't make a purse out of a sow's ear.' The guy is simply unscrupulous. He feels no obligation to do a real day's work. Yet I know the guy can do a good job, because for a long time he did. But in recent months he's slipped, for some reason, and his whole attitude on the job has changed. Why, it's even getting to the point now where I think he's inducing other employees to 'goof off' a few minutes before the lunch whistle and go down to the washroom and clean up on company time. I've called him on it several times, but words just don't seem to make any lasting impression on him. Well, if he keeps it up much longer, he's going to find himself on the way out. He's asked me for a transfer, so I know he wants to go. But I didn't give him an answer when he asked me, because I was steaming mad at the time, and I may have told him to go somewhere else.

Views of Misunderstanding

So much for the case. Let me start with the simplest but the toughest question first: "What is going on here?" I think most of us would agree that what seems to be going on is some misunderstanding between Hart and Bing. But no sooner do we try to represent to ourselves the nature of this misunderstanding than a flood of different theories appear. Let me discuss briefly five very common ways of representing this misunderstanding:

1   as a difference of opinion resolvable by common sense, by simply referring to the facts;
2   as a clash of personalities;
3   as a conflict of social roles;
4   as a struggle for power; and
5   as a breakdown in communication.

There are, of course, other theories too—for example, those of the inter-actionists, the field theory of Kurt Lewin, and even the widely held views of Adam Smith or Karl Marx. But for our purposes here the five I have mentioned will suffice.

Common Sense

For the advocates of common sense—the first theory, though most of them would not call it that—the situation resolves itself quickly:

> Either Hart is right or Bing is right. Since both parties cannot be right, it follows that if Hart is right, then Bing is wrong; or if Bing is right, then Hart is wrong. Either Bing should or should not be singing on the job, carrying two or three panels at a time and charging double or triple setup time, and so on.

"Let us get these facts settled first," say the common-sense advocates. "Once ascertained, the problem is easily settled. Once we know who is doing what he should not be doing, then all we have to do is to get this person to do what he should be doing. It's as simple as that."

But is it? Let us look again at our case. Let us note that there are no differences of opinion between Hart and Bing about some matters. For example, both would agree that Bing is taking double on triple setup time when he carries his panels two or three at a time to his bench for inspection. Both would agree that Bing sings on the job and occasionally leaves his workplace a bit early for lunch.

Where they differ is in the way each *perceives* these activities. Hart perceives Bing's activities as "cheating," "suffering from illusions of grandeur," "thinking he is Frank Sinatra," "interfering with Bing's efficiency as well as the efficiency of other workers," "disturbing the other workers," "inducing them to goof off," and "influencing them against [Hart]." To Bing, on the other hand, these activities are "perfectly legal," "something we've always been doing," "something that is not disturbing the other workers," and so forth.

Among these many different conflicting claims and different perceptions, what are the facts? Many of these evaluations refer to personal and social standards of conduct for which the company has no explicit rules. Even in the case of taking double and triple setup time, there are probably no clear rules, because when the industrial engineer set the standards for the job, he did not envisage the possibility of a worker doing what Bing is now doing and which, according to Bing, is a time-saving device.

But we can waste effort on this question. For, even if it were clear that Hart is not exploring the situation, that he is not getting these important facts or rules which would settle who is right and who is wrong, it would still be true that, so far as Hart is concerned, he *knows* who is right and who is wrong. And because he *knows*, he has no reason to question the assumptions he is making about Bing's behavior.

Now this is very likely to happen in the case of advocates of the common-sense theory. Significantly, Hart himself is a good advocate of it.

Does this have anything to do with the fact that he is not being very successful in getting Bing to do what he should be doing? Let us postpone this question for future consideration.

Clash of Personalities

For the second school of thought, what is going on between Hart and Bing can be viewed essentially as a clash of personalities—an interaction between two particular personality structures. According to this view, what is going on cannot be known in detail until much more information about these different personality structures is secured. Hence we can only speculate that what is going on may be something of this order:

> Neither Hart nor Bing feels too sure of himself, and each seems to be suffering from feelings of inadequacy or inferiority. Being unable to recognize, admit, or accept these feelings, however, each one perceives the behavior of the other as a personal attack upon himself. When a person feels he is being attacked, he feels strongly the need to defend himself. This, then, is essentially what is taking place between Hart and Bing. Because of his feelings of inferiority, each one is defending himself against what he perceives to be an attack upon himself as a person. In psychology, the feelings of each man are conceived as being rooted somehow in his "personality."

That this theory is pointing to some very important phenomena can hardly be questioned. Certainly I will not argue its validity. I am only concerned with what it is telling us and what follows from it. As I understand it, this theory says that neither Hart nor Bing is aware of his own feelings of inadequacy and defense mechanisms. These are the important facts that each is ignoring. From this it follows that there is little hope of correcting the misunderstanding without helping Bing and Hart to become aware of these feelings and of their need to defend against them. Short of this, the solution lies in transferring Bing to a supervisor whose personality will be more compatible with Bing's, and in giving Hart a worker whose personality will be more compatible with Hart's.

Conflict of Social Roles

Let us look at the third explanation. Instead of viewing the misunderstanding as an interaction between two invidual personality units, it can also be viewed as an interaction between two social roles:

> With the promotion of Hart to the position of a supervisor of a group in which he had been formerly a worker, a system of reciprocal expectancies has been disturbed. Bing is expecting Hart to behave toward him in the same way Hart did when Hart was a worker; but by telling Bing to stop "crooning his fool head off," for example, Hart is not behaving in accordance with the role of a friend. Similarly, Hart, as the newly appointed supervisor, is expecting that Bing should do what he tells Bing to do,

but by singing Bing is not behaving in accordance with the customary role of the worker.

According to this theory, as any recent textbook on sociology will explain, when two actors in a relationship reach differing definitions of the situation, misunderstanding is likely to arise. Presumably this is what is happening between Hart and Bing. The role-expectation pattern has been disturbed. Bing views his singing as variant but permissive; Hart views it as deviant. From these differing definitions of what each other's role should be misunderstanding results. According to this view, it will take time for their new relationship to work out. In time Bing will learn what to expect from Hart now that Hart is his supervisor. Also in time Hart will define better his role vis-à-vis Bing.

Struggle for Power

The fourth way of representing what is going on between Hart and Bing would be in terms of such abstractions as "authority" and "power":

> When Bing refuses to stop singing on the job when Hart tells him to, Bing is being disobedient to the commands or orders of a holder of power. When this occurs, Hart, who according to this theory is a "power holder," has the right to exercise or apply sanctions, such as dismissal or transfer. But the threat to exercise these sanctions does not seem to be too effective in getting Bing to stop, because Bing is a member of the union, which also has power and the right to apply sanctions. By going to his union representative, Bing can bring this power structure into play.

In other words, what is going on in the case is not merely an interaction between two individual or social personalities; it is also a struggle between two kinds of institutionalized power. It is an issue between the management and the union which may even precipitate a strike. Management will charge that it cannot have workers in the plant who are disobedient to the orders of their foremen. The union will charge that Bing is merely introducing a labor-saving device which the foreman has not enough sense to recognize. To avoid things getting to this stage, the struggle-for-power theory would recommend that if Hart and Bing between them cannot settle their differences, they should refer them to the grievance machinery set up for this purpose by union and management.

According to this theory, Hart got into trouble not because he had authority but because when he tried to exercise it and was unsuccessful, he lost it. Authority ceases to exist when it cannot be exercised successfully.[2]

Breakdown in Communication

The fifth way of stating what is going on would be to say that Hart and Bing think they are talking about the same things when in fact they are not:

> Hart assumes he understands what Bing is doing and saying; Bing assumes he understands what Hart is doing and saying. In fact, neither

assumption holds. From this "uncritical assumption of understanding," misunderstanding arises.

Thus, when Hart tells Bing to stop "crooning his fool head off," Bing assumes that Hart is talking about Bing's singing when Hart may in fact be talking about his difficulties in maintaining his position as formal leader of the group. Hart assumes that Bing is singing deliberately to flaunt his authority, whereas in Bing's mind singing may be a way of relating himself to people and of maintaining his conceptions of himself.[3]

According to this theory, Hart and Bing are not on the same wave length, and as a result communication bypassing occurs. Each is behaving in accordance with the reality as he perceives it to be, but neither is aware of the assumptions that underlie his perceptions. Their misunderstandings arise as a result.

This theory strikes a new note that I should like to explore further.

Roots of Misunderstanding

So far our theories have explained well why there is misunderstanding and conflict; they have not shown so clearly how any new behavior patterns on the part of Hart or Bing or both can emerge or be encouraged to emerge from the present ones. In them we have found no responsible actor, no learner, and no practitioner of a skill.

Could it be that what is going on between Hart and Bing results also in part from the fact that nobody is taking any responsibility for what is going on? May we not assume that people can learn through experience how to determine their relationships with each other as well as be determined by them? Let us therefore look at these interpersonal proceedings from the point of view of a person who is responsibly involved in them and who may be capable of learning something from them. I shall start with Hart and raise the questions: (1) "What is Hart doing to contribute to misunderstanding?" (2) "What, if anything, might he learn to do differently to minimize this effect?"

From now on I shall be chiefly concerned with Hart, not because I think Hart is any more or less guilty than Bing of creating misunderstanding, but because I wish to develop a useful way of thinking for persons in a position of responsibility like Hart. This way of thinking, I hope, will not be in conflict with our other theories. It will merely spell out what a supervisor must learn if he is to take into account the significant processes which these other theories say have been going on.

So, instead of viewing Hart in his dealings with Bing as a supervisor expressing his personality, playing a social role, or exercising power, let us view him as a practitioner of a skill of communication. Let us see what skills, if any, he is using. And if we find, as I fear we may, that he has not been too skillful, let us see if he can learn to become a more skillful practitioner, and how this can be done.

Hart's Trouble

When we ask ourselves what Hart is doing to facilitate misunderstanding, we meet again a number of different theories. Although I am not sure that these theories are pointing to different things, each uses a slightly different terminology, so I shall state them separately:

1. *Hart is making value judgments.* According to one view, the biggest block to personal communication arises from the fact that Hart is making value judgments of Bing from Hart's point of view. Hart's tendency to evaluate is what gets him into trouble. Not only is he evaluating Bing, but he is trying to get Bing to accept his evaluation as the only and proper one. It is this orientation that angers Bing and makes him feel misunderstood.[4]

2. *Hart is not listening.* According to another and not too different view, Hart gets into trouble because he is not listening to Bing's feelings. Because he is not paying attention to Bing's feelings, he is not responding to them as such. Instead, we find him responding to the effect of Bing's feelings upon his own. Not only is he ignoring Bing's feelings, but also he is ignoring the effect of what he is saying upon them. This kind of behavior also leads to Bing's feelings of being misunderstood.[5]

3. *Hart is assuming things that may not be so.* Still another point of view says that Hart is getting into trouble because he is making assumptions about Bing's behavior that may not be so. Hart is confusing what he sees with what he assumes and feels.

When Hart sees Bing leaving early for lunch, for example, he assumes that Bing is doing this deliberately, intentionally, and personally to discredit him and to test his authority. Because of this assumption he feels angry and his feelings of anger reinforce his assumption. Now if Bing's going to lunch a few minutes early is such an attempt to discredit him, then Hart's anger and his attempt to retaliate make sense. But if he starts with this assumption and makes no attempt to check it, then his anger makes less sense. Hart may be assuming something that is not so.

Again, Hart shows he may be making assumptions that are not so by the way he talks in trying to get Bing to stop singing at work or to stop inspecting panels two or three at a time. When he uses phrases like "crooning your fool head off" and "cheating the company," is he not assuming that Bing should feel about these activities in the same way that he himself does? And if Bing does not feel this way, then obviously, in Hart's view, Bing must be a "fool," "defective," or a "sow's ear." To Hart, Bing *is* a sow's ear. And how does one feel toward a sow's ear? Toward such an entity one must feel (by definition) helpless and hopeless. Note that Hart's assumptions, perceptions, and feelings are of a piece; each re-enforces the other to make one total evaluation.

In short, all of Hart's evaluations are suspect because he confuses what he sees with what he assumes and feels. As a result, there is no way for Hart to take another look at the situation. How can Hart check his evaluations when he is not aware that he is making them? By treating inferences as facts, there is no way for him to explore the assumptions, feelings, and perceptions that underlie his evaluations.[6] For Hart, Bing *is* the way he perceives Bing to be. There is no way for him to say that "because of the assumptions I make and because of the way I feel, I perceive Bing in this way."

4. *Hart is making his false assumptions come true.* A fourth theory emphasizes still another point. This theory says that the very kind of misevaluations which our last theory says Hart is guilty of must provoke *ipso facto* the very kind of behavior on the part of Bing of which Hart disapproves.[7] In other words, Hart is getting into trouble because, by his behavior, he is making his assumptive world come true.

Let us examine this theory first by looking at the effect of Hart's behavior on Bing. Very clearly Bing does not like it. Bing tells us that when Hart behaves in the way Hart does, he feels misunderstood, humiliated, and treated like a child. These feelings give grounds to his perception of Hart as "a sarcastic bastard," "a school teacher" pulling "kid stuff" on him. These perceptions in turn will tend to make Bing behave in the way that will coincide more and more with Hart's original untested assumptions about Bing's behavior. Feeling like a "marked man," Bing will behave more and more like a "sow's ear." Although he will try to "keep his nose clean," he will "slip it to [Hart], but good" whenever he gets the chance.

That this kind of misevaluation on the part of Hart will tend to produce this kind of behavior on the part of Bing is, according to this view, a fact of common experience. To explain it one does not have to assume any peculiar personality structure on the part of Bing—an undue sensitivity to criticism, defensiveness, or feeling of inferiority. All one has to assume is an individual personality with a need to maintain its individuality. Therefore, any attempts on the part of Hart which will be perceived by Bing as an attempt to deny his individual differences will be resisted. What Hart says about Bing is, from Bing's point of view, exactly what he is *not*. Bing *is* what he is from his own frame of reference and from the point of view of his own feelings, background, and situation. Bing *is* what he assumes, feels, and perceives himself to be. And this is just what Hart's behavior is denying.

In spite of the different terminology and emphasis of these theories, they all seem to point to certain uniformities in the interpersonal proceedings of Hart and Bing which should be taken into account regardless of the actors' particular personalities or social roles. For the misunderstandings that arise, Hart and Bing are not to blame; the trouble resides in the process of interpersonal communication itself.

Administrative Skills

Let us turn now to the second question: what might Hart learn to do differently in order to minimize the misunderstandings between him and Bing?

I also want to consider briefly the questions of what difference to Bing a slight difference in the behavior of Hart might make.

Problem of Involvement

So far it would seem as if we had made Hart the villain in the piece. But let us remember that although Hart has been intellectually and emotionally involved in what has been going on, he has not been aware of this involvement. All of our theories have implied this. Hart's ego has been involved; his actual group memberships have been involved; his reference groups have been involved; his feelings, assumptions, and perceptions have been involved—but Hart is not aware of it. If any new behavior on the part of Hart is to emerge—and *all* our theories would agree to this—Hart must in some sense become aware of and recognize this involvement. Without such an awareness there can be no reevaluation or no change in perception. And without such a change no learning can take place.

How can this change be accomplished? Some theories would seem to imply that misunderstanding will be minimized only when Hart *logically understands* the nature of his involvement with Bing. Hart will learn to evaluate Bing more properly only when he understands better the personality structures of himself and Bing and the social system of which they are a part. Only by the logical understanding and critical probing of his and Bing's feelings of inadequacy and defense mechanisms can he make a proper evaluation and bring about any real change in his behavior.

But there is another view. It holds that logical understanding is not of the first importance. Rather, misunderstanding will be minimized when Hart learns to *recognize and accept* responsibility for his involvement. Better understanding will be achieved when Hart learns to recognize and accept his own and Bing's individual differences, when he learns to recognize and accept Bing's feelings as being different from his own, and when as a result he can allow Bing to express his feelings and differences and listen to them.[8]

Let me explore this second theory further, for it suggests that Hart might possibly learn to do a better job without having to become a professional social scientist or be psychoanalyzed. Moreover, it coincides with some facts of common experience.

How Can Hart Be Helped?

Some administrators have achieved the insights of the second theory through the school of "hard knocks" rather than through the help of books or by being psychoanalyzed. So should there not be simple skills which Hart can be taught, which he can learn and practice, and which would help him to recognize and accept his involvement and to deal with it better?

Now it may be that Hart, because of certain personal deficiencies, is not able to recognize or accept his own feelings—let alone Bing's. That this holds for some supervisors goes without question. But does it apply to all? I do not think so, nor do I think it applies to Hart. Is it not possible that some supervisors may not be able to do these things because they have never learned how to do them?

The fact is, if our analysis up to this point is sound, that Hart does not get into trouble because he feels hopeless and helpless in the face of a worker who sings on the job, leaves early for lunch, and so on, and who refuses to stop doing these things when Hart tells him to. Any one of us who has had to deal with a worker behaving like Bing will recognize and remember feelings of inadequacy like Hart's only too well. We do not need to have very peculiar or special personality structures to have such feelings. Rather, Hart's trouble is that he assumes, and no doubt has been told too often, that he should *not* have feelings of inadequacy. It resides in the fact that he has not developed or been given a method or skill for dealing with them. As a result, these feelings are denied and appear in the form of an attribute of Bing— "a sow's ear."

In other words, I am suggesting that Hart gets into trouble partly because no one has assured him that it is normal and natural—in fact, inevitable—that he should have some feelings of inadequacy; that he cannot and *should* not try to escape from them. No one has helped him to develop a method of dealing with his own feelings and the feelings of Bing. No one has listened to him or helped him to learn to listen to others. No one has helped him to recognize the effect of his behavior on others. No one has helped him to become aware of his assumptions and feelings and how they affect the evaluations he makes.

Instead, too many training courses have told Hart what an ideal supervisor should be and how an ideal supervisor should behave. Both explicit and implicit in most of the instruction he receives is the assumption that an ideal supervisor should not become emotionally involved in his dealings with people. He should remain aloof, be objective, and deny or get rid of his feelings. But this goes against the facts of his immediate experience; it goes against everything upon which, according to our theories, his growth and development depend. Indeed, to "behave responsibly" and be "mature" in the way he is instructed to, without becoming emotionally committed, would be, to use the *New Yorker's* phrase, "the trick of the week!"

Is it any wonder, therefore, that Hart remains immature—socially, intellectually, and emotionally? He gets no understanding of how these frustrations and misunderstandings must inevitably arise from his dealings with others; he gets no help on how to deal with them when they do arise. He probably has had many training courses which told him how to recognize and deal with workers who are sow's ears. He probably has had no training course which helped him to see how his assumptions and feelings would tend to produce sow's ears by the bushel. He has not been helped to see how this surplus of sow's ears in modern industry might be diminished through the conscious practice of a skill. Thus he has not even been allowed to become intellectually involved and intrigued in the most important problem of his job. Yet there *are* training courses designed for just such a purpose, and they have worked successfully.[9]

Conclusion

Am I indulging in wishful thinking when I believe that there are some simple skills of communication that can be taught, learned, and practiced which might help to diminish misunderstanding? To me it is this possibility which the recent findings of general semantics and human relations are suggesting. They suggest that although man is determined by the complex relationships of which he is a part, nevertheless he is also in some small part a determiner of these relationships. Once he learns what he cannot do, he is ready to learn what little he can do. And what a tremendous difference to himself and to others the little that he can do—listening with understanding, for example—can make!

Once he can accept his limitations and the limitations of others, he can begin to learn to behave more skillfully with regard to the milieu in which he finds himself. He can begin to learn that misunderstanding can be diminished—not banished—by the slow, patient, laborious practice of a skill.

But we can expect too much from this possibility, so let me conclude by sounding two notes of caution:

(1) Although these skills of communication of which I am speaking deal in part with words, they are not in themselves words, nor is the territory to which they apply made up of words. It follows, then, that no verbal statement about these skills, however accurate, can act as a substitute for them. They are not truly articulate and never can be. Although transmissible to other persons, they are but slowly so and, even then, only with practice.

(2) Let us remember that these interpersonal proceedings between Hart and Bing, or A and B whoever they may be, are extremely complex. So far as I know, there exists no single body of concepts which as yet describes systematically and completely all the important processes that our separate theories have said are taking place and how they relate to each other. Let us therefore accept gracefully and not contentiously that these interpersonal proceedings, unlike the atom, have not been as yet "cracked" by social science. Only then can we as students of human behavior live up to our responsbility for making our knowledge fruitful in practice.

Notes

1. This case (names and places disguised) is adapted from a case in the files of the Harvard Graduate School of Business Administration.

2. For an elaboration of this view see Robert Bierstedt, "An Analysis of Social Power," *The American Sociological Review*, December 1950, p. 730.

3. For an analysis of this theory see Wendell Johnson, ''The Fateful Process of Mr. A. Talking to Mr. B,'' *Harvard Business Review*, January-February 1953, p. 49.

4. See Carl R. Rogers and F. J. Roethlisberger, ''Barriers and Gateways to Communication,'' *Harvard Business Review*, July-August 1952, pp. 46–50.

5. Ibid., pp. 50–52.

6. For a fuller explanation see Irving Lee, *How to Talk with People* (New York, Harper & Brothers, 1953).

7. For Example, see Hadley Cantril, *The Why of Man's Experience* (New York, The Macmillan Company, 1950).

8. For a fuller explanation see Carl R. Rogers, *Client-centered Therapy* (Boston, Houghton Mifflin Company, 1953).

9. See Kenneth R. Andrews, ''Executive Training by the Case Method,'' and F. J. Roethlisberger, ''Training Supervisors in Human Relations,'' *Harvard Business Review*, September 1951, pp. 58, 47.

33

How Much Stress Is Too Much?

HERBERT BENSON and ROBERT L. ALLEN

"There is no question that a certain amount of stress is good," says one of the chief executives quoted in this article. "If I have a particularly easy week, I can feel an ache or pain, but if I get really busy, I feel really much better." But when managers feel themselves under too much stress, the executive adds pessimistically, then "not only will they burn out in time, but they get erratic and their judgment goes all to hell." These insights reflect one of the authors' main themes: medical research finds stress productive up to a point (which of course varies with the manager), but beyond that point it can be disastrous. The trouble in corporate life seems to be that leaders appreciate the first part of the relationship but not the second. As a consequence, both individuals and organizations suffer—and suffer greatly. This penalty is unnecessary, the authors believe, because a newly tested, proved, and relatively simple approach to managing stress is available to any corporation that wants to use it.

A corporate medical officer reported to his president that there was rampant drug use during working hours throughout the company. In fact, he said, "Every single employee is on a drug," and, moreover, "no one of them can perform with maximum efficiency without this self-administered drug." The medical officer added, however, that on-the-job abuse of the drug was the principal cause of absenteeism, lapses of judgment, cases of heart disease and stroke, forced early retirement, alcholism, and occasional suicides. Translated into dollars, this drug abuse was having a substantially negative effect on profits. Yet, because the drug enhanced efficiency, its use was necessary to keep the company going.

Although the report is fictional, it portrays accurately the situation of

---

Published in 1980.

almost every sizable corporation. The self-administered drug—adrenalin—is secreted in employees' bodies as a response to stress. At proper levels of secretion, it is stimulating and beneficial. But with excessive stress, an "overdose" may be harmful to the individual and the business.

The need for a balance is clear. We benefit from the exhilaration of stress for business efficiency and well-being, but we must recognize and avoid the excessive stress that wastes human potential.

This article is based on years of medical research on stress and ways of coping with it.[1] But we also draw on the views of six chief executive officers who have looked at stress from a practical business standpoint: George F. Bennett of State Street Investment Corporation, Thomas S. Carroll of Lever Brothers, Albert V. Casey of American Airlines, J. Edwin Matz of John Hancock Mutual Life Insurance, C. Peter McColough of Xerox, and Edmond T. Pratt of Pfizer. We found the often intense, highly personal interviews helpful to our understanding of the advantages and costs of business stress.

One of the men we interviewed, often warned by his doctors to take vacations and avoid stress, has survived two heart attacks and endured major stress-related surgery in order to return to his desk. "In the daily routine, at least," he told us, "I am not aware of any stress—none whatsoever. I never feel exhausted from stress or strain." However, later in the interview he said: "Stress is here practically all the time. To be very honest with you, I don't know a time when we don't have it."

Another chief executive confronted stress early in his career when he quit a job before he was damaged. He told us: "I was getting that dirty brown taste; I was sure that I could get an ulcer. The damn company was great, and for me it was a great opportunity—but the stress was too much."

Other chief executives told us histories of business leaders who were forced into early retirement by stress or fired because they could not manage the stress of their jobs.

The executives we interviewed know the effects of stress on themselves and their colleagues. Even without data, they are quick to acknowledge the important dollar drain of time lost to stress. They appreciate the costs of retraining and replacement because of stress-related early retirement, illness, and premature death. They speak sadly of the high costs of inept decisions made by employees pushed beyond their competence by stress. And yet, for the most part, these chief executives do not try to deal with stress in their companies. In conversation, most convey only a rudimentary understanding of the problem, despite a flood of speeches and articles in recent years. Each understands an aspect of stress, but none has formulated a policy designed to manage it.

What should top management know about stress—both its value and dangers? What can managers do to balance the consequences of stress so that both individuals and their enterprises will benefit?

'Fight or Flight'

Stress is difficult to define and even more difficult to quantify. We believe that stress results from environmental situations that require behavioral adjustment—ranging from petty daily annoyances to such events as significant illness, death of a spouse, and divorce. The behavioral adjustments necessitated by stress are, in turn, related to specific physiological changes, including increased blood pressure and heart rate, sweating, faster breathing, and markedly increased blood flow to the muscles. These changes frequently occur in an integrated, coordinated pattern called the "fight-or-flight response."[2]

First described by Dr. Walter B. Cannon of the Harvard Medical School, this response has had great evolutionary significance. When used appropriately, it enables an animal to escape a threatening or dangerous situation by fighting or running. Many scientists contend that the long-term survival of human beings was made possible because of this response.

In our everyday lives, the elicitation of the fight-or-flight response is often associated with increased performance. Before an athletic event, competitors involuntarily elicit this response. Before an examination, students exhibit increased heart rate and blood pressure. Similarly, in today's business environment, the stimulus of the fight-or-flight response is often essential to success.

The same response, however, can also have undesireable effects. If the response is elicited frequently in a person who cannot fight or run—that is, cope in some appropriate way—the resulting stress is believed to be an underlying cause of high blood pressure, heart attacks, and strokes. High blood pressure affects about 60 million Americans. Related diseases of the heart and brain account for about 50% of the deaths each year in the United States, and during 1979 they cost society an estimated $35.1 billion.[3]

Counteracting the Effects

There are two proved ways of counteracting the harmful effects of the fight-or-flight response.

First, regular exercise is very helpful. The physiological changes of a fight-or-flight response prepare an individual for physical activity. Dr. Cannon believed that athletic endeavors could "burn off" the harmful physiological effects of the response. In other words, the person reacts in the manner nature intended.

The second proved method is the elicitation of the relaxation response, described in the publications earlier mentioned (see footnote 1). When a person elicits the relaxation response, the physiological changes are precisely opposite those brought forth by the fight-or-flight response. The overall metabolism of the body drops markedly, heart and breathing rates decrease, blood flow to the muscles stabilizes, and blood pressure falls. Dr. Walter R.

Hess, the Swiss Nobel Prize-winning physiologist, described this response in laboratory animals as "a protective mechanism against overstress."

The relaxation response is elicited by the use of age-old behavioral techniques, including Western relaxation methods, Eastern meditative practices, and certain types of prayer. The techniques contain four basic elements necessary to bring forth the response: a quiet environment; a comfortable position; the repetition of a word (for instance, the number *one*), phrase, or prayer; and the adoption of a passive attitude when other thoughts come into consciousness. The relaxation response is therapeutically useful in diseases related to stress and may also be useful in their prevention. It has been established as an effective therapy for high blood pressure, many forms of irregular heartbeat, and symptoms associated both with tension headaches and anxiety.

The usefulness of the relaxation response in a business setting has been well documented. As described in detail in "Time Out from Tension" (*HBR* January-February 1978), employees who regularly took a "relaxation response break" were compared with a group that sat quietly and with one other group that continued normal daily activities. Care was taken to ensure that all groups were similar at the beginning of the experiment.

The group instructed to take relaxation response breaks did so an average of 8.5 times per week for eight weeks, following which period this group had significantly lower blood pressure levels than the other two. In addition, the general health of the first group improved—as measured by reductions in such symptoms as headaches, backaches, nausea, diarrhea, difficulty in falling asleep, and nervous habits (all characteristic of stress). Daily self-ratings of performance also revealed that in the group taking the relaxation response breaks performance with significantly increased, while no such improvements were evident in the other groups.

There are a great variety of measures—good and bad— that a person can use to cope with the effects of stress. We feel that, for the maximum benefit, an individual should choose a repeated word, sound, phrase, or prayer that he or she feels comfortable with and believes in.

Yerkes-Dodson Law

To balance stress, we must understand the important relationship among the fight-or-flight response, the relaxation response, and exercise. Let us turn briefly to the Yerkes-Dodson law (see Exhibit 1).

The beneficial and deleterious effects of stress on performance and efficiency were first described in 1908 by Drs. Robert M. Yerkes and John D. Dodson of the Harvard Physiologic Laboratory.[4] These investigators demonstrated that as stress increases, so do efficiency and performance. However, this relation persists only to a certain level. If stress continues to increase, performance and efficiency decrease.

The beneficial effects of the fight-or-flight response occur on the left-hand upside of the curve. Here greater stress increases efficiency. The det-

Exhibit 1.   Yerkes-Dodson Law

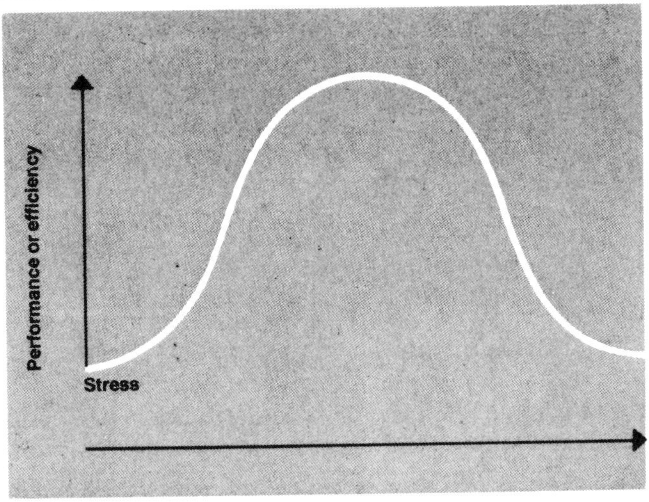

rimental effects take place on the right-hand downside of the curve; there the symptoms of excessive stress come into the picture.

Executives Look at Stress

In our interviews, we discussed the Yerkes-Dodson law with the six chief executives and asked for their thoughts. Peter McColough agreed about the positive effects of stress represented by the upside of the curve. He said: "There is no question that a certain amount of stress is good. If I have a particularly easy week, I can feel an ache or a pain, but if I get really busy, I feel really much better."

But he added a sobering thought about the downside: "My judgment is that when people get up here [pointing to the top of the curve], not only will they burn out in time, but they get erratic and their judgment goes all to hell."

Albert Casey quickly saw a problem in trying to "live" by the curve. He doubted that a supervisor could apply it readily—as when, let us say, a subordinate he called Joe is under great stress. Casey said: "In the first place, I wouldn't really agree that it's the supervisor's job to act in a little more reserved fashion for a while so Joe will be able to perform at a higher level for a longer period. That would be too much; it's attributing an awful lot of insight to ordinary management.

"I really think that's asking too much because, meanwhile, the supervisor has all sorts of pressures on himself for performance, so he has to divide those pressures and goals with the peole who work for him. I'll be honest with you, if the supervisor can see that Joe can contribute more in the near term, he's probably going to take advantage of that."

Most of the chief executives made it clear that their recruiters seek people who start out well on the upside of the curve. Thomas Carroll said: "We select out. When we go out to the business schools, we look for people who are highly motivated—kind of driven. Frankly, they have a lot going for them."

Impact of Incentives

And the companies work to keep stress present through incentive plans that reward achievement. Thomas Carroll commented on incentive-plan performance reviews as stress generators: "Some people say that performance reviews cause stress. Sure, they cause some stress, but, on the other hand, they help to reduce stress. We think performance reviews are helpful because they make clear what is expected. If you don't know where you stand, that is stressful. Without performance reviews, people don't know where they stand."

McColough agrees with the importance of the performance reviews. He said that almost everone at Xerox is on some type of incentive plan based on the growth of the company and that "there is a lot of stress generated." He added: "Some people have to leave the company because of stress, but I don't know that there would be less stress if they were on straight salary. We want to keep growing at least 15% a year and that causes some real stress. But we don't put people under stress just to make them better performers. Stress flows from our basic objectives, which we all share pretty much."

Edmond Pratt takes just the other tack on motivation of people who are on the upside of the curve. He said: "I don't believe in aggressive incentive pay schemes. The people in our key jobs are motivated enough already, and we aren't going to motivate them any more by putting tension on them to 'succeed or else.'"

Meeting Pratt partway on the question of stress and incentives, Carroll told us: "I don't think that an incentive program is a day-to-day incentive— most people forget about it during the year. I think their pride, their desires, what's expected of them matter more. For instance, take a group of six product managers. They know that the way to get ahead is to be a better product manager than the other guy. And when that promotion finally comes, I'll tell you, it generates stress in the other five for sure."

Role of Management Style

Different styles of management stood out in our interviews and were related to the personal beliefs of the chief executives. For example, George Bennett does his share of stress counseling. He told us: "In the investment management business, where you are dealing with markets that are changing moment to moment, nothing is very stable. It is always a footrace to keep up with what is going on. Therefore, it's a very stressful business.

"I have been running the firm for a little over 20 years and I've tried to major in people, bringing in just the best we can find. They have a lot of fine qualities, and the ability to deal with anxiety and stress is one of them. I am conscious that it is important to monitor their handling of stress all of the time."

One of the chief executives reported candidly about one of his officers who had left the company: "He couldn't live with me and I sure as hell wasn't going to live with him. He couldn't learn to live with stress. He couldn't adjust. He always lived by the manual."

Another chief executive spoke of a style that recognized only the upside of the Yerkes-Dodson curve: "I can think of one large company in which the chief takes real pride in the way he runs his organization. It isn't a question of "Let me see it by five this afternoon;' it's rather 'Stop everything, I want it now!' His monthly management meetings are so stressful that he frequently reduces his immediate subordinates and division heads to emotional collapse. And he is proud of his operation."

Each chief executive was aware that the way he copes with his own stress or the way he views his job and his relationship to the company inevitably gets transmitted throughout the corporation. For Edmond Pratt it can be summed up in one word: fun. He said: "I will never allow myself to work in circumstances where it isn't satisfying and enjoyable. Work can be challenging and tough, but you can love what you are doing.

"As far as I am concerned, we at Pfizer are trying to be one of the top, aggressive companies, but I want people to enjoy what they are doing. The best you can do at the top is to set the right example. I try not only to set the example, I talk about it. I say I think working at Pfizer should be fun, and I have never had anyone disagree with that. It's a little hard to disagree with it, if your boss says it."

For McColough, it is important to decrease stress periodically and shift back to the upside of the curve. He said: "I insist on taking vacations. I take vacations well above average, six or eight weeks a year—although never six or eight weeks at a crack. I always have one or two vacations scheduled beyond the next one. I sail in the summer and I ski almost every weekend in the winter. Around here it's not shameful to take a vacation; no one feels guilty about taking time off."

Xerox stands out with another enlightened style of its own. Said McColough: "We say over and over that we want people who are balanced— that we are not looking for workaholics. We expect our people to work hard, and we do work hard. We also do believe that there is a broader purpose to a good corporation than just making money. We try to bring balance to people's lives. We greatly encourage them to do outside activities so they can get some interests outside of business."

By "greatly encourage," McColough referred to a paid social service leave for employees and a sabbatical for executives. "The other thing we do to relieve stress and promote good health," he told us, "is to have gymnasiums at most major Xerox facilities throughout the world. If a gym can save just one heart attack a year, it pays for itself."

If Xerox does all that, why do executives leave because of stress? Here is McColough's answer: "Despite the climate here, which still has a lot of stress, some people just can't cope with it. I would say that some of the people who left didn't lead balanced lives. Some of them had no outside interests—their lives were totally business. If Xerox disappeared during the night, it would have been the end of the world as far as they were concerned.

"We have had people, for example, who drank too much and took pills to make them sleep at night. They got so they could not stand the pressure. Perhaps they were all right most of the time, but in a top business position you can't be all right just most of the time. If you go off the deep end a few times you can come back, but after that you are destroyed as far as the organization is concerned."

Stress in Middle Management

The chief executives clearly remember the stress of their middle management years. Matz said: "It is universal that middle management—and especially young middle management—should always feel discontented. They always look ahead and see no opportunities for promotion coming, and they complain that they are not consulted and don't know what is going on. In spite of all the attempts you make, you still get that story. We keep working at it, but it seems that we will never make much headway against that ingrained concern."

Carroll also commented about the uncertainties felt by middle managers that generate stress: "The managers in the business often don't know when the next opening will occur. They make book, of course. They may say: 'That Tom Carroll, I know his age. At the outside, he can't go beyond. . . . ' Everyone's aware of the transitions."

With the transition to the job of chief executive, some people seem to break into the clear. For Pratt, the headaches that had plagued him for years ceased. For Carroll, becoming master of his own schedule meant the freedom to play squash at noon—and dissipate some stress. "People used to say, 'You have to eat; why don't we have lunch and talk this over.' Now I say, 'I don't eat lunch, I play squash. If you want to see me, what about 10:30 this morning, 8:00 tonight, or a 7:30 breakfast tomorrow?' "

What Can Management Do?

Our interviews with the six chief executives taught us that most agree that stress is serious and demands attention. Further, it is clear to us that while stress will always be with businesspeople, it *is* manageable, and business is well positioned to use it effectively and to counteract its harmful effects. Because the majority of adults in the United States spend at least half their waking hours at work, outside of weekends, the workplace is a logical environment for programs that will decrease stress. Policy decisions should be made to enhance the beneficial aspects of stress and to minimize its harmful consequences. Whether stress is the responsibility of the organization or of the individual makes no practical difference. Too much stress is costly to both; the balancing of stress is mutually beneficial.

However, the information gained from our interviews and from numerous other conversations indicates that most top managers and directors are generally isolated from consideration of what stress means to their companies. We do not know of a single company that has formulated a policy to manage stress. Very few management committees have ever discussed stress, except in cases in which an individual is directly concerned and such questions arise as: "Can she handle this stressful assignment?" or "Is he taking early retirement because of stress?"

To balance stress, executives need first to understand the ideas described earlier in this article:

☐   The fight-or-flight response, which releases stimulants that prepare us to accomplish and achieve.

☐   The Yerkes-Dodson law, which explains that the stimulants increase our efficiency for an initial period but later decrease it.

☐   The great value of the relaxation response and exercise in rescuing us from the downside of the Yerkes-Dodson curve.

Executives who understand each of these elements and their relationships with one another have the tools necessary to manage stress productively—that is, to use it when it can be valuable and minimize it when it can be destructive.

The next step is for the chief executive to assign responsibility in the organization for investigating stress and developing guidelines. Because all managers know from direct experience what is stressful, a chief executive can rest assured that members of a "stress task force" will be sympathetic to the problem. A management group studying stress will be strengthened from the outset if it includes not only representatives from the medical and personnel departments, who have a recognized job-related interest in stress, but also managers from finance, production, marketing, and research, who might benefit personally from an understanding of stress and its effects.

Organizations that market stress-reduction programs may provide useful guidance as well. The task force can judge these programs by their understanding of the factors of stress and by their ability to present a plan suitable to the individual needs of a business.

Such a group will be alert to identify those operations that might benefit from being moved forward on the upside of the Yerkes-Dodson curve as well as to point out overstressed activities that suffer the results of slipping to the downside. Although the chief executive may form a stress force in the name of increased productivity, the potential benefits in job satisfaction, personal health, and happiness for employees carry rewards beyond measurement.

Suppose you take on the job of observing where stress is excessive and encouraging individuals to cope with it. What should you look for and do? How employees feel is a good indication of how they are balancing stress in their lives. As indicated earlier, stress is related to the symptoms of headaches, backaches, nausea, diarrhea, insomnia, and other nervous habits. The relaxation response and exercise generate a sense of well-being as they alleviate the unproductive, harmful aspects of stress. Therefore, provision should be made for regular exercise and for relaxation response breaks. Some individuals prefer exercise; others prefer the relaxation response. The individual can best determine which approach is personally most beneficial.

In one of our interviews, Bennett expressed his choice as follows:

> I have been an evangelical Christian all my life. I believe in prayer and reading the Bible daily. I realize the strength and the peace and tranquility you can get from taking your eye off the business ball for just a few minutes by praying or reading the Bible. I can see that others could get a similar—but, in my judgment, less effective—type of benefit from 15-minute interludes of meditation.

Despite the great potential of worthwhile methods of balancing stress, gymnasiums will be unused, breaks from work will be unproductive, the results of stress-alleviating programs will quickly fade, and desirable policy changes will never be fully accomplished if the chief executive officer is not an example of the effective balancing of his or her own stress. Further, he or she must have the conviction that stress influences the survival of the corporation.

An effective concern for stress demands a long-term view of the function of management. It is well beyond the sales and earnings reports for the next quarter, beyond next year's first board meeting, beyond the results of the five-year plan for new products. A concern for stress means a broad perception of the company and of the well-being of future managment generations.

Notes

1. See, for example, Herbert Benson, "Your Innate Asset for Combating Stress," *HBR* July-August 1974, p. 49; and Ruanne K. Peters and Herbert Benson, "Time Out from Tension," *HBR* January-February 1978, p. 120.

2. Herbert Benson, *The Relaxation Response* (New York: Morrow, 1975) and ''Your Innate Asset for Combating Stress,'' *HBR*.

3. American Heart Association, *Heart Facts 1979* (Dallas: American Heart Association, 1978).

4. See Robert M. Yerkes and John D. Dodson, ''The Relation of Strength of Stimulus to Rapidity of Habit-Formation,'' *Journal of Comparative Neurology and Psychology*, 1908, p. 459.

About the Authors

Robert L. Allen has been the executive director of the Henry P. Kendall Foundation in Boston since 1974. Previously, he was the assistant secretary of Dartmouth College and, for 10 years, he worked for the Kendall Company.

Michael Baker is vice president and research director at the Educational Fund for Individual Rights, a nonprofit research center. Among the current projects he directs are: a study of the effectiveness of company complaint and appeal channels for nonunion employees; research on technical, professional, and ethical disputes between scientists and engineers and their employers; a study of corporate responses to employee crime; and an assessment of the health implications of office automation.

Mr. Baker is a social scientist by training and a former university instructor. Over the past 15 years, his work has centered on how organizational decision-making affects individual rights and opportunities, with special attention to fair treatment in the workplace. He has advised the Privacy Protection Study Commission and the New York State legislature, working most recently on legislature to protect employees from reprisal after they have raised health, safety, and environmental issues inside their firms.

Mr. Baker is co-author of a number of books and reports including: The Changing Workplace: A Guide to Managing the People, Organizational and Regulatory Aspects of Office Technology, *with Alan F. Westin, Heather A. Schweder, and Sheila Lehman (Knowledge Industries Press, White Plains, New York, 1985);* Ethical and Legal Disputes Involving Corporate Engineers (Technology and Society, *June 1985); and* Are You Hearing Enough Employee Complaints and Concerns? (Harvard Business Review, *May/June 1984).*

Publisher's Note. Biographical information was not available on all authors at the time of publication.

Fernando Bartolomé *was born in Spain and obtained a Law degree and an MBA in his native land before going to the United States where he received a Doctorate in Business Administration from Harvard University in 1972. He then joined the faculty at INSEAD, the European Institute of Business Administration in Fontainebleau, France. He taught there for nine years before returning to the United States where he spent two years as a visiting professor of business administration at the Harvard Business School. As of September 1983, Professor Bartolome joined the faculty of Bentley College in Waltham, Massachusetts. Professor Bartolome has consulted and lectured widely in Europe and the United States, focusing especially in human resources management in the areas of interpersonal behavior in organizations and stress and the management of the interaction between professional and private life. He is the author of numerous articles in his field and a book titled,* Must Success Cost So Much, *with Paul Evans, that has been published in the United States and already translated into five languages.*

William G. Damroth, *once president of an investment company, is now a nature photographer and his own publisher. He has published four books and has another due out this fall. His nature books are distributed as a gift to young readers. Several printings have been distributed to children's hospitals in 39 states. Two printings have gone to Reading Is Fundamental, Inc., at the Smithsonian. To encourage reading, R. I. F. distributes the books through its many branches to school children.*

In The Executive Dilemma, *we have interviews with Mr. Damroth and Wheelock Whitney in the article entitled, "Don't Call It Early Retirement."*

Albert H. Dunn *is a professor at the University of Delaware, the College of Business and Economics, Department of Business Administration. He attended Amherst College where he received an AB, as well as receiving an MBA and a DCS at the Harvard Business School. He taught at Syracuse University, the University of Delaware, and IMEDE Lausanne and CEI, Switzerland. He is the author/co-author of four books on sales management, and the author/researcher (or supervisor) of writing for over 300 teaching cases. He has been director and/or instructor of sales management development programs at General Electric, Hercules, Westinghouse, and others. From 1965 to 1975 he was director of Field Sales Management Institutes (Sales/Marketing Executives International). He was also an instructor at the Graduate School of Sales Management and Marketing and a consultant on management training to companies and trade associations.*

Paul A. Lee Evans *is professor of Organizational Behavior at INSEAD, Fontainebleau, France and chairman of its International Program for Human Resource and Organization Studies. With a PhD in organizational psychology from MIT, his past research focused on career and management development and international management (e.g.,* Must Success Cost so

Much *(Basic Books 1980) co-authored with F. Bartolomé). He has been a visiting professor at several European and American universities, and was a visiting scholar at USC in 1983. He is active as consultant on human resource issues with many international firms.*

Jan Gypen holds a PhD in Organizational Behavior and is the academic director of the Executive MBA Program at the Handelshogeschool/Antwerp Business School, Belgium. He also serves as a consultant on organizational analysis and development to several firms.

Edward W. Jones, Jr. is president of Corporate Organizational Dynamics, Inc., consultants that specialize in enhancing corporate knowledge and understanding of the "Dynamics of Difference" encountered in diverse managerial cultures. He graduated in 1972 from H.B.S. as a Baker Scholar and has had 20 years of experience primarily as a line manager including large organizations of several thousands employees; a profit center of over $100 million strategic and market planning; reporting to CEO; heading an organization responsible for improving manpower training and utilization in New York City with a board of directors of 14 CEOs. In 1984 and 1985, he completed extensive research on the organizational dynamics encountered in diverse management teams. In 1985 he is writing an updated article for H.B.R. *and publishing a book entitled* The Dynamics of Difference: The C.E.O.'s Handbook for Understanding And Managing Diversity In A World Class Company.

Manfred F.R. Kets de Vries is professor of Organizational Behavior and Management Policy at the European Institute of Business Administration (INSEAD). He possesses an Econ Drs from the University of Amsterdam and an MBA and DBA from the Harvard Business School. He has held professorships at H.E.C. Montreal, McGill University, and the Harvard Business School. He is also a practicing psychoanalyst and a member of the Canadian Psychoanalytic Society.

    Dr. Kets de Vries has authored, co-authored, or edited five books and more than 40 scientific papers as chapters in books or as articles. He has been a regular consultant on organizational design and strategic human resource management to many American, Canadian, and European firms.

Edmund P. Learned, has been connected with the Harvard Business School for half a century. He received the Distinguished Service Award from the School at Alumni Day exercises. He is an authority on business policy and the use of statistics in management after having retired in 1967 as the Charles Edward Wilson Professor of Business Policy, Emeritus, after 40 years of active teaching and research. He received his BS degree from the University of Kansas in 1922. While at the University of Kansas he taught courses in economics and commerce while working toward his MS, which he received in 1925. He earned a second graduate degree, an MBA, in 1927 from the Harvard Business School.

Harry Levinson, PhD is president of The Levinson Institute; lecturer in the Department of Psychiatry, Harvard Medical School; and head, section on organizational mental health, Massachusetts Mental Health Center. He received his BS and MS from Emporia (Kansas) State University. He took his training in clinical psychology in the Veterans Administration—Menninger Foundation—University of Kansas program, which led to his PhD from that university. In 1954, Dr. Levinson created, and for the next 14 years, directed the division of industrial mental health of The Menninger Foundation. He has been a visiting professor in the Sloan School of Management at the Massachusetts Institute of Technology and in the School of Business at the University of Kansas. He was Thomas Henry Carroll—Ford Foundation Distinguished Visiting Professor in the Harvard Graduate School of Business Administration. Dr. Levinson is a consultant to and lecturer for many business, academic, and government organizations. In addition to many articles, he is the senior author of Men, Management, and Mental Health *and author of* Emotional Health in the World of Work *and* Executive Stress *among others.*

Rosabeth Moss Kanter, currently on leave from her position at Yale University as professor of sociology and professor of organization and management in the School of Management, is also chairperson of the Board of Goodmeasure, Inc., an international management consulting firm specializing in strategies for innovation, productivity, and effective human resource management. Her latest bestselling book, The Change Masters: Innovation for Productivity in the American Corporation *is a selection of the Fortune Book Club, the Macmillan Book Club, the AMA Book Club, and the Executive Program. Her 1977 book,* Men and Women of the Corporation, *received the C. Wright Mills Award for the best book of the year on social issues and was a selection of the Book-of-the-Month Club and the Fortune Book Club. Dr. Kanter received her BA from Bryn Mawr College in 1964 and a PhD from the University of Michigan in 1967. She is the recipient of many national honors, including the Guggenheim Fellowship.*

Eric H. Neilsen is associate professor of organizational behavior and director of the executive MBA program at Case Western Reserve University. He received an AB from Princeton, 1985; an MA, PhD from Harvard, 1970, in sociology. He has taught at the Harvard Business School (1970–1974), and the Catholic University of Leuven, Belgium (1983). He helped to start the MS Program in Organization Development at CWRU and was the program's director from 1975–1982. He has published articles in Human Relations, Harvard Business Review, Organizational Dynamics, The Organizational Behavior Teaching Review, The Academy Of Management Proceedings, *and numerous readers and anthologies. He recently completed a book,* Becoming an OD Practitioner *(Prentice-Hall 1984).*

Father Theodore V. Purcell, S.J. died on March 21, 1984. He was the research professor at the Jesuit Center for Social Studies and professor of management at the School of Business Administration at Georgetown University. He received an AB from Dartmouth's Tuck School of Business as well as a PhD in Social and Industrial Psychology from Harvard University (Wertheim Fellow). Among his numerous published books and journal articles are Blacks in the Industrial World: Issues for the Manager *and* Blue Collar Man. *He was affiliated with the American Psychological Association (Fellow, Division of Industrial and Organizational Psychology).*

Mary P. Rowe has been special assistant to the president of MIT since 1973. Originally she specialized in the concerns of women. In the late 1970s she became a general ombudsperson for students, staff, faculty, and employees who are not in bargaining units. Her doctorate, from Columbia University, in economics. Most of her writing is on management problems, especially in conflict management. In recent years she has consulted widely on intra- corporate dispute resolution. She helped to begin the Corporate Ombudsman Association. She is chairperson of the Ombudsman Committee of the Society of Professionals in Dispute Resolution and of the Ombudsman subgroup of the Negotiation Program at Harvard.

Warren H. Schmidt is professor of applied behavioral science and director of the institute for public-private partnership in the School of Public Admin- istration at the University of Southern California. He is a certified psy- chologist in California and a diplomat of the American Board of Professional Psychology. Dr. Schmidt's most recent book is Organizational Frontiers and Human Values. *In addition to producing many articles in management and psychology journals (including a* Harvard Business Review *classic on lead- ership), Dr. Schmidt has authored several widely used films and is general advisor for the CRM-McGraw-Hill Management Film Series. One of his films,* Is It Always Right to Be Right? *won an academy award in 1971 and was named "Best Training Film of the Decade" by the U.S. Industrial Film Board.*

Robert Schrank is presently a management consultant and visiting scholar at Cornell University School of Industrial and Labor Relations. From 1970 to 1982 he was a program officer at the Ford Foundation. He received a PhD from Union Graduate School in 1974, a MA from New York University in the Department of Sociology in 1967 and a BA from Brooklyn College, City University of New York, Department of Sociology in 1965. He is edi- tor/author of many publications including books such as American Workers Abroad, Ten Thousand Working Days, *and* Democracy at Sea.

Robert Tannenbaum is an Emeritus Professor of Development of Human Systems at the Graduate School of Management, University of California,

Los Angeles. He is also a consultant to industry, government, education, community health, and similar entities on organization development. He received his PhD from the University of Chicago. He has been an author and co-author of numerous articles. Human Systems Development: New Prospectives on People and Organizations *(Jossey-Bass, 1985) a book which he's co-editor of with two colleagues will be out in August of this year. He is a member of the Editorial Board,* Journal of Humanistic Psychology.

Wheelock Whitney is a graduate of Yale University from which he received a BS degree in applied economics. In 1976, he was awarded the honorary degree of Doctor of Human Letters by Hamline University, St. Paul. Since 1973, he has taught a course in management to seniors and graduate students at the University of Minnesota's School of Management. In 1956, Mr. Whitney joined J.M. Dain & Co., a local investment firm headquartered in Minneapolis, representative as a salesman. He became a vice president in 1958, and in 1963 he was elected chairman of the board and chief executive officer. In 1971, Mr. Whitney was president of the Investment Bankers Association of America, the largest trade association in the securities industry. He was also named Investment Banker of the Year in 1971 by Finance *magazine. In 1972, he left the investment company to devote his energies to human services, particularly in the areas of chemical dependency and health promotion. He and his wife, Irene, were founders of the Johnson Institute, a nonprofit organization in the field of alcoholism and drug addiction. He was its chairman for 13 years.*

Abraham Zaleznik is the Konosuke Matsushita Professor of Leadership at the Harvard Business School. He is also a psychoanalyst and an active member of the American Psychoanalytic Association. He is director of several corporations and a consultant to management. Dr. Zaleznik has written extensively on organizations and power. His most recent book, written with Manfred F. R. Kets DeVries, is Power and the Corporate Mind *(Houghton Mifflin).*

Author Index

Acton, Lord, 44
Alexandre, Philippe, 29
Allen, Robert L., 7, 433, 557–567
Andrews, Kenneth R., 556
Argyris, Chris, 17

Baker, Michael, 432, 491–505
Banks, Pamela M., 435
Barbour, Floyd, 152
Barnard, Chester I., 90, 219
Bartolomé, Fernando, 8, 223, 338, 339,
    401–418, 419–430
Baruch, Rhoda, 290
Bennett, George F., 558, 562–563, 566
Bennis, Warren, 52, 57
Benson, Herbert, 7, 433, 557–567
Berenbeim, Ronald, 191
Bierstedt, Robert, 555
Blodgett, Timothy B., 126, 153–183
Bradford, Leland P., 241, 327–336
Bray, Douglas W., 70
Brenner, Charles, 366
Brown, Jerry, 292
Buhler, Charlotte, 286

Campanella, Roy, 211–212
Campbell, Margaret, 152
Campbell, Richard J., 70
Cannon, Walter B., 559
Cantril, Hadley, 556
Cardoza, Vitória, 435, 463–466
Carroll, Thomas S., 558, 562, 564
Casals, Pablo, 277
Casey, Albert V., 558, 561
Clawson, James G., 238
Collins, Eliza G. C., 1–10, 153–183,
    223–238, 303
Coser, Lewis A., 520
Crook, Thomas, 375

Dalton, Gene W., 272, 275
Damroth, William G., 5, 240, 315–326
Darrow, Charlotte N., 302
Davis, Stanley M., 5, 9, 240, 256–275
De Gaulle, Charles, 19
Dodson, John D., 560, 567
Duggar, Benjamin, 277
Dunn, Albert H., 239–240, 243–255

English, O. Spurgeon, 366
Erikson, Erik, 13, 114, 122, 272, 273, 302
Evans, Paul A. Lee, 338, 339, 401–418, 430

Ford, Henry, 380–381
Fouraker, Lawrence E., 22
Franklin, Benjamin, 277
Frenkel-Brunswick, Else, 285
Freud, Anna, 366, 400
Freud, Sigmund, 106–107, 277, 347, 413–414
Freudenberger. Herbert J., 64, 70
Fulmer, William E., 57

Gabarro, John J., 223
Galbraith, John Kenneth, 278
Gardner, B. B., 90, 91
Gavin, James, 69
Golden, Clinton S., 90
Gould, Roger L., 5, 9, 240, 256–275
Grant, Donald L., 70
Gyllenhammar, Pehr, 46, 57
Gypen, Jan, 13, 112–124, 431

Hahn, Kurt, 130
Hall, Calvin S., 366
Heller, Joseph, 257, 272
Hess, Walter R., 559–560
Hitler, Adolf, 377
Hoover, J. Edgar, 3, 376–377, 378

Jacques, Elliott, 290
Johnson, Bobbette, 435, 457–458
Johnson, Wendell, 556
John XXIII, Pope, 289
Jones, Edward W., Jr., 10, 126–127
Jones, Frank S., 192, 200, 203, 208
Jones, Reverend Jim, 376, 377

Kanter, Jay, 432, 467, 476–482
Kanter, Rosabeth Moss, 7, 12, 43–60, 126
Kennedy, John, 70
Kets de Vries, Manfred F. R., 3, 10, 338, 376–389
Kissinger, Henry, 292
Klein, Edward B., 302
Kram, Kathy E., 238
Kuhlen, Raymond G., 2902

Ladd, Alan, Jr., 432, 467, 468–476
Lang, John A., 192, 199, 203
Lankenner, Wanda A., 303
Lawrence, Paul R., 25, 29
Learned, Edmund P., 6, 12, 30–42
Leavitt, Harold, 18, 26
Lee, Irving, 556
Levinson, Daniel J., 238, 272, 273, 302
Levinson, Harry, 2–3, 4, 6, 12, 61–71, 240, 276–290, 291–302, 337–338, 341–375, 390–400, 418, 433
Levinson, Maria H., 302
Lewin, Kurt, 546
Lloyd, William, 435, 444, 448–449
Lombardi, Vince, 70
Lord, Linda Bose, 153
Lorsch, Jay W., 25, 29

McClelland, David C., 54, 57
McColough, C. Peter, 558, 561, 562, 563–564
McDonald, Alonzo, 7, 11, 15–29
McGregor, Douglas, 90
Mack, Raymond W., 520
McKee, Braxton, 302
MacKinnon, Catherine A., 178
Marx, Karl, 547
Masarik, Fred, 520
Maslach, Christina, 64, 70
Mastalli, Grace L., 153, 180–183
Matz, J. Edwin, 558, 564
Mayo, Elton, 91
Menninger, Karl A., 375

Morley, Eileen, 256
Musham, William C., 192, 200–201, 205

Napoleon I, 15, 24
Neilsen, Eric H., 13, 112–124, 431
Neugarten, Bernice L., 290

Patton, George, 69
Pearson, G. H. J., 366
Pelz, Donald C., 57
Pierce, Chester, 152
Pratt, Edmond T., 558, 562, 563, 564
Price, Raymond I., 272, 275
Prouty, Margaret, 371, 375
Purcell, Theodore V., 8–9, 126–127, 192–209

Quinn, Robert E., 238

Raskin, Allen, 375
Read, Milt, 460
Robinson, Jackie, 210, 211
Roe, Anne, 282, 290
Roethlisberger, F. J., 3, 10, 12–13, 72–91, 433, 543–556
Rogers, Carl, 17, 91, 556
Rollins, Billy J., 243
Rowe, Mary P., 126, 140–152, 153, 184–191, 432, 491–505
Ruttenberg, Harold J., 90

Safran, Claire, 178
Sandburg, Carl, 277
Santayana, George, 277
Sartre, Jean-Paul, 152
Schmidt, Warren H., 432, 506–520
Schrank, Robert, 9, 10, 125–126, 129–139
Schulberg, Budd, 282–293
Schultz, William C., 433, 521–542
Smith, Adam, 547
Snyder, Richard C., 520
Sophocles, 106, 277
Stein, Barry A., 57
Sullivan, Reverend Leon H., 192, 199–200, 202, 204, 205, 206

Tannenbaum, Robert, 432, 506–520
Terkel, Studs, 1
Thompson, Paul H., 272, 275
Till, Frank J., 178
Titian, 277
Toner, Frank J., 192, 201, 202, 205, 208–209

Torell, Bruce, 71
Trainer, Cynthia, 463–466

Vaillant, George E., 272, 273

Weber, Max, 17
Whitney, Wheelock, 5, 240, 304–315
Wigan, Gareth, 432, 467, 482–490
Willett, Albert V., 243

Williams, Clarence G., 191
Wylie, Irene E., 192

Yerkes, Robert M., 560, 567

Zaleznik, Abraham, 7–8, 13, 92–111, 218,
  413, 418, 431
Zaphiropoulos, Renn, 8, 431, 435–466

Subject Index

Abrasive personality, 390–400
  need to be perfect, 399–400
  problem situations:
    boss, 397–398
    candidate, 398–399
    peer, 398
    you, yourself, 399
  profile, 392–394
  self-test, 400
  solving dilemma, 394–397
Absenteeism, 64
Acceptance, retirement, 328–329
Accessibility, complaint channel, 497–499
Achievement, retirement and, 329
Activity and passivity, 94
Adaptation, new job, 405–407
Adjudication, complaint system, 500,
  502–503
Administrative process, foreman's level,
  85–87
Administrative skills, interpersonal
  communication, 552–554
Adolescence, dynamics of subordinacy,
  104–107
  initiative and competition, 106–107
  intimacy and dependency, 105–106
  learning through conflict, 107
Adult development, 273–275
  stages in, 294–295
Advice and counseling, complaint channels,
  501
Affection, need for, 532
Affirmation, retirement, 329
Aggressive energy, channeling, 297
AIM (Action for Independent Maturity),
  334–335
Alliance Against Sexual Coercion, 188
Alliance vs. competition, 114–115

American Association for Retired Persons,
  334
Anger, 283–284, 350, 371
Anxiety, 4, 356–357
Attitude reversal, subordinacy and, 100
Authentic behavior, 428–429
Authoritarian pattern, top-management,
  22–24
Authority problem, 529–530
Avoidance of differences, 511–512

Backlash, 206
Balance:
  importance of, 270–272
  superego, 351–352
Barriers, overcoming, 431–567
  complaint channels, 431–433
  differences among people, 506–520
  friends working together, 467–490
  interpersonal communication, 543–546
  interpersonal relations, 521–542
  management philosophy, 435–466
  stress, 557–567
Behavior:
  occupational activities and, 296–298
  personality and, 337–430
    abrasiveness, 390–400
    folie à deux, 376–389
    success, 401–418
    suicide, 341–375
    work alibi, 419–430
Behavior symptoms, interpersonal problems,
  522–527
  communications, 522–523
  indiscriminate opposition, 524–525
  loss of motivation, 523–524
  operational problems, 525–526
  task distortions, 526–527

Biofeedback, 64
Blacks, 192–222
  as managers, 210–222
    color factor, 219–220
    initial exposure, 212–213
    job offer, 211–212
    lessons from experience, 218–219
    new challenges, 216–218
    on-the-job, 213–216
    problems of "fit," 220–221
  preferential treatment, 192–209
    case history, 192–198
    justifying preference, 207–209
    management deficiencies, 201–203
    qualification, 205–207
    query and commentary, 198–201
    underlying issue, 204
Breakdown, communication, 549–550
Bundy v. *Jackson*, 182
Burn out, 61–71
  characterizations, 63–65
  managerial jobs, 65–66
  prevention, 66–70
  situations, 61–63

Civil Rights Act of 1964, 180–182, 207
Civil suits, sexual harassment, 182–183
Clarifying expectations *vs.* second-guessing, 115–117
Clash of personalities, 548
Clearing the air, 540–541
Common sense, 547–548
Communications problems, 522–523
Compensation, defense mechanism, 359
Competence *vs.* inferiority, 118–119
Competition, adolescent, 106–107
Complaint channels, nonunion employees, 491–505
  accessibility, 497–499
  credibility, 499–500
  drawbacks of conventional approach, 494–497
  functions, 500–503
  systems approach, 503–505
  unconstructive *vs.* constructive options, 493
Complaint procedures, sexual harassment, 189
Compulsive subordinate, 97–100
  control through passivity, 98–99
  recurring themes, 99–100
Confidential complaint channels, 501
Conflicts:
  dealing with, 426–428
  learning through, 107

Constructive drive, 347–348
  handling, 367–368
Contact, maintaining, 110–111
Control:
  need for, 532
  through passivity, 98–99
Coping:
  with discrimination, 147–150
  new job, 405–407
Credibility, complaint system, 499–500
Criminal actions, sexual harassment, 183
Cynicism, 64

Decision, consensus for, 527–529
Denial, as form of repression, 358
Denial of responsibility, subordinacy and, 100
Dependency, 388–389
  in adolescence, 105–106
Depression, 374
  vulnerability, 375
Destructive drive, 347–348
Differences, 506–520
  basic assumptions, 507
  diagnosing disagreements, 508–511
    nature, 508
    stage of evolution, 509–511
    underlying factors, 508–509
  enriched problem solving, 515–518
  objectivity, 518–520
  selecting an approach, 511–515
Differentiation *vs.* identification, 119–120
Directoire, 24
Disappointments, learning from, 412–414
Discretion, organizational power, 45
Discrimination, as management problem, 140–152
  background, 140–142
  issues raised, 142–145
  learning from respondents' opinions, 150–152
  in organizations, 145–150
    coping, 147–150
    damaging effects, 146–147
Disillusionment, middle-age, 281
Displacement, ego defense, 360, 361, 368
Dominance and submission, 94
Doubt, compulsive subordinate and, 99
Drugs and alcohol, 64

Early retirement, 303–326
Ego:
  anxiety and defense mechanisms, 355–359
  and reality, 353–355
  see also Superego

Ego ideals, 295–296
Emotional drive, 348–353
  balance wheel, 351–352
  conscience and culture, 350
  home and job, 352–353
  self-image, 350–351
  superego and conscience, 349–350
Employees, changing needs, 239–336
  middle-age, 256–290
    adult development, 273–275
    balance, 270–272
    corporate mid-life crisis, 256–275
    indexes of health, 277–279
    managers, 276–290
    personal and organizational
      implications, 286–289
    subtle changes, 279–286
  new vs. traditional work values, 243–255
  overview, 239–241
  retirement, 303–336
    early (interviews), 303–326
    survival, 327–336
  second career, 291–302
Enjoyment misfit, 409
Equal Employment Opportunity
  Commission (EEOC), 155
Equality, preferential treatment to blacks
  and, 206–207
Executive suicide, 369–375
  early traumas, 371–372
  high aspirations and, 370–373
  prevention, 373–374
  threat of failure, 372–373
  vulnerability, 375

Failure, threat of, 372–373
Family influence, suicide and, 345–346
Family relationships, 284–285, 299
Fight-or-flight response to stress, 559–561,
  565
First-line supervisors, powerlessness of,
  46–49
Flexibility, as organizational value, 56
Folie à deux, 376–389
  dynamics, 379–383
    getting trapped, 380–382
    scapegoats, 382–383
  entrepreneurial dangers, 383–384
  management, 385–388
    checking out managers, 385–386
    peculiarities of organization, 386–388
  meaning of, 378
  paradox of dependency, 388–389
Followers, top-executive level, 18
Foreman, 72–91

administrative process, 85–87
  new concept, 88–90
interactions, 76–83
knowledge and, 74–75
position of, 73–75
restriction of freedom of action, 75–76
salient features, 83–85
social processes, 81–83
Foreman-foreman, 80
Foreman specialist, 79–80
Foreman superior, 76–79
Foreman worker, 80–81
Friends working together (Ladd Company),
  467–490
Führerprinzip, 24

Goals, retirement and, 329
Group compatibility, 533–537
Group development, 537–539
Growing apart, retirement couples, 333

Handling people:
  behavior, personality and, 337–430
    abrasiveness, 390–400
    folie à deux, 376–389
    success, 401–418
    suicide, 341–375
    work alibi, 419–430
  employees, changing needs, 239–336
    middle-age, 256–290
    new vs. traditional work values,
      243–255
    retirement, 303–336
    second career, 291–302
  introduction, 1–10
  overcoming barriers, 431–567
    complaint channels, 431–433
    differences among people, 506–520
    friends working together, 467–490
    interpersonal communication, 543–546
    interpersonal relations, 521–542
    management philosophy, 435–466
    stress, 557–567
  people problems, 2–10
  when job (not personality) is problem,
    11–124
    burn out, 61–71
    foreman's level, 72–91
    new executive, 30–42
    subordinacy, 92–111
    subordinate's predicaments, 112–124
    top management level, 15–29
  working together, 125–238
    blacks, 192–222
    canoe raft trip, 129–139

Handling people: (*Continued*)
    romance within same company, 223–238
    sexual harassment, 153–191
    subtle discrimination, 140–152
Hereditary factors, suicide and, 344–345
Hidden aggression, subordinacy and, 100
Hypochondriasis, 368

Idealization, defense mechanism, 359
Identification, ego defense, 357–358
  with aggressor, 389
Impulsive subordinate, 95–97
Inclusion, need for, 531–532
Indiscriminate opposition, 524–525
Influence, recognition-based, 26
Information factors, diagnosing
    disagreements, 509
Initiative, in adolescence, 106–107
Initiative *vs.* dependence, 117–118
Integrity *vs.* denial, 122–123
Interested parties, soliciting help of,
    387–388
Interpersonal communication, 543–556
  administrative skills, 552–554
  misunderstanding, 544–552
    case history, 544–546
    roots of, 546–550
    views of, 546–550
Interpersonal relations, 521–542
  applications of theory, 539–541
  behavior symptoms, 522–527
    communications problems, 522–523
    indiscriminate opposition, 524–525
    loss of motivation, 523–524
    operational problems, 525–526
    task distortions, 526–527
  common issues, 527–531
    authority problem, 529–530
    consensus for decision, 527–529
    problem member, 530–531
  covert factors, 521–522
  framework for behavior, 531–532
  group compatibility, 533–537
  group development, 537–539
  top-management, 19
Intimacy, in adolescence, 105–106
Introjection, ego defense, 357–358
Investigative complaint channels, 501–502
Irritability, 64

Job hopping, 93
Job itself (not personality) as problem,
    11–124
  burn out, 61–71

characterizations, 63–65
managerial jobs, 65–66
prevention, 66–70
situations, 61–63
foreman's level, 72–91
  administrative process, 85–87, 88–90
  interactions, 76–83
  knowledge and, 74–75
  position of, 73–74
  restriction of freedom of action, 75–76
  salient features, 83–85
  social processes, 81–83
new executive, 30–42
  Dashman Case, 32–35
  Dixie Case I, 35–39
  Dixie Case II, 39–42
  introduction, 30–32
overview, 11–14
subordinacy, 92–111
  business examples, 93–94
  impact on development, 104–107
  implications, 107–111
  patterns and dimensions, 94–104
subordinate's predicaments, 112–124
  self-protection, 114–123
  self-protective responses, 112–113
  taking action, 123–124
top management level, 15–29
  basic types, 18–21
  interpersonal relationships, 19
  organization, 21–25
  organizational underside, 25–26
  personal ambitions, 19–21
  responsibility, 26–29
Job security, 27

Leaders, top-executive level, 18
Learning through conflict, 107
Letter writing, dealing with sexual
    harassment, 186–187
Line/staff, top-management level, 24
Love affair, executives within same
    company, 228–232
  male's quandary, 231–232
  outsiders and, 228–230
  woman as scapegoat, 230–231

Management philosophy (at Versatec, Inc.),
    435–466
Management team approach, 25
Managers:
  blacks as, *see* Blacks, as managers
  middle-age, 276–290
    indexes of health, 277–279

personal and organizational
implications, 286–289
subtle changes, 279–286
"Mañana" attitude, 424–425
Marital difficulties, retirement, 331–333
Marriage conflicts, fear of confronting,
422–423
Masochistic behavior, 100–102
Mediation, complaint channels, 501–502
Middle age, changing needs, 256–290
adult development, 273–275
stages, 294–295
corporate mid-life crisis, 256–275
case histories, 258–270
importance of balance, 270–272
managers, see Managers, middle-age
personal and organizational implications,
286–289
facing crisis, 286–287
organizing for renaissance, 288–289
taking action, 287–288
subtle changes, 279–286
anger, 283–284
disillusionment, 281
family relationships, 284–285
obsolescence, 281
pain of rivalry, 282–293
personal goals, 285–286
point of view, 280–281
vocational choice, 281–282
work style, 280–284
Miller v. Bank of America, 181
Misunderstanding, 544–552
case history, 544–546
roots of, 546–550
views, 546–550
breakdown in communication, 549–550
clash of personalities, 548
common sense, 547–548
social role conflict, 548–549
struggle for power, 549
Moral misfit, 409
Motivation:
loss of, 523–524
top-management, 26–27
Multiple chief executive, 24–25
Mutual concern vs. self-interest, 121–122

National Commission on Working Women,
188
Negativism, 64
Neutralists, top-executive level, 18–19
New executive, 30–42
Dashman Case, 32–35

Dixie Case I, 35–39
Dixie Case II, 39–42
introduction, 30–32
No, ability to say, 411

Objectify conflict, 110
Objectivity, managerial, 518–520
Obsolescence, middle-age process, 281
Oedipus complex, 106–107
Operational problems, 525–526
Organizational values, broadening of,
414–415
Organizations, subtle discrimination,
145–150
coping, 147–150
damaging effects, 146–147

Passivity, control through, 98–99
Peer networks, 45–46
Perceived differential treatment, sexual
harassment, 164–170
Perceptual factors, diagnosing
disagreements, 509
Perfection, need for, 399–400
Performance appraisals, 416
Personal ambitions, top-management, 19–21
Personal communication, complaint system,
500–501
Personal goals, 285–286
Personality clash, 548
Personal work ethic, 252
Physical factors, suicide and, 345
Point of view, middle-aging process,
280–281
Positive spillover, 403–405
Power:
dealing with sexual harassment, 189–191
expansion and sharing, 53–57
job activities and political alliances, 45–46
loss, at retirement, 329–330
meaning of, 43–44
origin of, 44–46
Powerlessness, 43–60
first-line supervisors, 46–49
meaning of, 44
staff professionals, 49–50
symptoms, 53
top executives, 50–53
woman managers, 57–60
Power struggle, 549
Predictability, as organizational value, 56
Preferential treatment, minority employees,
192–209
case history, 192–198

Preferential treatment, minority employees
    (*Continued*)
  justifying preference, 207–209
  management deficiencies, 201–203
  qualification, 205–207
  query and commentary, 198–201
  underlying issue, 204
Président Directeur Général, 24
Pressures, organizational, 410–411
Private and professional life, separation
    between, 417
Projection, ego mechanism, 358–359

Qualifications, top-management level, 28–29

Raft trip story (men's need to impress
    women), 129–139
  deliverance analogy (navigating and big
    bureaucracy), 137–139
  on river, 131–137
  preembarkation, 129–131
Rationalization, defense mechanism, 358
Reaction formation, defense mechanism, 359
Reality, patterns of subordinacy:
  identifying and addressing, 110
  recognizing, 111
Rebellion, dynamics of, 96
Reciprocal pattern, subordinacy and,
    109–110
Recognition, organizational power, 45
Recognition-based influence, 26
Relating personally *vs.* relating
    impersonally, 120–121
Relevance, organization power, 45
Repression, 348, 358
  of differences, 512–513
Resonance effect, dynamics of subordinacy,
    110
Responsibility, top-management, 26–29
  core-qualifications, 28–29
  motivation, 26–27
  service, 27–28
Retirement, 303–336
  interviews with early retirees, 303–326
  survival, 327–336
    problems, 331–334
    programs, 334–336
    what one loses, 328–331
Reward ladder, 415–416
Role factors, diagnosing disagreements, 509
Romance between executives (in same
    company), 223–238
  introduction, 223–225
  love affair, *see* Love affair

opportunity and need, 225–228
  dynamics of relationship, 226–227
  transitions, 227–228
resolution of conflict, 232–237
  as conflict of interest, 233–234
  one must leave, 235–236
  outside help, 234
Routines and time, retirement and, 330–331

Safe system, for complaints, 499
Scapegoats, 230–231, 382–383
Second career, 291–302
  ego ideals, 295–296
  options and critical issues, 298–302
    family, 299
    freedom *vs.* constraints, 300
    joint expenses, 301–302
    present job, 299–300
    rebuilding, 300
    status, 300
    talk, 301
    year-long depression, 300–301
  reasons for, 293–294
  stages in adult development, 294–295
  work style and behavior, 296–298
Self-assessment, 411–412
Self-control, impulsiveness and, 96–97
Self-directed aggression, 373
Self-image, 350–351, 370–371
Self-management, subordinacy and, 108
Self-protection, subordinate's predicaments,
    see Subordinate's predicaments, self-
    protection
Sex role, retirement and, 332–333
Sexual harassment, 153–191
  amount of, 161–163
  as complex problem, 177–178
  dealing with, 188–191
    aims of individual action, 185–187
    effective complaint measures, 189
    employer's role, 188
    power relationship, 189–191
    practical approaches, 185
    special measures, 188–189
  disparities in perception, 163–172
    management, 171–172
    perceived differential treatment,
      164–170
    vignettes, sample responses, 166–169
    what woman can handle, 170–171
  EEOC guidelines, 155–156
    and company policies, 172–177
  legal context, 180–183
    civil suits, 182–183

criminal actions, 183
  Title VII, 180–182
meaning of, 156–161
survey approach, 179–180
survey of findings, 154–155
Socialization, retirement and, 328–329
Social roles, conflict of, 548–549
Societal attitudes, retirement and, 333–334
Sponsors, 45
Staff professionals, organizational
    powerlessness, 49–50
Stress, 65, 66, 71, 557–567
  fight-or-flight response, 559–561, 565
  impact of incentives, 562
  middle management, 564
  reducing, 564–566
  role of management style, 564
Sublimation, 358
Subordinacy, 92–111
  business examples, 93–94
  impact on development, 104–107
  implications, 107–111
    guidelines, 109–111
    self-management, 108
  patterns and dimensions, 94–104
    compulsive subordinate, 97–100
    control through passivity, 98–99
    impulsive subordinate, 95–97
    interpretation, 103–104
  masochistic behavior, 100–102
  recurring themes, 99–100
  role of self-control, 96–97
  withdrawn, 102–103
Subordinates, organizational power and, 46
Subordinate's predicaments, 112–124
  self-protection, 114–123
    alliance vs. competition, 114–115
    clarifying expectations vs. second-
      guessing, 115–117
    competence vs. inferiority, 118–119
    differentiation vs. identification, 119–120
    initiative vs. dependence, 117–118
    integrity vs. denial, 122–123
    mutual concern vs. self-interest,
      121–122
    relating personally vs. relating
      impersonally, 120–121
  self-protective responses, 112–113
  taking action, 123–124
Substitution, defense mechanism, 359
Subtle discrimination, see Discrimination
Success, 401–418
  coping with new job, 405–407
  learning from disappointments, 412–414

price some managers pay, 403–405
private and professional life, 417
right job and, 407–412
  ability to say no, 411
  absence of skill, 408–409
  different values, 409–410
  dislike of job, 409
  external rewards, 410
  lack of fit, 408
  organizational pressures, 410–411
  self-assessment, 411–419
what organizations can do, 414–417
  broadening values, 414–415
  performance appraisals, 416
  reducing uncertainty, 416–417
  reward ladder, 415–416
Suicide, 341–375
  case history, 341–368
    background, 341–343
    cautions, 364–366
    defensive process, 359–362
    ego and reality, 353–355
    ego's assistants, 355–359
    external factors, 348–353
    family influence, 345–346
    hereditary factor, 344–345
    internal drive, 346–347
    physical factor, 345
    reason why, 362–364
    warring drives, 347–348
    why it happened, 343–346
  corporate executives, 369–375
    early traumas, 371–372
    high aspirations and low self-image,
      370–373
    point of vulnerability, 375
    prevention, 373–374
    threat of failure, 372–373
Superego, 349–353
  balance wheel, 351–352
  conscience and, 349–350
  culture, 350
  home and job, 352–353
  self-image, 350–351
  see also Ego
Support systems, retirement and, 330
Survival, retirement, 327–336
  problems, 331–334
    marital, 331–333
    societal attitudes, 333–334
  programs, 334–336
  steps to take, 336
  what one loses, 328–331
    acceptance and socialization, 328–329

Survival, retirement (*Continued*)
    goals, achievement, and affirmation, 329
    power and influence, 329–330
    routine and time, 330–331
    support systems, 330
Susceptibilities, monitoring, 387
Systems approach, complaint system,
    503–505

Task distortions, 526–527
Title VII (Civil Rights Act of 1964), 180–182
Top executives, organizational
    powerlessness, 50–53
Top-management level, 15–29
  basic types, 18–21
  interpersonal relationships, 19
  organization, 21–25
    absolute ruler, 22–24
    line/staff, 24
    management team, 25
    multiple chief executive, 24
  organizational underside, 25–26
  personal ambitions, 19–21
  responsibility, 26–29
    core-qualifications, 28–29
    motivation, 26–27
    service, 27–28
Trusting relationship, establishing, 386–387

Uncertainty, reducing in organization,
    416–417
Upward feedback complaint channels, 503

Vocational choice, middle-aging process,
    281–282

White backlash, 206
Withdrawn subordinate, 102–103

Women managers, organizational
    powerlessness, 57–60
Workaholism, 420–421
Work alibi, 419–430
  capacity to change, 430
  enhancing home life and, 429–430
  potential solutions, 425–429
    authenticity, 428–429
    avoiding saying "mañana," 425–426
    dealing with conflicts, 426–428
  sources of problems, 421–425
    incorrect assumptions, 421–422
    legitimate distractions, 423–424
    "mañana," attitude, 424–425
    marriage conflict, 422–423
  versions of same story, 419–420
  workaholics, 420–421
Work ethic, new *vs.* traditional, 243–255
  as commentators see problem,
    250–251
  events, 254–255
  problem, 245–249
  sales organization schedule, 245
Working together, 125–238
  blacks, *see* Blacks
  canoe raft trip story, 129–139
    deliverance (analogy), 137–139
    on river, 131–137
    preembarkation, 129–131
  romance within same company, *see*
    Romance between executives
  sexual harassment, *see* Sexual harassment
  subtle discrimination, *see* Discrimination
Working Women's Institute, 188
Work reorientation, 388
Work style, middle-aging process, 280

Yerkes-Dodson law, 569–561, 563, 565